AF352449

GLOBAL YORÙBÁ

INDIANA UNIVERSITY PRESS

GLOBAL YORÙBÁ

REGIONAL AND DIASPORIC NETWORKS

TOYIN FALOLA

This book is a publication of

Indiana University Press
Office of Scholarly Publishing
Herman B Wells Library 350
1320 East 10th Street
Bloomington, Indiana 47405 USA

iupress.org

First Printing 2024

Cataloging information is available from the Library of Congress.

ISBN 978-0-253-07054-8 (hardcover)
ISBN 978-0-253-07055-5 (paperback)
ISBN 978-0-253-07056-2 (ebook)

To
Damilola Osunlakin
In Memoriam

Contents

     Contents

Maps

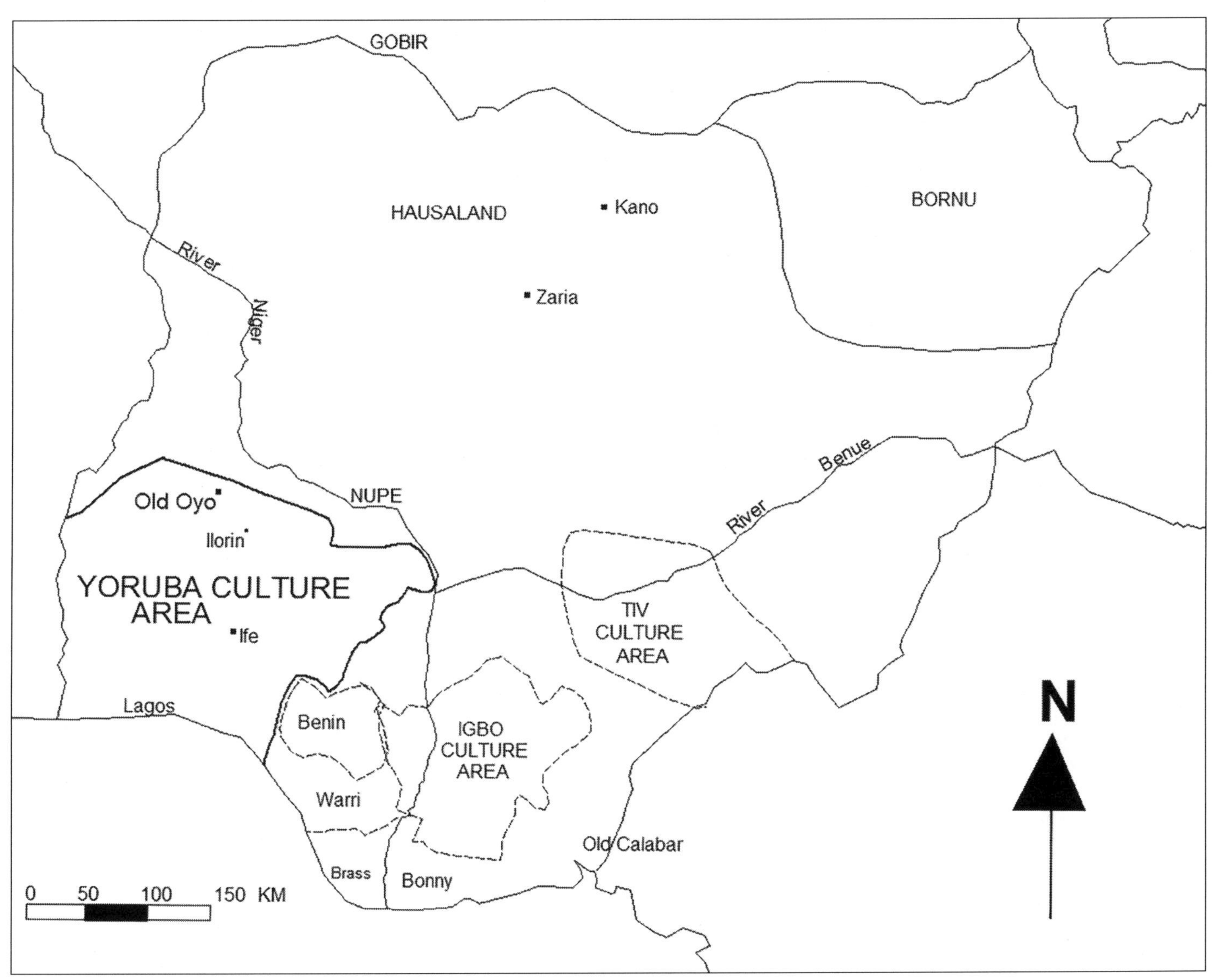

Map 1. Yorùbá Culture Area in Nigeria

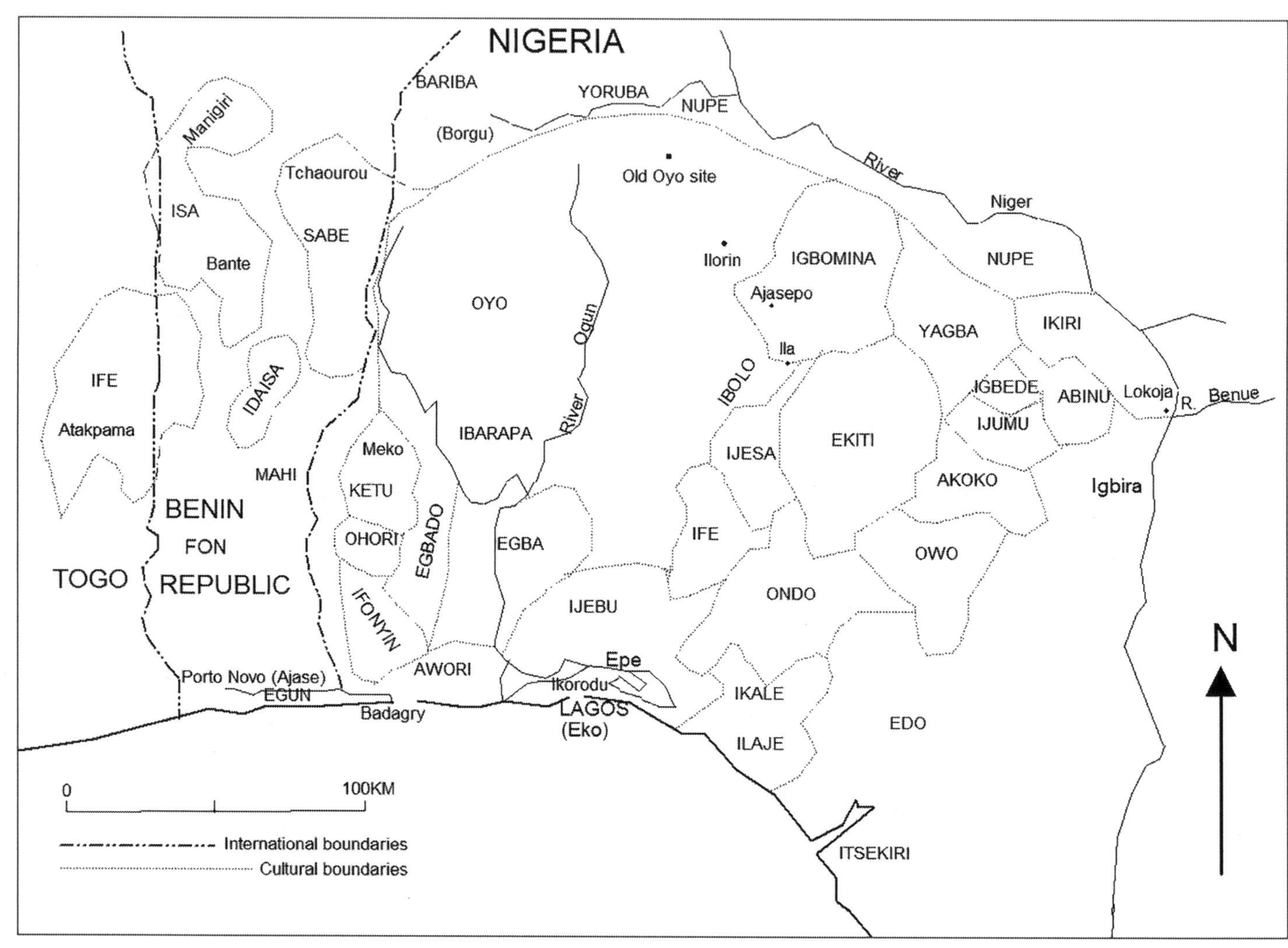

Map 2. Yorùbá Subgroups

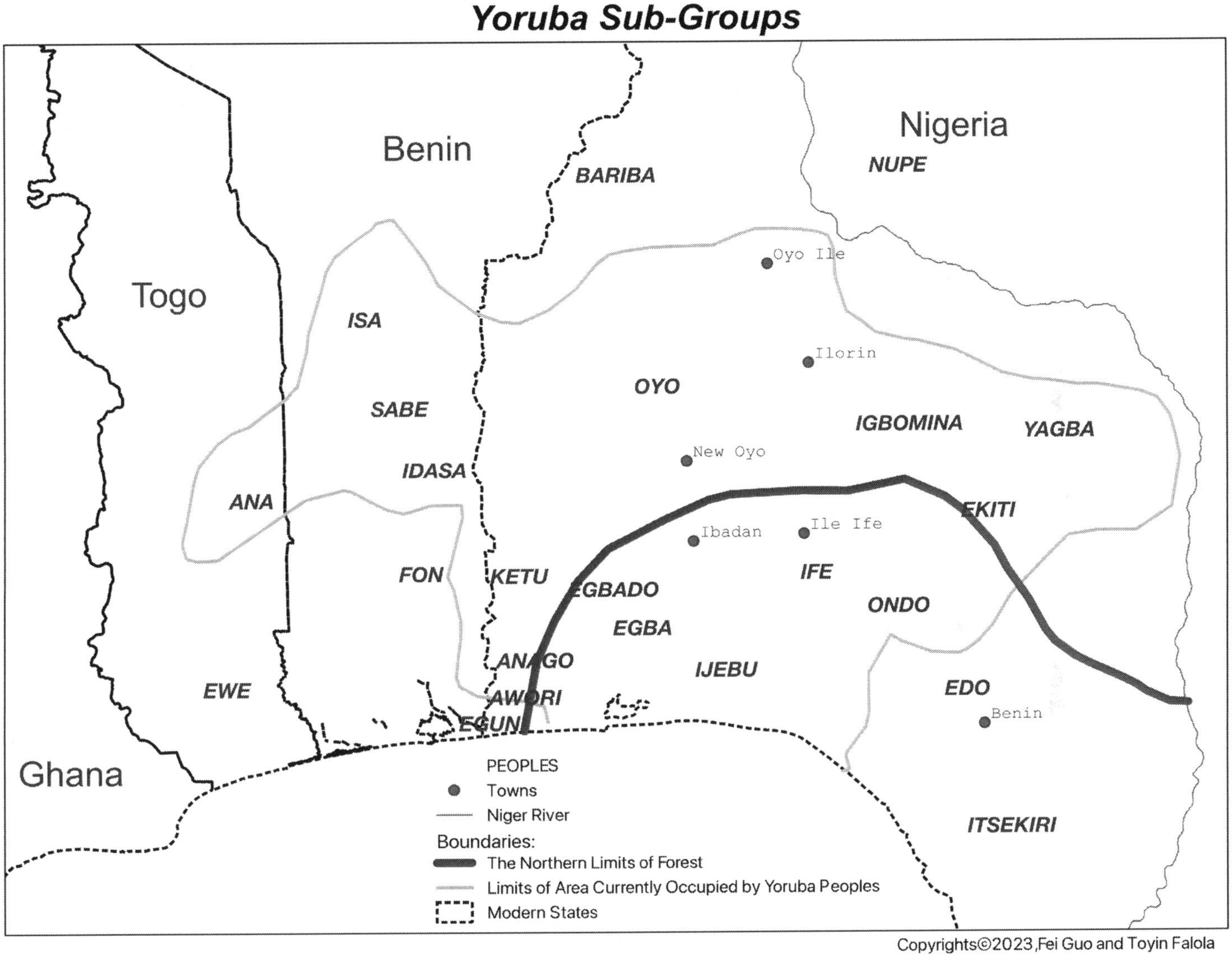

Map 3. Yorùbá Subgroups and Their Neighbors

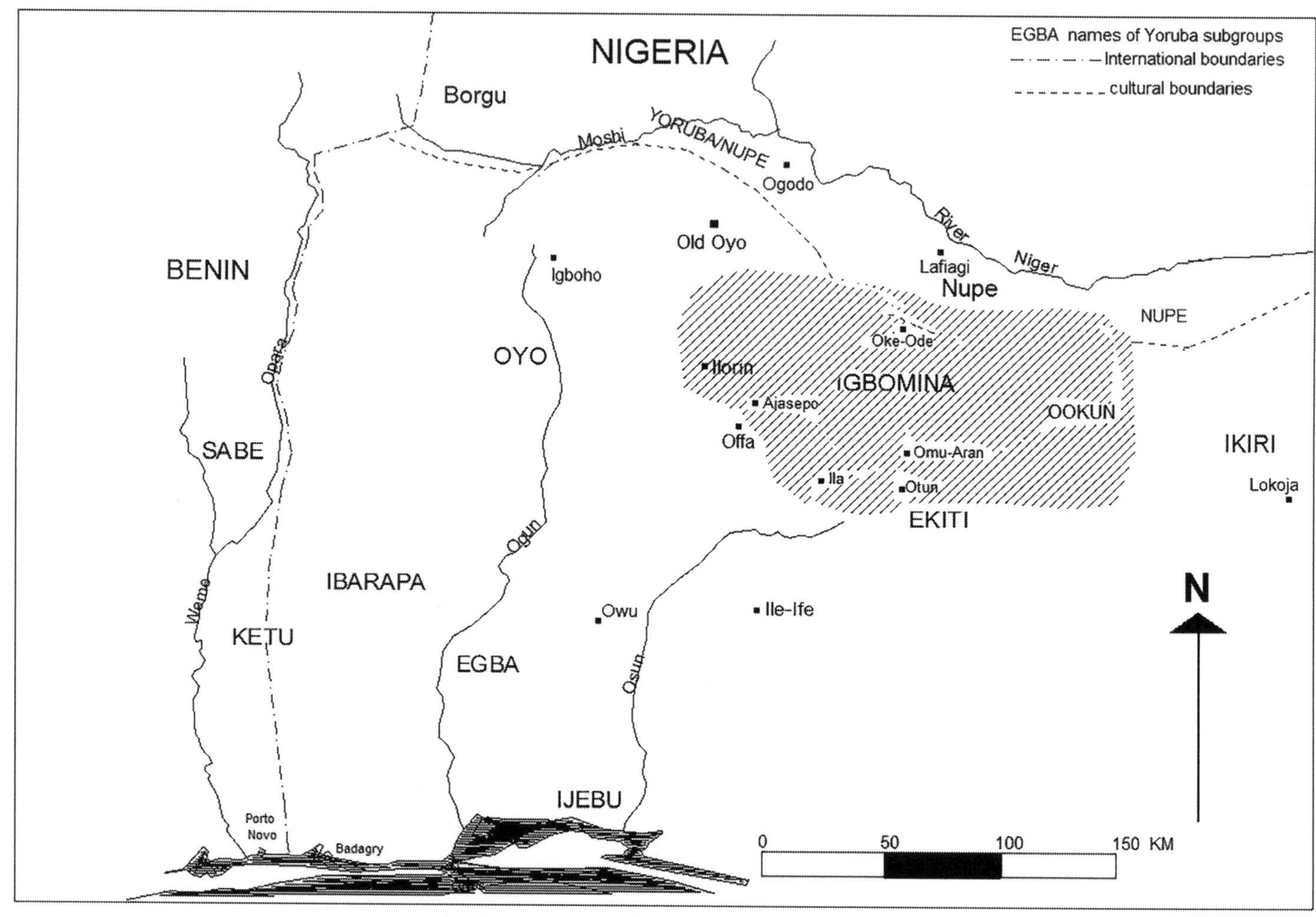

Map 4. The Northern Yorùbá

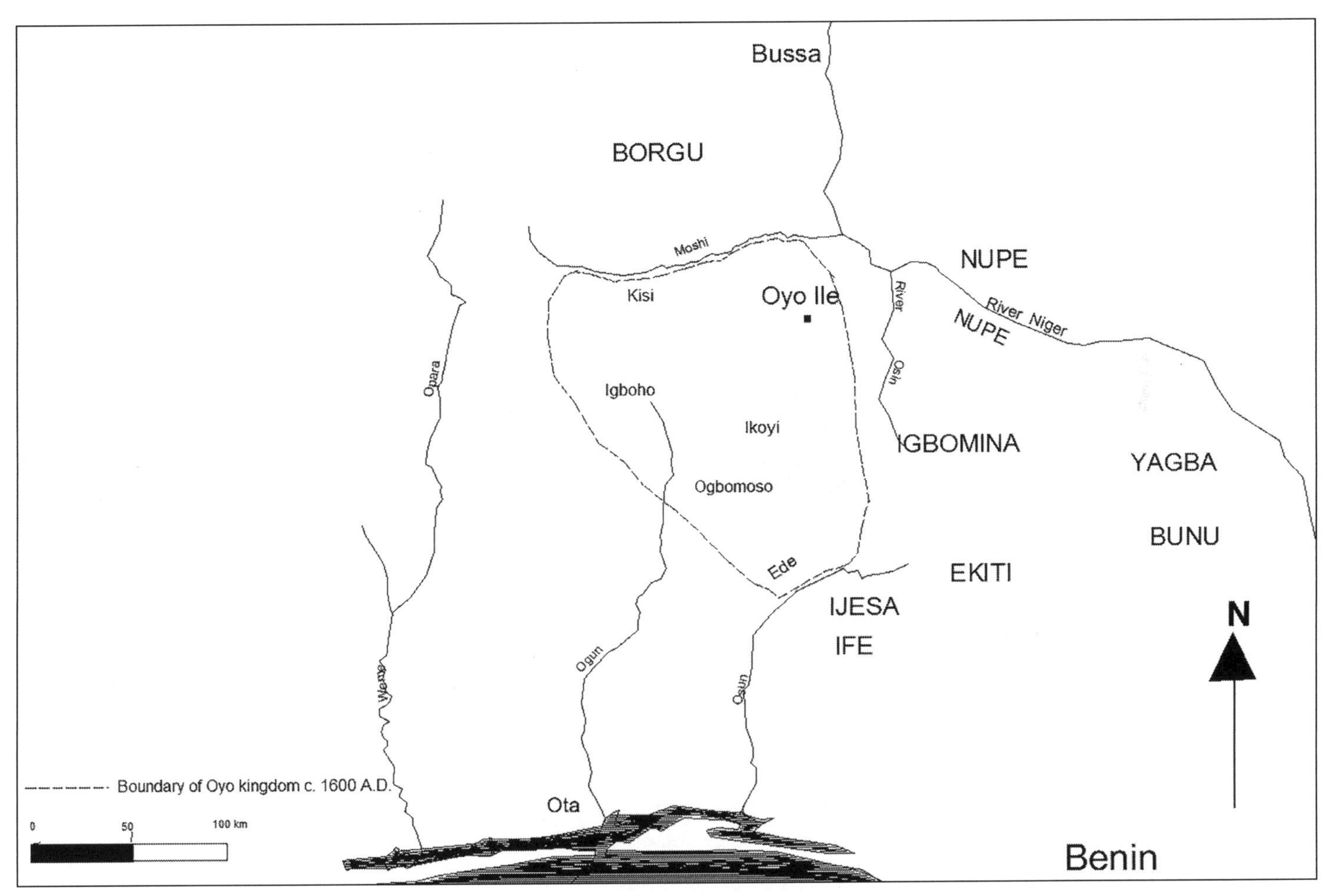

Map 5. Oyo Early Expansion

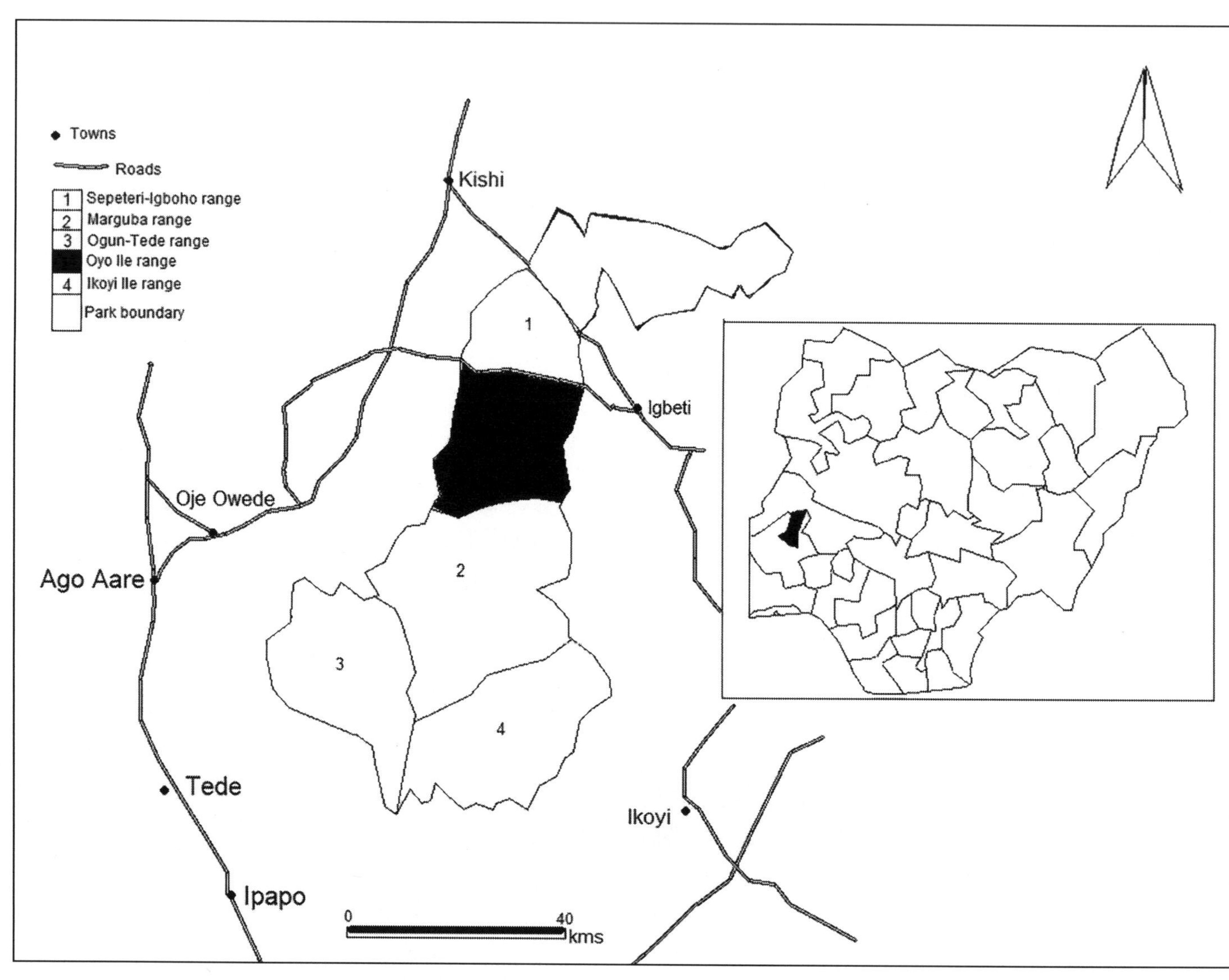

Map 6. Old Oyo Location and Neighboring Settlements

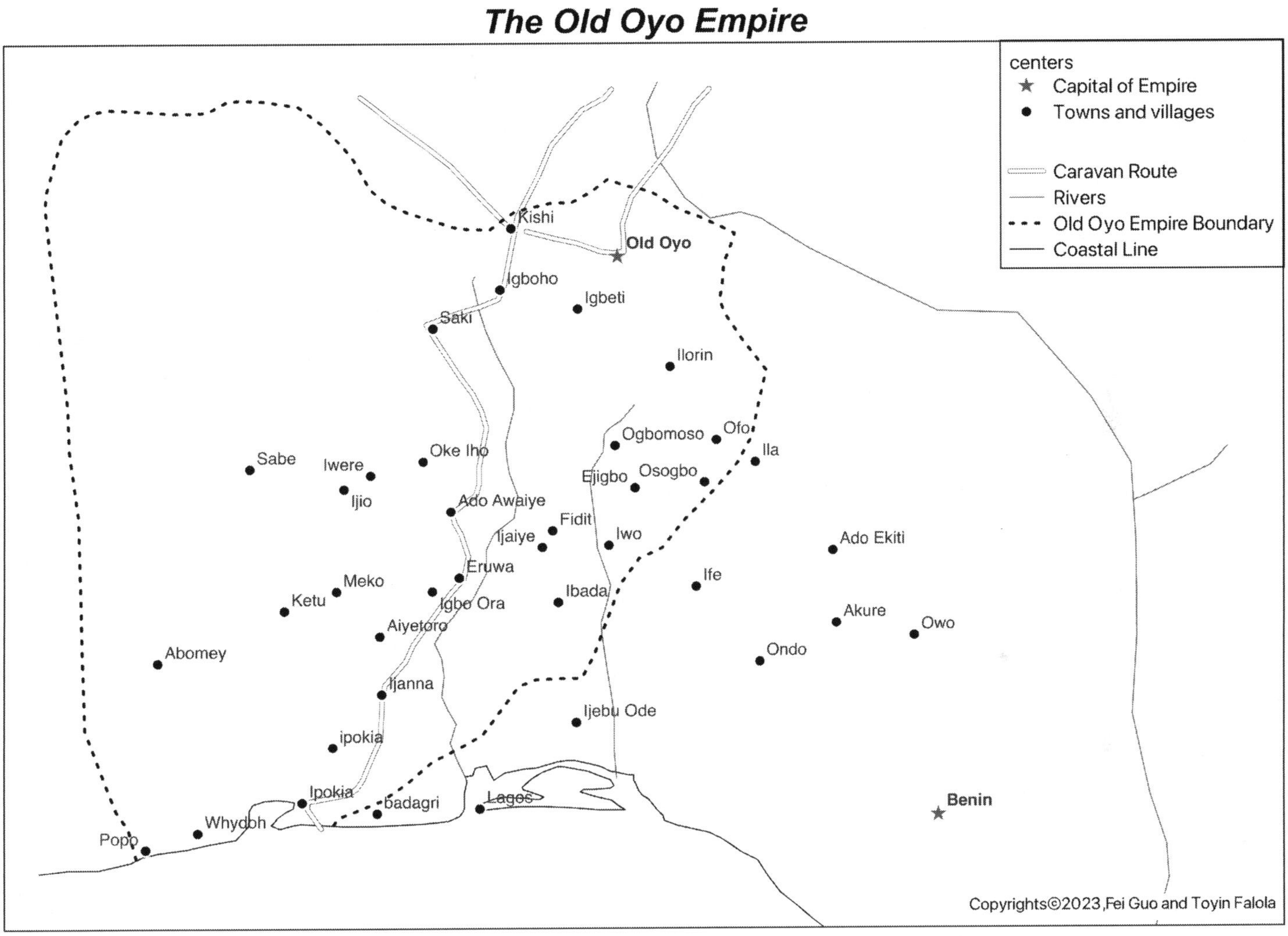

The Old Oyo Empire

Map 7. The Old Oyo Empire

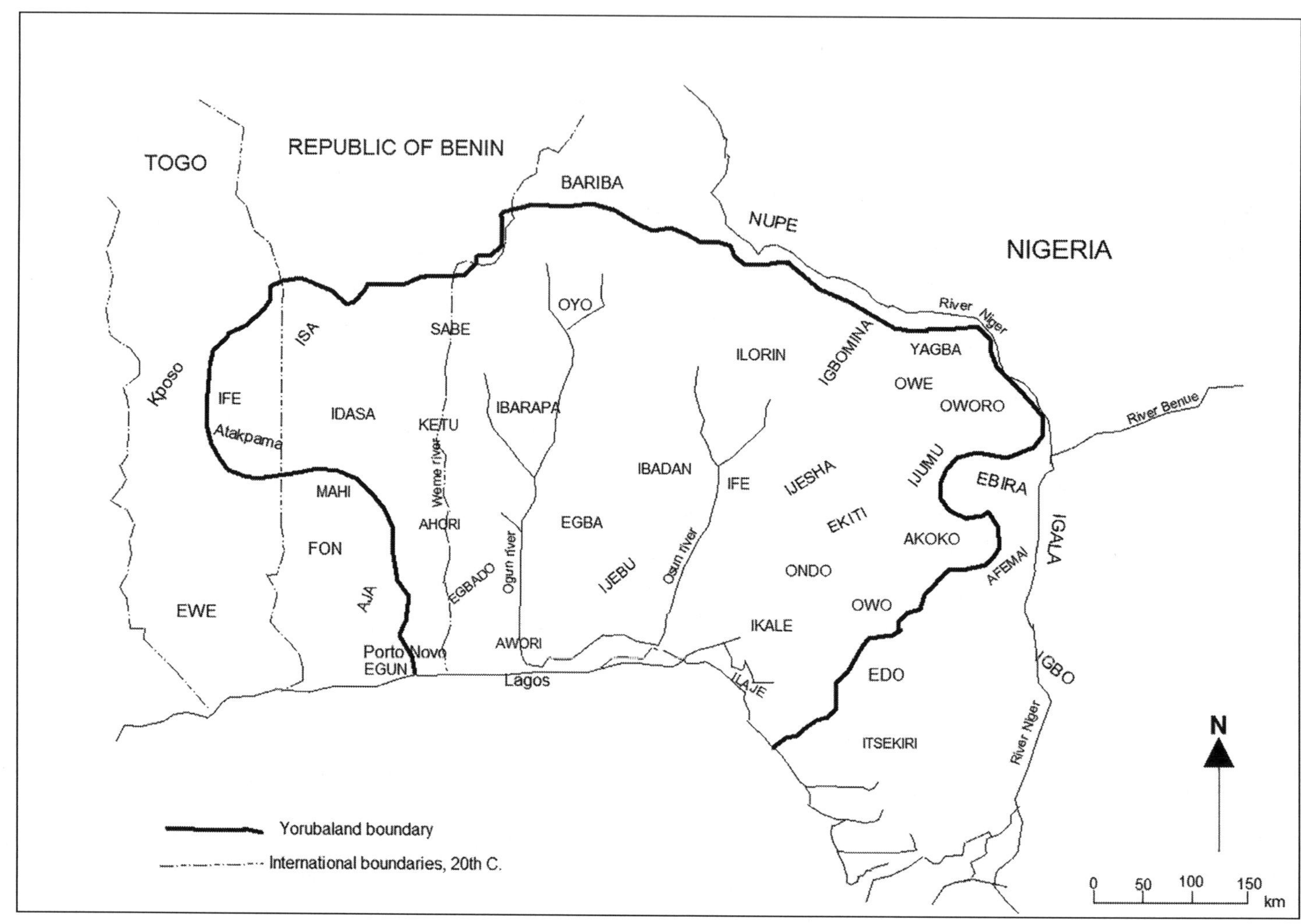

Map 8. Yorùbá and Their Neighbors

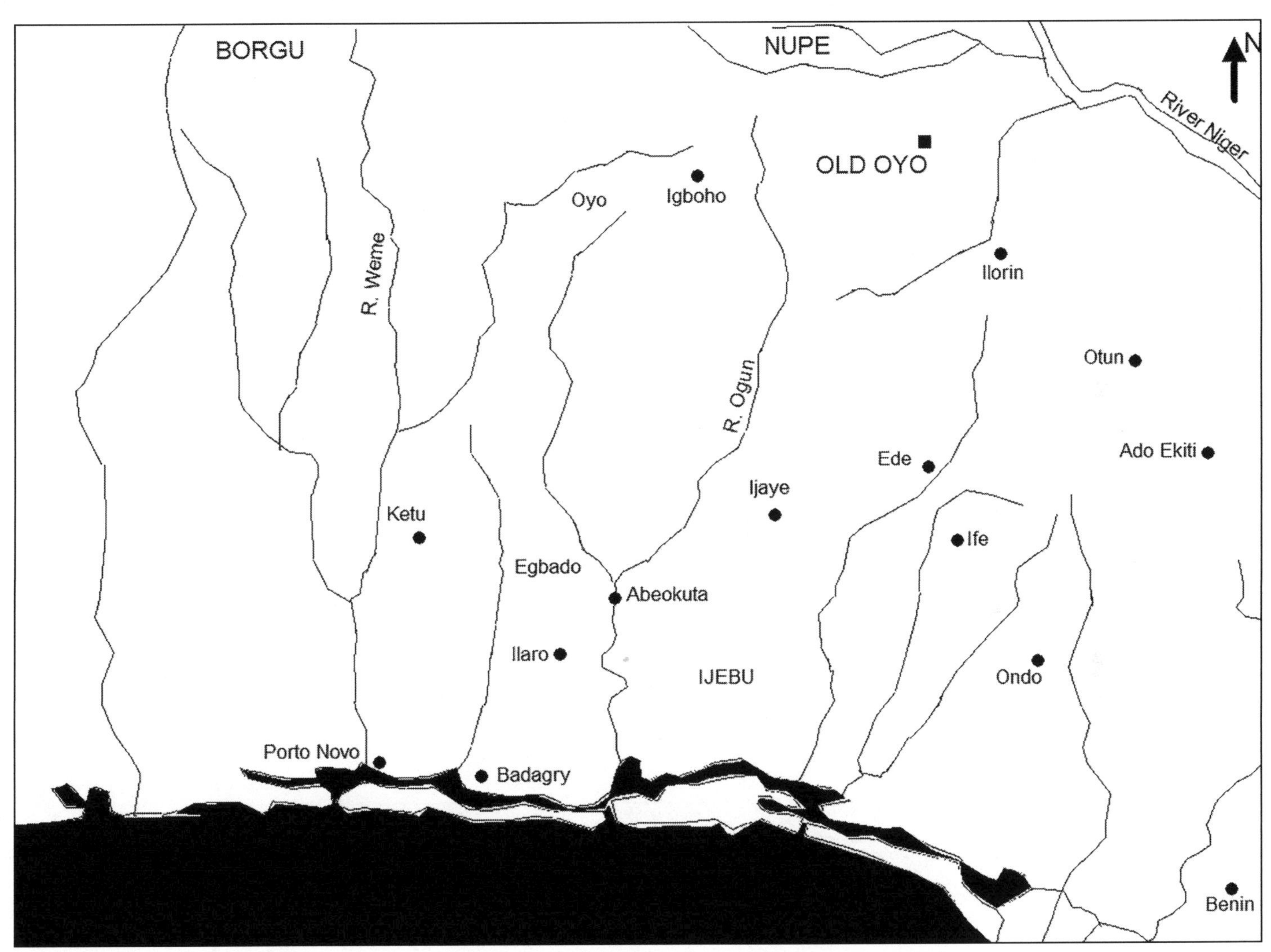

Map 9. The Yorùbá and Nupe Neighbors

Yoruba Wars of the Ninetheenth Century

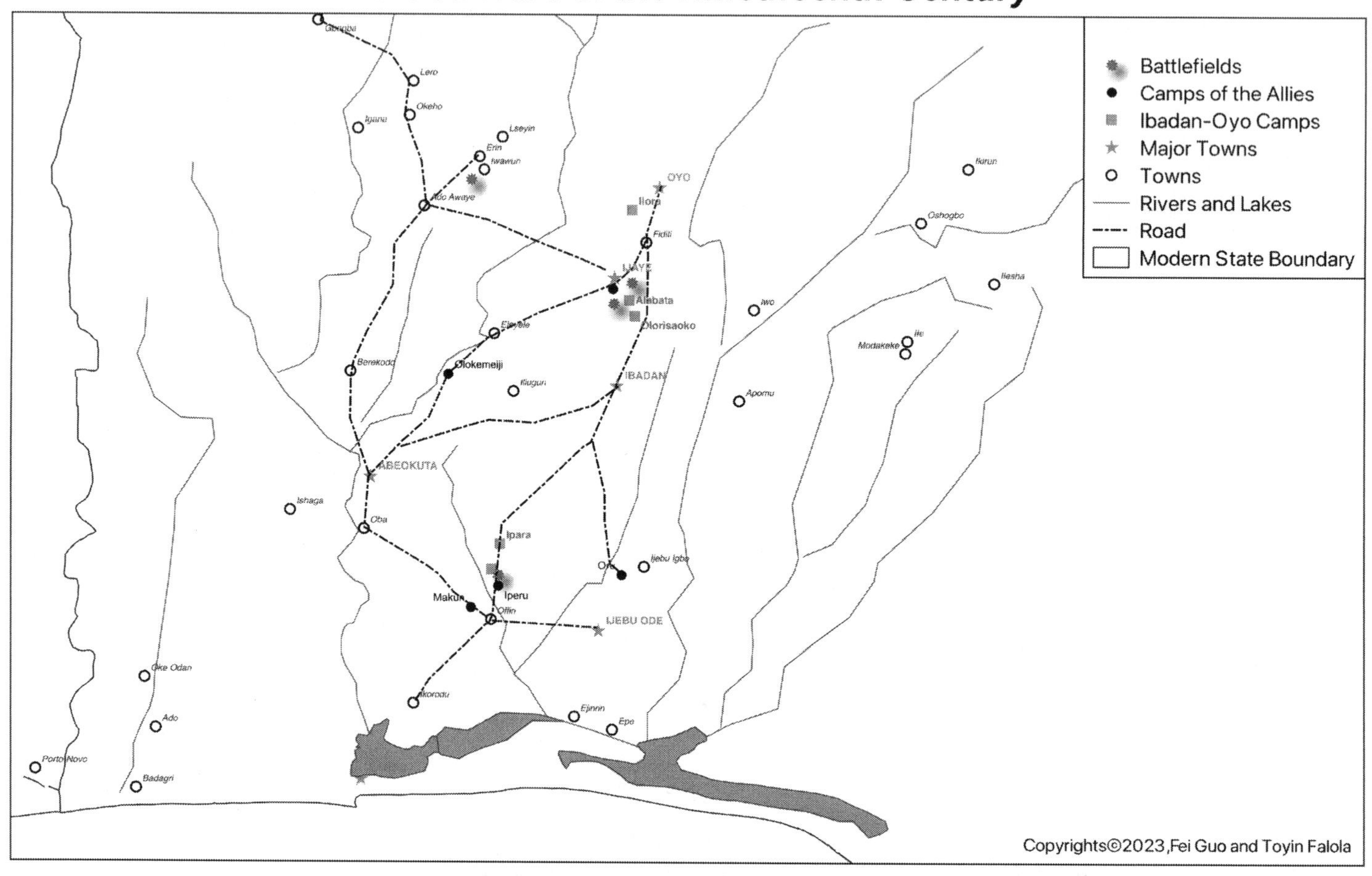

Map 10. Yorùbá Wars of the Nineteenth Century

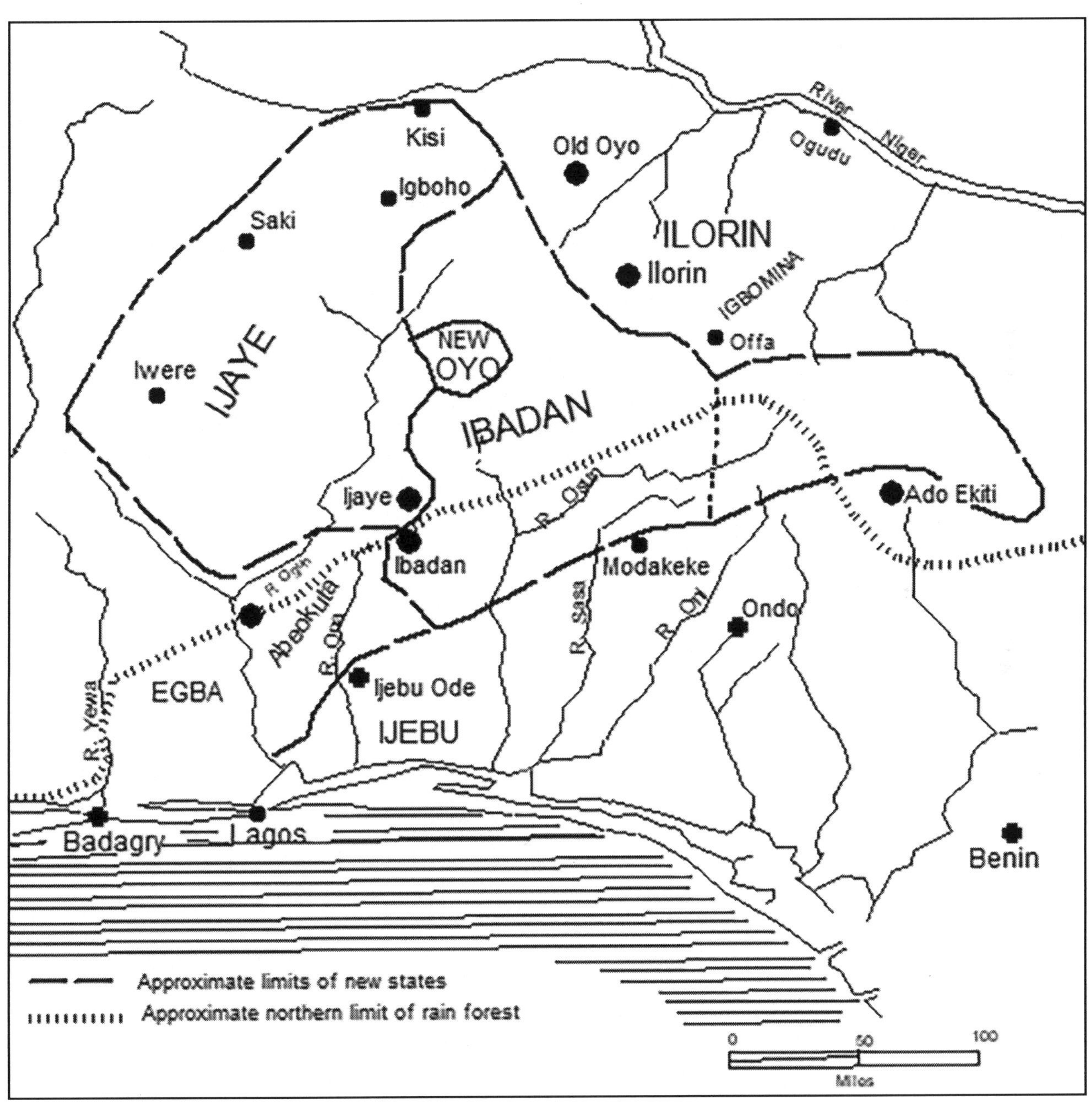

Map 11. New Yorùbá States in the Nineteenth Century

Yoruba Sub-Groups in the 19th Century

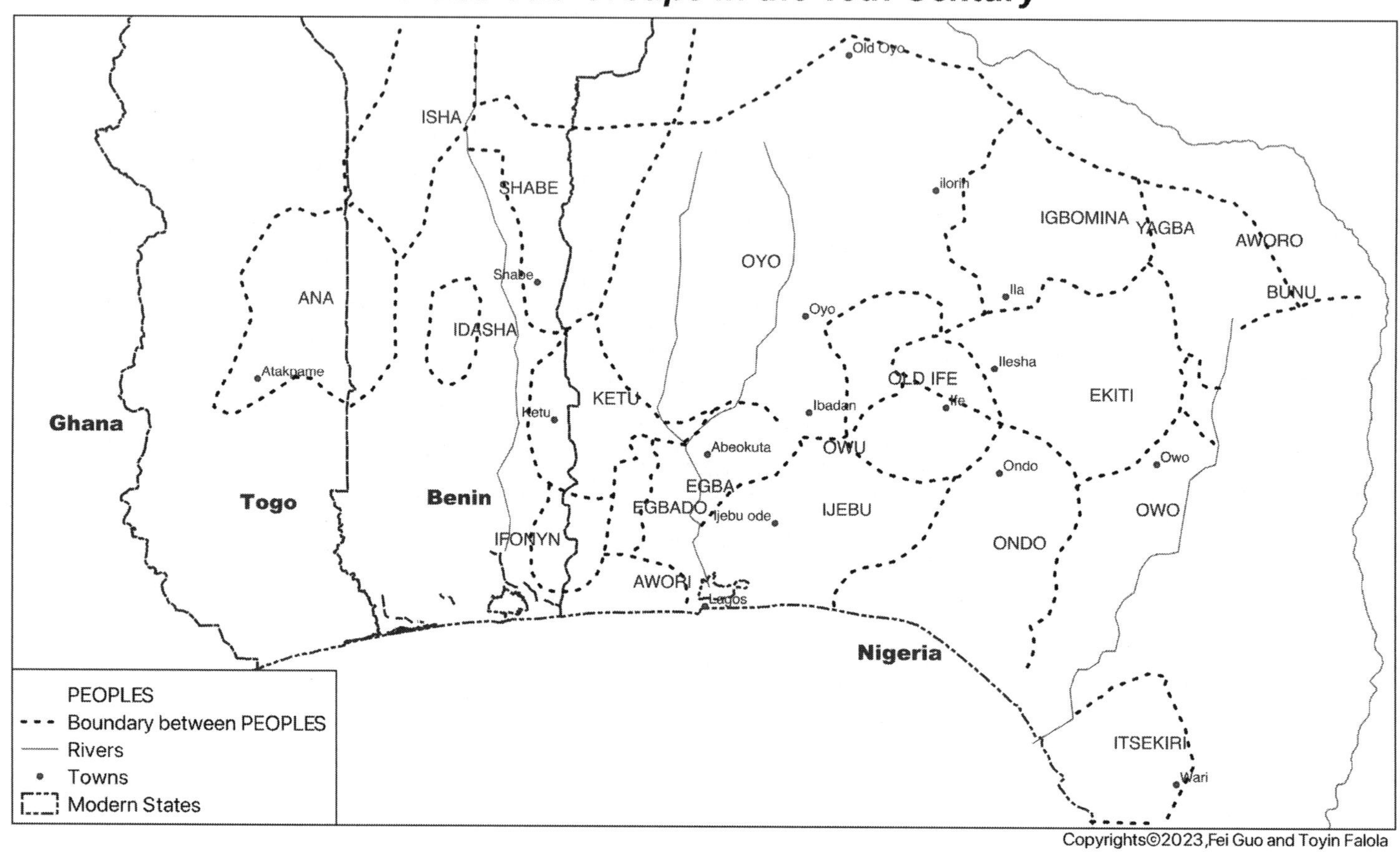

Map 12. Yorùbá Subgroups in the Nineteenth Century

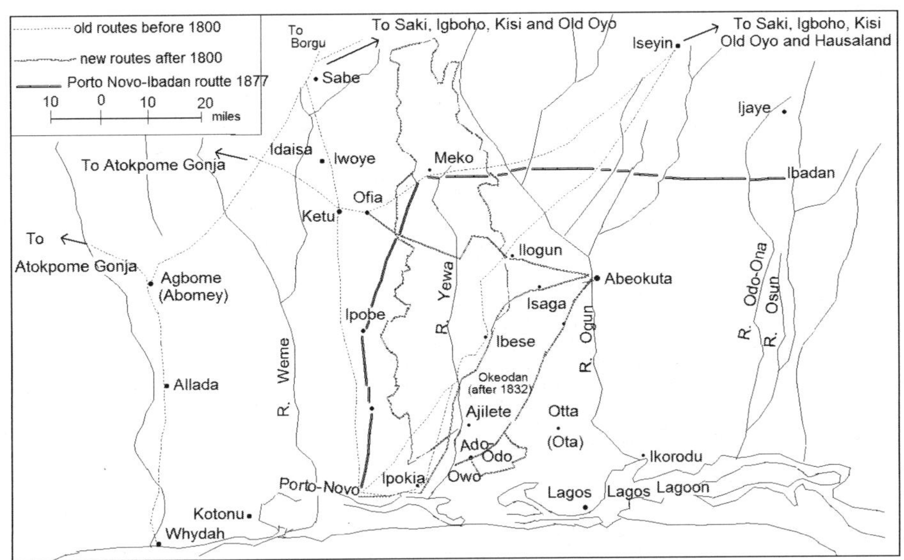

Map 13. Some Trade Routes from the Interior to the Coast

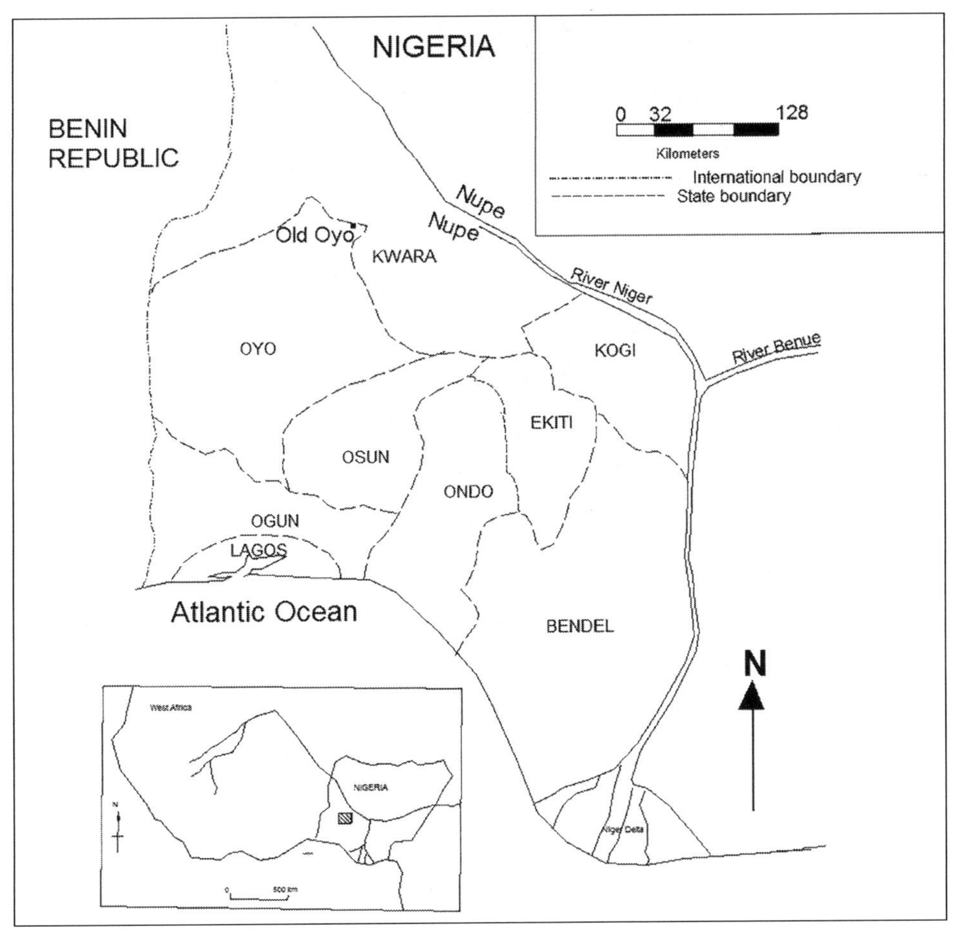

Map 14. The Yorùbá in Postcolonial Nigeria

Figure 0.1. The contemporary remaking of Ifẹ̀ Bronze Head, twelfth to fifteenth century. The bronze head is an iconic Yorùbá image, displaying the achievements of centuries ago. The remaking, an idea analyzed in chapter 18, shows the continuity in creativity and a continuous adaptation to changing ages. From the Toyin Falola Private Collection.

Preface[1]

This book is about the spread and globalization of Yorùbá life, ideas, and culture. It captures the Yorùbá people worldwide and the diversity of their experiences and ways of life in time and space. The reordering of Yorùbá geographic spaces and changing traditions in the wake of the historical moments of the nineteenth century impacted the people across different global spaces. The history of the Yorùbá as an identity and the "nationalization" of this experience is derived from a long process of creating "national" identities from clusters of multiple groups and subgroups. This explains why the agenda and process of converting a people to a cultural identity were consolidated and supervised by returnees from Sierra Leone and Liberia (and later with local elements) who had been exposed and acculturated to the alternative worlds created by slavery and the Atlantic slave trade, Islam, Christianity, education, and the knowledge of using cultural institutions for political mobilization.

Those integrated into the universal space of literacy and Western education successfully deployed the print media to shape the narrative of the Yorùbá as a nation. The same media used to write about the Yorùbá people was adopted by the nineteenth-century elites to create an intellectual domain for Yorùbá practices. Put simply, pages of the same pamphlets, newspapers, magazines, tracts, and other literature of this period, where the cultural industry of the people had been demonized to reinforce the need for colonization, were also used for the emancipation of the people with a success that culminated in the independence of Nigeria in 1960. This study is thus interested in how global cultural practices were adopted in the creation of a Yorùbá community across different places and spaces.

Since Samuel Johnson wrote his classic work on the Yorùbá in the late nineteenth century, more contributions have come to characterize the interest of scholars from various fields in the culture and civilization of the people. These works, without exception, have tremendously built on the efforts and contributions of these pathfinders and vanguards of Yorùbá history and culture. As a collective reference term, Yorùbá describes the Indigenous people of present-day southwest Nigeria and their descendants in West Africa (Republic of Benin, Togo, Ghana, and Ivory Coast) and across the Atlantic, regardless of their geographical location. Arguably, Yorùbá, as a language, language group, identity form, way of life, culture, and philosophical worldview, has been among the most studied by scholars since the advent of the academic study of societies, peoples, and cultures in Africa.

---

1. In line with the *Chicago Manual of Style* (CMS 17.7.53) guidelines for words in other languages, which states that once a term becomes familiar through repeated use, it does not necessitate italics in subsequent instances. Recurrent Yoruba words, such as Ifá and Òrìṣà, are italicized upon their initial appearance in a chapter and are not italicized thereafter.

The topics and themes in this book have been chosen to capture those areas considered key to understanding the Yorùbá in their global dimension, the progression of these thoughts, and ideas that have sustained it over time. The two dominant issues are what the Yorùbá receive from the outside world (as in the case of Islam and Christianity) and what they contribute to the world beyond them (as in the Òrìṣà in the Americas, Aládúrà/Pentecostal churches in Britain and the United States, and even Islam in the United Kingdom) through the auspices of Yorùbá organizations such as the Nasrul-Lahi-l-Fatih Society of Nigeria (NASFAT).

Despite all the attention to Yorùbá studies, none of the extant texts on the Yorùbá people covers the wide range and varieties of topics, themes, events, and paradigms of discussion that inform this book in its idea around Yorùbá globalism. This book does not claim to cover all aspects of the Yorùbá civilization, culture, and traditions, given their magnitude and many contours to navigate this process. However, in its twenty chapters divided into three sections, the book covers a substantial ground in this vast field of intellectual inquiry on movements and migrations of the Yorùbá people and their global implications within and outside their original home.

The question of origins, which will continue to bother archaeologists, historians, and scholars in related fields working on Yorùbá history and culture, opens the ground for discussion in the book, while colonial and contemporary themes that gave form to the notion of global Yorùbá are spread through the rest of the book. By so doing, the study adopts the Akan idea of *Sankofa*—that is, viewing and understanding the present from the past to delineate the key factors in the making of a global Yorùbá community and how this community has been projected over time and in different forms through diverse, unique ways of life.

Furthermore, the study follows the spread of the Yorùbá, particularly as an ideology—that is, as a worldview—across the Atlantic and other places often referred to as diaspora locations. This is a long period of history dotted with many events and consequences that shaped the form of a transnational Yorùbá community discussed in this book. From the mythical stories of origins on which consensus on Yorùbá identity and nation first emerged among the educated elites and missionaries of the nineteenth century to the fundamentals of Yorùbá lifeworld and meaning and other paradigms of knowledge that come straight down to the adaptability of the culture to the evolving world, the book gathers what could be called a dossier of approximately ten centuries of events that mirror the experiences of the people.

Over time, this experience has been shaped alongside their close and distant neighbors—the Borgu, Benin, Nupe, Dahomey, Hausa states, Ilorin, and the Mali and Songhai Empires. The Yorùbá people have been largely influenced by cultures outside the African enclave. Entering through the Maghreb as early as the seventh century AD, Islam had begun to make its indelible mark on African states and cultures. Through the Hausa states of Kano, Borno, and Katsina, and other places close to such powers as Mali along the trans-Saharan trade routes, this influence gradually spread to the Niger River plains, transforming the cultural practices of people in this region together with their political morphology.

Through the formidable Yorùbá imperial power, the Old Oyo Empire, Yorùbá civilization spread across a wider region. Oyo's history is related to those of Borgu, Nupe, and Islam. Although the exact time and events leading to Oyo's existence remain one of the debates that pervade the study of Yorùbá state formation, it is less debatable that Islam did not gain heavy ground among the Yorùbá people until late into the eighteenth century. The constitutional crisis that engulfed the Oyo Empire then and during the early nineteenth century, with its attendant economic crisis that left the people longing for relative peace, opened a space for the greater penetration of Islam. Owing to the time and way Islamic culture came into Yorubaland, unlike in the case of their neighbors through whom they inculcated this world frame, it never rapidly took a firm hold on the political structure (as in the case of how the jihad established a theocracy) but had a great impact on both tangible and intangible aspects of culture. Islam has a significant impact in such Yorùbá towns as Ede, Ikirun, and Iwo.

The hope of an in-depth inroad of the Islamic culture into the sociopolitical landscape of the people was slowed by the swift and spiral events of the nineteenth century. In its wake was the return of Yorùbá captives taken into slavery in the Americas, joined by Christian missionaries, and it ended with the colonial domination of the country. Besides the act of trading relations and social contact, the spread of Islam in Yorubaland had no grand plan that became more intensified as the century ran into the next when colonization fully took root. The Yorùbá were connected with dominant global forces: the trans-Saharan and transatlantic trades—the routes through which both cultural changes entered Yorubaland and the creation of the global Yorùbá space, bringing with them Western education, Christianity, and Western values, which set the society up for new transformations.

The first secondary school was stationed in the city of Abeokuta in 1908, where many of these returnees had settled, and offered flourishing Christian missionary activities. The Abeokuta Grammar School was built from the communal contributions of the people of the city, demonstrating their readiness to incorporate new ideas into their cultural practices and form. Their open-arms policy to the Christian missionaries, aided by the return of their kinsmen, put them on a pedestal in the emerging modern society that later became Nigeria. The products of Western education led to nationalist agitations and helped organize resistance against British rule in a nonviolent way.

Early on, such practices as *egúngún* (masquerade), the use of cavalry soldiers, the *Ifá* divination system, and the art of ironmaking and sculpture had been incorporated into the practices of the people at various times from cultures that included that of the NOK, Nupe, Borgu, and Ado (Benin). Expectedly, these cultural and technological advancements had been infused into the people's social ambiance, history, and existing cultural practices. Alongside these practices, they evolved conceptual readings that helped sustain their civilization, producing new ideas and reproducing older ones. Here lies the making of such a body of knowledge around Òrìṣà, which constitutes parts of the fundamental scopes through which the Yorùbá world was given its peculiar characterization.

One of these fundamentals was Ifá. As the discussion in the first section of the book shows, the history of Ifá among the people is hard to spell out. However, whatever the origins are, Ifá and other bodies of ideas around *Òrìṣà* grant us access to the pool of Yorùbá epistemic knowledge. The Ifá-Òrìṣà metaphysics provide a compendium to understand Yorùbá philosophy, cosmology, ethics, history, sociology, and much more, and have remained significant to date despite the infiltration of foreign cultural elements into Yorubaland. This book is also grounded in the incorporation of external ideas. The flexibility and adaptability of Yorùbá culture constitute the key reasons for the making of global Yorùbá.

Both within their homeland and in their diaspora spaces, the Yorùbá used these core cultural frames to define and emancipate themselves from the cultural domination of the Arab-Islamic cultural world and the Europeans. It is rather instructive that the same century that sent the Yorùbá into the Atlantic world, with the displacement of hundreds of homes, livelihoods, and polities, saw the transformation of their culture, community, and identity through the same displaced persons serving as agencies. Almost simultaneously, and on both sides of the Atlantic, the Yorùbá were making immense changes to the practices and functionality of the Yorùbá as a community of people, ideas, and philosophy.

As the book indicates, they were incorporating foreign elements into their religion for sustainability, acceptability, and, ultimately, reproduction and were also preoccupied with the task of bringing elements of the core Yorùbá practices that revolved around those tripodal epistemologies—that is, Ifá, Òrìṣà, and Orí. Ifá and Òrìṣà were taking their roots and shape in line with the experience of the people across the Atlantic, as Islam and Christianity were also doing in Yorubaland. Religion and cultural forms became tools for social mobility in West African homes and in the Atlantic spaces. As we enter the contemporary period, cinematography and the Internet in this digital age have been added to the changes, reinforcing the idea of transnational Yorùbá communities in the modern world.

Consequently, the Yorùbá metaphysical outlook manifests in places like Cuba, Brazil, Trinidad and Tobago, the United States of America, Haiti, and other parts of the Americas, while the Yorùbánized Christian form, the Aládúrà movement and, more recently, Pentecostalism, is rapidly gaining a foothold in their homeland. Through these religious beliefs and institutions, core elements of Yorùbá civilization have survived, although in mutational or hybridized settings. The same measure goes into the making and practice of Islam among the people.

Ultimately, the flexibility and adaptability of Yorùbá culture constitute the key reasons for the making of global Yorùbá. The book is grounded in the incorporation of external ideas, substantially contributing to the scholarly interest in understanding the Yorùbá people. It provides grounds for further discussion on the making of the Yorùbá communities and is set to create a new vista of conversation on the Yorùbá in the world.

Acknowledgments

Gratitude to Isola
Whose sources are covered in three calabashes
Hidden insights in the alley of wisdom at Oja'gbó
Unfathomable knowledge located on top of the
Òkè'Bàdàn
The eternal rock
Ìbà!

Salutation to Àwọn Ènìyàn Pàtàkì
Damilola Osunlakin, ọmọ wọn l'Óṣogbo
Luqman, ọkọ ọmọ Óṣogbo
Damilare, ọmọ Bello n'Íjẹbú
Bode Ibironke, Ìjẹṣà pọ́ńbélé
Kaosarat, Iya Mubarak, aya wọn ní Yewa
Oluwafunminiyi Raheem, Iwo odidere
Oritoke Alaba, iya n'Kano

Respect to Àwọn Àgbà Ọ̀jẹ̀
Baba Oladejo Afolayan
Alhaji Bola Dauda
Ọ̀jọ̀gbọ̀n Biodun Ogundayo
Alagba Julius Adekunle, ọmọ Ìgbòho
Mama Sotunsa, ìyàwó 'Jẹbú

GLOBAL YORÙBÁ

Introduction

The Making and Form of Global Yorùbá 1

The term *global Yorùbá* can provide multiple frames of reference. The global development of a Yorùbá identity is an outcome of globalized modernity, and its properties include iterations across spaces and Yorùbá cosmopolitanism as a lived experience. However, the circulation of worlds to and from the Yorùbá homeland must be contextualized to define the global within the framing of Yorùbá identity—culturally, politically, and socially—as well as the Yorùbá in the global practices of the people.

The global Yorùbá idea reveals Yorùbá culture, community, and worldview from the perspective of one who has traveled beyond one's local borders due to slavery, colonization, and more recent migrations driven by decolonization and globalization. This book focuses on the union of those who identify as Yorùbá and who truly have Yorùbá roots. This includes Yorùbá people living in different parts of Nigeria, West Africa, and the Atlantic spaces, who constitute what scholars have described as the "Yorùbá" in the homeland and the diaspora.

The idea of a diaspora population or community remains contentious among scholars,[1] principally based on the question of scope. Should this frame include the Yorùbá people residing in different parts of Nigeria, outside the southwestern geopolitical zone such as Kano or Enugu, and in other West African countries? The term was initially used to contextualize populations forcefully taken to new regions during the transatlantic slave trade. However, the concept has been extended to cover those involved in recent migrations to different parts of the world beyond the Americas.

In all its forms, the notion of diaspora is intrinsically made manifest in the transnationality of cultures, peoples, and ideas.[2] Populations migrated to their diaspora homes and brought local practices, forms, and philosophies, transplanting them into new spaces through different mechanisms that were affected by the extant social milieu of their locations. However, if one chooses to conceptualize the diaspora as a community of people and ideas outside their homelands, the most important point remains the extent to which the organic culture of the people is replicated or reduced.[3] This is the measure of local ideas taken beyond their borders and the forms in which they have survived.

---

1. Bose, "Dilemmas of Diaspora," 58–68; Braziel and Mannur, *Theorizing Diaspora*.
2. Nehl, *Transnational Black Dialogues*, 39–54.
3. Anteby-Yemini and Berthomière, "Diaspora," 262–270.

No part of this premise can be understood without illuminating the conditions that informed these ideas in their homelands and recognizing their replication in diaspora spaces. Migration always manifests new possibilities for hybridity and syncretism. The definitions, content, and spirit of Blackness and Pan-Africanism depend on interactions between multiple people, communities, ideas, and philosophies that can be framed in ethnicities, languages, and religions. Migration enables this dynamism and cannot be avoided—social contact and interactions along these lines are inevitable.

Beyond contact with other Black peoples in the diaspora, global Yorùbá also interacts with, contributes to, and borrows from other groups. The question can be asked: What made the Yorùbá Òrìṣà religious system a workable agency for a global projection of the Yorùbá world and culture in the Americas but not in West Africa? Carefully structured attempts have been made to shed some light on the question.

That the Yorùbá are one of the most researched sociocultural entities in modern Africa is a testament to their global popularity among scholars and communities of cultural enthusiasts. This book provides a myriad of information on why and how this came to be, identifying a momentum that has been richly sustained in a global measure. The trajectory of the Yorùbá people is charted through migration, state formation, political strife, and the rise and fall of powerful states, along with the emergence of new polities and power blocs.[4] Trade and geophysical features played important roles in the development of Yorùbá society,[5] and these events left an indelible footprint on the cultural form of their civilization. On material and spiritual planes, cultural forms have transformed in response to the dictates of emerging social milieus.[6] This book adumbrates how this process shaped the Yorùbá culture, world, and identity across three landscapes: epistemological, ontological, and cosmological. The ethical, historical, and metaphysical "truths" of the Yorùbá people are interrogated in the production of a transnational Yorùbá frame.

Myths and orality worked in tandem among the Yorùbá people; the latter was used to communicate the former and to ensure that it became tradition before the advancement of technology brought new agents for social transformation in Yorubaland.[7] Some of the present day's greatest ideas were communicated and entrenched in human consciousness through language and orality, which demonstrates the efficacy of oral traditions and the inevitability of communication in the evolution, production, and reproduction of human society.

This book covers Yorùbá history, people, tradition, environment, religion, spirituality, cosmology, culture, and philosophy, including the group's relationships with distant and immediate neighbors. It considers their position in the global space of modern history and their progress in advancing civilization through these transnational engagements. The book examines how people have adapted to their environment and tapped it to (re)invent their civilization, shape their culture and traditions, and inform their socioeconomic relations with their neighbors.

---

4. Bascom, *Yoruba of Southwestern Nigeria.*

5. Ogundiran, *Yoruba.*

6. Barber, *Anthropology of Texts.*

7. Agai, "Rethinking Yoruba Culture," 427–450.

These interactions have guided the Yorùbá philosophy that developed over time, expressing their conviction regarding society's evolution and the place humans occupy within it.

The Yorùbá people have mastered the science and technology of cultural production through the continual mutation and transplantation of foreign cultural elements, not only within but also outside their West African homes, including the Atlantic space, where they constitute an impressive community. They have borrowed elements from immediate and distant neighbors of their primordial space as well as components from those in the East (Arabs) and the West (Europeans and Americans). Yorùbá histories were shaped partly through trading relations and social contacts with the Nupe, Borgu, and Hausa states in West Africa, as well as Western imperial states like the United Kingdom, France, Netherlands, and the United States.[8] These external people and cultures brought their religion, art, and science, which have been successfully incorporated into the Yorùbá cultural system and territoriality.[9] Similarly, the Yorùbá are no strangers to the artful preservation of intellectual productions.[10] This book reiterates the consensus among scholars who have studied Yorùbá cultural and intellectual artifacts, narrating the modern development of a Yorùbá political unit in the face of necessity.[11] The book's first section attests to the historical exactitudes that created this political exigency.[12] This discussion is reinforced by the ready-made myths and traditions common to dozens of subcultural/dialect groups within the Yorùbá nation.

The first chapter considers mythical narratives that establish the Yorùbá people's origin, not because these narratives contentiously claim different sides of history but because historical facts may be located within regional backgrounds and knowledge systems. It is more concerned with the underlying messages embedded in these myths and traditions, which can be validated by archaeology and the sacred beliefs with relevant information.[13] Careful examination can establish core pillars entwined in stories that unify the Yorùbá as a nation, community of people, and body of ideas that reveal deeper regional and transnational connections.

This first part of the book highlights Ọbàtálá and Odùduwà, two prominent figures regarded as the progenitors of the Yorùbá race.[14] They represent two important eras in the people's history—the so-called golden age and the period leading up to it. Ideas from this golden age and the pregolden era can be linked to contemporary debates, contextualized in ideas like the Internet of Things, globalization, and Nollywood. To create the nation of Yorùbá people and its community of ideas, myths, and traditions were woven together as abridged syntheses of golden and pregolden eras populated with mythical characters, legends, and historical figures. In the case of Ọbàtálá, a connection was made between an unseen heaven and the visible world, which is treated as a form of cosmic globalism. For Odùduwà, mythologies that connect the

---

8. Ogundiran, "Of Small Things Remembered."

9. Jimada, *Historical Background*; Akinwunmi, "Oral Traditions," 49–73; Sundkler and Steed, *History of the Church in Africa*.

10. Adeeko, *Arts of Being Yorùbá*; Osunlakin, "Rethinking Cultural Diversity," 53–57.

11. Ogundiran and Ige, "'Our Ancestors Were Material Scientists,'" 751–772.

12. Peel, "Cultural Work of Yoruba Ethnogenesis," 67–89; Apter, *Oduduwa's Chain*.

13. Rosenberg, *World Mythology*.

14. Lawuyi, "Obatala Factor in Yoruba History," 369–375; Akinjogbin, "Growth of Ife," 51–61.

Yorùbá with the distant world in migrations represent the understanding of geographic spaces and a clear case of extensive interregional connections.

Between the twelfth century and today, major local, regional, and global events calibrated the transformation of the Yorùbá landscape as a philosophy, a community of people, territoriality, and identity.[15] Within this period, particularly the late eighteenth and early nineteenth centuries, the various connotations and manifestations of "Yorùbá" transitioned from a localized/regional functionality and entity to a global one.[16] The people and their ideas joined the global pool of social connections and intellectual discourse even as their primordial home was structurally infused into the global economy.[17]

This process was kick-started by successful efforts at using the mythical stories of Odùduwà to unify dozens of extant polities in the area later known as Ile-Ife.[18] The centralization of polities, otherwise known as the creation of nations, is a monumental period in the evolution of human society; it acted as a catalyst for developing new social orders.[19] In unifying the existing structures of diverse polities under a central political canopy, Odùduwà accomplished what other historical legends had created at different times and in different spaces. This culture surfaced centuries ago in a fashion similar to King Narmer's unification of Lower and Upper Egypt, making it a significant milestone for the Yorùbá civilization's political advancement.[20]

The expansion of the kingdom of Kush and its merger with Egypt, forming the Ethiopian–Egyptian polity/empire, was a similar political development. The Egyptian polity, situated at the center of great civilizations, epitomized the contours of such transformational forces.[21] In a similar pattern, Odùduwà created the "golden era" that lifted proto-Yorùbá people and communities above their autochthonous formation to bring cultural advancement.[22] Odùduwà did exactly what Narmer (an ancient Egyptian pharaoh who is regarded as the founder of the First Dynasty and the unifier of Egypt) and others did, unifying sovereign political entities to become the component units of a central government, which supports the view that the evolution of human societies differs only in their use of technology.[23] The dominant religious institutions of existing policies were consolidated into a central body attached to the royal cult. In Egypt's unification period, this created the single supreme entity named Amen-Ra—borrowed from Amen and Ra, gods of Lower and Upper Egypt—and a similar transformation brought Ọbàtálá into the royal cult of Ife. Whether as mythologies or actual historical experiences, they are products of intellectual imaginations drawing on ideas from diverse sources.

---

15. Akintoye, *History of the Yoruba People*.

16. Ogundiran, *Yoruba*; Akinjogbin, *Cradle of a Race*, 51–61.

17. Structurally, because long before the eighteenth and nineteenth centuries, Yorùbá people engaged in different relations outside of their homeland, West Africa, and even Africa. Aside from trading and social contacts with the Arabs, their relationship with Europe had been initiated at least three centuries before this was concretized in a structure evoked by their colonial experience. Hopkins, *Economic History of West Africa*.

18. Akinjogbin, *Cradle of a Race*; Biobaku, *Sources of Yoruba History*.

19. Atanda, *Introduction to Yoruba History*.

20. Diop, *African Origin of Civilization*.

21. Diop, *Precolonial Black Africa*.

22. Ojuade, "Issue of 'Oduduwa' in Yoruba Genesis," 139–158.

23. Ibidapo-Obe, "Battle of Three Ancestors," 33.

The first section of this book notes that this evolution fanned the embers of confusion and obscured clear historical pictures of Odùduwà and Ọbàtálá. Were they a single historical figure? Are they mythical or historical beings? Did they live at the same time? Beyond etymology, to what do the names relate? Many other questions have inspired the discussions within the body of this text. The dominant story explains that Odùduwà and a host of others migrated from somewhere around the Mediterranean. They usurped political power from existing leadership within Igbòmokùn communities (in present-day Ilé-Ife, southwestern Nigeria) that had been under the ministerial guidance of Ọbàtálá.[24] Like many other societies, the Yorùbá respect their ancestors, and similar narratives have been encoded in common creation myths. Here, mythologies are treated not as facts but as epistemology—a way to understand the world at a particular moment in history.

Chapter 1 validates the relevance of myths, without which all the chapters in part 1 of this book cannot stand. The various myths show how the Yorùbá perceived a transformational stage in their history—as if it were the beginning of the world. Some contested conclusions have linked these stories with events in the Mediterranean, especially during the seventh-century Islamic revolution. The composition of the Egyptian polity was altered by a liberal migration and settlement regime, and flourishing societies combined with influential geophysical fixtures, leading to the mythologies of migration of ancestors that laid the foundations of Yorùbá culture in all its different connotations. In this globalizing mythical narrative, Odùduwà is seen as a descendant of these migrants, leaving Egypt to settle on the banks of the Niger River, west of Egypt.[25] By creating polities with the pedigrees of gods, unification was achieved through the instrumentality of cults that turned religion into a device for forging loyalty and legitimizing the leadership's mandate; at that point, a ruler was claimed to be divine.[26] A divine kingship built on this careful frame can develop into a stable, prosperous hegemonic polity.

Information from this period is sourced from myths and legends among the Yorùbá—creation myths as mnemonic vehicles for historical evolutionary moments is a common practice among cultures, dating back to prehistoric times. The Yorùbá used this medium to preserve their historical past, demonstrating their innate ability to tap into this universal pool of knowledge largely responsible for the formation and advancement of human society.[27] These myths, which display the fundamental characteristics of world myths, consist of legends, metaphors, personifications, and other literary devices that enhance their presentation and highlight the attention that has gone into their preservation.[28]

Common elements of heaven and earth appear in creation stories from ancient civilizations all along the Mediterranean in Yorùbá myth.[29] The world's creation is attributed to a fundamental mission organized by a supreme being who delegates power and responsibility to individual

---

24. Beier, "Before Odùduwà," 25–32; Akinjogbin, *Cradle of a Race*.

25. Agai, "Investigation into the Ancient Egyptian Cultural Influences," 9.

26. Ojo, "'Heepa' (Hail) Òrìṣà," 30–59; Dianteill, "Deterritorialization and Reterritorialization," 121–137.

27. This will be another fundamental area in which the fallacy of Eurocentric writers like Hegel is readily faulted regarding African civilization.

28. Barber, *Anthropology of Texts*.

29. Beier, *Yoruba Myths*.

ministers (seen as gods). These stories reflect ancient Egyptian cosmology, describing the formation of human society with the phrase "As above, so below." Every aspect of ancient Egyptian civilization was built on this guiding principle. Subsequent civilizations and cultures adopted this system to organize their polities.[30] In cultures based on this idea and in Yorùbá mythologies, the gods are regularly discussed in the sociological frame of human beings and human societies. Their quest to organize human society ultimately provides historical context for human actions and their consequences—the world is perceived as an unchanging cycle of events. Religious tenets, political systems, educational models, social formations, ethical frameworks, and other structures are drawn from these circuits, which were both regional and global.

In the context of the Yorùbá people, creation stories are seen as ways in which people have mythologized their history's golden era, which began with the coming of Odùduwà. Stories of Osiris, Seth, and Isis were told with the same spirit in ancient Egypt, and adaptations have occurred with different characters in Roman and Hebrew myths.[31] Such myths have been used to explain the genesis of evil and envy among humans and the effects and consequences of nurturing such behavior. Another story circulating in cultures and civilizations worldwide describes the end of the first human civilization brought about by water.[32]

In cultures such as the Dogon of Mali in Africa and the Mayans in Latin America, the earthly world of humans is regularly visited by extraterrestrials whose arrival heralds a momentous leap into an epoch marked by advances in technology, governance, economics, nutrition, art, science, spirituality, and other components of civilization. In many respects, these stories enshrine the religious, social, and political character of the civilizations that tell them. Odùduwà, Ọbàtálá, and similar figures should be located within these global dynamics of myth creation and historical reproduction. In place of reading these myths literally, their essence should be examined through a deeper interpretation of the history they recount. Among the Yorùbá, these myths can be understood as the religious text of their global community. The *Ifá* corpus, the Yorùbá nation's holy book, is rife with stories that can provide clearer interpretations of popular myths and traditions.[33]

The Yorùbá gods that traveled to diaspora locations with their adherents brought stories shaped by these myths and legends. Symbols and other religious motifs were transplanted to new homes in the diaspora.[34] Odùduwà, Ọbàtálá, Ògún, Ọṣun, Yemọja, Ọya, and other Yorùbá deities and historical figures became globalized in this process, and their contributions to civilization have been used to forge new Yorùbá communities. The same has happened with the Ifá corpus, along with all the characters, towns, ideas, and the full body of epistemology that created this text, giving it meaning and form.

The Yorùbá worldview is encapsulated in the tripod epistemologies of *Orí*, Ifá, and *Òrìṣà*, which are explored in this book to understand their role in the global space. Ifá is equated to

---

30. Ibidapo-Obe, "Battle of Three Ancestors."

31. Saakana, *African Origins.*

32. Zielinski, "Ten Ancient Stories."

33. Bascom, *Ifa Divination.*

34. Bascom, *Sixteen Cowries.*

the spirit of wisdom that was with the Supreme Being during the creation of the world in the Judeo-Christian tradition.[35] Orí has parallels with the notion of predetermination. The idea of Orí is central to the art and practices of the Yorùbá people—it is a cultural and philosophical system resembling the idea of monism, a belief that all forms of existence and phenomenon can be reduced to one principle.[36] The production of Yorùbá Òrìṣà has followed the process that permeates ancient civilizations around the world.

Òrìṣà went global: it enabled the syncretic practices of the Yorùbá community in Cuba and Brazil, where Yorùbá gods were substituted for Catholic saints.[37] In different traditions and under different circumstances, Òrìṣà figures have been canonized at various times in ideological and cultural enclaves. While many traditions discuss mythical beings and entities from the extraphysical world, precolonial Yorùbá civilization developed under a system of divine kingship. Odùduwà and Ọ̀rànmíyàn (the founder of Oyo) came to be seen as embodiments of these ideas. Both figures established and nurtured this governance model throughout Yorubaland and Benin. These transitions brought social stratification, state formation, political morphology, epistemologies, mythologies, pedagogy, art, and science. They also contributed to the general making and deterritorialization of Yorùbá history.

The structure of Yorubaland's indigenous governance system deserves careful consideration, belonging to a set of topics that includes the formation of new polities, their religious institutions and belief systems, the fall of Ife hegemony and the rise of Oyo, and the making of a transnational Yorùbá community. In all these histories, liberal economic and migration policies played a vital role among the Yorùbá, propelling the changes and transformations that took place in each period.[38] The Ijebu were exceptionally outgoing, but most Yorùbá polities never fully pursued isolationism—they were in perpetual contact with regional and global states, maintaining relations and treaties with multiple state and nonstate actors.[39]

The full extent of Yorùbá history to be uncovered depends on the depth of available sources,[40] and little is known about the hegemonic days of Ife, aside from suppositions regarding its contact and relations with the Nok culture in present North Central Nigeria.[41] Most knowledge of Yorùbá cultural contacts and impact is derived from the years of Oyo's ascendancy. The Old Oyo Empire was a powerhouse of Yorùbá cultural production and perseveration, and its heritage characterized most relations until the late nineteenth century, when the British government, controlling the so-called Lagos protectorate, was encouraged to intervene in Yorùbá politics.[42] As the largest polity in Yorùbá country—until the 1830s, when it was reduced to shadows of its former self—Old Oyo behaved as if it was the central authority for external

---

35. Eason, *Ifá*.

36. Balogun, "Concepts of Orí," 116–130.

37. Vega, *Altar of My Soul*.

38. Smith, *Warfare & Diplomacy*.

39. Adeoti and Adeyeri, "War and Peace in Eastern Yorubaland," 1–7; Sofela, *Egba-Ijebu Relations*; Biobaku, *Egba and Their Neighbours*.

40. Falola and Genova, *Orisa*.

41. Obayemi, "Between NOK, Ile-Ife and Benin," 82–100.

42. Law, "West African Cavalry State," 1–15.

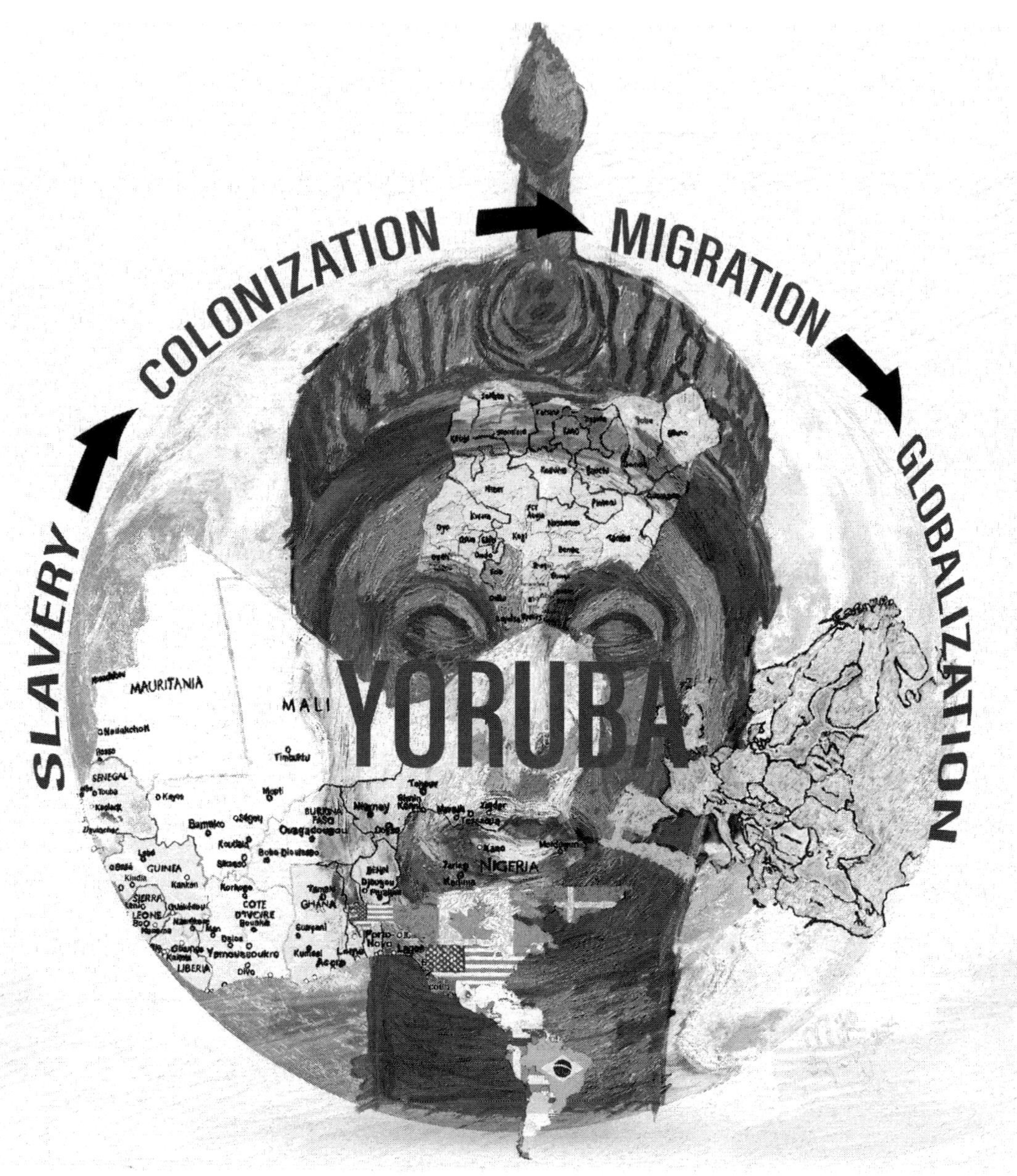

Figure 1.1. The Yorùbá in global networks takes its course based on four phases—slavery, colonization, migration, and globalization. These four phases can be viewed from the period when contact was established with European slave raiders and, subsequently, the invasion and forceful subjugation of the people, creating migration streams worldwide. Sculpture by Michael Efionayi.

contact and activities that could be described as foreign relations. Imperial narratives tend to subdue those of others, as it was clear that the Àwórì and coastal communities were connected to the Atlantic system.

The transition of power from Ife to Oyo can be read as the global dynamics of state formation, where a mother polity or major civilization dissolved after transplanting innovations and ideas into new territories, often creating subsidiary cultures.[43] This phenomenon, which is encapsulated in a Yorùbá saying (*bí ógẹ́dẹ́ kú, á fi ọmọ ẹ̀ rọ́pò*) about a new banana plant replacing the dying tree that birthed it, speaks to the transformation of existence from human to human or nonhuman entities. In Europe, ideas and civilization are believed to have originated with the Greek civilization and the Roman Empire. As Anta Diop, Senegalese historian and anthropologist, argued, these advancements emerged within the ancient Egyptian civilization and were brought to Greece, Babylon, Syria, Meroe, and other early African civilizations. In Africa, Europe, and the Middle East, the cultural circulation that produced the earliest iterations of human civilization was reproduced in various geographic spaces. In Greece and the Roman Empire, for instance, political concerns applied to the production and reproduction of history circulated well, as seen in the impact of Ife traditions in West Africa. By the time the last great Egyptian civilization succumbed to external aggression, falling to Islamic forces in the seventh century, its ideas and some aspects of its civilization were replanted in many different political spaces, where they adapted to their new environments and social milieus.

In the early part of the nineteenth century, the collapse of the Old Oyo Empire led to a flood of migrants. This was like the fall of the ancient Egyptian civilization, although the Egyptian people were spread across lands beyond North Africa and reached some areas still unknown. Former citizens of Oyo remained within Yorùbá territory, where they scattered among their kinsmen. Geography and the contextual causes for each polity's collapse played a key role in the distribution of people and global knowledge systems.

Both civilizations (Egypt and Oyo) suffered from similar afflictions, including a weakened central authority and Islamic jihadists who exploited their weaknesses. The collapse of empires, kingdoms, and civilizations tends to follow this subjective pattern—dwindling political exactitude and threats from external actors (usually longtime rivals) ready to take advantage of the situation. Although Ife might be one of the few exceptions, this is related to its location; it was the only advanced civilization in the region until about the fifteenth century and the rise of Benin, Ilésà, and Oyo. The recession of Ife's hegemony would have involved external forces ready to dismantle its political power if larger polities existed nearby. However, Ife hegemony was built on intellectual fecundity instead of military prowess. This endeared it to its subsidiary cultures, and they had no cause for aggression until late in the nineteenth century. At that time, the country's cultural history began to be rewritten through the instrumentality of war.[44] The wars related to the Atlantic economies that received slaves in exchange for guns and gunpowder, as well as other commodities and ideas.

Yorùbá civilizations created a palace system, divine kingship, and transformational art forms that involved sculpturing, carving, orality, and performance. All the polities formed by the "seven principal descendants" of Odùduwà replicated these developments. Of all these polities and their subsidiaries, Oyo transcended its origins to become an empire and evolved a kingdom structure. By the time the Ife hegemony declined around the fifteenth century, Old Oyo had begun consolidating its influence along the Niger River.[45] A strong singular empire

---

43. Denton, *Fall of Empires*.

44. As Ajayi and Smith (*Yoruba Warfare*, 9) put it, "War was the progenitor and accelerator of change."

45. Law, *Oyo Empire*.

emerged in Yorùbá territory, headquartered in the capitals of Old Oyo. The Oyo Empire became the bastion of Yorùbá civilization, and its founder, Ọ̀rànmíyàn, was recognized as its apostolic forerunner. In the eighteenth century, at the height of its political grandeur, Old Oyo covered an area roughly the size of Nigeria's current southwestern geopolitical zone.[46] At forty-five thousand square kilometers, the empire's size exceeded that of modern European nation-states such as Switzerland, Turkey, Denmark, the Netherlands, and Bosnia.

The loosening political grip of Ife had granted political autonomy to polities like Benin, and Yorùbá cities and kingdoms proliferated in subsequent years. Turmoil in the nineteenth century brought the decline and fall of Old Oyo, which led to the emergence of new polities and experimental governments in Yorubaland.[47] More importantly, participation in the slave trade enabled the creation of global Yorùbá communities in Europe and the Americas.[48] The history of the Yorùbá from the fifteenth century focuses on the Old Oyo polity, which justified the adoption of an Oyo identity when describing the peoples and cultures within the entire region. This continued even into the late nineteenth century when Oyo's power had waned. Oyo created the Pan-Yorubana with cultural varieties that reached the Gambia in the North Atlantic.

The rise and fall of states in Yorubaland were entangled with global and regional histories—the fall of Ife hegemony cannot be disconnected from the climactic changes of the period that equally destroyed the Mali Empire. The rise of Old Oyo cannot be discussed without understanding how the region's geophysical fixtures shaped political development. Geography was a key factor in the establishment of Oyo and its ongoing development, and it was essential for state formation at every level. While Ife's political relevance was in decline, Oyo's was on the rise, which follows common global trends for the early formation of states: the demise of an old polity paves the way to new ones.[49]

Oyo grew in military prowess, becoming a major power in politics and the West African slave trade by the close of the seventeenth century.[50] In the following century, at the height of its power, Oyo's influence extended as far as present-day Ghana, Togo, and the Benin Republic, collecting taxes and levies. Representatives of the Aláàfin, supreme leader of the Oyo, were stationed in these remote locations to act as eyes for the king.[51] These representatives reflected a regional way of thinking: some were citizens, some were slaves, some were Yorùbá, and many were drawn from the Hausa population under the Aláàfin's control. They visited the capital at least once a year, reporting on their stewardship for the Aláàfin. The strength of Oyo's strong army relied on its cavalry prowess, and many lands and political formations in and around Yorubaland were utterly routed. After Oyo's decline and eventual collapse in the first half of the nineteenth century, the entire Yorùbá nation was left in turmoil; its political hegemony had

---

46. Johnson, *History of the Yorubas*.

47. Atanda, *New Oyo Empire*.

48. Falola and Childs, *Yoruba Diaspora in the Atlantic World*.

49. Burrow, *History of Histories*; Yandaki, *State in Africa*.

50. Morton-Williams, "Oyo and the Atlantic Trade," 25–45.

51. Johnson, *History of the Yorubas*, 198–210.

   GLOBAL YORÙBÁ

ensured relative peace and reduced political maneuvering.[52] The history of Yorubaland and its people is incomplete without a careful study of this evolution.

The establishment and evolution of the Old Oyo polity include many unresolved issues, such as the influence of northern neighbors—notably Borgu[53] and Nupe[54]—on its formation and institutions. Although many studies have been conducted on these topics, their limitations have failed to bring absolute clarity to the subject. This book does not pretend to have all the answers, but it takes discussions further and offers clarifications from new interpretations linked to a core theory: all were part of an extensive regional and global network.

Oral traditions of the empire seem to challenge popular beliefs about the establishment of the Ifá in Yorubaland.[55] Ifá is a popular geomantic system of divination among many African cultures, although it is known by different names and involves varied procedures. The system that the Yorùbá call Ifá is referred to as Afá among the Ewe of Togo and Fá in Dahomey. Yorùbá communities in Cuba and Brazil have retained the Ifá signature in their diaspora homes.[56] Different variations are also found among the tools and objects used to prepare this cosmic luminary system. They have been built in different patterns using similar objects, and one such tool is the divination chain. The Yorùbá refer to the chain as Ọ̀pẹ́lẹ̀, the Jukun call it Noko, and it is known as Eba in Nupe. Similar systems are found among the Kamuku and Gbari (Gwari) of northern Nigeria and among cultures and societies in the southeastern corner of Côte d'Ivoire and the coast of Ghana.[57] Mediterranean civilizations, including the Egyptians, the Phoenicians, and the Assyrians, were also at the center of this divination system's ubiquitous spread.

The incorporation of Ifá into the royal cult of Oyo, and its emergence as a principal deity for the polity, is said to have been the work of a priest from Adó (Benin, to the east). This followed the people's experience during the reign of Aláàfin Onígbògi, who refused the advice of his mother, an indigene of Ọ̀tà (a location near modern Lagos, close to the Atlantic), during his preparation for office. This story, cloaked in typical metaphoric symbolism, describes the Ifá cult's rejection in Oyo and its acceptance at Adó, leading Oyo to incorporate it into its religious system later.

This narrative, and its implication in a regional and global network of religious practices, is reinforced by the flexibility that cultures use in adapting to the dictates of events and historical developments. It was not the only addition made to the royal cult of Oyo during the period; the *Egúngún* cult from Nupe was brought into the same royal cult system around the same time.[58] The migration pattern of West African cultures suggests that differences in the practice of Ifá divination emerged through centuries of migration and countermigration. The core of the practice has been retained and reproduced in tandem with environmental and historical developments.

---

52. Falola and Oguntomisin, *Military in Nineteenth Century.*

53. Akinwumi, "Oyo-Borgu Military Alliance," 159–170.

54. Jimada, *Nupe and the Origins.*

55. Lijadu, *Orunmila!*

56. Kumari, *Iyanifa Woman of Wisdom.*

57. Bascom, *Ifa Divination,* 3–5.

58. Adebowale, "Significance of Egúngún."

As noted in this book's discussion of epistemologies, parts of the Ifá corpus relate to the environmental conditions of their surroundings. Additional graphemes for the Ifá literary corpus, originating in places like Trinidad and Cuba, incorporate the Atlantic experience of practitioners during the grand ritual sessions of devotees.[59] It is likely that the induction of Ifá into Oyo systems used the same processes that influenced the history and experiences of its people. Additions to the Ifá body of knowledge were not fully integrated when they became entextualized, but they became mythical, allegorical, proverbial, metaphorical, and historical fuses that were given plot in the Yorùbá environment. This suggests that Ifá, like the Egúngún cult, became a dominant metaphysical force in Yorùbá sociology through Old Oyo—not through Ife, as previously assumed. Tradition treats all Yorùbá polities in the ẹbí framework,[60] dotted with instances that portray Ilé-Ife as the cradle of the Yorùbá race and strengthens Old Oyo's claim to Ife heritage but does not disconnect from expanding geographical networks as argued by Robin Law[61] and established connections with Benin (Adó).[62]

Such a development would authenticate claims that the hermeneutic lens offers insights into the evolution of complex cultures, and such claims have been made by scholars, including Andrew Apter and John Peel.[63] These studies contextualize cultural history within its core frame and social milieu, just as this book agrees with the school of thought that "the historian is to observe, contemplate, and enjoy the incredibly glorious richness of the human experience. He is to look for human greatness and creativity everywhere, even in periods that might seem alien and distant from him."[64] Apter and Peel are anthropologists, but their perspective emphasizes the formation of the Yorùbá as a cultural and intellectual entity. Beyond the politics of nationalism that formalized the idea of a Yorùbá entity in physical, abstract, and geographic forms—it was concretized over time—the history of various identities, called "tribes" in Eurocentric literature, that composed the nation have been intensely enmeshed with one another for a long time.

Oyo's participation in the transatlantic slave trade can be traced to an event that is recorded in oral history as the unfortunate disappearance of about eight hundred people bearing gifts dispatched to the king of a Western imperial empire.[65] Their destination was most likely Portugal or the Netherlands. This event dates Oyo's participation in the slave trade to around the 1630s, offering details about the trade's conduct and organization at the time. There is no way to validate this oral history, but its essence—the construction of a global story—can be validated.

Historians such as Kenneth Dike and Saburi Biobaku published their pioneer works on *Trade and Politics in the Niger Delta* and *The Egba and Their Neighbours* in 1955 and 1957, respectively,

---

59. An example of this is Ìrẹtẹ́ Ìká, which was added by the Alasuwada conference in Trinidad, where the plot took hold of their Atlantic experience. Castor, *Spiritual Citizenship*, 156.

60. Ẹbí systems survive among the Yorùbá people as a form of filial or kinship bond. See Shitta-Bey, "Family as Basis of Social Order," 79–89.

61. Law, *Oyo Empire c. 1600–c. 1836*.

62. This position is juxtaposed and given in the first section of the text.

63. Apter, *Oduduwa's Chain*; Peel, "Cultural Work of Yoruba Ethnogenesis."

64. Burckhardt, *Judgments on History and Historians*, xviii.

65. Adewale, "Ijanna Episode in Yoruba History."

drawing attention to the significance of comprehensive study that illuminates neighboring cultures around their areas of research. Such studies have largely been classified as intergroup relations by subsequent scholars looking for ways to unite Nigeria after the civil war (1967–1970). Studying a society through its neighbors can reveal different aspects of cultural borrowing and intellectual sharing that stem from trade relations, political interactions, and social engagements. Collectively, these reveal the nature of a society in terms of its geographical features, neural faculty, societal composition, and socioeconomic morphology. Many cultures and peoples that share boundaries with the Yorùbá people were shaped, to some extent, by imperial conquests of the Old Oyo Empire.

In effect, the Oyo Empire extended to the limits of Yorubaland; it was instrumental in naming places and people with that designation after Ife provided its cultural basis. Most activities involving Yorùbá territory and its neighbors involved relations between Oyo and the people of Nupe, Dahomey, Benin, and others. This occurred on a macro scale and at the micro level, including with relationships between each community in Yorùbá territory, such as the eastern Yorùbá community of Ekiti, along with Benin, its powerful neighbor. The totality of the experience of the Egba with their Dahomey neighbors provides additional nuance to the narrative. As in other cultures, these relationships were characterized by the realities of war, conflict, and cooperation that enabled the exchange of ideas between these cultural groups.[66] Old Oyo's relations with these polities survived on the macro scale due to the magnitude and scope of its interactions, which defied geographical barriers.

Oyo's placement at the center of Yorùbá history is inevitable, especially when one explores the relationship between the Yorùbá and their neighbors. Oyo traders and trading networks dominated economic relations in the West African region until the post-1830 era and the rise of new economic and political power blocs—primarily Abeokuta and Ibadan. During this time, new social formations erupted in places like Lagos and Abeokuta through the effect of American and European antislavery laws. This introduced new actors into the system, eventually strengthening new trading patterns that displaced Old Oyo. By this time, Oyo had become like the metaphorical body of Osiris: broken apart and ideologically reassembled by its survivors at home and in the diaspora space. Much of its population had become scattered among kinsmen on the continent or across the Atlantic in plantations. Major neighbors, such as Borgu, Nupe, and later Dahomey, had no significant Yorùbá rival other than Oyo. After the empire's decline, they struggled for dominance over each other.

The rationale for discussing Benin as a neighbor and not part of Yorùbá territory is justified by the idea that present-day boundaries have been colored by the epistemic creation of the colonial government; this idea is discussed in the introduction to the chapter on the Yorùbá and their neighbors. The chapter's clarification of Yorùbá peoples and boundaries is important not only for a complete understanding of history but also for further debate regarding the actual geographic borders of Yorùbá territory and the criteria used to define it. The chapter examines patterns of relations between those defined as Yorùbá and their neighbors in various

---

66. Biobaku, *Egba and Their Neighbors*; Ikime, *Can Anything Come Out of History?*; Ajayi, *History and the Nation*; and Akintoye, "North-Eastern Yoruba Districts," 539–553.

regions, including North Africa. Trade and commerce are twin catalysts for cultural change, and these activities brought major transformations to Yorùbá territory. Most of these changes came through Oyo, the gateway empire.

The chapter "Oyo Heterogeneity" discusses the events that culminated in the creation of Yorùbá communities in different parts of the Americas. These populations were predominantly found in Cuba and Brazil until the 1830s, when they were brought to Sierra Leone and Trinidad and Tobago. This migration was driven by the so-called abolition acts implemented by Europe and the Americas.[67] This population flowed back to Africa, Sierra Leone, and Liberia from this period until the late nineteenth century.[68] From there, these people returned to the homelands from where they had been abducted.[69] This population, which had been removed on slave cargo ships, returned without bitterness; the people were invigorated by the idea of transforming these spaces with their newly acquired Western values. One explanation for this attitude is how the slave trade was conducted in Yorubaland during their captivity.

Many enslaved Yorùbá people considered themselves victims of war rather than thinking they had suffered from betrayal or evil of their own on the part of their kinsmen. This narrative explained enslavement as an unfortunate consequence of regularly selling captives in different markets. Some victims had maintained households before their captivity, and their slaves had contributed to various economic activities. Some of the former captives engaged in the trade and acquisition of slaves after gaining their freedom, and others had owned slaves of their own before captivity. These individuals were familiar with local practices and returned with the understanding that they could not obliterate this part of their history without engaging with society's highest echelon. They went from being returnee ex-slaves to movers and shakers within the emerging society, looking to make their presence known. J. F. Ade Ajayi accurately described the transformation of this group's identity as a shift from Anglophobe to Anglophile.[70] They championed restitution through the replacement of Yorùbá traditions with Western modernity. They also joined the wave that shaped patterns of West African migration among the Yorùbá people, which is discussed in chapter 6.

The inhabitants of major Yorùbá population centers are inherently inclined to trade. Today, anyone with remarkable trading acumen or who is perceived to be obsessed with material acquisitions to the point of selfishness is regarded as an "Ijebu" among the Yorùbá people. This label dates to the precolonial activities of Ijebu traders, who were known for long-distance trading.[71] This subset of Yorùbá built their reputation as merchants in all varieties of trade, including that of human beings, agricultural products, and crafts. The Old Oyo Empire was populated by people from a variety of cultures who engaged in varied occupations, and trade was the most lucrative economic enterprise in which it engaged.

Nature does not concentrate on human needs within a specific geographic region, and the cloth, produce, and other commodities traded by the Yorùbá were in demand across the entire

---

67. Lovejoy, *Prieto*.

68. Lindsay, "Transatlantic Journey."

69. Kopytoff, *Preface to Modern Nigeria*.

70. Osuntokun, "Professor Jacob F. Ade Ajayi," 300.

71. Sofela, *Egba-Ijebu Relations*.

West African region. This encouraged mobility among people in the West African region before the colonial invasion. Yorùbá traders were in contact with the people of present-day Ghana, Togo, and the Benin Republic—even the Mali Empire, to some extent—through Borgu. Colonization expanded the geographic reach of the Yorùbá people, influencing migration patterns along this corridor. After the colonial experience, the Yorùbá population had extended to places like Côte d'Ivoire, and patterns of relations had been modified to recognize itinerant residents.[72] The technological revolution was at the heart of this transformation, with profound impacts on transportation; land reforms and their economic implications; colonial policies, particularly regarding infrastructure and industrialization; and local responses to these developments. These praxes and their socioeconomic and political implications influenced the course of the transformation of Yorùbá civilization, affecting the spread of its culture and ideas across borders.

Scholars have examined diaspora communities in various locations and identified a resilient capacity for reproducing the Yorùbá worldview; it is an agency for self-emancipation and creating a biosocial community. The chapter "Cosmologies and Epistemologies" explores these worldviews and the philosophies they encountered. Concepts and ideas considered to be pillars of the Yorùbá lifeworld manifest in dimensions that transcend their epistemologies, becoming ontological, sociological, and metaphysical "truths." These ideas are explored in a global frame, tracking their trajectory from the corner of West Africa to their reproduction in the Atlantic world. The Yorùbá worldview is broadly examined through three powerful forces: Ifá, the witness to the primordial choice of individuals; Orí, the primordial choice itself; and Òrìṣà, the ancestral beings venerated for harmony between humans and the primordial choice. The relationship between these concepts reflects how they have been aggregated, engaged, and understood at different times and in different locations among communities. These ideas can stand alone, but none can be fully explored without the others—they depict an overlapping structural notion of human existence.[73] They explain cosmological views while providing insights into sociology, philosophy, ontology, and metaphysics.

Within Yorùbá epistemologies, the idea of Ifá (a system of divination), Orí (inner essence), and Òrìṣà (deities) are intertwined to symbolize the totality of the Yorùbá worldview. They transcend social relations to define aspects of spirituality. By interrogating these concepts and phenomena, readers can understand how the Yorùbá people came to dominate and represent African spirituality in the "new world." This is significant because they were mainly in the minority among Atlantic farm plantations, living among enslaved Africans from other regions. The Yorùbá people believe in opposing forces, seeking the temerity to navigate them successfully. These interactions are found among more than 401 Òrìṣà, as Ifá often talks about "Òkànlénírínwo irúnmolè tó t'ìkòlé ọrun bọ wá s'ílé ayé" (the 401 deities that descended to the earth from the abode of the gods). Some accounts present this number as 201, but the logic behind the number is supported by the belief that apotheosis is an infinite process.[74] Yorùbá Òrìṣàs regenerate at intervals, especially when an elderly member of society transitions to the

---

72. Skinner, "West African Economic Systems," 77–88.

73. Abimbola, *Sixteen Great Poems of Ifa*.

74. Abimbola, *Yoruba Culture*.

world beyond; that person is believed to attain extraterrestrial status. The world beyond is an important part of daily life because these entities can influence the actions and conduct of individuals. The Yorùbá universe is governed by energies (spirits) consistent with these beliefs, and their configuration requires no specific structure. Despite this unpredictability and complexity, people understand that these energies can be manipulated through propitiation.[75] These ideas, which constitute the cosmologies and metaphysical landscape of Yorùbá society, inform and are framed in Yorùbá epistemologies.

After covering the broad array of background information regarding the construction of a global Yorùbá community, this book interrogates the transatlantic experience of people through the agency of their culture, traditions, and practices that have hybridized with modern elements—Western components. In the Atlantic world, the Yorùbá created a unique religious experience for themselves due to their understanding of religion as an individual's spiritual encounter. Environment, history, and traditions are taken as an individual's experience to which supernatural forces are to be annexed or drawn.[76] In the Yorùbá metaphysical world, the Supreme Being is best invoked within cultural practices. As a result, Yorùbá became experts in acclimatizing foreign religions to Yorùbá culture; they evolved a system blending traditional Yorùbá beliefs with Catholicism. Elements of Yorùbá belief systems were infused into Christian and Islamic practices, recreating indigenous belief systems within the Christian frame for use in Atlantic locations. The resilience of the Yorùbá people is largely due to their adaptability,[77] as many returnees were forcefully converted to Christianity and given no other choice during their Atlantic confinement.

The largest number of Yorùbá captives entered transatlantic markets during the twilight of the Old Oyo hegemonic presence. The constitutional crisis of the late 1700s, which began with Baṣọrun Gáà, had snowballed into a major displacement crisis by the first half of the following century.[78] Much of this population was taken between the 1790s and 1830s.[79] The slave trade was outlawed during this influx of Yorùbá captives, and the bulk was smuggled into Atlantic spaces on cargo ships that evaded antislavery patrol ships. Major slave traders began encountering frequent problems with the antislavery authorities in the 1830s, but this remained a period of displacement.

Patterns of slave trading had shifted from the days when the Old Oyo had tremendous power. Raids and kidnappings had become lucrative military expeditions. Military leaders acquired greater relevance and began reshaping governance, administration, and economic production within society. Ibadan, which had emerged from the ruins of Old Oyo, experimented with a large army as it reorganized the Yorùbá polity within a political framework of meritocracy.[80]

The Yorùbá territory was also undergoing a subtle transformation due to the adoption of Islam. Centuries of trade with Hausa states, and the presence of Hausa slaves in Old Oyo, had

---

75. Akin-Otiko, "Significance of Sacrifice," 17–24.

76. Bascom, *Ifa Divination*.

77. Lovejoy and Ojo, "Lucumí, 'Terranova,'" 353–372.

78. Law, "Constitutional Troubles of Ọyọ," 25–44.

79. Ojo, "Organization of the Atlantic Slave Trade," 77–100.

80. Awe, "Ajele System," 47–60.

converted many Oyo residents to Islam. This population of converts joined other disaffected elements in the empire and contributed to its eventual implosion.[81] Although this population brought Uthman dan Fodio's jihad into Yorùbá territory, its people were still vulnerable to being sold into slavery as victims of war—the Muslims considered it an aberration to be enslaved by "unbelievers." Yorùbá captives exhibited differences based on their place of captivity. Elements of Islamic traditions were not strong in many parts of the Americas, but they were a major social vehicle in West African homes developed for returnees from the Americas and people rescued from slave ships.[82]

In Sierra Leone, the Islamic identity was zealously guarded in the presence of dominant Judeo-Christian traditions. Some Muslims crossed to the area later known as Senegambia as part of efforts to escape Christian domination and freely practice their religion. The basis of each group's worldview meant fundamental differences in religion, social life, and education. One group maintained an Arab-oriented sociocultural consciousness, and the other cultivated a Western frame of consciousness. The return of freed slaves led to the emergence and spread of Christian missions in Yorubaland.[83] Conversely, Islam continued to thrive in trade and social interactions, the vehicles it had originally used to penetrate the heart of the nation. Muslims maintained a sympathy for those who had brought its culture to their homeland. By the time slaves were taken to Sierra Leone and freed, society exhibited Arab-influenced cultural patterns, including clothing, and Yorùbá Alfas (Islamic scholars) had emerged.[84] These scholars inculcated the Islamic doctrine just like anyone else who had been converted in their homeland, using religion as a source of liberation and enlightenment. Christian returnees were also bringing a new way of life. Their novel ideas were heralded as the next civilizing stage in society's evolution, supported by the increasing presence of Western imperial states and ties to capitalism. In this evolving social milieu, Christian adherents felt emboldened to champion their cause among their kinsmen, unlike their Muslim counterparts.

The wider spread of Islam and Christianity was enabled by the Yorubanization of each religion. This was more pronounced with the spread of Islam until the emergence of African churches that had broken loose from established Christian missions. Each religious effort incorporated elements of Yorùbá belief systems into their practices, which assisted their ecumenical endeavors. An emerging class of elites and the introduction of Western education initially generated tremendous amounts of attention and an air of respectability among the Yorùbá. This enthusiasm did not spread to all, as many people realized that the new religion's tenets were difficult or almost impossible to follow in their localities. Many maintained superficial involvement, continuing practices from their traditional belief systems that opposed the church's tenets.[85] These shifts began in the late nineteenth century and occurred throughout the twentieth century.

---

81. Smith, "Little New Light."

82. Bassia, "Marriage Rites among the Aku," 251–256.

83. Ajayi, *Christian Missions in Nigeria*.

84. Alade, "Examination of the Contributions of Muslim Clerics," 565–584.

85. Falola, *Cultural Modernity*.

Yorùbá-based churches were established as a tool of decolonization, creating balance and allowing the adherents to have a voice in their spirituality.[86] However, many converts were disappointed to see that their socioeconomic conditions had not improved. Instead of finding relief, their situations were exacerbated by colonial pressure and exploitative economic policies. Maintaining a household became even more difficult for those who got married, and the church's requirements sometimes failed to recognize the reality of local existence. These problems were seen as failures that the Aládúrà churches emerged to address; they adapted the Judeo-Christian ontological concept of opposing sides—good and evil—to resonate with traditional notions of a binary ontological world.[87]

This perspective saw good and evil as stand-alone entities, perpetually opposed to each other, which meant that existing Yorùbá beliefs had to be modified. One example is the case of *Èṣù*, the Yorùbá god of intersection/crossroads who wields the power of manifestation.[88] Similar deities can be found in the metaphysical landscape of every culture and civilization, but *Èṣù* was equated with the biblical Satan. This process stripped *Èṣù* of his original status, and the Aládúrà churches gained popularity for their ability to organize intense prayer sessions that could oppose the "wicked" acts of this invented devil.[89] Orthodox Christian institutions accused Yorùbá Òrìṣà of appeasing the devil, and prayers replaced sacrifices for supernatural protection.[90] These changes were appealing because they fed into the belligerent nature of local adherents, addressing their desperation to overcome imposing challenges and pandering to extant beliefs about supernatural forces that impeded their progress. Although these converts suffered under obnoxious, self-serving, and contradictory colonial policies, they preferred to look for metaphysical explanations.[91] Prayer sessions and other activities organized by the new churches made vigorous attempts to disassociate the people from ancestors who had been at the core of their spirituality and religious institutions. This reduced the scale of local practices that venerated ancestors, but some of the instruments and performances involved in their veneration were incorporated into the emerging Christian practices.[92]

The modes of worship adopted by the Yorùbá-derived churches, which included dancing, clapping, and drumming, had previously been clamored for by many voices in their congregations.[93] These performance elements made Christian gatherings more appealing, but these components troubled white missionaries, who regarded some practices as paganistic.[94] Over time, the traditional organization of Western churches became less dynamic enough to gain new adherents. Orthodox churches saw that they were losing members to emerging churches and their new doctrines, and some were forced to adapt to these changes. However, substan-

---

86. Ayandele, *Missionary Impact on Modern Nigeria.*

87. Crumbley, "Indigenous Institution Building."

88. Falola, *Esu.*

89. Omojola, "Singing Yoruba Christianity," 133–135.

90. Ogungbile, "Comparative Study of Revelation."

91. This is not to deny the role of the supernatural in the governance of earthly activities but to stress the over-stretched nature of this reality vis-à-vis the sociopolitical milieu in which the individual lives.

92. Adejobi, *Observances and Practices.*

93. Falola, *Cultural Modernity.*

94. Cornelius, "'We Slipped and Learned to Read,'" 171–186.

tial differences remain among different denominations. Some areas of disagreement include gender roles, polygamy, marriage traditions, and the extent to which traditional practices have been integrated into Christian worship.[95] These changes continued from the colonial period through the postcolonial period.

In a paradox of historical development, the faith brought from Europe and America was taken back to these spaces as a refined African development.[96] Immigrant populations generally accepted these changes in Western cities, and African churches became avenues that allowed immigrants to construct social networks. Whether singing from hymnals, praying, dancing, listening to the choir, or engaging in other performances during church, people within and outside the Yorùbá identity have become acquainted with alternative, culture-based practices. In the contemporary era, people from around the globe have begun engaging in pilgrimages to places like Lagos, Ibadan, and other Yorùbá locations where these churches have been established. The internet has created a bridge between Yorùbá culture and the rest of the world, and religion has integrated the people into the shrinking space metaphorically described as a global village.

Before their return to Africa, which began in the early nineteenth century, Yorùbá captives on farms and plantations in the Atlantic world created communities of people who were more closely united through their ideological inclination—framed around a Yorùbá identity—than by bloodlines or filial relations. The Òrìṣà cult system of spirituality united these communities and an identity framed in origin stories, fictional kinship, and new notions around ethnicity. The chapters in the section on religions explain that these captives included people skilled in occupations other than farming. Some were regarded as Ifá priests versed in divination art and science. Sculptors provided necessary objects and symbols of worship to replace the paraphernalia left in their African homelands. Poets recited the praise poetry of the gods, performing other mnemonic rituals and often doubling as singers. Drummers provided rhythms and contributed energy to religious gatherings that often scared plantation owners. Others also offered their services to re-create an African homeland in the Atlantic space. Elders retained their elevated status in captivity, although most captives were younger. Elders in their various Atlantic homes worked to preserve the sanctity of this community, reproducing their Yorùbá traditions and recounting their Atlantic history. During this process, the hybridization of religious practices became an important conduit for transmitting messages and making an impact. In some Atlantic spaces, they embraced elements of Christian Catholicism and incorporated elements from other African traditional religions, predominantly those of the Yorùbá, to create Candomblé, Santeria, and other religious cult structures.[97] Such practices were most common in Brazil and Cuba, where Yorùbá populations were the largest.

The impact of religion and its spread across different places can be seen in the continued dominance of Yorùbá communities in Trinidad, which has been accomplished through the

---

95. Brennan, *Singing Yoruba Christianity*.

96. Adogame, *African Christian Diaspora*, 169–189.

97. Herskovits, "Social Organization of the Afrobrazilian Candomble," 147–166; Murphy, *Santería: African Spirits in America*.

instrumentality of Yorùbá religious cult systems.[98] Yorùbá captives first landed in Sierra Leone before being shipped to Trinidad as "indentured" workers—their label was different, but their situation remained almost completely unchanged. Some of those who remained in West Africa chose to identify with Islam, while most allied with Christianity.[99] This phenomenon shows the extent to which Islam had permeated the social fabric of Yorùbá society and influenced the social conditioning of different geographic locations. Ifá, Òrìṣà, Ògún, and Ọya are some of the popular Yorùbá divinities who were transformed into agents of resistance, opposing white domination in the Atlantic space and the Americas.[100] These deities constituted a common body through which the population in Trinidad and other Atlantic places could form organic communities. In these groups, they were emancipated in mind/spirituality, politics, economy, and culture. By venerating these spirits, they could reenact their shared history[101] in ways that restored their human dignity.[102] This was unnecessary in Sierra Leone because "biosociality" was formed around Islam and Christianity. When Muslims felt disadvantaged compared to their Christian counterparts, they traveled to Muslim-dominated Gambia. In some Atlantic cities today, Yorùbá religious cults constitute a dominant force in the Afro-Atlantic religious space. These dynamics are investigated in the section on religion, examining the lifeworld of the people vis-à-vis the creation of a global Yorùbá community. As if reconnecting with the globalization of mythologies, some scholars have treated Yorùbá deities as resembling those of ancient Egypt.[103]

If Europeans were trading African bodies in the previous centuries, the nineteenth and twentieth centuries saw an increasing wave of expansion through the coastal population to meddle in African affairs into the hinterlands. The new "civilization" envisioned by the Yorùbá returnees was incubated in a colonial state.[104] In 1900, around fifty years after returning to their ancestral homes, colonial rule was formally established in the area that became Nigeria.[105] Although pockets of resistance remained in many parts of this colonial leviathan, the major wars of resistance in Yorùbá territory had been fought and terminated. Despite the crisis of the nineteenth century, Yorubaland's political culture enabled virtually all the cities, villages, and kingdoms to be controlled by the British protectorate in Lagos, unlike the armed resistance that was mounted in many parts of the area that became the northern protectorate.[106]

Ijebu and Lagos were exceptions to this development, which explains why political culture was an important factor. Neither city was under the hegemonic power of Old Oyo, even though the empire's presence was a major impairment to the cities' activities. The conflicts between these states and the British government were due to imperial calculations. Lagos was

---

98. Castor, *Spiritual Citizenship*.

99. Gijanto, "Abolition and the Rise of the Aku."

100. Omari-Tunkara, *Manipulating the Sacred*.

101. Usman and Falola, *Yoruba from Prehistory to the Present*.

102. Falola, *Alternative History*.

103. Oduyoye, *Vocabulary of Yoruba Religious Discourse*; Saakana, *African Origins*.

104. Ayandele, *Educated Elite*.

105. O'Hear, "Carnegie's Letters," 330–331.

106. Mohammed, *European Trade*.

Figure 1.2. Yorùbá religion and the images that represent it are part of regional and global networks. Yorùbá gods are represented in texts (Odu Ifá) or verbal renderings (*oríkì*) and wooden images that are spiritually charged and ritualized with sacrificial materials during periodic religious festivals or commemorations. From the Toyin Falola Private Collection.

bombarded in 1851 by British naval forces responding to slave traders who had violated the abolition act, which was enabled by collusion with its king, Kosokó.[107] The attack on Ijebu took place about four decades later, following an alleged violation of the 1886 treaty that ended internecine Yorùbá wars. The treaty had ensured the free flow of trade between all polities in the region, and the invasion of Ijebu opened a trade route that linked it with Lagos in 1892. This was hailed as a positive development across the social strata of Yorùbá society.[108]

The Ijebu invasion was welcomed by every group that would benefit from a shorter route linking the rest of Yorubaland with Lagos—traders, travelers, and foreign and domestic Christian missionaries. It did not lead to the immediate installment of a British colonial structure, unlike the wars fought in northern states. The Lagos protectorate had been prompted to invade by unceasing pressure from British traders and reduced government revenues, independent of any action from the colonial office in Britain. It was a "Lagos affair," promoted by mercantilist interests from subjects of a European imperial state[109] who spearheaded the effort almost entirely on their own. Yorùbá kings mounted a subtle resistance to British colonial domination, protesting what they considered unfair manipulation and the theft of their traditional roles; they felt their sovereignty had been diminished by the agreements they had signed. This meant minor opposition in the form of petitions and letters that had little support from the public—the emerging educated elites saw these developments as the advancement of political civilization.

Educated Yorùbá elites arranged for the Lagos government's intervention in their war-torn country's politics, culminating in the 1886 peace treaty.[110] The Aláàfin of Oyo reinforced—or rather, illustrated—the importance of this elite in the changing society by requesting their help to secure British intervention in the seemingly intractable Lagos crisis. Yorùbá politics during this period meant that the British government's intervention in Lagos made it impossible to mount violent armed resistance against colonial domination. The existing political culture meant that a larger state's submission to colonial rule also meant the subordination of other outlying polities. This arrangement focused on the country's dominant political units, and these areas became provinces and divisions in the colonial administrative structure.[111]

The next phase of Yorùbá resistance to colonial rule came from the people, and emerging educated elites opposed the entrenchment of British authority. Influential citizens such as Herbert Macaulay wrote petitions, organized meetings for political action, and represented Nigerians—including kings—in different forums that included courts, panels of inquiry, and meetings within and outside the colony.[112] The colonial state's structure gave power to traditional rulers in ways that were difficult to quantify; debates continue as to whether their powers

---

107. Smith, *Lagos Consulate*.

108. Flint, "Nigeria," 239.

109. Flint, "Nigeria."

110. Chief Oladiran Ajayi, Otun Asiwaju of Modakeke, on July 15, 1989, at Modakeke High School Hall in a Special Commemorative/Mid-year Lecture to Mark the Creation of Ife North Local Government Area, 8.

111. Ballard, "Administrative Origins," 333–348.

112. Cole, *Modern and Traditional Elites*, 110–112.

were amplified or diminished.[113] The extent of these two outcomes is also debated, but both scenarios were as vivid as they were palpable.[114]

Colonization left a lasting imprint on social structures. The depletion of local populations through the transatlantic slave trade meant little in comparison to the colonial superstructure established in pursuit of complete control. The goal was absolute mastery not only of the region's natural resources but of its people. After the abolition of slavery, the British imposed a more comprehensive agenda on their captured territories, including the many cultures that existed in the region later known as Nigeria. British colonization began a new phase of their supremacist plan to dominate the population.[115] Their reasons were more economical than political—Europeans understood that their economic gains in the African world relied on a consolidation of power. The greatest profits could only be obtained by administering the political structures of these colonies, which meant there was an urgent need for political consolidation. In the early days of the nation's integration into the global politics of nation-states, the Yorùbá people needed to make cultural and political adjustments to address the sociopolitical realities of the time. This book examines how emerging Yorùbá elites weaponized their initiation into various aspects of Western civilization, including education, socialization, religion, and political systems. Their work in navigating this nascent space was essential for the emancipation of their people.

The entity known as Nigeria entered the "modern" era as its people watched and participated in the transformation of their traditions and material culture. Their politics changed, but not all their political culture. The Yorùbá was linked with the European world through Western education, Christianity, and new forms of elitism. Many emerging elites had studied at Fourah Bay College in Sierra Leone and different cities in Britain and the United States. They had read Western books and, to some extent, were initiated into aspects of Western society.[116] Initially, there were low numbers of African students in American and British universities. Their numbers increased substantially after World War II. Up to this period, Yorubaland's nationalist scene was shaped by returnees and their descendants.[117] They brought global debates about welfare, labor unions, democracy, governance, and human rights into the Yorùbá political space.[118] Some of these individuals ventured into journalism, becoming thorns in the side of Nigeria's colonial government.[119] Their positions as intermediaries between their Yorùbá homeland and the British colonizers made them influential in the implementation of Western ideals. Returnees and their descendants ushered society into a new age of civilization, placing themselves at the fore of nationalist agitations.

---

113. Lawal, "Positions of the Chiefs," 69–87; Bitiyong, "Chiefs," 145–155.

114. Vaughan, *Nigerian Chiefs*.

115. Pétré-Grenouilleau, *From Slave Trade to Empire*.

116. Odubajo and Alabi, "Elite Factor," 121–139.

117. Adeboye, "Diaries as Cultural and Intellectual Histories."

118. Okonkwo, "Nigeria Civil Service Union," 609–622.

119. Lawal and Jimoh, "'Missiles from Kristen Hall,'" 41–62; Okigbo, "Nigerian High School Students," 907.

These elites inspired subsequent nationalists, and their early indoctrination with Western education[120] allowed them to craft nascent institutions that perceived and resisted the injustice in the colonial system. Scholarships and funds to advance their studies were provided by the colonial government, missionaries, and community contributions. Others received financial support from their families. These elites transformed Nigerian society, culminating in nationalist movements that gained momentum after World War II. Nigerian nationalism and nationalist agitations were led by those based in Lagos and parts of the western region.[121]

In a common pattern with African colonial states and their Western colonizers, leaders of independence movements had received their advanced education in Britain or the United States. They were acquainted with the ideals of Pan-Africanism that were popular with Black students, and they developed the same charismatic aura that was shared by leaders of the movement. When Obafemi Awolowo and others returned to Nigeria, they established media networks that could communicate their ideas to the public for enlightenment and mass mobilization. The use of such media had been initiated by early nationalists, but its reach and presence later became ubiquitous.[122]

Professional journalism was a foreign institution that had been brought into the Yorùbá social system before colonial rule.[123] This occupation was especially attractive during the colonial administration because it allowed people to express themselves and reach massive numbers of people. Lawyers, teachers, doctors, clerks, engineers, and others with the basic ability to communicate in the Queen's English also felt the urge to join this industry. Not every journalist was critical of the colonial government. Some admired the British presence, voicing support for the colonial project and its continued implementation in Nigeria. Others vented their disgust for the government and advocated for independence. The latter adopted and nationalized the global Pan-African campaign in Yorubaland. Influenced by the works of Marcus Garvey and W. E. B. Du Bois, they formed associations determined to emancipate Black people from every type of subordination and created new groups that could meet their country's needs. The West African Students' Union (WASU) and the *Ẹgbẹ́ Ọmọ Odùduwà* functioned within both categories.

The WASU focused primarily on the welfare of West African students in the United Kingdom who were committed to the emancipation of Black people.[124] The group supported the education of those who worked toward liberation by providing hostels and creating a single community for discussing the ideas of decolonization and Pan-Africanism. The Ẹgbẹ́ Ọmọ Odùduwà was a sociocultural solidarity group whose political sentiments leaned toward cultural exactitude.[125] Both were established in Britain by Yorùbá students, sustaining the momentum for Nigerian nationalism in the coming years. In the post–World War II years, greater numbers of nation-states in different regions of the world participated in global poli-

---

120. Ajayi, "Development of Secondary Grammar School," 517–525.

121. Coleman, *Nigeria*.

122. Babalola, "Newspapers as Instruments," 403–410.

123. Enemugwem, "Impact of the Lagos Press," 106–114.

124. Hakim Adi, *West Africans in Britain*.

125. Ayoade, "Party and Ideology in Nigeria," 169–188.

tics—that is, modern international relations. During this period, the increasing demand was unprecedented. Members of the Ẹgbẹ́ and WASU brought the Nigerian colony and the Yorùbá world into this discourse.

The forces at work in Nigeria differed from the ideals of humanity and governance that were taught in school. The double standards that the British government and other imperial powers used to run their colonies were a central part of this awareness and agitation. Although western Europe claimed to lead under the banner of liberty, equality, and fraternity that marked the French Revolution, these virtues were absent from the Nigerian colony. Herbert Macaulay had resigned from the colonial service in the Survey Department due to the system's injustice. Many educated Yorùbá elites shifted from romanticizing English culture to questioning these cultural entities. Within their Anglophile scope, the elites initiated a drive for decolonization in the colonial state, especially on the cultural plane. Politically, they supported the colony's status and structure. In other parts of Africa, such as Ghana, Congo, and Tanzania, leading nationalists advocated for a return to precolonial communal systems that were reconceptualized under different names (e.g., Ujamaa). However, none of the leading Nigerian nationalists advocated for the decolonization of their state's political economy. This book's discussion of Awolowo shows that they employed a philosophy that Africanist scholars now describe as Afropolitanism, adopting aspects of the African past that are relevant to the politics of the time.[126] Under Afropolitanism, these aspects of the past are incorporated into the vision of a modern state assembled from cultures inside and outside Africa. Although this hybridization was successful at mobilizing political support, it failed to address the flaws in the nation-state that had been created by the colonial government.[127]

Nationalist politics in Yorubaland—an area called the Western region after the Richards constitution of 1946—was advanced by sociocultural bodies promoting ethnic allegiance, placing the agenda of cultural nationalists squarely in its political frame. Although the Ẹgbẹ́ Ọmọ Odùduwà was established in 1945 by Awolowo and other students of Yorùbá descent in Britain, earlier efforts by Mojola Agbebi, Sapara Williams, Samuel Ajayi Crowther, Isaac Oluwole Delano, Samuel Johnson, and others had championed the idea of a Yorùbá nation.[128] Cultural nationalists advanced their agenda for the Yorùbá nation along different dimensions: the use of writing, adoption of a standard Yorùbá alphabet, names, interest in Yorùbá clothing and fashion, promotion of micro and macro histories of the Yorùbá people, and the emergence of independent Christian churches as a significant institution in the colonial state.[129]

Written publications distributed by the emerging press addressed a growing community of literate Africans, and other engagements addressed the colonial structure of modernity. Through these efforts, individuals in Yorubaland showed local and global communities that their culture was relevant in emerging society. The chapter "Cultural Icons" affirms the influence of the individuals who engineered the modern Yorùbá identity through deliberate efforts to resuscitate and sustain the debate over the relevance of culture for national development.

---

126. Mbembe, "Afropolitanism," 26–30.

127. Olaopa, "Yoruba Nation," 594; Falola, *Violence in Nigeria*.

128. Falola and Genova, *Yoruba Identity*.

129. Falola, "Samuel Johnson," 89–103.

A study of Chief Obafemi Awolowo explains the modern democratic practices of the Yorùbá people. The works of Chief Isaac Oluwole Delano, D. O. Fagunwa, Adebayo Faleti, and Akinwunmi Ishola demonstrate the literary progress of the Yorùbá. These individuals have also shown an ability to make the most out of every opportunity that has come their way, including Western education. The establishment of the Ẹgbẹ́ was an important legacy for these historical figures. It became a rallying ground for the Yorùbá people, allowing them to express and pursue their political views. In 1951, the Ẹgbẹ́ was transformed into the Action Group, a political party.[130] Sociocultural groups in other regions of Nigeria metamorphosed into similar groups, preparing to administer the autonomous regions granted by the McPherson constitution that same year.

The final section of this book discusses the archetypal roles played by Chief Obafemi Awolowo and the city of Ibadan. It also examines colonial encroachment into Yorubaland politics, recounting how the people, led by nationalist leaders, adopted the spirit of the French Revolution—the revolution was a watershed moment for the progression and formation of modern nation-states, described by Francis Fukuyama as the end of history.[131] This section examines how educated Yorùbá elites engaged in political activities during the 1950s and beyond. Along with their fellow citizens, they localized the raging global resistance against colonial domination, calling for a reordering of international relations. These demands were supported by the idea of a modern state, supposedly enshrined in the ethical and legal codes of the Western cities where they had acquired their education.

Yorùbá cities and towns became global spaces that bred cosmopolitan populations. This book discusses the impact of multiple cities and urban centers in Yorùbá territory during the British colonial project and under the postcolonial government. European occupation reordered the economic landscape of every colonized society, including the societies in Yorubaland, and these shifts had massive implications. Not only did they enable the colonial government's social rewiring but they also drove a massive and continued migration of people. Young men and women moved into the emerging Yorùbá cities of Ibadan, Abeokuta, and Lagos, as well as other emerging cities in places like Kano, Kaduna, and Enugu. Their movements introduced new cultures and social behaviors to the Yorùbá people, and these settlements attracted migrants from all over Yorubaland, including people from other cultures.

Migrations changed the face of urbanization and the composition of cities. Advances in transportation, modern architecture, and telecommunication facilitated the development of infrastructure that led to the emergence of modern cities and urban centers. The economic boom enjoyed by these new centers drew a migratory population in search of opportunities. Towns and villages became cities and urban centers that blended different cultures. Railways, telecommunications networks, and roads expanded during this period. The proliferation of European and indigenous firms, along with other urbanization or modernization projects that involved new construction, created new jobs in these locations. Young people abandoned rural areas in favor of urban centers, and the culture created in these cities became a yardstick for

---

130. Nolte, *Obafemi Awolowo*.
131. Fukuyama, "End of History?"

civilization from this period onward. These changes had severe consequences for traditional institutions and the organic aspects of popular culture. Cities became the new incubators for the culture that governed the emerging social space. Ibadan emerged as a major cultural capital, and the university located in the city became a global space.

Nigeria's political independence in 1960 added another dimension to the global history of the Yorùbá people, even as they continued their role as the creators of new intellectual products in the developing nation-state. Chapter 17 presents Yorùbá films (Nollywood) and introduces readers to the discourse surrounding Nigeria's pop culture industry. Nollywood Yorùbá has gone global, heavily watched in many African countries as well as Brazil and Trinidad. Yorùbá artists have played a pivotal role in these developments, and an academic discussion of literary and intellectual production focuses on their contributions. New media has helped to produce and reproduce global Yorùbá culture and traditions on a pluriversal scope—this has been enabled by the internet and the community of bubbles. Although the internet can pose threats to the preservation and production of organic Yorùbá culture and traditions, it is also capable of reproducing, popularizing, and preserving the culture, traditions, and history of the people for generations to come. The popular culture that drives the internet community does exhibit universalist tendencies, but distortion can also be recognized as the mutational tendency of culture, which has been expressed over many centuries.

Nollywood's importance as a cultural industry has increased dramatically through the internet, which has been heralded as the technological breakthrough of the millennium. It has enabled a cyberculture predominantly composed of youths connecting over large geographic distances. The development of Nollywood and the internet in the twentieth century added another dimension to the borrowing, creation, and distribution of cultural products. Culture and traditions are now transmitted through a medium that is easier for people to consume. Nollywood has grown far beyond its initial expectations, and this growth was exponentially magnified by online culture—the industry's increasing popularity has allowed people throughout the world to participate in a global market for the sharing of ideas.

This study concludes with an exploration of the ways that Yorùbá culture can be integrated into contemporary life, identifying ways to reinforce these values to promote a Yorùbá identity in the present day. The naming culture of the Yorùbá people is one such example because it has bent in the cultural whirlwind to achieve adaptation instead of destruction; Yorùbá people who follow Christianity bear names that combine a signal of their Yorùbá identity with a prefix or suffix that suits their faith. The process of transformation can protect the people's customs instead of destroying them. Yorùbá values can conform to contemporary reality with and without distortion or manipulation, and there is a genuine reason to accept developments like the appropriation of traditional names for the Yorùbá Òrìṣà, such as "Ọlọ́wọ́gbọgbọrọ" or "Aríìróàlà," to suit the Christian religion. Such changes, which may be done out of ignorance, can also be done in hopes of impressing the new faith. Either way, it indicates that Yorùbá culture has infiltrated a newly circulating culture. These instances should spur an examination of other ways through which cultural practices are negotiated.

The overarching interest of this book and the body of ideas woven together in its chapters will introduce readers to the making and form of a global Yorùbá community. A sojourn through the earliest Yorùbá history, which links to contemporary developments and central epistemic descriptions, can holistically explain the idea of Yorùbá in the global world of cultures and ideas. This fruitful engagement seeks to answer the question of what it means to refer to the idea of a global Yorùbá, along with other inquiries that revolve around the transnationality of the Yorùbá lifeworld. The Yorùbá identity and form have gained both a global dimension due to increased attention from global scholars and a momentum that has been used to inform and frame a global intellectual discourse on Africa, religion, and culture. These effects can be viewed as the cumulative result of the Yorùbá stories, myths, traditions, and cultural artifacts studied in different parts of this text.

The globalization of Yorùbá culture is framed along dual lines: the importation of cultural forms into native practices and the exportation of cultural inventions into foreign elements. The global intellectual discourse about this cultural and historical community has been framed through this dual landscape over time, discussed in its many dimensions in the following pages.

PART 1

Pan-Yorubana

Mythologies 2

Introduction

What makes the beliefs in society or commitment to upholding the ideals of such society is the clear understanding of the ideas that run through the fabric of societal constructs. Mythology is one of the ideas that has driven Pan-African advocacy and reflection throughout history. Convictions about mythologies did not begin with contact with Western civilization or literacy to understand the English words for them. Mythologies predate the colonization of Nigeria and the subjugations of the Yorùbá systems and leadership under the foreign overlords, which persisted through their rules and are still evident in the face of societal interactions in the post-colonial dispensation.[1]

The struggles among the Yorùbá groups and between the Yorùbá societies and other ethnic groups and societies and the successful creation of a Pan-Yorùbá world over the centuries are connected in many ways to stories and traditions we tend to dismiss as fiction. I approach mythologies in the four chapters that follow as evidence of the making of a society, as they tend to protect the interests and integrity of the value system, and many remain reflective in contemporary societies.[2] The approach includes the resistance to the imposition of foreign and strange ideologies that have tended to eradicate or diminish the importance of Yorùbá belief systems. Mythologies from previous centuries have remained connected to contemporary nationalist agitations and advocacies during the colonial system as well as the protection of the place of the Yorùbá societies in colonial social systems.[3]

In understanding these ideals and the frameworks upon which Pan-Yorùbá draws its ideological and theoretical strength both in ancient and contemporary societies, references are made to what constituted the understandings of both metaphysics and ideas that radiated around the questions of reality, social norms, cosmologies, epistemologies, and understandings. So, to support Pan-Yorùbá ideologies, one must understand these questions and establish factual claims particular to Yorùbá. In doing this, Yorùbá mythology must be understood and juxtaposed with facts and science. The link between understanding Yorùbá society and

---

1. Falola, "Pre-colonial Origins," 3–24.
2. Falola, "Ethnicity in Nigerian Politics," 148–166.
3. Ajala, "Yoruba Nationalism."

mythology is inspired by the reality that every society cannot be separated from myths and belief systems, whether scientifically substantiated or based on mere societal unconscious and conscious subscriptions based on cultural dictates. This leads us to the realization that mythology and society are inseparable insofar as society has a history.[4]

All societies have histories; as such, no society could be too scientifically motivated to alienate itself from mythological principles and the disposition of its social atmosphere. Many societies must have had a way of explaining their origins or that of the world, their place in the cosmological setups of the universe, the constructions of their social systems, their social justification of rules and laws, the explanations of different realities and occasions, and general conception.[5] These perspectives are fundamental in African societies.[6]

Mythology, in this regard, refers to the collections, bodies, or descriptions of myths and mythical beliefs that exist in society. It is also the examination, evaluation, and analysis of myth from different perspectives, plugging it into different societal realities. Myths are often narratives with symbolic attributes emanating from traditional conceptions of the people or a preponderance of beliefs that dictate general social behaviors. They tend to link reality and ideological, supernatural, or other beliefs that are primarily eccentric to scientific justifications but have justifiable roots in other myths or factual understandings.

Mythology is often contrasted with reality and thus encompasses not only the explanation of some super beings and origins of humans but also the conceptualization of a particular thing. Often, the state of that thing is seen as reality, and the perception of it that has no scientific or critical rooting is seen as a myth.[7] While this may not be entirely wrong, it should instead take cognizance that in many cases, mythical accounts are attempts to understand reality itself or the reality of a thing and might not have intended to contend with such reality. However, seeing it from the angle of contrast with a scientific or critical explanation could properly expatiate the analysis of factuality. We, therefore, ask questions like whether the Yorùbá's understanding of the cause of a life experience, which in itself is a reality, is justifiable by science and fact. The life issue is real to the extent of its existence, but its perspectives reflect the contentions between myth and science.

Another question is whether myth and mythology should be placed in opposition to science and fact.[8] Would it not amount to over preempting the ability of science to explain all things and provide a universal or unquestionable statement of reality and understanding of it? After all, what distinguishes science is its certainty and protracted finality.[9] However, we are aware that scientific facts previously held are often displaced by subsequent research and understanding, making the previous fact a myth.[10] This writer does not intend to displace the role of science in providing certainty to inquiries but states that mythologies should be seen

---

4. Gotesky, "Nature of Myth and Society," 531.

5. Jaja, "Myths in African Concept of Reality," 9–14.

6. Jaja, "Myths in African Concept of Reality," 9–14.

7. Vignoli, *Myth and Science*.

8. Wells, *Icons of Evolution*.

9. Norton, "Science and Certainty," 3–22.

10. Bauer, *Scientific Literacy*.

Figure 2.1. "Existence." Humans and objects are interlocked in a universe of mysteries. Drawing by Moses Ogunleye.

as an invitation for scientific exercise rather than as the opposite of science. This is because we cannot assume perfection from scientific or mythical perspectives.

Social values are people's collective customs, cultural dispositions, and shared philosophy about a particular thing.[11] These elements, including trauma, are often built from conscious and unconscious collective experiences. They are the societal explanation of things. Social values are sometimes built on myths that may not be substantiated by scientific inquiries and establishments.[12] What constitutes an understanding of society and its pattern of behavior includes myths, which have heavily influenced social structure. Hence, myths are reflected in society, and by society, they are in everything we see and do. They are core elements of society and may never be separable from the conception of any society.

Mythology of Everything

Since mythology is an approach toward understanding reality originating from shared beliefs, no matter how wrong, it is applicable or identifiable in many areas of society and issues. There is often a mythical conception in every aspect of discussions, occurrences, and the existence of things. It goes from understanding the world, the origin of people's social constructs, communications to the profession, and virtually everything. This is why a mythical approach to the discussion of the Yorùbá people would be incomplete without a theoretical appreciation of mythical social conceptions.

Different political systems in the world were built on the presumption that there is a spiritual blessing or endowment to the position held, and as such, disrespecting such authority is a disrespect to the supernatural being.[13] This conception can be traced to antiquity; in fact, great empires like Rome exhibited these traits.[14] The world has seen the dependency of the British monarchy and other world-old political systems and monarchies on theocratic ideologies and spiritual responsibilities.[15] The British monarch is the titular head of the Church of England and the supreme governor of the Church of England.[16] The monarch is also the defender of the Christian faith in the realm.[17] The implication of this system and practice, especially before the contemporary era, is that there is a higher propensity to hold the monarch in high esteem and thus depose to the recognition of the monarch's authority. This is the situation in other old empires that have related spiritual factors to political authorities. The history of political leadership, at least in the sense of a sophisticated and organized system, is closely related to some spiritual responsibilities and authorities so that such authorities are consciously and subconsciously respected.[18] Many Arabian and Middle Eastern societies have a long history

---

11. Naylor, "Social Custom Model," 201–216.

12. Idang, "African Culture and Values," 97–111.

13. Finn, "Politics of Spirituality," 333–345.

14. Mitchell, *History of the Later Roman Empire.*

15. Bonney, "Monarchy, the State and Religion," 199–204.

16. Bonney and Morris, "Tuvalu and You," 368–373.

17. Bonney and Morris, "Tuvalu and You," 368–373.

18. Audi, *Democratic Authority.*

of marriage between politics and religion. In Saudi Arabia, for instance, many political positions have spiritual and religious implications.[19] Their judicial system is more inclined toward observing current Islamic rules and practices.[20]

Notably, this is not to disparage these various authorities, governments, and their political philosophies, but where myth is counterpositioned against science and reality, spiritual inclinations pass as myths and make belief convictions. These practices are also reflected among Africans, particularly the Yorùbá, because there is a heavy link between traditional political systems and traditional religious systems, to the extent that they cannot be separated in many cases. The *Aláàfin* is seen as *Aláṣẹ Èkejì Òrìṣà; Ikú Bàbá Yèyé.* The Aláàfin of Oyo is second only to the gods and has the authority of the gods.[21] He is seen as death and life itself, possessing the ability to spare someone from death or life, and is expected to be a powerful force in the spiritual paraphernalia of the Yorùbá society. It is also found in several traditions and societies in Africa.

There is indeed a mythical property in many of these political systems and setups worldwide. Singling out African societies and their dispositions toward legitimate gods and religious beliefs as the pillars of their social and political structures is to blow both hot and cold. Hence, there are predominant mythologies of politics worldwide, especially concerning spirituality. Today, the world has moved toward the coast of logic, science, certainty, and secularity, and one would expect a reflection of the same in contemporary political practices. While it is agreeable that the systems, in many cases, are moving away from spiritual embellishments, major contemporary civilizations still have strong traces of mythical influences.

At that time, humans were often afflicted with diseases and illnesses for which there were no viable solutions or treatments. This string of instances emphasizes that mythology will always be a feature of every society. In terms of health, it was deployed to maintain social sanity, unity, and understanding in the face of such uncertainty.[22] In medical history, diseases or pestilences, for the sake of social emphasis, always come before cures. Hence, both preventive and curative methods are sought afterward. While scientific inquiries tarry, society attempts to create a perception of such diseases, giving space to the generation of myths.

When there is a long period of indefinite scientific cures for diseases, the myths become social solutions, and behaviors toward them and those that suffer from them develop from the respective myths. In the case of early HIV infection in some parts of the world, including African societies, there was a heavy experience of social stigmatization, harassment, and segregation based on health; many believed that a mere close interaction with victims could lead to contracting the virus.[23] In addition, many subscribed to the myth that every case of HIV/AIDS resulted from sexual impurity, accompanied by unnecessary condemnation.[24] Before the virus was controlled, it became an outbreak that caused death and the unpleasant appearance of

---

19. Al-Turaiqi, *Political System of Saudi Arabia.*

20. Al-Turaiqi, *Political System of Saudi Arabia.*

21. Oladiti, "Religion and Politics," 72–84.

22. Clift and Rizzolo, "Vaccine Myths and Misconceptions," 21–25.

23. Mawar et al., "Third Phase of HIV Pandemic," 471.

24. Sivelä, "Dangerous AIDS Myths or Preconceived Perceptions?" 1179–1191.

Figure 2.2. "Ancient Cosmos," by Michael Efionayi. In the Yorùbá world, prehistory belongs to the knowledge zones of mythical imaginations. The mandate and power of earthly creation were handed down to Odùduwà through a chain and other sacred materials.

some of those who contracted it. It became increasingly difficult for scientists, virologists, and health care practitioners to convince society that HIV/AIDS was not terminal and to rebut the presumption that became myths and disguised reality to the people. These sentiments and stigmatization still exist in many African nations today. Although the apprehensive attitudes and myths toward those managing the virus have subsided, owing to aggressive orientation and handling of such cases, there are still cases of apprehension and stigmatization.

At a point during Africa's early contact with the Western world, West Africa, in particular, had no established treatment for malaria and other local sicknesses that were foreign to the biological and body systems of Europeans.[25] There was no enlightenment or discovery of qui-

____

25. Cole, "Sanitation, Disease and Public Health in Sierra Leone," 238–266.

nine, but the local people had developed both a biological system that was immune to the illnesses to some extent and locally made solutions and cures that might have been strange to the foreigners.[26] Regions were known as "the white man's grave" since several explorers and colonizers got sick and lost their lives.[27] The beliefs became myths before the definite discovery of both preventive and curative measures against malaria.

Medical myths are not things of antiquity; they can occur in any era and time in society. In contemporary society, we have seen instances whereby people were led to and held several contrasting beliefs, even if there were the right solutions. In the 2014 Ebola virus outbreak, especially in Nigeria, different myths and philosophies developed about the disease and curative and preventive measures toward it.[28] Some people believed that the ultimate solution to the virus was the excessive use of salt. Hence, several Nigerians were bathing in salt water, applying salt to many things, and embarking on other socially developed solutions to the virus.[29] This became even more widespread among the people as social media, a contemporary element of global society, became instrumental in disseminating misinformation.[30]

An analysis of social media engagement on Ebola during its outbreaks shows that only about 38.3 percent of the tweets on Twitter regarding the virus were true and incorrect medically, but others were without any validity or were medically correct.[31] They were made with either negligence or qualified intentions. Unfortunately, several literate and educated people held many of these beliefs, which were supposed to be the hallmarks of the required orientations. Similar issues occurred during the global coronavirus outbreak, as several people used different unverified and uncertified means of treatment as an alternative.[32]

Society rests on its culture in evaluating what should constitute reality, the rightness of a subject matter, and the perspective in comprehending everything. This is why there will always be a mythology for everything because culture influences every aspect of society. The constructions of cultural beliefs are unquestionably the result of consistently used and surviving myths and facts.[33] Hence, separating mythical perceptions would be almost impossible in every human society. Understanding this creates a more explicit rationale for engaging theoretical frameworks and paraphernalia related to mythology in Yorùbá societies. Primarily, it is important to reiterate that mythological beliefs are not qualifications of barbarism or underdevelopment; the biggest civilizations in the contemporary world have held on to several myths in their values based on some level of conviction. Importantly, understanding these myths allows exposure to people's thinking processes, hence its necessity.

---

26. Darkwa, "Missionaries and the Politics of Quinine," 115–128; Headrick, "Tools of Imperialism," 231–263.

27. Curtin, "End of the 'White Man's Grave'?" 63–88.

28. Iliyasu et al., "Multi-site Knowledge Attitude," e0135955; Wilkinson and Leach, "Briefing: Ebola–Myths, Realities," 136–148.

29. Kaoje et al., "Awareness, Knowledge, and Misconceptions of Ebola Virus Disease," 105–111.

30. Balami and Meleh, "Misinformation on Salt Water Use," 175.

31. Balami and Meleh, "Misinformation on Salt Water Use," 175.

32. Isah, et al., "Corona Virus Disease 2019 (COVID-19)," 24–37.

33. Kajiru and Nyimbi, "Impact of Myths," 1–27.

Also, there is a mythology to business practices and professional conduct.[34] For instance, the widespread misconception of lawyers as liars, although generated from the angle of sarcasm, has formed the subconscious orientation of several people who are not ready to listen to the strength of logic that dispels such assumptions. Social conversations and interactions,[35] education,[36] sexualities,[37] religion,[38] politics,[39] and several other social facets have developed mythologies, even from the most ancient times.

Mythology in Ancient and Contemporary Society: Social Norms and Ethics

To maintain the core of the primary conversation in the first part of this book, one must draw a connection between establishing an ideological description of the Yorùbá and its relevance on the contemporary and global stage. Would it be out of place to state that despite the level of exposure to Western culture, globalization, and cultural adaptation and diffusion over the years, there are values drawn from the basis of ethnic conception that determine the Yorùbá in general? Is our ancient perception of things sustained among the people today? If this path is not threaded carefully, it could lead to the conclusion that the agitations and consciousness for the retention of African ideologies, values, and culture in contemporary engagement and social development are the promotion of mythologically informed values. Should Pan-Africanism and other Afrocentric advocacies end with the outcome of sustaining unsubstantial principles, it would be a waste of time, career, and an expression of widely shared folly.

Hence, this chapter seeks to establish that, despite notes derived from Western civilizations and orientations, African ideas, cultures, and orientations are not only mythically influenced. Where there is mythical evidence in some of these perceptions, there is evidential justification in the face of history that could substantiate events and practices,[40] which brings us to state the relevant correlation of ancient beliefs and myths to contemporary ones. This demonstrates that the continuing practice of some cultures that some would see as myths or that run against fact and science is not wrong based on their African origin and the inability of Western conceptualization. Where similar Afrocentric standards of evaluation are used to view practices that are now seen as legitimate in the West, similar conclusions may be reached as if they were valid.

Today, what constitutes the social norms in Chinese society will always have genealogical traces to the past, thus defining them.[41] Yorùbá people are defined not just by historical relationships and connectivity but also by enduring shared beliefs passed down consciously and subconsciously. These shared beliefs would form part of contemporary values, even if they were generated from myths of the past or strengthened by myths of the present. You cannot separate

---

34. Trevino and Brown, "Managing to Be Ethical," 69–81.
35. Campbell, *Myth of Social Action*.
36. Hughes, "Myth and Education," 55–70.
37. Levine and Troiden, "Myth of Sexual Compulsivity," 347–363.
38. Avis, *God and the Creative Imagination*.
39. Wilson, *Myth of Political Correctness*.
40. Wambua, "African Perceptions and Myths about Menopause," 645–646.
41. Chen, *Modern Chinese*.

Figure 2.3.
In precolonial Yorùbá society, an elder passed down legends, myths, and folklore of the people to a younger generation; this generation was expected to imbibe the lessons drawn and pass these to the next generation. Drawing by Dr. Kazeem Ekeolu.

a society from its past; where it is heavily influenced by a diffused foreign culture within its system, it would instead transform the practices of the new culture and create a hybrid.[42] In essence, no matter how far back in history, past myths and cultural subscriptions are important in contemporary society because they form part of contemporary social norms, values, and ethics.

Hence, if one would understand and advocate for the knowledge of Yorùbá epistemology, cosmology, heterogeneity, and other distinguishing attributes of the people as seen in their social norms and ethics, one cannot avoid discussing the strings of logic, including the myths that formulated them. Social norms are the informal or unlegislated policies and rules that determine the behavioral orientation of society.[43] These social norms serve different functions and have different effects depending on the group. These functionalities are traced to the shared beliefs that persist beyond time. To capture how the past can be identified in the totality of the social norms of the Yorùbá, to give a clear pathway into seeing the influence of mythology, one must understand that the conceptualization of social norms transcends the evaluation of recurrent patterns and the observable behavior of a particular people. They both serve as reliable means of evaluation, but this could be misleading if there must be a right capture of the heterogeneity and complexity of behaviors influenced by norms. As a result, it is necessary to look beyond the obvious into the submerged energies and beliefs.

For instance, the strength of past African social contracts that depicted general cooperation and collectivity in the progress of every member of this society still exists.[44] The Yorùbá society is far from individualism, although there is evidence of tilting toward it. They are still subconsciously collective in character. This is why there will always be a presumption of hospitality toward another Yorùbá man or woman and even some level of tolerance.[45] The depiction of a fellow countryman as "ọmọ ìyá mi," even if there is no blood relationship but a shared ethnicity in the current dispensation, says a lot about it. This reference will prepare readers' minds for the concepts represented in "Yorùbá Mobility," especially in West Africa, with the envious connectivity of the people even in a strange land. There is a bond created by past experiences, traumas, and excitement, even when they were only known by generations beyond. A similar orientation is seen among the Igbos in contemporary society. There is a tendency for an Igbo man or woman to call the other "nwanne," which means brother or sister. This affinity may not occur when an Igbo man sees a Hausa or Yorùbá man in the context of someone of his ethnicity.

Yorùbá traditional beliefs always emphasized understanding supernatural beings, witchcraft, and extraterrestrial powers that could change reality by harming or making a situation or person better.[46] Similar beliefs exist in other religions, including Christianity, so nothing is demeaning about that. For example, in Christianity, it is believed that differences among the people are evident in their current religions and practices. Nigeria has become one of the worldwide centers of Christianity and Islam, and the Yorùbá people have been instrumental in their

---

42. Latour, *We Have Never Been Modern*.

43. Bicchieri, Muldoon, and Sontuoso, "Social Norms."

44. Tarrow, "Mentalities, Political Cultures, and Collective Action Frames," 174–202.

45. Olayinka, "Religious Heritage and Values Perfecting Peacefulness," 103–121.

46. Jegede, "Yoruba Cultural Construction of Health and Illness," 322.

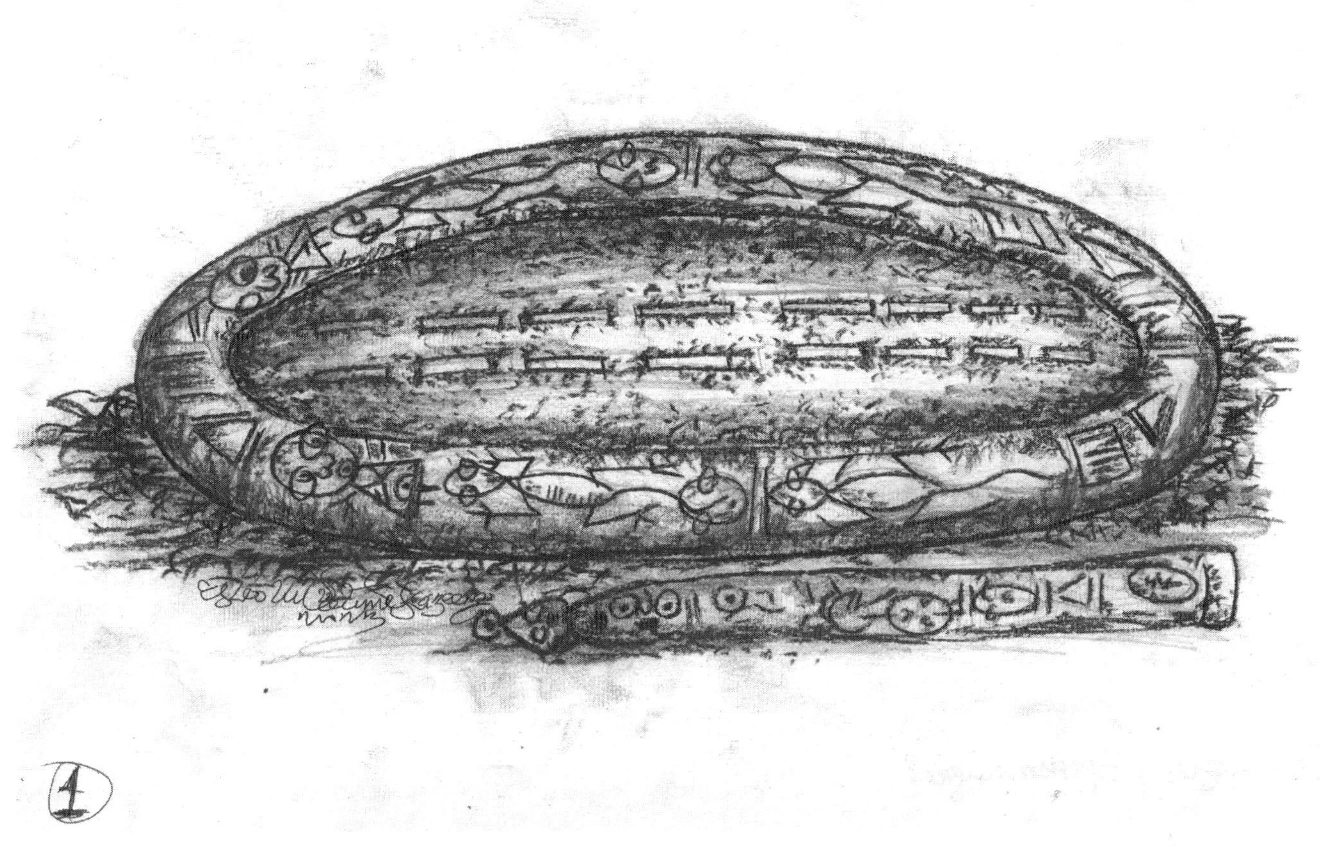

Figure 2.4. "Ifa and Ogbe," by Dr. Kazeem Ekeolu. Divination tray and symbols used for cosmic interpretations. Divination trays offer windows to deeper knowledge about mythology and the esoteric. Symbols are interpreted to reveal a hidden meaning. The Yorùbá diaspora holds this tradition in many of the traditional Afro-Brazilian/Cuban religions.

transformation and development. The advancement of Christianity to large groups of Pentecostal faith today has a lot to draw from the Yorùbá movements and ideas.[47] The postflu development of Christianity in the world was exemplified in the creation of the Aladura churches.[48] Today, hundreds of Pentecostal churches have expanded across the world. At this point, the failure to quickly get a definitive and widely distributed cure for the flu has reinvigorated some of the traditional beliefs that found fertile ground in the current religion. Those things have been adopted so much that most people might not notice their cultural background.

The myth of seeing a ghost, the effects of dreams, and other spiritualties that could be regarded as myths or superstitions have been the source of strength in the religious perspective of people today. There is, therefore, a point at which traditional beliefs have merged with new

47. Marshall, "'Power in the Name of Jesus,'" 21–47.
48. Crumbley, *Indigenous Institution Building*.

ones to form contemporary belief systems. Hence, the religions that form social norms among the Yorùbá people of today are influenced by the cultural, religious, and traditional backgrounds of the people.[49] The versions of contemporary religion among Yorùbá people form the social norms; old values influence the versions, and the old values are influenced by beliefs, part of which could be regarded as myths.

The normative values of the Yorùbá people are still strongly shared, even among those who have lived in the diaspora for a long time.[50] One can still see the resistance some of them form to the ideological and value developments in the world. There is still evidence of reservations stemming from how women were influenced by the social structure that existed during pre-Western civilization in Nigeria. This aspect has been vitiated by changes that have made us see women in strategic positions and allowed them to realize independence, which is why many people still have higher modesty expectations of women, expect their submission to patriarchal structures, and in some extreme cases, do not expect leadership from them. However, cultural respect and reverence for women in Yorùbá's old societies allowed for easy transformation to change such orientations.

The Yorùbá people's social expectation of sexuality is that an individual is heterosexual. However, one cannot emphatically say that there have been no instances of homosexuality in the past. Instead, such is regarded as an abomination.[51] The promulgation of the Same-Sex Marriage (Prohibition) Act in 2013 and its rise from the immense resistance to same-sex marriage in society is another reflection of the cultural background in the formation of social norms and social expectations.[52] The act was both a cultural and moral statement of the people on sexuality; this would build an expectation of how an average Nigerian, particularly a Yorùbá man, would see same-sex relationships. Hence, there is still continuity between the old and contemporary social expectations. Where such apprehension of other sexualities is seen as abysmal, the beliefs would be considered myths. There can be a conclusion drawn that the mythical conceptions of the past, in many cases, can dictate today's social expectations.

Social norms are the drivers of individual behaviors, either from the angle of conformity or defiance. This provides the context for the ideologies represented in this book, allowing readers to understand Yorùbá from local and global networks. There are some wide presumptions of attitudes expected of a Yorùbá person, subject to attribution and behavioral rebuttals. They are subsumed into the ideas of Yorùbáness and gradually inform the concept of Pan-Yorùbá movements. Whether created or influenced by myths, the Yorùbá's behavioral patterns and cultural orientation have adjusted to realities with time, making them conform to current global expectations without necessarily sending the initial values into extinction. These are what Pan-Yorùbá ideologies try to bring to the surface and protect from death due to ignorance.[53]

---

49. Peel, *Religious Encounter and the Making of the Yoruba*.

50. Adefarakan, "Yoruba Indigenous Knowledge."

51. Ajibade, "Same-Sex Relationships in Yoruba Culture and Orature," 965–983; Aderibigbe and Johnson-Bashua, "Yorùbá Traditional and Contemporary Cultural Perspectives," 279–301.

52. Ajayi-Lowo, "Same-Sex Marriage (Prohibition) Act in Nigeria," 71–92.

53. Falola, "Ethnicity in Nigerian Politics."

Myths and the African Society: Justification for Yorùbá Mythical Beliefs

The explained necessity of myth and society and its reflections in old and contemporary societies serve as a primary justification for the Yorùbá's reliance on mythology to understand certain realities. However, the relationship between African society and mythology is unarguably pronounced because of the nature of the continent's history. Africa is mentioned in the same breath as culture and traditions, which are the components that uphold mythology.[54] African cultures are part of the considerations that separate the continent from others. Africans have always created myths because they cannot leave questions unanswered, especially when these questions concern reality, existence, and things that affect them. The concentration of this mythical explanation becomes a part of African cultures, making myth creation a core element in the formation of African cultural beliefs.

African philosophy, in its uniqueness, could not be engaged without the establishment of premises and statements that form wisdom that is appealing to the people.[55] They became the foundations for African knowledge and philosophies, in addition to evaluating the understanding of humans, society, and existence.[56] Seeing that myth became the root of African epistemology and other aspects of philosophy, the Yorùbá society cannot be an exception but has become one of the strongest examples of the same, as seen in its proverbs and pearls of wisdom. In the epistemological construction of an average African society, myth became the carrier of the people's past experiences to the present, forming values and norms for the people to follow.

Moral education is premised on myths to reinforce the effects of an act or make people desist from doing it.[57] In some Yorùbá societies, children are educated to wash clothes, grind pepper, sweep the floor, pick beans, or remove the shells of white-seed melon (egusi) at night.[58] These instructions were intended to ensure cleanliness, prevent danger, and provide personal protection. The mythical repercussions have been the possibility of one's mother dying, seeing things in a dream, annoying the gods, or envisaging other scary problems that may arise.[59] Some mythical accounts are also designed to teach more sophisticated general lessons and set norms that guide interpersonal interactions. There are stories of the endeavors of Ọ̀rúnmìlà, Ògún, and other Yorùbá gods that have formed a set of lessons for people to learn from.[60] The legends of historical figures among the Yorùbá people, in whatever ways they are told, often carry some mythological properties that enact moral lessons and solutions.

Mythology is core to African philosophy and the conceptualization of things. It has helped the African nations manage their perspectives and rarely failed them until recently. Seeing the preponderance of mythology in African culture and philosophy, one would understand why there is a need to build a theoretical framework around Yorùbá mythologies.

---

54. Mudimbe, *Idea of Africa*.

55. Jaja, "Myths in African Concept," 914.

56. Jaja, "Myths in African Concept," 914.

57. Jaja, "Myths in African Concept," 914.

58. Wahab, "African Traditional Religions," 1–9.

59. Wahab, "African Traditional Religions," 1–9.

60. Parratt and Doi, "Some Further Aspects of Yoruba Syncretism," 252–256.

Conclusion

It is impossible to separate people from myths, which prevents them from forming cultures and norms for the people. Hence, it must be a core part of every society, and no matter the prejudice that may be held, it explains the composition of the people, their past, and the reflection of those experiences in the present. Mythology forms the basis of Yorùbá philosophy; hence, any understanding of the Yorùbá people must first generate or erupt from an understanding of their philosophical orientations. In the chapters that follow, I ground historical origins (iṣẹ́ṣe) in mythologies, explain how mythologies form the basis of epistemologies that spread regionally and globally, develop the spread of these ideas around the Oyo Empire, and show the existence of Pan-Yorubana.

Early History and Mythologies of Networks 3

Introduction

"If there is anything primordial about ethnicity, it is not the blood-based body of affective affiliations that plagued an earlier generation of modernization theorists, but rather, as Comaroff . . . revisiting Barth . . . maintains, 'the act of drawing boundaries among population.' The context in which such demarcation occur are of course crucial to their social and historical significance, whether they are motivated by politics, resource competition, class formation, marketing, immigration, religious encounter, or the apocalyptic violence of state-directed genocide."[1]

Since early in its history, the framework of Yorùbá origin has been woven around the "global" in multiple ways—namely, stories of connections to the Mediterranean; mythologies of connections to heaven; accounts of migration and state formation; the transformation of myths into political tools; the making of Yorùbá in all its broadest contemporary meanings and the production of a transnational Yorùbá community; the continued agitation for the creation of the Odùduwà Republic; the very concept of ìṣẹ́ṣe (origin), which grounds multiple cultural practices across the globe; and many frames, phenomenon, and ideas that transcend the scope of discussions in this chapter. One will be saying the obvious, then, to mention that the very idea of writing Yorùbá history is intrinsically woven with global history and common stories that have shaped human civilizations around the world. Many of the questions, contradictions, dynamics of events, phenomena, and motives that spur the curiosity of many writers to study the Yorùbá past share the same motivations with others elsewhere.

As in the Sumerian texts and myths from Mesopotamia, Assyria, Egypt, Rome, and other ancient civilizations around the world, among which the Yorùbá belong—namely, the Igbo, Hausa, Akan, Wolof, Kikuyu, and Luo, to mention a few—understanding the history of their founding or, rather, fundamental traditions that birthed the idea of Yorùbá, which has gained global legitimacy, lies in combing myths and legends that have circulated among them. Whether written as texts or presented as oralities, mythologies are the key to understanding the emergence of Yorùbá subcultural groups that made up the nation. After all, it is a well-known fact that accounts of "prehistoric" civilizations are encapsulated in oral traditions. The very idea of

---

1. Apter, "Yoruba Ethnogenesis from Within," 135.

oral tradition and its varieties of genres, thus, readily deconstructs reference to the precolonial past. Human beings predated the invention of writing and written texts.

Yorùbá history did not begin with African contact with Western imperial powers and their agents—travelers, explorers, missionaries, merchants and trading companies, and colonial administrators. Attempts at alternative documentation and reconstructions have been a common factor in exhuming the tales, myths, legends, stories, and other organic materials—read, artifacts—among Yorùbá cultures. Myths and other traditions on which this chapter lays the basis of its analysis are entextualized materials known to encode and animate historical moments in the life of the civilization. As with other mnemonic instruments, myths and legends teach generations about their history by way of presenting mythologies in a literary sense.[2]

The intrinsic literary value of these stories has given room to their reproduction in multiple cultures, using different characters and, in some cases, varying plots.[3] The themes are, however, always constant. The mythical founders of the Yorùbá—Odùduwà and Ọbàtálá—could, therefore, be replaced by different characters among the Ewe, the Zulu, the Fon, and other cultures, with their story given life within their environment and life experience.

It is in this understanding that one finds in these myths the navigation between heaven and earth and constant dialogue between the material and the immaterial worlds in the creation and evolution of human society. In them, the two worlds exist in one another. [4] The cosmology and other cultural frames of these cultures are so linked as they are derived from the same pool of ideas.

Mythologies supply insight into the structure, form, and thoughts that inform the analyses and conclusions in this chapter. Owing to the generic nature of materials from which information is sourced, deductions and conclusions made from the "historical accounts" explored fall within the realm of extrapolations and speculations, as several significant events therein lack a substantial degree of certainty and clarity. Since they are made and preserved as mnemonic vehicles, they communicate the past to generations in ciphers as they adopt metaphors, personifications, allegories, and other literary tools to write history and sometimes conjoin and compress different histories together. One cannot think this less than the need to reduce the existential threat of forgetfulness, distortion, and even total loss of these traditions. This is further necessitated given the distance of the past they communicate and the multiple generations with which they are meant to have this conversation. Committing these traditions to heart, which was the only way they could be preserved, meant that large-scale events were whittled down into the barest minimum symbolic narratives, fascinating enough to be recalled by different generations for the reproduction of history.

The extent to which one could distill meaningful thoughts from mythologies thus lies in the access to other traditions within and outside the studied culture, as well as the familiarity of the scholar with other works that have been conducted on the topic and the culture. Archaeological, botanical, genomic, and other fields of science, including physics, have been incorporated

---

2. Rosenberg, *World Mythology.*

3. Asante and Mazama, "Ogun."

4. Page, *Encyclopedia of African History and Culture.*

    GLOBAL YORÙBÁ

into the search for the rationality of some of these stories by historians and anthropologists.[5] Sure, there is no question about the potency of oral traditions in historical reconstruction and other matters of, inter alia, anthropological, sociological, and literary concerns. However, for social archaeologists, whose primary preoccupation includes pursuing data to their possible and logical "end,"[6] the thought of getting hold of, say, Ọbàtálá's "memoir" (or that of his followers in their ancient abode known as Igbòmokùn) or that of the legendary Odùduwà (or his supporters/lieutenants) crosses the mind for the weight such documentation carries.

This is to understand not only the identity of the individuals in question but, of equal importance, the social milieu in which they lived. Left with oral textuality that includes myths, legends, stories, and other traditions drawn from the political exigencies of the time, the social archaeologist is left with some loops into the past, which must be refined for some measure of rationality.[7] This does not mean written texts, like oral memoirs, could be produced without the effect of the political exigencies of the time; indeed, the political effects, as well as the rationality of a narrative, have always been the primary preoccupation of the social archaeologist, regardless of the topic at hand.[8]

Again, in a sense, since events are being interrogated that occurred at a time described by historians as a "pre-history"[9] in the evolution of the Yorùbá people, it is not hard to tell how these traditions—the myths, proverbs, rituals, performances, stories, songs, tales, and all other genres of orality—have served as a nucleus for the reproduction of the civilization and its history. Myths and these traditions form a substantial part of the preservation and reproduction of history in all human civilizations. As subsequent discussions will show, and as the title of the chapter suggests, aside from their mythological representation, neither of the progenitor figures among the Yorùbá exhibits an exact historical identity; rather, they connote symbolic characters. Part of the confusion common to both is whether the names they are known with today were their real names during their lifetime, since we are made to believe from the traditions that they lived as men who became only powerful enough to reach apotheosis leading to their deification by clusters of cultural groups that now refer to themselves as Yorùbá.[10] Another major problem encountered in this endeavor lies in the migration stories, starting with where they migrated from and the circumstances that surrounded this.

Various proto-Yorùbá groups included people in places such as Ile-Ife, Oyo, Owu, Egba, Egbado, Ikale, Ekiti, Ondo, and others. The term *Yorùbá* itself never existed widely before the

---

5. Odey, Nengel, and Okpeh, *History Research and Methodology*.

6. Armstrong, "Collection of Oral Tradition in Nigeria," 12; Imbua, et al., *History, Culture, Diasporas and Nation Building*.

7. Falola, "Ritual Archives," 703–728; Ki-Zerbo, *General History of Africa*, 4; Odey et al., *History Research and Methodology in Africa*.

8. Finnegan, *Oral Literature in Africa*; Akporobaro, *Introduction to African Oral Literature*.

9. The term *prehistory* is not used with the Eurocentric universalist intent that history begins with writing culture and that anything before this time existed in the dark, laid without form like the beginning of times. Rather, it is used with the understanding that recovering events during this period are heavily dependent on "folk" accounts preserved only in oral traditions.

10. This is further supported in Èjì Ogbè, one of the Ifá corpus, where Ọ̀rúnmìlà is seen talking about the essential features that make a deity.

seventeenth century and was not adopted as an ethnonym until the latter part of the nineteenth century when these groups metamorphosed into an ethnic community. To this extent, the people strictly maintained these distinct identities before the nineteenth century; even then, these primordial clusters of attachments were, at best, only relaxed, not eliminated. One source claimed that Yorùbá itself as a name was coined by a Timbuktu scholar, Abu al-Abass Ahmad Baba al Timbuktu, in his 1615/16 writings and later popularized by a Sokoto Caliph, Muhammad Bello, in his nineteenth-century writings. It was also claimed that Yorùbá became adopted by missionaries and subsequent others to describe these clusters of groups from the nineteenth century onward.[11] Before the widespread adoption of Yorùbá, it was used to describe only a subgroup, the Oyo. This was at a time when the Old Oyo Empire was positioned as one of the great imperial powers in the region.

Several protests by different Yorùbá subgroups against the use of Yorùbá as a generic identification were ignored, as a single name came with advantages: it was administratively convenient for the missionaries and the colonial government to use a single label; it was politically viable for social mobility and mass mobilization among the emerging Yorùbá elites in the nineteenth century; and it became theoretically useful for a large-scale scientific study of the people by colonial anthropologists and others. The buildup of the Yorùbá identity, beyond the mythologies and legends, could thus be seen as a frame that has a long history in regional networks facilitated by global trade and regional contacts.

Speaking to Apter's submission in the opening excerpts, the population of the people forcefully taken into captivity in the Americas and the Caribbean also began organizing themselves around this common identity in a resistance bid that led to the first phase of deterritorialization of the Yorùbá community.[12] Although they were not always known as Yorùbá in various Atlantic locations, and their formation around this identity took a different turn that incorporated other ethnic identities—especially from West Africa, such as the Hausa, Fula, Mandinga, and the Fon—they represent the extension of Yorùbá culture and the reproduction of its traditions.[13] Following the common trend in the transplantation of elements of culture in another environment, Yorùbá pantheons and the practice of the Yorùbá Òrìṣà religion in the diaspora took after the environment of the captives, as did the collective identity they adopted—namely, Nago, Mina, Aku, and Lucumi.

The Yorùbá nation in Nigeria, where the people are largely concentrated, is located below the confluence of River Niger to the west and used to stretch from the southern heights of the same river; Dahomey, Benin, Nupe, Bariba, and Aladah shared this boundary with them. They fought most of their wars and engaged in cultural exchanges with these neighbors. The great Oyo Empire had suzerainty over the larger part of this extension and, as such, fought many of the wars and acted as the conduit for the cultural borrowings until its decline in the first half of the nineteenth century.[14]

---

11. Jimada, *Nupe and the Origins and Evolution of Yoruba*, 9.

12. Lovejoy, *Prieto*.

13. Lovejoy and Ojo, "Lucumí, 'Terranova,'" 353–372; Falola and Childs, *Yoruba Diaspora in the Atlantic World*.

14. Akinjogbin, Abiodun, and Adebayo, *War and Peace in Yorubaland*.

Scholars such as H. A. S. Johnston, Maurice Delafosse, H. R. Palmer, and others have at various times subscribed to the theory that all African ruling dynasties migrated from the Middle East, while others have referred to them as Judeo-Syrian migrants.[15] Among varying other suppositions, another described them as the "children of Canaan" who were of the "tribe of Nimrod" but driven out of Arabia by a prince called Yaa-Roba.[16] But the reflections of the origin of the people or their progenitor, as this chapter will show shortly, can only lie in a dual origins paradigm. As such, the "nationality" of Odùduwà, where he migrated from, and the root of the Yorùbá nation and people, as well as the identity and role of Ọbàtálá in the unfolding events of the time, are explored here. These stories are deployed as part of earlier attempts to connect people and places in a pan-regional way of thinking.

Odùduwà

To start with the popular view of scholars of Yorùbá history, Omari-Tunkari explained that "exhibiting diversity and organized into at least twenty-five discrete, semiautonomous monarchies, most Yorùbá speakers maintain a sense of unity by tracing their common descent through Odùduwà—a deity and an ancestor/ancestress."[17] One important question that emerges from this is the gender of the progenitor figure, Odùduwà, which has remained murky in Ife history and the minds of the Yorùbá people at large. Even the very name, Odùduwà, is very less likely to be the name of the supposed progenitor of the Yorùbá nation who supposedly migrated from somewhere in the Mediterranean and settled at Ile-Ife. If there is anything that nonacademic chroniclers of Yorùbá history agree on, it is that the group that came to unify and initiate the basis of the Yorùbá identity migrated from somewhere around the Mediterranean, a region encompassing the Phoenician territories, Egypt, Syria, Nubia, and Yemen.

In another way, as it appears, aside from the middle word, which could be interpreted as "to create"—*dá*—the name Odùduwà consists of two principal words that are integral to Yorùbá civilization. These are *Odù*, which in Yorùbá cosmology implies the embodiment of wisdom in the realm of the extraterrestrial, thereby inaccessible to humans unless through *Ifá* divination and revelation, and *Ìwà*, which in the sociology of the people connotes character. It cannot be out of place to suggest that this was the name used to denote, symbolically, that great figure who united the proto-Yorùbá autochthonous communities in the area later known as Ife and initiated what scholars have called a "golden age" among the people.[18] This golden age brought about the fusion of preexisting cultures and ideas in this region with new ones that seem to be advanced and enduring from hundreds of miles away. Insofar as this is picturesque of how ethnic identities and nationalities are formed—that is, the fusion of different cultures, traditions, cultural groups and practices, and peoples over time—it is hard to tell the extent of this fusion, as societies are constantly evolving. Nevertheless, the Ife traditions and that of the Igbòmokùn

---

15. Apter, "Yoruba Ethnogenesis from Within," 135.

16. Bascom, *Yoruba of South Western Nigeria*, 9.

17. Omari-Tunkara, *Manipulating the Sacred*, 27.

18. Obateru, *Yoruba in History*.

people, also known as Ugbo or Ìgbò, suggest a seamless integration that appears only as an expansion of the existing structure.

The Igbòmokùn people are recorded in history as the aborigines or the earliest settlers who settled Odùduwà and his group of migrants in their quarter upon arrival at the place later known as Ile-Ife.[19] Primarily through the works of archaeologists, conclusions have been reached as to some cultural elements that separate the period before and after the golden era. One such conclusion is found in the objects used in making artworks and religious symbols represented by stones in the Igbòmokùn civilization, while the new era was marked by brass. By implication, objects, including gods represented in stones, are alluded to the former, and brass for the latter. Leaders of the Igbòmokùn communities rotated leadership among themselves in a kind of confederacy and maintained no sacred or divine kingship.[20] The special arrangement among the people saw the selection of a leader from heads of one of the communities who only acted as one among equals. Odùduwà transformed this system and established the culture that sustained it. Therefore, from autochthonous arrangements somewhat equal to a decentralized state, these communities were transformed into a centralized polity bringing about the mystification and deification of kingship in Yorubaland. With this, the villages were turned into quarters in the new order, where the heads continued to enjoy some substantial measure of autonomy and authority.

Taken from the account of Ade Obayemi, the very term *Olóyè* ("chief"), for instance, could be said to have emanated from the word *Oòyè* or the acclaimed lieutenants of Odùduwà who followed him on his journey to the area later known as Ile-Ife.[21] The term came to represent deputies or those who held important offices in the central administrative system that was being put in place after they subdued the resistance elements among the Igbòmokùn communities. It has since been used to refer to cabinet members who advised the king on administrative matters in all of Yorubaland. The term Oòyè, however, has been attributed to another event of a more mythologic nature and an adaptation of the deluge account in the religious texts of the Abrahamic faiths and common among cultures around the world.[22] In one of the Ife traditions, Oòyè refers to those who came out of a historic flood that once took over the whole earth with Odùduwà, including his children. In this tradition, which is less acceptable or popular among the Yorùbá people, Odùduwà and the people arrived on earth through a chain after the flood and moved to establish Ile-Ife. They were thus referred to as the saved ones, which could also translate as Oòyè in Yorùbá terminology. In any of the traditions that sought to trace the etymology of the word Oòyè, one certainty is that the term emerged during Odùduwà's time to imply his lieutenants, advisers, followers, or loyalists.

---

19. Beier, "Before Odùduwà," 25–32.

20. Indeed, as Atanda pointed out with supporting evidence from the likes of Beattie and Frazer, political power in present-day Nigeria before the appearance of centralized states was largely a military exploit with no spiritual underpinnings to gaining legitimacy. The ritual aspect of power brought about dynasties, as it left no room for such rotational leadership that had existed in the predynastic era. Atanda, "Kings in Nigerian Society."

21. Obayemi, "Phenomenon of Odùduwà in Ife History," 70–71.

22. Fabunmi, *Ife Shrines,* 4.

In the inaugural lecture of J. A. Atanda, he explored the trajectory of the kingship system in Nigeria from the very time central states began to surface among cultures around this area, illuminating how myths and traditions were coined by the people to consolidate, concretize, preserve, and reproduce what might be called elite history. In this context, although both the myths of descension from heaven and the Near East traditions agreed to the fact that the Odùduwà assumed his role in Yorùbá civilization and the world, by extension, having triumphed Ọbàtálá, none of these sources bothered to dwell on the details of the skirmishes that enabled Odùduwà to take advantage of Ọbàtálá's lapses. Such silence is expected considering that the myth of descension from heaven follows the adaptation of the traditions from the Near East and events at Ile-Ife during the evolving saga. More importantly, all the traditions and myths evolved to legitimize the Odùduwà dynasty; the oldest so far is tied to migrations, ostensibly without arousing bad memories that could jeopardize the continuity and endearment of the new order to the people.

According to the Ife tradition, Odùduwà and his entourage were welcomed to Ile-Ife by the likes of Ọbàtálá, Ọrànfẹ, Orofioye, and other heads of the Ugbo/Igbòmokùn commu-

nities, who settled them at a place known as Idio.[23] Perhaps, one of the situations that facilitated the emergence of a centralized state from small village-states and communities adumbrated by Atanda could shed light on the making of Odùduwà heritage in Yorùbá history: this might include natural disasters like drought, famine, war, and other situations that challenged the collective fate of the society, demanding for the intervention of a heroic figure.[24] In this way, the hero became the rallying point of the people. It could have been that it was in assuaging these situations that Ọbàtálá failed, as the head of the confederacy at the time Odùduwà took over, a scenario that is captured in the myth where Ọbàtálá got drunk and could not continue the journey of creation.

---

23. Adediran, "Early Beginnings of the Ife State," 89.
24. Atanda, "Kings in Nigerian Society," 378.

Whatever the situation, Ife traditions maintain that like every other place where a centralized state had emerged, the Odùduwà dynasty and its phenomenon did not succeed in taking hold in the area until it was able to contain rebellions and dissenting voices from some Igbòmokùn population that was incorporated into the new administrative system. This took the use of force and diplomacy as seen in rituals and performances, the wars that were waged from both sides, and the chieftaincy composition of the Odùduwà dynasty. For instance, Obadio, one of the leading heads of the Igbòmokùn communities and one whose community Odùduwà resided upon arrival, became the Onísòrò—that is, the traditional keeper of the Odùduwà shrine. Òránfióyè, another Igbòmokùn chief who welcomed Odùduwà into Ile-Ife, played a major role in the coronation rituals of an Ọọni-elect; in the long run, Ọbàtálá was deified and incorporated into Ife pantheons and the royal cult.

The reforms and gestures at establishing and reproducing the Odùduwà dynasty have seen to it that all Ọọni of Ile-Ife, regardless of their peculiar trajectory in the polity, are counted as Odùduwà's descendants. This is not particular to the Ọọni but to the entire Yorùbá people, with traditional accolades like *Ilẹ́ Oòduà* (the land of Oòduà) and *Ọmọ Oòduà* (offspring of Oòduà) used in making this collective identity. In the very case of the Ọọni, however, he is referred to as the Àrólé *Oòduà* (one who stands in for Oòduà).[25] These traditions are given mythical representations to consolidate the evolving sociopolitical morphology and conditioning of society. The mystification of these traditions or historical accounts is instrumental to the making of a divine kingship to which Odùduwà ascended.[26] With the mystification of the kingship came several other practices and structures to protect the legitimacy and integrity of the throne.

Together with the evolving traditions among the people, myths were used as an essential tool to bring about such structural and systemic changes grounded enough to keep reproducing themselves in society.[27] In a divine kingship, the figure whose praise and legendary was being explored was mythologized and presented to society to be larger-than-life. All over the world, this became possible because the king, now an embodiment of the state, its traditions, and culture, also doubled as the patron of intellectual production and development of the society.[28] He simply was the civilization. This "civilization," as myths presented it, was regional and global, while stories reflect local adaptations.

One such adaptation was the creation of a palace system, described in traditions as *Ajẹwọ̀*. Transforming the *Àjẹwọ̀* palace system into the tradition of an official "state house" (the palace system) and the rituals and ceremonies that come along with the installation and reign of the king, including the royal regalia that consisted of the crown, staff of office, horse tails, beads,

---

25. Oòduà is another way of spelling Odùduwà. In the same manner, the name of the town, Ifẹ, has been given differently at different times, perhaps, depicting the changing use of language among the people. Ile-Ife, Ife, Ufe, Illife, Iffie, Uhe, and Ise, are noted by Obayemi to be among these variables. One of the problems faced by historians in locating the historical developments among the Yorùbá people cannot be isolated from the ambiguous use of words and an obsolete version of some of words in the traditions. In the case of ambiguity, a single figure could be referred to in different names and at the same time, the different names given to this historic figure could take the life of their own as different traditions could also be developed to explain their role in history. Obayemi, "Ancient Ile-Ife," 152.

26. Feeley-Harnik, "Issues in Divine Kingship," 273–313.

27. Barthes, *Mythologies*; Falola and Jennings, *Africanizing Knowledge*.

28. Diop, *Precolonial Black Africa*.

and the best fabrics available at the time, constituted some of the practical paradigms through which the myths and traditions came to serve their purpose.[29] Indeed, given this trajectory, it is believed that the Ọọni's crown, *Adé Arè*, is the oldest symbol of kingly authority in Yorubaland; through this, others draw their legitimacy. The establishment of divine kingship saw to it that kings were seen as only next to the gods in Yorubaland through rituals that transformed this Ọba or the Ọba-elect from ordinary to an extraordinary being. Hence, given the significance of this figure in the Yorùbá civilization, it can be suggested that Odùduwà, or the infinite wisdom or cosmic intelligence, if you like, that constructs the norms and traditions that govern existence, was a mythical name set forth to describe the role of this figure in this transition. An intellectual history was created by framing a being as a cosmic figure with resemblances to others in a globalized world of kingship.

An Ifá verse in *Èjì Ogbè* goes thus: *Ọ̀rúnmìlà wí: Ènìà ní í d'Òrìṣà! Mo ní ènìà ní í d'Òrìṣà. Ó ní, Odùduwà tí ẹ rí hun, ènìà ni; nígbà tí ó ṣe ohun rere sí Ayé, ni wọ́n fi n bọ ọ́, ti wọ́n sì júbà ré.*[30] This translates to "Ọ̀rúnmìlà said, 'It is human beings that are transformed to become Òrìṣà!' I responded; human beings become Òrìṣà. He said that legendary Odùduwà was a human; he became revered and deified because of his good works while on earth." The good works the Ifá verse refers to can be located within the historical accounts that have been recorded in the Yorùbá traditions, parts of which have been adumbrated in the foregoing discussion. This feeds into the common structure and system that have produced ancestors and initiated ancestral worship among cultures around the world. It bears noting that after this influential figure, only one other character in the Yorùbá world of traditions is referred to in his infinite wisdom. This is Olódùmarè—the Yorùbá term for God. This is close to what the English speakers would call the Supreme Being. Both figures are described in the Yorùbá traditions as the originators of the Yorùbá world and the entire human civilization by extension. Two important considerations breathe some rational sense of life into this myth and adumbrate, ostensibly, how familiar and informed the people were about their environment and the world around them.

For one, the theory of Ife as the cradle of human race is understood as a metaphoric expression used in referring to Africa as a region of the world now scientifically proven to be the home of the earliest humans that went on to populate other regions of the world.[31] On the other leaf, the place of Ife, aside from political reasons, which, of course, is a recent development, has never been called into question even when it was sacked and its people were forced to take refuge elsewhere for at least three years. Through its decline and the rise and fall of the Oyo Empire, Ife remained the most revered of all the Yorùbá cities and towns, not because of its standing army (which it lacked), formidable market, or peculiar expertise of the people in the trade or a profession but through the foundation laid by Odùduwà during the golden age. The reference to Mecca in the traditions by some local historians and palace historians, before the interrogation of this tradition by scholars who have yet reached an authoritative conclusion on an alternative origin, are commonly cited in explanations that point to the Near East and the Mediterranean world common among the Yorùbá people at the time these traditions were developed.

---

29. Akinjogbin, *Western Yorubaland under Colonial Rule*, 57; G. Ojo, *Yorùbá Palaces*.

30. Sowande, *Ifa*, 43.

31. Smythe, *Africa's Past, Our Future*.

Accordingly, the people could be said to have had an idea of where their progenitor migrated from, but not the exact location, which they chose to adduce to Mecca, a prestigious Arab civilization that became the heart of Islamic peoples, cultures, and states from the seventh century onward. The very mythology itself does not fully reside in truth verification but in epistemology. Once a story is created, it brings consequences. Therefore, the "pain" of locating the exact place of migration of Odùduwà, and by extension, the Yorùbá people, has been a long one that modern technology and increasing knowledge of this region—that is, civilizations around the Mediterranean—have not been able to definitively pin down. It is a quest, and the search may even be fruitless, but not the idea itself. If the specific origin of the people in the Mediterranean cannot be authoritatively ascertained, as it may simply be referencing the knowledge of geography and a globalized world, evidence abounds that speaks to the place of Ife among the Yorùbá people. And tellingly, whatever authenticates the history of Ife has a huge bearing on what is known about the Odùduwà legend.

Distinguished pioneer historian Adeagbo Akinjogbin, in his introduction to the study of Ile-Ife, noted several quotations from eminent individuals in Yorubaland and a visitor who had hitherto commented on the status of Ife in that area. Among those quoted were the Ibadan "authorities," Balógun Ogunsigun of Ijebuland, and David Hinderer, a missionary. Most notable were the comments attributed to various forces within the several Yorùbá groups who could have contested the authority of Ife, especially during its days of tribulations and decline. Perhaps a look at one of these quotes would bring this to a clearer point of conclusion on how much the Ife tradition is revered among the people: A war had broken out between different factions in Yorubaland, in the name of the Kirìji-Èkìtìparapò War in the second half of the nineteenth century. In the bid toward making peace, the Ọ̀ọni of Ife in 1882 accused the Ibadan authorities of not being sincere in the peace process and wanting to attack Ile-Ife. This allegation was said to have been made to Samuel Johnson, the renowned scholar of *The History of the Yoruba*, who, in his professional conduct, demanded the response of the Ibadan authorities on the issue as raised by Ọ̀ọni Derin. The Ibadan authorities responded thus, as reported by Johnson: "I was assured by them (Ìbàdàn) that this was a false allegation, that even their descendants dare not carry war into Ife country for the following reasons (a) Because the Ifes were the power from whom they inherit the spirit of war and their war banner was made by them; (b) that the king of Ife is considered superior to their lord, 'The King of the Yorubas,' to whom His Majesty of Oyo pays homage, Ife as it is believed being the place where all nations of the earth have sprung from."[32]

This notion has remained largely unchallenged by any of the people, aside from the part that contends that nations have emerged from the great city, a position explained earlier in this chapter.[33] More so, it has remained the oldest Yorùbá town without consistent shifts due to war-induced problems or natural causes like other cities and towns in the area. Tellingly, the Yorùbá existed as a nation of people with several traditions that predated its solidification, a

---

32. Akinjogbin, *Cradle of a Race*, xii.

33. Several other works that point to the relationship between Yorùbá towns and kingdoms, and the making of the Yorùbá identity, include Law, *Ọyọ Empire*; and S. Johnson, *History of the Yorubas*.

process that was influenced by Christian missions, the missionaries, colonialists, and the educated and political elites of the nineteenth century.[34]

The solidification of the relationship that had existed between the various Yorùbá cities and villages by this emerging class of people in the social stratification of the society was necessitated by administrative needs. The Christian missionaries needed an indigenous language of communication among the people for the propagation of their religion.[35] This led to the reduction of the language into writing in which out of the dozens of its variants, the dominant Oyo variant survived this process, with others remaining as what are now called local dialects. The primacy given to Oyo on this particular note and in others, including the term Yorùbá, also comes from the administrative needs of the missionaries and the colonial government, which it was able to provide successfully given its administrative advantage over Ile-Ife at the time.[36]

In his critique of the 2004 publication of *Analysis Magazine* written by Bala Usman, Jimada Sha'aba, and Barira Mohammed, Fwatshak revisited the history of various groups in the Plateau area of Nigeria.[37] There, salient paradigms of considering ethnic identities, particularly as it relates to the indigene/settler question that is fundamentally germane to our understanding of the Yorùbá people and the role of the mythical figure, Odùduwà, in the formation of this identity, were raised. Among many of these daunting questions, consider this: "Are the places identified as the cradles of different ethnic groups mentioned above those ethnic groups' ultimate places of origin? In other words, did the Berom come from Wukari, the Ngas, and Geomai from Borno, the Kofar from Kano, etc.?"[38] Extend this to the Yorùbá, and the search for the exact place of dispersal of their progenitors becomes even more daunting.

Historians have taken to archaeological findings and relied on historical artifacts like the Ọ̀pá Ọ̀rànmíyàn (the obelisk now present on the supposed grave of Ọ̀rànmíyàn) with its so-called Phoenician inscriptions, the Ife marbles, and other sculptures, some of which are said to be present in the Egyptian court, to conclude on the Egyptian or Phoenician origin of the Yorùbá people.[39] Others have traced their root to the Jews, Etruscan, Mecca, and Yemen, while the myth maintains its heavenly origin. Instructive in the daunting task of locating the cultural extract or place of migration of Odùduwà must consider double, if not multiple, origins of the people where the existing information about this place has led scholars to find evidence linking

---

34. Peel, "Cultural Work of Yoruba Ethnogenesis," 67–89.

35. Peel, *Religious Encounter*.

36. History shows that from the late 1600s, Ọyọ had become a formidable empire stretching to the boundary of the Niger River, where another powerful culture, Nupe, thrived, to places like Dahomey, Allada, Badagry, and almost the entirety of the Yorùbá country. Until the coming of the freed captive returnees from Sierra Leone, Christian missionaries, and the colonial government, Yorùbáland was palpably burning under the leadership void that the decline of the Old Oyo in the early part of the nineteenth century had left behind, with different groups jostling to fill the void. Already, given its expansive administrative reach during its imperial days, its traditions, only next to that of Ife, must have influenced the larger portion of the groups later identified as the Yorùbá, thereby making it easy for the proponents of a Yorùbá identity to find a foundation already laid by Oyo during its heydays, combined with the existing Ife traditions. For more on this, see, for example, Law, "Constitutional Troubles of Ọyọ," 25–44.

37. Fwatshak, "Reconstructing the Origins," 122–140.

38. Fwatshak, "Reconstructing the Origins," 127.

39. Akintoye, *History of the Yoruba People*.

these cultures. This is more so for the suppositions that tie the Yorùbá to Egypt, Upper Nubia, and Phoenicia.

Following his submissions in his work on the "Origin of the Yoruba People,"[40] Saburi Biobaku argued from the works of Herman-Hodge and others, including the traditions of origin of Yorùbá people, in *The Egba and Their Neighbors, 1842–1872*, that "it is safe at any rate to say that whatever the various suppositions and deductions is true of the Yoruba is equally true of the Busawa, that they both probably migrated from Arabia (having migrated from north Africa) and that religious troubles were responsible for their flight across Africa."[41]

Biobaku maintained the view that of all the groups that migrated from Sudan, the Yorùbá went southward from Nupe in search of better and more promising opportunities. From there, they migrated to Ile-Ife, where the aborigines welcomed them; after settling, they formed the Yorùbá nation. This Nupe origin theory is the most recent of these postulations into the origin of Yorùbá. Surely, none of these submissions could be dismissed for their thoughtful explorations and the intuitive room they provide us for further summation. Moreover, most of these conclusions were reached based on sculptures, artworks, historical artifacts, oral traditions, and other visual and oral textual repositories found in Ile-Ife. They may be misleading as "facts" but not as a body of knowledge.

Whereas the common idea of Odùduwà shared by the popular traditions and myths of the origin of the Yorùbá people pictured Odùduwà as a male figure, in what seems like an isolated or rather less recognized tradition that linked the origin of the people to Nupe, Odùduwà is recognized as a female figure and the wife of Ọbàtálá, otherwise known as Sẹ́tílù. One of the major proponents of this school, Idris Sha'aba Jimada, in his PhD thesis titled *The Nupe and the Origins and Evolution of the Yoruba c. 1275–1897*, took the argument from the geographical proximity of the Nupe and the Yorùbá, which made interactions possible between them, to show how the Nupe culture produced what later became known as the Yorùbá civilization.[42] The entirety of the text is dominated by the influence of the Nupe on the origin and evolution of the Yorùbá people vis-à-vis culture, traditions, religion, economics, and politics. Aside from the commonality of their gender description of Odùduwà as a male figure, the popular traditions, as in many other cultures in Africa, have been related to the Hamitic hypothesis propagated by Eurocentric writers who are of the view that whatever history or advancement African states and peoples had witnessed in the past before the coming of the Europeans must have been engineered by cultures outside Africa.

This assumption has led to the description of Egypt not as an African civilization but as one birthed outside the region. It is this civilization that inspired the Nupe origin theory of the Yorùbá people. Using several primary accounts, this tradition debunks the Hamitic view of human formation in various parts of Nigeria, but as a scattered people of several origins, Jimada took the turn of laying to rest the Odùduwà legend in the evolution of the Yorùbá people. Ọbàtálá, the supposed husband of Odùduwà according to the Nupe tradition, was a blind migrant from Nupeland with mystical power who later came to influence Ife society with this advantage via

---

40. Biobaku, *Origin of the Yoruba*.

41. Biobaku, *Egba and Their Neighbors*, 2.

42. Jimada, "Nupe and the Origins."

the Ifá divination.[43] The *Egúngún* traditions and the Ifá cult, attributed to the Nupe origins, have led some to the conclusion of the Nupe origin of the Yorùbá people. However, this can best be understood as the effect of intergroup relations among people who had lived together for some substantial period.[44] Intergroup relations yield knowledge on regionalism and globalization.

---

43. Jimada, "Nupe and the Origins," 29.
44. Akinwunmi, Okpeh, Je'adayibe, *Inter-Group Relations in Nigeria.*

The geography of the area, a mixture of savanna and rain forest, together with its lowness of land and abundance of water, might have attracted the earliest habitation of people in that area, including the proto-Yorùbá and proto-Nupe groups. Given the richness of that area, can it be said that this place was inhabited by a group of people who later dispersed to their current locations? If it is agreed that this auspicious location was occupied by peoples of different origins and clusters, what evidence is there to prove the Nupe first resided in that area and that the various influences recorded in this tradition on the Yorùbá people were not another cultural adoption and adulteration by either of these groups—the proto-Yorùbá and proto-Nupe groups—or both of them at different stages, from other cultures within and without that territory? Even though an authoritative answer might elude one at this point concerning the second question, the first has been clarified by existing historical evidence that forms part of the subsequent analysis in this study.

The fusion of autochthonous communities and civilizations with later migrants invariably led to ethnic identities. The Yorùbá is here noted as people of multiple origins who share the same culture, language, and traditions, as they are bred in the same civilization. What is more is that, if at all we can trace where Odùduwà and his group migrated from, it is only a starting point to his origin, which might not necessarily be from this location but elsewhere, near or far. And his group of migrants, or entourage, as one of the traditions would have it, cannot be said to be of the same root. What Jimada adduced to the Nupe origin of the Yorùbá people, Banji Akintoye explains thus: "The proto-Yoruba and proto-Nupe language sub-families seem to have migrated from a little further up the Niger, slowly expanding towards the confluence, and that during that process each finally became differentiated from a mother language group. The clear implication of all this is that the origin of the Yoruba people as a linguistic and ethnic group belongs in the process of slow differentiation of proto-groups which occurred in the Middle Niger and around the Niger—Benue confluence, beginning about 4000 BC and continuing for thousands of years."[45]

During what has been described as its "New Kingdom," spanning between 1570 and 1085 BC, "Egypt improved on its standing army and engaged in successful wars against Palestine, Syria, and Nubia to the fourth cataract. Wars were fought with the Hittites of Turkey and the Libyans."[46] As with every successful military expedition where war captives were taken by the triumphant faction, an infusion of people of other cultures and civilizations into the Egyptian traditions followed. And before this time, from round 5000 BC, the Sahara region of North Africa had begun to dry up due to changes in the climatic condition of the area, affecting the living conditions of peoples and cultures that had flourished in the region. This must have informed another form of migration from this area for the population of other new settlements, or an existing state developed enough to secure the needs of the people who must have suffered economic hardship and political instability for years. The foregoing speaks to the truth in migration studies that suggests that the formation of states was characterized by waves of migrations by people of different origins.[47] Moreover, this becomes further illuminating when

---

45. Akintoye, *History of the Yoruba*, 22.

46. Falola, *Key Events in African History*, 37.

47. Vansina, *Oral Tradition as History*.

we consider that "in this world, an individual identified himself first and foremost as a Jew or a Christian (or later a Muslim), rather than as a Roman, let alone a Syrian or an Egyptian. The Near East inherited by the Muslim Arabs was more than anything else a mosaic of religious identities, the pieces of which were colored but distinct traditions."[48]

The muddle has risen from locating the supposed place of migration of Odùduwà and understanding why these cultures could have migrated to the western portion of the region to continue their cultural practices, from whence Ife was noted to have constituted the largest concentration of these pantheons. One thing that is repeated by the proponents of the linkages with an external world about this past is that the progenitor of the Yorùbá country had his roots in the Mediterranean culture, Egypt, they insisted, owing to its strategic location and influence in this area as well as the time these groups were said to have migrated to settle at the Niger River basin.

Another question that comes to mind in complicating the stories is whether the progenitor figure, Odùduwà, was the one who left this location to reach Ile-Ife. Or was he the son of a migrant to the West African region from Egypt who joined many others to settle at the Niger River before the dispersal of many of the cultural groups that make up the Nigerian state today? The migration of these groups, such as the Phoenicians, Nubians, and Egyptians, to the bank of the Niger River probably coincided with the seventh-century political catastrophe and natural disasters in parts of the Mediterranean. Berkey reviews events around this place at the time thus:

> Both historical and, especially, archaeological evidence suggests that, from some point in the early- or mid-sixth century, cities such as Antioch, Aleppo and Latakia experienced economic decline, depopulation, and a contraction of that civic space and life which had supported a flourishing urban life in late antiquity. The decline affected as well Roman defenses on the southern desert frontier, where forts were abandoned (to be occupied, in some cases, by solitary monks) and security turned over to nomadic or semi-nomadic tribes (like the Ghassanids) . . . The Roman emperor's unsuccessful attempt to force their wholesale conversion in 632 is just as telling, if less dramatic, a sign of the culmination of the process of resolving religious identities which had characterized late antiquity as the Arab conquests which followed rapidly upon the death of Muhammad in that same year.[49]

Nothing sparks migration like crises. The admixture of drought, external invasions, internal political shenanigans staged on a religious pedestal, and the expected economic decline and social fatigue are enough ready-made prerequisites for mass migration of people away from a region to populate another land, surely far from the uncertainties and precarious condition of the states around the Mediterranean basin and beyond. The confusion and possible mixture of cultural groups notwithstanding, myth creators are of the view that the elasticity of the term *offspring*, or children, at least during the period under study, could be expanded to

---

48. Berkey, *Formation of Islam*, 52.
49. Berkey, *Formation of Islam*, 52.

include slaves and subjects. This way, it would not matter where Odùduwà or his ancestors had migrated from to the place where they took a flight to the West African region. Neither would it matter if those on the entourage were from the same culture in this area. More so, this conclusion offers a better understanding of the reference to Odùduwà as a prince from Yemen, Syria, Mecca, or other places adduced to his migration. Accordingly, Odùduwà must have taken the identity of the ruler of the place from which he migrated, the same way those that followed him on the journey to their West African location took after his own identity and down to the entire Yorùbá civilization as it was later known.

By AD 640, the first major conquest of Islam was recorded in Egypt and "other parts of the fertile areas of the lower Nile."[50] If we were to establish the Egyptian root of Odùduwà, it cannot be out of place to relate his supposed migration from this area to this period. The choice of this period is not to imply that the Nile valley occupied by the Egyptians had been a sort of El Dorado during this period that could have prevented the migration of peoples around this place.[51] Rather, this is considering the probable period the group was said to have migrated to the Niger–Benue confluence, down to the place later known as Ile-Ife. Moreover, if there is anything common to all the traditions, it is that the migration of this group of migrants was instigated by religious displacement. Whether this religious displacement had occurred in the Middle East, Mecca, as one of the traditions has it, cannot also be authoritatively ruled out in the creation of a global mythology, considering that this was around the same period Prophet Muhammad died, ushering the spread of Islam through invasions. Among the evidence used to establish an extensive connection include references to the tremendous explosion of peoples around the Mediterranean during this period, overwhelming linguistics and archaeological evidence that takes us back to the Egyptian roots.[52]

When we consider the long duration of migration taken by this group that later populated the banks of the middle Niger, mostly in the areas of the Niger–Benue confluence and above it, and their evolution in this location that later saw the development of dozens of linguistic groups that scattered around the area now known as Nigeria (e.g., the Nupe, Igbo, Igala, and others), we are looking at centuries of relations among different ethnic groups in Nigeria as we have it today before their independent formation of cultural clusters. Consequently, the notion that Odùduwà as the figure who migrated from the Near East to Ile-Ife to establish a dynasty cannot pass the test of (historical) rationality unless this time line is adjusted, or we believe that Odùduwà lived for centuries.

Relating the migration of this group to their West African location to the Islamic invasion of Egypt and surrounding states can also be taken from the tradition that narrates these migrants as the subjects of the Egyptian conqueror, Nimrod, of Phoenician origin, whom they followed on several missions of conquest going as far as Arabia, where they had to settle for a while.[53] As it is customary for a conqueror to have some of his subjects reside in the conquered territory

---

50. Falola, *Key Events in African History*, 85.

51. Indeed, studies from this region, some of which have been quoted above, have variously shown this region to be a place of strife for political and religious dominance long before this time.

52. Oduyoye, *Vocabulary of Yoruba Religious Discourse*.

53. Johnson, *History of the Yorubas*, 6–7.

for consolidation and administrative purposes, so was it expected for some elements in a conquered territory to escape the alien rule when given a chance. Whether the foregoing could explain the relationship between West African migrating forces and the Near East cultures remains a matter of speculation.[54] However, given existing historical evidence, the various groups of persons that left this area to settle in the Niger River basin could not have engineered the sociopolitical changes that appeared later in this area, which historians have put to around the eighth century.[55] Perhaps, their descendants could have. It is even less likely that the same generation of people made it to the Niger basin, let alone established the centralized states in this part of West Africa. In a way, this explains their gradual cultural detachment from cultures in the Near East as they developed through these cultures to engineer new cultural frames that only retained parts of the Near East traditions that must be meticulously examined by scholars.

An essential feature of a prosperous human society has been linked to access to water. Leaving the crisis-prone Mediterranean and volatile Nile regions for an auspicious location that could offer relatively the same comfort as this area before the crises must have influenced the continued migration of the people, in addition to the need for security. At the bank of the Niger River, where this was found, dozens of cultural groups that made up the modern Nigerian state settled. Linguists are of the view that Yorùbá, Ebira, Igala, Nupe, Idoma, Edo, Igbo, Gbayi, and Kakanda share the same cluster of the Kwa language subgroup. Laying credence to how the Niger basin has engineered the birth of new civilization in this part of West Africa, the Kwa language subgroup is just a microcosm of a larger family of languages known as Niger-Congo (or Nigritic).[56] Adding to this, the separation of Igala, Idoma, and Edo from Yorùbá is said to have occurred about two thousand years ago.[57]

At this point, mention should be made of the postulation that "the ancestors of the Yorubas, hailing from upper Egypt, were either Coptic Christians or at any rate that they had some knowledge of Christianity"[58] posed by Johnson and buttressed by Lange in his "lost tribe of Israel" theory[59] and others in their works. This might not be so true in that evidence of the relatability of Yorùbá myths and accounts of existence to the Bible or Israel are nothing more than the dominant traditions used for social reproduction in the Mediterranean but adapted into the cultural peculiarities of these ancient civilizations. Johnson's reference above suggests the version of this tradition he was familiar with, as in others like him at his time,[60] most essentially as a Christian priest, where he thought the people had adapted many of their myths and traditions.[61] One instance of the transfer of the historical narration of the story of the deluge in the

---

54. In any case, the same Nimrod takes up another character as he is given another role in a different version of this tradition that seeks to establish the Near East origin of the people.

55. Atanda, "Kings in Nigerian Society."

56. Akintoye, *History of the Yoruba People*, 22.

57. Apter, "Yoruba Ethnogenesis from Within," 135.

58. Johnson, *History of the Yorubas*, 7.

59. Lange, "Origin of the Yoruba," 579–595.

60. Oduyoye, *Vocabulary of Yoruba Religious Discourse*.

61. By not bringing this view of a common myth and traditions among civilizations built around the Mediterranean into proper consideration, Doortmont, in his review of Samuel Johnson's works, made the same error as Johnson when he assumed that some elements of the traditions of the Yorùbá people, primarily the Oyo, were adapted from Muslims

holy books from the Abrahamic faiths into the Yorùbá world of cosmologies made the children of Noah symbolic figures for obedience and guidance among the people—so much so that they put the norms of social relations within the conceptual frame of *Ọmọlúàbí*. However, we do not know when this idea became part of Yorùbá traditions, and like the Yorùbá Ifá corpus, it is hard to tell which part of these traditions is mythical and which is factual.[62] In a Yorùbá version of this tradition, Noah has been replaced with Odùduwà as the deluge is presented as the genesis of the creation of the world by Odùduwà.[63]

But like every account in these texts, this is an example of local traditions that survived in the Mediterranean civilizations in which Odùduwà and some of his men must have been grounded. Thus, what appears to be the dominance of Judeo-Christian traditions in Yorùbá mythologies and traditions blurs the fact that such traditions also exist in Islamic and Sumerian texts and are indeed indigenous to cultures around the Mediterranean. Like Samuel Johnson, Lijadu also relates these traditions to the Judeo-Christian traditions, while indeed, they are meticulous modifications of the popular traditions in the Near East. Yet as far as these traditions could be adduced to the Judeo-Christian heritage, others would relate Ọ̀rúnmìlà with Jesus of Nazareth[64] and the Oyo dynastic traditions as ancient Near East traditions in which Ọ̀rànmíyàn represents the biblical Jacob, Àjàká as Isaac, and Olugbogi as Jeroboam II; among other prominent characters in Yorùbá traditions, Bașọrun (vizier) Gáà is likened to the Assyrian ruler Tiglath-Pileser.[65] The latter set Oyo traditions as some form of transplantation of an Israelite-Assyrian tradition to West Africa. What seems like a mishmash of historical "irrationality" highlighted all through these myths and their traditions constitute, indeed, a form in which social archaeologists can begin to understand and interpret the myths and traditions of the Yorùbá people, as in other preliterate societies.

What this means is that an attempt must be made to locate these myths in the traditions of the people. Only in the same way can it be seen clearly how these myths are a symbolic representation of the real-life events, phenomena, or practices they were launched to preserve and buttress, albeit in a more colorful manner. Traditions from the Mediterranean bring further clarity:

> Religious divisions are strong within the Middle East; and for many persons religious and sectarian fidelity even replaces nationality, so that it is frequently possible, on asking an Arab to what country he belongs, to receive the answer "I am a Christian," a "follower of Islam." A remarkable feature of the area, possibly connected with its geographical

---

who came from the north (up Niger River). This would imply that these traditions only developed after the penetration of Islam into the land, which has been dated to around the late eighteenth century, with little effect until later in the first half of the nineteenth. Nevertheless, as Doortmont has shown in his criticism of Johnson, the only world Johnson knew from the time he was born in Sierra Leone until his death was that of the Christian world garnished alongside the history of the Greeks and Romans, both of which were designed to lay claim to these traditions. Doortmont, "Concept of Yoruba History."

62. Adegbindin, "Interface between the Written and the Oral," 19–40.

63. Fabunmi, *Ife Shrines*, 4.

64. Sowande, *Ifá*, 63.

65. Lange, "Origin of the Yoruba," 589–590.

Figure 3.3. "Oduduwa," eponymous founder of Ile-Ife, creator of the centralization of political authority, and adopter of a beaded crown as a symbol of royal authority among the Yorùbá. In the Yorùbá world, all Yorùbás are believed to be descendants of Odùduwà. The image shows a sculpture of Odùduwà in the private collection of Prince Yemisi Shyllon, Lagos, Nigeria.

function as a meeting-place of peoples and ideas, is that three great religions of the modern world—Judaism, Christianity, and Islam—have risen within its limits; and that others, notably Zoroastrianism (now confined almost entirely to the Parsees of Bombay), Manichaeism, and Mithraism (of great influence in the later Roman Empire) should also be associated with the Middle East.[66]

While it is true that "what several groups of Yoruba say or think on almost any subject consist of infinity varied ideas and concepts, including those that are mutually exclusive and irreconcilable with one another,"[67] the immersion of those who came to reinforce the Yorùbá identity in Mediterranean cultures and the purpose, considered significant, that myths are meant to represent, gives this liberty to the people. Therefore, they adopt the same mythical narrative in different contexts, changing the characters and modifying the settings to suit the current matter.[68] In this way, for example, the narrative accounting for the mission of creation of the world where Odùduwà is a central figure could choose to include Ọbàtálá, from whom Odùduwà took over the mission of creation, or remove both mythical figures altogether and replace them with Èlà and Èṣù or Ọrúnmìlà. The tradition could go on to relate the mission of creation to Ọrúnmìlà, or Èlà, neglecting the Odùduwà narrative.[69]

These myths were developed in response to different historical situations to explain different phenomena or practices. This explains the changing character and modified narratives but the same plot in which the myths are set. For instance, while the Odùduwà/Ọbàtálá myths tend to establish the origin of the Yorùbá civilization and the entire world by extension, the Èlà/Èṣù narrative is primarily concerned with the creation of the world, the making and meaning of the days of the week in Yorùbá worldview.[70] In slightly the same manner, infusing Ọrúnmìlà into this narrative serves the purpose of explaining the creation of the world and the role of Ọrúnmìlà, which the biblical account refers to as the spirit of wisdom present all through the process of the creation of the world by God. Ọrúnmìlà is thus referred to as *ẹlẹ́rìí ìpín* ("Witness to the Choice/Predestination"), *Igbákejì* Olódùmarè (Deputy to the Supreme Being).

Meanwhile, Odùduwà is said to have given birth to one son, Ọkànbí, who begat seven princes and princesses, the first of whom was a lady who later married a powerful warrior and priest that established the kingdom of Òwu. This is followed by the mother of the Aláketu of Kétu, the king of Benin, the Ọràngún of Ìlá, Onísàbẹ of Sàbẹ, Olúpópó of Pópó, and the Ọrànmíyàn of Oyo. This conventional tradition poses some form of confusion in that if the era of Odùduwà in Yorubaland occurred around the tenth and eleventh centuries, as many historical works have suggested, it would be hard to believe that Ọrànmíyàn lived in the Yorùbá traditions till around the fifteenth century when Oyo was formed as a small settlement, or that his so-called siblings whose kingdoms were established around the same time could be the grandchildren of Odùduwà, who lived approximately two to three centuries before their time. The rationality of

---

66. *The Middle East* 1957, 4.

67. Sowande, *Ifá*, 5.

68. Indeed, this is not unique to the Yorùbá people but a common practice in oral traditions in Africa and elsewhere. Blier, "African Creation of Myths," 41.

69. Lijadu, *Orunmila!*

70. Lijadu, *Orunmila!* 35–45.

this tradition becomes even more complicated when we come face-to-face with another version of the tradition that depicts these figures as Odùduwà's children, not grandchildren.

The elasticity of the term *children* to subjects of a royal or noble family in Yorubaland is regarded in mythologies as a tradition transferred from Egypt and other Near East cultures to the Yorùbá. The complex composition of the Odùduwà dynasty, which sees the incorporation of other families from the Igbòmokùn communities in this tradition, all of whom are regarded as the descendants of Odùduwà, shows a complex web of relationships in multiple spaces. These figures might not necessarily have a direct link to Odùduwà but to the earliest rulers of the reformed state, like Ọbàlufọn Aláyemore, the ruler who changed the title of the Ife monarch from Olófin, which it was called during the time of Odùduwà, to Ọọ̀ni. Relating the establishment of the principal Yorùbá towns and kingdoms to those with a blood link to Odùduwà should be seen as a way of welding the Yorùbá identity better through the traditions. In any case, the political culture and structure that evolved with the reign of Odùduwà, which gave equal room to the Igbòmokùn chiefs and peoples, must have ensured that brave men within the nascent state, with loyalty to the Odùduwà throne, went on to establish new settlements. And by the elasticity of the term *Ọmọ Odùduwà*, this could have assumed the role of the sons and grandsons of this progenitor figure until this tradition was further reinforced by the colonial government, missionaries, and elite project in Yorubaland.

Ọbàtálá

Like Odùduwà, Ọbàtálá (also referred to as Òrìṣà ńlá or Àgbọnìrègún) is credited with the creation of the world in the Yorùbá origin myths and traditions. Ọbàtálá is said to be among the *Òrìṣà*—deified beings—that were sent to the earth for creation by Olódùmarè. Before, the world was in shambles and without form, filled only with water. The numbers of these *Òrìṣàs* vary from one tradition to the other, but the common number is often given as 401: "*Òkànlénírínwo irúnmọlẹ́ tó t'ìkọ̀lé ọrun bọ̀ wá sílé ayé*," which is a common line in Yorùbá metaphysical poetry. It means, "The 401 deities that descended from the abodes of the sky to that of the planet earth."

According to the traditions, on the mission, which included Odùduwà, Olódùmarè gave the deities some quantity of sand kept in a snail shell, one chicken, and one palm nut. Where Ọbàtálá got his palm wine from is not known, as the tradition was silent on this. However, the traditions relate that Ọbàtálá did get hold of a calabash full of palm wine and drank himself into a stupor. This drove him to sleep on this journey, leading to anxiety among his lieutenants. To save the mission, Odùduwà is said to have taken over the mantle of leadership from Ọbàtálá and headed to the earth with others on the journey. Odùduwà got to earth and perfected what Olódùmarè had instructed. He thus became the originator of the world in the traditions of the Yorùbá people.

This account could be, and has indeed been, related to different characters and in different contexts within and outside Yorùbá traditions, reaching the Sumerian civilization. In these traditions, myths construct bigger realities. To this extent, the same myth could be and has been used in a different context with different characters. Historical traditions of Ife, especially from the pre-Odùduwà times when those referred to as the Igbòmokùn communities had thrived, have proven the above to be one of the mythical representations that sought to explain the condition of the Ife society during the arrival of Odùduwà and his group of migrants. The above myth, a common one, constitutes an effort to explain how Odùduwà took hold of the reins of governance and administration in Ife from the existing Igbòmokùn communities, which numbered more than thirteen. It sought to establish the notion that the world as we know it originated from this location. Combining this notion with the power tussle between Ọbàtálá and Odùduwà establishes the role Ile-Ife is meant to serve in the cosmological world of the Yorùbá people.

The Ọbàtálá legend establishes the pre-Odùduwà tradition in the place later known as Ile-Ife. According to Ife traditions, about thirteen communities had existed at Ile-Ife before the arrival of Odùduwà. Among these communities were Ido, Iloromu, Ideta Oko, Iraye, and Iwinrin.[71] These settlements had evolved a political system and administrative structure that sustained their collective fate before the coming of Odùduwà. Ade Obayemi, historian and archaeologist, suggests that the people had "evolved a local political system in which leaders took titles prefixed by the word Ọba and perhaps Olú. Among these chiefs were Ọbawinrin, Ọbarenà, Ọbariyùn, Ọbalárà, Ọbamerí, Ọbagede and one Ọbàtálá who appeared to be supreme or at least had a higher status as Primus inter pares."[72] Although Obayemi could be right about the common choice of Ọba as a prefix to the names of the leaders of each of the communities, other titles equally formidable during this period included Ònpetu, Lokore, Apata, and Fegun. Whether the adoption of the "Ọba" prefix was influenced by the reorganization of these communities by Odùduwà or had been in existence to describe leaders of these communities, one cannot say. Together, these chiefs and their communities concretized the link between the surviving political culture in Ife and its prototype—that is, the predynastic/pre-Odùduwà and pre-urban system.[73]

Historians have come to believe that these settlements evolved a political system in which there was a political power at the center that was selected among their leaders. This power was rotated among the communities, as the government was a confederacy, to use the modern term.[74] This myth could be seen as playing into the role occupied by Ọbàtálá at the time the power tussle between both parties emerged. At the time of Odùduwà's migration, Ọbàtálá happened to be the symbol of unity among the autochthonous communities in this area. This position could be seen in the aspect of the myth that relates to us the will of Olódùmarè to hand Ọbàtálá the mission of creation. Drawn from the practice and rituals of the Ọbàtálá worshippers, it could also be suggested that due to his excessive palm-wine intake, Ọbàtálá failed to defend the mission entrusted to him by the Igbòmokùn communities. Accordingly, among other things, neither an Ọbàtálá priest nor the worshippers are permitted to consume palm wine, the same way Muslims, for instance, are prohibited from consuming certain meats.

---

71. The exact number of these communities remains a matter of speculation by historians, as scholars tend to give different numbers for their existence. In the edited work by Akinjogbin (*Cradle of Race*), which serves well as a groundwork on history of Ile-Ife, the number of these communities is consistently put at thirteen.

72. Obayemi, "Phenomenon of Oduduwa," 70.

73. Obayemi, "Phenomenon of Oduduwa," 71–72.

74. Beier, "Before Oduduwa."

   GLOBAL YORÙBÁ

Taboos are another form of social control among ingroup members. While some came because historical experience prevented reoccurrence, others evolved from mere observation. Social cohesion is important in these considerations.[75]

Given that Odùduwà succeeded in his civilizing mission in the vast region later known as Yorubaland by taking control of the administration of the Igbòmokùn and surrounding communities, trust in Ọbàtálá's leadership ability must have waned considerably among the people. This, in every sense, feeds into the conditions adumbrated above to be responsible for the emergence of many central states in the area later known as Nigeria—as elsewhere—which began around the ninth century. The same conditions are responsible for the emergence of new dynasties and, in some cases, the search for a messiah. It is on record from Ife traditions that several attacks were staged by a faction of the Igbòmokùn communities that rejected the rule of Odùduwà, signaling continued instability for the Odùduwà dynasty. The new regime made diplomatic gestures and incorporated important Igbòmokùn traditions and figures into the highest echelon of the emerging kingdom's administration, including access to the throne built on the Odùduwà dynasty and the recognition of Ọbàtálá as a national deity. This suggests that the continued resistance of remnants of the Ugbo community would be tentative.

Betraying this logic, the struggle between the two has continued to our modern history.[76] The animosity between Ife and some of the Ugbo communities suggests that instead of the sacking of the Odùduwà dynasty by the Ugbo people, as some historical accounts have recorded, powerful elements in the pre-Odùduwà era were incorporated into the dynasty that has been designed to be thoroughly elastic enough to assuage the anger of major stakeholders. Consequently, Ọbalùfọn Aláyémore, who is said to be the son of Ọ̀sángangán Ọbamakin, the king who reigned after Odùduwà and a prominent figure among the aborigines, had a close association with heads of pre-Odùduwà communities such as Eteko, Olorogbo, and Akire.[77] This suggests that the Odùduwà era in Ife did not commence with a war of conquest per se but by other means, which resulted from the choice of some factions of the aborigines who were enchanted by his leadership, capacity, and knowledge that could be used in addressing whatever predicament they were faced with at the time. An Ife tradition would suggest that Ọbamakin was one of the children of Odùduwà and the elder brother of Ọ̀rànmíyàn and that the absence of Ọ̀rànmíyàn during his death led to the succession of the throne by his son, Alaiyemore.[78] This can only be taken as another attempt by the traditions to synchronize the list of Ife kings into the Odùduwà heritage, as was expected of a dynasty. The structure of administration initiated after this period and the socioeconomic potential of the new polity brought many more to the Odùduwà side of the divide and left some of the Ọbàtálá faction in the resistance drive. For instance, even though Ọbawinrin was one of the major leaders of the Ọbàtálá

---

75. Apter, *Rituals of Power*.

76. Evidence of this continued rivalry surfaced in the form of a supremacy battle between the throne of Olugbo of Ugbo and the exalted throne of the Ooni.

77. Adediran, "Early Beginnings of the Ife State," 90.

78. Obayemi, "Ancient Ile-Ife," 156–157.

Figure 3.4. Oduduwa image by Lamidi Fakeye, Obafemi Awolowo University, photography by Ademola Fakeye.

faction, his Iwinrin quarter later became the place where others who decided to join the new polity from the Ugbo resided after leaving the area.[79]

Unlike in the usual occurrence of events during the unification and expansion of small states during which the autonomy of the authority and the communities were reduced considerably or revoked altogether, what surfaced at Ife was the quarter administrative system. In a way, this quarter administrative structure was not too different from what was obtainable in the pre-Odùduwà era, where the head of a village oversaw the affairs of his constituency and represented this constituency in general discussions that affected settlements around this area. Their authority might have been reduced, as all the decisions taken by a quarter chief could be reversed by the central authority, but the power to administer these areas remained largely with these village heads turned quarter chiefs. Moreover, the change from a village head to a quarter head is only a matter of syntax, as the same territory that made up a village in the past now became a quarter under the expanding kingdom. This structure of administrative accommodation has since been adopted by virtually all Yorùbá towns and villages to reflect the diversity of the society, maintain political stability, and promote swift development.[80] Maintaining this tradition, Yorùbá communities are arranged in clusters of groups of related traditions.

Therefore, the continued attacks staged by the Ugbo people against the people of Ife should be seen as a kind of internecine rivalry between factions of the same civilization and not between strangers who came to usurp power from the people and the aborigines. The transformation of the Ọbàtálá cult into a national one that has taken different forms and names in different Yorùbá towns—like *Oòṣàkirẹ̀* in Ìkirẹ̀, *Òrìṣàoko* at Òkò, *Òrìṣàògìyán* at Èjìgbò, and *Òrìṣàjàiyẹ̀* at Ìjàiyẹ̀, to mention a few—attest to the continued duality of Yorùbá origins—that is, an admixture of the pre- and post-Odùduwà traditions. The deification of Ọbàtálá after his death, although political power in Igbòmokùn civilization was based on military valor and not rituals or divine mandates, supports the summation of Apter on the nature of the Yorùbá *Òrìṣà* system as he sought to theorize the political function and social-communicative strength of *Òrìṣà* worship among Yorùbá people.

According to this reasoning by Apter, "Òrìṣà rituals and masquerades are also arenas of political action in which important statuses are publicly negotiated through the distribution of praise and shame."[81] Again, it is believed that deities, also known as oracles, are made through "natural or logical outgrowths from divination or from the need to receive mystic advice from supernatural sources."[82] One aspect of the Igbòmokùn civilization that must be made clear at this point is the process of the making of gods in this society before the coming of Odùduwà. If Odùduwà created the tradition of divine kingship among this population and surrounding areas, did he also initiate ancestral worship? In as much as an authoritative response to this is important for understanding these village groups, including their religious practices, the extent to which the post-Odùduwà era was shaped as an extension and termination of previous practices, and the deification of Ọbàtálá; such information eludes our knowledge. Available

---

79. Ikuemonisan, *Kingdoms "Olugbo of Ugbo" and "Ooni of Ife."*

80. Peel, "Kings, Titles, and Quarters," 110–135.

81. Apter, "Comparative Study of Orisa Worship," 3.

82. Obichere, "Contribution to the Study of West African Oracles," 4.

evidence does suggest, however, that ancestral worship was one of the practices introduced, or at least substantially transformed by, Odùduwà, who established an advanced culture, complex religion, and centralized system of government in Yorubaland.[83]

The Ife tradition of Ọbàtálá contradicts the version that is related to Nupe. Unlike the Ife tradition, which characterized Ọbàtálá as one of the original settlers in Ile-Ife, both in myths and traditions, Nupe traditions described this figure as a later migrant from Nupe. The Nupe account of Ọbàtálá adduces his migration from Nupe to the area later known as Yorubaland to the effect of the increasing spread of Islam and Islamic teachings in this area, which saw the Ifá divination system of Ṣẹ́tílù, better known as Ọbàtálá, as a threat for its popularity among the people. In this tradition, Ṣẹ́tílù was born blind and was a source of concern for his parents, who thought of killing him until they saw him display extraordinary powers that led to the development of the Ifá divination system through which he, even at a tender age, made predictions for his parents and other people that came to him. Ṣẹ́tílù grew in strength and wisdom at Nupe but without sight, until he was forced out by the Muslims. He took his journey through Ekiti down to Ile-Ife, where he settled.

As is customary with these traditions, the period this took place is unknown. More curious is that this journey was undertaken only by Ṣẹ́tílù, who at the time had gained many followers to the supposed dread of local Islamic authorities, although another version of this tradition is silent about the reason for his migration from Nupeland to Ife. This brings into question the epoch in which Islam began to make an impact around the area vis-à-vis the time Odùduwà is projected to have lived in Ife. This tradition also suggests that the same Ṣẹ́tílù was a husband to Odùduwà. The tradition goes further to surmise that whereas the earliest means of divination Ọbàtálá/Ṣẹ́tílù used in consultation with Ifá were pebbles, this was changed to palm nut at Ife. By this reasoning, Ifá divination came to Yorubaland through Ṣẹ́tílù/Ọbàtálá, who took the tradition to the people. This tradition fits into the Obichere's second submission on the making and understanding of deities. As he explained, "There is the probability that oracles 'just happened,' that is, that they came into being directly and independently because of their basic indispensability to religious man,"[84] a practice he noted to be common to the Nupe people.

This is the same with the Ife tradition, which in a bid to establish Ọbàtálá in the pre-Odùduwà order and the differences between the two eras, mentioned Ọbàtálá as one of the gods represented in stones by the Igbòmokùn people alongside other deities like Òrìṣà Ijugbe. This gives

---

83. Some of these include the Ifá verse, Èjì Ogbè, quoted earlier, and the multiplication of gods among the people. The latter has brought about the concept of +1 in the Yorùbá metaphysical system—that is, the continuous production of gods among the people. In this case, scholars are quick to mention 201 or 401 as the numbers of Yorùbá pantheons as Odùduwà came to transform the religious practices of the people; hence, on every single day, at least one of these gods was worshipped in Ile-Ife, and the kingdom as the spiritual and cultural headquarters of the nation was established. Despite the varying numbers often adduced to Yorùbá pantheons, as seen in the above numbers, none of these submissions could explain the question without giving room for the yet-to-be-made-gods in Yorùbáland, represented by the +1. The +1 phenomenon also included those ancestors of little or no national significance revered by their community/family. Therefore, if at all ancestral worship had been practiced among the pre-Odùduwà civilization in Ife, this was transformed into a ground philosophy, form, and system with the restructuring of the polity. Abimbola, *Yoruba Culture*; Omari-Tunkara, *Manipulating the Sacred*.

84. Obichere, "Contribution to the Study of West African Oracles."

the impression that Ọbàtálá was a living being and a deity at the same time, represented in stones like other deities worshipped by the people. Among other things, the confusion lies in the representation of other deities mentioned alongside Ọbàtálá in this tradition—namely, Òòṣ àkirè—which is another version of the deity peculiar to the Ìkirè people. It remains to be seen, at this point, how a deity represented in stone could simultaneously fight for a leadership role in the evolving polity of the time. This brings us to the conclusion of his deification after his demise. Meanwhile, if pebbles were to be used for divination in the past and only transformed into palm nuts later on, could it not have been that the Ifá divination system had been with the Igbòmokun people before the golden era or arrival of Odùduwà since their religious symbols and items were largely represented in stones?

But the history and spread of Ifá in Yorubaland go beyond this, as discussion on "Oyo Heterogeneity" will show in chapter 4.[85] Besides, the Yorùbá god of divination is not Ọbàtálá/Ṣẹ́tílù but Ọ̀rúnmìlà. In the Yorùbá cosmological and metaphysical view, each god has functions given by Olódùmarè to deputize him in different conditions. While Ọ̀rúnmìlà serves as the infinite wisdom always present with Olódùmarè, Ọbàtálá is characterized as one responsible for the molding of humans. Upon coming to the earth, Ọ̀rúnmìlà is said to have acted as the loop through which humans made contact with cosmic bodies that could help in navigating situations thought to be beyond earthly grasp. Ọ̀rúnmìlà is therefore synonymous with Ifá divination, while Ọbàtálá is synonymous with human creation in this world of tradition. This way, every deformed person is regarded as a special being under the exclusive protection of Ọbàtálá—ẹni òrìṣà.[86] This version of the Yorùbá myth that relates deformity with Ọbàtálá feeds into the Nupe-Ṣẹ́tílù story, which portrayed this figure as a blind man, but for some clear inconsistencies that have been previously addressed. Provided with the materials for the creation of humans by Olódùmarè, it is believed in the traditions, sometimes Ọbàtálá decided to mold certain humans with disabilities for reasons sometimes related to punishment for a sin committed by the child's parents. This myth, indeed, tells a lot about Ọbàtálá with his deformity while alive but is less likely in the Nupe version.

Since the Ṣẹ́tílù tradition of the Nupe was set to dislodge the Odùduwà tradition among the Yorùbá people, it is important to add the following points that discredit this tradition. Historical accounts from Nupe record that until the fifteenth century, when Tsoede was said to have arrived among the people of Nupe, a centralized state never emerged among the people, but pockets of villages came together to form a small state as existed before the arrival of Odùduwà in Ugbo/Igbòmokun. The Tsoede transformation would be about three centuries after such polity had been replaced or transformed, rather, into a centralized state in Yorubaland. The question now would be who and where the Nupe migrant got the idea of such a massive organization that completely restructured Ife politics and how the people had been divining before this time.

---

85. Here, the circumstance and situation that warranted the introduction of Ifá into Yorùbáland through Ado upon its rejection at first in Oyo comes along with the history and evolution of Oyo as presented to us by Johnson. Meanwhile, the Nupe origin tradition also affirmed that Ifá got to Ado before its spread in Yorùbáland but related this story in another way that continued with Setilu's journey, who crossed the town on his way to Ife.

86. Lawuyi, "Obatala Factor in Yoruba History," 373.

The Ọbàtálá faction that continued to resist the new political order migrated further eastward into the Yorùbá country, where they are settled and located today.[87] This was after they were subdued by the Odùduwà faction through the help of the Ife princess, Mọ́remí, who exposed their war tactics. Movement further eastward would be in their determination not to be part of the new political order. Here, they have maintained, to some extent, some form of cultural distinction, which includes language. Yorùbá states located in this area share more political connections with Benin than Ife. This, however, was primarily because of their geographic location, as in others at the end of the northern part of the Yorùbá country now classified as part of the people of northern Nigeria.[88]

Leaning on the version of the tradition of the Ugbo/Igbòmokun people as espoused by the faction of the culture that exists in this area, the crisis that led to the overthrowing of preexisting order in Igbòmokun civilization was propelled by an interregnum caused by the lack of an heir to the leadership of the Ugbo people, as Ọbàtálá, the heir, was too young to assume this position.[89] His eventual installation as the king of the Ugbo people weakened his power position. Watching events from his quarters, Odùduwà took advantage of the situation, the peak of which was the intoxication of Ọbàtálá to enthrone himself.

From what we know from other traditions that have been explored so far, the society was at the fourth stage of the evolution of states identified by Atanda—that is, at the point when village groups that had evolved from hitherto autonomous lineage groups and clans and began organizing into small states,[90] as these were autochthonous communities. If we are thus to go with these traditions, the society had at this time begun to evolve hereditary leadership, as the conglomeration of clans and lineages would have warranted social stratification along some primordial lines. Although illuminating, this tradition, however, can only be taken as another modified form of the traditions that have sought to explain the relationship between Ọbàtálá and Odùduwà, including the myths that put the plot in a heavenly abode.

The best takeaway from the tradition would be the reiteration of the political decline and social distress witnessed in Igbo communities at the time the Odùduwà dynasty was enthroned, which captured the political condition of the polity that created the ground for Odùduwà's emergence. At this point, it would not matter if the account of interregnum and Ọbàtálá was presented accurately or should be understood for its plain/basic meaning. Like the rest of the myths and traditions we have treated so far, the tradition attests to the existence of a pre-Odùduwà civilization at Ile-Ife, which had developed a certain structure of political administration that was at the time of Odùduwà in the care of Ọbàtálá but restructured and extended by Odùduwà due to the character flaw of the latter. The weakness that Ọbàtálá exhibited after his installation as the head of the Ugbo communities should be understood only in terms of the rate at which he consumed the local palm wine, which has been attributed to his failure to hold together the Ugbo communities, and not in terms of military valor and other manners of character needed to deify a figure. It is this character flaw that his devotees and followers have tried

---

87. Ikuemisan, *Kingdoms*.

88. Ogen, "Exploring the Potential of Praise Poems," 77–96; Paul, "Migration Patterns," 108.

89. Ikuemisan, *Kingdoms*.

90. Atanda, "Kings in Nigerian Society."

to avoid by systematically turning the use of palm wine in sacrifice, close to the Ọbàtálá shrine, or consumption by adherents, into a taboo.

Conclusion

The controversies that surround these significant characters in Yorùbá history are not isolated from the generic aura mythical stories and prehistoric characters exhibit in every culture. In most cases, locating the etymology of the names of these characters could be the major leap one needs to find the true picture of their contribution to history and, more importantly, civilization. The account of state formation that gave us Ọbàtálá and Odùduwà in the traditions of the Yorùbá people, as noted in the introductory chapter to this book, depicts the multiple contours from where global and regional narratives could be located in the creation of the community. For one, the common knowledge among the people about the trajectory of the nation from Odùduwà, which is often silent on the pre-Odùduwà era, is a testament to the Victorian narrative found among cultures, most recent of which was perpetrated by the Western imperial powers in different parts of Africa. And telling this story fits into the contemporary global intellectual movements aimed at decolonizing the writing of history, especially in Third World countries. As seen in the Ife traditions, state formation is hardly engineered in space with no existing civilization. When this is understood, we can begin to look at identity groups in their true fluid and evolutionary character.

Whereas the foregoing has reviewed some aspects of the Ọbàtálá and Odùduwà traditions, one of the many questions that remain unanswered is how the Ọbàtálá cult managed to spread across the Yorùbá nation more than the triumphant Odùduwà cult. Today, the chronology of kings in Ife describes all Ọòni of Ife as those with direct blood relations to Odùduwà, even though they came from different backgrounds that have, since the time of Ọ̀ságangan Ọbamakin, extended to the Aborigines. Generally, the soft approach to the enthronement of the Odùduwà dynasty must have been responsible for the long duration of time the dynasty and polity had existed. The sociopolitical morphology that surfaced after the enthronement of the central administrative system headed by Odùduwà does not suggest a conquest; rather, it suggests other means that involved the participation of a faction of the Ugbo communities. The Yorùbá nation has come a long way, and even at this point, the process of adaptation and acculturation of peoples of several other cultural groups in and outside of the nation is still taking place. In their diaspora homes in West Africa and across the Atlantic, for instance, the global Yorùbá community is characterized by people of other cultural groups in West Africa, the top among which are the Hausa, Fon, and Mandinga.

Reconstructing the history of the Yorùbá people during this period, characterized by limited data and mythical bodies, is based on assumptions derived from the few facts available to the writers at the material time and space of recording such intellectual records. This is more so considering the different conclusions often reached. As the foregoing has shown, they all open debates on the possible origin of the Yorùbá people, and this argument will continue as new evidence and techniques for interrogating this past surface. This study suggests a compilation of the various praise poems of different groups that are today known as Yorùbá and see the nexus that might be hidden within this art common to them all if only to ascertain the authenticity of the Ile-Ife supremacy and the migration story of these groups. This could be another step toward tracing the union of the Yorùbá race.

However, one thing that is certain in all these studies is that the Yorùbá, like other groups of people, emerged as a function of incessant migrations, conflicts, wars, intergroup relations, and regional networks. While it is true that some groups among the Yorùbá race adduce their direct trajectory to Oyo and other acclaimed cities of the seven sons of Odùduwà, others trace their direct ancestry to Ile-Ife, ostensibly in a bid to put themselves in a similar position with the likes of Oyo, Egba, Ijebu, Ila, and other acclaimed original descendants of the Ife dynasty.[91] This trend has continued with them in their diaspora space, where the Yorùbá community of Oyotunji in North Carolina has tapped into the Oyo traditions for legitimizing its Yorùbá origin and its king among other Yorùbá kings. Through this and other rituals, Ile-Ife has remained the recognized mother culture of the Yorùbá people, as it is seen as a symbol of unity among the various Yorùbá groups, irrespective of their location, through the mythical figures discussed in this chapter.[92] Through its political exploit, Oyo shares a larger part of this charter in the global Yorùbá community. In all, the Egyptian origin of the people, as suggested in a mythology, should be taken as the ancient root, and the Niger River basin as the immediate, with the latter being the most probable place from where Odùduwà and his group of migrants journeyed from as several other protoethnic formation groups in various parts of contemporary Nigeria were setting out to form larger polities as known today.

91. Asiwaju, "Political Motivation and Oral Historical Traditions," 116–121.
92. Apter, *Oduduwa's Chain*; Falola and Genova, *Orisa*.

Cosmologies and Epistemologies 4

Introduction

Epistemologies are conceptual frames of ideas, traditions, and thought systems through which cultures and civilizations understand and communicate their world. Fundamental in this makeup is the lived experiences of the culture, which in turn is a subject of the social and physical environment. We come to know epistemologies and cosmologies and other forms of knowledge production through the study and interpretation of the environmental forces by the inhabitants. These structures of knowledge production constitute the ground upon which civilizations are built, sustained, reproduced, and made distinct from others. The ideas represented in this chapter examine the nucleus of Yorùbá culture and traditions. Within the epistemic pursuit of Orí (the essence of human personality, fate, and the locus of existence), the philosophy of the people is encapsulated, and through *Ifa's* thought system, this understanding is encoded and transmitted. The paradigm upon which these two philosophies exist is based on the notion of Òrìṣà, venerated spirits or Yorùbá saints. Yorùbá *Òrìṣà* is produced out of Yorùbá cosmology, which sees most things as connected to the will of unseen forces.

The fundamentals of every ancient culture are built around their religion and religious institutions. Religion itself is a larger construction for humans to keep up with myriads of challenges around them and a loop between the seen and the unseen world. Some elements of a religion are found in different places and cultures, perhaps with some modifications that consider the experience of the people where the religion originated. Tellingly, the three concepts considered as the core of Yorùbá civilization to be discussed in this chapter could be framed in two global structures: some elements are inherently found in other cultures of the world, while, on the other hand, they have traveled around the world with generations of Yorùbá migrants. Globalizing these cultural conceptual frameworks along these dual pedestals enables us to appreciate how much the Yorùbá have leaned on global ideas in the creation of their world and the spread of their inventions over the years in this global space. The former reiterates how interconnected the human world is and its shared trajectory.

Further, even though Ifá has traveled to the Atlantic along with Yorùbá migrants starting with the Yorùbá captives, especially those of the eighteenth and nineteenth centuries, the concept of Ifá is not alien to some other cultures, indigenous or otherwise, in these Atlantic spaces. Like Yorùbá Ifá, civilizations throughout immemorial history have developed systems of divination and access to cosmic space. This is likewise the *Òrìṣà* and the idea of *Orí*. None of these concepts could be rightly said to originate only among the Yorùbá; rather, an adaptation of common cosmologies and metaphysical beliefs have circulated among cultures and cultivated civilizations for thousands of years. Characterized by fixtures of ancestral worship system ubiquitous among indigenous cultures, Yorùbá *Òrìṣà* signifies the reenactment of the history of the people as well as the reproduction of their traditions.

Alongside other frames of ideas woven around Òrìṣà, epistemologies keep the conversation between the material and the immaterial worlds open. As an extension of the human community, the extraterrestrial world is conceived as a unit of the living world where ancestors reside to help tailor the experience of the people. Therefore, no indigenous culture exists without the structure of consciousness that made up the paradigm of discourse in the following analysis. Furthermore, as in the case of the Yorùbá, they have all been kept as the pillars of the cultural heritage of these civilizations. Hence, in addition to the myths, histories, and legends of Odùduwà and Ọbàtálá, these ideas and traditions have been cast as the philosophical bond that defines the Yorùbá community in the diaspora.

It should be emphasized that religious ideas can start as local—as in Christianity and Islam—but they become global. The Bible and Quran, centuries-old documents, have become the most globalized holy scriptures. It is the same with aspects of Yorùbá beliefs, formulated at a time that we cannot date but which have now spread widely. Thus,

1. Many of the cosmologies and epistemologies discussed here have become global.
2. Over time, Islamic and Christian ideas have modified their contents.
3. Yorùbá, as migrants, have been the couriers of these cosmologies and epistemologies, which can be found in different parts of the world.
4. Cosmologies and epistemologies shape perceptions of how people relate to their spaces.
5. The ground notions of *ìṣèṣe*—fundamentalist organic practices—have endured the test of time.

The *Òrìṣà* guides the Orí—the personality soul—in making good choices, while Ifá points in the direction of both forces for individuals to be aware of the cosmic configuration that affects their situation and how to go about aligning with this formation. The Yorùbá people value responsibility, honor, respect, hard work, peace, patience, contentment, integrity, and communalism. These virtues characterize what it means to be Yorùbá; they are the ideals governing the existence of society. Ifá teaches polarity and balance in Yorùbá religious theology, which comprises cosmological and metaphysical paradigms of operation/interaction. Its literary corpus is a documentation of Yorùbá classical thought and philosophy. Many turn to this text for fuller access to the inner workings of the Yorùbá civilization.

Orí in Yorùbá Cosmology

Orí is the consciousness and inner essence of every human, and it characterizes the being and what others know of it. By implication, Orí is believed to be the spiritual space or entity that governs individuals' conduct and rites of passage. Awo Fa'lokun Fatunmbi defines it as the

"Yoruba word used to describe the vessel that can process conscious thought."[1] If Orí were to be a blacksmith, like *Ògún*, the patron deity of blacksmiths, it would be both the workshop and the blacksmith, only it would not be forging swords for warriors or machetes for farmers or any other metal implement. Rather, in this capacity, Orí would be the workshop and the blacksmith that shape the identity of the warrior, the farmer, the chief, the craftsman, the diviner/priest, and the Yorùbá pantheon of gods.[2] The idea of Orí among the Yorùbá thus pushes the conscious need for consistent spiritual alignment between the individual and their inner essence to the fore. Put another way, the concept of Orí embodies Yorùbá peoples' notion of predestination, providence, character, and all that characterize the living conduct and expectations of the people.

In the Yorùbá belief system, all these are governed by the binary dimensional reality of the terrestrial and the extraterrestrial.[3] Actions taken in the former are believed to have implications in the latter, and whatever is manifested in the former is understood as a causation of the latter. So individuals embark on every endeavor in the terrestrial world as it has been designed, set, or inspired by the subterrestrial forces that their inner essence, since before birth, has been tasked to negotiate and bargain with in the transparent world. While this idea is not exclusive to the Yorùbá people, it manifests through the conceptualization of their belief system and its adaptation to their cultural framework and lived experiences. Explaining this pointedly would be the biblical reference to Yahweh telling Jeremiah the Prophet that he knew him before he was "formed in his mother's womb."[4] In the Yorùbá metaphysical landscape, the personality soul—Orí—of an individual emerges after creation by Olódùmarè, who gives the individual the first platform to be human—that is, to make a choice. This choice would come to be the Orí, the personality soul of this fellow. *Orí ni àkúnlẹ̀-yàn*, meaning "Orí is one we select with reverence," is a popular saying among the Yorùbá people. In a way, it suggests that the Yorùbá believes both in free will and predestination. Free will is, however, exercised at the time before the Orí was involved or had not yet been invoked into the individual's conduct, and only at this time of critical selection does it surface in the affairs of humans. Following the selection by free will, predestination takes over the unworldly and earthly conducts of the individual; consequently, in the event of contemplation over an important task or endeavor, the person is asked to *bere lọ́wọ́ Orí ẹ* (ask your Orí).

At this point in the arrival as a child, the individual is launched into the deep ocean of forgetfulness through which he is brought into the earthly world as a baby. Owing to this process, the oracle could be consulted to foretell the destiny of an unborn child. Putting this in the context of the Yorùbá belief that *Olódùmarè ni ó ń ṣe ọmọ*—that is, it is the Supreme Being that gives us our children—the choice that a child would be born to a family is determined by Olódùmarè using the spiritual indexes—which also counts as the Orí, as it is made up of different particles of energy operational in the multidimensional world—of members of the family,

---

1. Fatunmbi, *Ifá Theology*, 26.
2. Fatunmbi, *Orí*.
3. Fatunmbi, *Orí*.
4. Holy Bible, Jeremiah 1:5.

Figure 4.1. Obatala descending from heaven to create the world, with a chain to create land for the Yorùbá people. In Yorùbá mythology, he was given a rooster, a bag of sand, and other materials by Olódùmarè to create the earth but subsequently slept off in the middle of the mission after consuming palm wine. Drawing by Dr. Kazeem Ekeolu.

the community, and that of the child. To this extent, the Ifá priest could predict the birth of a child to a certain family at a particular time. Orí thus becomes the first deity of every individual in a "traditional" Yorùbá setting anywhere below or across the Atlantic or elsewhere.[5] We can then see how in a diasporic space like Trinidad and Tobago, where the Yorùbá Òrìṣà system is practiced and its principles observed, the rite of cleansing or what might be called purification of the congregation for magnetic readiness for divine energy starts with reverence notes to the inner essence of congregants and continues with reverence to the Yorùbá pantheons and other important characters in the making of the Yorùbá metaphysical space:

> We pay homage to our Orís, and we thank our Orís for bringing us here this morning.
> *Orí* it is you and only you who would guide this destiny of ours,
> And we ask you for blessings this morning.[6]

Nothing happens without the cooperation of Orí. Through the significance attached to this deity, the basis of the religious belief system and structure of the people, as well as their social conduct and form, is carved.[7]

Ifá is consulted to inquire about events and circumstances that Orí has brought to one's life and to know its demands for spiritual alignment. Likewise, the countless—usually mentioned 201 or 401—gods of the Yorùbá were conceived as forces through which Orí could negotiate and make a pact on behalf of the individual.[8] This engagement can be triggered in the physical world due to unpleasant occurrences, or at the time a critical action must be taken, the individual is directed by the Ifá priest to appease any of the deities or the inner essence. This tradition has been adopted in Nigerian Pentecostalism, especially by the Aládúrà section of it.[9]

Without these gods, Orí cannot navigate the cosmic space of its carrier and bring about palatable manifestations. Without the Orí, there would be no Yorùbá spirituality or gods, for humans would have continued to live on free will and not a predestined choice. By predestined choice, we mean those choices left in that predestined box at the point of choosing one's path on the earth, the primordial choice. In any case, Yorùbá pantheons of Òrìṣà, other than their adaptation from observation of environmental elements and phenomena, are made of men and women whose sophisticated personality soul is counted among those worthy of emulation, reverence, and adulation.[10] By doing this, their followers are implicitly consulting the wisdom, character, and nature of the deities. Consequently, after divination, the individual is told which of the deities to offer sacrifice. In the case where such a person is told by the Ifá priest to offer a sacrifice to his Orí, we see Orí acting in the capacity of a mini-Èṣù.

Èṣù in Yorùbá theology is the mythical character that acts as the principal of the loop that exists between the human and the nonhuman world where prayers, supplications, and wishes

---

5. Kamari, *Mapping Yorùbá Networks*.

6. Quoted in Castor, *Spiritual Citizenship*, 72.

7. Olajubu, *Iwe Asa Ibile Yoruba*.

8. Abimbola, *Sixteen Great Poems of Ifá*, 34.

9. Brennan, *Singing Yoruba Christianity*.

10. Fadipe, *Sociology of the Yoruba*, 262.

are communicated and passed on for manifestation.[11] The refusal of Èṣù to grant this access makes the task of manifestation even more daunting. In its form, the conflict between the inner essence and its carrier blocks the road to the manifestation of tangible sacrifices in the material world of the individual. It means the foundational loop of cosmic communication is closed, or at best, on very low energy. Nicholaj De Mattos Frisvold explicitly describes Èṣù thus: "Ifá considers Èṣù to be the custodian of mystery, as the owner of the crossroads that both binds and separates the visible and the invisible. . . . As linguist, Èṣù serves as a bridge and mediator in all realms, and enables communication between spirit and man, man and plant, beast and spirit. Èṣù is also the warden of truth and embodies the principle of choice: therefore he is identified with roads and crossings."[12]

Èṣù and Orí work best among the Yorùbá Òrìṣà. Consequently, for one not to become unfortunate, for instance, it is both forces that are strategically in alignment with the individual. In this epistemic stretch, disappointments could be attributed to the refusal of the inner essence to work in favor of its carrier—*Orí ẹ ta kò ó* (One's Orí is in opposition to one), they will say. There is no better recipe for great disaster than a persistent opposition of Èṣù and Orí against the carrier.

The physical head is portrayed as a symbolic representation of the inner essence of an individual. In this capacity, the physical head serves as the point of contact between the physical being and the inner essence. Hands are laid on the head for blessing, or the head is washed with special preparation. During the coronation of a king in Yorubaland, the process is not complete without the ultimate ritual that decorates the head of the chief with a special leaf called *Ewé akòko*.[13] Tagging this on the head of the chief symbolizes the power that now inhabits his body from the cosmic world. Furthermore, the act of paying homage to an older person or someone in authority by way of prostrating or kneeling signifies reverence to the personality soul embodied by the individual. This way, honor shown toward monarchs is expected to be at a higher degree compared to any others in a community since they are believed to embody great personalities and souls rolled over the years from their ancestors who established the town or settlement.[14]

The same symbolic expression is extended to the members of a royal family. Hence, the mode of social stratification that exists in the community. Such homage could be transformed into veneration as these figures become deified. By venerating the spirit of these figures, the Yorùbá culture creates its form of ancestral worship, which had been initiated earlier in the social relations of the society long before the death of an elder. This practice, ubiquitous in African cultures, is an ancient one that can be traced to the belief in the underworld or world beyond where elderly or powerful figures reside after their deaths. Indeed, it is not uncommon for people to refer to some figures as having descended from this unknown subterrestrial dimension of reality. Myths and traditions found among different Yorùbá communities, like other ancient

---

11. Abimbola, *Ifá Will Mend Our Broken World*.

12. Frisvold, *Ifá*, 19.

13. Falola, *Collected Works of J. A. Atanda*.

14. Vaughan, *Nigerian Chiefs*.

civilizations around the world, are littered with these figures.[15] Given this, there is a continued conversation between the multidimensional world of reality, among which the one occupied by this physical body is only one. And because the cosmic energy of the ancestor who has gone to this other dimension and that of the people who have entrusted their fate to their ancestors' hands, either by relations or followership, are connected, "cosmic bubbles" become frequent. It is believed that auspicious vibrations that could enhance the personality soul do occur. Ancestral worship built on the doctrine of interfate connection is, therefore, a cardinal element in the Yorùbá cosmological space.

Informing the social makeup of the people, Orí is linked to the identity of the individual, and its exploits are encrypted in poetic lines known as *Oríkì*.[16] In a simple expression, Oríkì will pass as the description of the inner essence of a person whose praise is heralded. As with the *Odù Ifá*, which leads a diviner into the history of a client's challenge(s) to divine a possible remedy, praise poetry among the people in its various forms acts like a dossier of an individual of Yorùbá descent.[17] The first call of Oríkì is to identify the sex of the subject of attention, especially in the case of humans, as praise poetry among the Yorùbá people transcends this realm to animals, trees, food, and other animate and inanimate objects.[18] This determines the name and personal praise poem of the child who has accumulated exploits and experiences that are acknowledged by poets in the panegyric. Other expressions tied to the inner essence of the fellow could dominate the rest of this oral creative art. However, the sex of the figure is usually the basis of all others.

This is an example of the Yorùbá people's notion of *àkúnlẹ̀yàn* or predestination when a human was without a permanent biological makeup but took up a physiological frame from the primordial lot chosen; gender is thus given on earth by extension. Not only does a primordial lot earnestly influence the family and community of birth but it also speaks forcefully in the name of the child. Names like Àbìkẹ́, Àmọ̀kẹ́, and Àṣàkẹ́ are given to a child by the first consideration of being a female. Àkànmú, Àkàngbé, and Àlàbí, on the other side, are given to a male child. Depending on the family of the child and time of birth, prefixes like Akin, Adé, Ògún, Ifá, and many more follow other names given to the child. These prefixes have different connotations that range from warrior, royalty, blacksmith, and divinity/priesthood, respectively. Meanwhile, upon birth, the predestination of the child has been divined by the Ifá priest.[19] The tradition is usually followed to ascertain the part the child is to follow in life. Essentially, what the oracle looks into in most cases is the personality soul of an ancestor that has returned. Knowing this allows the parent to ensure the child does not commit the same errors made by this ancestor. It is incumbent upon the parents of the child to guide the baby through the path of their ancestors.

Ilé là á wò kí á tó sọmọ lórúkọ translates to the circumstance of birth that influences the choice of names given to a child. As a symbolic mark, the child is usually given the panegyric

---

15. Rosenberg, "Creation of the Universe and Ife."

16. Babalola and Alaba, *Dictionary of Yorùbá Personal Names*.

17. Babayemi, "Oríkì Orílẹ́ as Sources of Historical Data," 110; Awe, "Praise Poems as Historical Data," 331–349.

18. Olademo, *Gender in Yoruba Oral Tradition*.

19. Ellis, *Yoruba Speaking Peoples*.

Figure 4.2.
"Mother of the World"
depicts a mythical
story of creation tied to
motherhood, fertility,
and productivity.
Women in the
Yorùbá worldview are
considered guardians
of the power that
governs and hold all
other elements of the
society's universal
experience, whether
in the sociopolitical,
economic, or religious
planes. Drawing by
Moses Ogunleye.

this ancestor was known with. The idea of Orí portends the ability to moderate social relations and teach the virtue of patience and contentment among the Yorùbá people in the same way that the Ifá divination system does. It enhances the social bond and collective existence within which an individual's fortune and misfortune affect many. This brings us to the notion of kinship and the *ẹbí* system among the Yorùbá. The communal landscape of the society was primarily built as a constellation of the personality soul of members of a lineage, extending to other lineages and clans as the society developed. We can see this clearly in the ancestral worship system and the making of gods in this part of the world.[20] Born into a family and belonging to a particular community brings the cosmic frequency of the individual in an intertwined position with others in this environment. This is where the environment shapes the lived experience of every member of society. With their conceptual and philosophical frame of Orí and epistemic framework discussed in this chapter, the Yorùbá have been able to moderate these relations harmoniously.

We can say Orí is the spiritual energy carried by the individual. In Yorùbá's metaphysical view, human consciousness consists of nothing more than particles of cosmic energy. Whereas Orí acts as the magnetic force that attracts and amplifies this energy in one's life, Ifá provides the direction for this action through divination.[21] The Ifá priest uses his analytical tools, known as the divination materials, to reach these cosmic energies and advise the client on how to better engage this entity with the help of his cosmic energy/personality soul. This way, misfortune, often associated with bad energies and unfavorable cosmic configuration, could be transformed into fortune, and fortune could be multiplied. Represented in mythology, at the point that the Yorùbá pantheons were to come to the earth for the creation and to set the stage for the reproduction of humans and their environment, Olódùmarè charged Orí with the responsibility of superintendent over their paths on earth. This would include, fundamentally, the geographic location in which they would reside and explore. Established in their various locations, these gods maintained extensive relations among themselves, ranging from enormity to friendship. The same Orí made them patrons of their different professions. Ògún went into blacksmithing, Òrúnmìlà into divination, Ọya into tie and dye, and the list goes on. This myth, it should be noted, symbolizes the Yorùbá worldview about the role of the cosmic self in human existence.

Ifá and the Art of Divination

"The ambition of first generations of deep thinkers, in all known human cultures, was to search for, and discover knowledge and wisdom, useful for understanding and the management of every aspect of nature, human life and existence."[22]

As in the ancient civilizations of Egypt, Persia, and Greece, the Yorùbá world is built around gods and goddesses that are worshipped daily.[23] As an essential tool of every civilization, religion has been the medium through which human societies have maintained social cohesion

---

20. Barber, "How Man Makes God in West Africa," 724–745.

21. Oguntola-Laguda, *Divinities in West African Religion.*

22. Oluwole, *Socrates and Òrúnmìlà,* 15.

23. Apter, "Rituals of Power."

and consequently kept their traditions and cultural values. Although not entirely a religion, Ifá represents the pillar of the Yorùbá civilization.[24] It is not only integral to their day-to-day activities as a guiding spirit but also to the curriculum through which their world could be accessed. Although not a religion in itself, it is a geomantic divination system that establishes, among other things, the Yorùbá Òrìṣà worship system. The notion that the Yorùbá Òrìṣà religion is built on the principles of monism and pantheism is worth exploring, even though there is a clear picture of a Supreme Being in the culture, packed into the concept of Olódùmarè. For one, as a cultural and theological system built on the notion of monism—that is, the reduction of all forms of existence and phenomena into one principle—Orí comes at the center of the art and practice of Ifá, the complete treaty of the people. It is the central variable within which all ideas are embedded.[25]

Orí influenced Ifá's teachings on the virtue of patience and character and advice on which of the gods to propitiate. Again, regardless of their conception of God, the pantheistic aspect of the Yorùbá religious system heralds the structure of the Yorùbá pantheon of divinities. In this sense, there is a multiplication of the sense of god among the people with the adaptation of environmental forces, phenomena, and persons believed to be special due to their cosmic frequency and makeup into their religious practices.[26] Therefore, in addition to their conception of Olódùmarè, Yorùbá developed a cosmological and metaphysical paradigm that leans on the forces of creation to reach this supreme entity. This, as briefly mentioned above, explains why the Babaláwo (the Ifá priest) consults the Ifá for some pattern that allows him access to the cosmic condition of the client, and in some cases, the god(s) responsible for this condition, either for appeasement or devotion.[27] Ifá, in this sense, is the system that helps locate the spiritual authority among the bodies of the forces of creation whose cosmic energy is needed to resolve a situation, build a future, or make an important decision. Among other things, Ifá provides the human world with sociological, historical, geographical, theological, anthropological, ethnological, psychological, musical, artistic, philosophical, medical, ethical, mathematical, and economical aspects of the Yorùbá world, in addition to adding their theogony into its teachings and revelations. By so doing, and given the composition of these pantheons and the belief system that sustains them, the Yorùbá religion, in which Ifá represents the nucleus of order, subscribes in part to pantheism.

The practice among the Yorùbá is credited to Ọ̀rúnmìlà, a figure whose form is yet to be ascertained by historians and social archaeologists, whether as a mythical or historical entity. This confusion follows the pattern of other figures in Yorùbá traditions.[28] One cannot get less confused when Ọ̀rúnmìlà is said to have lived about two thousand years ago, around which time the sixteen principal Ifá corpus was developed by his sixteen students, including his eight children, following his demise;[29] yet, in these sixteen principal Ifá texts, he is often quoted

---

24. Lijadu, *Ọ̀rúnmìlà!*

25. Bascom, *Ifá Divination.*

26. Falola and Akinyemi, *Culture and Customs of the Yoruba.*

27. Bascom, *Ifá Divination.*

28. Rosenberg, *World Mythology.*

29. Abimbola, *Sixteen Great Poems.*

to have made witty references to characters like Odùduwà, Ọbàtálá, and others postulated by social archaeologists to have lived much later, between the eighth and twelfth centuries.[30] In particular, these two figures, at least with the evidence we currently have access to, are the grand patrons of the Yorùbá civilization and identity. If Ọrúnmìlà had lived before these figures and their social milieu, reference to these characters in Ifá corpus could only establish the mythical symbolism and metaphoric representations its teachings connote.

Like other holy scriptures, ancient texts, and philosophers, Ifá uses poems, metaphors, personifications, prose and narratives, parables, and myths as vehicles of communication.[31] The use of different characters, regardless of their social form and the social milieu in which they might have lived, is used to capture their message, preserve it, and perpetually reproduce it across time.[32] The supposed discrepancies in this literary corpus do not necessarily invalidate the narrative, nor can one ignore, even in the rational sense, the lessons and teachings of this traditional Yorùbá body of wisdom and civilization. The narratives, as they seem, were not conceived for their nonfictional purpose or to be taken as such but rather to put the reality of the long, day-to-day experience of man into a philosophical frame, since generations of humans are known to always return to this planet earth with the same sets of problem.

Aside from the sixteen principal *Odù Ifá*, also known as *Méjì Odù*, credited to the sixteen followers of Ọrúnmìlà, the minor 240, otherwise known as *Ọsáàtúrá*, are additions, added over the years. *Ogbèyẹkú* is said to be the most important of these 240 minors, with the sixteen majors marked by the *Méjì* or *Èjì* signature.[33] These are extensions and interpretations of the sixteen original texts put in the specific social order of the period as the problems were encountered within the social context of each generation and space they occupied. About two decades ago, when the diasporic Ifá community wanted to preserve and reproduce a common consciousness across the Atlantic world, in line with Ifá teachings, the Alasuwada conference in Trinidad added a new verse called Ìrẹtẹ Ìká to this body of knowledge.[34] Going further to express the nature of the mythical figure, Ọrúnmìlà, and the form of his text, Sophie Bosede Oluwole writes that "there are two sources of notable differences in the same verse rendered by various Babaláwo. The first is the existence of different Yorùbá dialects and local experiences. This explains the use of different words, symbolisms and illustrations in the same text, depending on where it comes from. The second is that the systems itself allows for these variations and new additions as long as the main thesis is kept intact."[35]

The additions can only be done by those who have attained the highest echelon in the Ifá cult and are inspired by collective vibrations emanating from the spiritual energy charged during a ritual performance. If Ifá speaks of Èṣù, Ọya, Ògún, and other Yorùbá gods, some of whom are known to scholars as the adaptation of environmental forces but related in the Ifá corpus as humans that lived at the inception of time and others noted above to have lived roughly

---

30. Akinjogbin, *Cradle of a Race*.

31. Morton-Williams, Bascom, and McClelland, "Two Studies of *Ifá* Divination," 406–431.

32. Barber, *Anthropology of Texts*.

33. Abimbola, *Sixteen Great Poems*, 14.

34. Castor, *Spiritual Citizenship*, 168.

35. Oluwole, *Socrates and Ọrúnmìlà*, 13.

around twenty centuries before now, it will not be out of place to describe Ọ̀rúnmìlà as the infinite wisdom that transcends time and space. Therefore, Ọ̀rúnmìlà cannot be located within a fixed time or space, as it represents ancient knowledge and mystery. What we can endeavor to uncover, however, is how it became the neural body of Yorùbá civilization—that is, the historical body that embodied this cosmic energy and initiated others in Yorubaland in the particular form it has taken among the people.

In the previous chapter, we mentioned the need to reconcile the narrative of Ọbàtálá being one of the deities that existed among Igbòmokun people and his deification after his demise by his Igbòmokun/Ife followers. Among other questions that could be resolved through this would be the question asked in the concluding part: How did Ọbàtálá, the leader of a belligerent faction supposedly overthrown by Oduduwa, leading to a new dynasty and the creation of a Yorùbá country, become a national deity among the Yorùbá community across space, with the triumphant party, Odùduwà, only known to few, maybe in Ilé-Ifè? The two angles have been remembered and mentioned in history, and they seem to suggest that Odùduwà was a deified political figure, while Ọbàtálá was a spiritual figure. In discussions about the political unity of Yorùbá, mention is made of Oduduwa, but for the spirituality of the people, Ọbàtálá quickly comes to mind, at least before Odùduwà.

A major bone of contention in locating these figures precisely in history is the names they take up in these traditions. In the previous chapter, one of the questions raised, which is considered instructive here, is whether these names are mythical, eponyms, sobriquet, or their actual names. Breaking down the etymology of the name, Ọbàtálá, Oduyoye would later relate this to the Arabic word *tal*, meaning "tall," "high," and combined with the Oba prefix to mean "exalted king."[36] In this context, Ọ̀rúnmìlà is seen as taking the eponymous name, Ifá, and in another pseudonym, Ẹlàasòde, also known as Èlà. Implicitly, Ọ̀rúnmìlà could be referred to with any of these names. However, one wonders if anyone could be called "divine illumination," because this is what all these names imply.[37] Again, can we add that the choice of the title of the Ifá verse, Ọ̀sá Méjì, which tells the story of Ọ̀rúnmìlà and the establishment of the Ifá cult, was inspired by the dual identity of the historical figure that embodied this abstract form? Perhaps unveiling the identity of this figure lies in uncovering his other identity.

In a similar vein, whereas Ìkirè traditions relate the history of its Oòṣàkirè, the principal deity worshipped by the people, to another myth situated within their history, Oòṣàkirè is another version, a localized version, so to say, of Ọbàtálá, who had taken up different names and form in different space where it has been adopted, including the Atlantic locations.[38] But removing the chaff from the grain to ascertain these traditions, as in the Oòṣàkirè and many others, lies in gaining access to substantial data for juxtaposition, a luxury that the social milieu these figures lived has not always afforded us. On the one side, one could begin to think of Ọ̀rúnmìlà as the same figure as Ọbàtálá given some of the similarities they exhibit (mainly in the use of white garments and their love for drinking) and the Ṣẹ́tílù narrative, which relates

---

36. Oduyoye, *Vocabulary of Yoruba Religious Discourse*, 29.

37. Fatunmbi, *Ela*.

38. Osunlakin, "Oral Traditions and the Making of Identity."

Figure 4.3. "Rituals" are important prescribed procedures and customary observances for conducting religious ceremonies in the Yorùbá world. They serve as key categories of religious and cultural behavior for protecting, cleansing, or maintaining peace and stability in the Yorùbá society. Rituals are performed at any specific period and are evidence of the Yorùbá people's close affinity with religious codes and practices. Drawing by Moses Ogunleye.

the Yorùbá Ifá divination system to Ọbàtálá.[39] This is somewhat nullified by different taboos related to their cults and the argument given in the previous chapter against the Nupe Orígin of the Yorùbá people within which the Ṣẹ́tílù narrative was invoked. It should also be recalled that in the Ṣẹ́tílù tradition mentioned in the previous chapter, on his way to Ile-Ife, he called at Adó. Something of this nature also features in *Òsá Méjì*. It can be extrapolated that the art and practice of Ifá got to Adó before taking root at Ile-Ife.

The Ifá verse establishing the genesis of divination in Yorubaland referred to Ọ̀rúnmìlà explaining to his followers that his presence at Adó was not because he originated there; rather, he was there to enlighten the people in the ways of Ifá. One could then wonder who Ọ̀rúnmìlà was and the historical milieu in which he lived. Oluwole provides us with three fundamental traditions within which this figure could be situated: Ọ̀rúnmìlà as a mythical figure, corporate collection, and historical figure.[40] These three levels are germane to our understanding of this figure, as they share the same matrix that allows for some tentative suppositions. Albeit presented as a historical figure with unknowable origins, Ọ̀rúnmìlà, as a mythical figure and corporate collection, is fully established in Ọ̀sá Méjì, one of the Odù Ifá said to be the most important. In this verse, Ọ̀rúnmìlà was a powerful itinerant figure who possessed the ability to maintain peace and order in the world due to his wisdom, as ordained by Olódùmarè. He had eight children and had been to many different places for different purposes, often related to divination and trade. Being a powerful man of wisdom with divination power and wealth, he caught the attention of many who became his followers. On one fateful day, Ọ̀rúnmìlà invited his eight children who had gone to establish different settlements, alongside his followers, for the *Ifá* festival.

The youngest of his sons, the Ọlọ́wọ̀ of Ọ̀wọ̀, disrespected him at the event by refusing to pay homage to him, claiming the two had become equal because they wore the same regalia and possessed the same knowledge of Ifá. Ọ̀rúnmìlà could not help but give in to anger. He "de-robed" the insolent son and left this planet, never to return.[41] His absence on Earth, however, brought about immeasurable pain, loss, and anguish through famine, infertility of man and animals, diseases, and more. Ọ̀rúnmìlà was called upon by his followers and the people to return, but he refused. Instead, he gave them sixteen palm nuts as a piece of him through which he could be consulted anytime, especially when the people needed his wisdom in times of uncertainty, confusion, and calamity. This, known as Ikin, has since become the sacred symbol of the *Ifá* cult.[42]

Another has Ọ̀rúnmìlà living at Ilé-Ifẹ̀ around 500 BC at Òkè-Ìgbẹ́tì; he had eight children with wives and concubines that included Olùkun and Ìwà. He sent Ìwà away for her dirtiness but later pleaded to have her back, having come to the realization that life without Ìwà (character) is doomed. How he died and the *Ifá* cult established does not bother this tradition because,

---

39. To be sure, white cloth is not only peculiar to these two mythical figures, but of all the Yorùbá male deities of national significance, only these two are represented in white and revered as benevolent, alongside female ones like Ọ̀ṣun.

40. Oluwole, *Socrates and Ọ̀rúnmìlà*.

41. Fabunmi, *Ife Shrines*, 51–67.

42. Fabunmi, *Ife Shrines*, 51–67.

GLOBAL YORÙBÁ

in truth, it had established the intended narrative, which will be discussed soon. The same Ọ̀rúnmìlà is also explained in a myth that brings him among the deities sent by Olódùmarè to engineer human civilization. He is said to have been present with Olódùmarè all through the process of creation, as he represents the spirit of wisdom. He was also present at àkúnlẹ́yàn—that is, the point of choosing which inner soul an individual brings to the world. Hence, he is also known as ẹlẹ́rìí-ìpín, witness to one's life choices. Sent alongside other deities, his responsibility was to ensure order in the world and peace among the deities, all of whom were prone to conflict. Disappointed by the level of chaos and disorder in the world and constant impediment from the people (the deities he sojourned with to the earth) to intervene, Ọ̀rúnmìlà returned to heaven and, again, never came back.

If there is anything insightful about all these traditions and myths, it is their insistence on the neurologic role of Ọ̀rúnmìlà in the reproduction of human life. In Ọ̀sá Méjì, he rebuffed every insinuation of where he came from even though that opportunity could have allowed him or those said to have been present during his time to inform us of his, say, Nupe origin. Consistently, he rebuffed every claim of this origin to explain his mission in those places. Upon being told he came from Iléṣà, Ọ̀rúnmìlà explained that he only went there to teach the people how to trade so they could overcome their poverty. Graphically painted in that *Ifá* verse, the poverty of the people of the land is illustrated with the king and chiefs who wore similar clothes without prestige. In the same manner, but on a different mission, he went to Offa to heal the people of their sickness, and the list goes on to give a picture of Ọ̀rúnmìlà that is of a corporate collection. Ọ̀rúnmìlà in these stories could be likened to the biblical spirit of God who hovers above the earth for creation. The same scripture talked about this spirit as the spirit of wisdom. Given that the version of this account accessible is in English and not in the original language in which the text was developed, liking this spirit to wisdom could be a distortion of the expression and representation of the spirit. This consideration notwithstanding, the meaning is expected to be closer to this.

Explaining this in Jules Verne mythology, *The Nautilus* and *Drunken Boat*, Roland Barthes writes that despite the typical contradiction, irrationality, and excessive use of expressions in hyperbole, "the basic activity in Jules Verne, then, is unquestionably that of appropriation. The image of the ship, so important in his mythology, in no way contradicts this. Quite the contrary: the ship may well be a symbol for departure; it is, at a deeper level, the emblem of closure. An inclination for ships always means the joy of perfectly enclosing oneself, of having at hand the greatest possible number of objects, and having at one's disposal an absolutely finite space."[43]

This speaks as much to the preponderance of metaphoric expressions in the creation of myths as it explains the context in which we can begin to understand Ọ̀rúnmìlà. Laying credence to this would be the role in which Ọ̀rúnmìlà was said to have been designated by Olódùmarè in the Yorùbá mythology mentioned earlier. By his role, nothing exists outside the sight of Ọ̀rúnmìlà, making him omniscient.[44] From the creation of the world to its maintenance and

---

43. Barthes, *Mythologies*, 66.

44. Lijadu, *Ọ̀rúnmìlà!*

exploration and the activities of man and the gods, Ọ̀rúnmìlà's prying eyes never close. Nothing eludes him. This explains why all mysteries and secrets are uncovered through a diligent inquiry from him. Wande Abimbola made a helpful reference in this regard when he posited that the word Ọ̀rúnmìlà could be taken to connote ọrun ló mọ ẹni ma là—that is, only heavens know individual's destiny. What is more is that Èlà, relating to (divine) illumination, comes as a major tool in consulting Ọ̀rúnmìlà. Thus, both the mighty and low are subject to his power and influence. One of the earliest Christian converts and priests in Yorubaland explained that *Ifá* (Minerva) is the God of intelligence and wisdom, with its priests imposing upon even kings and chiefs and divining and deriving their support from them.[45] He installs kings, dethrones chiefs, and determines the life path of the ordinary people, in this context, through a carefully placed mathematical algorithm derived from the complementarity of the tools used in divination.

Anyone familiar with the biblical story of the Holy Spirit can easily spot the similarities between one of the Ọ̀rúnmìlà traditions earlier noted. Following the crucifixion of Jesus of Nazareth and when he was bound to transform, he told his disciples not to weep for him but to remain strong in the Holy Spirit that he was going to send to replace him. This Holy Spirit could be taken as the palm nuts Ọ̀rúnmìlà was said to have given his followers. Considering that many of the Yorùbá pantheons are mostly revered patrons and vanguards of a particular occupation, the historical figure through whom this tradition came into Yorubaland could have been given the name Ọ̀rúnmìlà out of reverence, like when the title of "pastor" replaced the real name of a missionary lost to history. Ọ̀rúnmìlà's supposed Òkè Ìgbẹ̀tì home in Ilé-Ifẹ̀ can best be described as the residence of this historical figure who first taught this art—the art of Ọ̀rúnmìlà—at Ilé-Ifẹ̀. The figure could be used in the mythical narratives meant to establish this infinite cosmic energy that is presented in the myth.

While the Ewe people of Togo call it Afa, the Fon of Dahomey refers to it as Fá. In the diaspora, where millions of people are influenced by this Yorùbá tradition, it follows the same name as that of the Yorùbá—that is, *Ifá*. This is a common practice not only in West Africa but also in communities that dot many parts of the ancient world, especially around the Mediterranean, from where many of the cultural groups that emerged in West Africa claimed to have migrated.

Ugbo, whom we noted in the previous chapter to have populated the Niger River basin together with the proto-Yorùbá group, also practice divination with palm nuts. A similar system can also be found among the Kamuku and Gbari or Gwari people in northern Nigeria. The system exists from present-day Ghana, Côte d'Ivoire, down to faraway lands across the Atlantic Ocean and Europe. With slightly different forms, the divining chain referred to as Ọ̀pẹ̀lẹ̀ among the Yorùbá people is known as Noko, among the Jukun, Eba among the Nupe, Agbigba among the Yagba Yorùbá, showing the prevalence of this system in West Africa.[46] The above suggests that *Ifá* divination is only one of the numerous ways in which this cosmic energy has been attracted by civilizations over the years. In *Ọ̀sá Méjì*, one could see the position of this study playing out in the discussion, which we take to be between the historical figure that

---

45. Ajayi, "General History of the Yorùbá Country."
46. Bascom, *Ifá Divination*, 3–4.

established the tradition among the people and his disciples. This was an attempt to establish Ọ̀rúnmìlà as the all-seeing, all-knowing, and ever-present spiritual energy that the Babaláwo, the apostolic descendants of the mythical Ọ̀rúnmìlà, can only reach through the established principles of the *Ifá* system.[47]

The sixteen palm nut practice among the Yorùbá, also known as Ikin, was used in divination, and one speculation was that the first divinations were conducted on plain sandy ground. With considerable time, the sixteen original texts were carved as the curriculum for all who wanted to learn the art of *Ifá*. This was structured in the usual informal educational settings of the people. Students stayed with their teachers (the priests) in their homes and followed them around to learn the art and practice of divination in a process that could take longer than it takes a medical student in the modern world to graduate. After this period, which could take up to a decade, the student, though now an initiate and professional, remains a student for life while he also mentors others. As Frisvold mentioned, "*Ifá* has no monasteries and no universities; the *Ifá* School of learning is the extended family where everyone takes on the responsibility of being a mentor and teacher to younger generations."[48]

During the long period of training, the student is expected to have memorized a substantial volume of the *Ifá* literary text, which, as it stands today, has over four hundred thousand verses each, spreading across the 256 Odù. This structure has been described by various scholars and interested observers as a "computerized storage" of Yorùbá worldviews and thought in compartmentalized folders holding each file of related texts. Principal paraphernalia used by the *Ifá* priest (the Babaláwo, "father of esoteric knowledge") includes two different sets, depending on the preference and magnitude of importance of the matter at hand: using the Ẹ̀là system, the *Ifá* priest engages his ọ̀pẹ̀lẹ̀, àpò Ifá (divining bag), and a mat or any object upon which the *Ifá* priest could sit and throw the material. Ọ̀pẹ̀lẹ̀ is a reasonably long rope or chain material with a satisfactory type of pod indicating the convex and concave parts carefully tied in four rolls each on both sides of the rope/chain, with other materials like beads, cowries, corn, buttons, and rings attached to the tail end of the divining chain, ostensibly to allow the eight half pods a soft landing to increase the chances of an accurate prognostication. Usually, this is done in such a way that the left and right sides of the material are known to the Babaláwo to the extent that he knows how to perpetually throw it for divination.[49]

Built on a binary system of mathematical calculation, the pods on either side communicate a different but complementary message used in exploring appropriate *Ifá* graphemes.[50] This system is noted to have been initiated later in the history of the *Ifá* system among the people at the time the older one, the *Ikin* system, became somewhat difficult for subsequent practitioners to accurately divine. The *Ikin* system requires sixteen palm nuts, Ọpọ́n Ifá (divining plate), Iyẹ̀

---

47. Lijadu, *Ọ̀rúnmìlà!*

48. Frisvold, *Ifá*, 27.

49. Ọ̀pẹ̀lẹ̀ is described further by Chief Onliu as the "primordial computer of Yorùbá origin, which handle spiritual data and concerns generated from the in-depth subconscious mind if the client (cosmic energy).... Ọ̀pẹ̀lẹ̀ is a super oracle in nature due to its multipurpose functions as divination and physical therapy instruments." See Onilu, "Opele = Ifá Divination Chain."

50. Onilu, "Opele = Ifá Divination Chain."

Figure 4.4. "Captured in a trance," by Dr. Kazeem Ekeolu, is an abstract image of a man lost in a trance. This is a common phenomenon in some Yorùbá cults in West Africa and the diaspora, where "hot" deities form an inherent part of their past. Drawing by Dr. Kazeem Ekeolu.

rẹ́-osùn (yellow powder sand usually taken from termites' nests), and *Àpò Ifá* (divining bag). The importance of the *Iyẹ́rẹ́-osùn* and the divining plate is principally to encode or register the encrypted message of Òrúnmìlà passed through the binary frame with sixteen dialed cowries. The binary algorithm produced through this process is passed through the neural nerves of the *Ifá* priest, who picks from the large store of the *Ifá* repository learned over the years to address the concern(s) of the client. The argument is that, whereas both methods arrive at a similar point at the end of a divination process, engaging the *Ikin* system could embarrass an *Ifá* priest who is not well-grounded. Even then, arriving at an accurate result is always difficult, sometimes taking longer compared to *ọpẹ́lẹ́*. Since the practice of divining involves predictions dialed with the object of divination, "the law of probability" also applies. It is in this way that the *ọ̀pẹ́lẹ́* system became ubiquitous because the probability or odds of making errors are considered lower compared to the *Ikin*.

As the older and original version of the art among the Yorùbá people, the *Ikin* system is adopted when consultation is to be made on a crucial matter, mostly of community importance. Thus, the mythical servant-apprentice of Ọ̀rúnmìlà became prominent for the art of divination among the Yorùbá people. Both systems could be adopted to ascertain the predictions. Fatunmbi captures this thus: "Divination is a problem-solving tool and not a fortune-telling gimmick. *Ifá* does not make arbitrary predictions; the oracle explains the consequences of specific behavior by explaining the consequences of specific actions. There is nothing magical in telling a person if they sit in a fire they will get burned."[51]

Deepening this understanding, Oluwole writes, "The act of *Ifá* divination is, therefore, not a process of speaking directly to God like a medium. The goal is that of choosing relevant verses from a large expanse of oral texts stored in a computer-compactible binary coding system. The technique formulated by Ọ̀rúnmìlà is one in which predictions are arrived at through the use of mathematical probability."[52]

The binary algorithm calculation and predictions or not, the whole process is, of course, believed to be divinely inspired. To ascertain this, the divination process is cast eight times during the binary algorithm combination and is arrived at for further inquiry by the Babaláwo. One can be sure that there is a myth establishing the use of ọ̀pẹ́lẹ̀ for divination because it is a common practice for important transformations and events like this to be preserved through this medium, necessary so that when young ones raise questions on such a topic, there is something sufficient to say. Some of these myths and the mishmash representation or transfer of another event with the hope of bringing extra to the ordinary event cannot be overemphasized.[53]

Quite instructively, ọ̀pẹ́lẹ̀, whose name was Ìrere while alive, is described at once in this myth as a servant of Ọ̀rúnmìlà who was bought from Èjìgbò market. His responsibility was to clear the weeds around Ọ̀rúnmìlà's divining shrine. Ìrere turned out to be a talented diviner who learned how to divine by listening and watching his master. Ọ̀rúnmìlà allowed him access to the divining material for this reason, and he became an apprentice. In his usual itinerant mode, Ọ̀rúnmìlà left Ilé-Ifẹ̀ for divination elsewhere when Odùduwà needed him for the same purpose. The king's messengers met Ìrere, who assured them he could perform the task, as his master was away. On agreement, Ìrere performed the divination successfully, to the chagrin of everyone. He became boastful and insulted the elders at the palace. Hearing about this, Ọ̀rúnmìlà sought to talk to him, but the former remained adamant. Annoyed, Ọ̀rúnmìlà hit Ìrere with the Ìrọkẹ́ (a symbol of authority found in the hands of the *Ifá* priest). This turned Ìrọkẹ́ into four pieces of Èlà pods. Separated into parts, the pods became the eight pieces with two faces, often attached to the ọ̀pẹ́lẹ̀ chain for the binary algorithm result that takes the Babaláwo to the portion of the 256 *Ifá* corpus and over four hundred thousand texts relevant for the wisdom and remedy to the situation at hand.[54] Hardly can anyone store such a volume of work in memory. Nonetheless, *Ifá* priests are required to attain substantial levels of proficiency in them.

---

51. Fatunmbi, *Ifá Theology*, 13.

52. Oluwole, *Socrates and Ọ̀rúnmìlà*, 48.

53. Afigbo, "Fact and Myth in Nigerian Historíography," 81–90.

54. One *Ifá* grapheme could contain up to twelve "chapters."

This myth reinforces what we already know—that is, the *òpèlè* system was brought about by one of the disciples of the historical figure cloaked in the Òrúnmìlà myth. It became generally acceptable due to its level of accuracy. To be a seeker is to be the servant or apprentice of Òrúnmìlà. So "Ìrere" could have been a servant or apprentice in the service of any notable diviner in history. All human religions are invariably built on some sort of secrecy without which their mythical adaptations and beliefs cannot be sustained. Covering this secrecy, they plead on the invocation of the spirit of faith in (prospective) adherents to explain and understand that which cannot be taken in sync with the rational mind. To this extent, priests and religious leaders, the custodians of these traditions and their esoteric knowledge, have been at the vanguard of the social cohesion needed for engineering civilization. Religious power, in this sense, is interlocked with political reality and authority.[55]

The Yorùbá Babaláwo is an expressive representation of this role. The Babaláwo maintains the secrets that keep *Ifá* traditions in reproduction and relevance across time and space, the same way his counterparts in other religions do. This gives the religious leader the liberty to muddle the myths, abstract entities, or metaphors with factual expression. Moreover, both in philosophy and theology, only a very thin line exists between fiction and nonfiction. Major terminologies surrounding this practice include the following: Odù, category of *Ifá* divination poetry or *Ifá* graphemes; *rírán Ifá*, the process of gaining confidence and mastery of sacred literary corpus; *ṣíṣí-òpèlè-já*, the ceremony that heralds the complete lecture and grasp of manipulating the divining chain; *ojú Odù*, the sixteen primary chapters; *ọmọ odù*, also known as *amúlù*, the 240 minors; *Ìrọkè*, the carved ivory rattle; *Òpẹ Ifá*, the palm tree that produces the four-eye palm nuts.

No Babaláwo would want to divine wrongly; therefore, both the divining chain and the sixteen palm nuts are objects of worship for *Ifá* priests. Today, the presence of the Yorùbá *Ifá* cult in the diaspora, especially in places where Yorùbá captives were taken during the inhumane transatlantic slave trade, dwarfs its presence in the southwestern part of Nigeria, where the people are primarily located. It has grown a substantial number of followers and remains popular in many transatlantic circles.[56]

Patrons, Power, and Agency: Yorùbá *Òrìṣà* across Space

From the foregoing, it appears there are multiple levels of the Yorùbá pantheon, and they follow in order of importance, which is encoded in *Ifá* verses and other traditions. The first, the *Orí*, is followed by one's parents and family, with other Yorùbá pantheons beneath this level. The importance here does not relegate the Yorùbá pantheons; instead, it suggests that they do not act until there is some kind of harmony in the other realm. This was earlier explained as the propitiation of one's *Orí* in the case of an individual's alignment with destiny. The Yorùbá religion being a way of life cloaked the second level in the sociological framework of the *ẹbí* system. Kinship is seen as the nucleus of the human community, and as such, it is no small

---

55. Falola and Genova, *Òrìṣà*.

56. Vega, *Altar of My Soul*.

   GLOBAL YORÙBÁ

amount of effort that goes into building one. This is to see to it that, in the end, the frontiers of the community traditions are carefully expanded, among other means, through the production of ancestors of certain characters/personality souls. In Yorùbá settings, reconnaissance is conducted from both sides of the family to be sure of the cultural reproduction about to be made. Cultural reproduction here does not necessarily relate to ethnic identity but to family traditions and composition.

The creation of ancestors is integral to the Yorùbá culture, just as the family is seen as the pillar of its traditions.[57] Built on an intensive binary impulse, the cosmological understanding of the people places the ancestral world within the human world. In all cases, the former is regarded as an extension of the latter and its inhabitants (among which are the ancestors) as revered members of the human community. These ancestors are believed to watch over the affairs of the loved ones they left behind in the human world. The veneration of ancestors in Yorubaland stems from the practice of social stratification that gives primacy to age. Elders are revered for their age, wisdom, and experience, with which they nurture the mind of society and negotiate their engagements with environmental forces.[58] Seen as part and extension of the human community, in Yorùbá metaphysical belief, elders do not die; instead, they transition into ancestors where they continue to live and influence society. The belief in ancestors, ancestral power, and the ancestral world creates, among other things, the Yorùbá notion of the afterlife. The afterlife is conceived as a space for envisioning how the totality of the Yorùbá worldview is grounded in binary oppositions.

To be sure of the weight this carries among the people, one needs not to look further than their concept and practice of *Òrìṣà*. As earlier mentioned, depending on whom one meets, the preference of the fellow, and what comes to mind at the material time, Yorùbá pantheons have been counted to be around 401, 201, and in some cases, 801. While the numbers seem to be in apparent disagreement, they relate a common message at a deeper level. Thriving on a tradition broken into strategic levels of spirituality that recognize the role of each environmental and productive force in the advancement of human society and a classical philosophical approach that emphasizes harmony between and among these forces, a static religious system or structure cannot be expected from the people. In any case, scholars of the Yorùbá study have argued that, indeed, what we know as the "traditional" Yorùbá religion, until recently, which could count from the colonial era, was not just a religion but a way of life.

Like culture and cultural practices, the formation of the Yorùbá pantheons has been an ever-evolving one that slowed recently in the face of modernization. My argument is that the end of the formation of older pantheons probably ended with the emergence of the new ones after the 1940s with the rise of the nationalist and prominent Nigerian political figure Chief Obafemi Awolowo, who became, over time, transformed into a "god."[59] Traditionally, new deities were added at the national, community, and lineage levels. Although, as just mentioned, with the massive inroad of the Abrahamic faiths into Yorubaland, one hardly can talk about the continued multiplication of gods in recent times, although the elusive count of the Yorùbá pantheons

---

57. Willis, *Masquerading Politics*.

58. Osunlakin, "Rethinking Cultural Diversity," 54.

59. Falola, "Yorùbá Writers," 157–158.

still subsists significantly. A community could have more than a dozen deities, among which one serves as the principal deity of the community and others with either national or lineage importance. The principal deity is usually enshrined in the peculiar history and traditions of the community.[60] Invariably, many of the traditions belong to the royal families. In other words, the traditions of the royal families are the traditions of the towns.[61]

In most cases, such deities are localized versions of one of the existing national deities, as in Òòṣàkirè in Ìkirè, Òrìṣà Àgìyàn in Èjìgbò, and others, who came as the localization of Ọbàtálá in the production and reproduction of life in their respective domains. What, therefore, populates the hall of hundreds of Yorùbá pantheons is the lineage and communal deities, some of which are adaptations of the prominent ones. In any case, the formation of a lineage, family, or lineage deity has never led to the abandonment of the dominant national deities like Ògún, Ọ̀ṣun, Ṣàngó, and others. Rather, these dynamics have been used to reproduce and reinforce their efficacy.[62] Quite revealingly, this process of localization of the Yorùbá Òrìṣà and their reproduction in many spaces have gone beyond the southwestern geographic entity in Nigeria, where the Yorùbá civilization was birthed, to different locations across the world.[63] Through the Atlantic experience of the Yorùbá people, Yorùbá culture and traditions traveled along with the people.[64] What is not expected, however, is that the core aspect of their culture, which is the Òrìṣà worship system and the complementary philosophy and traditions, could be ingrained to permanently change and shape the social landscape and configuration of these societies.

Many enslaved and freed African slaves in different parts of the Atlantic location, from the Caribbean to the Americas, turned the Yorùbá pantheons into an agency for social emancipation and political liberation. As the major system through which the Yorùbá civilization evolved and around which its traditions and norms were given, embracing these pantheons in several diasporic spaces like Cuba, Haiti, Brazil, Trinidad and Tobago, and the United States meant the adoption and reproduction of the entire Yorùbá culture and traditions in these locations.[65] The debate as to whether the Yorùbá Òrìṣà worship system could be taken as a religion or tradition before the colonial event necessitated its designation as the former will have to consider the clear-cut difference that lies between the two. For one, if anything, the effectiveness of the communal configuration of traditional Yorùbá society made the traditional practices of the people, which they called *àṣà ìbílẹ̀* or *ìṣẹ́ṣe*, as effective as a religion, even though this was not always called *ẹ̀sìn*—that is, religion. The etymology of the word *ẹ̀sìn* is said to lay primarily within the expression of slavery, which the people thought the Abrahamic faiths to be among them. This was particularly the case with Islam, which they considered a hard doctrine—*ìmọ̀ lílé*, later modified into *ìmàle*.[66]

---

60. Apter, "Rituals and Power."

61. Barber, *I Could Speak until Tomorrow.*

62. Murphy and Sanford, *Osun across the Waters.*

63. Marta, "Yoruba Orisha Tradition," 201–206.

64. Falola and Childs, *Yoruba Diaspora in the Atlantic World.*

65. Gonzalez-Wippler, *Powers of the Orishas*; Kamari, *Mapping Yorùbá Networks.*

66. Oduyoye, *Vocabulary of Yoruba Religious Discourse*, 17 .

Figure 4.5. "Abalaye," by Moses Ogunleye, depicts the agelessness of "origins" of humans and civilization, as represented in mythologies. From the Toyin Falola Private Collection.

The term used to describe the Yorùbá belief system remains *Ìṣẹ̀ṣe*, even though some are beginning to use terms like *ẹ̀sìn ìbílẹ̀* and *ẹ̀sìn àbáláyé* to connote the practice as a traditional religion. This reveals a certain confusion of form that exists in this cultural space. Nevertheless, the Yorùbá cosmological belief system has been used as a tradition and religion among the people, as it serves the dual role of communicating with the spirit realm by way of attracting ancestral powers and the ultimate purpose of social cohesion among the people, irrespective of their location.[67] When they got to their various Atlantic locations as captives, the latter was the first basis of the organization of the Yorùbá people, joined by others from different parts of Africa, Central and West Africa in the main. Traditional Yorùbá worship system began in these locations, from farm plantations where the captive population took to their folk songs and in their wrenched homes where they organized themselves after the work of the day and other home traditions embedded in their memory.

These traditions captured their struggles against the dehumanization of their persons in their repressive Atlantic conditions, highlighting the flexibility of the Yorùbá culture, modeling the nature of the making of Yorùbá pantheons, especially the major ones, and turning these traditions into rituals and performances that took the form of the social milieu in which the Yorùbá captive population lived. Santeria, Lukumi (Lucumi), Candomblé, and many different other names have been used to depict the Yorùbá Òrìṣà worship system and its adherents in places like Brazil, Cuba, Trinidad and Tobago, the United States, and other diasporic places. In these locations, the Òrìṣà tradition, more than any other thing—either in cultural symbol or economic materialism—created a distinct African community in the diaspora, to the extent to which one could talk about "spiritual citizenship." Undoubtedly, the visibility of this community took no short period to materialize.

The nineteenth century was a decisive period in the history of Africa and what remains of its culture. The totality of the cultural experience of the people was under immense threat from Western modernity, which turned everything African into so-called voodoo science and thus inconsequential. This was the same package of prejudice to which their kinsmen in the Atlantic world were subjected. The performances, rituals, and other religious rites associated with the Òrìṣà were engaged secretly. In this way, before the second half of the twentieth century, when the Yorùbá Òrìṣà tradition began to experience exponential growth in the diaspora, the "spiritual citizenship" now somewhat ubiquitous in these locations was, in many places, a hidden one.[68] Both at home (southwestern Nigeria) and in the diaspora, this population engaged in a significant transformation, so to say, particularly during the nineteenth century. The Òrìṣà system among the Yorùbá was the basis of their civilization.[69] The political morphology of the country depended on it, its social form was cultivated on it, and the economic giving was tamed along with this. The folk songs and chants with which the Yorùbá captives in the diaspora began the practice were attached to one religious rite or the other. At home, the process of leadership selection rested on this cultural institution.

---

67. Valdés-Cruz, "Black Man's Contribution to Cuban Culture," 244–251; Siedlak, *Seven African Powers*.

68. Alonso, *Development of Yoruba Candomble Communities*.

69. Ojo, "'Heepa' (Hail) Òrìṣà," 30–59.

Consequently, the attempted "purification" of the people in Western culture by Christian missionaries in Yorubaland and slave masters in the Caribbean and the Americas signaled the systemic collapse of the Yorùbá civilization. For obvious reasons, all related to the different social ambiance of those at home and in the diaspora, this endeavor succeeded more in the homeland than in those diasporic locations. Social mobility was integral in these dynamics. The Òrìsà tradition could not thrive back home with a colonial experience where all that the people could hope to become entrapped at the bottom of the taxonomy of European civilization. In their peculiar social milieu, they were needed to aid the colonial enterprise by serving in the colonial administrative structure. Clerks, catechists, messengers, teachers, railway workers, and others employed in their colonial service were invariably those who had gone through this process of Western purification, including its religious beliefs. To a great degree, social mobility was assured by imbibing Western philosophy, as its very basis became the template for social relations.[70]

The role of the returning captives from Sierra Leone in this transitioning period cannot be overemphasized. Many of the returnees were already Christian converts who had been indoctrinated in Western civilization and used this as a currency to negotiate their movement on the social ladder. This section of the population was the epitome of the new reality in which most people wanted to live. Yorùbá traditions, including the Òrìsà system, were thus referred to as the "old tradition," downgraded to "paganism," while Western traditions were regarded as the new (civilized) traditions.[71] On the contrary, no amount of indoctrination in Western traditions could alleviate the conditions of those in the diaspora, especially those in different Atlantic locations. As captives whose conditions have been justified in the moral codes of the society, they found themselves in the same moral codes enshrined in the religious belief and philosophy of their captors, a form of self-enslavement. Unlike their kinsmen back home, the ability to read, write, speak their master's language and worship his God, and share the same worldview with him did not guarantee them a better place in the Atlantic world, where the only reason they were able to have the opportunity to be acquainted with these things was primarily for them to be converted into Christianity. Their masters, increasingly anxious about their social practices and organization, especially during their evening gatherings when they engaged in rituals, dance, and performances that seemed strange to the masters, attempted to convert this population to Christianity by teaching some of the slaves how to read the Bible.

If few could succeed in being literate, they could teach others, religion could spread among the people, and there could be an end to their mysterious practices that appeared to be a precursor for slave revolts. Ironically, this turned out to be a way of arming the people, as their literary skills were deployed in rejecting Christianity while adopting parts of the biblical teachings in their traditional Yorùbá practices. Their ability to read the Bible allowed them to access the words of the sacred text and digest appropriate information as they understood them to be and

---

70. Falola, *Cultural Modernity*.
71. Pallinder-Law, "Aborted Modernization in West Africa?," 65–82.

not as interpreted by their masters. This marked the beginning of the adoption of the Catholic holy order in the Yorùbá Òrìṣà religious system.[72]

Yorùbá pantheons, in this view, shared lots of similarities with the Catholic saints, who were only canonized after their death in recognition of their contributions to the growth of the church and in reverence of their spirit. In Yorubaland, both the gods that lived and deified and those who emerged from the study of environmental forces have several myths and traditions establishing their existence. This population then began to use the similarities found in Catholicism to express its religious beliefs secretly, disguised as honoring the Catholic saints. The shrines were dressed in Catholic style for the same reason the tradition was organized around Catholic saints in disguise. Together with elements of Catholicism and other African traditions like those of the Bantu and Ewe, the Yorùbá Òrìṣà religious system was transplanted into the diaspora for social resistance, identity formation, and social mobility, not only among the Yorùbá in the Atlantic diaspora but also among other African populations.[73] It became the rallying point for biosociality and the growth of African spirituality in this diasporic space.

Since the 1960s, when the practice emerged in America, with the migration of African slaves following the Cuban revolution of that time, the religion has witnessed tremendous growth, with attendant criticism from its detractors.[74] The major conflict between Yorùbá and Western cosmological views lies in their representation of morality rooted in their interpretation of mythical and religious symbols. In many parts, they shared the same mythical symbols. Hence, the Yorùbá Èṣù was equated to the Western notion of Satan as encoded in biblical narratives.[75] In a similar vein, the accusation of Òrìṣà worship system as witchcraft and magical invocations has not left the community of adherents in their various locations. Accounting for hundreds of millions of adherents in these diasporic places, the Yorùbá Òrìṣà religious system has become a significant vehicle for the continued reproduction of Yorùbá culture. In the abstract, these deities are still countless, but in reality, they have now been reduced to a considerable number among the diaspora population who now follow this ancestral link through the principal Yorùbá pantheons like Ọ̀ṣun, Ògún, Ọya, Ṣàngó, and Ọbàtálá. Ifá is integral to the workings of this system. As such, among the adherents of the Yorùbá belief system, it remains the loop through which these deities are consulted and adherents initiated into the religious practice.[76] In the same manner, Oduyoye describes Yorùbá Òrìṣà as patrons, pathfinders, first among equals, and vanguards of discoveries. Also, Fatunmbi asserts that "In *Ifá* emanation from Source is called Òrìṣà, meaning select consciousness. Òrìṣà is the specific quality of consciousness found in a given Force of Nature."[77]

<hr>

72. Cornelius, "We Slipped and Learned to Read," 171–186.

73. Omari-Tunkara, *Manipulating the Sacred*.

74. Garcia-Navarro, "Brazilian Believers."

75. Falola, Èṣù.

76. Kumari, *Isese Spirituality Workbook*.

77. Fatunmbi, *Ifá Theology*, 24.

Conclusion

Yorùbá beliefs have been transformed into a global phenomenon that attracts the outside world to this West African culture. It is, indeed, an irony drawn from the social environment that the Yorùbá civilization is being appreciated and reproduced more in the diaspora than where it originated from in Africa. This is the force of globalism. The terms of social cohesion, emancipation, and identification in both the slavery and colonial experience were quite different, bringing about different reactions. By implication, how culture was used by different groups—Africans/Yorùbá people under colonial rule and slavery—in pursuit of their interests were different. While a cultural identity built on these cultural inscriptions emerged among the people in southwestern Nigeria for political contestation and inclusion in the political process, the same process took place in the diaspora but emerged as a tool of distinction, a symbol of independence, and an expression of fundamental human rights through the self.[78] In this context, the Yorùbá cosmological space has been a form of sanctuary for several cultural groups and individuals in the diaspora, regardless of their background or race, who seek spiritual experience and enlightenment outside the more conventional religious systems. Indeed, "to risk a little exaggeration for the purpose of making a point, there is no land on earth where some people, no matter how few in number, do not strive to be Yoruba,"[79] and these cosmologies and their epistemic expressions have been pivotal to this reality.

---

78. Alonso, *Development of Yoruba Candomble.*
79. Adeeko, *Arts of Being Yorùbá,* xiv.

5 Oyo and Its Heterogeneity

Introduction

Oyo heterogeneity can be framed on two strands: the Old Oyo as a major empire and key player in West African politics and economy; and as the arbiter of Yorùbá culture. Through these strands, the empire was right at the center of the production of a global Yorùbá community and the transnationality of the Yorùbá identity and form. Oyo traditions reinforce the notion that the emergence of a name, frame, or taxonomy gives meaning to what had existed with its peculiar characteristics and form, which, if carefully observed, animates the reproduction of this entity in such a way that can be scientifically explored.[1] Of course, when it comes to culture, cultural practices, and cultural clusters, arriving at this junction does not occlude the possibility of nuances and some dynamics: these are indeed expected as a significant sign that symbolizes a vibrant entity of discourse.[2] Put differently, coming face-to-face with the static notion of the African past in some quarters, the existence of palpable dichotomies within the similarities among subcultural Yorùbá groups, like other cultures, attests to the perpetual preoccupation of the people with the reproduction of their cultural forms as influenced by their geophysical location, and the degree to which they will desirously protect them. Taken from historical developments in Central Sudan, the rise of polities and states like Benin, Urhobo, Ijo, Itsekiri, and others following the Odùduwà[3] model and heritage suggests a distorted frame of Yorùbá identity by the time it became a conceptually defined entity that had to be recognized by others.[4]

This chapter employs mythologies to add complexity to existing narratives and also attempts some possible historical reconstructions. In both approaches, people and places interact in physical spaces and how they construct their ideas and events. The limitations in the characterization of Yorùbá identity appear to speak readily to the effect of empires, empire building, and powerful states in the making of a substantive civilization. The Benin civilization anchored by the Benin Empire, by its geophysical location and proximity, had closer (imperial) relations

---

1. Barth, *Ethnic Groups and Boundaries*; Jenkins, *Social Identity*; Peel, "Cultural Work of Yoruba Ethnogenesis," 67–89.

2. Apter, *Oduduwa's Chain*.

3. See chap. 1. Odùduwà was regarded in mythology as a divine king, the first to govern at Ifẹ, who became the ancestral primogeniture of the Yorùbá.

4. Akinola, "Origin of the Eweka Dynasty of Benin," 21–36.

with polities and states in the eastern part of Yorubaland to a significant degree but had even more with its other neighbors settled around the great network of waters and a vast array of land known as the Bight of Benin.[5] The Kingdom of Benin became so great simultaneously with Oyo around the late 1500s, primarily with the coming of Portuguese and Dutch merchants, that it could absolve itself from the shadows of Odùduwà for political currency in the areas of its expansion in later years. If anything, going by the logic of political legitimacy, inheritance, and ancestral claim, the Benin traditions—and by implication, its metropolitan and outlying states—could lay claim to Odùduwà's heritage through his son/grandson, Òrànmíyàn (in various texts, it is not uncommon to adduce the role of a son to Òrànmíyàn; in another, a grandson[6]). It is recounted that Òrànmíyàn played a significant role in reforming the Benin polity, establishing the ruling dynasty that exists into the present day, in the same manner as his grandfather and father in the place later known as Ile-Ife.[7] But this was not the case, further crediting the dual origin theory of cultures, societies, and peoples. This would have given another form of nuance to what became the Yorùbá as a language group, cultural entity, geographical space, polity, and philosophy.

Adding political currency to the making of ethnic identities in this context is evident even in the characterization of Lagos as a Yorùbá state. The coastal city is recorded to have been established as a military camp by Benin forces to protect its growth and expansion as a military state in the unfolding eighteenth century around its part of the Atlantic coast.[8] This trend would indicate that had Iléṣà, another powerful Yorùbá state that emerged alongside Benin and Oyo, been successful in its attempts at territorial expansion to the magnitude of building an empire simultaneously with Oyo and Benin, Yorùbá identity would have been even further altered. Being the sole empire in the whole of the area later known as Yorubaland following the fifteenth-century decline of Ife political hegemony, Òrànmíyàn, the legendary founder of the Oyo traditions, could be correctly said to have preserved the Odùduwà traditions and values and, most importantly, the dream of an ideal state, sociopolitical morphology, and expansion.

One could see the keen persistence with which the intrinsic dialogue between these two legends of Odùduwà and Òrànmíyàn—whose names have survived and reproduced more in mythical forms as well as the periods in which they lived—shaped the sociopolitical policy of the Old Oyo Empire with a huge effect on its religious identity.[9] Tellingly, this—the Yorùbá religious cult of Òrìṣà—is one aspect of Yorùbá culture that has been instrumental to the reproduction of substantial elements of the civilization, which in turn has paved the way for the characterization of a Yorùbá deterritorialized community in the diaspora, particularly in the

---

5. Ryder, "Reconsideration of the Ifẹ-Benin Relationship," 25–37.

6. This is a consistent contradiction even in what came close as a primary data narrating the history of the people produced by Reverend Johnson.

7. Ryder, "Reconsideration of the Ifẹ-Benin Relationship."

8. Mann, *Slavery and the Birth of an African City*.

9. It is instructive to note that some of the Yorùbá pantheons of gods were transplantations of Mediterranean gods the ancestors of the people from this region adopted in navigating their daily living experiences and in response to their environment. This process of continued adaptation and incorporation of new elements into these practices and beliefs based on the specific environmental givings of their location have remained into the Atlantic world. Diop, *Precolonial Black Africa*, 216; Omari-Tunkara, *Manipulating the Sacred*.

Atlantic world.[10] It was the basis of the social and political bond that birthed the idea of Yorùbá among the diaspora of West African captives during the inglorious years of the slave trade.[11] And if there is any sense of truth or rationality in the submission made by Erwan Dianteill about the political role and exigencies of religious cults themselves, then the Old Oyo Empire cannot be dislocated from the center of the reproduction of the notion of Yorùbá in diasporas on either side of the Atlantic, as in the homeland. As he wrote, "If we are to put the concept of religious territory into operation in social science, we should not simply conceive of it as representing the relationship between living space and 'the administration of the sacred' by a human community. Using this concept also implies combining it with at least two other dimensions of community life: kinship and political organization."[12]

Oyo came to represent the latter two through the years of its glory and even afterward as it became the single political entity in the collective memory of those identified as Yorùbá captives in the Atlantic.[13] Because of this, one cannot be sure what became the faith of captives taken and sold by the kingdom of Benin. Due to proximity, Oyo's influence, and some cultural similarities, these populations could indeed adopt the Odùduwà currency in their search for social emancipation and political expression in the Atlantic world where cultural transplantation by proxy was rife. This is more so considering the magnitude of Yorùbá captives that were victims of this trade between the 1790s and the mid-nineteenth century and the possibility of members of a minority group taking up the identity of a dominant group for visibility and expression of a substantive culture.[14] Many of the captives from this part of the West African slave trade had been under the direct suzerainty of the Aláàfin as far back as their grandparents could remember; hence, their personal lives had been shaped by the changing events in the capital, Oyo-Ilé.[15] As such, as Ife symbolized the "administration of the sacred" of the Yorùbá pantheons, the Old Oyo Empire symbolized the kinship and political construction.[16]

In a careful selection reflecting other bodies of work on Yorùbá history, Akin Ogundiran classified its sociopolitical and economic trajectory into six basic epochs: Archaic (300 BCE–CE 300), Early Formative (250–750), Late Formative (650–1050), Classical (1000–1420), Intermediate (1400–1570s), Restoration (1570s–1650), and Atlantic (1630–1840).[17] Of these periods of historical development, Ile-Ife, the cradle of Yorùbá, held sway as a powerful force in all spheres of human and community development in the whole of Yorubaland during the Classical period (1000–1420). By the turn of the Intermediate years (1400–1570s), the powerful kingdom of Ifẹ—built not on military prowess but on intellectual fecundity embodied in its cultural spread—began to lose its political grip and influence, giving way to the rise of new

10. Tsang, "Art of Sweeping Sickness and Catching Death," 292–316.

11. Castor, *Spiritual Citizenship*.

12. Dianteill, "Deterritorialization and Reterritorialization of the Orisa Religion," 121.

13. Lovejoy and Ojo, "Lucumí, 'Terranova,'" 353–372.

14. Barth, *Ethnic Groups*.

15. Hence, in their various Atlantic locations, they took up those forms of identification with which the Oyo were known by their earliest contacts like Lucumi and Anago, and the overall would be the Yorùbá form. Owomoyela, "Pragmatic Humanism of Yorùbá Culture," 126–132.

16. Ojo, "'Heepa' (Hail) Òrìṣà," 30–59.

17. Ogundiran, *Yorùbá*.

and powerful polities. As the discussions in chapter 1 have shown, before the Classical Age, what existed were proto-Yorùbá autochthonous communities that had grown to a meaningful degree of sociopolitical organization by the Late Formative years of 650–1050 when the revered progenitor figure of the civilization emerged superintendent over developments in the epoch that succeeded this.

Following this Classical Age, the sociopolitical foundation and traditions laid by Odùduwà became instrumental to the tremendous rise of Oyo, Iléṣà, and Benin during the Restoration period until the Atlantic Age when they all collapsed, paving the way for a new political order built on the old but extant social order. During these periods, especially for the better part of the Atlantic Age, the Old Oyo held the northern part of Yorubaland firmly under the control of the Aláàfin, with some measure of penetration into the eastern and southern flanks of the country where its competitors, the Ìjẹ̀ṣà in the southern region and Benin far into the eastern region, held sway. Quite revealingly, Ọ̀rànmíyàn was instrumental to these three rising polities of the Classical Age. More interesting is that their growth and decline were simultaneously driven. Oyo heterogeneity thus investigates those areas in which the historical developments of the Old Oyo Empire inspired the twenty-first-century notion of Yorùbá identity and its diasporic implications.

Ọ̀rànmíyàn and the Expansion of Ife Traditions

One of the fundamental areas of conflict in the study of Ọ̀rànmíyàn lies in his relation to Odùduwà. To consciously navigate these two divides, over the years, the former has created a bridge on which the two traditions could meet by describing him as the last born of Odùduwà. But to lay to rest the contradictions from either of these traditions is to be certain of the period in which Odùduwà lived and the time other principal towns in Yorubaland were established, since Ife princes supposedly left Ile-Ife for creating sovereign political entities for themselves at the same time. The contradictions do not get better with the tradition of the seven grandchildren of Odùduwà, who first spread out to establish various sovereign territories of their own patterned after the Ife traditions, first described by Samuel Johnson, creating the genesis for the reproduction of Yorùbá history. The Yorùbá tradition that transcends to Benin was charged by Ọ̀rànmíyàn, the same legendary character who established the Oyo tradition from the Pàràkòyí, south of Ife.[18] This tradition notwithstanding, the account of the seven grandchildren of Odùduwà relates these two figures.

The implication of the seven grandchildren theory would mean that this was never intended to be understood as a relation by blood but by selection based on relation to the Ife tradition. Indeed, the traditions of these polities suggest that they were established around the same period. Samuel Johnson and many other Yorùbá scholars have attested to the fluid manner in

---

18. This could have (partly) induced the decision of Ọ̀ọ̀ni Abeweila centuries after to settle the displaced people from the fall of the empire in this direction. Document Extracted from Lecture Delivered by Chief Oladiran Ajayi, Otun Asiwaju of Modakeke on July 15, 1989, at Modakeke High School Hall in a Special Commemorative/Mid-year Lecture to Mark the Creation of Ife North Local Government Area, 8.

which the idea of "children" is conceived by the Yorùbá people.[19] Even Odùduwà himself is portrayed as the son of Olódúmarè. While this would explain the liberty in the way Òrànmíyàn has been depicted in Yorùbá history regarding his relation to Odùduwà, it does not explain the kind of reverence the idea has enjoyed among Yorùbá monarchs, said in one of the traditions to have been as a result of his position as the last child of Odùduwà. In a way, there could be some truth to this. What is certain is that when put in the biblical context, much of which is reproduced among the Yorùbá, Òrànmíyàn would be St. Paul—the faithful disciple of Christ whose contributions to the making of Christianity are unquantifiable when compared with his equals.

Òrànmíyàn practically took the sociopolitical template and thoughts of Odùduwà and implanted them in his political career all through his long, glorious years. What the circumstances of time, most significantly, deprived Odùduwà, Òrànmíyàn explored excellently, saving Ife traditions in the process by the time Oyo had reached its political nadir. Fundamentally, the restoration and preservation of Ife traditions were anchored on this figure. Another character, the last in the era before the colonial incursion, whose historic imprint could be seen in a similar light, was Aláàfin Abípa. Before him, Oyo was a striving kingdom incessantly forced to evacuate its capital to places like Ajàká, Gbere (in Ibariba country), Kusu, and Igboho. With his foresight and tenacity to implement his father's policy of a return to the old capital, Abípa engineered what could be called the golden age in Oyo history. This period witnessed a thriving Oyo kingdom expanding into an empire that spread over a land area almost the size of all southwestern Nigeria, standing at precisely forty-five thousand square kilometers by the early eighteenth century, with a population of around a million people. Of course, as with all golden epochs in the history of civilizations, the Oyo golden age was followed by a decline.[20]

Nevertheless, all that needed to be done by this time to mirror the peculiarities of what later became Yorùbá country and identity had developed into a form in which they could be reproduced anywhere and at any time. Consequently, as Oyo was falling and Yorubaland was in disarray, their culture, traditions, and forms were fossilized and reproduced in the Atlantic world.[21] The great Yorùbá pioneer historian Samuel Johnson divides the periods leading to the foregoing into seven historical episodes: Mythological Kings and Deified Heroes; Historical Kings; Kings of Oyo Igbòho; Despotic Kings; Basòrun Gáà, His Atrocities, and Abiodun's Peaceful Reign; the Age of the Revolution; and the Rise of the Fulani to Power. These periods spanned the Classical and Atlantic periods—in this case, from about the thirteenth century to the mid-nineteenth century.

Part of the Odùduwà tradition alludes to a religious conflict in the Far East in which Odùduwà lost to the Islamic parties in the war leading to his displacement alongside his followers and lieutenants and their relocation to a place later known as Ile-Ife. In a continuation of this tradition, Oyo accounts posit that, owing to the inability of Odùduwà to avenge this fate before his demise and the enraging animosity that persisted among Odùduwà's children and

---

19. This has even been explained in their epistemic stretch of the idea of *ile* (home) and kinship. See Apter, "Yoruba Ethnogenesis from Within," 356–387.

20. Law, *Oyo Empire c. 1600–c. 1836.*

21. Falola and Genova, *Orisa*; Kumari, *Iyanifa Woman of Wisdom.*

followers toward the incident, Oyo was established in the process of a retaliatory attack led by Ọ̀rànmíyàn. Described by many as a renowned hunter and restless warrior, Ọ̀rànmíyàn mobilized his brothers, who by this time had established the various principal Yorùbá towns, to plan the invasion of the mythical location, probably an area among the Borgu. In what would later seem as the transfer of a much later event into this myth, of all the children of Odùduwà, only the Ọwá of Iléṣà refused to join the invading army of Ọ̀rànmíyàn. This would come to be seen in the refusal of the Ọwá of Iléṣà to celebrate the reconstitution of the capital of its powerful rival to the north of the country in its old location at Oyo-Ile during the reign of Ọbalokun, who began the reign at the old site, as Aláàfin Abípa passed on before they got to this location.[22] The circumstance and timing of this tradition, like others, were developed based on the grand historical picture they gave, and this is unrelated to the role of Islam in the fall of Oyo and the social status of Johnson, which was inclined to the local feelings at the time.

Meanwhile, bringing the Ọbàtálá-Odùduwà tradition of palm wine into this account, the revenge mission was summarily terminated at a place called Ìgángán due to a conflict that ensued over a pot of beer. In this tradition, Ọ̀rànmíyàn's army was to march through the Nupe territory from whence they could cross the Niger River to make their way to Arabia since the old route they took on their departure to the western part of the continent was inaccessible and inauspicious for traveling, but some factions of the Nupe communities denied them this opportunity. As seen in chapter 1, because all these people constructed a mythology that they were victims of the same sociopolitical development in the Far East leading to their western wave of mass and multiple migrations, it betrays common logic that Ọ̀rànmíyàn forces were rebuffed on such a mission, if it had existed, by the Nupe. More instructively, until after the establishment of the Old Oyo Empire, there is no historical record adumbrating any form of hostile relations between Ọ̀rànmíyàn and the Nupe. But for whatever reason, his brothers now returned to their various towns and kingdoms in this tradition, and Ọ̀rànmíyàn and his lieutenants moved to Bàrìbá. Mythologies should not be taken at face value, but they show extensive intergroup relations.

A young crown prince and astute warrior, Ọ̀rànmíyàn's urge to settle with his people on a separate and sovereign land led him to request the assistance of the king of Bàrìbá in pursuing this impulse. Tradition has it that the king gave him a boa snake to lead his way to the space where he could fruitfully settle his people and reign as a sovereign king. Since there could be no verbal communication between Ọ̀rànmíyàn and a boa, the boa led him with a sign, and the sign was that during the sojourn, the boa would stay at a place sometimes for the people to take a rest and ultimately, to indicate the place of settlement for the entourage. The latter came at a place later known as Oyo-Ilé, where the boa stayed for seven days before disappearing. Scholars like Akintoye suggest that older Yorùbá towns like Àdìkún, Òwu, and Ogbòro were settled around this place at the time, implying an existing civilization and people in this area.[23] The mission of Ọ̀rànmíyàn in this place, as in Odùduwà in Ife, would have been to bring together different polities in this area under a central government with its headquarters at Òkò. This signaled a

---

22. Johnson, *History of the Yorubas*, 168.
23. Akintoye, *History of the Yoruba People*, 247.

great deal of threat to its powerful neighbors, the Bàrìbá and Nupe, who feared at various times the danger a stable Oyo polity portended for them.

In another tradition that is even more mythical, Ọ̀rànmíyàn, not Odùduwà or Ọbàtálá, was the one given the mission to create and expand the world. This direction depicts the understanding of how the Yorùbá people see themselves and project themselves in the metaphoric form of the "world," a kind of Yorubaland as the centerpiece of the world policy preserved and expressed in myths. There is no question that these three figures fit into this mythical character substitution on the criteria of their roles in the development and expansion of the Yorùbá political morphology at significant moments in their history. Hence, at various times and in different locations, Olódúmarè gave these ancestors objects with which they were to create and expand the human world. These objects could also be interpreted as the political sagacity, intellectual fecundity, bravery, and other skills needed to achieve the purpose for which Olódúmarè is believed to have brought them into society. So, like his forebears, Ọ̀rànmíyàn was given a tray of sand with twenty-one pieces of iron and a cork for the mission of creation. The sand lay on the waters, the cork did the spreading, while the irons were to give meaning to the process under what they connote as the natural treasure of the earth for the engineering of the intended civilization. Having completed this task and given the centrality of land to the activation and exploration of their potential, his brothers were made to pay him for portions of the land to cultivate and live. Consequently, they brought goods and produce from principal Yorùbá towns to the Aláàfin. As territorial expansion later became well pronounced, this was extended to other Yorùbá towns and peoples.

If the mythical mission of creation led him to Ife or Oyo, the tradition did not indicate. But the message is clear: Ọ̀rànmíyàn created a new polity of order next only to Ife in Yorubaland, and as we know, this was in Oyo and Benin.[24] During these early years, Ọ̀rànmíyàn left Òkò, the then-Oyo, in the hands of his son, Ajuan, who took up the eponymous name of the later settlement, Àjàká, where Aláàfin Ṣàngó relocated the capital during a crisis. Ostensibly, this was to allow him to formerly depart from Ile-Ife, as was the tradition. On getting to Ile-Ife, he launched toward the eastern part of the country to reach Benin, on the invitation of the people, where, like his father/grandfather, Odùduwà, he reformed and transformed the Benin polity to the same pedestal with Ile-Ife and Oyo, after which he birthed a new dynasty, put his son, Eweka, at the helm of affairs, and sought to return to Oyo. Crisscrossing this large expanse of forest is daunting; together with his mission on these sojourns, it was expected to take a few years. On his return to Òkò, his son, Àjàká, had been properly installed as the Aláàfin instead of the acting position in which he left him. With this development, Ọ̀rànmíyàn decided to go back to Ife. There, he retired as a private citizen. Some accounts claimed he died at Òkò and that his body was only taken to Ife for burial, being an Ọ̀ọ̀ni before abdicating the position for his political crusades. Whatever the case might be, following his return, nothing significant is noted of this historical figure.

This is curious in that all through the political maneuvering that ensued after his reign and possible return, which saw his choice of acting-Aláàfin deposed forcefully for his brother,

---

24. Akinjogbin, "Oyo Empire in the 18th Century," 450.

     GLOBAL YORÙBÁ

Olúfinràn, alias Ṣàngó, Òrànmíyàn was never mentioned to have played any role, especially in putting the polity back on the right footing. The only plausible reason for this is that Òrànmíyàn passed on earnestly afterward or he only returned after the crisis, compelling him to retire to private life. But even then, until after the eventual cracks in the settlement, the likes of Olówu, Alákétu, Ọwá, and other acclaimed brothers of the Aláàfìń honored him with gifts, making him the richest among his equals. This position is explained in different traditions, one of which has been mentioned above regarding the mythical creation of the world. Other theories that have been developed explaining this practice include the last-born theory and Òrànmíyàn's choice of heirloom. Starting with the latter, the itinerant hunter-warrior is said to have been absent when their father died; hence, he took what was left of their father's property, which was land, as his inheritance, while others shared the wives, cloth, shoes, beads, cowries, and everything else among themselves. As the owner of the land where his brothers could explore, live, and reproduce, the tributes from other Yorùbá kings to Oyo are deemed as a payment for this purpose, as in a relationship between a landowner and a tenant.

On the other hand, the last-born theory adduced this to his position. In this case, tributes to the Aláàfìń by the principal Yorùbá kings are only a measure of a kind gesture to their youngest sibling so that he could maintain himself and feel the abundance of riches of the country whose foundation their father had laid. But then, a somewhat similar scenario could be seen in Ìjẹ̀ṣà traditions where Obòkun (a name supposedly derived from the assignment accomplished by the progenitor of the people who volunteered to fetch seawater to cure Odùduwà of eye infection) was given a sword known as Idà Àjàṣẹ́ (sword of victory) by Odùduwà, having been away when his siblings were given emblems for the establishment of new territories.[25] Subsequent kings of Iléṣà would later use the sword to expand their territorial reach and exert authority, especially in central Yorubaland. It would also be used to check the southward spread of Oyo. The how and when Oyo began to enjoy tribute collection from other principal Yorùbá towns is a history shrouded in speculation, the best of which could be adduced to its rapid but inconsistent growth and expansion during the Classical Age and common practice of exchanging gifts among Yorùbá kings at the time.

Hence, while the Ọwá of Iléṣà, for instance, was in the practice of sending gifts of mats, cowries, and agricultural produce from the fertile lands of his rain forest region, the Aláàfìn sent goods like cloths and other refined materials it has been trading with its close and distant neighbors. Already, between the Classical and Intermediate periods—the earliest formation of Oyo from around the twelfth to late sixteenth centuries—the town had witnessed considerable growth that threatened even those who helped the people in settling in the space they occupied, notably the Bàrìbá and the Nupe, who before this time had been launching attacks on pre-Oyo settlements of Òwu, Kétu, Ìlá, Àdìkún, Ogbòro, and others, pushing them southward. Although at one time the Oyo were made to pay tributes to the Nupe, they were never perpetually or completely subjugated. Consequently, as seen in the events that led to the dethronement of Àjàká and the enthronement of Ṣàngó, who resuscitated the militarist nature of the polity shortly after their father, Òrànmíyàn, had left the political scene, no sooner had Oyo

---

25. Akinjogbin, "Oyo Empire in the 18th Century," 112.

been established as a human settlement in the savanna region of Yorubaland than it became a formidable force for many polities around. This brings to bear the aura that the founder of the town, Ọ̀rànmíyàn, espoused.

Several connections could be made as to how and why the Aláàfins were treated with honor and respect shown in tributes and courtesy offered to them by other principal Yorùbá cities. Among these, and laying the foundation for others, would be the stature of the founder as a renowned warrior king whose political achievements were next to only that of Odùduwà. Earlier, Ọ̀rànmíyàn was likened to the biblical Paul in keeping the traditions, teachings, and spirit of his father/grandfather. In this way, one can begin to appreciate the reverence he enjoined during his days as not just Odùduwà-incarnate and mouthpiece but a renowned warrior with about 150 well-trained bodyguards.[26] Building on this factor would be laying credence to the two traditions (heirloom and last-born theory) meant to explain this, albeit fusing elements from both. In a way, both traditions speak to the late settlement of Oyo among the principal Yorùbá towns of Ìlá, Òwu, Kétu, and others, as well as the allowance given to Ọ̀rànmíyàn to establish Oyo on a vast expanse of land that brought together old settlements in the area.

So, as the youngest and the most powerful of all, he was revered and made to coordinate the fate of these communities at various times. Although the traditions would make this process seem to have occurred in one fell swoop, the historical process of the settlement shows this occurred into its golden age when it took its final form. When Oyo took over the Ìgbómìnà region of Yorubaland, it preserved the sanctity of Ìlá. In another turn of events, after the demise of Ọ̀rànmíyàn, attempts were made by the Olówu of Òwu to stop this "family tradition,"[27] which is said to have been responsible for the birth of the ẹbí system in Yorubaland and more importantly among Yorùbá kings.[28] In the subsequent practice, upon the death of any of the principal Yorùbá kings, their property was shared among other principal kings in the country. When we consider the assertion that Ọ̀rànmíyàn met some communities around this space that he incorporated into the larger and central administrative center at Òkò, it explains further why he was consistently attached to land in the traditions as well as the various myths that seek to illuminate the history that legitimizes the tributes collected by Oyo and the influence it established.

Furthermore, Oyo traditions reinforce the dual origin theory of the Yorùbá civilization in that historians and social anthropologists are yet to ascertain the true link between Ọ̀rànmíyàn/Oyo and the Bàrìbá, on the one hand, and Nupe and Oyo/Ọ̀rànmíyàn on the other. Oyo traditions are conspicuously dotted with events and traditions of these two places. In a way, this could help postulate on Ọ̀rànmíyàn's choice of a northern migration from Ife. Aside from the political undertone noted earlier, one could make sense of the account that suggests that Ọ̀rànmíyàn's choice of northern migration was to march an army to Arabia as a story

---

26. Johnson, *History of the Yorubas*, 143.

27. None of these polities was able to restructure the polities of places they occupied like Oyo did. For instance, Ila never exerted political authority over settlements that had existed in the Igbomina region the way Odùduwà did in Ife, and Ọ̀rànmíyàn in Oyo and Benin. Usman, "Ila Kingdom Revisited," 130.

28. Akinjogbin and Ayandele, "Yorùbáland up to 1800," 121–133.

attempting to mythologize his deliberate choice of that route to establish a sovereign entity with a mandate of reproducing and expanding the spread of Ife/Odùduwà civilization to the reach of the Niger River from whence his ancestors had dispersed for Ile-Ife. Considering the distance of Oyo to Ife and the strategic geophysical space it occupies, Òrànmíyàn's choice of this area could not have been by chance but by a strategic military and geopolitical calculation.

It was noted in chapter 1 how many of the different cultural groups in present-day Nigeria once settled at the banks of the Niger River following their dispersal, according to their myths, from the Far East. All through the centuries before modern transformation that terminated the competitions, rivalries, and wars of expansion by precolonial societies in this part of the Niger, the greatest threat to the survival of the Ife traditions would come from this very northern region of the kingdom. Òrànmíyàn must have been aware of this—that is, the development of equally powerful states—plus the need to expand the reach of the Ife traditions as far as possible to set the boundary for the southern expansion of polities in that area.

Taking the mythologies at face value, Òrànmíyàn must have been aware of the trajectory of his ancestors in Ile-Ife from the Far East; the lives they led in the Niger River valley with other groups that have equally left the area to establish civilizations elsewhere; and the age-long tradition that has kept polities expanding, influential, and powerful in the area they are situated—a situation that led to the dispersal of his ancestors from the Far East. Accordingly, instead of going to Arabia to avenge his ancestors' displacement, Òrànmíyàn left Ife to establish a sovereign entity of Ife heritage, to serve as a buffer between Ife and its northern neighbors for the preservation of Ife traditions.

In this way, as with the relationship between Ẹdẹ and Oyo, Oyo was meant to be the frontier of Ifẹ́ against northern incursion, and preservation of Ife traditions, which included its geographical spread. One can relate this further to the reason for Òrànmíyàn's navigation of that area only to hand over power to his son and move back to Ife from whence he headed to Benin, perhaps another part of the country he thought would need to be secured. Òrànmíyàn, in this process, became the apostle of Odùduwà in that with his skills—both in military and intellect—he was able to secure Odùduwà's vision of a new civilization below the Niger. Another important area in this intellectual inquiry would be the relationship that existed between Ife and these polities before the migration of Òrànmíyàn to found Oyo. Among other things, this could offer a clearer picture of the roles of these settlements in the establishment and growth of Oyo. It does not get more interesting when Oyo traditions further reveal that Ṣàngó, one of Òrànmíyàn's sons, was from a Nupe woman, and at various times, the Aláàfins and their subjects found refuge in the Ìbàrìbá country. In any case, there were deep cultural mixtures among cultures in this region, as Oyo married from notable neighbors like the Bàrìbá and Nupe. Several practices came into Oyo traditions through these cultures. Cross-cultural breeding aided close relationships but did not avert wars and rivalry. In contrast to what later became the practice of war and warriors in the Atlantic Age, wars were at this time fought not for spoils and captives taken as commodities but principally to exert authority and for territorial expansion.

Invaded territories were preserved and protected by the invading forces against another great power in that area.[29]

Again, it is quite instructive that Oyo traditions could grant us some insights into *Ifá* practice in Yorubaland. That it took a major crisis in which the people of Oyo thought their rejection of the advice of Arugbá-Ifá, the mother of Aláàfin Onígbògi, was responsible for the calamity that befell them from their Nupe neighbors before the Ifá system was incorporated into the Oyo traditions suggests that Ifá had not become a dominant force in Ifẹ̀ traditions during the greater part of the Classical Age when Odùduwà and Ọ̀rànmíyàn lived. Before Onígbògi, about six Aláàfins, including Ọ̀rànmíyàn, had reigned in Oyo, the longest reign of which has been attributed to his immediate predecessor, Olúàso, who allegedly reigned for almost a century. If there is any truth to this, Olúàso must be among the few who reigned from a very young age and enjoyed a long and healthy life. This situates the reign of Onígbògi to the Intermediate Years in the Yorùbá calendar of history, which brings us to around 1400 to the 1570s, when the Restoration period was activated under Aláàfiń Abípa, alias Ọba Mọrọ̀.[30] The Classical Age, which most likely ended with the reign of Olúàso, was, according to Johnson, terminated on a peaceful and prosperous note. Olúàso had prudently built on the efforts of his predecessors to establish a politically fortified city and prosperous empire.

With the removal of Àjàká during the reign of deified kings due to his alleged political and military weakness and the emergence of Olúfinràn, who became defied as Ṣàngó, Oyo politics was tilted toward militarism, as subsequent aláàfins were considered for their bravery and ability to protect the town. Even Àjàká himself came back to the throne after the controversial death of Aláàfin Ṣàngó, stronger and better than his previous reign. He was credited to have launched a successful attack against the Nupe. That Àjàká came back to become the Aláàfiń after Aláàfiń Ṣàngó's demise confirms the assumption that the latter's reign was short-lived, as he passed on at a young age. If anything, the reign of deified kings showed the people the towns and kingdoms they were to contend with if they were to fulfill the purpose for which the settlement was established in the first place. Until the Atlantic Age, these forces were predominantly the Nupe and Bàrìbá. Since the time of Aláàfiń Ṣàngó, the capital of the settlement oscillated between different locations that included Òkò and the likes of Oyokorò (also known as Àjàká), Bàrìbá, Kusu, and Ìgbòho.

To avoid the incessant attack by their powerful neighbors, Oyo, like every other people who had suffered the same fate,[31] adopted and developed the military tactics of these neighbors. Part of this included the introduction of poisonous arrows and surprise attacks. Horses and cavalry soldiers with which their enemies had been routing them were introduced during the Intermediate age as contact with the Hausa states was established. Together with these, warriors were followed to battles by masquerades. With this strategic rearrangement of the military network and structure of the kingdom, Aláàfiń Ọ̀ròmpọ̀tọ̀ and his immediate successor, Ajiboyede, defeated Bàrìbá and Nupe forces in different battles and at different times, signaling

---

29. Ajisafe, *Iwe Itan Abeokuta*.

30. Johnson, *History of the Yorubas*, 164.

31. Makar, *History of Political Change among the Tiv*.

   GLOBAL YORÙBÁ

the rise of Oyo as a sole dominant force and "largest ever in the history of the tropical forests and grasslands of West Africa South of the Niger."[32]

These and the economic prosperity as well as the political stability guaranteed helped Olúàso achieve tremendous success as the longest-reigning Aláàfín. Although still ruling from Àjàká, Olúàso's immediate predecessor, Kori, had consolidated previous political successes of the past, most significantly by establishing a military outpost for the empire in a northeastern settlement called Ẹdẹ under the leadership of a military warlord known as Tìmì. Somewhat, Ẹdẹ in Oyo traditions became what Oyo was to Ifẹ́, just under a different circumstance. The establishment of Ẹdẹ was to check the expansion and growing power of Iléṣà in the southern forest of Yorubaland. Both Oyo and Iléṣà in Yorùbá country were the contending power for political dominance at this time, as Ifẹ́ was on the verge of collapse and its influence dwindled largely due to drought and the ambition of its mini cultures like Iléṣà and Oyo.[33] As Ẹdẹ was to stop the Ìjẹ́ṣà forces, in case of confrontation, before advancing further into Oyo territories, so was Osogbo carved by the Ọwá of Ìjẹ́sà to check the Oyo. This military organization shows how far Oyo, and indeed, Yorubaland, had come. Ìkòyí and Igbàjà were later added to the important military outposts of the empire. The capital remained at Àjàká, and the people lived relatively peacefully until the demise of Olúàso, as none of their enemies could stage a successful attack against the growing empire until the next reign.

Upon Onígbògi's enthronement, his mother—whose name was given as Arugbá-Ifá, a name derived from her role in the Ifá cult—came from Òtà with the hope of guiding her son through the system of governance. However, her advice for the installation of Ifá as a principal deity in the town was rebuffed by her son, the Aláàfín. Arugbá-Ifá soon left Oyo with her Ifá followers, who wailed their way out of Oyo heading toward a place known as Adó, where they were stopped by the head of the community, Aládó, who invited them to practice and teach the people the Ifá system. Years into his reign, Nupe forces attacked the new capital again with success after centuries of relative peace at Àjàká. This development moved Oyo to Gbérè in the Bàrìbá country, where they proceeded to Kusu for a final strategy at reconstituting their lost settlement. The people, including the king, thought this to be a result of their attitude toward establishing the Ifá system into their religious cult, while indeed, this had been caused by the early fifteenth-century recalibration of the Nupe polity. During this period, Nupe emerged as a stronger neighbor under the central administrative government of Tsoede, making the army even more formidable than what his predecessors faced.[34]

Given the historical makeup of the communities in this area, it is likely that in the previous wars and times of peace, various Nupe communities could have taken different sides as events suited their purpose. This could also explain why despite giving one of his daughters to Òrànmíyàn, obviously as a measure of goodwill and ostensibly as a way of protecting its interest in the emerging polity by producing the Aláàfínate, Nupe forces harnessed and attacked Oyo several times. With another Òrànmíyàn figure in the Nupe country, it is only expected

---

32. Akintoye, *History of the Yoruba People*, 242.

33. Ogundiran, *Yorùbá*.

34. Atanda, "Kings in Nigerian Society."

that he experimented with its age-long rival. The combined forces of the Nupe country with well-trained cavalry soldiers took the pleasure of displacing the people after about a century's attempt. Unfortunately, Arugbá-Ifá died before the calamity befell them. The only person to help them in this process was Aládó, who gladly obliged their call. In what seems like an ironic turn of events, during the same period, the Egúngún cult was introduced into Oyo traditions from Nupe. To date, the Alápini who heads the cult in Oyo is derived from a family that originates from the Nupe country. These marked the two fundamental changes Aláàfiń Olúgbógi introduced into the Oyo polity as it was about to be reconstituted at Ìgbòho. Both Egúngún and the Ifá cult became so important in Oyo traditions that they led conquests and took leading roles in the administration of the empire.

Implicitly, Ifá was established in Adó before it came to Oyo. The same conclusion was reached in the case of Ifẹ̀ (in chap. 2 of this work), which was backed by Odù Ifá Ọ̀sá Méjì, bringing us close to the possible period Ifá was brought to Yorubaland and leaving us more confused as to its presence during the time of Odùduwà, as dominant Yorùbá traditions would have us believe. By incorporating these systems into the sociopolitical structure of the state, leaders believed that future wars would be averted or prepared for through Ifá divination, and wars could be won through the support of ancestors whose ancestral energy was believed to reside within the masquerades. Onígbógi also added one more cabinet seat in his government that later became one of the most important in the Aláàfińate. The title was *Òsì'wẹ́fà*, and it was first conferred on the son of Gbọnka Ajanlapa, who disguised himself as the Aláàfiń when the Nupe forces entered the palace during the invasion that took them to Bàrìbá country. Putting on the regalia of the Aláàfiń, Gbọnka Ajanlapa stayed back in place of Onígbógi, whom he convinced to flee. As the political system was reconstituted, he instituted the Òsì'wẹ́fà title to compensate the soul of this good servant of his. Òsì'wẹ́fà acted in place of the Aláàfiń when circumstance demanded such. Thus, Oyo politics was reconfigured at Kusu and transferred to Ìgbòho when they finally moved to this new location.

Ìgbòho was another site where the people enjoyed relative peace until Aláàfiń Ajiboyede thought it wise to move the headquarters of the administration back to its original home, a wish executed by his son, Àtìbà, at Òkò. Before this time, the Oyo polity became so strong at Ìgbòho that it entertained no fear of relocating to its ancestral location from possible attack from Nupe or any other peoples. The period at Ìgbòho was not only peaceful but prosperous, so much so that many of the nobles and chiefs made several attempts to weaken this position. They could not part with the glory of living in the capital, their fixed properties, or businesses, which had included participation in the trans-Saharan trade with the Hausa states from where they got their luxury items and horses. Here began another regime of conspiracy in Oyo politics, a precursor to the decline of the Atlantic Age. This dragged on during the time of Ajiboyede until his demise and when his son, Abípa, rose to power. Unable to convince Aláàfiń Abípa to change his mind on the matter, the chiefs sent those referred to in Yorùbá traditions as *àkàndá ẹ́dá* (specially made beings) or *ẹni òrìṣà* (people that belonged to the gods) to the location when it became clear that the king was sending an advance team to collect information on the viability of the place and what needed to be done before relocation, since this was a ruined homeland long abandoned.

Each of the chiefs donated one of these special beings for the mission. These characters included a hunchback, an albino, a person with leprosy, a dwarf, a person with an unspecified physical disability, and a person with prognathism. The role of these special beings was to create a phantom reality of a spirit-infested area not habitable for the advance party. With their flashlights, they displayed their notoriety on a hill close to this location as they shouted, "*Kò sáàyè, Kò sáàyè!*" ("No space, no space!"). For days on end, these "phantom spirits" tormented the location from the hills. The advance team returned to Ìgbòho to give its report to the king, who immediately sensed foul play. He requested his hunters to go and rally these creatures and bring them to him. It turned out that the king was right, but he decided not to kill these characters. In place of punishment, he called a feast where he invited the chiefs, who were then served by their "spirit" messengers thought to be running their errands on the hill of Òkò. Thus, Abípa took the sobriquet, Ọba Mọ̀rọ̀, "the king who arrested ghosts."[35] Upon their return to this old site, which came only after the reign of Abípa, who died before they inhabited the reconstituted headquarters, the people named this place Oyo Oro (Spectral Oyo). Accordingly, Abípa fulfilled the wishes of his father, Ajiboyede, whom he succeeded, and by so doing, he engineered or rather triggered the period of growth, expansion, and great glory of Oyo by insisting on the reconstruction of the capital in its ancestral location. Through festivals like the *Bebe*, which often lasted for three months, Oyo brought many Yorùbá towns and kings together in a single place as they strengthened their cultural bonds, although this was mostly related to those within the core of the administration of the empire.

In addition to this, it is said that no Ọba in Yorubaland could order the execution of anyone without being so commissioned through a sword of justice known as Idà Ọ̀rànmíyàn located at Ile-Ife alongside other rituals expected to be performed on an Ọba-elect (not bale) at Odùduwà's grave and rites by the Ọ̀ọ̀ni of Ife.[36] These rituals brought the Ọba-elect to the rank of these two significant figures in the political history of Yorubaland, a rank that conferred legitimacy and continuity,[37] and this is only concerning the principal Yorùbá towns and monarchs. In any case, as the crown proliferated and many joined the league of Ọba-Alade (crowned Ọba) in the subsequent epochs, this tradition was torpedoed. One could begin to understand the basis on which Ọ̀rànmíyàn became prime among other Yorùbá principal lords, even though some, like the Òwu, Kétu, Ìlá, Pópó, and others, had been in existence before Oyo.

In what followed, Oyo witnessed tremendous growth under what Johnson described as despotic rulers. This was the age Oyo expanded in territorial reach, grew in access to trade networks and trading activities, became fully kitted for political hegemony, and spread its social institutions across cultures. At this period, both old and new settlements in Yorubaland were steadily under the suzerainty of the Aláàfin. From Popo, Dahomey, Nupe, Ẹ̀gbá, Ẹ̀gbádò, Ìbàrìbá, Ìdásá, Ìgbómìnà, Ìbọlọ, and O-kun to the Asante and Ga in Accra and many other near and distant lands, ancient and emerging, Oyo grew into an important empire in the whole of West Africa, collecting tributes with varying arrangements from thousands of territories. At

---

35. Johnson, *History of the Yorubas*, 165.

36. Agai, "Samuel Johnson on the Egyptian Origin of the Yorùbá," 238.

37. Asiwaju, "Political Motivation," 116–121.

the time, Aláàfin̄ Abiodun reportedly met with his namesake, Adegolu, the Baálẹ́ of Akala, toward the end of the glorious years of the empire to save the polity from the destructive cloud of Baṣọ̀run Gáà; sixty-six hundred towns and villages were said to be under the control of Oyo, which itself was under the control of the Baṣọ̀run and his sons.[38]

As he did in Benin, the legendary Ọ̀rànmíyàn created a central administrative system in the northern part of Yorubaland by bringing together several polities in that area, which became a major threat to its neighbors, managed from different centers of administration by his descendants and transforming to become the most powerful and important polity in the whole country until the colonial period. As complicated as the preceding narratives are, mythologies produced a history of state formation, interlocking spaces, and shared ideas that developed over time. This mythology should be read as the creation of a regional and Pan-Yorùbá history.

The Rise of Oyo, c. 1630–c. 1790

The absolute geographical reach of the Old Oyo Empire remains a matter of speculation, as historians and archaeologists have sought to understand this from areas that held some levels of allegiance to the empire. Indeed, this has proven to be difficult; not only has the boundary consistently shifted over time, but the great empire had several forms of relations with both small and powerful polities in West Africa. More importantly, as tactically raised earlier in the case of Benin, the question would be how many of these cultures could be referred to as Yorùbá. This would later be a critical question in the magnitude of those identified as Yorùbá, even in the variants of the name, in the transatlantic slave trade, and the background of the Yorùbá community in the Atlantic diaspora.[39] In the meantime, however, going along this line within the area today considered part of Yorùbá identity, Morton-Williams writes, "That eastern and north-eastern Yoruba tribes do not have those political and religious institutions which distinguish Oyo cultural influences throughout the western and southern parts of the Oyo empire supports the view that the eastern area was rather a slave reservoir than under Oyo administration."[40]

This also applies to Oyo's relationship with the Ìjẹ̀ṣà, which was corrupted into Ìjẹ òrìṣà ("food of the gods"), the premise on which they were hunted among other Yorùbá communities and groups thought to be their (Oyo) subjects to whom they could do as they wanted. Hence, the stereotypical angle to the extension of the legitimacy of the Aláàfin̄, which fueled the multiple directions it marched its soldiers for expansion or exertion of this fictitious idea. Coming close to this were those slaves sold to Oyo from other cultural groups and those who were transported through its territories. In addition to this would be the subject of tributes, also discussed earlier, especially with places like Iléṣa, Kétu, and other principal Yorùbá towns and settlements. What is certain in this consideration, however, is that building on the political sagacity and hegemony deeply rooted by their predecessors, particularly the immediate

---

38. Johnson, *History of the Yorubas*, 183.

39. Lovejoy, "Yorùbá Factor in the Trans-Atlantic Slave Trade," 40–51.

40. Morton-Williams, "Oyo and the Atlantic Trade 1670–1830," 27.

ones at Ìgbòho, Oyo despotic rulers, as Johnson described them, despite their character flaws and political misadventures, presided over the largest polity in the whole of the Niger area. In the previous age, the kings at Ìgbòho had put the Nupe and the Bàrìbá—their only formidable neighbors—in their place in order to dominate the geopolitical ambiance of the Niger area. Like the Nupe, Ifá divination—the use of masquerades to accompany warriors consisting mainly of cavalry formations with poisonous arrows to war, and sometimes involving a surprise attack—had been adopted by the Aláàfìń during the reconstitution efforts that began at Ìgbòho, culminating into the reign of Òfinràn. These could be dated to around the late 1500s to early 1600s.

Described by Ogundiran as the "period of restoration," this era saw the massive expansion of Oyo as an empire. The developments of Iléṣà, Benin, and Nupe as hitherto great polities of the previous centuries, like Ifẹ́ to the south of the Niger and Kanem to the north, were on a steady decline, leaving their ruins for new settlements and existing but small towns to build in their various geophysical spaces and regions.[41] The formidable growth of Oyo under the Aláàfìń since their "exile" at Ìgboho—the new capital after they left Gbere in Ibariba country under their Wasangari cousins—left it a dominant force replacing the grandeur of the Ifẹ́ kingdom in the extreme north of the country till the collapse of the empire in the early part of the nineteenth century. By the end of the fifteenth century, Ife was on a steady decline due to the climatic condition of the region of Central and Western Sudan heralding droughts; limited harvest; starvation; trade; and economic disruption, depopulation, and ultimately political maneuverings, leading to instability in the polities of the then-powerful states in the region reaching the great Mali Empire. As should be expected, all these political purges had their socioeconomic and trade implications.

In the Yorùbá country, as in Kanem, Mali, and others at the time, dominant trading routes and advantages shifted to the younger state to the north. Oyo became the embodiment of Ife traditions, reproducing and giving meaning to the cardinals of its sociopolitical hegemony. This made the reach of Ife traditions and Yorùbá country extensive and complex, as Ogundiran splits into three key levels: ideas drawn from the Orisa pantheon, the ebi fraternity, and kingship.[42] However, Oyo's style of dominance and governance were substantially different from that of Ifẹ́.[43] Some of this, as related to their military reordering, has been discussed earlier. It is here important, however, to note the political frame of these changes. The military posture of Oyo's growth and frame of its contribution to the formation of Yorùbá identity is not unconnected to this political morphology. Unlike Ifẹ́, Oyo was at this time built on alliances from different forces, villages, and peoples across its northwestern side, where they saw a ready alliance with the Wasangari, Mossi, and Djerma, and toward the south and northeast with both older and new Yorùbá towns. Be that as it may, this would be the revenge expedition to Arabia encrypted in the Ifẹ́-Oyo traditions noted earlier. These forces, regardless of their peculiar individual interests, were bounded by the overarching interest of resuscitating Ife political

---

41. Ogot, *General History of Africa*.

42. Ogundiran, *Yorùbá*.

43. Law, *Oyo Empire*.

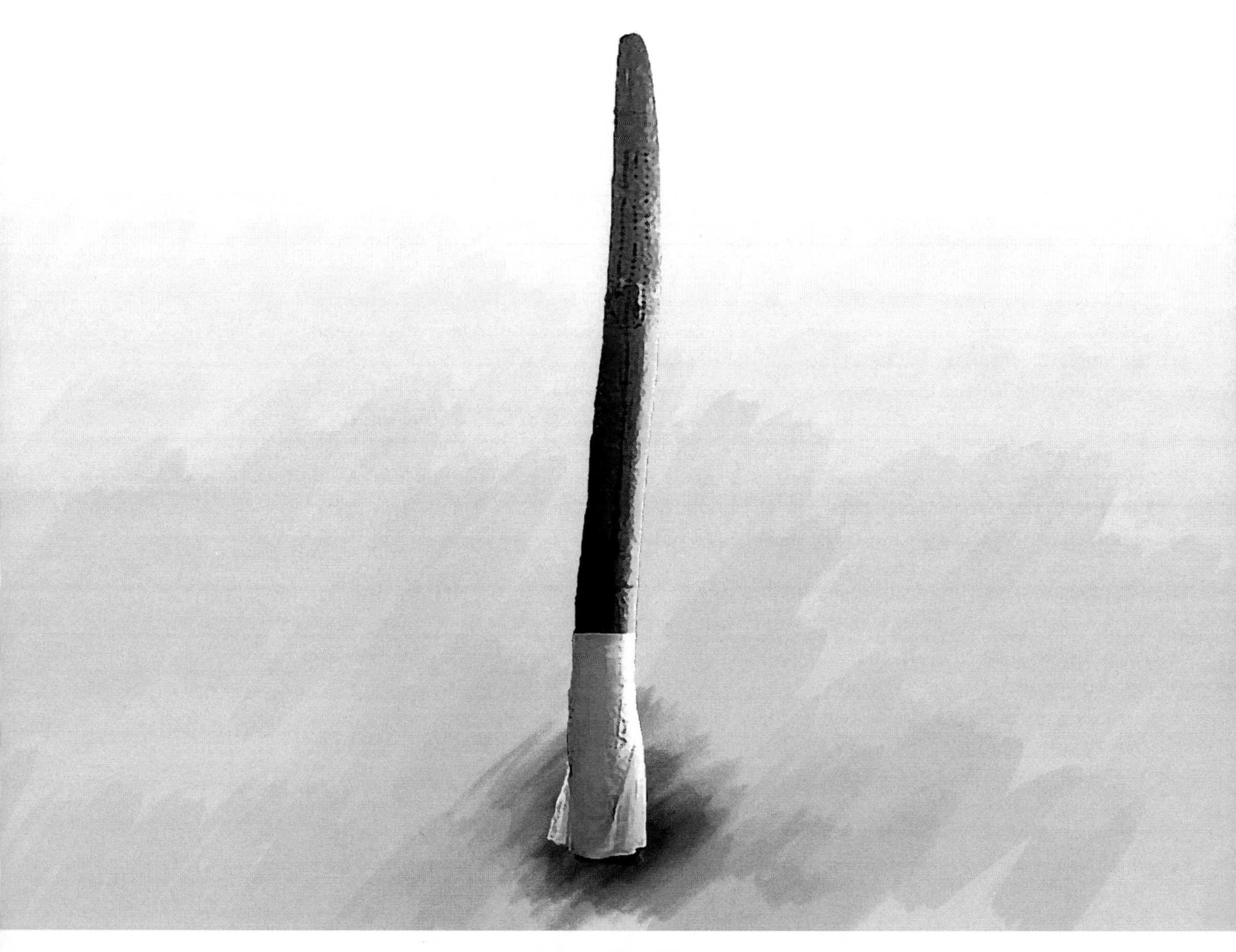

Figure 5.1. Opa Oranmiyan, eighteen feet high, located at Ile-Ife. It is described as the mythical "walking stick" or obelisk of the founder of the Oyo Empire, created many centuries ago. Ọ̀rànmíyàn's legacies can still be felt in neighboring Yorùbá communities such as Benin. From the Toyin Falola Private Collection.

hegemony to the southwest of the Niger River through Oyo due to its political trajectory and strategic geographical location to the expanding Nupe government across the river.

By the time Àjàká was attacked by Tsoede's valiant cavalry, Ife was on the decline, and many of its tributary states were ransacked and kept under the dominance of the Nupe. This would include the Yorùbá nations of Èkìtì, Ibọlọ, Ibàràpá, and Ìgbómìnà. It was the same period that

  GLOBAL YORÙBÁ

Ifẹ́/Yorùbá traditions began to decline in Benin with the usurpation of the Eweka dynasty.[44] Oyo thus rose to dominance and structured its political morphologies along these advantages as the ransacked states rallied around its growing military power. This particular period, circa 1630 to circa 1790, saw the consolidation of these gains as the capital was moved back to Oyo-Ilé, from where it continued to expand. The same period witnessed the establishment, growth, and expansion of trade in human cargo as an organized trade.[45] As the government expanded, the Aláàfin sent his representatives to monitor the activities of chiefs in their domains for the collection of all that was due to him, including the tributes and honor. Oyo also engaged in the extensive use of slaves in its administrative system, among which these representatives were chosen. This system used in ensuring the political stability of the growing empire was the same pedal upon which it secured its economic growth from the seventh to eighteenth centuries.[46]

Immediately upon the reconstitution of the old capital, the kings became despotic, feared, and resented by their subjects. Johnson noted how Ọbalokun—the Aláàfin who eventually led the people back to their ancestral homeland—sent eight hundred men to a particular port, as will be seen later, presumably Little Ardra, to show his appreciation to the European crown, which Johnson reasonably related to be Portuguese, but they never returned. As Johnson reports in his account of the event, "This king was said to be in friendly relations with the king of France (probably Portugal) with whom he had direct communication. It was said that the King sent 800 messengers with presents to that European sovereign, but that they were never heard of again. Tradition says that the sounds of bells ringing in the skies was plainly heard in the Akẹ́sán (King's) market and it was conjectured that it was the voices of the unfortunates speaking to them from the other world to their fate."[47]

It is difficult to accept this narrative as a coincidence of which Aláàfin Ọbalokun was not aware. Going by this narrative of bewilderment, Akintoye ascribed the nonuse of firearms by Oyo forces to this episode that brought about skepticism and suspicion of the white man in Oyo.[48] But going by the events of this period, part of which climaxed into the military reforms and traditions invented by the successor of Aláàfin Ọbalokun that saw to the creation of the office of Are Ona Kakanfò, the dispatch of four simultaneous expeditions under its four most powerful military chiefs, the tradition of an Aláàfin naming an enemy to be attacked in a grand ceremony that heralded the season of invasions, and the introduction of salt amusedly referred to as *dùn mọmọ* (i.e., very sweet) before being popularly known as *iyọ̀* during the time of Ọbalokun, one could deduce that those eight hundred men were part of the earliest sets of Oyo captives sold to the Europeans, certainly either the Portuguese or the Dutch. The people of Oyo, and all of Yorubaland by extension, were only getting the first taste of what was coming for them under the new political dispensation in the event Johnson described in the above excerpt.

---

44. This reached its peak late in the colonial era. See Akinola, "Origin of the Eweka Dynasty," 27.

45. Ojo, "Organization of the Atlantic Slave Trade," 77–100.

46. Biobaku, "Historical Sketch of Egba Traditional Authorities," 40–42.

47. Johnson, *History of the Yorubas*, 168.

48. Akintoye, *History of the Yoruba People*, 257.

It bears recalling that before the decision to return to the ancestral capital of the growing empire, successive Aláàfin at Igbòho had established Oyo as a formidable and dreadful power in the Niger area. Even though it was not located at the coast, this gave Oyo, among other things, access and control over the earliest trading routes to the coast of Little Ardra, Whydah, Allada, and Popo.[49] The history of slave trading shows that the dominant suppliers of captives were the powerful kingdoms of the hinterlands who annexed coastal states under their suzerainty.[50] Until this mechanism of collecting trade from the hinterlands for the coastal market was established, the trade in human cargo around the Bight of Benin was at its lowest ebb. The first European ship in this axis of coastal trade in West Africa berthed at the coast of the small communities of Itsekiri and Ijaw in the mid-fifteenth century, occupied by Portuguese merchants and merchandise. Their contact with Benin, their suzerain and largest polity in the area, was not until late in the century, around 1487.[51]

Even then, trade was low, as the Portuguese' favorite trading interest, human captives, could not be met by this power centered in the hinterlands due to its reluctance in the heinous trade. These dynamics further cast the seismic impact of the sociopolitical eruption of the sixteenth century into concrete light of subsequent events all through the centuries leading to the twentieth, not only in Yorubaland but around the world. This impact illuminates the folly of the static past comment on Africa. The main differences in the events going on across the Atlantic and below it at this time were in the magnitude, characters, and region. Like the Benin and traders at the Elmina trading port in Gold Coast, the Portuguese and other European imperial states now chased off the Mediterranean slave trade by the Ottoman conquest of Constantinople, who were now driven to sub-Saharan Africa in search of labor for their plantation fields, especially the newly "conquered" lands in the Americas.[52] The European quest for human captives could not, therefore, be met by the hinterland powers controlling the earliest coastal trade of Elmina and Urghoton, let alone their vassal states at the coast.[53] These traders, especially the ones at Elmina, prized human captives over any other commodity brought to them by the Portuguese. Hence, they exchanged gold for human captives to work in the mines and other fields of production, farmlands not occluded.

This put the Portuguese in dire straits, adding to the fact that new trade routes in Southeast Asia had already been opened for some of the goods from these ports. In the early sixteenth century, the Portuguese and the Dutch made contact with Ijebu coastal fronts. But as enterprising as the Ijebu were, they could not assuage the appetites of their Portuguese friends. Given the magnitude of their involvement in the trade in human cargo in later years after the decline of Oyo, it cannot be gainsaid that the presence of Oyo and Benin in the areas the Ijebu could have raided for slaves was instrumental to their inability to meet the demands at the time, and not because of principle or state policy, as in the case of Benin. This event could also have tilted the unraveling geopolitical dynamics of the fifteenth to sixteenth centuries in favor of the Ijé

---

49. Law, "Lagoonside Port," 32–59.
50. Saupin, "Emergence of Port Towns," 172–184.
51. Ryder, "Trans-Atlantic Slave Trade," 238.
52. Curtin, *Rise and Fall of the Plantation Complex*.
53. Feinberg, "Reviewed Work," 405–410.

bú, who had access to firearms and better military hardware. Although, as it would be seen, imported European military gear could not deter the avid Oyo archers, described in oral traditions as the best in the whole of West Africa.

As time went by, the Portuguese interest in the West African market was waning, seeing, for instance, the decision of the Portuguese crown to sell his interest in the area to private trading companies as well as the new American colonies lying wasted for want of labor. The effect of the foregoing was the tendency of the Portuguese king to make handsome proposals and extend his hands in fellowship, as he did to Ọbalokun, for trading relations with groups along the route leading to the estuaries.

The shift of the Portuguese to Little Ardra in the early sixteenth century contributed to the establishment of Lagos as a military camp by Benin, which wanted to continue control over coastal trade to the Atlantic. At Little Ardra, Oyo sold its human captives through the Yorùbá kingdom of Kétu. The road leading to this emerging port that passed through the Ẹgbádò country was now predominantly under Oyo control. In 1668, Olfert Dapper observed that from Oyo, "many slaves partly taken in the wars, and partly made such as punishment for their offenses" were sent to "Little Ardra, and were sold to the Portuguese to be transported to West Indies."[54] Trade in human captives began to grow around the Atlantic coasts around the time Oyo was returning to its ancestral capital, shifting the flow of the trade away from the trans-Saharan route to the Atlantic. Assuredly, the Atlantic was not even the only trading route where slaves were needed; instead, the fifteenth-century crises had redistributed prominent interregional markets and trading routes to favor the Atlantic route.[55] It should be recalled that Oyo's alliance with its Ibàrìbá neighbors, the Djerma of the Songhai Empire and the Mossi, was partly due to the closing of its access to the trans-Saharan trade through the Hausa states, by the Nupe. As with the Nupe, human captives were used in the purchase of horses used in prosecuting Oyo wars that subdued the Nupe and captured distant lands.[56] Accordingly, by the time the Atlantic route was opened, Oyo, reacting to the pressure of its geophysical space and adopting some of the measures of its powerful neighbors, was not new to the trade in human captives so much so that the king of Portugal or the Dutch, who, so mesmerized Aláàfiń Ọbalokun, would have lured him into forfeiting eight hundred men to him in the name of exchanging pleasantries and gifts.

That Ọbalokun was the first confirmed Aláàfiń to be mentioned with the transatlantic slave trade is further supported by Dapper's observation, which established that Oyo had been in the trade before 1668. More so, the same picture painted by Johnson could be seen in the early days of the trade in human captives in Benin. Between 1487 and 1507, when contact was built between the emerging empire and the Portuguese, trade was only carried out between the king of Benin and the king of Portugal through their agents, and slaves transported from Oyo yearly averaged merely 250. The possibility of the Ọbalokun's European imperial friend being the Dutch crown despite early Portuguese domination of the trade is that with the establishment of the Dutch West Indies Company in 1621, the Dutch had begun to make a substantial

---

54. Cited in Morton-Williams, "Oyo and the Atlantic Trade," 26.

55. Ogot, *General History of Africa*.

56. Law, *Contemporary Source Material*.

impression on the trade in human cargo in the West African ports of the Bight of Benin. Around the 1630s, large-scale shipments of human captives were transported to the plantation fields in the Americas, including Brazil.[57] Going by Oyo traditions, including its chronology of kings, the reign of Ọbalokun and the return of the people to Oyo-Ile falls within the early seventeenth century. Salt, which was introduced into Oyo during this period, was certainly an item of European trade in addition to luxuries like cloth, drinks, cowries, copper, and others.

Morton-Williams wrote that "what is certain is that before 1670 the Oyo had begun to supply a proportion of slaves exported through Little Ardra (near modern Porto Novo). What they got in return apart from salt and luxuries, is less certain."[58] The Djerma and Mossi horses were now needed for raids and conquest more than ever before to meet the growing demands for human captives in West Africa, where European merchants from Spain, Portugal, the Netherlands, and later France and Britain were jostling for trade in human cargo. It was through their horses, and later through those imported from the Hausa states after the Nupe were subjugated and made to pay tribute to Oyo, that the Aláàfiń conquered more land and took more human captives to feed the European/Atlantic market on the coast. Men from these places, especially the Hausa, became principal slaves in the service of the Oyo Empire for their special skill in maintaining the stables—the arsenal of Oyo's military and the nucleus of its hegemony that later reached parts of contemporary Ghana, Togo, present-day Benin, and the greater part of the Niger River basin in Nigeria.[59] Until the rise of Dahomey, which became an albatross of this great empire from around the first half of the eighteenth century, its dominance remained largely intact with no serious threat to its political hegemony vis-à-vis the coastal trade.

Dahomey symbolized an albatross not in the rise of Oyo per se, as its growing army could not withstand that of the latter, which was at its peak at the time. However, it did constitute an unyielding nuisance to Oyo's trading relations and economic policies.[60] To pursue this effectively to their advantage, Dahomey adopted some sort of guerrilla war strategy, as it did what it could to avoid confrontation with the Oyo forces. Evidently, from the early 1600s, Ouidah and Allada ports of Little Ardra and Jacquin served Oyo slave-trading purposes until the 1720s when Dahomey forces from the west of Oyo sacked the coastal communities and, by implication, seized control of the ports.[61] Reinforcing the nonessential external threat to the Oyo kings since their return to their ancestral home until the rise of Dahomey, as against the practice in the later years, Oyo did little or nothing to control the trade at the coast. The closest it came in this regard was the establishment of a commercial state along the trade route that led to the trading ports of Alladah and Whydah and close to Kétu in 1700. Ifonyin or Ifonyin-Anago, as the settlement was called, was headed by Elehin-Odò, appointed by the Aláàfiń; his title indicated the geophysical feature of the settlement: "the lord behind the waters." The responsibility

---

57. Slave Voyages, "Trans-Atlantic Slave Trade Database," *Slave Voyages*, accessed December 4, 2020, https://www.slavevoyages.org/.

58. Morton-Williams, "Oyo and the Atlantic Trade," 25.

59. Biobaku, "Historical Sketch of Egba," 35–49.

60. Law, "Lagoonside Port in the Eighteenth Century."

61. Falola and Heaton, *History of Nigeria*.

of this settlement and the ruler was to coordinate and protect Oyo's trading interest to the coast.

The Elehin-Odò, by the late 1700s, had grown so wealthy performing this responsibility that Baṣọrun Gáà became jealous of his ability to match the grandeur of the Aláàfìń; during a ceremony, he ordered an invasion of Ifonyin and the beheading of the Elehin-Odò. Dahomey's sacking of Whydah and Allada was a sort of "collateral damage," as its only interest in the polity of the coastal states was trade. Lending further credence to this, Oyo cavalry forces had grown powerful and famous by the later 1700s. Eye-account testimonies attest to how Oyo was feared by their neighbors and enemies, and on more than two occasions before the second half of the seventh century, it gave the Dahomey people a taste of this dreadfulness, forcing them to abandon their homes, treasures, and properties a couple of times, as many kingdoms and towns at this time would do. Oyo chose to abandon the trade along this route as it moved its operations to the newly founded towns of Whydah, Alladah, and Weme, displacing peoples in a place known as Badagry.[62] Whereas Dahomey continued to monopolize trade along these ports, as it ensured its regulation of the trade deterred others from direct transactions with European merchants plus exorbitant taxes and tariffs, Oyo's dominance was maintained not by conquest, as Dahomey did, but by the use of liberal trade regulations that favored many communities. Badagry became a major port. With the Dahomey disruption of trade in the name of regulations at Whydah and Alladah markets, and in place of beating them into submission, Oyo moved its trading activities to its eastern flank, where Porto Novo and Badagry markets were growing.

Again, before the end of the eighteenth century, the same Dahomey forces were instrumental to the movement of trade from these ports to Lagos. Lagos thus became the last bastion of slave trading in the whole of the Bight of Benin, with its growth coinciding with the sociopolitical burst in Oyo.[63] By implication, dominant characters and states in the trade in Lagos from the hinterlands were certainly less of the Oyo Empire than several independent states in Yorubaland, some of which had been Oyo subjects until this era.

Three factors could be attributed to the rise of Lagos as a major slave-trading port of the late eighteenth century until the effective termination of the trade in the following century: the first was the monopolistic trading policy of Dahomey through unfavorable regulations of the market in the old ports; the second was the focus of the prying eyes of the British-French anti-slavery naval ships in the direction of the old ports following the 1807 Abolition Act; and third, the reign of a free-for-all and massive sociopolitical implosion that erupted not only in Yorubaland but across the Central Sudan, in which the Sokoto jihad was also instrumental. In addition to the relationship between Dahomey and Oyo, it is important to note that Dahomey had been a tributary state to Oyo from around 1747, even when the grandeur of the latter was waning, persisting until 1827, a few years before its final devastation. The only reason Oyo could have yielded to Dahomey's activities, and in some cases, atrocities at the old ports, was the economic

---

62. Law, "Lagoonside Port in the Eighteenth-Century."

63. Law, "Career of Adele at Lagos and Badagry," 59.

calculation that indeed favored a shift. In this process, it is evident that until it got to Lagos, the trade was steadily shifting closer to Yorùbá country and Oyo territory in particular.

This suggests that the rise of the Lagos port was to serve a temporary clandestine purpose for the trade, which was abolished shortly after a gradual shift to the port by slavers. The temporality of this purpose is not unrelated to the simple logic that it is only a matter of time for the antislavery patrols to figure out this new diversion and direct their search lens in its direction. Toward the end of the first half of the nineteenth century, this became the dominant trend, culminating in the diversion of slave ships to Sierra Leone and Trinidad[64] and the notable bombardment of Lagos in 1851. In the meantime, however, the Lagos port served its purpose as intended by King Akinsemoyin in the 1760s when he opened the trading port of Lagos and extended his invitation to slave traders in major ports, especially at the growing Porto Novo market. Even then, that was after the antislavery squadron had focused its sights on the Lagos port. Trade records of the time showed that, in most cases, most of the embarked ships from Lagos disembarked safely and profitably in their Atlantic destinations.[65] More so, through the Lagos port, wealthy merchants were continuously expanding their wealth on both sides of the Atlantic. Philip Curtin wrote in his exploration of the topic of abolition: "By treaty with Britain, the Portuguese slave traders were safe from British cruisers south of the equator until 1839, and Brazilian slavers enjoyed the same privileged sanctuary until 1845. The end of the general legality for the trade, however, marks the end of regular and official shipping data from the slave-trading nations. If such exist, they remain buried in the archives."[66]

Despite the intermittent bickering between Oyo and Dahomey, Robin Law noted that "by the 1770s many of the slaves sold through Dahomey were supplied by the Oyo, who brought them to Abomey Calavi, on the western bank of Lake Nokoue, which served as a neutral 'free fair' for trade between Dahomey and neighboring countries."[67] The kings of Dahomey at this time were recorded in history to have pursued a trade policy that encouraged the diversion of Oyo captives for trade eastward, where they were sold at its Whydah-controlled port. This way, even its archrival in the expansionist quest and imperialistic endeavors expressly acknowledged its significance in the continued reproduction of this trade all through the century. It should be recalled that the kingdom of Dahomey was a special tributary state to Oyo at this time. In a way, ambitious Dahomey needed Oyo's services to survive as a kingdom, which had depended almost entirely on the trade in human cargo, and maintain the ports it had forcefully taken some years earlier. Adding to the dependence of Dahomey on Oyo slave imports would be the displacement of communities around it where it could seek slave captives and the relocation of these communities to areas securely protected by networks of water and the lagoon difficult to navigate by Dahomey's land army.

---

64. "Liberated Africans," accessed February 17, 2021, http://www.liberatedafricans.org/.

65. This is evident in the 5:20 ratio of intercepted ships to those that successfully disembarked in their various Atlantic locations. Implying that until the effective abolition of the trade, for every five ships seized on the waters, about twenty more made a successful voyage. See Ojo, "Slave Ship Manuelita," 360–382.

66. Curtin, *Atlantic Slave Trade*, 232–233.

67. Law, "Lagoonside Port on the Eighteenth-Century," 45.

Meanwhile, in these new locations, such as Badagry, Porto Novo, and Epe, the trade in slaves remained on the rise as the new settlements were built on this lucrative business.[68] Toward the end of the century, however, it did penetrate some of these coastal states, sacking their capitals and further displacing some of the people. But this was not until the alliance among the communities was broken, with different sides helping to plot against the other.[69] The instability of one meant the diversion of trade and relevance to the other. This was the case between Badagry and Porto Novo late into the eighteenth century.

Again, Oyo showed the typical trait of great empires and kingdoms in its rise and march toward the precipice that ended finally in its relaxed hegemony in the 1830s. The late 1700s was filled with the irreversible accumulation of the political decisions and actions of successive Aláàfin, especially those after the final relocation starting with Ọbalokun. By the time of Onisile, the last of the despotic kings, around the late eighteenth century, the Aláàfin had grown so powerful and wealthy that the vices of absolute power and wealth could not be divorced from their actions and inactions with dire consequences on their relations with their subjects. With growing despotism and greed among successive Aláàfin, up to Onisile, who, against advice, decided to experiment with a leaf that resulted in lightning that rendered him incapacitated, it became a conversation among Oyo nobles to prevent subsequent Aláàfin from passing on naturally or reigning for a long period. In a way, the increasing wealth of the empire could also be related to the excesses of the crown princes at the time, leading to the tradition that warranted their death along with their father, the Aláàfin, since they both enjoyed the privileges of the Aláàfinate.

Adding to this was that the arrangement understood the implication of the action of both men on the polity. Generally, the response of the Oyomèsì to the despotic culture and excesses of the Aláàfin from Ọbalokun to Onisile was the leeway given to the Baṣọrun, as the most senior chief in the council, to grow political wings in an unprecedented manner. Ostensibly adding to the prominence and role of Baṣọrun Gáà in Oyo polity was the choice of an unpopular prince to replace Onisile. Labisi, the prince who succeeded Onisile, could hardly be called Aláàfin, and neither can his episode in Oyo history be referred to as a "reign" since he neither completed the rituals that would have legitimized this honor nor did he wear the revered crown of the Aláàfin, which was the royal, ancestral, and untransferable symbol of the authority of the Aláàfin. Since none of these was performed on Labisi, the best he would be was an Aláàfin-elect. Thus, Labisi had his hope of reigning as the twenty-fourth Aláàfin of Oyo reversed when Soyiki, alias Esuogbo, the then-Baṣọrun, passed on, seventeen days into his installation process, and Gáà took charge. The Baṣọrun appointed another Aláàfin—this time, Awọnbíojú, who reigned for about 130 days before his demise at the instigation of the Baṣọrun. In both cases, there was no evidence that the people were displeased with Gáà, as they saw it as a payback to the Alaafinate for years of their despotic rulership, exploitation, and injustice. Gáà was the hero of the time, and he exploited the resentment of the people toward the Alaafinate to enhance his feasibility and power.

---

68. Law, *Contemporary Source Material*.

69. Law, "Career of Adele at Lagos and Badagry," 35–59.

At the risk of overemphasizing the point, Oyo had grown to its limit by the late eighteenth century, and the only remaining extension would be to the forest region of Ìjẹ̀ṣà and across the Niger River, two missions that would see it reconstitute its military structure and system. But within the current system, it was a peaceful period with no significant wars—that is, to the magnitude that could threaten its hegemony or existence as in the early years and, as would be seen in the years after this period, significant trade expansion and attendant wealth. These— that is, the peace and prosperity of the time—would either continue to be controlled by the Aláàfìn and his slaves, mostly of Nupe and Hausa origin, or shift to Baṣọ̀run Gáà. But significant power shifted to the Baṣọ̀run, and it was through him that three successive Aláàfìn, as well as Labisi, the Aláàfìn-elect, drew their breath. Hence, the latter scenario prevailed, and it was under the command of the Baṣọ̀run, "assisted" by his children, that the vast wealth of the empire was controlled, distributed, and appropriated.

In the growing resentment of the past before the rise of the Baṣọ̀run, who can rightly be described as the nemesis of the Aláàfìnate, successive Aláàfìn, especially during this period, mastered the use of servant-slaves to reconstitute their political morphology, enhance the sophistication of the administration, and ensure a stable polity with minimal suspicion of betrayal.[70] Of course, this gave the Aláàfìn a better advantage over their ambitious chiefs while limiting their opportunity to access state treasure. Aside from their traditional role, the servant-slaves, especially those skilled in writing, reading, and documentation, were placed higher than the Oyomesi. The case of the *Òsìwẹfà* title instituted by Aláàfìn Onigbogi, as noted earlier, was a case in point on how slave servants could be placed above the Oyomesi. But the influx of Hausa slaves into Oyo from northern Nigeria, since the reopening of the trading route along the Nupe country after the consolidation of Oyo's hold of the Niger basin, further complicated the matter for Oyo chiefs. The Aláàfìn, whose economic and political security was bolstered by these elements, were thus encouraged by the despotic rulership.

The initial acceptance of Baṣọ̀run Gáà thus came as a welcome development to redistribute power in Oyo politics and give more responsibilities and roles that could increase the economic fortune of the Oyomesi. Given their composition as consisting of principal lineages in Oyo and the excesses of the Aláàfìn, it was not surprising that the people of Oyo took the side of the Oyomesi through Baṣọ̀run Gáà. Having instigated the death of Agbólúajé and his brother Májẹ́ógbé on this premise, the aberration of the Baṣọ̀run was reverted by Aláàfìn Abiodun. Both men, Agbólúajé and Májẹ́ógbé, reigned for more than a decade, compared to the 130 days recorded for their predecessor, Awọ́nbíojú. The period attributed to Agbólúajé and Májẹ́ógbé was in regard to events and activities ascribed to their reigns in which a three-year Bere festival was conducted by the former whose Baṣọ̀run, Gáà, also celebrated Owara afterward, which lasted for three months, and the politicking that followed, which led to the invasion of Ifonyin and eventual his suicide.[71] This gives us approximately five years of rule. The brother of the Aláàfìn who succeeded him is said to have gone into a prolonged battle with Gáà, though how prolonged is unknown. This conflict could as well have lasted for at least five years. The longest

---

70. Law, *Oyo Empire*.
71. Johnson, *History of the Yorubas*, 180.

Figure 5.2.
"Oyo and its neighbors." At its height, Oyo's imperial expansion covered client and tributary states, gift-giving associates, areas in the heartland, and frontier zones, with an estimated 60,000 to 140,000 people resident in the capital by the turn of the eighteenth century. Dahomey in the present-day Republic of Benin was one of Oyo's subjugated territories; a large Yorùbá diasporic presence has existed there over the past century. Drawing by Dr. Kazeem Ekeolu.

serving Aláàfin of this era, Abiodun, most likely came into power around the 1770s. This is going by the reduction of Dahomey to an Oyo tributary state during the reign of Aláàfin Ojigi, an encounter historians have dated to 1747.[72]

Between this period and Abiodun's reign, about seven successive kings reigned in Oyo, two of whom lasted less than five months and others an average of about five to ten years. Together with the kings during the years of Gáà, the historical kings who supervised the final expansion and consolidation of Oyo's strides over the centuries were described to have been short-lived in their reigns. This brings us closer to circa the 1630s, attributed to the return of the people to their ancestral capital during the reign of Ọbalokun in earlier submissions. The eventual demise of Agbólúajé after the Bere festival ostensibly brought to fruition the oft-referenced *Iku* ceremony (funeral rites), marking the last years of the long reign of the Aláàfin, who often passed on shortly after. How long Agbólúajé spent on the throne is unknown, aside from speculation, which takes into consideration how long he could have stayed on the throne to think of such an event and how long it lasted.

Although the prolonged battle between the Baṣọrun and his predecessor had left the former largely incapacitated, given his charms and political networks, he was still the man to be feared. The Baṣọrun, under his de facto leadership, created the ground for Abiodun to defeat his powerful prime minister. A decade was enough time to juxtapose their condition and the political temperature of the empire under the de facto rule of the Baṣọrun and de jure rule of the Aláàfin. This position added to the chances of Abiodun to defeat the powerful Gáà, who, like the kings before him, had attracted resentment and dread among the people, a situation compounded by the penchant of his children to exploit and deride their subjects all over the empire. Another decisive factor that tilted the ensuing political maneuvering in favor of Aláàfin Abiodun was his popularity among the people, which in a way, could have been the making of the Baṣọrun through his inactions and unpopular actions, especially since the invasion of Ifonyin for the head of the Elehin-Odò after a desperate plea by the Aláàfin and others. The Baṣọrun's actions also forced Aláàfin Agbólúajé, who had just celebrated with the people and brought a comfortable ambiance of relief and leisure that came with festivity, to commit suicide.

Never in the history of Oyo or Yorubaland until this period and the ones that followed would a cabinet chief declare war on another town, let alone go to war without the permission of the king. Gáà was the first to do this, and even though he succeeded, it cost him his popularity among the people, as evident in the alliances that defeated him and the support of the people on the ground. The only popularity that remained for him by the time of Abiodun was premised not on the resentment of the Aláàfin but on the fear of the Baṣọrun's ever-dangly sword of death (not justice). This created a huge precedence for states that emerged in Yorubaland after this period. With the defeat of Baṣọrun Gáà by Aláàfin Abiodun's shrewd alliance, the political waters were settled and there was a peaceful reign, which, in any case, could not prevent the collapse of the empire in the nearest future. Abiodun could not address the various grievances and diverging interests of his chiefs both in the capital and the metropolises. The only strength left for the empire was the presence of the Aláàfin Abiodun himself, whose

---

72. Law, "Lagoonside Port in the Eighteenth-Century."

figure at this time was perhaps more respected than the Aláàfinate. As Johnson noted, Aólẹ, the Aláàfin that followed, "was unfortunately saddled with the ill fate of the nation."[73] The people decried his short stay in power as a period of disaster that impoverished them.

Fundamentally, the rise of Oyo signaled the pattern of the transatlantic slave trade, which would later become a significant factor in the making of Yorùbá identity, including its territoriality and transnationality, thanks to its geophysical advantage that gave it access to the trading ports and antecedents in this space. This became so much so that by the end of the current period, it was dangerously illuminating that regardless of the outcome of the heavy gathering cloud of political shenanigans over the great empire, the political atmosphere in the capital would continue to dictate the pattern and temperature of the trade.[74] If Oyo came out of the brewing crises stronger, it would continue to dominate the trade till its effectual abolition. On the other hand, if it came out weaker, its dependent states, and those whose stakes in the trade had been significantly limited by its participation and keen interest, would now have no imperial Oyo figure in the whole of the southwestern basin of the Niger River. Whereas the former might not have brought about a significant change in trade patterns, this cannot be said about the latter possibility, as it meant a reign of a free-for-all, a kind of liberalization of the slave trade in which more and new characters were injected onto the stage. As the following shows, the latter took charge of events in the subsequent years.

The Age of Independence and the Rise of the "Go with Him" Phenomenon in Yorubaland, c. 1790–1886

The trade along the Atlantic coast was growing at the same rate as the sociopolitical condition of the polities in the hinterlands, the largest suppliers of human items. The hotter the politics, the higher the frequency and magnitude of the trade. So until the abolition of the slave trade by the British Act of 1807,[75] the political intrigues in the hinterlands all through the eighteenth century, when the trade picked up significantly, were good for the imperial plantations in Fernando Po, Cuba, Brazil, and Haiti. Trinidad was later added to these colonies but was not active in disembarking captives from this part of the Atlantic trade until well after the abolition of the trade when it served the same purpose, but in a different structure, as Sierra Leone.

There have been speculations as to the sources of the human captives sold by Oyo forces since the reign of Aláàfin Ọbalokun, around the 1630s, when the trade began to take form with the participation of larger polities like Oyo. Such speculations, taken from the events of this period and the participation of Oyo forces therein, bring us to places like the Nupe country and people invaded and conquered by Oyo-Mossi-Ibariba-Djerma forces, and later parts of Yorubaland, particularly the eastern and southeastern communities where loyalty to the Aláàfin was either divided with another powerful state like Benin and Nupe or altogether absent. Territorial expansion was certainly a multiple win for empires, and among the low-hanging fruits were the human captives. More so but in an expectedly limited magnitude, human captives sold to

---

73. Johnson, *History of the Yorubas*, 188.
74. Ajayi and Smith, *Yorùbá Warfare*.
75. Curtin, *Atlantic Slave Trade*, 231.

European slavers were victims of various crimes and atrocities. Since the territory of the Oyo empire until around 1790 had extended its limits to the bank of the Niger River, incorporating parts of Nupe and Ibaràpá lands to its eastern and western flanks, respectively, and the various places mentioned above, one can imagine, on the one hand, the magnitude of human captives sold into the Atlantic trade through this vast empire, and on the other, how its politics in times of strength and weakness shaped the Yorùbá Atlantic community. Yet it is worth noting that the magnitude and frequency of this trade during the referred period were remarkably lower than what later became the trend, all, or at least in the main, courtesy of the political developments in the great empire.[76]

On different occasions, Aláàfin Aólẹ felt slighted by his chiefs, adding to the list of his enemies, real or imagined. Assuredly, the goodies of the transatlantic slave trade and the exigencies of their environment had made frequent raids traditional for Oyo monarchs and their chiefs. Indomitable and dreaded, they launched out every dry season to claim more lands, extend territories, and gather more captives for sale, while the rainy periods were used for planting and other activities. This tradition coincided with the emergence and growth of the transatlantic slave trade and the reign of Ọbalokun. Again, we mentioned that at the time Agbólúajé took reigns of the Aláàfinate, there were no wars to fight either for territorial gains or hegemony. This had not changed significantly by the time Aólẹ ascended the throne, even though some of his predecessors had to check Dahomey's actions intermittently. But wars must be fought, if only for raiding purposes.

Human captives not sold to the Atlantic market were useful in the local industry and domestic fronts. Since raids were conducted in the dry season, it would not be out of place to retain some slaves for the next planting season. Later, known historical figures like Ẹfúnṣetán Aníwúrà, Madam Tinúbú, Baṣọrun Olúyọlé, and others were popular for growing their wealth from this form of labor. Those from the Hausa states not sold to the Atlantic market were engaged in barbing, horse-keeping, rope making, herding, and recordkeeping for Oyo merchants, since they were knowledgeable in Arabic, medicine, farming, and in the court of the Aláàfin. Their Yorùbá counterparts were also engaged in some of these occupations. This phenomenon was in the process of changing the demography of the empire, particularly the capital city, with an impending effect on the loyalty of the people to the Alaafinate or the Yorùbá heritage.

Hence, in the usual practice, after a grand ceremony heralding the raiding season, Aláàfin Aólẹ was asked who his enemies were. Conventionally, this tradition allows the Aláàfin to revenge for any wrong anyone had done to him in the past, the implication of which affects all and sundry in the said community and in the market for the Atlantic trade. On this occasion, the Aláàfin had no one in sight aside from the Baálẹ of Apòmù, who had offended him by preventing him from selling his trusted servant and friend into slavery at Apòmù market and sending his powerful Kakaǹfò into the frontier settlement of Ilorin, Àfọnjá. Apòmù market was at this time popular for its strategic trading location, alongside others in Erúnmú and Ìwì, the latter gaining prominence with the liberalization and rise of the slave trade along the

---

76. Lovejoy, *Prieto.*

Atlantic. Consequently, like these other markets, it grew to become one of the major local markets where Yorùbá traders from all over the country traded their goods. Since the demand dictates the direction of trade, the traders in this market were adjusting to the lucrative and highly demanded human captives at the coast. Aólẹ́ was responding to this call when he sold his confidant to slavers at the market. But the timing brought about the precarious situation that led to the animosity he (Aólẹ́) nurtured against the Baálẹ̀ of Apòmù. Although Aláàfin Abiodun was able to stem the rising tide of Baṣọ̀run Gáà and bring the polity back to the full arms of the crown, he could not, perhaps, live long enough to use his political stature to unite different sections of interest in the polity. Yet the Baṣọ̀run he defeated still had some supporters within the polity, even though many had fled or were killed during the imbroglio. This development further aroused the interest of its tributary states in securing their independence.[77]

This was the state of the empire when Aláàfin Abiodun was to grapple with the development at Apòmù market. Oyo had been a principal actor in the transatlantic slave trade in the whole of West Africa and the Yorùbá country. It considered all the people as its subject to whom it could do as it pleased, including selling them into slavery for European luxuries. The trade was growing to the extent at which traditions have it that any slight offense was met with banishment, a term used for taking victims away from the public eye and selling them into the slave market. If Oyo people, especially those from the capital, had been sold into the trade in the past, they were criminals and offenders in the above category. By the late eighteenth century, trade liberalization was becoming increasingly visible because of political intrigues that threatened to consume the empire. This would see to the tradition of raiding for slaves even among traders along the route to Apòmù market, among which were the people of Oyo. The empire's ego was bruised by the development. As such, the Aláàfin rose to the occasion by instructing the Ọ̀ni of Ifẹ́ and Olówu of Òwu, as the two closest principal traditional rulers in that area, to check the activities of slave raiders at and around the market. The instruction was then passed on to the Baálẹ̀ of Apòmù, whose settlement emerged consequent to trading activities here.

This scenario is typical of the structure of government in Yorubaland.[78] These principal chiefs around Apòmù were to be the eyes of the Aláàfin in that important axis of the Yorùbá country, and through them, important instructions like this were to be executed. That this instruction took hold to have humiliated an Oyo prince mirrors the sense of influence and hegemony still enjoyed by Oyo at the time of Abiodun. The policy at Apòmù market, therefore, was never to attack or sell anyone from Oyo to the slavers when Aólẹ́ sold his companion. As he could not be given the capital punishment that such an offense attracts, he was flogged and left to find his way back to Oyo. Avenging this encounter instigated by the burgeoning slave market and the political weaknesses in Oyo, all of which stemmed from the rise of Oyo into a powerful and prosperous empire, the Baálẹ̀ of Apòmù committed suicide at the wind of the impending doom to avoid the invasion of his town by Oyo forces. A few years later, when the revolution

---

77. According to Adeyemi, whose view was expressed by Ibiloye, the people of Oyo province of Igbomina accounts that they voluntarily allied with Ilorin due to the fear of slave raiders, and the political situation in Yorùbáland epitomized in the ensuing crisis in Oyo. A competing tradition from Ilọrin claims the people were outrightly conquered and brought into the emirate during this period. Ibiloye, "Enduring Impact of the 1804 Fulani Jihad," 105–106.

78. Falola, *Collected Works of J. A. Atanda*.

gathering at this stage had been unleashed, his fear came to light as Apòmù, Ìkirè, Akínbótó, Iwàtà, Ìtaàkùn, Gbòngán, Ìséyìn Orò, and many other communities on Ifè territory were displaced by the Olówu, this time on the instruction of the Adégún, the Oníkòyí of Ìkòyí and the Tóyéjè, and the Baálè of Ògbómòsó, who also doubled as the chief of army staff (Kakanfò) to the declining empire after the Àfònjá fallout.

That the Baálè had committed suicide never suited the Oyo forces, who were accustomed to the raiding tradition in the name of revenging their monarch. Such expenditures were an easy source for human captives and looting, and they were used to feed the restless nature that the Oyo army had grown into over the years of political consolidation and hegemony. As would be seen in the later years, this same trait pervaded Ibadan politics, the close successor of the Oyo Empire.[79] Following this event, it was time for the execution of the reluctant will of the Aláàfin, to have his sword pointed in the direction of his chief of army staff, Àfònjá. However, given the circumstances at the time, two of his powerful military chiefs and others in the military rank opposed him. It was a dangerous decision to make, if not suicidal. Yet animosity was brewing in and outside the capital among some of the chiefs, between some of the chiefs and the Aláàfin, between the Aláàfin and his subjects, and between the provincial rulers/chiefs and the Aláàfin. It was a tinder box waiting for a touch to explode and expose years of acrimony.[80]

In a mission cloaked in the illusion of an attack on Gbeji, the tip of the territory in which the last expedition had stopped, Àfònjá; Owota, a powerful slave-servant (èsó) in the service of the empire; and the Basòrun—the three powerful military chiefs thought to be against the Aláàfin—were led to an impregnable town of Ìwéré, with the hope of ending their lives in the herculean task. Alliances were forming along different lines, and that of the military chiefs was among the most dreadful, as it consisted of the most powerful forces from within and without the capital. The dynamics of events during this period suggest that the choice of Gbeji, since previous invasions had ended there, was only a diversionary tactic used to lure these anti-Aláàfin allied forces into a preconceived doom. Even though the empire was living its last glory and dragging the last of its breath of affluence, it had the capacity to launch simultaneous attacks on its enemies. But it did not. To the invading army led by Àfònjá and his men, they were heading to Gbeji, but on the king's instruction, they were taken through another route thought to get them there faster and safer. The situation was clearer to this advancing team when the men sighted the impregnable walls of Ìwéré.

This is a town that had not been successfully invaded for years due to its defense networks and structures. The message was clear to these anti-Aláàfin allied forces that they were on a suicide mission, as the chief of army staff had to successfully take down a besieged territory and return to the capital within three months or perish and have his head brought to the Aláàfin. This was the immediate beginning of the end to the great days of the empire so feared by all. The king's army that took them through this route was executed, and the clandestine plan of these forces to stage an attack against the Aláàfin was hatched from this moment on. Aólé died in the process through suicide. Indeed, this was the way most Aláàfins who reigned after the

---

79. Awe, "Ajele System," 47–60; Falola, *Political Economy*.

80. Falola and Oguntomisin, *Military in Nineteenth-Century Yorùbá Politics*.

return to the reconstituted capital joined their ancestors. Abiodun was among the few who died naturally.

The nominal king appointed to fill the void of governance after Aólẹ́ spent only 130 days on the throne till he was thrown out of the palace by death. The revolution had thus begun, spreading across Yorùbá country and taking new forms that characterized the whole country vis-à-vis its identity, morphology, practices, and geophysical limitations.[81] No subsequent Aláàfìn, or any single political figure/entity, could hold the empire together. As Aláàfìn Aólẹ́ reportedly projected in his last words, the empire fell like the body of Osiris, scattered across the land, only to be fused and given form, against his wishes, by the Isis of collective symbols, practices, rituals, performances, traditions, language, and history that make and connect the Yorùbá people regardless of location. As the last bastion of the Ifẹ́/Odùduwà traditions, millions of African captives in the various Atlantic locations who identified with the Yorùbá heritage took this identity form directly or indirectly from Oyo.[82] According to Olatunji Ojo, "Slave production in the interior raised exports from Lagos tenfold, making it West Africa's leading slave port. The most accurate trade figures are found in the Trans-Atlantic slave voyage database, which put the number of slave exports between 1776 and 1850 at 308.800. Of that number only 24.000 slaves were shipped before 1801, while 114,200 and 170,600 were sold during 1801–25 and 1826–50, respectively."[83]

As Yorubaland was imploding, so were the Hausa states in the northern part of the Niger River and many of their neighbors reaching the boundary of Yorubaland in the Nupe country, with tremendous benefit for the transatlantic slave trade, slavers, and transnationalization of Yorùbá identity.[84] By virtue of the withdrawal of the British and French governments from the slave trade following the 1807 abolition act, there was a tremendous increase in the chances of the Spanish slave merchants in Cuba and the Portuguese in Brazil[85]—hence, the emergence of a significant number of Yorùbá captives in these two Atlantic locations. After 1807, Cuba became the second-largest destination for captives leaving the West African market, the bulk of which came from Oyo territories produced from the evolving crises.[86] The magnitude of captures from the Yorùbá hinterlands contributed significantly to the frequency with which slave ships embarked at the Lagos port and the difficulty of the British-French governments in enforcing the abolition of the trade.[87]

Àfọ̀njá of Ilorin and Opele of Gbogun became the first to proclaim independence after the demise of the nominal king, Prince Adebo, with others following through in subsequent months and years.[88] Knowing he had no right to the Aláàfìnate, Àfọ̀njá was determined to

---

81. Ojo, "Organization of the Atlantic Slave Trade," 35.

82. Barcia, *West African Warfare*.

83. Ojo, "Organization of the Atlantic Slave," 80.

84. Falola and Childs, *Yoruba Diaspora in the Atlantic World*.

85. Alonso, *Development of Yorùbá Candomble*.

86. Toward the tail end of the effective termination of the trade, there are indications that more than 90 percent of liberated slaves were identified as Yorùbá. See Ojo, "Slave Ship Manuelita."

87. Curtin, *Africa Remembered*.

88. According to Obayemi, by 1837, all the political structure on which the empire was built and given form had collapsed, especially in the Okun region. See Obayemi, "Sokoto Jihad," 64.

isolate the capital and replace its grandeur with Ilorin. To execute his plot, he developed a prudent strategy of statecraft that involved the invitation of a military warlord with a professional army, horses, and all that is needed to acquire more lands, as well as a wealthy merchant rich enough to finance the mission, which would require feeding a large army, maintaining equally large stables, expressing grandeur to allay the fears of those who might want to change their allegiance from the Aláàfìńate, and all.

These brought the itinerant Fulani warlord and Islamic scholar believed to own real charms that could sway the tide of war in one's favor and a large army of disciplined soldiers into the Oyo debacle.[89] Alimi, the said Fulani man, and his family moved to Ilorin on this premise. Solagberu, Àfọ̀njá's wealthy friend from Kurwo, was to join him as well. There were two fundamental conflicting cultural principles in this alliance. Soldiers, like every other human, react to primordial impulses stemming from such identities as religion, language, and culture. Àfọ̀njá would not convert to be a Muslim, probably so as not to be seen as a stooge of Alimi in the hands of the alliance he was stretching across Yorubaland, but his friend, Solagberu, was already a convert and was the first to create this divisive consciousness in geographic terms, probably in the whole of Yorubaland. His home and quarter of the town were stationed at a place known as Òkè Súnà—that is, the hill of the faithful ("faithful" implying Muslims). We mentioned earlier how Hausa captives were engaged deeply in the administration and regular daily activities in Oyo. The 1804 Uthman dan Fodio jihad that started from Gobir brought more Muslims and non-Muslim captives into Oyo. The outpour was even greater with the failure of the jihad, which saw to the sale of Muslims into the trade by their fellow faithful and continued raids for increasing political exertion and its material givings that came from the exploitation of the people within the caliphate and outside it, in the case of those sold into slavery.[90]

Meanwhile, many of these displaced Muslims had converted owing to the religion's social mobility currency. They thus resented their treatment both in their ancestral homes and Oyo. It is believed that a Muslim must not enslave a fellow faithful, just as it is an aberration for a non-Muslim to enslave a Muslim; however, a Muslim has all the rights there are to enslave a non-Muslim. Indeed, it was a good indoctrination that was meant to fill the converts with pride. And it did work. If this those in this population had lost their homes and properties, this value propelled and prepared them for the opportunity Àfọ̀njá would later offer them, albeit inadvertently. By the time Àfọ̀njá was taken out of the picture through Alimi's men, not even his friend, Solagberu, could save him, as the alliance had tilted against him.[91] Earlier, Àfọ̀njá had been saved at the point of death by the party that had disguised itself to be on the side of his enemy, only to turn against him at the decisive end. This was the time Agunbambaru, one of Baṣọ̀run Gáà's sons, returned from the Ibàrìbá country to avenge the death of his father and to take a leading role in the country after the demise of the nominal king and usurpation of government vacuum.

Agunbambaru also formed alliances with the ones he rode with from Ibàrìbá. His first call of action and the army he rode with had registered a great deal of fear in the people of Oyo;

---

89. Law, *Oyo Empire*, 245–299.

90. Falola and Heaton, *History of Nigeria*.

91. Smith, "Little New Light," 42–71.

everywhere he turned to for alliance, he got it, albeit mostly as a precautionary measure against his sword and army. Dozens of Oyo chiefs and nobles and others supposedly loyal to Àfọ̀njá or who supported the invasion of his father's compound were massacred. All the communities and people on the path of the army were displaced and ransacked. The brutality of the army vibrated across the land so much so that those who cried for the return of Aláàfiń Abiodun during the reign of Aólẹ, claiming they had packed their things to flee their homes due to the precarious atmosphere of the time, now had to finally move those properties. But this was only if they were lucky enough to have packed those properties.[92] Many were caught in the process and sold into slavery, while others were killed.

Agunbambaru and his army reached Ilorin and almost got Àfọ̀njá, but factions of the Yorùbá army with invading forces turned against them once reinforcement came from Ìkòyí, another party that entered into the phantom alliance with him. The invasion of villages and displacement of peoples along their path had little consequences for the phantom Yorùbá allies of Agunbambaru. If anything, this created an auspicious ambiance for greater participation in the transatlantic slave trade. The thick atmospheric condition in Oyo would soon meet with the jihadist expansion from the north, and all would be set for the reconstitution and reformation of the whole of Yorubaland, its identity, and future reproduction across space.[93]

What follows this period is the continued massive implosion and invasion of communities, depopulation of some Yorùbá towns and the population of others, reconstruction of some old and new polities (elsewhere), massive displacement and enslavement of peoples, incessant internecine wars, jostle for the replacement of an Oyo figure among Yorùbá warlords and surviving powers, the rise of military states, increasing presence of the Yorùbá in the Atlantic diaspora, the fall of the empire (as epitomized by the independence of its tributary states), and the eventual collapse of the Yorùbá project into the colonial structure.[94] By the time the empire began to implode, those who would identify themselves as Oyo—people, villages, and towns—were in the thousands and millions. According to the testimony of Ali Eisami, a native of Bornu, who was a slave at Oyo during the time of the Hausa-led Muslim revolt in Oyo and whose evidence was recorded by S. W. Koelle in Sierra Leone around 1850, portrays the event to have commenced in 1817.[95] This was another remarkable moment in the myriads of different but interlocking dramatic events leading to the 1886 treaty mediated by the Lagos consulate among Yorùbá rulers, warlords, and communities that guided the peace efforts of the time.[96] By now, it was clear to the Aláàfiń that his old power could hardly be restored without such an alliance with the British government in Lagos, just as it was becoming clear to observers of the time that a search for another power to replace Oyo might altogether consume the tradition

---

92. *Laiye Abiodun l'afi Igba won 'wo, Laiye Aole l'afi adikale* (During the time of Abiọdun money we weighed by Calabash in the time of Aólẹ we packed to flee).

93. Ajayi and Akintoye, "Yorùbáland in the Nineteenth Century."

94. Akinjogbin, Abiodun, and Adebayo, *War and Peace in Yorubaland.*

95. Curtin, *Africa Remembered,* 212.

96. Smith, "Little New Light."

that Oyo had inherited and saddled with the responsibility of preserving, transforming, and reproducing across lands.[97]

Conclusion

The making and transition of Yorùbá identity in modern times can be divided into two long epochal periods and events characterized by the arrival and departure of the Odùduwà/Ifẹ́ traditions, as well as that of Oyo/Òrànmíyàn. These periods spanned about seven centuries, from the Classical Age to the Age of the Atlantic. The search for and the reproduction of the Oyo figure did not end with the 1886 peace treaty. Since the idea of Yorùbá had endured so much under the tutelage and legacy of Oyo, its reproduction became a seed to be planted in any environment—hence, the revival of the quest to resuscitate this tradition alongside its political symbols in the North Carolina village of Oyotunji in the United States by a man known as Walter King, who later became Adefunmi Osejiman.[98]

The discussion on the role of the Oyo Empire and its traditions in the making of Yorùbá identity and form becomes clearer when we consider that the "link between an orìṣà, a lineage and a place," which constitute the cardinals of the reproduction of Yorùbá identity in the diaspora, "had . . . already been partially weakened by the wars of conquest and the institution of an imperial political entity in Yoruba territories."[99] This imperial political entity was none other than the Old Oyo Empire, which choreographed the deterritorialization process of the Yorùbá community of people and ideas. The foregoing thus illuminates how the empire had played this role through the years that spanned the early period of its formation to the latter years when its decline scattered Yorùbá people across the world, ultimately consolidating this process. In chapter 6, we will see how this also affected the West African migration of the people. Next, we will examine contact, relations, and exchanges between the Yorùbá country and their neighbors.

97. Atanda, *New Oyo Empire*.
98. Clarke, *Mapping Yorùbá Networks*.
99. Dianteill, "Deterritorialization and Reterritorialization," 135.

The Yorùbá and Their Neighbors 6

Introduction

On my first field trip I discovered that change is acceptable and constant to the Yoruba. Their ready acceptance of the new is manifested everywhere: in changing fashions of dress and in the contemporary design of buildings. . . . Nothing was adapted that could not be used in an old pattern, but with greater efficiency or meaning . . . form can change constantly, but the Yorùbá patterns remained constant.[1]

Relations between neighboring civilizations have been an important aspect of state formation and the evolution of human civilizations. These relations, which range from trade, politics, diplomacy, conflict, and wars, have been instrumental to the continuity of these civilizations. Often, the collapse of a civilization does not mark the end of its traditions and heritage. Hence, when the physical structures are devastated and in ruins, the ideas and motifs live on as they are reproduced in various forms in other places, especially among their neighbors. The expositions in the preceding chapters have shown how this cycle has been affected at various times in history, from the ancient civilizations, most notably Egypt, to contemporary West African civilizations, such as Ife. Following this trajectory, which saw to it that these cultures survived their collapse, the previous chapter adumbrates how the collapse of the Old Oyo consolidated the heterogeneity and deterritorialization of Yorùbá in all its forms and connotations. This chapter explores how the interaction between Yorùbá people and their neighbors shaped their cultural practices over time.

The relationship between Yorùbá and their neighbors is as complex and intricate as it is daunting to give a defined and absolute geographical shape in all sense of history and traditions. Among the many instances of controversies and debatable areas in the history of the Yorùbá people that cut across discussions in the preceding chapters, ones surrounding the status of the great Benin Empire emerge as other key points in this history. Several symbols, practices, and traditions connect what could ordinarily be called Benin and Yorùbá civilizations,

---

1. Cordwell, "Art and Aesthetics," 56.

almost to the point of inseparability.[2] Generically, geography and politics played a decisive role in the long history of Yorùbá and their neighbors. As shown in studies like this, and as part of the nitty-gritty of the discussion of this chapter depicts, eastern and southern Yorùbá communities and peoples, among which are pockets of coastal communities, share more with the Benin Empire than their kinsmen in other parts of the Yorùbá country, particularly to the north. Meanwhile, the Benin tradition itself is built on Odùduwà/Òrànmíyàn traditions. In describing what constitutes Yorubaland, a few scholars have included Benin and the Aja, Sabe, Fon, Popo, Ketu, and other kingdoms that stretch far and wide into parts of present-day Ghana, Benin Republic, and Togo in West Africa.[3] In this history lies extensive regional connections within West Africa and a much broader one to the Atlantic economy.

As the discussions in the previous chapter have shown, many of these polities share traditions with the Old Oyo Empire. However, some cultural practices and traditions came into Yorubaland through the relations of these kingdoms with their non-Yorùbá neighbors. From here, we can begin to cast a wider reach to examine the entire region. Then we have the Itsekiri, Urhobo, Ijo, towns like Onitsha, and other cultures mainly around the creeks of southern Nigeria, heavily influenced by Benin traditions; these polities, together with Benin, share the same ancestral link to Yorubaland, making them traditionally part of Yorubaland but for the absence of the influence of the Old Oyo Empire which came to encapsulate the Yorùbá ideology and polity in these areas. In contrast to this bearing, Yorùbá communities around the Niger–Benue confluence, known as the Okun, are included in Yorùbá despite their closer ties and cultural similarities with the Nupe, Ebira, Idoma, and Igala and less cultural affinity with Yorubaland.[4]

The contemporary approach to the study of Yorùbá is oriented around three decisive events in the making of the Yorùbá nation and identity: the decline of Ife political hegemony from around the fifteenth century, the rise of new dominant polities—the Old Oyo Empire, Benin, and Iléṣà—and the colonial incursion. As the might of the Old Oyo Empire could not (deeply) penetrate the southern and southeastern spheres of the country, primarily for geographical reasons, as it did in the savanna region of the northern, northwestern, and northeastern spheres, the presence of a strong Ife kingdom in this seemingly impregnable region would have been a place of convergence of the Yorùbá civilization. This way, while the tide of Oyo political might have stopped at the garrison town of Ede, Ife maintained its influence all through the forest region of the country down to Benin, reaching the creek states of the Niger Delta region and beyond. In the absence of such an arrangement, which led to the rise of Benin, Oyo, and Iléṣà jostling for political power and hegemony, the colonial government adapted the evolving structure it met on the ground, welding and breaking cracks where necessary. The emerging educated class played no small role in what became the seemingly latent picture of these precolonial cultures as we know them.[5]

The structure of the colonial polity gave rise to ethnic politics by introducing vague ethnic consciousness in the political culture of these societies—this was, in many ways, the proverbial

---

2. Egharevba, *Short History of Benin*.

3. Biobaku, *Egba and Their Neighbors*.

4. O'Hear, "History of the Okun Yorùbá," 111–126.

5. Nolte, *Obafemi Awolowo and the Making of Remo*.

   GLOBAL YORÙBÁ

straw that broke the camel's back. The political expediency of traditions and easy administrative advantage now supplied the ideas to construct cultural boundaries and ethnic structures.[6] This history has defined the rapport between core Yorùbá towns in the present southwestern part of Nigeria and their kinsmen in the western flank of the Yorùbá country, now in Togo and Benin Republic. Scholars like Geoffrey Parrinder have noted that the obstruction caused by proximity and language have been major barriers in maintaining such communication with communities in former French colonies.[7]

Due to this history of colonial interference, Yorùbá and Benin are treated in this chapter as separate nations that maintained close cultural relations during the precolonial epoch. Besides its popular usage in contemporary times, due largely to the influence of the Old Oyo Empire after the implantation of the Eweka dynasty, this approach is adopted in this study of the transnational history of Yorùbá peoples and their culture. Indeed, in all the forms these have taken in the diaspora, particularly in the Atlantic, they have been characterized by Oyo cultural signature.[8] This will follow Fredrik Barth's notion of cultural identities and the social theory of identity.[9] It is in this view that we can begin to understand the preponderance of the Old Oyo Empire and its traditions in mapping what constitutes Yorùbá as a people and an ideology, particularly in the precolonial times and in their relations with other cultures. Ideas, symbols, practices, and all that came to be part of the Yorùbá culture were diffused through the instrumentality of the relations between the Old Oyo Empire and its neighbors, which, before the emergence of Alladah, Porto Novo, Dahomey, and Badagry in the early seventeenth century, were limited, principally, to the Nupe, Borgu, and the Hausa states.

Through these neighboring polities, distant cultural practices from North Africa were incorporated into what became known as the Yorùbá civilization. The great Oyo Empire could not afford to have many powerful neighbors because of its ambition that saw to the incorporation of old and new settlements around the Niger basin under its political hegemony, leaving it in intermittent contention with the powerful Nupe and Borgu. These long-existing polities date as far back as ca. 100 and AD 700, in the case of the latter. This falls within the pre-Odùduwà epoch in Ife/Yorùbá tradition. Leaving out the period in which the Wasangari dynasty was initiated by the flight of Kisra-led migrants from the traditions called Persia, the traditions of the Bàrìbá mirrored those of the Yorùbá. More of this, and the implications of the close location of Oyo to this country on the Yorùbá culture and civilization, shall be discussed soon. The influence of the relations between the two would reach distant Yorùbá cultures in Ketu, Sabe, and Aja and many more across the Yorùbá country like the Egbado, Igbomina, Ibolo, Okun, and Egba, all at varying levels.[10]

The erudite scholar of these boundaries, I. A. Asiwaju, provides a brilliant taxonomy of Yorùbá identity that could help reach a broader view of the country and the task at hand. Navigating the study of western Yorùbá cultures through this illumination, R. T. Akinyele writes,

<hr>

6. Ogundiran, "Filling a Gap in the Ifẹ-Benin Interaction Field," 27–60.

7. Akinyele, "Historiography of Western Yorùbá Borderlands," 98.

8. Dianteill, "Deterritorialization and Reterritorialization," 121–137.

9. Barth, *Ethnic Groups and Boundaries.*

10. Usman, "Ceramic Seriation," 149–169.

A. I. Asiwaju illustrates this point by using three concentric rings to describe the Yoruba culture area. The innermost ring depicts the core area, beginning from southwestern Nigeria stretching through the southern and central parts of the Republic of Benin and terminating at the Ufe and Atakpame areas of central Togo. The middle ring embraces groups that are related to the Yoruba by language, culture, and traditions of origin such as the Edo, Itsekiri, Borgu, Igala, and the Aja. I. A. Akinjogbin has widened this middle ring to include the Nupe, the Fon of the Republic of Benin, and the Gaa, Krobo, and Adangbe of modern Ghana. The outer ring, as identified by Asiwaju, is formed by the Yoruba diaspora communities in Sierra Leone, Cuba, Brazil, Haiti, Jamaica, and other places.[11]

Even though what constitutes the difference between the criteria for the core and the middle rings remains very thin, considering that the same factors that characterize the latter also framed the former, this classification is quite useful. Perhaps, after the publication of this text, the renowned scholar must have added to some of these communities and cultures, especially those in the middle ring, which omits the likes of Onitsha and Urhobo. And yet, the list is sure to elicit concern among some of the listed middle ring cultures and communities, particularly the Nupe and the Borgu. The inclusion of the Aja people in the middle ring also raises the question of the designation of Dahomey, being a polity that sprang up from a faction of the Aja communities.[12] Such is the complexity of the full contours of Yorùbá boundaries. It cannot be overemphasized that Oyo not only dominated the core ring; the extensions to the middle and the outer rings have been made possible through Oyo imperialism in West Africa for about two centuries—circa 1630 to circa 1830.

Although other Yorùbá subcultural groups like the Egba had their separate encounters with Dahomey, these encounters amounted to two things: territorial expansion and security.[13] The Egba took neither the warring tradition of the Dahomey, which involved the use of Amazons, women fighters, nor part of their sociopolitical bearings. In subduing the Dahomey menace, the Egba chiefs had to engage with the lessons of war they cultivated from the Oyo, such as the use of calvary, which was earlier introduced into Oyo traditions from both Borgu and Nupe. This form of encounter grants some nuances to the general relations of the Yorùbá country with its neighbors. This leads us into a discussion in this chapter that examines close and far neighboring polities such as Benin, Dahomey, Nupe, Borgu, Hausa, the Songhai Empire, and the Mossi, as well as port cities like Little Ardra, Badagry, Epe, and Lagos.

The Sociopolitical Aspect of Relations and Exchanges

Through centuries of long encounters, both cooperative and competitive, Yorùbá communities formed several levels of relations with their neighbors. Not only were these relations formed in different stages and times, but the intensity of their marks on the growth of the Yorùbá nation

---

11. Akinyele, "Historiography of Western Yorùbá Borderlands," 96.

12. Akinjogbin, *Dahomey and Its Neighbours.*

13. Biobaku, *Egba and Their Neighbors.*

and identity varied significantly. Whereas what could be regarded as the relations between Yorubaland and Benin emerged with the Ọ̀rànmíyàn-engineered Eweka dynasty around the late twelfth century, the very beginning of the Old Oyo Empire was christened by both Nupe and Borgu traditions so much so that some traditions would regard Oyo as a hybrid of Yorùbá, Nupe, and Borgu.[14] With the level of the relations that existed between the Old Oyo and Nupe, on the one hand, and the Borgu, on the other, this tradition has come to question the authenticity of Ọ̀rànmíyàn traditions beyond the mythical narrative intended to extend Yorùbá traditions, stemming from Odùduwà heritage, to the massive empire.[15] In place of a historical function, Ọ̀rànmíyàn constituted a political expediency. Whatever the biological makeup of Ọ̀rànmíyàn was, wherever his ancestral home led, and in whichever form this historic figure existed, he played a pivotal role in defining Yorùbá as a geographic space and idea. As the previous chapter has shown, the relationship between Oyo and Nupe, as well as Oyo and Borgu, started when the former was established as a sovereign political entity, with Nupe rebuffing this attempt, which was aided by Borgu.

According to Oyo traditions, Ọ̀rànmíyàn was given a magical reptile, a boa, to accompany him on his quest for sovereign settlement. In the tradition Robin Law and others have questioned, this was after he both migrated from Ile-Ife and met antagonism at Nupe, a country where he was said to have taken a wife. From this time on, the relationship between Yorubaland, through the Old Oyo Empire, and these polities had seen intermarriages, cultural exchanges, wars, economic cooperation, military aliments, and all sorts of conceivable manner of relations. Oyo kings and nobles married from Nupe and Borgu, integrating these cultures into the core of Yorùbá civilization. It is quite ironic and yet a testament to the complexity of human nature that as this cooperation began, these marriages did not guarantee the absence of war among these parties. It did, however, give refuge to the people of Oyo during the days they became overwhelmed by Nupe attacks. On different occasions since its inception, the Old Oyo had to ward off the threats of domination, at best, and extermination, at worse, by Nupe and Borgu forces before it grew into a formidable empire. In one of these instances, the people of Oyo were pursued from their homes to take refuge in Borgu, and a couple of others evacuated their capital to other locations. As the youngest of the polities around this Niger River basin at the time, Oyo territories were raided for slaves to feed the trans-Saharan trade market and political exaction by their powerful neighbors. Even when the polity grew into an empire and could no longer be dabbled around, these two remained the neighbors to watch out for.

Prominent among Oyo figures that married from Nupe, according to Oyo traditions, was Ọ̀rànmíyàn, whose Nupe wife gave birth to Olufinran, Aláàfin Ṣàngó. The skepticism that has pervaded the identity of Ọ̀rànmíyàn in some intellectual circles becomes clear: Ọ̀rànmíyàn migrated from Ife and married a Nupe woman, whose son would come to stabilize and rejuvenate the polity that was helped put in place by a Bàrìbá king. Among many things, the practice of facial marks inscription among the Yorùbá was attributed to this tradition—that is, the marriage between Ọ̀rànmíyàn and the daughter of Eléǹpe of Nupe. Following the return of

---

14. Johnson, *History of the Yorubas.*

15. Law, *Ọyọ Empire.*

Ọ̀rànmíyàn to Ile-Ifẹ, where he took another mission to Benin, Ṣàngó was put in place of his brother, Àjàká, who proved to be a weak Aláàfin. In this tradition, which comes rather as a myth than a fact, Àjàká, ostensibly opted for basic rites and rituals, choosing less confrontation, in a bid to settle his problems and consolidate his rule. It was claimed in the traditions that the Aláàfin sent two messengers, one Tetu and a Hausa slave, to Nupe to fetch him the name of his mother. Intoxicated and confused by the reception accorded them by their Nupe contacts, one of the messengers, the Hausa slave, got the name wrong, while the Tetu provided the name Torosi, Iya Gbado. In anger, the Aláàfin instructed that the former be punished in a way he thought would make him deformed, while the latter was awarded bountifully. This led to the marking of the body of the Hausa slave with 122 razor cuts by Babajegbe Ọ̀sán and Babajegbe Òru, the traditional Olowola (markers) of Oyo.[16]

By the time the wounds healed up, however, they were seen as attributes of beauty and elegance, as they added radiance to the man's looks. Fascinated by this, the wives of the Aláàfin requested the same; jealous, the Aláàfin asked to go first in the markings. Lacking the strength to withstand multiple cuts, the Aláàfin stopped the *Olowola* at the stroke of two cuts, which have remained the distinctive badge of royalty in Oyo. According to the tradition, this resulted in the appellation of the royal family as Akẹyọ; the mark known as ẹyọ is drawn from the shoulder to the wrist. This led to the practice of facial marks in Yorubaland, as other communities began to adopt the practice not only for beautification but also for identification and rituals. But then, evidence suggests that the practice of facial marks predated Oyo or Ṣàngó, as similar marks could be found among the Borgu, Aswan of Egypt, Kanuri of Borno, South Sudan, Ethiopia, and others, some of whom were at this time not alien to the Yorùbá people. This remains an extant practice among the Aswan, who still etch their children's faces with the same marks found among the Yorùbá people.[17]

Considering the history of the Yorùbá, which has been traced to the Mediterranean cultures around Egypt, it is not unreasonable to suggest that the Yorùbá, like other protocultural groups around the Niger and other places in modern Nigeria who traced their ancestry to this region, had been acquainted with the practice of body adornment. Lending further credence to this is evidence from the attributes of their artworks, their sculptures in particular. Archaeologists and art historians believe that both Nok and Ife artwork share many stark similarities, with the former having a great influence on the latter as an older civilization. These Nok artifacts wear facial marks similar to those found at Ife.[18] Meanwhile, the Nok civilization had maintained measures of relations with Bàrìbá communities centuries before the advent of the Oyo polity.

Given this, cultural spread from the Nok culture, which embodied the most advanced civilization in the region at the time, to Yorubaland must have taken this route, making the implantation of a Yorùbá polity in this axis even more imperative. Oyo thus became a repository of this cultural spread across Yorubaland. This became evident in its advancement in art and sculptors alongside Ife. Yorùbá art forms were characterized and became diffused through the instrumentality of these states and their relations with other advanced cultures like the NOK

---

16. Johnson, *History of the Yorubas*, 150.

17. Edward and Abayomi, "Understanding the Socio-Cultural Identity," 8.

18. Edward and Abayomi, "Understanding the Socio-Cultural Identity."

of central Nigeria. As such, the admired marks on the faces of these artworks that predated the emergence of Ife as a political model could not have been inspired by the irresponsibility of a so-called Hausa slave. If anything, it was a familiar tradition that the said incident could only have revived, at best, or meant for another unknown purpose, at worse. Either way, this tradition affirms the role of intergroup relations between Oyo and its neighbor in the making of one of its essential traditions. More so, the traditions surrounding this practice have never been homogenized but speak to different events. This notwithstanding, it is discernible from the practice of the preponderance of Oyo in the spread and form of the culture in Yorubaland.

Marriage also forged an alliance between the Oyo and the Borgu to counter the rising tide of Nupe. The military reorganization of Oyo, which took practices from both Borgu and Nupe, was only made possible through the alliance between Oyo, Borgu, the Djermas of Songhai, and the Mossi, which brought the polity back to its feet for subsequent military reforms. This alliance saw the safe return of Oyo from Gbere in Bàrìbá country to Igboho, after which Oyo forces began to invade Nupe instead of the previous practice where invasions were usually conducted by the latter. Oyo forces were at this time trained by Borgu calvary soldiers, who were supplied horses by the Mossi and Djermas, with their stablemen drawn from these cultures. The success of this alliance and the return of Oyo from Bàrìbá country to Kusu and Igboho ensured that the use of calvary soldiers became an integral part of Oyo war traditions. However, this did not indicate the introduction of horses into Yorubaland, as the animal had been a rare and luxurious means of transportation by nobles in the country. It became largely synonymous with war and militarism, so much so that from the information available to Snelgrave, an English slave merchant who visited Whydah and Alladah in 1734—after Oyo had launched a calvary attack that demystified the Dahomian king around 1727—Oyo military consisted only of calvary soldiers, "for they never use infantry."[19]

In an attempt by a mulatto Portuguese in the Dahomian court at Allada to describe the powerful polity around the Niger River, he referred to as J-oe (Oyo) where he had gotten the "two pretty horses, each about thirteen hands (52 inches) high, which is very much better than those we had seen at Jaqueen (Jakin)."[20] By this period, characterized by the rise of the Oyo Empire and its hegemony around the Niger River reaching parts of Ghana, Nupe, Togo, Bàrìbá and the Republic of Benin, Oyo had dominated major markets coming from the Maghreb through the Hausa states and Nupe kingdom at the lower end of the Niger River. Access to the best horses and other products from these areas can only be expected. It was among these that the mulatto Portuguese and Dahomey forces stole their "pretty horses" as part of the spoils of war between Oyo and Dahomian forces, where some among the former were killed or left their horses to flee after a surprise attack by the latter after a four-day siege of the Dahomey country by Oyo.

The alliance between Oyo and the Bàrìbá, which brought about the fundamental changes in the Oyo military composition, was formed before the consolidation of the Borgu polity under the Wasangari in the seventeenth century. The politics of the Wasangari aggravated the political tension between Oyo and the Ìbàrìbá, culminating in the intermittent wars between the

---

19. Law, *Contemporary Source Material*, 14.

20. Law, *Contemporary Source Material*.

two. With the rise of the Wasangari, as in the case of Tsoede in Nupe earlier in the fifteenth century, the decentralized states of the Bàrìbá country were consolidated into larger and more centralized kingdoms. Together with the events in Nupe, including the coming of Tsoede, and Borgu and the arrival of Kisra, meant that Oyo was faced with a far greater threat from its neighbors. In this sense, the privilege enjoyed by Oyo during the time of evacuation to Ìbàrìbá would be difficult because of the disharmony of the polity, which has Ife with all forms of divisions that could be exploited. As in the case of the Yorùbá people, rulers of Borgu traced their ancestry to a common progenitor, Kisra, through whom they enjoyed legitimacy. A similar case of political consolidation in Nupe had influenced the outcome of the military restructuring in Oyo, signifying how political developments in one state affected the other.

Because of its proximity to Borgu, Oyo quickly developed the art of blacksmithing, providing it with the needed instruments of war like swords and javelins. But as Oyo was responding to these external stimuli, so were the Wasangari during the time of their political usurpation. The Wasangari were known for their use of magic and witchcraft, and armed with the art of guerrilla warfare, they continued with the use of poisonous arrows of the indigenous Bàrìbá people. By the time the administration of Oyo was moved to Ìbàrìbá country, the relationship that existed between the two involved marriage connections, and the two could be regarded as relatives. This is evident in the case of Òfinràn, the Alaafin who finally removed the administration of the empire from Ìbàrìbá to Kusu, where it was eventually taken to Igboho. Moreover, it would have been unthinkable for Òrànmíyàn to be accorded such support by the king of Borgu during the early days of the Oyo polity without the latter not securing his support by giving one of his daughters in marriage to Òrànmíyàn or his children. The mother of Òfinràn is said to be a Borgu woman, which contributed to the decision he took to relocate the capital of the empire (then barely a kingdom), as he could not endure the treatment by his kinsmen. In a way, this close relation guaranteed the option of residing in Ìbàrìbá country and exiting at will.

As Oyo was incorporating calvary into its army, it also adopted the masquerade tradition of the Nupe and the poisonous arrows of the Bàrìbá in battles. These would prove to be the most significant sets of reforms in the Oyo military structure and war strategy, influencing its traditions and altering the sociopolitical morphology of the Yorùbá polity. The Nupe masquerade tradition was used both in times of war and in the absence of it; it was believed that the powers and support of the ancestors could be annexed through them in pursuit of peace and prosperity as well as in prosecuting wars and defending their sovereignty. Whereas the former was performed during one of the most important festivals of the people, the latter was conducted during military expenditures as Nupe forces were accompanied to battlefronts by these masquerades. In addition to the spiritual support they imparted, these rituals also served as a distraction and instrument of fear to their enemies at war. Like every other cult, it had its priest and followers dedicated to the veneration of the ancestral spirits.[21] It was this tradition that Oyo adopted as it was reconstituting its polity and society at Igboho.

Masquerades, which became known as *Egúngún* (that is, skeletal piece of a departed ancestor or ancestral spirit) in Yorùbáland, followed Oyo armies to wars and were incorporated into

---

21. Willis, *Masquerading Politics.*

     GLOBAL YORÙBÁ

the royal cult. This tradition, particularly as related to the latter purpose, soon spread across the polities and communities in Yorubaland through centuries of Oyo imperialism and the crises that ravaged Yorùbáland in the nineteenth century, leading to the displacement and migration of Oyo populations across different parts of Yorubaland with their cultures, traditions, and practices. Two rites are considered a sine qua non and integral to the production and reproduction of the traditions, practices, and culture of Yorùbá communities in splendor. One of these is the *Egúngún* rite, followed by that of *Orò* (bullroarer). Although both serve the same purpose, their practices and rites are different, and this cannot be divorced from how the former was incorporated and the peculiar tradition it represents.

Both are considered ancestral spirits meant to cleanse society from anomalies and avert impending disaster. This could include natural occurrences like floods, droughts, and discouraging harvests or man-made crises like wars and raids. But since masquerades were used in wars—and it was in fact because of this, at least the prime factor in its adoption—which was witnessed by all, regardless of age, status, or gender, its civil performance could not have been restricted, as in the case of the bullroarer. So while the bullroarer rite takes place in the dead of night, with strict instructions for the absence of female characters, the masquerade rite is conducted in the glaring eyes of all during the day. In many Yorùbá communities, it is the most celebrated festival, lasting for months in some communities.[22] The head of the cult in Oyo, the Alapini, is usually drawn from a family originating from Nupe, thereby sustaining the tradition of its emergence. Samuel Johnson explains the situation as follows:

> The Egúngún mysteries also were hitherto unknown to the Yorubas, by this means the Tapas have long imposed upon them, they believing in the reality of the so-called apparitions. On the hill Sanda at Kusu the secret was made known to Saha the King's head slave. The first Alapini with the other Egungun priests the Elefi, Olohan, Oloba, Aladafa, and the Oloje, emigrated from the Tapa country to Yoruba, joining the remnants returning from the Bariba country. These became the first priests, and instructed the Yorubas further in the Egungun worship; therefore, the honours and emoluments to be enjoyed in this worship by right belong to them and their successors unto this day.[23]

Since the fall of the Old Oyo Empire, this tradition has lost its military purpose. Aside Oyo in Yorubaland, another tradition that came close to using masquerade-like characters in wars is found in the Igbòmòkun communities of Old Ife, long before the establishment of Oyo polity. Outside of Yorubaland, aside from the Nupe, the Dahomey Amazons were also reported to have taken to this tradition in the later years, which came around the nineteenth century when this tradition had already evaporated from Oyo with its colossal collapse. Even then, how these masquerade-like characters were used in rebellious Igbòmòkun tradition and the Dahomey army was different from that of Oyo and the Nupe. In the former two, soldiers were cloaked in masquerade gear to make their enemies think they were fighting with spirit beings while they were the actual fighters. However, in the latter two, these "spirit beings" only escorted the army

---

22. Drewal, "Arts of Egungun," 18–19, 97–98.
23. Johnson, *History of the Yorubas*, 160.

to war and performed the same rites they perform in civil matters—that is, cleansing and clearing the path from all evils that could impede the success of the people—while the soldiers are left to do the fighting.

One common element to these two rituals is that they function more as a form of fear-mongering during wars, leaving the timid soldier demoralized and confused. Even though there is no specific account of how this strategy worked in Oyo war expenditures, the advantage it accorded the Dahomey army and the rebellious Igbòmòkun people is on record. In the case of the latter, it took a suicidal reconnaissance mission on the part of Moremi for the people of Ile-Ife under the leadership of Odùduwà to decipher how to respond to the Igbòmòkun attacks. Likewise, it took a desperate effort on the part of Egba military chiefs to overcome the Dahomey menace in their new settlement of Abeokuta. Consequently, the military strategy of masquerade helped tremendously in winning wars in the precolonial days, and its role in strengthening the Oyo army could not have been different. Left to its civil role after the decline and fall of the Old Oyo, the tradition became ubiquitous across Yorubaland and more popular with those areas where the great empire had immense influence—that is, the northwestern and northeastern states from whence others incorporated the practice.

While traditions mentioned the incorporation of this practice into Yorubaland to lead the Oyo army into war, it is not certain that they were used for a long period. If this were to be the case, several eyewitness accounts describing the various wars fought by the Oyo army would have found this fascinating to add to their reports, but none exist. Also, the tradition had been relegated in the war strategy of the Nupe by the time war traditions around this area became the subject of record by European merchants and explorers from the eighteenth century. Since the details of the Egúngún practice at war is not known, two things could account for the absence of the practice in European reports replete with accounts of the use of horse, bows and arrows, and other weapons and tactics of war: either the practice had been abolished by this time for reasons unknown, or the masquerades were only used in the opening of a war with the rest of the army fighting on, while they returned home without catching the attention of European observers. Whatever the case, their role at war had so much diminished that they had no place in the European diaries as an instrument of awe when describing the war and tactics of war prosecution. Given this, the fall of the Old Oyo would then only mean the final blow to the hope of resuscitating the tradition.

However, it remains highly significant in the civil administration of towns and kingdoms in Yorubaland. Throughout the Egúngún festival, the masquerades are usually divided into hierarchies and paraded to the public through every nook and cranny of the community, with followers playing the drums and plenty of pomp and pageantry that often feature poetic performances in praise of the ancestral soul by poets as well as glamorous dancing by those in masquerade.[24] The tradition has expanded so well in Yorubaland that in the same way in which there are families devoted to the worship of Ògún and other pantheons of Yorùbá gods, specific families are also in devotion to this spirit. Now, while the festival is celebrated by the whole

---

24. Okediji, "Art of Yorùbá," 175.

community, these families are responsible for maintaining the social code, traditions, and practices of the cult under the headship of a chief priest, given different names in different Yorùbá towns. Unsurprisingly, owing to the immeasurable influence of Oyo in the making of Yorùbá culture and identity, this tradition has found its way into the Americas, where Yorùbá culture has been reproduced since the nineteenth century.[25] This practice can only remain symbolic in these locations, as they can hardly express, to the fullest, the functionality of the tradition and the rites that accompany it.

Aside from being a large cult, requiring families with their masquerade to which they are dedicated and through which the festival is performed, the social construction of their geographical space offers a great impediment. Nevertheless, this tradition lives on as an integral part of the Yorùbá society and ideology. It bears mentioning that the planting season in a Yorùbá community that practices Egúngún begins only after the celebration of the Egúngún festival. In other words, the festival heralds the planting season, which is traditionally regarded as the beginning of the cycle of a new year. As it cleanses the community, the growing season is meant to be smooth and harvest bountiful, with adequate rain, sunlight, and peaceful and healthy existence for the people to enjoy.

Perhaps nothing adumbrates the complex web of entanglements between Yorùbá people and their neighbors more clearly than what could be described as a wrestling influence these cultures, especially along the Niger River, wielded upon themselves at various times. Oyo had to ward off its powerful neighbors to build a prosperous empire. All through these years, culminating into the fall of the empire in the nineteenth century, Oyo was either a tributary state to any of these neighbors or it was doing the same to the Alaafinate. In his annotated piece drawn from primary accounts of events in Oyo around the late eighteenth century, Robin Law documents vital information that illuminated this intricate relationship from the account of Norris in 1789:

> The borderers on this kingdom [Dahomy] are the Eyos or Eyoes on the eastern side, between Dahomy and Benin; the Mahees, on the western; and the Tappas, whose country lies contiguous to the Eyos. The latter are a very spirited nation, and first gave a check to the ambitions of Guadja Trudo. . . . Their form of government is not very different from that of Dahomy, from which their despot, until very lately, exacted a yearly tribute for many years, as the price of peace. They cultivate cotton, and a species of grass, and manufacture both into clothing, for the use of the natives. Their traders deal likewise in slaves, which are disposed of the factors of Dahomy. . . . Of the Tappas, but little is known. . . . This nation, however, must have acquired considerable importance, as they drew a regular tribute from the Eyos. . . . The King [of Dahomey] pays a considerable yearly tribute, in cowries and merchandise to his formidable neighbour the King of Eyeo, part of which is defrayed from the contributions levied upon those states which are tributary to Dahomey.[26]

---

25. Ọyọtunji African Village, http://www.oyotunji.org/.

26. Law, *Contemporary Source Material*, 53.

At various times, these neighboring powers had weakened the stability and position of one another, as one acted as a check on the rise of the other, and this would come to later define the geographical coordinate of Yorubaland. Whereas Oyo had decisively checked what it considered the excessive rise and activities of Nupe from the seventeenth century until the eighteenth century when it is said to have been paying tributes to the same Nupe, its eventual collapse was a matter of interest of powerful neighbors that included the Nupe and Dahomey, and they played their roles in ensuring this.[27] Around the same period recorded in the excerpt, which falls within the twilight of the reign of Aláàfin Abiodun, there was a war between Oyo and the Bàrìbás under the leadership of Sabi Agba's four thousand bowmen and fifty horsemen that resulted in the defeat of Oyo forces, further weakening the polity.[28] This was in 1783. By implication, by the late eighteenth century, Oyo had lost its political hegemony over Nupe and Bàrìbá.[29]

Borgu traditions reveal that, whereas many of the Borgu communities had submitted their authority to the Kisra-led Wasangari group, with others led into the union by way of the sword, leading to the emergence of the three main kingdoms and dynastic rule, "the second wave founded the numerous chiefdoms in southern Nigerian Borgu in the eighteenth and nineteenth centuries."[30] The creation of numerous chiefdoms here should be taken as a substantial expansion of the reach of the three kingdoms. Oyo thus became the second wave of political formation and expansion of states around the Niger and those in Yorùbá hinterlands. The inability of Oyo to have initiated or extended its new political reform in the Bàrìbá country despite the role the people played in the formation of the polity, and how the polity was an incorporation of existing communities into a union of a centralized state, would only suggest that the autochthonous polities rallied round by Kisra in the seventeenth century included remnants of those that had hitherto refused the Oyo union but instead remained as they were.[31]

After the fall of Oyo in the early nineteenth century, many Yorùbá towns and kingdoms, especially those in the western part of the country, fell under the control of Dahomey, with Idaisa joining this league in 1881, Sabe in 1885, and Ketu in 1886. With the weakening of Oyo's authority, Egba, Ijaye, and Ibadan, the emerging powers in Yorubaland, had sporadically raided these western Yorùbá towns, probably for slaves, and certainly for the expression of their political agenda. Not long after its encroachments into these parts of Yorubaland, Dahomey came under the subjugation of French colonial rule in 1892.[32] Up to the time of its final collapse and despite its earliest access to European trade along the Atlantic coasts, the Oyo army prosecuted wars using bows and arrows, javelins, and swords, all suitable for its calvary. The battle between Oyo and Dahomey in the early eighteenth century took the form of European firearms against

---

27. Law, *Ọyọ Empire*.

28. Adekunle, "Wasangari," 438.

29. Falola and Oguntomisin, *Military in Nineteenth Century*.

30. Falola and Oguntomisin, *Military in Nineteenth Century*, 437.

31. This is a common phenomenon in the formation of larger polities, as evident in the case of Odùduwà and the Igbòmòkun and much later in the instance of Kisra in Borgu, where not all existing polities would agree to join a new union to the extent that such an endeavor often resulted in intermittent wars.

32. Akinyele, "Historiography of Western Yorùbá Borderlands," 101.

locally made weapons in which the former was adequately dealt with. Even more dramatic, during what could be referred to as the late eighteenth-century tidewaters, Oyo had stretched its tentacles beyond Dahomey to capture an estimated twenty thousand Mahee slaves.[33]

In the eastern region of the country, Nupe, Benin, and Oyo vied for the control of these pockets of villages, some of which were later grouped under a confederacy in the Ekiti area to become a powerful force of protection. This was following the fall of Oyo and the weak attempt of Ibadan to continue Oyo's intermittent activities in the region in contention with Benin.[34] Both Benin and Oyo served as the overlords of these communities; Benin easily wielded direct authority over many of the polities due to its proximity.[35] Given this, corresponding patterns of sociopolitical structure and forms could be found among these cultures and Benin. The absence of a powerful Yorùbá polity around this place saw to it that relations between Benin and the Yorùbá consisted less of the intrigues and adventurism of the north, between Oyo and others. Many communities in this area were constituted in small settlements, with some located in places where it is naturally impossible to expand for maximum political impact. The choice of such a settlement pattern by these communities was caused by their concern for safety and defense.

Therefore, rather than settle in fields where they could spread and communicate about the possibility of growing to become a well-established political hegemony, they looked for naturally protected locations, mostly characterized by rock formations, to settle. Not only was this obstructive to external invasions but it also made communication and exchange among these communities daunting. This experience suggests that true to Peter Morton-Williams's postulation, this area was once the raiding reserve of Oyo to feed its Atlantic market.[36] Such was the case with the Okun people at the periphery of Yorùbá country. In response to incessant raids from their powerful Nupe neighbor, many of these communities shifted their homes to the hills, while others found new homes and settlements in caves, rock shelters, and other rugged terrains impenetrable to calvary, never to return until the twentieth century.

Benin activities in this area, like other places, were more of political exaction than raiding for slaves. It collected tributes in exchange for protection. Some of the palm oil and farm products the empire traded with the Europeans were derived from this part of the Yorùbá country, which produced these in large quantities at substantial quality. A Dutch visitor to the empire's capital as early as the sixteenth century was so impressed by the level of development he saw that he compared it to Amsterdam. Subsequent developments provided the impetus to the magnificence of the Benin Empire until the tide turned elsewhere in the nineteenth century. Until the coming of the Europeans in the fifteenth century, Benin's biggest trading partners lay in the Yorùbá country, and even after this period, its most powerful and important neighbors were located here. This makes some of the cultural and sociopolitical influences of the empire in eastern Yorubaland subject to perspective and supposition since the Benin culture itself leans heavily on Yorùbá culture. For instance, the use of a living person to impersonate

---

33. Law, *Contemporary Source*, 65.

34. Awe, "Ajele System," 47–60.

35. Asiwaju, "Dahomey, Yorùbáland, Borgu and Benin," 699–723.

36. Morton-Williams, "Ọyọ and the Atlantic Trade," 25–45.

Figure 6.1. "Strangers in Bed," by Dr. Kazeem Ekeolu, depicts two people, unknown to each other, who could sleep together, as in coexistence and peaceful relationships. The Yorùbá value system emphasizes the need for hospitality, even to strangers.

the deceased in Benin, which is said to have been introduced from the empire to eastern Yorùbá towns like Owò and the Ipeku tradition and impersonation by masqueraders in the Yorùbá *Egúngún* cult, has been identified as a twin culture.[37] Since the time of Eweka until recently, the deceased body of an Ọba of Benin was taken to Ife for proper burial.

This tradition followed the instructions given by Eweka, who demanded to be buried with his ancestors at Ifè after his death. In following this tradition, given the logistic delays in carrying out the instruction, the people of Benin developed ways of preserving the deceased bodies. This culture of preservation also deals with the issue of logistics on the part of the ordinary people of Benin to give their loved ones befitting burials. Deceased bodies were therefore

---

37. Poynor, "Ako Figures of Owo," 82.

preserved by smoking and drying, the use of effigy, and impersonators. In a tradition found among eastern Yorùbá towns like Owo, both the impersonating figure and the funeral ceremony for the Queen Mother, the Ọba and nobles in Benin are referred to as *Ako* (*arha* among the commoners). This becomes the alternative since the body of the deceased cannot be preserved perpetually. While the body is buried as early as possible, the deceased is represented by an impersonator when his or her demise is to be celebrated. This falls within the range of ancestral worship, as it is hoped that the deceased live on, and in celebrating them on earth, they are venerated to perform their watchful responsibilities from the other world. In a similar practice, the Ijebu also preserved the body of the deceased person until arrangements were made for the burial, whether on the arrival of the family of the deceased or for any other reason. To this extent, the culture of preserving the body of a deceased person by smoking and drying is not unique to Benin, even though its very form of adopting this practice must have influenced that of the eastern settlements. Describing this tradition as it relates to the Yorùbá people in form of *Egúngún* rites, Robin Poynor explains that

> Impersonation is also found in Benin.... Although there were no real second burial ceremonies, some funeral ceremonies might be delayed for years until the family had collected enough money to carry them out with due magnificence. In such a ceremony, a living person is dressed up to represent the deceased.... This ceremony, the arha, takes place on the sixth day after death. A close relative wearing fine clothes, and adorned with beads, receives the salutation of his descendants, blesses them, and dances with them one last time. Bradbury interprets this as a final leave-taking and as the reception of the father by his kin who have preceded him to the invisible sphere occupied by deities, spirits, and an elder among the various groups of collective dead.[38]

Similarities and various versions of these similarities between Benin and Yorùbá traditions are expected, given the long years of relations between the two. Aside from the funeral rites instructed by Eweka, which has since resulted in Ife becoming the final resting place of the Ọba of Benin, Ife was kept in the loop of the administration of the empire. Important developments and decisions were relayed to the Ọọni for his advice, support, and prayers.[39] In a way, this relationship could be said to have commenced even before the establishment of the Eweka dynasty by Ọ̀rànmíyàn. According to Benin traditions supported by that of Ife and Oyo, Ọ̀rànmíyàn went to Benin on invitation by the people who pleaded with the Ọọni to help save their polity during a major political crisis among its ruling class. This further confirms the position of this study regarding Ọ̀rànmíyàn in the previous chapter, given as a foremost apostolic follower of the Odùduwà heritage. If the traditions were anything to go by, Ọ̀rànmíyàn was sent to Benin for this purpose, having set the train for the Oyo polity. He only left Benin after he could not bear some of the practices of the people, a decision that made him put his son, Eweka, in his place, as he did in Oyo. Until recently, part of the important information Ife had to hold included the installation of the Ọba of Benin.

---

38. Poynor, "Ako Figures of Owo."
39. Akinola, "Origin of the Eweka Dynasty," 21–36.

Whatever revolved around the conduct of the office of the Ọba was important and must be relayed to Ife: deposition, demise, burial, festivals, and other conceivable roles as a suzerain and closest principal center of civilization. The rituals and rites for the installation of the Oba start and end at Ilé-Ife in that the process for the installation of a new Oba could not be activated in Benin without the knowledge of the Ọ̀ọ̀ni, who would give the go-ahead, and the final installation was not complete until gifts and homage were paid to the Ọ̀ọ̀ni. This was typical for relations between a paramount ruler and a lesser sovereign.[40] It is clear from the traditions of Oyo that Ọ̀rànmíyàn did in Benin what he did in Oyo, and as stated previously, geography and a weak grip of Ifè political hegemony have created a peculiar bond that has historically defined the relationship between these two entities—thus, the discussion of Benin as a separate cultural entity and Oyo as a part and parcel of the "family." The nineteenth-century ordeal of the kingdom did not help matters; rather, it aggravated the purge of its political power and hold on to previous traditions.[41]

Another time when this bond could have been reignited came when the whole of Yorubaland was recovering from incredible turmoil in 1897 during the British invasion. A decade before, the British had signed a peace treaty between Yorùbá communities and warlords. It was an each-to-itself affair, typical of the colonial political form. It was with the decline in the political hegemony of Ife that Benin took control of southern and southeastern Yorùbá polities, as it grew alongside Oyo as the protégé of Ife. In this area, only Ilesa, another strong polity that emerged from the ashes of Ife, stood in between Benin and Ife. In other words, Ijesaland stood as the Ife–Benin cultural corridor. According to Obayemi, "The development of a kingship institution at Ile-Ife helped to widen the interactive networks in the region, an historical process that culminated in the trend toward regional cultural homogenization between the thirteenth and sixteenth centuries."[42]

In the same manner, "Old Oyo's relations with north-central Yorubaland seem to have initiated change, evident in large chiefly elites sites, large enclosed wall systems, an increase in ritual activities, and stylistic similarity in pottery decorations shared with Old Oyo."[43]

In a way, the role of Ife in Benin polity goes beyond the Ọ̀rànmíyàn tradition when it is considered that this was the cradle of civilization and the most prestigious institution in that area before the fifteenth century. This, combined with the Ọ̀rànmíyàn tradition, sealed the relationship between the two polities, as far as the theory of affiliation to a prestigious institution is concerned in the traditions of African polities.[44] In the same manner, Benin followed Ife political enlightenment because of its grandeur, chieftaincies, and political structures. Each adapted its political form from traditional rulers in the Yorùbá area where it dominated. Court rituals and rites were drawn from Benin, even though many were rooted in the influence of Ife. It bears mentioning that what constitutes Yorùbá culture and ideology today is an intricate web

---

40. Oyemakinde, "Chiefs Law," 63–74; Atanda, "Kings in Nigerian Society."

41. For the first time, during this period, the polity was dissolved following its confrontation with the newly constituted town of Modakeke. See Akinjogbin, *Cradle of a Race*.

42. Obayemi, "Between NOK, Ile-Ifẹ and Benin," 82.

43. Usman, "View from the Periphery," 43.

44. Vansina, *Oral Tradition as History*.

of contoured practices and rituals. As such, most practices, including arts and sculpture, that formed the basis of cultural exchanges between Benin and these cultures could be seen as the Edo variant of these traditions, as in Oyo, Ketu, Popo, Sabe, Ijesa, and others.[45]

Whereas classical Ife art dates as far back as the ninth century, records of Benin date back to around the fifteenth century. Reinforcing the close link of Benin to this southeastern Yorùbá states, this style of Benin classical arts was obtained in Owò.[46] This notwithstanding, it enjoyed the patronage and reverence of these communities so much that some of their traditions have been mistaken, and could be, if not carefully navigated, for Benin origin, in place of Ife.[47] Some of Ife arts and practices that went through this corridor were refined and reintroduced to these polities. Another part of these relations, which has generated unresolved controversy, is in the title of the Benin monarch. *Oba* is a generic term used to describe a Yorùbá monarch, but while some trace the etymology of the word to Benin, others aver to its Yorùbá route. One could draw from this that since the term itself preceded the time of Odùduwà, as it could be found among Igbòmokùn chiefs, among which were Obawinrin and Obatala, it is either this polity (Benin) shared the same heritage with the Igbòmokùn communities in terms of trade or traditions, or the name/title emerged after the intervention of Òrànmíyàn. In any case, both share the same kingship tradition and maintained a familial relationship until recently.

At the Niger–Benue confluence area of the Yorùbá country were those referred to as the Okun-Yorùbá, with communities spread across difficult terrain in small villages. These communities suffered a lot from their Nupe neighbors. The influence of Nupe in this axis did not allow for a proper political organization of these communities. They formed the frontline relations of the Yorùbá country with the Ebira, Igala, and Idoma, exchanging cultural practices that included burial rites. Common among these cultures is the use of red cloth for burial purposes.[48] This population is known for their cloth weaving, which they taught Nupe women as slave captives.[49] As earlier noted, the predicament of these communities is somewhat like that of the people of Ekiti, which once served as the slave reserve of the Old Oyo. As the slave reserve of Nupe, they were constantly vulnerable to raids, leaving the communities deserted at different times with devastating implications for their economy and trade. Given the direct relations between Oyo and Nupe, as well as the marginal role of these periphery Yorùbá communities, it is unlikely that significant cultural productions entered Yorubaland through here. The reverse was rather the case, as seen in the case of the women who taught Nupe women how to weave, a practice cultivated from Oyo.

Socioeconomic Engagements

Through trading relations with the Nupe, Hausa merchants, Borgu, Mossi, and the Songhai Empire, nobles' use of horses became popular in Yorubaland. Located in the savanna region

---

45. Ryder, "Reconsideration of the Ifẹ-Benin Relationship," 25–37.

46. Quoted in Obayemi, "Between NOK, Ile-Ifẹ and Benin," 82.

47. Ogen, "Exploring the Potential of Praise Poems," 77–96.

48. O'Hear, "History of the Okun Yorùbá," 116.

49. O'Hear, "History of the Okun Yorùbá," 113.

of the country and close to powerful kingdoms and empires in the West African region, with access to markets from across Africa reaching the tip end of the continent in the Maghreb region, which links Africa to other continents, Oyo was placed above other Yorùbá towns and kingdoms in matters of trade, goods, and productivity.[50] Cloths; livestock, including horses, goats, and cattle; ivory; human captives; farm products, including onions, groundnut, and cotton; dairy products; salt, leatherworks; craftworks; ironware; and palm oil and palm products were all exchanged in these markets.[51]

Whatever Oyo merchants traded in impacted other Yorùbá communities. Of course, Yorùbá merchants in these markets were not limited to the Oyo. Distant and nearer Yorùbá towns and peoples joined this enterprise at various times and varying levels. As polities were evolving and dissolving at every turn because of wars of conquest and expansion, political instability, and related affairs of this period, Yorùbá actors were also changing. Before the second half of the nineteenth century, the likes of Abeokuta and Ibadan that later dominated the trade, along with the introduction of new trade, were absent.[52] The latter had been on the rise since its establishment as a military camp in the 1830s when it was reported to have grown to a population of over twenty thousand, the largest in the whole of the Yorùbá country. This number, though admirable for a young polity like Ibadan, was nothing compared to what the Oyo Empire must have been.

Certainly, the reality of the Ibadan and other Yorùbá communities of this period is a product of the demise of the Oyo rule in the land. Contrary to the diminishing role of Oyo in Yorùbá external trade, the Ijebu were able to maintain their involvement in the trade from the previous years to this period and beyond. The trading policy, or rather trading culture (as it goes beyond a policy), of the Ijebu was somewhat responsible for this. Among the Yorùbá groups not penetrated by the radiating force of Oyo were the Ijebu.[53] As in other forest states of the Yorùbá country, the Ijebu were naturally protected from the Oyo calvary, which they relied upon so heavily. But the Ijebu were no fans of the liberal open market economy. The trading policy of Ijebu was restrictive, thereby preserving their organic cultures and primordial formation for many years until they were forced to open up by the British colonial encroachment. What has been described as the policy of isolation of the people was so much of a burden to Yorùbá trade that it took a major defeat of the Ijebu army by the British forces for trade to begin to flow across the town.[54]

Not only was external trade "forbidden" in the Ijebu communities, visitation from outside peoples, which included their neighboring Yorùbá communities, was tightly restricted. As the polity of the Yorùbá country underwent an intensive recalibration, Ijebu remained one of the few enduring Yorùbá polities. The demise of the threat of the Oyo Empire did not result in the establishment or involvement of Ijebu in the Yorùbá trade, unlike in the case of Abeokuta and Ibadan. The demise of Oyo did, however, strengthen their position. Even before the final blow

50. Akinjogbin and Ayandele, "Yorùbáland up to 1800," 121–133.

51. Ekundare, *Economic History of Nigeria*.

52. Falola, *Political Economy*, 2.

53. Ayandele, *Ijebu of Yorubaland*.

54. Smith, "Nigeria-Ijẹbu," 175.

that collapsed the empire in the 1830s, Ijebu had assumed the overt position of the Old Oyo in the transatlantic slave trade and, by implication, in the collection of slaves in Yorubaland.[55] Indeed, this resulted in the Owu war and contributed to the spiraling damages that befell the Yorùbá polity of the time.[56]

Of particular interest in this area is the clothing culture of the people, particularly males, which has since become largely an adulteration of Arab-Hausa cultures. In style and design, Yorùbá clothing tradition is markedly derived from the indigenous clothing tradition of the Hausa people and those the Hausa adopted from the Arabs. There is no question that the sub-Saharan trade played a fundamental role in the evolution of African cultures.[57] The power of trade is such that items in demand shape the social fabric of the society, and there is no limit to how its subtle lens could change the culture and cultural practices of the people—both the sellers and the buyers. The presence of Arabs in Africa is a long history that precedes the fall of Egypt to Islamic jihadists of the late seventh century.

By the time the likes of Kanem, Borno, Mali, Songhai, and Ife, among others, became powerful states in the sub-Saharan region of the continent from around the twelfth century, Arab influence in Africa had spread from the Maghreb. These polities were the main call of contact in the sub-Saharan region, and by the time they collapsed, the influence of this culture on African traditions had transcended religion to language, fashion, manners, and customs.[58] In some instances, as in the case of the Yorùbá, where Arab loan words crept into the vocabulary as a result of the contacts between Oyo and Hausa merchants, these traditions were diffused by second parties from African cultures, invariably through trade and trading relations. This clothing style included robes and male gowns (popular among which is agbádá) and Arab-style trousers that included *atu, kanki, salubaki,* and *kembeku.*

Going by how the intellectual productions of preliterate societies were preserved, especially in this part of Africa, not much information on this tradition is known except the careful exploration of the oral traditions and the creative orature of the people. Of course, scholars are drawn to retrieving these traditions, and a great deal of effort is provided by Akinwunmi in one of his articles. From the panegyric of Akintokun Akintola, the Balógun of Ibadan from 1897 to 1899, and Ọba Folasade Ajiga, to that of the Àpetumodu monarch and others that come as good as cogent notes on traditions and evolution of clothing, and cloth in Yorubaland, Akinwunmi provides anecdotal insight into how virtually all the male clothing style in Yorubaland was inspired by Arab traditions. As he sums from the panegyric of Akintola and Ajiga,

> In this poem, Akintola was a warlord who dressed in *guru,* a trailing cloak (toga) made of a large prestigious fabric and draped over an under tunic or robe. The draping was done thus: an end of the fabric was laid against the chest, then carried over the left shoulder and around the back and brought under the right arm to the front. Next it was draped

---

55. Ryder, "Trans-Atlantic Slave Trade," 238–250; Law, *Oyo Empire,* 247–275. See also the accounts of Osifẹkunde and Crowther in Curtin, *Africa Remembered.*

56. Ajayi and Smith, *Yorùbá Warfare in the 19th Century.*

57. Ogot, *General History of Africa.*

58. Mazrui, *Africans.*

over the left shoulder, and finally tied in the back. This arrangement was made in such a way as to leave the right arm free. The draped toga further enhanced the stature of the wearer of *girike*, *gbáríyẹ́*, *dàndógó*, or *agbádá* robe. The toga can be classified into two types. When the toga left a trail of about 3 meters on the floor, it was known as *guru*. If an elegant one almost touched the ground, it was known as *gogowu*. The horse-riding knee breeches, *kẹ̀mbẹ́*, were usually a part of their dress ensemble, as demonstrated in this poem. . . . Beside going in clogs and wearing gogowu or guru over the Arab-styled robes, some monarchs appeared in other dress combinations. They wore over any Arab-styled robe a waistband made of sizeable number of strung beads to show more affluence.[59]

It is evident from these summations, which are similar to information derived from other praise poems like this, that before the influence of Arab-Hausa cultures began to refine the clothing traditions of the Yorùbá people, the society subsisted on untailored clothes. Justin Cordwell explains that "before Yoruba men adapted the northern style of robe (the agbada and its variations) during and after the Oyo wars of the first half of the 19th century, their traditional skirt wrap fell from a heavy roll of cloth around the waste, down to the ankles."[60]

While these changes were taking place in male clothing long before the colonial period, serious evolution in the clothing tradition of women did not emerge until the eve of the colonial period as missionaries and Yorùbá captive returnees from Sierra Leone were preparing the ground for the remodeling of the society and culture. Among the historical implications of this is that the social effect of trade impacted more men than women, because men dominated the trade. The Arabs, the Hausa merchants, and their Yorùbá partners were mostly male, with the only exception being Yorùbá women from Ijebu, Oyo, and other parts of Yorubaland. Fabrics exchanged that women could use were tied as wrappings; soon this moved to headgear and other Christian-inspired looks that saw to the (ìró) wrapper being complemented by Buba. In this evolution, cloth and other body adornments, including beads, and hairstyles thus served as an important aesthetic expression of the Yorùbá art and social stratification.

Arranged in caravans—a sort of market syndicate of itinerant merchants along long-distance routes and markets—Yorùbá traders took their activities to markets in Nupe and Hausaland, including the Koolfu market in Kotangora.[61] This arrangement helped the traders to bear the loss of their investment and time gracefully while all leveraged one another to make a successful trip. This ensured a safe route and, more importantly, guaranteed limited risk of loss and the fortitude to bear the long-distance journey. Unlike in the case of the Arab traders and those in the Maghreb down to the Sahel who used camels, Yorùbá caravans consisted of only humans, which included few slaves for the transportation of goods. Such trips, depending on the distance, could take months or weeks. Whatever the case, the merchants could usually be sure of profit. The number of traders in these caravans expanded as they passed other villages.

The use of caravans along the market in the Borgu territory from Yorubaland and other places that included Nupe, Hausaland, and the Songhai Empire did not surface until around

---

59. Akinwunmi, "Oral Traditions," 59–60.

60. Cordwell, "Art and Aesthetics," 58.

61. Falola, "Yorùbá Caravan System," 188.

the seventeenth century. Despite their similar traditions, there is no account of economic relations between the Bàrìbá and the Yorùbá until this period. This would be centuries after the establishment of the Oyo polity, which brought the Yorùbá country nearer to the Niger River. Like the Ijebus for so many years, the Borgu people traded among themselves as they jealously protected their cultures and practices and restricted outside contact. This made the spread of Islam difficult in the country.[62] It is instructive to note that, just as in the case of the Old Oyo Empire, the Borgu polity under the Wasangari rulers began to witness hiccups at its peak.

This led to the "highway princes" phenomenon along the trading route that led to Nikki, the Bàrìbá trading capital, which was only opened after the Songhai Empire finally subdued its rulers. Trading activities here did not gain impact far into the kingdoms and empires in West Africa until the seventeenth century with the stability of Oyo polity at Igboho and its continuous spread around the Niger reaching Ghana, Togo, Benin, and, exclusively, almost half of the Yorùbá country. Yorùbá merchants and others traveling to the Nikki market were faced with banditry from Nikki princes who were bent on diverting the trading frequency away from Nikki to their newly formed settlements in the southern part of the country situated close to the Yorùbá country.[63]

The situation of caravan trade along this route was further compounded by the fact that these acts of banditry were not limited to the princes for their political calculations. Common criminals also engaged in highway robbery, leaving Yorùbá merchants at the mercy of Oyo soldiers. Expectedly, this trade added to the pulse of the Oyo Empire. Tolls were collected on every passage, and taxation within the empire increased because the people joined the burgeoning economic opportunities to expand their production and trading engagements. As it is with any other society, this practice came with its implication in the social fabric of the Yorùbá country. Yorùbá artisans were involved in calabash carving, mat weaving, basketmaking, blacksmithing, pot making, embroidery, leatherworks, sculpture, and many more activities that characterized their industrial output. Clothes, ironware, craftworks, and varieties of farm produce, including kola nuts, thus accounted for much of the Yorùbá trade. Yorùbá women were skilled in producing pottery and clothes dyed in brilliant colors, some of which they traded in these distant markets, up to Mali, where archaeological findings at Tellem burial caves reveal caps "bearing the extant and popular Osu Bamba motif common in the àdìrẹ art of the Yoruba."[64] Even with the advent of colonial rule, which limited the taste for local art and industrial produce, their clothes were in demand in Ghana and elsewhere.[65]

The geophysical environment of the empire, which gave it access not only to trade from distant lands but to an advanced culture of the NOK people, ensured its development in art, which influenced others around the country to the extent that by the nineteenth century, it became a common saying that *B'Onírèsé ò fín gbá mọ́, èyí tó ti fín sílẹ̀ ò lè parun* (If Onírèsé no longer carves calabash, the ones he has made cannot go into extinction). During the reign of Aláàfin Abiodun at the twilight of the empire, close to a thousand artworks were produced by Lagbayi, an Oyo

---

62. Julius, "Borgu and Economic Transformation," 1–18.
63. Adekunle, "Wasangari," 442.
64. Areo and Kalilu, "Adire in South-Western Nigeria," 352.
65. Areo and Kalilu, "Adire in South-Western Nigeria," 364.

sculptor, alone, with all adorning the palace of the Aláàfin.[66] With this level of advancement, the Oyo prided themselves as dwellers of a great city with advanced civilization compared to their kinsmen in the hinterlands whose works have been influenced by Oyo. Thus, the saying *alárà, Oyo màrà ju ará oko lọ* (the owner of creative force, Oyo who knows creativity more than people in the suburbs).[67] But this will not be the only area in which the empire benefited from its location, culminating in prominence in Yorubaland and the whole of its West African neighbors. The mastering of iron smiting or processing by the people also came from this advanced NOK culture through the Bàrìbás, which contributed in no small measure to the advantages enjoyed by the Old Oyo polity.

There is no question that precolonial African societies were neither static nor absent of innovations. Even though instruments of economic actions were crude, society consistently moved and adapted to its changing environment. The discovery and mastery of the art of iron processing brought gravity to the socioeconomic composition of African societies, with tremendous effects on their political morphology. From farm implements to weapons of war, objects of everyday use to ritual objects, the Iron Age revolutionized African societies.[68] In the sub-Saharan region, Oyo occupied a peculiar position in the production of iron, so much so that its people traded in ironware with distant cultures and neighbors that included the Nupe.

No doubt, Anthony Hopkins has provided us with a meticulously illuminating piece regarding the question of economy and economic relations in West Africa during the precolonial epoch. His comment on the production and use of iron in Yorubaland is instructive: "In 1904, one of these settlements had a population of between 100 and 120 all of whom (including women and children) were engaged in the various stages of iron mining and manufacturing. The output of this settlement supplied an area which covered several hundred square miles. . . . An analysis of samples carried out in 1904 showed that producers had selected the best possible flux, and that the finished product was paddled or forged steel, and not simply wrought iron."[69]

Given the ubiquity of iron smelting in Oyo, it is not out of place to relate the origin of Ògún, the Yorùbá god of iron and the patron deity of blacksmiths, to this place. Their kinsmen in the forest region of the country recognized the preeminence of this deity through their engagement with metal objects produced from this region in their daily economic activities like hunting and farming. This does not contradict the position of Odunyoye, who attributed the making of Ògún among the Yorùbá to the understanding and reaction of their ancestors to the volcanic eruptions experienced in many parts of the Mediterranean, from where they migrated.[70] It only follows that since the belief in a volcanic god was conjured to appreciate and make meaning of the volcanic eruptions, as well as the conversion of its power into the use of man, as in the making of iron and refining other industrial materials if at all the practice was to be

---

66. Akintonde and Areo, "Art and Craft of the Old Ọyọ," 54.

67. Akintonde and Areo, "Art and Craft of the Old Ọyọ."

68. Vercoulter, "Discovery and Diffusion of Metals," 706–729; Porteres and Barrau, "Origins, Development and Expansion," 687–705.

69. Hopkins, *Economic History of West Africa*, 89–90.

70. Oduyoye, *Vocabulary of Yoruba Religious Discourse.*

reinvigorated in their West African home where they eventually migrated, it would be at a place where this phenomenon and its adaptation thrives.

The communities noted in the above excerpt were mostly surrounded by woodlands. Accordingly, they lacked nothing in the reproduction of the art, as they were armed with logs to create charcoal for the processing of ironware. This knowledge and its products spread across the Yorùbá country, and it is not unlikely that they contributed to Benin's art and smithing tradition. The practice and prominence of Ògún in Yorubaland cannot be discussed fully without understanding the input of Oyo and its ironworkers. Trade always has its way of molding society along the lines of the objects of trade as they portend the function of a signifier toward which the culture and society gravitate. This is true in all levels of cultural production: organic culture, high culture, pop culture, and so on. [71] The prominence of Islamic culture in Africa, for instance, did not begin with the activities of Islamic missionaries and the later jihadists but with economic exchanges and the cultural entanglements that inevitably followed. Considered as a form of high culture, identifying Arab wares, fashion, and taste in many cultures, from contemporary northern Nigeria to the southwest of it where the Yorùbá populate, will now take a meticulous study.

For a long time, Oyo, through which Islam could have penetrated Yorubaland well before the crisis of the nineteenth century, like its Ìbàrìbá kinsmen, had resisted its growth or adoption as a state religion as it was in Hausaland and Songhai. This, nonetheless, did not make the people averse to their innovations and goods. Whereas the Bàrìbás under the Wasangari militated against this through a trading policy that prohibited Muslim traders from the Songhai Empire, the Wangara, from trading in its kingdoms until the successful invasion of the empire, which saw the reversal of the policy, Oyo had always maintained a liberal economy. This enabled the spread of Islam within the empire. In what has been a slow spread of the culture and religion in Yorubaland, as evident in the above text from the panegyric of some prominent Yorùbá figures in the nineteenth century, this accelerated from the eve of the eighteenth century when Arab culture came to influence the social form of the society, especially in the aspect of fashion.

Through its trade and trading relations with distant cultures and polities, the Oyo Empire was, at various times, able to extend the reach of provinces under its control to territories touching those West African countries mentioned above. For instance, it was in a bid to control the routes leading to the lucrative emerging markets in Porto Novo and later Badagry that the Egbado nation of several polities was subjected to the empire's rule. Fortunately for these polities, this ensured that they were secured against the threat of their powerful Egba, Dahomey, and Benin neighbors. Indeed, Oyo imperial moves of the early seventeenth century to the early nineteenth century, built on past achievements, can be attributed to the complex nature of understanding the proper framing of Yorùbá boundaries, especially on the middle-level taxonomy of Asiwaju.

At the dawn of the transatlantic slave trade, the focus of external trade in Yorubaland shifted to coastal cities. This, again, and far more in proportion compared to that along the Sahara through Bàrìbá and Nupe, gave impetus to the role and place of Oyo in the traditions of the

---

71. Danesi, *Popular Culture.*

Yorùbá country and its relations with neighbors and the outside world. Already, among those items of social changes from trade across the Sahara were new seeds for plantations from Asia Minor, together with the transatlantic trade, many conduits for cultural diffusion into the interior of Africa through powerful centralized states like Oyo. Rice, cassava, and new species of crops like cotton were introduced into society. Although in the case of the former, the Europeans dealt with traders at port cities, the bastions of the cultural mixture and diffusion, Oyo controlled these ports and the cities at various times. The relationship between Oyo and its neighbors was like an intricate wrestling match, particularly so with the various accounts recorded in relation to its encounters with Dahomey in the eighteenth century.

Some of these accounts draw some basic questions, one of which was raised in the previous chapter. Several accounts allude to the rise of Dahomey in the eighteenth century, so much so that it sacked the trading port city of Whydah, used by Oyo in 1727 under its ruler, Agaja. This event is often reported to have forced Oyo to move its trade to newly formed port settlements of the displaced peoples of Whydah, Alladah, Weme, and others around the early port cities, which included Badagry and Epe.[72] The activities of Dahomey in these port cities, which equated it to the degree of an albatross on the state, would later push Oyo to the Lagos port, at least it seemed. After the whole road to conquest by Dahomey, it became a tributary state to Oyo while it was supposedly on the rise and leaving Oyo with no option but to scamper for alternative trading routes to European markets.

In fact, after the successful invasion of Weme, Dahomey gave substantial gifts to Oyo to avoid a situation where it would support the sacked town with its army. That Dahomey was not even a fit to Oyo during this period is evidence of the strategy often adopted by its forces during Oyo attacks, where they often fled their towns together with their kings, only to return after the Oyo forces had left.[73] Guerrilla war tactic, as it is called. This did not change until the troubles in Oyo brought it to the lowest nadir of its political influence and power in West Africa in the later eighteenth century. It can be surmised, therefore, that, among other things responsible for Oyo's reaction to the expansion of Dahomey, Oyo saw opportunity elsewhere for its trade to continue to boom. Trade records of this period—dominated by human cargo—demonstrate this well.[74]

A more dramatic turn hovers above this discussion even further when it is assumed in some quarters—first promoted by Akinjogbin in his thesis on Dahomey[75]—that the Agaja sack of Whydah in 1727 was an attempt at putting a stop to the practice and trade in slaves, but only turned to continue with the trade and monopolize the market after realizing he needed the support of European powers through their merchants and merchant companies, to counter the power of the Old Oyo.[76] If this was Agaja's position, it never worked, as the kingdom continued to remain subservient to Oyo. All through this period, Dahomey took frantic steps to control

---

72. Law, "Lagoonside Port," 32–59.

73. Law, "Lagoonside Port."

74. Ojo, "Organization of the Atlantic Slave Trade," 77–100.

75. Akinjogbin, *Dahomey and Its Neighbours*.

76. Hopkins, *Economic History*, 156. Thankfully, Hopkins also drew a caveat on this submission as he noted that "there is not complete agreement over the interpretation" of this aspect of Dahomey tradition. It is here added that,

trade with the Europeans, leading to its further pursuit of the newly constituted polities of those it had displaced earlier, Badagry and Epe, and the eventual check of its rascality by Oyo during the reign of Aláàfin Abiodun. The involvement of Yorubaland with the transatlantic trade saw to its relations with port cities polities in Little Ardra through Ouidah and Whydah, Badagry, Epe, and Lagos; the last three within the Yorùbá country. In other words, the rascality of Dahomey rulers pushed the trade further and further to Oyo, showing a tremendous increase in the number of transacted slaves.[77]

Trade in human cargo was no doubt an important factor in the wealth of states and societies in precolonial Nigeria, both across the waters and the desert. Between the time of the Uthman dan Fodio jihad and the eventual collapse of the Old Oyo Empire, there was a massive increase in human trafficking in West Africa, with Yorubaland acting as the effective loop through which most enslaved people were transported. This circuit made Lagos a regional trading center for the whole of sub-Saharan Africa.[78] Expectedly, this brought about an increase in the wealth of Yorùbá slave merchants and their states while simultaneously resulting in the participation of more peoples and polities in the heinous trade that displaced many communities and families. Among those who resisted the abolition of the West African trade in human cargoes were Yorùbá chiefs and nobles. The trade was expensive, requiring a concentration of military resources and political might, which only the chiefs, nobles, and kings could guarantee. The trade, as in the European capitals, was organized around these state powers.

The Alaafin dominated the trade before the eighteenth century by using his designated representatives, mostly slaves. In fact, as a general practice, the kings of Lagos also adopted this structure of trading administration. For instance, accounts of the exploits of Oshodi Tapa and the Oba Ehinlokun's family are still resounding in the history of the trade. At least three decades after the 1807 British abolition, trade in human cargo continued in Yorubaland and its ports. If anything, abolition increased the frequency with which slaves were embarked in the Bight of Benin, Lagos in the main.[79] The activities of Benin in the eastern and southeastern regions of Yorubaland were more a political exaction than a raid for slaves, as in the case of Oyo, and, later, Ilorin. But while it is true that the slave trade increased the wealth and power of states in Africa, Benin was an exception.

Its reluctance to respond to the demand for human captives by Portuguese merchants who first landed on its shores as early as the late fifteenth century when trade in farm products turned to demand for slaves, steadily shifted the merchants' attention to Porto Novo, where slave traffic from Oyo sustained the trade.[80] Benin maintained this policy to a considerable degree all through the period of the slave trade across the Atlantic. Southern Yorùbá, located in the forest region where animals like elephants could be found, was used to supply Benin's ivory to the Europeans. Ivory and palm oil flowed from this region to Benin down to its ports for European

---

perhaps, other parts of the traditions of the kingdom during this period have been faced with misinterpretation. See also Brenner, "Reviewed Work," 300.

77. Lovejoy, "Yorùbá Factor," 40–51.

78. Coquery-Vidrovitch and Lovejoy, *Workers of African Trade*, 65.

79. Law, "Trade and Politics," 321–348.

80. Feinberg, "Reviewed Work," 405–410; Curtin, *Atlantic Slave Trade*.

engagement. So while Oyo and other northern Yorùbá towns maintained an economy framed on transactions in human cargo, Benin and southeastern Yorùbá peoples flourished on the so-called legitimate trade even before abolition. The abolition of the slave trade and the rise of legitimate economic trades only reinforced the position of these polities.

As it became apparent that the trade in slaves could not continue with the increase in the activities and tentacles of the British naval squadron, marked by the invasion of Lagos in 1851, many of the chiefs and nobles involved shifted their attention to the production of farm products in demand using slave labor. This way, while the abolition act stopped the trade in slaves, as their labor was no longer needed in the increasingly industrialized Atlantic cities and farms, it could not prevent the practice in the "native countries." Here, more than before, their labor was now needed.[81] Among other things, it makes no economic sense for these imperialist states to keep importing slaves to produce what could be produced and imported from Africa to feed their emerging industries. This, together with the need to decongest the cities and moderate the economic fortunes of the emerging industries, fueled the urge to return people to Africa. The impacts of this in the Yorùbá country have been well-documented.[82]

The close association of Benin with coastal states and the Europeans ensured its access to salt, which it also traded with its Yorùbá neighbors in exchange for the farm products from the Yorùbá forest region and goods like leather and other items from the Sahel from Oyo. Talking about its geophysical environment and the relations of Yorubaland with its neighbors, it is worth noting that the geographical advantage enjoyed by Oyo brought it on the pedestal of a buffer between these neighbors and other Yorùbá communities. To appreciate the role of Oyo in writing the transnational history of Yorùbá peoples and ideas, one needs to understand the extent to which streams of cultural practices flowed from this area to other parts of Yorubaland and the presence that constitute this transnational community. In relating some archaeological finds of selected northern Yorùbá towns toward the Niger River, Obayemi explains that "pottery types from Old Oyo became known in Ìgbómìnà probably as early as the thirteenth century AD, and continued to occur in some areas until the late eighteenth century. The presence of Oyo pottery in Ìgbómìnà has important implications for the understanding of Oyo's relations with the northern Yorùbá group and the frontier position of Ìgbómìnà during the Old Oyo Empire."

As a frontier state of the Yorùbá country, its relations with neighbors had a significant impact on many Yorùbá communities and peoples. Aside from the area of clothes and clothing tradition, trading relations between Yorubaland through Oyo and the Hausa states brought about the introduction of onions into the former's recipes. Tellingly, "the Oyo northern link also predisposed the supply of leather used for the production of puffs, hand fan, bag, purse and other leather items. The link also must have brought the diffusion of northern motifs in the designs and pattern of the Oyo leather work. These motifs were also employed in gourd and calabash carvings."[83]

---

81. Coquery-Vidrovitch and Lovejoy, *Workers of African Trade*, 69.

82. Pallinder-Law, "Aborted Modernization in West Africa?" 65–82; Peel, *Religious Encounter*.

83. Akintonde and Areo, "Art and Craft of the Old Ọyọ," 52.

However, this also came at a cost for the empire. It was noted in the previous chapter how the relationship between Oyo and the Hausa states resulted in the influx of the Hausa population into the empire as captives and traders. The continuous arrival of this population into Oyo equally saw fundamental changes in the social formation of the society. Since approximately the eleventh to twelfth century, Islam had become a major factor in Hausaland, governing all spheres of the state. Many had converted for economic and social advantage. Consequently, the influx of Hausa populations into Oyo meant the gradual penetration of Islam into Yorubaland. In the same way, trade brought about the influence of Islam into Hausaland through Arab traders and their Muslim neighbors. Hausa traders, along with their trading activities, began to infuse Islamic knowledge and teachings into the social fabrics of the Old Oyo Empire.

Already the Hausa captives had become valuable for royal duty at the time, taking care of stables, acting at the highest echelon of the administration of the empire, and of course, with others as drawers of waters and hewers of woods.[84] Those given the former privilege would have been educated in Arabic, giving them some level of literacy. They were later joined in this faith by their Yorùbá hosts. This created, for the first time, a fundamental shift in the religious ideology and identity of the state that became clear in 1817 when this population rose to revolt against the Alaafinate, leading to the decisive loss of the grip of the empire on its subjects.[85] It is apparent from the events that culminated in the Bașọrun Gáà debacle and the Aláàfin Abiodun's reign that by 1789, the Old Oyo was teetering.

Society at this time was fundamentally arranged around what economic historians have called contractual relations over kinship ties.[86] This implies the reorganization of society and labor beyond household and familial ties to consideration of expertise and skills. From the seventeenth century, the Hausa captive population in Oyo enjoyed this privilege, as it not only guaranteed the leaders the security needed for them to be sure their interests were adequately represented but also saw to it that skilled traders, communicators, and other needed skills were harnessed appropriately for an economically buoyant empire and a booming polity. Other slave populations in the state also enjoyed this privilege. Essentially, as the polity grew, labor organization fell on an ever-expanding and ever-adaptive household made up of extended relations, slaves, and visitors. The construction of the home and arrangement of the family compound also adapted to this expansion. Hence, John Michael Vlach argued that socioeconomic needs rather than environmental conditions played a leading role in the construction of homes in Yorubaland.[87]

The level at which trade in sub-Saharan Africa had grown in the nineteenth century is even more tremendous, with great effects on the cultural circulation by trade. From the inception of long-distance trade, this practice has been added to the calendar of cultures around this region. Given that they had to balance their farmwork with trading and considering the condition of the road that would lead them to their destinations, this falls in the dry season. During this period, there was massive traffic on the trade routes. By the nineteenth century, not only

---

84. Ojo, "Atlantic Slave Trade," 73–100.

85. Smith, "Little New Light," 42–71.

86. Hopkins, *Economic History*, 154.

87. Vlach, "Affecting Architecture of the Yorùbá," 48–55.

was the practice of family enterprise, in the form of collective investment in an enterprising member, becoming conspicuous, but the circle of trade was also incredible with the inclusion of the practices like hoarding. Hausa merchants would hoard tobacco until the time favorable for their sale. This practice was common among the merchants from the Hausa states of Katsina, and they would purchase livestock like goats and cattle at Zinder and Agades, where they had disposed of the hoarded products.[88] From here, the livestock was transported to Yorubaland, where they were sold at Ibadan, Ilorin, and Abeokuta for further trade in kola nut.

Because kola nut was produced from these interior locations in Yorùbá, from whence they were taken to Lagos, it is unlikely that they moved beyond these interior markets for kola nut, which they sold on their way back home. This is more so considering that Ibadan had by this time produced a substantial number of large farm owners whose produce could meet the increasing demand for kola nut in the Hausa states of this century.[89] Saying this, of course, would be shuffling aside large and petty farmers in the forest region of the country, whose products fed the Lagos market. In any case, the sale of livestock to Yorubaland shaped the face of the society and the diet of the people. Interestingly, the pattern in which this livestock was sold into Yorubaland still subsists, only that some breaks have been witnessed in the chain since the demand for the goods that made up the chain collapsed. For instance, the demand for kola nut has reduced compared to the past, and a lot has changed in trading routes and mechanisms of trade. Previous routes have been rerouted through railways and the construction of bridges and roads using modern transportation systems. What has remained in this practice is the continued movement of livestock from Katsina and other parts of the Hausa states to Yorubaland. Over the years, they have been joined by Yorùbá traders.

Conclusion

Essential to the foregoing is the idea of cultural circulation propelled by centuries of cultural and economic exchanges and relations among cultures.[90] Indeed, the idea of cultural circulation, which is responsible for the assumption of the Nupe-root of some aspects of Yorùbá civilization, explains the skepticism that has greeted the identity of Òrànmíyàn and his link to the Odùduwà tradition, as well as other complexities encountered in the description of Yorubaland vis-à-vis its neighbors. The interaction between the Old Oyo Empire and its neighbors, which has impacted other parts of Yorubaland greatly, is such an interesting and intricate one that it could justifiably make the skepticism of the Òrànmíyàn identity worth a second look, if only to strengthen his Yorùbá origin. And it is again here recalled the Benin tradition that alluded the rise of the Eweka dynasty to the invitation of the people to Ife for a political revival, a call to which Òrànmíyàn happened to have acceded.

Trade and politics played a major role in the interaction between Yorubaland and its neighbors, with one reinforcing the other. Among many deductions from the above discussion, it is evident that, as in modern state relations, developments and events in one polity take their toll

---

88. Vlach, "Affecting Architecture of the Yorùbá."
89. Falola, *Political Economy of a Pre-Colonial African State.*
90. O'Hear, "History of the Okun Yorùbá," 111–126.

    GLOBAL YORÙBÁ

on the other, the measure of which is determined by the level of relations between the states and the capacity of the other state to take advantage of such situation.[91] From Oyo to Borgu, Nupe to the Hausa states, Benin to Dahomey, and to some relative extent as events would come to prove later, Yorubaland and Ilorin,[92] this factor has played a significant role.[93] The role and place of Ilorin is another knotting area in defining this discussion. Although a garrison town of the Old Oyo, it fell to the Fulani in the early nineteenth century, and even though there are substantial extant Yorùbá traditions in the town, its relations with its kinsmen (Yorùbá people) have been subjected to a sort of neighboring cultures, building a relationship of constant strife and suspicion.

This, like others, ended with the colonial sharing of boundaries and peoples, which has removed this polity from Yorubaland in tandem with the practice on the ground that brought it under the Sokoto caliphate. The kingdom of Borgu also suffered the same fate, and what is left of these precolonial formations is only a subject of colonial mapping, revealing less of their traditional and historical context. In any case, as the opening excerpt of this chapter indicates, change is a constant occurrence in the life of individuals and society. This chapter has shown how this has come to characterize Yorubaland, its people, and culture up to the dislocation of its population across different lands and the world. These places are distinguished by their cultures and traditions, molded over centuries of cultural circulation among their neighbors. As a community of people known for their adventurism and enterprising inclinations, the people have taken advantage of the colonial intervention and policies to expand and deepen their presence among their neighbors in the West African region. Through this process, precolonial historical ties are recalibrated and reproduced in their contemporary relations.

---

91. Obayemi, "Sokoto Jihad," 64; Ajayi, *General History of Africa*.

92. The case of Ilorin is, to some extent, similar to that of the crisis in the Aja part of the Yorùbá country where rebel factions displaced existing polities to establish what later became the Dahomey kingdom. With Dahomey renouncing the *ebi* system that ideologically ties the region and its people to Yorùbáland, with policies advanced toward this, Dahomey is hardly recognized as having its root in the Yorùbá civilization, with established links to Ife, sustained by Òyó hegemony.

93. Law, "Constitutional Troubles of Oyo," 25–44.

7

Mobility within West Africa

Introduction

I returned to Monrovia and decided to spend a day looking through the main market there. Normally, the market in African setting serves as an economic center for the buying and selling of all basic commodities and articles; a social center; a political center of some sort; a recreational center; a learning center; and, importantly, a communal center. It is also a center for measuring the pulse of the community. . . . For most of these reasons, my visit to the Monrovian main market was desirable. Unperturbed, undisturbed, and incognito, I walked my way through the market. I was savoring the sights, the pleasure, the cacophony, and the noise of the market when I heard a market woman hailing another market woman within shouting distance, saying, "Mama Fike, se e ni change nibe yen? (Fike's mother, can I get some small change from you?") It was as if I was in a market in any Yoruba town in Nigeria. It was an eye-opener for me, realizing how much Nigerians, particularly women, are part and parcel of the economy of all West Africa.[1]

If there is any one sentence that sums up the discussions in the preceding chapters, and judging from the image projected in the excerpt, it is Muhammad Mukhtar's analysis that trade and commerce are twin catalysts for cultural and societal transformation.[2] Since the ancient civilizations of Kush, Egypt, Nubia, Carthage, and Axum, African states have engaged in dynamic relations with their immediate and distant neighbors, with trade and commerce driving these arrangements.[3] Hundreds of units of towns and settlements could be produced and reproduced from a single polity through migration and countermigration. However, through trade and commerce, contact is maintained, and other forms of relationships capable of facilitating cultural exchanges are forged.[4]

---

1. Obasanjo, *My Watch*, 230–31.

2. Mukhtar, *Ancient Civilizations of Africa (General History of Africa)*

3. Ibid.; Diop, *African Origin of Civilization.*

4. In the ancient Egyptian knowledge system, the Supreme Being, Amen-Ra, is a matter made of Nun with the immense capacity to reproduce itself in various forms. Saakana, *African Origins*; Ajayi, *General History of Africa VI.*

If markets unified disparate peoples and places of commerce, politics and social exchange encapsulate all these through different organs and structures of the state. Of course, at the center of this is the question of migration. Migration facilitates trade and state formation. The concern here would only be the distance of migration, which, in turn, influences the economic nature of the people. Since time immemorial, groups and individuals have migrated from one place to another in search of political stability and economic prosperity. These often go hand-in-glove; a politically stable entity is usually a harbinger of economic growth and prosperity that attracts several categories of migrants far and near.[5] Parts of the discussions in the previous chapters have shown how this reinforced the dominance and collapse of the Old Oyo. It is in this light that one must recall the role of geography in this history. Geography determined the patterns not only of trade but also of migration. Migrant laborers moved to places where their services were needed,[6] just as traders traveled to both near and distant lands to locate their market interests.[7] This meant a shortage of supply and consequent demand for their goods and services in these markets.

Not all migrations were related to commerce. Mobilization for war, hunting, and decongestion of existing polities all drove these dynamics as well. Anything aside from this, people migrated as they tried to escape situations that posed threats to their well-being and livelihood. This could be internal political wrangling, external attack/invasion, and natural disasters, common among which were drought and famine that produced abysmal harvests.[8] While these forms of migration persist till contemporary times, new trends have emerged, as seen in migration by social networks. This explains the ubiquitous presence of Yorùbá migrants in West Africa and the swelling of this population wherever they are located. In search of a habitable home where they could reproduce their customs and traditions, Yorùbá migrants have, over time, stretched the boundary of their homelands from different points in the present southwestern part of Nigeria to present-day West African states that include Benin, Togo, Côte d'Ivoire, Sierra Leone, Gambia, Liberia, and Ghana.

Mobility within the West African region has been a recurrent phenomenon in the evolution of cultures, peoples, and polities.[9] Before the boundary demarcations that resulted in the emergence of colonial states, transportation of goods and the movement of peoples within West Africa had been seen as a form of mobility within a single community, not necessarily in terms of political rights but economic opportunities and social freedom.[10] No restriction was placed on trade, even though modern arrangements of taxes and customs duty were also put in place, among other things, to assert the sovereignty of the state.[11]

---

5. Yandaki, *State in Africa*.

6. Coffee, cocoa, cotton, and other farm products, as well as construction sites and mining fields, pulled the highest numbers of this migrant population across West Africa. Hopkins, *Economic History of West Africa*.

7. Hopkins, *Economic History*.

8. Bangura, *Falolaism*, 63.

9. Bangura, *Falolaism*, 162.

10. Ajayi, "Towards an African Economic Community," 298–299.

11. Falola, *African Diaspora*; Ikime, *Can Anything Good Come out of History?*; Ajayi, "Towards a More Enduring Sense of History," 1–3; Ajayi, *History and the Nation*.

Migration has been made possible by leveraging social networks of communal or familial relations in which a member of a community or family invites other relatives to partake in the opportunities offered by their new location. Additionally, the abolition of the slave trade played a significant role in redirecting African captives from the Americas and Europe, rerouting slave cargoes to the peninsula of the newly established farmlands in Sierra Leone for resettlement. These developments saw the swelling of the Yorùbá community and mobility in the West African region. Affirming the logic of the free movement of persons and goods that existed among states in the region during the precolonial days, the regional body Economic Community of West African States (ECOWAS) has set measures in place to reactivate the region as a community of peoples from its postcolonial structure of a community of states. In other words, article 27 of the treaty establishing the commission is aimed at creating a platform for closer people-to-people relations, community citizenship, and integration through free migration across the region.[12] How far this goes in terms of implementation depends on the political will of states. In the meantime, however, through both legal and illegal social networks, Yorùbá migrants have continued to increase their stake in West African mobility; in the process, they have contributed substantially to the economy of this region of over three hundred million people. This chapter historicizes this migration trend of Yorùbá people across West Africa, and patterns and implications of this on transnational Yorùbá form are explored.

Mobility across this region has faced major transformations over time with implications for the pattern it exhibits. This includes the trading routes, items of trade, mode of engagement, and spatial differences. Therefore, while the chapter on Oyo heterogeneity sheds insights into the production of the Yorùbá community in the Atlantic, discussions here are framed at locating their presence in the West Africa region.

Trade, Commerce, and Migration

From Oyo, Ijebu, and Ilesa to Osogbo and later Ibadan and Abeokuta, Yorùbá traders had organized themselves in caravans for long-distance trading across West Africa, reaching places like Mali.[13] Effectively dominating the trading engagements of the region, within and without, were Oyo merchants who controlled about half of the whole of Yorùbá country, including the Egbado, Ibolo, and Ìgbomina regions. By so doing, the Old Oyo produced the highest number of Yorùbá merchants in West African markets, so much so that other Yorùbá traders in the entourage were identified with Oyo.[14] Again, as with the question of Yorùbá and their neighbors, the issue of mobility of the Yorùbá people in West Africa must be understood from the colonial context of the production of boundaries that characterize this region and the states. Before the colonial demarcations, for instance, many parts that constitute the present Benin Republic were polities under the influence of the Old Oyo, like little parts of Togo and Ghana. Correspondingly, the level of interaction that existed among precolonial West African states

---

12. Adepoju, "Creating a Borderless West Africa," 161–173.

13. Falola, "Yoruba Caravan System," 111–132.

14. Law, *Contemporary Source Material.*

   GLOBAL YORÙBÁ

ensured the free flow of trade, ideas, and people across cultures.[15] The pattern of Yorùbá trade, especially with its transnational dimension, speaks somewhat to a syndicated business morphology.

This was only as crude and advanced as the societies that evolved through the unveiling of their inherently latent capitalist forms. Yorùbá traders were not short of the type of ideas that produced the European syndicates that stole their profits and created trading imbalances. What they lacked was the capability to meet the financial strength of European syndicates. The fundamental factors influencing this imbalance were the economic structures that produced both. Whereas Yorùbá syndicates had emerged only through family and communal means of generating capital, such as loans and contributions through the *èsúsú* (thrift society), pawn systems, progressive unions, cooperative societies, rotational joint contributions, and household financial donations—a pattern that has continued well into the colonial and postcolonial era—European businesses and syndicates were bankrolled by European banking systems and their home states.[16] As in other African polities, access to banks and bank loans did not emerge among the Yorùbá people until the colonial period, and even then, the system was skewed against the people to favor European merchants because these were European banks established to protect European interests.[17]

The different capitalist inclinations between Europeans and Yorùbá affected the participation of Yorùbá merchants in West African trade as the big companies took the place of African states and peoples in the construction and dictates of commerce. As many local artisans could not compete with these companies or against foreign goods and items, a new pull of migrant populations was produced by the colonial state. Compounding the economic situation that fed the pull of labor migrants in the region during this period were the two world wars. The earlier abolition of the slave trade and the return of African slaves back to Africa meant a pull of labor to service the growing industries in Europe. As Francois Manchuelle puts it, "The most important phenomenon following slave emancipation in West Africa was not a definitive exodus of slaves away from their regions of captivity, but their entry into periodic migration as a means to economic and social advancement."[18]

Against the humanitarian conditions given for the abolition of the trade in human cargo by Eurocentric apologists, Africanist scholars have argued for the political-economic considerations that propelled the abolition act.[19] The pull of labor for farm production no longer existed at the height of the industrial revolution in Europe. If anything, such a labor force was only relevant to the extent to that it could contribute to the growth of these industries at little cost and responsibility for the European merchants and the states. Two factors were involved in promoting abolition: the decongestion of European capitals and the production of a labor and consumer force in Africa. By effect, these returnees were to be the archetypal figures in the evolving African polities, even if only by implication and not necessarily by design. Their

---

15. Adepoju, "Creating a Borderless West Africa."

16. Skinner, "West African Economic Systems," 77–88.

17. Lawal, *Nigeria Culture*, 165–194.

18. Manchuelle, "Slavery, Emancipation and Labour Migration," 100.

19. Omasanjuwa and Phebean, "Acrimony in Colonial Liberia," 1–38.

presence in Africa was instrumental to the sale of European culture in the region through their lifestyle and promotion of signifiers of Western civilization. Everywhere they migrated, as Manchuelle mentioned, they carried along with them their hybridized culture: their items of trade were usually manufactured products from Europe, and their culture was a blend of Western and African taxonomies.

Cultures transform along the lines of trade and trading items since these are intrinsic carriers of the cultural productions of civilizations. To this end, the British government led a negotiation with the local chiefs in Sierra Leone for the purchase of a large peninsula. In 1822, President James Monroe of the United States, after whom the Liberian capital, Monrovia, was named, negotiated a deal that would lead to the repatriation of freed African American slaves. The first set of returnees from the first negotiations, numbering about four hundred, arrived in the newly acquired acres of land that would become Freetown in 1787.[20] This was followed by several other waves of returnees, many of whom could not survive the conditions of the peninsula. The steady and conspicuous presence of this population in West Africa began to take hold about five years after, in 1793, when slaves from Nova Scotia in the settler state of Canada were relocated.[21] Although there is no evidence that Yorùbá people were among these first waves of returnees, they formed a formidable portion of later returnees, between the 1830s and 1880s, both in Sierra Leone and Liberia. This period is even more particular in the case of Liberia, owing to what has been described as the nineteenth-century internecine wars and political instability in Yorubaland.[22]

Although not the only repatriated population in their West African state, the Yorùbá were inherently able to use their culture and traditions as an agency for a peculiar form of visibility that reinforced their dominance in these states. This is so in the case of the Aku in Sierra Leone, who relegated the earlier returnees who regarded themselves as superior to all other sociocultural groups in the country. Study of this population provides another level of understanding of the mobility of Yorùbá people across West Africa. Consequent upon their activities, together with this population, was the colonial reordering of the socioeconomic and political space of African states and that of the Yorùbá country. During this period the trading pattern of the country was liberated, as young men and women could now engage in trading activities of their own, not necessarily those sanctioned by familial heritage. The introduction of wage labor further changed the characterization of production among the people and expanded their participation in trade.[23] As the need for manual labor on European farms and capital was declining, it was in steady demand in Africa.

Massive regimes of slave labor for economic production were used throughout the nineteenth century in this region. Colonization, however, came with the demand for civilization and modernization, which were nothing more than European universalism. In this context, rhetorically, this meant that, as in Europe, the world had reached the age where all human beings were to be dignified and treated as free men and women. Pawnship and slavery had

---

20. Bassia, "Marriage Rites Among the Aku," 251–256.

21. Bassia, "Marriage Rites Among the Aku."

22. Law, "Constitutional Troubles in Ọyọ," 25–44; Akinjogbin, Abiodun, and Adebayo, *War and Peace in Yorubaland*.

23. Freund, *Making of Contemporary Africa*.

provided the pull of labor to fill the void of those drawn from within their families and these practices were condemned and criminalized by the colonial government. Many with big farms, usually nobles, were by the later nineteenth century dependent on slave labor.[24] The abolition and criminalization of slavery in Yorubaland, as in other places, marked the beginning of migrant labor mobility in West Africa.[25]

The opening of trade along the Atlantic route had expanded the economies of precolonial African states in ways that built on previous contact with the Arab world along the Saharan route.[26] This trade activity was incompatible with the economic transformations of the colonial period. The economic opportunities of this new era were responsible for the rate at which the individual elements of the communal bonds of the society became conspicuous. Both slaves and the freeborn demanded wage labor as well as participation in the emerging trading schemes. New opportunities were created by revolutions in the transportation industry. A journey of months was reduced to a few days with the use of lorries and, later, other forms of automobiles. Not only did this save time, but faster transportation also ensured a better turnover, as goods and communication crisscrossed destinations more swiftly. These changes in the flow of commerce gave rise to a class of Yorùbá traders that did not need to rely on the caravan traders of the nineteenth century. In many cases, however, trade mobility during this period was premised on preexisting networks now under reconstitution by the colonial project, which meant new trading opportunities that could be navigated through historical and social ties.[27] Some traders also invested in the transportation industry. While this was successful and became a big industry for the Yorùbá community in Côte d'Ivoire, the reverse was the case in Ghana, where they faced challenges related to the conduct of their employees, drivers in particular. With the new transportation system came new trade routes and the emergence of new markets and market cities.

Two basic migration patterns along the West African trading corridor have been identified by scholars. According to Abner Cohen, "At one end are migrants who form only segmental, temporary, tribal groupings. At the other end are migrants who form autonomous, multipurpose tribal communities."[28] The former occurred where trade and mobility by Yorùbá people across West African states had begun long before the colonial period through the activities of caravan traders. Goods were taken from Yorùbá country to other places across West Africa; there they were traded for other products, which were in turn sold on the migrants' way back home or in their communities. From this pendulum trend, which aided short-term investment, they made their returns from where they reinvested for another trip.[29] Such a trip was usually taken during the dry season that comes after the period of harvest. In many cases, it was through the farm products from their communities that they entered the regional trade. The colonial reconfiguration of polities in this region and the consequent increase in participation

---

24. Falola, *Political Economy*.

25. Pecoud and De Guchteneire, *Migration without Borders*.

26. Ajayi and Alagoa, "Nigeria before 1800," 224–235.

27. Manchuelle, "Slavery, Emancipation and Labour Migration," 94.

28. Cohen, "Politics of the Kola Trade," 18.

29. Cohen, "Politics of the Kola Trade," 18.

and frequency of mobility of persons, goods, and services along this West African corridor changed this trading landscape. Expressly in this arrangement, the colonial state strengthened the process of job specialization already taking effect in society.

Over time the organization of trade and other activities became less dependent on agriculture. Many moved out of farming to engage in trading and other emerging sources of livelihood. Communities that produced farm products became rural areas and were depopulated as the labor force moved into other aspects of the economy.[30] In most cases, traders were traders, railway workers worked in their stations, and migrant laborers worked in their employers' fields. In some cases, however, though farming was no longer attractive to the new generation, it was still combined with other occupations but at a lower scale, irrelevant to the organization and calendar of the emerging cities where most workers resided. Consequently, long-distance trading activities were conducted regardless of the season. Markets expanded, and the trading routes became busier. This ended in the second phase of the development identified by Rouch, where these immigrants began to take up residence in other West African countries where they conducted their trade. Some became produce agents for multinationals and hired laborers, while others became traders of cloths and other goods.

Individuals and groups who had decided to remain outside of their homestead were fond of inviting their kinsmen to their new homes for economic reasons and for the continued reproduction of their traditions and culture. They established themselves within the communal frame of their kinsmen in their homestead. Whatever structure they evolved, which, until recently, was placed within the prism of gerontocracy, provided social security for its members. The difference at this time was the frequency with which individuals were placed at the center of this migration and the pattern of integration into their host communities.

Until the 1930s, Yorùbá cloth merchants only went to transact and return to Nigeria to prepare for another trip. The increase in the demand for Yorùbá clothes in the quasi-state, especially after World War I, made the West African colony a point of attraction to many Yorùbá traders. *Àdìrẹ, kampala,* and *aṣọ-òkè* were among the Yorùbá fabrics in demand, to which Yorùbá traders from Ogbomoso, Osogbo, Abeokuta, Iwo, Ejigbo, and elsewhere responded, swelling the presence of Yorùbá people in this location and the frequency of trade along the Nigeria–Ghana corridor. The effect of this increase was the emergence of a Yorùbá community in Tamale. Tamale was at this time the preferred destination of Yorùbá migrants due to its status as a promising urban city with basic amenities and infrastructure, both military and civil. This ensured that Tamale was as secure as it was economically viable. Virtually all the large corporations and companies in the country, which were, of course, owned by Europeans, had their branches in the city of Tamale.

Here, Yorùbá labor migrants came to look for jobs in factories, mining fields, construction sites, coffee plantations, and other emerging fields of labor. This came in addition to those who engaged in trading activities like purchasing produce and selling tires, clothes, slippers, and home accessories. Almost a decade after the economic decline in the country and the consequent return of some Yorùbá immigrants, they are said to have constituted three thousand of

---

30. Mabogunje, *Urbanization in Nigeria.*

Figure 7.1. "Road Travels" by Dr. Kazeem Ekeolu. Road travel has been the most common in the region since the twentieth century. In previous centuries, head porterage was the most visible.

the sixty thousand people in Tamale by 1969.[31] Similarly, of the estimated fifty-five thousand Nigerians in Côte d'Ivoire in the mid-1950s, 85 percent were not only Yorùbá but of Ejigbo origin. As in the old migrations, Yorùbá immigrants in these West African countries were propelled by the economic opportunities provided through the government's policies of each period of their immigration.

From their newly constituted West African base in Sierra Leone and Liberia, Yorùbá returnees and recaptives, like their kinsmen in other West African states, grouped themselves into a cluster of people with shared traditions, culture, and heritage.[32] In the former, they became known

---

31. Eades, "Kingship and Entrepreneurship," 169.
32. Falola and Akinyemi, "Introduction," 4.

as Aku. Owing to the magnitude of displaced populations produced in nineteenth-century Yorubaland, which coincides with the abolition of the slave trade, many of this population were recaptives whose slave ships had been diverted to Sierra Leone for embarkation instead of their Atlantic destinations. On a single trip in 1833, virtually all the 523 captives on board a Cuban slave ship, Manuelta, intercepted by the joint British-French naval patrol, were either from Yorubaland or of Yorùbá origin.[33] Between this period and the bombardment of Lagos in 1851, several thousands of Yorùbá captives were on board the apprehended slave ships that landed either in Sierra Leone or Liberia in West Africa—that is, if not indentured to the Caribbean.[34] The sociopolitical conditions in Yorùbá country were responsible for driving the trade from the beginning of the nineteenth century, leading to the forceful displacement of the population around the world. Their numerical strength, coupled with their enterprising and adventurous delight, became responsible for their domination of trade and politics of the country.

In the later years, with cross-cultural blend and identity infused into the Aku identity from other returnees and recaptives, they were referred to as Kreole. This was after their exploits in trade, economy, and politics of the country forced some of the earlier returnees from Nova Scotia, in particular, to go back to the Americas. They could not bear sharing status with those regarded as primitive. Despite the broadening of the Aku identity to encompass other cultures making up the Kreole, Yorùbá and Western elements dominated the cultural form. Most of this population was divided between Christianity and Islam but used Yorùbá cultural agency to make their mark and thread the sociopolitical and economic space. This population was also referred to as Okun. The difference is very evident in the circumstance of their return. Those from the Americas were either Catholics, as in the Agudas from Brazil, or had joined the emerging Protestant movements of the Anglican, Baptist, and others. Those who identified with Islam were primarily the recaptives. The Yorùbá community in Sierra Leone held about three identities: Aku, Okun, and Kreole. Although English is adopted as the official language of the state, Kreole is widely spoken as a national language, even though the Kreole population constitutes only about 4 percent of the population.[35]

While other returnees and recaptured slaves brought to Sierra Leone left Fourah Bay, their place of arrival, to other towns in the country, Yorùbá elements of the population stayed back. From there, some of the people, especially the Muslims among them, launched through the waters to Senegambia, where they again flourished. Some of this population also left Sierra Leone for their Nigerian homes. The bulk of this population was from Egba, a large cluster of villages and towns now in Abeokuta. It was in this location that those who returned met them as they were removed from the Egba forest by the same series of events that culminated in their enslavement.[36] Once they were able to get information about the new location, and the affair of their kinsmen, some of the returnees directed their social networks to return home. Others

---

33. Ojo, "Slave Ship Manuelita," 360–382.

34. As Omasanjuwa wrote about this period, "Between 1821 and 1867, during the era of the abolition of slave trade, about 13,000 slaves rescued from the high seas joined the Liberian settlement." See Omasanjuwa and Phebean, "Acrimony in Colonial Liberia," 4.

35. Ogundayo, "Diaspora," 92.

36. Curtin, *Africa Remembered*.

were from Oyo, and on their return to the homeland, they found their new homes in the emerging cities, especially Lagos.

The Yorùbá community in this West African country was at the highest echelon of society, especially in trade. With some arrangements facilitated by their kinsmen or organized for them by the government of Sierra Leone, this afforded many of them the security to pass through Nigeria unscathed. In their new homestead of Abeokuta, these returnees were referred to as Egba Saro, indicating their subcultural identity among the Yorùbá returnees from Sierra Leone. Dominating the Yorùbá Saro identity, aside from the Egba, were the Ìjẹ̀sà. Some of these returnees stayed in Badagry or Lagos, while others moved on to Ibadan and Iléṣà. Anywhere they were located during this period, they were agents of change, transformation, and Westernization. Following their return, they established a trading route between the Yorùbá country and Sierra Leone. Those that returned to their homelands kept in touch with their Sierra Leonean contacts. Communication between those that remained in Sierra Leone and their kinsmen in Nigeria was also opened, as people from places like Abeokuta, Lagos, Badagry, and Ibadan visited their kinsmen and vice versa.

Yorùbá Migrants and the Challenges of West African Mobility

In the course of increased contact with European markets, items of trade along West African markets by Yorùbá traders evolved from farm products, textiles, metals, and craftworks to industrial products mainly imported from Europe. In Côte d'Ivoire, Yorùbá migrants, dominated by Ejigbo traders, took advantage of the influx of French products into the country to become middlemen. The open market economy of the state not only facilitated the French market on its streets but also enhanced the participation of immigrants who were given the same civil rights as Ivoirians. Attaining citizenship status gave Yorùbá immigrants the legal boost to conduct their activities and expand their reach in the state's economy.[37] The question of the motive for the migration choice of the Yorùbá people in places where they are found today in West Africa is a genuine one that falls back on the economic viability of the host country. For instance, ordinarily, it is quite unthinkable to describe Côte d'Ivoire as the "capital" of the Ejigbo community in Nigeria in the face of proximity, culture, and language. Ejigbo is a Yorùbá town in present-day Osun State.

Until the fall of the Old Oyo, it was under the control of the Aláàfin; after this period, it fell under the Ibadan before the British colonial conquest. Although Yorùbá traders were involved in long-distance trade, their relations with and presence in Côte d'Ivoire were minimal. There are little or no historical ties that bind these two communities other than the colonial trade. The story is a bit different in the case of Ghana, Benin, and Togo, where Yorùbá merchants had established long-term relations with the people. Indeed, parts of these modern states were under the suzerainty of the Old Oyo. But then, as in other West African countries where they are found, history and historical links are not enough to secure the well-being of the people. Aside from familial links, this opened the route to Sierra Leone and the frequency with which

---

37. Adeniran, "Migration and Integration of Ejigbo-Yoruba," 144–157.

this route was serviced by Yorùbá migrants. What is common to this trend is the economic opportunities offered by these countries at various times through their economic policies and infrastructural developments.[38]

These two—policy and infrastructure—affected the place they reside in these countries. This is usually the center of market and trade, equipped with necessary modern structures that make possible the ease of conducting one's business. Hence, the choice of Abidjan, Tamale, Accra, and Monrovia, among other West African cities and capitals. But this did not come without its challenges. They faced both healthy and toxic competition, first with the Indigenous peoples of these places, then with other migrants of different cultural backgrounds. Although some successful Yorùbá traders were able to diversify their investment in Ghana after the post–World War II rush for Yorùbá clothes that began in the 1950s, they could not enter the foodstuff market, which was firmly controlled by the locals. At various times, they were perceived as a threat to the well-being and livelihood of their host communities. This is more so in the face of limited resources, which ironically and unfortunately became the common theme of post-colonial African states. Postcolonial disillusionment vis-à-vis the euphoria of independence was ubiquitous in Africa.[39] And at various times, when this reaches its crescendo, migrant communities become the target of the Indigenous peoples, as they are accused of hijacking limited resources.

Regardless of their ethnicities or cultural orientations, Yorùbá or not Yorùbá, migrants are usually prone to taking the lead in the economy of the state where they reside. The case of the Yorùbá in these cities is only well pronounced because of their sheer number, organizational strength, and wealth, which made them a formidable force among other migrant communities. No sooner had Ghana gained independence than the country began to slide into several crises. The first effect of this on the Yorùbá community in the country was the demand for their much sought-after clothes, since the economic downturn meant limited purchasing power of potential consumers. This signaled the beginning of the crisis to be faced by the Yorùbá community in the newly independent state. With a dwindling economy and the low purchasing power of the population, divestment was even riskier. Many Yorùbá migrants lost their investment and joined the wage labor pull, while others simply returned home—that is, to Nigeria. As the economic situation worsened, the expulsion of migrants became an official state policy under the Alien Compliance Order and Exodus of 1969.[40] The tone and effects of the order betray the very fundamental ideals that birthed the Ghanaian state—Pan-Africanism—in every respect.

This was a country that for decades was among the top destinations for migrants, especially migrant labor, in West Africa. The postcolonial disillusionment reflected in the case of Ghana sent many in the Yorùbá community packing their things, with some selling their properties for relocation. Decades later, it was the turn of the Ghanaians in Nigeria, mostly domiciled in the southwestern home of the Yorùbá people in the country, to be sent home due to the economic crisis of the 1980s. By this time, many Ghanaians fleeing the wanton condition of their country had migrated to Nigeria, especially during the oil boom of the 1970s.

---

38. Shack and Skinner, *Strangers in African Societies*.

39. Adebanwi and Obadare, *Encountering the Nigerian State*.

40. Ogundayo, "Diaspora," 92.

In Côte d'Ivoire, where the hospitality of the people is regarded as one of the essential pull factors for Yorùbá migrants, the relationship between economic reality and the host community's attitude toward migrants was no different. As it appears, Ivoirians pursued the project of migrants' expulsion from their country with the same vigor with which they welcomed them. The Yorùbá community was particularly affected by this, owing to the social capital they had acquired over the years, which had translated to some political power, and they remained relevant in the economic production of their host state. During the millennium political crises that ravaged the country, first with the military coup that opened this new era and then the subsequent events that culminated in election crises and power tussles among major political powers in the state, Yorùbá migrants were made the scapegoat by Ivoirians. Due to their economic prowess and social networks, their detractors believed they had contributed to each of the crises either by commission or omission.[41]

This trend, as first seen in Ghana in the 1960s and later in Nigeria in the 1980s, signaled a precursor to the later rise of xenophobic attacks in South Africa. It is in this context, especially as adumbrated in the extreme twist of events of the Ivoirians in the latter years, that such attacks should be seen for their economic undercurrent. Crisis of this nature subsists at an intermittent level today in West Africa, especially in Ghana, with a palpable threat to the ECOWAS protocol on the free movement of people and goods across the region.[42] But this is not the only challenge to the community of people's vision and project of the regional body, even though this cost the migrants their property, investments, and livelihood.

Following the independence of states in West Africa, several measures were put in place, building on the colonial structure, for the continued interaction among these nascent states.[43] The level of interaction across this divide during the colonial period was minimal, as each colonial power operated an exclusive policy of their area of influence, adopting different policies to run their colonies and ensure maximum exploitation.[44] It was in a bid to recalibrate this amorphous structure and bring the people of the region back to the precolonial ties that the ECOWAS commission was formed in 1975 following years of negotiations and experimentations. Trading routes were rerouted by the colonial government to link colonies that fell within their area of influence for better administration. This meant that the pattern of mobility across the region had gradually changed in conformity with the modern system of migration.

Whereas traders and other migrant groups have always been in the practice of paying tolls to each sovereign territory they crossed and taxes on traded goods for the merchants, the colonial states "redeemed" this structure through the introduction of customs duties, police systems, and cash economies. Consequent to the postcolonial states in this region, this very structure became the first obstacle migrants experienced on their way through this new world of transnational trade. Several reports by migrants navigating this corridor are clear by the extortion, double charges, and unnecessary delays caused by the security architecture of these states.[45]

---

41. Raji and Adebayo, "Yoruba Traders in Cote D'Ivoire," 134–147.

42. Adepoju, "Migration in West Africa."

43. Ajayi, "Towards an African Economic Community."

44. Akinjogbin, *Western Yorubaland under European Rule.*

45. Barka, "Border Posts," 6.

This promoted a substantial network of illegal migration in the region as traders attempted to bypass the corrupt state legal structure and make more profit from their transactions. As such, despite the challenges of this regional trade and migration, the Benin–Nigeria border remains the busiest in the region, with hundreds of Nigerian migrants, mostly traders, navigating this corridor daily, legally, and otherwise.

This history highlights the huge gap that exists between the ratification of treaties, protocols, and agreements and their implementation. In the most recent case, the alien Nigerian community in Ghana, which is populated by migrants of Igbo and Yorùbá groups, had their rights stifled by the Ghanaian government and faced threats of deportation. Whereas the government had cloaked this in a legal toga as it accused these migrants of nonconformity with the legal framework that allowed aliens to trade in the country, not few are convinced that this measure was taken in a bid to assuage the economic strains hitting the host communities hard. The reason given comes as an incarnation of Kofi Abrefa Busia's expulsion notice of 1969, where the "alien" community was required to seek stay permits in the country within two weeks or face deportation. Busia was the president of Ghana when the Alien Compliance Order was charged by the state, and his template has been used in executing these plans in the subsequent years.

In any case, however, the trend that began with Yorùbá migrants of the colonial period in the 1830s when they began to take up residence in the country and forge a community of people, had continued unabated in the postcolonial state, although this time around with stock of other Nigerian cultural groups, especially the Igbos, joining them in taking the advantage offered them by the market and government policies. In his account of the subject, J. S. Eades writes, "The town had two main markets: The older central markets was the main stronghold of the Yoruba traders; a third of the 700 stalls owned by the Tamale council were rented by Yoruba, and a further 200 Yoruba had built stalls for themselves on land allocated by the council."[46]

As they continued to own more stores and dominated the market, ostensibly to the detriment of the Indigenous Ghanaians, Yorùbá communities became the target of xenophobic attacks. Meanwhile, their kinsmen in Côte d'Ivoire were equally making waves in the economic and sociopolitical spheres, even long after the former had reached the point of decline in its influence. The community remained a formidable force in the post–military coup crisis in the country, a situation that first led to their own "Alien Compliance Order and Exodus." What we see here is a case where the Yorùbá community in Côte d'Ivoire was, and still is, not only an extension of their various primordial homelands in southwestern Nigeria but more essentially in the case of the Ejigbo people who constitute the majority in the community population, the country shares the signifier of their cultural and historical heritage with the southwestern home of the global Yoruba community. In the absence of a viable Nigerian state that is responsive to their concerns, both the Ejigbo community in Nigeria and Côte d'Ivoire regard this Francophone country as their capital.

---

46. Eades, "Kingship and Entrepreneurship," 169.

Figure 7.2. Yorùbá markets are as old as the people. Markets have been a site of power and commerce and were mostly sited close to the traditional ruler's palace. They were mostly dominated by women who controlled and regulated the activities within. The *Iyaloja* is the most senior-ranking member within the social hierarchy of any Yorùbá market. From the Toyin Falola Private Collection.

Even though the routes and pattern of migration across this region have evolved with time, elements of the old still subsist. On the one hand, it is the organization of transportation, on the other, the operation of trade. Migrants still bond themselves in groups like the caravans as they meet for the sojourn at a place generally known to all on a designated day of the week. Like the old caravans, this allowed for a more organized communal trading network in which traders shared the burdens of the journey. Despite the revolution in the transportation industry of this region, journeys through places like Côte d'Ivoire take days of tedious labor, even though these migrants were seated in a bus.

Much of this population travels by road. The trade is organized in such a way that Yorùbá migrants from these countries, especially where they have substantial numerical strength, with a long distance to cover, like Côte d'Ivoire, travel to Nigeria for various purposes in groups, mostly for visitation and trade, and usually return in the same manner. Ibadan and Lagos constitute their popular point of departure and embarkation. From these cities, Ejigbo traders in Côte d'Ivoire, for instance, bought slippers, shoes, electronics, and other items of trade to be sold in Abidjan and other Ivorian cities as well as towns like Bassam, Marcory, Adjame, Port Bouet, and Temidire. Due to the special relations that exist between Ejigbo and Côte d'Ivoire, unlike other Yorùbá migrant communities in West Africa, there is constant communication, not only by mobile communication but travel, between these two. This explains why this community dominates the discourse on Yorùbá migrant community in the region with so much dynamism. Adding to this is the success they have recorded in their investments in the transportation industry, which is different from the scenario that played out among their kinsmen in Ghana.

Regardless of the expulsions and threats by Ivorians, in a 2008 hip-hop hit in the West African music industry, this community represented the theme of expression of wealth and affluence. Rajomovic eulogized Yorùbá big men in Abidjan, who mostly consist of Alhajis—a title for Muslims who have successfully made their pilgrimage to the Holy Land, Mecca. In the music video, the Ivorian artist could be seen popularizing the Yorùbá culture through fashion traditions. Depicting how successful this community has been in the country, many of these Alhajis are known to be younger—hence their popularity in the social circle of the country.

Other challenges faced by this community are related to the issue of currency and language. Whereas the latter could be said to have been surmounted through years of relations or residence in the host community and the adoption of the lingua franca of these states as a common medium of communication, it remains a challenge for newcomers. West Africa consists of states that recognize English, French, or Portuguese as their lingua franca. English and French share the highest stake in this language domination. Expressly, to transact in countries colonized by France, for instance, migrants from ex-British colonies must understand basic French words and terminologies, or at least have with them an interpreter, an option that limits their access to the market. In all the places where Yorùbá traders are located in West Africa, like other migrant communities, access to information is cardinal to their exploits. This networking demands that they rely not only on their kinsmen but on others outside of the community of their kinsmen.

Here, the lingua franca of the host country comes in as a unifying force. It is, therefore, a good measure of the integration of Yorùbá migrants into their host community. In addition to the language difference is currency. These two remained at the heart of trade and commerce anywhere in the world. As a community of multiple governments and fiscal regimes, migrants along the West African trade corridor remain in business through the constant exchange of currency. Language has always been a barrier in West African trade, as the old traders usually engaged the service of interpreters to conduct their trade; fiscal barrier epitomized in currency difference is a recent development that forms part of the colonial alterations of historical trading patterns.

Before this time, Yorùbá caravan traders and their counterparts across Africa transacted through a generally accepted medium of cowries.[47] By the twentieth century, the currency used in West Africa had shifted from the exchange of goods (the barter system), cowries, and coppers, all of which were standardized across the region, to European currencies regulated by the West African Currency Board, in the case of the British West African colonies where the condition of migration of Yorùbá traders and others was engineered.[48] While the former was dismantled for each sovereign state in the region to develop its fiscal policy, the structure remained in the former French colonies—the Francophone countries. This has continued as a medium of building a closer tie among these Francophone countries, on the one hand, and the French government, on the other.[49] In both cases, the arrangement has left the region polarized on the monetary note and fiscal policies.

The Yorùbá and West African Migration

One noticeable trend in Yorùbá mobility in West Africa is the level at which they were able to blend their culture and traditions with the evolving modern cultures and that of their host communities. In one instance, as in the case of the Aku in Sierra Leone, in their hybridized form, this community was able to use Yorùbá traditions and practices to dominate the cultural frame that became known as Creole. Largely, some of the members of these communities were either Christians or Muslims, a situation that comes in contrast to that of their kinsmen in the Americas for a few reasons. The making of a transnational Yorùbá community in Sierra Leone has been mentioned above to be in response to the 1807 abolition of the slave trade in European markets through the instrumentality of the British Parliament. In their homeland in present southwestern Nigeria, this was during the period when the Old Oyo Empire was in decline—unprecedented because until the seventeenth century, it had always been a battle for a stable polity, moving between dominance and devastation—with a spiral effect that counts on the sociocultural formation of the people.

Across the Atlantic, aspects of this population went through the process of acclimatization that has transformed them within Western cultural forms. Some of these returnees might have been converted to Christianity in Sierra Leone, given the different conditions in which religion and culture were used as an agency for social change and resistance in the two locations—the Americas and Sierra Leone. In their various locations in the Americas, Yorùbá captives, together with others from various parts of Africa, weaponized their culture and traditions as a bulwark for making their existence in this Atlantic world known to all, most importantly the slave masters, the imperial states, and the system bent on incarcerating them through the systemic denunciation of their culture.[50] It is here that the Old Oyo Empire resuscitated, culturally, and not in the West African community of Yorùbá migrants. Many vigorously resisted

---

47. Hopkins, *Economic History*.
48. Abdel-Salam, "Evolution of African Monetary Institutions," 339–362.
49. Abdel-Salam, "Evolution of African Monetary Institutions."
50. Shittu, "Ethnographic Reading," 187–204.

indoctrination into Christianity; instead, they converted Catholic symbols, practices, systems, and rituals into use within their Yorùbá belief system.[51] Acting under the social milieu in which they found themselves, this allowed for a kind of peculiar sociopolitical contest and negotiation in the Atlantic locations, a situation not present in Sierra Leone.

In fact, unlike in the Americas, where their thought process mattered not and their conversion to Christianity served them no better social status, these became the vehicle for social mobility in their new West African home.[52] Among these populations were the Aguda from Brazil in Yorùbá cities like Lagos, Iléṣà, and Abeokuta. Many others were Saro, some who never really crossed the West African waters before they were taken to Sierra Leone. Among them were those supposedly liberated but taken into another captivity in the newly acquired farm plantations in Trinidad and Tobago. Together with others whose affiliation to Yorùbá was only relative at the time due to Oyo's influence, this population forged a new Yorùbá community in Sierra Leone. Hence the hybridization of Creole with dominant Yorùbá and Western elements. As it was in the Atlantic world, and as it would soon be uncovered in their homeland, the former was used to pursue and navigate various aspects and structures of the latter such as religion, education, fashion, and language.

Back in the homeland, the process of social transformation that would shape the West African transnational Yorùbá community had begun with the increased relations between the Old Oyo and Hausa states: The presence of Bàrìbá to its western flank had prevented the spread of Islam from Mali and the Songhai Empire.[53] This process was exacerbated by a series of events within and without the Oyo Empire, among which was the influx of Hausa captives into the empire as a result of the jihad from the north, the Alimi factor, the increasing presence of Muslim Hausa merchants in Oyo markets and society, persistent contact between Muslim Hausa merchants/captives and their Yorùbá hosts, and the weakening of Oyo political hegemony, which was involuntarily ceded and decentralized among stronger Yorùbá polities like Ilorin, Abeokuta, Ijebu, and Ibadan.[54] In chapter 3, where the heterogeneity of the Old Oyo was discussed, mention was made of Oyo as the last central bastion of Odùduwà heritage.

It became clear in the nineteenth century that the Old Oyo polity was on to its final collapse, with tremendous effects on its economy. The people resorted to different means by which they could assuage their predicaments. This also gave adequate room for alternative opinions to thrive in the empire. Together with Hausa captives coming from the North were Arab clothes and objects.[55] The Muslim uprising of 1817, aided by the presence of Alimi, an Islamic cleric and Fulani warlord in Ilorin, speaks to how much ground Islam had gained in the Old Oyo in the early part of this century, when Yorùbá captives became ubiquitous in the trade.[56] The Yorùbá portion of loads of slaves embarked at the Lagos slave port, the largest at the time, was on an

51. Gonzalez-Wippler, *Powers of the Orishas.*

52. Pallinder-Law, "Aborted Modernization in West Africa?," 65–82.

53. This is contrasted by the position of scholars who date Islam in Yorubaland to the fourteenth century. See, for instance, Alade, "Examination of the Contributions of Muslim Clerics," 567.

54. Falola and Oguntomisin, *Military in Nineteenth Century Yoruba.*

55. Akinwunmi, "Oral Traditions," 59–60.

56. Akinjogbin, "Ọyọ Empire," 449–460; Falola and Childs, *Yoruba Diaspora in the Atlantic World.*

unprecedented level all through the early nineteenth century until the bombardment of Lagos in 1851 by British naval forces. Between this period, many made it to the Atlantic lands, as their ships were either successfully smuggled past the antislavery patrols or embarked during the early years of the abolition when the Lagos route was just coming into prominence with the attention of the antislavery squadron diverted to other West African ports.[57]

Others, like Samuel Ajayi Crowther, spent brief periods across the Atlantic before they were returned to Sierra Leone.[58] Aside from Islam, which some of the freed captives took along with them as part of their identity, none of this population was Christian at the time they were enslaved or recaptured for emancipation. Their Christian identity evolved in Sierra Leone, and from there, they influenced their kinsmen in their homelands. Owing to the presence of Europeans in this location, Christianity was favored above other religions, with a population that was more than 80 percent of the state's demography. However, the Yoruba/Aku Muslim population in this community, the Okun, swelled by Hausa and others, resisted this attempt. Some of this population soon found closer ties with the people of Senegambia (now Senegal and Gambia), who were predominately Muslims. Although culture had contributed to their closer ties, trade played a major role. Manufactured goods from Europe, like torches, umbrellas, shoes, and other items of luxury, were taken to this place by Creole traders, mostly the Okun section. With time, some of this population took residence in this location and have grown so well that, even though they constitute a minority in the state polity, about 2 percent of the population, they remain a force to be reckoned with in politics, the economy, and society. This community soon became the elite operating at the highest echelon of society and led the independence movement of the state.[59]

For fear of usurping the power and privileges of the Indigenous people of the Gambia, attempts to install a king among the people were met with stiff resistance from the government, admonishing them to concentrate on contributing to the economic growth of the country and respecting the traditions of the Indigenous people of the state.[60] On the other hand, their kinsmen, who had converted to Christianity and moved onward to their homelands in southwestern Nigeria, quickly created a new class of elites and social formation that would come to characterize the modernization of the society. Many from the Americas had been taught how to read and write; through their daily engagements with the Atlantic environment, they were acclimated to European ways of life.[61] The literacy process was a bit different in the case of their kinsmen, who were recaptives and never made it out of West Africa. While the former acquired literacy largely informally, the latter took a former frame in Sierra Leone. Religious literature in hymns and sermons, as well as in historical and cultural texts that open the Yorùbá world and heritage to the modern world, was essential to this process.[62]

---

57. Slave Voyages, "Trans-Atlantic Slave Trade Database"; Law, "Lagoonside Port," 32–59.

58. Curtin, *Africa Remembered*.

59. Gijanto, "Abolition and the Rise of the Aku."

60. Tine, "Gambia."

61. Cornelius, "'We Slipped and Learned to Read'" 171–186.

62. Falola, *Cultural Modernity*.

It is quite revealing that the opening of the Sierra Leonean route to their homelands in Nigeria, followed by their decision to return permanently to this place, opened a new vista for these experiences in Yorubaland.[63] Those that settled in Abeokuta brought with them the "modern" system and structure of government with which they organized the Egba polity and set the nascent town on the path of statehood. In a way, the constitutional monarchy under the Egba United Government and other experimental paradigms helped stabilize the rocky political terrain in the town of many polities and groups. In every respect, this population of the Yorùbá community in Sierra Leone brought with them Western culture and civilization, which transformed the social fabric of Yorubahood. Since the mid-1820s, this community in Sierra Leone has installed its kings and administered their affairs alongside other communities and the country at large.

In the long run and by implication, this development shaped subsequent Yorùbá mobility and community in the West African region. Matching with the Yorùbá identity in their respective West African communities took this hybridized landscape differently from what was obtainable among their kinsmen across the Atlantic.[64] Rooting their indoctrination in Western and Arabic cultures within the fundamentals of their organic culture brought with it the nuances in practice with which they were able to dominate the socioeconomic and political landscape of their host states and communities. For instance, while it is believed that married women would follow the purdah ritual in Islamic rites, thereby keeping them enclosed and shielded from public view, Yorùbá Muslim women seldom take to this practice. Among other things related to human rights and their ability to socialize, this practice goes without its huge economic deficit. The women were deprived of the right to make a living while they remained full-time housewives and mothers with many restrictive parameters set on their movement and conduct.[65]

This practice is contradicted by Yorùbá social values and principles that emphasized the dignity of labor for all levels of the social stratification of the society. One could quickly add that as against the Western gender model, Yorùbá women could rise to the highest echelon of society with this principle, as this traditionally accounts for their roles as priests, chiefs, respected traders, mothers, and wives.[66] In their positions regarding the last two, their ability to help formulate policies and steer the political waters of their communities through their sons and husbands cannot be divorced from their socioeconomic role as well. Among those on the caravans that routed West African markets were Ijebu, Oyo, Iléṣà, Ibadan, and Abeokuta women. They were engaged in short- and long-distance trade as *aláróbò* and *alájàpá*, respectively.[67] Since the caravan journey was taken during the dry season when farm work ceased, married women whose grown children could take care of the home and their husbands in their stead took parts of the farm harvest to these markets, while their husbands went hunting or engaged

---

63. Ajayi, *Christian Missions in Nigeria*.

64. Castor, *Spiritual Citizenship*.

65. For more on this, see Yusuf, "Purdah," 238–245.

66. Falola and Yacob-Haliso, *Gendering Knowledge in Africa*.

67. Sofela, *Ẹgba-Ijẹbu Relations*, 9.

in any other activities—hence, the form of Islam they practiced. The trend remains that Yorùbá women dominate West African migration.[68]

From the Gambia to Côte d'Ivoire, this gave Yorùbá households an advantage to leverage. These two countries have Muslim majorities, and it was possible to compete with their women in highly commercial trade, leaving room for Yorùbá migrant women to occupy. Yorùbá households in these places are structured in such a way that every member contributes to the wellbeing of the family by connecting in different ways to the business venture of the head of the family, which is usually the family business. The head of the family establishes a business enterprise, and the whole family is expected to rally around it, thereby producing a plethora of corporate family businesses among members of this community. In this way, the head of the family rents a stall; the wife takes a space in front of the stall where she sells stuff of her choice, while a relative who stays with them or their children is sent out to collect goods for the business and run other important errands; this serves as the relative's apprenticeship.[69] Shall one add that this structure is responsible for the rate at which this population has grown and expanded in their West African homes?

Starting their businesses was facilitated primarily by short-term credit facilities that included *èsúsú* (rotating credit associations), daily contribution collectors, communal contribution through town unions, reciprocal stall-minding that ensured that customers were connected to the stall of their fellow kinsmen, and leveraging on the social network and strength of their kinsmen.[70] Latter migrants, usually younger relatives who acted as assistants to their forebears, gained training and capital from their more established relatives. Through their wealth, they built places of worship, usually the first in such places as Gambia, Sierra Leone, and Côte d'Ivoire, where they worshipped and led the community of their faith. Their social networks were also used to help others outside of their community in these places. This further endeared them to other cultural communities, with some referred to as aliens. This was particularly the case with the molding of Creole in Sierra Leone. This community simply had the necessary social network to expand within other cultures and communities and form a new cultural body, as seen in Aku, Creole, Lucumi, Anago, and others on the two sides of the Atlantic.

This aside, they maintained the Yorùbá tradition of circumcision, naming, and wedding ceremonies. These, together with their mannerism, food culture, and fashion, would come to distinguish them in their West African homes. Even though they had to adopt the lingua franca of their host country, the Yorùbá language is mostly used as a medium of household and community communication. This explains the vivid picture painted in the chapter's opening excerpt. The feel within the community remains largely that of Yorubaland, bridging space and time in

---

68. Adepoju, "Creating a Borderless West Africa," 3.

69. Eades, "Kingship and Entrepreneurship," 174.

70. This constitutes one of the models through which the Yoruba sociological framework has been replicated in almost an exact form in West African states. In a typical example in their ancestral homeland, see Mbanga, "Utilization of Community-Based Association," 255–266. In a way, one could add this to the effect of the social milieu of their location on the extent to which diaspora Yoruba communities have reproduced Yoruba culture and philosophy, as this is contrasted from the organization and practice of the community in the Americas. Clarke, *Mapping Yoruba Networks*.

a linguistic and social atmosphere. Yet, their inoculation in the cultures of their host country offers a loop into transcultural exchanges across the region of West Africa. As catalysts for the rapid growth of the economy of Côte d'Ivoire, especially during the economic growth of the 1970s to 1980s, produce agents for multinationals; labor; and traders of clothes, shoes, and other accessories were from the Yorùbá community resident in the country.

Added to other fascinating experiences of members of this community with their hosts and host country, the people of Ejigbo, who dominate this community, have since deconstructed the notion of home and state in modern times. Back in their homeland, miles away in Nigeria, children communicate in French better than in English. English is the lingua franca of Nigeria but not of Ejigbo, at least informally. Further, Naira is the official Nigerian currency; aside from a few places in Nigerian cities, Ejigbo is about the only Nigerian community where CFA is recognized as a medium of transaction. A French learning center was established in Ejigbo, Nigeria in 1969 by Côte d'Ivoire–based Ejigbo indigenes. Interestingly, the inscription on the center's entrance—"learn French for better tomorrow"—is conspicuously indicative of the significance of such language to the functioning of the Ejigbo society as a whole, though English is the lingua franca in Nigeria.[71]

Learning French has proven to be a good path to the future of the people of the town as they migrate to the West African country at various stages of life. Deserted and most occupied by the frail and old, mostly women, the increasing intensity of the relations between Ejigbo and Côte d'Ivoire, despite the previous threats, can only be imagined. Like their kinsmen in other parts of West Africa, they have contributed substantially to foreign remittances flowing into their homeland; unlike these kinsmen, many of these remittances have gone into infrastructural projects that have remained empty and without correlating activities worth their value. As early as the 1960s, the presence of the Yorùbá population in Côte d'Ivoire had increased tremendously; a Yoruba-Abidjan Traders Association was formed for the operation of Yorùbá traders and others in the city. In the 1980s, when the economic growth of the country was still on the rise, they established the Yoruba-Abidjan International Transport Union. This made their investment in the industry secure with yielded interest in profits, unlike their Yorùbá kinsmen in Ghana.

The frequency at which this route was also traveled tells of the success they had in the business. This population is scattered in towns like Bassam, Marcory, Port Bouet, Adjame, and others, with a heavy concentration in Abidjan. Innovatively, as in the North Carolina Oyotunji Village in the United States, this community has since coined for themselves, and of course, for other interested parties, a community they called Temidire. In furtherance to this practice and paradigm of reproducing the Yorùbá sociological frame in their respective abodes outside their ancestral homes, Yorùbá in Hastings, Waterloo, and Benguema—the three dominant Aku communities in Sierra Leone—began appointing a king in the mid-1820s.[72] Several decades after, this stride was replicated in Abobo-Abidjan by their kinsmen.

---

71. Adeniran, "Migration and Integration of Ejigbo-Yoruba," 152.
72. Fyle, "Yoruba Diaspora in Sierra Leon's Krio Society," 369.

Conclusion

Trade, migration, livelihood, and geophysical fixtures can be easily identified from the above as constituting the industrial complex that produced human relations and reproduced their legacies. The changing dynamics of societal formation during the colonial period transformed the pattern of migration of Yorùbá migrants across West Africa. Meanwhile, as a major event in the political implosions of the nineteenth century in the region, the massive displacement of the Yorùbá population from their ancestral homes to places across the Atlantic, as well as on transit to these locations, created a viable ground for the dictate of these migrations. Until the return of these populations to their ancestral homeland in present southwestern Nigeria to influence the sociology and history of the people, the common identity frame with which these communities have been discussed in this chapter was, at best, only in the building process.[73]

Through the instrumentality of the printing press, media, and literacy, they brought about what could be referred to as the first known case of "brain remittance" in the history of Yorubaland. It was in this pursuit that they went from being Anglophiles to Anglophobes, using their Yorùbá culture as an agency for resisting European cultural imposition and characterization of the people.[74] Splendid as the pattern of Yorùbá migrants along the West African trading corridors could be, it is worth noting that, as with other parts of Africa, it is not as robust, at least in the financial sense, as the traffic outside the region. Fundamentally, this speaks to the veritable role of the condition of livelihood and other factors mentioned above in the making of migrant populations. However, it can only be expected that with the ratification of the African Continental Free Trade Agreement by West African governments and their counterparts in other regions of the continent, the trend will be boosted in the coming years. This expectation will imply looking away from the saggy full takeoff of the West African free movement agreement and other extant measures of regional integration within the region and others on the continent. With improved economic conditions in the region, Yorùbá migrants are expected to experience a less xenophobic atmosphere.

As this chapter has shown, unlike the mobility across West Africa, the presence of the Yorùbá community in the Americas has been sustained partly by the reproduction of Yorùbá metaphysical thoughts and their cosmologies. This discussion is explored in further detail in the next section.

---

73. The "idea of describing all the subgroups as Yoruba and using a standard orthography is one of the principal achievements of the nineteenth century Yoruba intelligentsia." Falola, "Yoruba Town Histories," 67.

74. Osuntokun and Oloruntimehin, "J. F. Ade Ajayi and His Intellectual Contribution."

PART 2

The Yorùbá in the World of Religion

Òrìṣà 8

SPIRITUAL NETWORKS AND PRACTICES

Introduction

The four chapters that form this section of the book can be described as studies of the impact of global trends on the making and understanding of the Yorùbá religion over time. Thus, the effects of globalization and modernization are essential, as they explore how this community of people and ideas has been navigating these structures through the agency of their culture. Yorùbá culture has survived partly because of the hybridization of its organic elements with external borrowings. In this part of the book, elements of this cultural hybridization and the condition of its production are brought to the fore.

This chapter illuminates factors that have contributed to the spread of the Yorùbá culture and religion in the form they have taken in several Atlantic locations where they have been transplanted over the course of a long history. The mobility of Yorùbá traders and others around the West African region resulted in some aspects of the Yorùbá culture being transplanted into these locations. However, the little aspects of the Yorùbá culture that have been nursed in these places have largely been adulterated with Islam and Christianity. As it has been argued, Yorùbá *Òrìṣà* involving pantheons of deities has been symbolic of a Yorùbá community's presence in the Atlantic world.[1] The Yorùbá people's movement across these two geographical locations, one within the region and the other across the Atlantic, was different in circumstance, purpose, and time. These posed a major influence on their composition and impacts in various places.

Although trade and trading relations were instrumental to their mobility in both regional and Atlantic spaces, their position in such an economic enterprise was quite different. Whereas the former traded goods ranging from craftworks to farm products, the latter traded commodities in exchange for European goods like textiles, lanterns, gin, mirrors, and other significant and insignificant trading items. In other words, while the former constituted traders, the latter traded items. More revealing is that by the time this population was forcefully taken to these various Atlantic locations as captives, many of them had limited contact with foreign religious practices. Although Islam was already making its presence known in the country by the late eighteenth century when many of these populations were taken into slavery, it remained a marginal force in the sociology of many Yorùbá groups. Islam's impact on many segments

---

1. Apter, *Oduduwa's Chain.*

of the population was, thus, not tangible at this time. Many resisted becoming institutionally acquainted with Islam and Christianity in the Americas, instead riding on their cultural peculiarities to navigate their way through difficult living conditions and the limited social ladder of their new political environment. Together with other captives of African descent, some Yorùbá captive communities in these places resisted the religious aspect of Western culture and organized themselves around their African belief system, in which the Yorùbá *Òrìṣà* worship system played a key role.[2]

In this process, the Yorùbá Òrìṣà worship system became known as Santeria, Candomblé, Lukumi, and other forms in the Americas where Yorùbá captives were taken, with various modifications that went as far as incorporating elements of Catholicism in practice while retaining the core of its philosophy and theology.[3] Today, this paradigm has been created in various locations across the Atlantic through "spiritual citizenship." Yorùbá culture is more effectively reproduced in these diasporic spaces than it is in Nigeria, where the practice originated. These dynamics are examined in the following sections.

Universal and Local Religions

The philosophical legitimacy of indigenous religions, such as the Yorùbá Òrìṣà, has long been debated. Controversies abound in such discussions, not because conferring legitimacy on religious identity is a divine responsibility of any people or civilization but because of a racially skewed assumption that Africans were irredeemably erratic, lacking the intellectual capacity to interpret nature and interact with the cosmic intelligence. Regardless of how skewed these assumptions were, they were driven by some reality's worth investigating. The competition about the supremacy of (their) God between followers of the Christian faith and those of the Islamic religion stretches back to earlier centuries. Each of these two religions was immersed in its own religiously orchestrated fantasies that any civilization or an expression of human identity whose ontological existence differed from theirs was a departure from what should be acceptable and, as such, should be marked for immediate redemption. Due to the understanding that any religious design that commanded a larger audience could control global politics to a certain degree, the decision for religious expansion through proselytization became necessary for these Abrahamic religions. This invariably forced them to consider exploring the countries around them until they reached Africa.

Underneath this arguably false thinking was the impression that Africans were inferior humans and thus found self-examination difficult. Perhaps by some natural coincidences, these religious explorers discovered that African religions and "gods" varied proportionately, so much so that the "god" worshipped in a geographical setting could differ from what their contiguous neighbors believed in or shared. Instead of seeing a structured religious democracy, Muslim and Christian missionaries concluded that the African perception of the Supreme Being was inferior. The superficiality, or perhaps irony, of this thinking was that while they were usually

---

2. Cohen, "Orisha Journeys," 17–36.
3. Boaz, *Banning Black Gods*, 1–10.

predisposed to suffocating rivalries and incessant controversies over the supremacy of their God, until recently, Africans, no matter how religiously diverse, were peaceful religious neighbors. They did not engage in friction because of the dissimilarities of their faiths, nature, or the type of religion they professed. Africans were ridiculed alongside their religions as part of the European encounter. Because the success of external proselytization depended on the extent to which they promoted their religious beliefs and the God represented in them, and, thus, the extent to which all the African gods and religions were maligned, religious expansionists addressed these African religions in degrading terms, to achieve their ominous agenda.

The focus of this work is not to establish the legitimacy of African religions, as that has been carried out by experts in religious and anthropological studies.[4] Instead, the chapter is inclined to establish the validity of the Yorùbá religion as having a similar pattern of preservation and making as many other religions. This will lead us to the focus of this chapter, which is the reasons and ways by which the religion was preserved in the Atlantic world. According to contemporary development in religious circles across the world, the Yorùbá religion is breaking boundaries in the Atlantic and several parts of the world.[5] This is primarily because the custodians of the religion orally transmitted their indigenous ontological realities into the places where they found themselves during the transatlantic slave trade. The presence of cultural exporters in the Atlantic was linked to the Atlantic slave trade, which caused a significant number of people to flee their ancestral homes. The Yorùbá were a sizable number among the people, and the fact that they were well-grounded in their religion gave impetus to the creation of their religious identity in the Atlantic.[6]

The Òrìṣà religion was built on the ontological perception that it is a global religion that extends to all parts of the earth, heaven, and everything in between. This is why the functions and interactions of the gods/goddesses and their worship took on universal characteristics even before the exposure of most people to the existence of Islam and Christianity.[7] Ile-Ife was the crust of creation and there is a core relationship between the *orí* of everyone and universal forces. "*A d'ífá fún Òrúnmìlà, nígbà tó ń ti ọrun bọ wá ayé,*" an inference to Òrúnmìlà when he was coming from heaven to earth, makes Ile-Ife the site of reception and beginning of creation.[8] However, despite the centralization of creation, Ile-Ife is considered a universe beyond those readily occupied by the people.[9]

Despite its universal philosophies, the carriers of the religion, especially before the Yorùbá people were exported to Europe and the Americas as enslaved peoples, did not attempt to universalize doctrines and practices in such a way that would assimilate cultural diversity, create a superiority posture, and impose the religion on everyone. Christianity followed a similar trail, beginning in Israel as an extraction from the Jewish religion practiced by the apostles.[10] Although many could key into several of the doctrines similar to Òrìṣà worship, there was not much of a global face at that time. The globalization process of Christianity could be said to have originated in the AD 325 Council of Nicaea convened by Emperor Constantine I.[11] The Council of Nicaea changed the theological perception of the religion, resolved some issues, and made new creeds that have further helped its permeation to many parts of the world after

---

4. See, for instance, Patterson, "Religion and the Rise of Africa," 181–196.

5. Chirila, "River that Crosses an Ocean," 116–151.

6. Sandoval, *Worldview, Orichas, and Santeria.*

7. Thompson, "Proliferation of Yorùbá Religion," 1–16.

8. Akinjogbin, *Cradle of a Race.*

9. Majasan, "Folklore as an Instrument of Education," 41–59.

10. Johnson, *History of Christianity.*

11. Clark, Oxenham, and Plumptre, *History of the Christian Councils.*

several understandings were projected on the religion to attain the universal posture needed. There was the creation of a trinity principal with the redefinition of the position of Jesus Christ, the Father, and the Holy Spirit, resulting in an orthodox stance. The Arian heresy on the divinity of Jesus was countered with the portrayal of Jesus as being made "of the same substance" as God, who is the Father.[12] They further explored the organizational and administrational construction of the church and faith and created an allusion to the Bishop of Rome as the head of the Western Church.

Even since its diaspora has spread, the stakeholders of the Òrìṣà religion have not taken a universal posture of practices or decided its canon for the world. This could be attributed to several factors, including the failure to seek settlements beyond the reach of the Yorùbá and their immediate distant environs; the lack of early international reputation; nonparticipation in international politics, which made the proselytization of Christianity easier; and the inability to establish a global political empire. The political standing of many of the Christian nations made the gravitation of Christianity, and even Islam, accessible to other parts of the world, a luxury that Òrìṣà development did not enjoy. In addition, the act of writing was not such that it was to be relied on in the religion. For instance, the Bible, Quran, and other religious texts and doctrines were produced in writing, making their adaptation easier. This was not a similar situation for the Òrìṣà religion.

However, the spread of Òrìṣà religion across the horizons of the Atlantic was made possible by the interaction of the Yorùbá nations with foreign powers, slave trade, colonization, migration, cultural diffusion, and many other mechanisms. But since its deposition across the coasts of the Atlantic and far beyond, the religion has been resisting the overwhelmingness of the adoption of some universal doctrines. Although many of them passed through some syncretic processes so that the religion would take a posture of local religion that fit in with the social construct of the people, there was nothing much done in establishing universal doctrines as seen in the Council of Nicaea. Following the diaspora exposure to the rest of the world and understanding of systems that helped the progression of the Òrìṣà religion elsewhere, the religion started taking a "world religion" posture similar to Islam, Christianity, and Buddhism. The practices in the Caribbean, the Americas, and West Africa are having globalized influence, and scholars who are devotees have juxtaposed the religion with others. Also, subject to its methods and diversity, scholars have been able to advance arguments that the religion is at par with others.

Òrìṣà religion has equipped itself with the gift of writing, and many of its teachings and doctrines have been adapted to reflect modern changes.[13] There are texts on several of the religion's principles ready for potential devotees to explore. In addition, several of the endeavors of some of the scholars have exposed the positive truths about religion, theoretically and realistically providing an alternative to the general religious subscriptions of people. The religion engages people intellectually through several papers and books that posit higher logic convincing enough to proselytize those who encounter them. Another factor that makes it easy is the

---

12. Abogado, "Anti-Arian Theology," 255–286.
13. Ilesanmi, "Traditional Theologians," 216–226.

adaptability of contemporary practices to people's free will and the ability to exercise a level of inquisitive minds. Several of these works are doctrinaire and proselytizing, either directly or indirectly. Many of them advance arguments that Òrìsà worship is superior to Christianity and Islam.

Furthermore, attempts to decolonize Africa extended to the religious convictions of the people. Efforts are being made to free the minds of the people from the fallacious inclinations that have rendered the African traditional religions inferior. The propaganda clouds are clearing, and if people continue to follow Abrahamic religious practices, many will see the permeated propaganda and understand the place of African religions. Globally, the drivers of this consciousness have used arguments around myths and histories recorded in other religions and traditions vis-à-vis the Yorùbá religion to show the religious politics that have been promoting one religion over the other without such overbearing justifications. So, while the Òrìsà worship grows and is exported to other parts of the world, the Òrìsà-influenced syncretized Islam and Christianity also help with the advancement of the consciousness.

One characteristic that distinguishes a religion as universal is its adaptability to the particularism of some people, their culture, and social structure.[14] There is Christianity, but aside from the common features of the religion that everyone may share, it is difficult to arrive at one generic whole of Christian doctrines without some striking differences based on locations. Christianity at the Vatican is entirely based on the principles of Roman Catholicism, while Christianity or even Catholicism practiced in Kenya are unlike the Vatican's Christian practices. This is the same situation with Islam and other religions. Likewise, Òrìsà worship has adopted universality attributes, with several practice systems that vary. The religious cultures of Cuba, Puerto Rico, West Africa, Brazil, and those in the Americas are different from one another. For instance, when the Oyotunji Village in North Carolina was created, the leader faced the challenge of acknowledging Santería and other practices with the claim of maintaining religious purity, focusing his attention on the practice as seen among the Yorùbá people of Nigeria.[15] Hence, for it to have a universal consideration, it must be seen to have a diversity of local religions, and people must be able to trace the root of their beliefs to it.[16]

A fundamental challenge that may reduce the prospect of achieving full-fledged universality of the language is the decline in learning and speaking of the Yorùbá language among the devotees. Although this should not be as disastrous as many scholars have anticipated, the command of religious language allows the maintenance of the major relevant principles, creates deeper understanding, and exposes the philosophies and epistemologies of the religion to devotees. Despite its susceptibility to local cultures, languages, and even religions, Arabic has always been a characteristic of Islam across the world.[17] The language is maintained for specific religious purposes to allow for easy engagement with the tenets of the religion. Only Christianity has been able to complete the total language adaptation with the original Hebrew texts interpreted into local languages, including semantics that are not far from those encoded or

---

14. Sharma, *Concept of Universal Religion*, 1–9.

15. Ilesanmi, "Traditional Theologians," 216–226.

16. Hunt, *Oyotunji Village*.

17. Baalbaki, *Arabic Lexicographical Tradition*.

intended in their original form. In other words, an English translation of the Bible could have a similar meaning to that of its Hebrew version, and, as such, the knowledge retained in the textual formation of Hebrew versions is maintained. Unfortunately, there is no Bible or Quran to be interpreted in Òrìṣà worship; instead, several of its tenets are locked up in the depth of its language construction, making the language important and not merely incidental to the engagement with the religion's epistemology. Therefore, accessing the religion without doing so under the knowledge base of the language may be quite detrimental, allowing the erosion of many of the religion's primary principles, which should not be compromised.

Yorùbá Spirituality in the Atlantic World: Relationship and Intertextuality

As pointed out in chapter 3, epistemologies do matter, for ways of knowledge can instigate actions. Ideas around spirituality have the capacity to move with people from one location to another. The conceptualization of Yorùbá spirituality begins with the deconstruction of the universalist conception of life. From close observation of the religion's operations among the Yorùbá, one finds that it began from their self-reflection on the essentiality of life, asking fundamental questions such as "Why are we here?" and "Who or what is responsible for human creation?" This does not suggest that other forms of spirituality were constructed without corresponding self-reflection by the people who introduced them. Instead, it seeks to pinpoint the fact that Yorùbá ontological design had primacy in their understanding and interpretation of the universe. Several scholars have argued that the Yorùbá worldview identifies two planes of existence: the visible and the invisible.[18] The visible plane covers only the planets, including those modern scientists have yet to account for. The assumption that the Yorùbá have an ontological understanding of the universe that influences their awareness of planets that have not yet been identified is not spurious or vague. Regarding their knowledge of cosmology, the universe is made up of planetary types that cannot be accurately predicted with mathematical accuracy. To understand this, consider their description of "God," called "Olódùmarè," the custodian of an infinite universe.[19]

Consequently, the planets fall into the category of visible planes if they can be discovered and occupied by living organisms. For example, Earth is inhabited by humans, plants, and animals. Also, some beings with no material realization coinhabit the visible plane with humans, animals, and plants, yet they have the power to alter the arrangements of the world. These beings can manipulate animals, plants, and even humans or use any of these three living organisms to disrupt the activities of others. In the Yorùbá worldview, the visible planes house those things that cannot be identified with human eyes or seen with contemporary scientific aids. However, the invisible or nonvisible plane is purely occupied by the things humans cannot see, and they also cannot disturb its organization. In this category are Olódùmarè, the "brain box" of the universe, and the primordial beings (irúnmọlẹ̀) that were sent to make internal arrangements in the planets. This is where there is a little controversy. Some scholars believe that occupants of

---

18. Drewal, *Yoruba Ritual*, 103–104.

19. Idowu, *Olódùmarè*.

Figure 8.2.
"Orisa," by Dr. Kazeem Ekeolu. An abstract sketch depicting two head figures. In the Yorùbá world, it is *orí*, the "head," that determines one's destiny in life. Some persons, whether man or woman, have been specially selected to become like gods because of the feats they can achieve beyond ordinary humans, so much so that they are honored and revered. The abstract has a male and female with their organs intact. Òrìṣà does not come by chance but by predestination, as foretold by *Ifá*.

the invisible planes are invisible because they cannot be seen; however, beings like Olódùmarè are invisible no matter the seeing aid (scientific or indigenous). For example, Obatala and other irúnmọlẹ́ cannot be seen nakedly, no matter how hard a worshipper tries, while some creatures in the visible plane can be seen through some spiritual conjuration. *Iwin* (gnomes) are the closest description of these creatures.[20]

The contention is not about the visibility or otherwise of these beings, whether they have material existence or not, but rather the category to which they belong. Having made the distinction on the logicality of oral materials, it is equally important to clarify that Yorùbá people still maintain a commensurable bond with both physical and spiritual beings. The Yorùbá believe that Olódùmarè, their Almighty Mega Force, is spatially distant from humans. Given the inherent complexity of managing the universe, the Yorùbá people believe that Olódùmarè should be venerated and persuaded to grant their request.[21] This means that the communication between Olódùmarè and the other beings is based on a boss–subordinate relationship. Olódùmarè is not directed to carry out a spiritual assignment for humans because this has already been determined, but He oversees granting its execution, which the Yorùbá call àṣẹ. Those beings with no material nature, which are said to loosely inhabit the visible plane (because they have unhindered access to the two) with the humans, animals, and plants, are usually the ones invoked to carry out a particular assignment. This is after propitiating Olódùmarè, the Supreme Force, to grant the request. The idea of sacrifice, worship, and veneration comes into play when these beings succumb to human invocation. As they have their existential focus, or perhaps assignments, they are usually induced by some actions before they can yield to human demands.

The occupants of the visible plane that cannot be seen are identified by Yorùbá people as ẹbọra, iwin, and irúnmọlẹ́ (which are unseen but can be invoked for personal or social reasons). However, there are Òrìṣà who are also dwellers of the invisible planes and the link between Olódùmarè and humans. These beings are flexible with their roles. As emissaries of Olódùmarè in the creation of the universe, they overlap between the visible and the invisible planes to carry out the cosmological duty assigned to them by Olódùmarè.[22] Because human activities can alter the arrangements of the world, such as the increase in global emissions that usually results in increased radiation and the weakness of the ozone layer, these Òrìṣà are dedicated to managing human excesses so that the planet does not die prematurely. The Òrìṣà are even programmed to listen to human yearnings and serve as intermediaries between them and Olódùmarè. Each of them has a unique assignment. For example, Èṣù is the gatekeeper who determines the success or otherwise of man's appeasement to Olódùmarè, as man's messages can be delivered or not. In essence, people are persuaded to appeal to Èṣù if they still encounter problems after a series of unsuccessful attempts to appease Orí or Olódùmarè.[23]

Other Òrìṣà also have direct access to Olódùmarè, but they could be disallowed if they have problems to settle with Èṣù. As a result, Òrìṣà such as Ọṣun is venerated, especially by those

---

20. Medine, Aderibigbe, and Aderibigbe, *Contemporary Perspectives on Religions*, 16.

21. Idowu, *Olódùmarè*.

22. Neimark, *Way of Orisa*.

23. Falola, *Esu*.

who are her disciples, and Ṣàngó is worshipped by those whose ancestral lineage supports him. The Yorùbá people believe that all living organisms on the planet come from a source to which they return after the end of their spiritual assignments. Let us consider water, for example. The transformation of water from one position to the other does not mean that it is dead. Once the substance to which it is transformed exhausts its living elasticity, it will return to the component it is naturally meant to be.[24] Likewise, humans began as sperms at conception; after their physical form during their existence, they transform and live in another manifestation or realm after their death. The Yorùbá believe that after one's death, the next plane of existence is not the invisible plane that is occupied by Olódùmarè and the Òrìṣà. Instead, one is believed to become other realizations in the visible plane and can be seen through spiritually devised means.

It cannot be overstretched that the Yorùbá became victims of the transatlantic slave trade that transported them to the other world. The enslaved Yorùbá were disconnected physically from their cultural and religious backgrounds but were inseparable from their internalized religious philosophies. The transplantation of the people did not come without their exposure to destructive social and political weaknesses. They experienced increased internal conflicts in their quest to make meaning of their conditions in the diaspora.[25] The tormented Africans faced unending slavery escapades in the hands of the European merchants so much that many families of lower social status who had no power to challenge the slave raiders would have prepared their children in ancestral worship and devotions so they could rely on spirituality in case of unforeseen emergencies.[26]

Enslaved Africans in the Americas reconfigured their existence through spiritual empowerment. Their experience provided a window for critical reflection as they were forced to abandon their cultural and spiritual origin, where they could have realized their full potential and transported to a place with constrained freedom. What was left for them was to seek appropriate ways to acclimatize to unfavorable conditions for self-realization. Their reversion to their spirituality in Africa was more of a necessity than a choice. In the psychology of traumatized humans, there is an urgent demand for consolation and freedom from whatever is holding them in situations of naked bondage, destruction, degeneration, and disrespect. Enslaved Africans had little or no prospects of escaping the harsh reality, and the best option was to rely on their spiritual reinvigoration. Many of them considered the veneration of their ancestors and invoked the spirits of their Òrìṣà to intervene in their challenges and bring succor to their spirits. Several Yorùbá slaves who were groomed in their indigenous religion conjured spirits and evoked the presence of their supernatural beings, who were persuaded to make their journey less difficult and more productive.

In essence, the conjuration of spirits among the Yorùbá is viewed as having an intertextual appeal in the Atlantic environment. African American magical practices featured the indigenous spirituality that exists among the Yorùbá people. Christianity in some places in the Atlantic environment witnessed some elements of Yorùbá and African spirituality, as in cases

---

24. Raheem, "Cosmic Perception of Water in Yorùbá Belief."
25. Fuglestad, *Slave Traders by Invitation.*
26. Chireau, *Black Magic.*

     GLOBAL YORÙBÁ

where religious leaders designated special attention to deities of African origin.[27] For example, Bishop Charles Harrison Mason, the founder of the Church of God in Christ, linked elements of African spirituality to his understanding of Christianity. His fascination and subsequent possession of uniquely formed natural objects demonstrate the psychological attachment he had to African religion. As the invocation of these beings helped in the revalidation of their humanness, Africans in the transatlantic environment reconnected with their African roots through the association of spiritual credibility to some symbols. Although they found themselves in a society with a different spiritual trajectory, they were dispirited by the feelings of losing touch with their ancestral sources and devised a solution to the problem. The Yorùbá at home conjured to heal, and in some other cases, they did so to invoke luck. All these were equally practiced among those who found themselves in the Atlantic. The Yorùbá religion, which survived in the Atlantic, was an instrument of creating consciousness.

The crux of the Atlantic reinvention of the Yorùbá religion and spirituality centers on the exchange of cultural traditions and praxes by the human agency through the transatlantic slave system. Those in the New World were constrained to function within an economic environment that delegitimized their identity through the restrictions of their material importance to economic value. Humans can function in various forms, part of which is the construction of an in-grouping mechanism through which their existence is validated. Whereas hegemonic power prioritized several expressions of identity from the political world to the social systems, the enslaved were interested in creating an identity that facilitated the rejuvenation of their Africanness and brought to them the legitimacy of their self-awareness and self-consciousness. Religion was necessary in this regard. Several slaves who were not well-grounded in the indigenous spirituality were ineluctably sold to it, knowing that the dictates of the new environment required their bonding and then interdependence.

Economic relationships sometimes overlap with the political system, and the construction of an identity that comes from it usually becomes the basis for differences. Africans who found themselves in the Atlantic were unified by their similar appearance, and the fact that Europeans became successful in transferring Africans from their countries to the Atlantic world immediately created in them a sense of valuation that manifested in inferior or superior thinking of oneself.

---

27. Noel, *Black Religion.*

These were some of the underlying issues that contributed to introducing their indigenous spiritual ideas in the New World, knowing that this could be their most assured strategy to coordinate themselves culturally and spiritually. Here, religion offered a remedy. The pronounced countermeasure to existential racial inclinations stemmed from the invocation of their ancestors, who may have died (interpreted as "sacrificed their lives") during the journey, to the conjuring of spirits culturally identified by their parents and acquaintances while they were in Africa. This became the politics of the New World. This gradual infusion resulted in the formation of a permanent religious identity based on the Yorùbá epistemological framework. In what would be expanded later, in the Yorùbá world, gods such as Ṣàngó, Ògún, Oṣun, and Yemoja, among others, found archetypal calibrations in similar fabrications in the Atlantic environment. As such, the semblance between the worship methodologies of these divinities in the Yorùbá and the Atlantic world speaks to the relationship between them. The systems of devotions found among some Christians in the Caribbean, Barbados, and Rio de Janeiro share compelling similarities with the ways indigenous Yorùbá worships are organized.

Gods and Humans: The Road of Convergence

Perhaps to understand the Yorùbá concept of God and its place in the structure of the universe, we must go back to Melville Herskovits's hypothesis, where he associates the immersion of Africans into religious inclination with unmistakable emotionalism. The dialectics of African religious identities was conceived as customarily mandated by the emotional reaction to the physical and social frustrations to which Africans were exposed in the Atlantic. In Herskovits's words:

> The prominent place held by religion in the life of the Negro in the United States, and the special forms assumed by Negro versions of Christian dogma and ritual, are customarily explained as compensatory devices to meet the social and economic frustration experienced by Negroes during slavery and after emancipation. Such explanations have the partial validity we have already seen them to hold for various phases of Negro secular life but, as must be emphasized again, cannot be regarded as telling the entire causal tale. For underlying the life of the American Negro is a deep religious bent that is but the manifestation here of the similar drive that, everywhere in Negro societies, makes the supernatural a major focus of interest.[28]

A careful examination of Herskovits's position reveals the wide difference between the African conception of God and religion and the Western understanding of cosmic intelligence. While the Black people conceive God as an absolute entity that remains regardless of shifting variables or emerging trends, some other civilizations see God and religion as unstable and even discardable as people have more knowledge and understanding. Herskovits did not create the impression that Africans were unaware of the complex politics of universal entities and the

---

28. Herskovits, *Myth of the Negro Past*. He was writing at a time when the use of the word *negro* was not considered inappropriate.

fact that their awareness triggered in them the construction of methodical institutions through which communication between them could be established. It is revealing that all Africans were perceived primarily as emotional, whose circumstantial frustrations were taken out on religious or similar modalities. Herskovits concluded that Africans aligned with religious philosophies rather than becoming pragmatic where needed. There were sociological reasons that facilitated their association with religious philosophies in the Atlantic world. Many Africans in these environments were helpless; the only apparent motivation and encouragement they got was the establishment of a foundation that would solidify their patrilineal bond, and religion was the main available agency.

These clarifications are made to understand the African thinking about God and Africans' condition as partakers in the activities of the universe and not dispersible articles. For a race of people who maintained a reasonable level of mutual understanding and peace that helped to stem the tide of fundamentalism capable of erupting social contradictions, Herskovits concluded that "in an age marked by skepticism, the Negro has held fast to belief."[29] This was with the underlying assumption that while others have mentally and politically evolved, the "Negroes" were stuck in the euphoria of emotional ululation.

The Yorùbá were religious but considered their social unification as equally important. There are different proverbial sayings among the Yorùbá, which reinforce their mutual deference to themselves and the divinities. The misinterpretation of this mutuality triggered Karin Barber to assert that the life span of Òrìṣà depends on the strength of its devotee's loyalty.[30] Let us consider a certain Yorùbá proverb that supports Barber's statement: *"Òrìṣà bóòle gbè mí, ṣe mí bóoṣe bá mi,"* which is loosely translated as "If a deity cannot add to human development, it should not complicate one's situation." This gives the impression that the Yorùbá people are very religious but do not substitute critical unthinking in the process. They identify the place of the Divine while simultaneously understanding their ingenious positions in the scheme of things. Some Igbo proverbs add seasoning to the current argument. For example, there is a saying that "if a deity is making excessive demands (from people), it would be shown the wood from which it is carved." This is self-explanatory. As noted by Herskovits, Africans were not immune to reasoning; they were just calculative and contextually conservative. According to Herskovits,

> from the earliest times of slavery, it has been the less inhibited, more humble denominations which have attracted Negroes in the United States. Perhaps because this is so striking, a formula which explains it in terms of simplicity, naivete, and emotionalism has attained a certain currency among students. Thus, the worship of the Negro is of the simplest sort. He has no appreciation of elaborate rituals, of services consisting of forms and ceremonies. Hence the great mass of colored races has united with either the Methodist or Baptist Churches. These churches have the simplest, least complicated forms of church services, and the Negro naturally gravitated toward them.[31]

---

29. Herskovits, *Myth of the Negro Past.*
30. Barber, "How Man Makes God in West Africa," 724–745.
31. Herskovits, *Myth of the Negro Past.*

People whom one accused of being excessively religious would not seek "less complicated" forms of church services, as they gravitated toward the mainline churches if they were truly religious. They would consider church denominations that had different ecumenical activities, which they could consider as archetypes of their African religions and would identify with them. We cannot accuse the Africans and, by implication, the Yorùbá people in the Atlantic of being exceptionally religious while also claiming that they gravitated toward other religious denominations. The reason for the misrepresentation is that not many understand differences in the idea of God among different people. God, regardless of being interpreted as the Supreme Intelligence or seen from the African angle, means different things to different people and cultures. Interestingly, this does not excuse or call for the imposition of one perception over the other, for it shows the epistemic perception of different cultures. Arguably, there is a philosophical meeting point between the conceptualization of God in the Western sense and the religio-cultural configuration of the same entity among the Yorùbá and African people. The ascription of Supremacy to God indicates a people's sociocultural interpretation of the world around them.

It is important to examine the cultural and religious representation of God in the psychology of the Yorùbá because their understanding of that Being determines, to a large extent, the philosophical image and social relationship they constructed. Yorùbá believe Olódùmarè to be the Cosmic Force that initiated the planetary existence and the very energy behind all the creatures in the universe. However, Olódùmarè's limitation is evident if we rely on the oral traditions of the Ifá corpus where a verse alludes that Olódùmarè consulted an Ifá priest on what it needed to do for the enhancement of its immoral status. After performing his divination, the Ifá priest, precisely Ọ̀rúnmìlà, prescribed a sacrifice for Olódùmarè, who conceded to the instruction, following the prescriptions with immediate actions.[32] It is from this oral account that we conclude that the association of absolute Supremacy to God is not done without some caveats. Èsù wields some spiritual power that one would think he rivals that of Olódùmarè.

There is a tenable contention about the semantic consistency of the word *Supreme* when we evaluate the Christian and Islamic God. This is because just as the Yorùbá people have the understanding that God is not entirely absolute or exalted without a considerable degree of dependence on humans, we have the impression that the Abrahamic God shares a similar conception. In one Yorùbá interpretation of the Bible and the Quran, we are intimated about the painful regret of God after the creation of humans. For example, in Genesis and Surah-al-Baqarah, the Abrahamic God expressed disappointment after creating humans and seeing their inelastic capacity for self-destruction and untamed frivolity. In annoyance, the Christian God destroyed humans in preparation to create other species, while the Islamic God showed regretful signs.

As a Yorùbá practitioner once explained, if we ascribe the status of supremacy to the Abrahamic God as all-knowing, omnipotent, and omnipresent, it betrays the simple logic that this Being would have no foreknowledge of the destructive capacity of His creatures. Even if, as some religious fundamentals would always try to use eschatological explanations to justify

---

32. Gbadegesin, *African Philosophy.*

Figure 8.4. Yemoja, literally "mother of fish," is a transnational female water deity associated with several water bodies and known for fertility, aquatic communication, and female power, among other powerful attributes. Drawing by Moses Ogunleye.

the situation, why then show any regret when He had prior knowledge of what these creatures would become? From close observation, therefore, one would see the compelling semblance or inevitable meeting point of both African and Western perceptions of God.

One can interpret the consultation of Ọ̀rúnmìlà (Ifá) as a signal of long-standing democracy or checks and balances that humans are enjoined to follow in Yorùbá epistemology. If it is culturally believed by the Yorùbá people that Olódùmarè created the lives and organisms on the planets, it is, therefore, consistent with the assumption that He has a higher status above the creatures. However, Olódùmarè chooses to be an embodiment of the general moral ideals of the people. It is a relationship between the leaders and the led, where the former is expected to have a moderate sense of reverence for the latter because their interrelationship determines the peace in society. Without such cooperation and commitment, the planet is exposed to avoidable challenges that would increase the misery humans would encounter. It is on this basis, therefore, that even Olódùmarè took a position about respect and consented to the prescription of its subordinate, Ọ̀rúnmìlà. For Ifá devotees, this developed in them the ethical behavior and principles that compelled them to consider their fellow humans not as competitors but as individuals with whom they must cooperate in their quest for the common and collective good. As stated above, the place of communalism and social togetherness is validated by the single action of Ọ̀rúnmìlà consultation.

In the aim to quickly find a meeting point between the prevailing belief system from the postexposure to Abrahamic religions, it became a trend to state that the Òrìṣà were intermediaries between human and Olódùmarè, creating both a monotheist and polytheist approach in the theological appreciation of the religion. People with Yorùbá roots acknowledge the existence of an Olódùmarè with an authority over everyone but do not always see it as a point of finality. Against the general beliefs, many of the Òrìṣà are regarded to provide final solutions to issues tabled before them without any need to consult or refer them to Olódùmarè.

When one delves into the local practice of the Yorùbá religion and the worship of Òrìṣà, it becomes clear that several of the people see their particular Òrìṣà to be some independent deities or nature god and approaching them would not come with some reference to a Supreme Being. Thomas Makanjuola Ilesanmi points out many of these instances to show the general erroneous generalization of intermediary positions of the Òrìṣà when he states that

> Osun worshippers in Oluponna, Osogbo and Iponda, see their deity as the only point of reference, and not as an intermediary or mediatrix between them and another superior being. Sango is ubiquitously treated as the supreme controller of all the activities of his advocates. The worshippers of Ogiyan in Iragbiji believe that their deity does everything for them; they do not send him to any Olodumare. Babarake controls the traditional life in Igangan without any reference to Olodumare; while Ogun wields total divine power in Ondo, Ipole, Ire Ekiti, and in many parts of Yorubaland, without his advocates feeling that he refers their cases to a superior deity. The Ikere people in Ekitiland in Ondo State have a nature god—Olosuta—who they believe does all things for them without alluding to any other power. The catalogue can be extended copiously.[33]

---

33. Ilesanmi, "Traditional Theologians," 221.

The supremacy of the Olódùmarè might not be in such striking finality that it is severally portrayed by many scholars. This could be another pointer to the Yorùbá mythological reference to democratic practice among the pantheons of Òrìsà. The term Òrìsà as a generic name for all the gods and deities has been identified to be more of a contemporary adoption to the gods who were supposed to enjoy some levels of independence from each other in many instances.[34]

According to the Yorùbá, humans are inherently powerful. The attribution of this power develops from the observation that humans have the capability to influence what happens to other living organisms, either consciously or otherwise. Let us consider the postcreation reactions of the Abrahamic God, in a Yorubanized construction, after finding out that humans masterminded destructions of surprising magnitude. When thoroughly examined, a God who was aware of their destructive potential yet observed with (unsuccessful) efforts to avert the potential aberration creates the notion that people may be difficult to manage when they decide to exert their human power. It allegorically happened in the Christian Garden of Eden in the Bible when the society chased the Prophet of Islam away from his cultural and social environment. These two cases would not have been the intentions of the Western-derived meaning of God. Also, the consultation of Òrúnmìlà means that Olódùmarè is aware of some ingenious capabilities of humans that need recognition. This summarizes the idea that the exaltation of humans among the Yorùbá people comes from the evaluation of human capacity and the awareness of their inherent power. It manifests in the exaltation of any being with extraordinary contributions to humanity.

How does this come to play even in the Atlantic world? When Yorùbá people die, they are usually not considered dead—as in the finitude of existence, a semantic implication that is associated with the Western (Christian) death. Instead, the Yorùbá commonly say they have transformed—that is, they have changed from one manifestation of matter to another. In line with the explanation made at the initial stage of this chapter, their dead are invisible but they still occupy the visible plane, which means they could be invoked and even seen by specialist diviners.[35] It was this sense that Lorand Matory means when he said that "their gods, and their priests are not things of the past but our co-residents in the great cities of the US, Latin America, and Europe, which host a lively industry devoted to the making and the maintenance of Afro-Atlantic gods."[36] It is in the understanding that the dead ones among them are still around in different manifestations that they invoke, appease, and call them whenever they are in danger or in a celebrative mood. In Caribbean spiritism, the senior house slaves, a ño and a ña, are worshipped, and their statues are generally referenced. A religious message of such immortalization of these individuals is that the worldly deprivations and suffering of humans, especially those Africans that were shown racial and political prejudices in the Atlantic, do not prevent them from being useful and eventful to those they leave behind. Modern science came close to this conclusion when it established that humans genetically transfer attributes to their successors.

---

34. Ilesanmi, "Traditional Theologians," 221.

35. Qláléyè and Òkédòkun, "Concept of Death," 111–128.

36. Matory, *Fetish Revisited*.

The Belief in Afterlife

Every society needs a moral reenactment and compact that would create some subconscious social contract to put everyone in check. Historically and universally, religion has been one of the hallmarks of these moral ideologies.[37] Christianity, Islam, and many modern religions served this purpose, and the Òrìṣà worship has a fair share of the moral protection of its local society. This brings us to the understanding of the concept of the afterlife and the protection and promotion of the operation of good and evil by religion.

Among the Yorùbá people, especially in West Africa, the afterlife is both a complex and nuanced concept.[38] The death of people is believed not to be a finality to their existence but the transformation and transcending to a life on earth that could interact with immediate society.[39] Ọ̀run and other ancestral planes of the dead are often connoted with an ambiance of peace, happiness, and fulfillment, with some accompanying rewards for an individual's deeds and accomplishments. Many of the dead are worshipped and revered, especially those who have had a significant contribution to the lives of the people or who led legendary lives. For instance, the deified Ọ̀ṣun, Ṣàngó, Ògún, and others were once heroes and heroines to their people who associate divinity with their abilities when they were on earth and enjoyment of same at their ascension.[40]

Many believe that Ọ̀run is not a plane for everyone, as there must be a point of reckoning for the subscription to either evil or good on earth. Would the spirit of an evil man be worshipped or revered after his demise? It is a question that points to the promotion of good over evil in Yorùbá society. "*Orí ìyá mi, gbè mí n' íjà*" (loosely "the personal god or deity of my mother should support or reinforce me") portrays the ready belief of the people in a reinforced afterlife and the acquisition of some celestial power over the terrestrial plane by the dead. Yorùbá worship their ancestors and the ancestors are not supposed to forsake them. Many believe them to be some guidance stars after their transformation. "*Bàbá má sùn o*" (father, do not sleep) is another Yorùbá statement that shows the deification of the dead.

Going to the root of the conception of human nature through the ontological understanding of the Yorùbá people, at least from some of the perspectives offered by the Ifá corpus, human is of dual nature.[41] The body and the soul make a man both an ephemeral and physical entity. When one lives on life at the current plane, death becomes a transformative factor to enable one to live in the spiritual phase as a soul. The transformation happens in this life but in a different form. M. A. Makinde explains understanding the soul thus: "Immortality in Yoruba language means '*aiku*' '*Emi*' (soul) is immortal. The creator of *emi* is *Olodumare* (*Ajalaorun*, *Olorun*, or God etc.). Thus, while *emi* (soul) is immortal, its creator, *Olodumare* is also immortal.

<hr>

37. McKay and Whitehouse, "Religion and Morality," 447.
38. Akomolafe, "Yoruba Ontology," 33.
39. Awe, "Existentialist Concerns in Africa," 41–48.
40. Ilesanmi, "Traditional Theologians," 216–226.
41. Akomolafe, "Yoruba Ontology," 33.

Figure 8.5. Ògún, one of the "hot" deities in the Yorùbá pantheon known for preparing the path for all deities to enter the earth. He is the deity of iron and patron of hunters, drivers, smiths, warriors, and others who work with iron. He is active in the West African Dahomey and Gu religions and Haitian Vodou. Sculpture by Ademola Fakeye.

Both are also spirits. While the soul as an immortal spirit is known as *aiku*, *Olodumare* is known as *Oba aiku*, i.e. the deathless or immortal king."[42]

The Yorùbá have a strong belief in the immortal soul of their ancestors that they believe is a reality and does not depend on the living's remembrance of them. They have some abilities, and it is only their physical forms in the pretransition stage that are susceptible to death. Beyond the duality structure of man that permeates into the understanding of the afterlife, other conceptions understand a man in three to four components. Examining several scholars, Mohammed Akomolafe creates an interaction with these understandings thus:

> Man, to the Yoruba, has as part of his compositions: *ara* (body), *emi* (soul) and *ori* (destiny), *ese* (journey/path) and *okan* (heart or mind). This position is corroborated by Makinde (2007:54) who affirms that, "in the Yoruba conception of human personality, a person may be said to consist of three parts viz, *ara* (body), *emi* (soul) and *ori* (inner head)." According to Segun Gbadegesin, in the worldview of the traditional Yoruba (2004:134), "*Emi* is a non-material force responsible for life. Its presence ensures life and its absence means death. But the *emi* is itself immortal, and it may reincarnate in another body." *Ara* is used to explain all the physical parts of the body which include hands, chest, blood, veins, legs, head (*ori ita*), etc. In the words of Gbadegesin (2004:154); whereas *okan* as another component of the human person is to be interpreted as "the heart or the mind (the home of consciousness)"; "*ori* is the bearer of a person's destiny as well as the determinant of one's personality" (Gbadegesin 2004:134).[43]

To resolve the divergence, it could be said that ẹ́mí and ara could be interpreted as manifestations of the human being. Orí, a personal god, serves as a guardian while on earth and could also take the place of destiny.[44] The ẹsẹ́ represents the path that would be taken by the person as dictated by orí. In essence, orí and ẹsẹ́ are more like instigators of the affairs of humans, both as ara or ẹ́mí, while ara and ẹ́mí are two manifestations of human nature. Theologians also believe in three components of human beings, including the body, the soul, and the spirit, all coexisting to form the personality of humans and link them to the spiritual plane.[45] Like ẹ́mí, although used to capture both soul and spirit, the soul and spirit leave the body, which is termed as corruptible or mortal. 1 Thessalonians 5:23 states, "May God himself, the God of peace, sanctify you through and through. May your whole spirit, soul, and body be kept blameless at the coming of our Lord Jesus Christ." Hebrews 4:12 also states, "For the word of God is alive and active. Sharper than any double-edged sword, it penetrates even to dividing soul and spirit, joints and marrow; it judges the thoughts and attitudes of the heart."

The above verses are evidence of the biblical foreground for the componential existence of the human. The Christian afterlife depends on the good behavior and life of a person before it can permeate to what is known as *ọrun rere* among the Yoruba people or heaven. Jesus describes

---

42. Makinde, *African Philosophy*.

43. Akomolafe, "Yoruba Ontology," 33.

44. Akpan, *Yoruba Concepts of Ori*.

45. Akomolafe, "Yoruba Ontology," 33.

the afterlife of a Christian as his Father's life when he states in John 14:2–3 that "my Father's house has many rooms; if that were not so, would I have told you that I am going there to prepare a place for you? And if I go and prepare a place for you, I will come back and take you to be with me that you also may be where I am."

The dead who had a bad life or subscribed to evil would be in eternal punishment or hell, and those who were righteous would have eternal life or paradise as seen in Matthew 25:46 and Luke 23:43. Jesus Christ described the transformation in 1 Corinthians 15:51–52 thus: "Listen, I tell you a mystery: We will not all sleep, but we will all be changed—in a flash, in the twinkling of an eye, at the last trumpet. For the trumpet will sound, the dead will be raised imperishable, and we will be changed."

This means that the transformation happens in a rapture, during which the dead who were waiting would rise, and the living would be caught up in the rapture. Although there are no known traces of the Òrìsà worship subscription to a rapture or doomsday of the world, there is a similarity in the transition and transformation of human nature upon death. Death is not the end, as taught in the Christian faith, because they both acknowledge the existence of a spiritual realm different from the permissible parameters of the world and continued existence after death. They both have some spiritual obligation to allow a favorable afterlife for the dead. In Islam, the soul of the dead leaves the body in a state of waiting called "Barzakh," until judgment day.[46] However, the soul is not able to have any conversation with or be summoned by human beings. The Quran states in Surah al-Baqarah verse 186: "And do not speak of those who have been killed in the way of Allah as dead; rather they are alive, but you perceive [it] not."

Guidance is to be sought from Allah and the attempt to have a conversation or consult with the dead could be regarded as *shirk*, which is tantamount to polytheism, an abomination for the faith.[47] The dead communicate with those who are listening. The Yorùbá do not believe in the finality of existence but strongly believe in the reality of the transformational state. Depending on the age and the circumstance of the death of the person, the spirit of the dead could be summoned for different purposes through different rites. This means that a meaningful conversation could be instituted with the dead to discuss the physical issue. This practice is often used to determine how the deceased died as well as the person or persons who caused the death.

Ríró òkú is another rite that is used to incite the dead to take revenge and kill the persons responsible for their untimely death.[48] This is done to people who died untimely, indicating that the Yorùbá people do not necessarily see death as evil except when the deceased died in an unfavorable circumstance or when young. This follows the culture of celebrating the dead after many rites and the sober and solemn atmosphere and procedures that follow the death of a young one.

Although there is a form of syncretism with the Islamic religion, there are also practices whereby some sacrifice, ritual, or rite is done for the dead at some point in time or when there is a directive that a member of the family should do it. An example is *yíyí òkú padà* (turning the

---

46. Tesei, "Barzakh," 31–55.
47. Sirriyeh, "Modern Muslim Interpretations of Shirk," 139–159.
48. Adebajo, "Oku-Riro."

dead) to appease the dead and show recognition of its continuing existence. Another is *sàárà*, a more syncretic practice with Yorùbá Islam, where the community is fed with mostly àkàrà (beans cake), and some of the pieces are dropped on the burial ground or around the vicinity of the house. Among the Yorùbá, it is common that when an old person dies, the body is buried close to the house. However, when it is a young person, the body is buried somewhere far where the parents cannot locate it. The burial ground's proximity reenacts the belief in the protective power of the dead and how they continue to be a part of the family.

A similar practice, although quite fundamental in the Christian faith, is how Saul summoned Samuel's spirit through a medium. In 1 Samuel 28, Saul was not able to overcome his fear and desperation against the war with the Philistines and could not get any message from the Lord as guidance. After meeting the Witch of Endor and performing the rituals as required, Samuel's spirit was called, and he told Saul that he and his sons would be defeated in the next day's battle. Something similar happened at the Mount of Transfiguration when Moses and Elijah, who had died centuries before, appeared and spoke to Jesus in Matthew 17, Mark 9, and Luke 9.

The concept of the afterlife could also mean some form of life again. This means that the afterlife must not necessarily be in the spiritual plane but could reincarnate in a new form or body according to the metaphysics in the Yorùbá knowledge base. The metempsychosis, or àtúnwá, is a conduit of the ancestor's soul, which could be born as a new baby or reappear somewhere else as àkúdàáyà or some form of àbíkú. Names such as Babatunde, Yewande, Yetunde, and Iyabo are given to children as an expression of the strong belief of people in the reemergence of their ancestors to take the role of protector, continue their legendary in the previous life, or satisfy other reasons believed to have been the purpose of their reemergence. A similar *àtúnwà* allusion to the Bible was when Jesus Christ referred to John the Baptist in Matthew 11:14 thus: "And if you are willing to receive it, he is Elijah who is to come." This meant that John the Baptist was some form of reincarnation of Prophet Elijah who had died hundreds of years ago, which is in tandem with the prophecy of Malachi in Malachi 4:5–6: "See, I will send the prophet Elijah to you before that great and dreadful day of the Lord comes. He will turn the hearts of the parents to their children, and the hearts of the children to their parents; or else I will come and strike the land with total destruction."[49]

Òrìṣà Traditions

An important point regarding the importance of Òrìṣà traditions in Yorùbá was that most people were culturally associated with a certain Òrìṣà, regardless of their awareness of it. There was an Òrìṣà attached to a lineage or town as part of communal identity. The belief that every human, regardless of their acceptance, awareness, disagreement, or orientation, had a connection to one Òrìṣà divinity or the other was even more astounding, especially because of the Òrìṣà essence in them. The inherent capacity of Ifá, the harbinger or source of Òrìṣà traditions, to accommodate differences was the only viable way to reinforce its legitimacy. Yorùbá religion thrived in the Atlantic environment because of its extraordinary flexibility and not

---

49. Malachi 4:5–6 NIV.

because people proselytized the religion. The religion was usually nonjudgmental, which was underscored by its flexible character and by its amenability to cultural and political situations where it was practiced. Some practitioners believed that Òrìsà religion avoided making ethical decisions for humans, and by maintaining this principle, it did not force guilt on humans. Humans were subjected to their social ethical definitions, and their observance of social codes determined their relationships to spiritual forces.

There were primordial characters who were effectively instrumental in the establishment of universal entities, helping and acting on the instructions of Olódù marè. Obàtálá, Èsù, and Òrúnmìlà, among others, were in this category and were nonhuman manifestations that were part of the universal organisms. There were also exceptional humans with supernatural characteristics who contributed to the development of the material nature of people and were, thus, venerated to the Òrìsà status, worshipped, and revered at chosen seasons. The manifestation of their extraordinary deeds prompted their exaltations among the people, and their earthly exploitations became the reasons for their eventual veneration and deference. In this category were divinities like Sàngó, a once-upon-a-time Aláàfin, the king of Oyo; there was also Oya, and there was Osun. These individuals were exalted to a divine status because they represented the cosmic forces while they were on earth. Perhaps it was realized more in an archetypal manifestation that these individuals embodied spiritual forces

that were recognized by all humans who were aware of their greatness. Considering the magnitude of their deeds, each of them was remembered through the organization of events that brought their memories to life, and the occasional invocation fulfilled some social purposes that could not be disregarded. The veneration of these Òrìsà transformed into the religion practiced in the Atlantic.

There was an assumption among the Yorùbá that everything was connected. Humans and animals had spiritually symmetrical points; plants and animals, people and nonliving entities were also connected. This was philosophically expressed in the relationship that the Yorùbá had with their surroundings. As such, those who had gone to join the ancestors were celebrated, and those culturally identified divinities were worshipped. During worship, however, the Yorùbá used semiotic materials as an agency of communication with the spirits invoked. Many Òrìsà devotees were united in their statement that they were happy people. It is a feeling that probably comes from the observation of how they socially and emotionally react to issues of utmost emotional turbulence. They see themselves as reasonably happy. Humans tend to export their social attitudes to whatever indulgence they are associated with, and the demonstrated attitudes that people express in their works and other activities can be employed to understand how they are socially perceived. The Yorùbá extended this cheerful disposition to their religious practices and systems, and they used objects and icons that would facilitate their happiness during worship. They drummed, clapped, danced, and made merry. Religious activities among them were garnished with sufficient practices that triggered what they defined as "happiness."

In what would be ridiculed by slave owners who had no cultural understanding of the religious activities of the Yorùbá, the Òrìṣà devotees were subjected to dehumanization, ridiculous evaluations, and subjective examination. They were seen as objects without verbal activeness, dubbed as uncivilized and acutely primitive, and subjected to unquantifiable disrespect because of their worship system. It is important to state that the use of symbols and signs as representational objects for different Òrìṣà propelled them to misrepresent the religion and even decided to frustrate them through demeaning remarks. Meanwhile, the creation of symbols of these divinities was a process of religious communication, as the focus was not on the created symbols but on the divine entity culturally and religiously attached to them. These symbols functioned as agencies of communication that facilitated easy access to the divinities and performed other sociocultural functions.[50] Contrary to the blatant misconception about these symbols, the icons of religion, such as the symbols of Ṣàngó, Ọ̀ṣun, and Yemoja, were not intended to represent the absolute manifestation or physical realization of these divinities; rather, they were the agency of accessing them. In this way, when people organized worship sessions and used drums or other designated icons, they intended to make these divinities happy to curry their favor.

Sadly, the Atlantic slave trade changed the course of Yorùbá history and disrupted their social and spiritual lives, subsequently influencing their religious growth. The terror of the Middle Passage reconfigured the sociopolitical and socioreligious ideas of the people. Among the victims and survivors of the excruciating experience of slavery were princes, chiefs, diviners, market women, sculptors, farmers, and others. Helplessly extracted and callously dragged into the ships bound for the Americas, the victims took little or no material possessions along, and on some brutal occasions, their clothes were stripped off them. Despite having no physical or material possessions en route to the New World, these transported Africans went with something more significant—their intellectual inheritance that was used to create innovations in different aspects of life. The farmers among them went with the knowledge of crop rotation and land tilling; those who were herbalists went with the knowledge of herbs and plants that could be used for their medical wellness; and more importantly, the diviners were armed with the knowledge of Ifá so much that many of them would unmistakably recite hundreds of Ifá verses by rote.[51] They went with the epistemological ideas presented in chapter 4.

---

50. Onipede, "Yorùbá and Their Symbolic Means of Communication," 145–160.
51. Matory, *Fetish Revisited.*

Subsequently, when the Yorùbá arrived at the Portuguese and Spanish colonies in the Atlantic, they were constrained by a social decree that gave them a limited choice of options between the existing Christian religion, predominantly the Catholic denomination, or facing more serious and cruel treatment with their "paganism." The reason for this choice was not for the salvation of their souls or the introduction of a better religious identity, for there appeared to be no relationship between enslaving people, subjecting them to harsh treatment in the process, and showing any moral interest in their salvation. Slave owners were going to crush the spirit of enslaved Africans regardless and, in the process, disrespect their human essence in their quest to make them work on plantations. It was, therefore, considered more appropriate if they opened the opportunity of choosing the Christian religion to them, as this would result in a new worldview that could be adapted to capitalism.

Due to the constraints imposed on them by their status as slaves in these colonies, it was impractical that they would share their knowledge and expertise among themselves. Slaves did not have the right to own themselves, much less own material possessions. This meant that those with skills would seek the means to function. Relevance could be generated among slaves, as in diviners becoming the cultural and religious icons whose work was to educate others of the knowledge of Ifá, even within stringent conditions. Slaves did not have time for themselves, except when allowed, but despite this existential challenge, the *babaláwo* among them trained apprentices and spread the knowledge of Ifá so that the legacy of Yorùbá religion would be retained and transferred to succeeding generations.[52] They reconstructed an environment that was socially suitable for the enhancement of Òrìṣà worship; thus, the Òrìṣà found themselves reincarnated in the Atlantic environment by conscious re-creation.

Back at home in Africa, they beat drums, sang, danced, and clapped when they observed their religious worship or rituals. Most of these objects, independently, had their social and religious significance. For example, there were drums used to evoke spirits, and there were others that were mainly for cultural aesthetic purposes.[53] However, this system would not be allowed in the Atlantic environment. Drums and rattles were strictly religiously outlawed in the churches' activities, but no one could impede Africans from making adjustments and compensation for the activities that were rejected. In Catholic churches, where they had an impressive presence, it was soon noticed that the enslaved Yorùbá and Africans had smuggled a foreign practice into the church's culture. To explain how these have introduced their special styles, Herskovits explains the following regarding the Baptist Church:

The change from Baptist ritual to the African-like "shout" during a given service is gradual, for, as is often the case in Africa itself, even the leader does not know when the spirit will come and possession will occur. Restraint, in the European sense, may reign for an hour or two after the beginning of a Sunday night ceremony, as was the case in at least several services visited. But sooner or later the restraint is broken–unless, that is, the service is one where no "shouting" can be indulged in because of danger from the police–and then the scene turns into one entirely comparable to those witnessed

---

52. Matory, *Fetish Revisited*.

53. Adegbite, "Drum and Its Role in Yoruba Religion," 15–26.

Figure 8.7. Ṣàngó, king-god associated with thunder and lightning and popularly considered the fourth Alaafin of Oyo who would subsequently abdicate his throne and commit suicide. He is also popular in many Afro-American communities. Drawing by Michael Efionayi.

in West Africa or the New World wherever African patterns of worship have been preserved. Drums and rattles, forbidden in Christian rite, are naturally absent, but the deficiency is compensated for by handclapping and the improvisations of rhythm taking the form of a vocal "rum-a-tiddy-pum-pum" sung in the bass by men who have the power needed to make their contribution heard above the blanket of choral singing.[54]

Even when it was apparent that the Yorùbá in the Atlantic world were religiously disadvantaged, they took charge of their situation and found ways by which they could syncretize their indigenous religious beliefs with the ones available to them. While they could not bring many of the religious items that were used to invoke the spirit of their ancestors and divinities, they clapped, danced, and made sure that their religious activities portrayed their African identity. As the Yorùbá religion was used at home to facilitate deep interrelationships among the people, the Yorùbá in the New World used the available religious identity to facilitate their common unity and strengthen the bonds between them. Since they were tied to certain social and political (in)actions, legally backed by the injunctions that prevented them from achieving their potential, they dissipated their energies to do more profitable things; before long, they could establish the rudiments of Yorùbá religion in the New World. Consequently, the society accommodated their religious identity and tenets, and they recorded success in changing the dialectics of the Yorùbá religion in the Atlantic.

Òrìṣà and Atlantic Archetypes

In the Yorùbá pantheon, there were diverse irúnmọlẹ̀, as many as 401 of them.[55] However, not all the irúnmọlẹ̀ could be said to be divinities that the Yorùbá routinely worshipped. Some Òrìṣà groups maintained that Ọ̀rúnmìlà, one of the versatile and efficient intermediaries between Olódùmarè and the people, did not have a prominent place of worship. One argument was that the creation of iconic characters that would be consulted or physically and materially accessed was primarily to exalt the very entity to which they naturally represented. As such, some groups would claim that the Yorùbá did not worship primordial beings, with the exclusion of Èṣù, who needed to be appropriately propitiated before he would grant àṣẹ to one's spiritual demands. There were some Yorùbá with superhuman attributes whose existence was filled with a history of mythical contributions to the advancement of the collective. These were the individuals who were mostly associated with and appealed to during worship. Any situation of religious veneration of these superhuman creatures signaled the conscious intention to keep their legacy alive. Some of these outstanding divinities were Ọ̀ṣun, Ṣàngó, Yemoja, and Ògún, among others. Every settlement among the Yorùbá was attached to the history of outstanding exploits they had done in relation to the town that adopted them as their god. For example, there was Ṣàngó in the history of Oyo, and there was Ọ̀ṣun in the history of Osogbo, both of which are discussed in what follows.

---

54. Herskovits, *Myth of the Negro Past*.
55. Matory, *Fetish Revisited*.

Ọ̀ṣun

Ọ̀ṣun was a goddess and one of the most beautiful in the Yorùbá pantheon. Myths and legends described the place of Ọ̀ṣun in the history of Osogbo, each of them revealing the extraordinary efforts she made in the protection of the people and their possessions.[56] Indigenes of the city were constant victims of natural and human challenges that threatened their existence. Although there were different expropriations of mythical explanations attached to the history of the city, many of them were contentious. However, they were united in their claim that the city was founded by a migrant prince from Iléṣà, a nearby settlement, to expand his socioeconomic reach.

Offered here is one version of the mythology. Called Láaróyè, the Iléṣà prince had settled in a village called Ìpọ̀lé, which had a close connection to Iléṣà township. During a particular period at Ìpọ̀lé, scarcity of drinkable water made survival difficult and almost made the people lose their domestic possessions, to the point of it triggering a famine. Láaróyè, alongside Olútìmẹ́hìn, took some strong men, and they set out on the voyage to get water. The people experienced hardship in the process as they searched for water unsuccessfully. When they were losing hope, they discovered a serene river; its water was healthy for consumption. Because there was drought, Láaróyè and his emissary, Olútìmẹ́hìn, were advised to relocate their people to the riverbank so they would avoid the recurrent challenge of drought. Láaróyè's father, Owate, declined for undisclosed reasons, but he ruled that his son and Olútìmẹ́hìn should consider relocating to the place. And because they were both in their adolescence, they accepted the advice and soon took to the place.

Barely a year after their relocation, the river flooded. The situation was so threatening that Láaróyè consulted the oracle, as was the custom when the Yorùbá faced consuming emergencies. The oracle prescribed sacrifice for the people and implored them to move away from the riverbank, as that was an invasion of the territory of the Ọ̀ṣun River. Expectedly, the sacrifice was offered, and Ọ̀ṣun showed the sign of acceptance by sending an underwater character, *Iko*, to reveal herself to the people. To the amazement of the people present, the character was a beautiful sight, and the appearance was irresistible. The king received her with an open heart, and so he established a bond between the people and the goddess. That action became the foundation for the establishment of Ọ̀ṣun annual worship, which usually coincided with the celebration of the royal family too. From that time, the Ọ̀ṣun goddess has remained the spiritual guide of the Osogbo people, and they have always offered their respect through worship in return.[57]

Notably, Ọ̀ṣun's archetype is orthographically represented as Ochun but shares similar pronunciation with the one among the Yorùbá.[58] In Afro-Cuban *oricha*, the Òrìṣà divinities and their overlapping meanings manifested in complex realizations because they were works in progress. While they were understood to have a beginning, they were equally projected to have a defining end. But in between the path was the process of adaptation and change, which

---

56. Esguerra, *Oshun Diaries*.

57. Murphy and Sanford, *Osun across the Waters*.

58. De La Torre, "Dancing with Ochún," 113–134.

reiterates the fact that the *oricha* were dynamic, as they were compelled to function within the environment in which they were found because they inherently had the potential through the potency of *àṣẹ* and the dictates of their destiny. As the Ọṣun divinity was associated with protection and support for the people, the path of *Ochun*, as conceived in the sociocultural setting of the Cuban environment, was that she represented the spirit of hard work, which invariably meant she supported productivity and the joyful and young in reasonable degree. In this Atlantic environment, Ochun's path manifested in different but ideologically complementing ways. In all her manifestations, she was associated with the river and controlled wealth in certain situations. She supported humankind and emphasized affection in the process. She was endeared in Cuba to take charge of all humans' erotic components because of her disposition to adornments and association with affluence and materialism.

The collective aspirations of the people were supported by the goddess as she equally responded to the social and political dynamics of the Atlantic world. Despite having experienced the naked savagery of the Middle Passage, enslaved Africans in the Americas identified the spiritual support of the goddess, which further stretched their perseverance, persistence, and preservation. Finding an archetypal strength in the rivers, Ochun became the navigating compass of individuals who had faced all manners of human degeneration. Surprisingly, Ochun undertook the spiritual assignments of the other Òrìṣà, using the power of productivity that water could always ensure. While not changing her spiritual potency, the process of adaptation and change remained a veritable basis for promoting her worship in the New World. Because of their manner of responses, these Òrìṣà had shown that their capacity for transformation was not to be undermined, as they would come to the rescue of their adherents if they maintained mutual understanding and created a peaceful atmosphere for this relationship. On several occasions, the cross-border interchange of the spiritual essence of Ọṣun strengthened the sociocultural understanding of the *oricha* in the New World.

Yemọja/Olókun

Yemọja was one of the divinities in the pantheon of the Yorùbá. She manifested in the duality of cultural representation because, despite her extremely feminine traits, she also had a considerable degree of masculine disposition.[59] Culturally, she appeared more in her feminine form, and except in situations where there was the need to demonstrate the more forceful aspect of herself, Yemọja was associated with peace, tranquility, and succor. The mythical narrative around the identity of this divinity was that during the early time, when the earth was circumscribed in water and was without a particular form, Olódùmarè commanded the sun to descend on the planet, and as the sun came out in fulfillment of this command, Yemọja was invaded and felt uneasy. Thereafter, new changes were made, and after birthing several Òrìṣà through her procreative power, Yemọja became the "Mother of the Earth." Because she was structurally construed as a woman, the water coming from her breast became clean streams and lakes. She demonstrated the Olokun characteristics of the aggressive storm from the sea whenever she

---

59. Otero and Falola, *Yemoja*.

was angry. She was a well-celebrated Òrìṣà among the Yorùbá people of Nigeria.[60]

Watermelons, grapes, palm oil, squash, beer, gin, rum, candy, kola nuts, flowers, and coral, among others, were sacrificed to this deity.[61] This was especially important as the gift of procreation for people seeking children. Yemọja's devotees understood that the dominant cultural and spiritual philosophy that their deity represented was the calmness of human character and the exemplification of affection, as these were conceived as the foundation for every harmonious relationship that would be the agency of progress generally. The concentration on being peaceful, however, did not condemn the decision to take to anger, especially if it was estimated that one's peaceful disposition was taken for granted. Yemọja was represented by rivers and sea, like the Ogun River, but its archetype in Brazil and Cuba has the ocean as its abode. She was overtly motherly and used her strong will to protect her children against foreseeable dangers. As her devotees proclaimed, during their time in the Atlantic world, she came to the protection of her children when invoked, and because of her extreme sensitivity to their plight, she comforted and cleansed their sorrow.

However, one thing is understood from the adaptation of Yemọja in the transatlantic environment. Unlike in the Yorùbá origin, where the dual attributes of Yemọja remained dominant, it was quite different in the diaspora, where Yemọja was separated from her Olókun spiritual binary. Scholars like Phillip Neimark raised concerns about this separation of the Yemọja divinity. According to him, the separation of the deity into Yemọja and Olókun potentially tends to reduce its spiritual import and impact.[62] Without the complementary contributions of the two qualities, there would be an observable reduction in the agility and vibrancy of the individuals that have the qualities of this Òrìṣà. In truth, all Òrìṣà have their spiritual manifestations in all individuals because humans are part of the creative force of the universe. Therefore, separating one from the other would always come with some consequences that, in the long run, would challenge the spiritual

---

60. Murphy and Sanford, *Osun across the Waters.*
61. Murphy and Sanford, *Osun across the Waters.*
62. Neimark, *Way of Orisa.*

essentialism of divinity. Perhaps because of the issue of cultural discontinuity, Santeria, Candomblé, and related religions have their justifications for this development.

Ṣàngó/Xango

Ṣàngó was a male-like deity, considering his strong characteristics and intemperate nature.[63] Two narratives explain the existence of Ṣàngó. First is that he was part of the original set of deities, having a familial relationship with Yemoja. The latter, according to this oral account, was his mother during the project of transformation that Olódùmarè had commanded. Another of the narratives, which is mostly attributed to the history of Oyo, is that Ṣàngó was once a king, the fourth ruler of the historical Oyo city-state.[64] Ṣàngó was tempestuous, temperamental, and quick to rage. One thing that foregrounded his vociferous temper was the transformation of his words into fire whenever he was deeply angry and fumed in annoyance. According to the mythology, he was unintentionally bestowed with this magic by his lovely wife, Ọya, whose fondness for her husband was the reason for this show of limitless affection. The feeling was mutual, as Ṣàngó was reported to have loved Ọya considerably. The natural force associated with Ṣàngó was lightning and fire, while his prominent symbol was *oṣé*, a double-headed battle-ax that remains the legacy of his disciples.[65]

Advised by Ọya to cast a spell between his two generals, Gbonka and Timi, to initiate destructive conflicts capable of weakening them, Ṣàngó acted hurriedly, following his wife's advice. Sadly, however, Gbonka survived the brawl, showing superior capacity and control over Timi. The consequence was that Gbonka, the survivor, became more powerful and insisted on driving away Ṣàngó from the stool of power. Defeated, Ṣàngó became angry, abdicated power, and embarked on self-banishment. In the journey to exile, he examined his leadership overindulgence and was contritely remorseful for his actions. Thus, he hanged himself from an *ààyán* tree. After the news about his action reached his admirers in the Oyo kingdom, they tried to recover his body to give him a befitting burial worthy of a brave warrior. Surprisingly, they could not find his body. He had disappeared and transformed into something different. From then on, Ṣàngó devotees designated special attention to him and worshipped him with utmost dedication.

In the Santeria religion, Chango is the archetype of the West African Ṣàngó deity, and it was one of the most feared and revered gods in followers' cultural engagement.[66] He was equally worshipped as an important deity in Haiti. However, in the Candomblé religion, people recognized him as Xango; united in their dedication to him, they believed that through the associated spiritual power commanded by Ṣàngó, they had the propensity to forge ahead in their ways, relying on his protection and support. Since Ṣàngó was said to have hung himself in response to his dejection after self-examination and his body was not found at the scene of the action, there was a controversy around the originality of the news. His loyal devotees believed

---

63. Tishken, Fálọlá, and Akínyẹmí, *Sàngó in Africa*.
64. Murphy and Sanford, *Osun across the Waters*.
65. Murphy and Sanford, *Osun across the Waters*.
66. Canizares, *Shango*.

that he transformed into something different and that there was no way he would have taken his own life. This was what brought about the popular praise-chant line *"Ọba kò so"* (the king did not hang) when evoking the Ṣàngó spirit. The line rejects the popular misconception about the circumstances of his death. He was popularly accepted in the transatlantic world because of the efforts of enslaved Yorùbá to immortalize him there.

Acculturation of Òrìṣà in the Transatlantic Environment

Brazil

Brazil was one of the transatlantic places where the bulk of enslaved Africans were transported, and as a result, it became the spatial force that connected the West African peoples. As the Yorùbá found themselves in the same condition in Brazil, they reignited their religious identity and began to syncretize it with the one available—Roman Catholicism. Consequent upon their unification of interest, a religious identity emerged called Candomblé, a religion whose spiritual philosophy was founded on Òrìṣà traditions where Olódùmarè was considered responsible for the creation of the universe through the Òrìṣà.[67]

As the Yorùbá religion that birthed the Candomblé archetype was founded on the understanding that Olódùmarè was supreme, the crux of spiritual engagement was the veneration of the Òrìṣà to appeal to Olódùmarè. Because the religion was syncretic, the Òrìṣà was linked with the Roman Catholic saints, sharing compelling attributes that made the devotees attain a spiritual balance. In fact, despite being sourced from different Africans, the revelations were complementary and reinforcing. The fortification of Òrìṣà among the Candomblé devotees was underscored by the erection of statues for the Òrìṣà they adopted.

Cuba

In Cuba, they practiced Santeria, the appropriation of the worship system of the Yorùbá into Cuban society.[68] Although this religion shared unique characteristics from the Yorùbá and the Christian religion, especially Roman Catholicism, it was believed to be polytheistic in practice. In Santeria, it was believed that every individual was associated with a particular Òrìṣà that was designated to them at the point of creation. Guided by the Òrìṣà, humans functioned to their fullest potential when they carefully aligned their thoughts and reasoning to that of their chosen divinity. The Yorùbá recognized the place of human capacity for social relationships, as the decisions made had corresponding results on the generality of humankind. For this reason, followers were encouraged to be in good standing with their Òrìṣà so that their world would be in good shape. Enslaved Africans who found themselves in the Atlantic were dispossessed of any material, especially concrete ones. This exposed them to limitless challenges in the New World,

---

67. Alonso, *Development of Yoruba Candomblé Communities.*
68. Brandon, *Santeria from Africa to the New World.*

but they were determined. The religio-cultural inheritance lodged in their minds helped them in the re-creation of their identity and they joined the Catholic Church.

After choosing the Christian religion, as many did reluctantly, they gradually introduced the Yorùbá system, consequently creating a hybrid religion. This explains why the Santeria religion made use of drums, dance, and songs in their quest to attract the blessings of Òrìṣà. Santeria shared the attributes of the Yorùbá religion in that they offered sacrifices and paid homage to the dead as commonly done among the Yorùbá of West Africa. They made offerings to the Òrìṣà in the forms of fruits and the blood of sacrificed animals, among others. Their special immersion in the tenets of Christianity notwithstanding, they made different attempts toward divination, especially through Ifá, from which they interpreted and deciphered messages of the Òrìṣà. They believed in natural healing and, in most cases, they used traditional means of healing that did not involve herbal remedies.[69] Their worship was done through the adoption of the Yorùbá language, called "Lucumi."[70] The growth of Santeria in Cuba was credited to the determination of its devotees amid several years of ceaseless repression and marginalization.

Trinidad and Tobago

In Trinidad and Tobago, there was the Trinidadian Òrìṣà, the adaptation of Ṣàngó. The religion was developed by taking attributes of the Ṣàngó worship in Nigeria and merging them with the Christian elements to produce a more powerful force. Because of the presence of baptism in Christianity, Trinidadian Òrìṣà incorporated the doctrinal elements of indigenous worship so that the combination of the two generated a contextually reinforcing spiritual impact.[71] Several religious scholars have considered the religion as being eclectic because it chooses from various religions of the world to become its current realization. Just like others of Yorùbá origin, there was a practice of song and dance accompanied by drums and claps. These were special religious practices used to unlock the key to abundance through their communication with the spiritual forces. The orientation of the religion stemmed from the understanding that the world was controlled by some forces in which humans were intertwined. Therefore, mutual understanding between the Òrìṣà, through invocation, was needed for human sustenance.

Conclusion

The presence of Yorùbá religion in the Atlantic environment is a testament to the reincarnation of epistemic principles of the Yorùbá. As tough as the Atlantic slave trade was, those who were deprived of taking material possessions along with them in crossing the Atlantic were experts in various fields. The situation warranted that they fell on their intellectual properties as instruments to re-create themselves in the New World. Those who were diviners began to teach others and spread the indigenous knowledge, especially to their offspring, as a way of preserving

---

69. Barnet, *Afro-Cuban Religions*.
70. Wirtz, *Performing Afro-Cuba*.
71. Houk, "Orisha Religion in Trinidad."

their identity and surviving the harshness of their new but strange environment. Yorùbá epistemologies and Òrìṣà became part of the Afro-Atlantic religion, and the gods and goddesses of West Africa moved to the Americas.

As the Yorùbá also accepted Christianity, a project of translation and localization followed. Christianity had to embrace aspects of indigenous worship system that recognized drumming, dancing, and singing as acts of worship. Gradually, the Yorùbá began to substitute drumming with clapping and light dances with heavy ones characteristic of Òrìṣà style. When slavery ended officially in the nineteenth century, they began to further promote their indigenous religious characteristics. Emboldened by the success they had in the process of introducing the Yorùbá religion, they became confident to consolidate their practices. As a result, some religions in the transatlantic environment were embedded with African systems, and this created a hybrid religious system that became a success in some parts of the New World. Interestingly, as the community was going through this process across the Atlantic, their kinsmen in their homeland were engineering a Yorubanized Islam and Christianity that later traveled across the world, as in the case of contemporary Pentecostalism. Here, elements of Yorùbá practices were infused into Islamic and Christian practices. This discussion informs the explorations in the next two chapters.

Introduction

The influence of Islam as a religion and culture continues to penetrate many places, and the religion is used as the vehicle for driving many transformations. There is an underlying interest in making Islam a global practice, and this orientation has been at the center of Islamic propagation and its positive image for many people. The situation is sometimes complicated by minority fundamentalists who continue to create problems for the religion in their interactions with both secular states and Christianity. As an illustration, several countries in the world, especially in the Global North and sometimes in Asia, view Islam with skepticism.[1] Not a few anti-Islam activists speak with hatred—their impassioned distance comes from the prejudicial evaluation of the accumulated behaviors of minority extremists. This prejudice is based on the idea that some Muslims are supportive of incidences of extremism.[2] Whatever image these skeptics have created for the religion, it must be registered that Islam has not only broken difficult boundaries but has also made itself a positive global force.[3] Islam, which is now part of the religions associated with the Yorùbá people, is not a new religion among them and much older than Christianity in many places.

Islam has penetrated the Yorùbá religious and cultural space for centuries, partly because of geographical proximities and the successful activities of its missionaries.[4] Economic interactions historically necessitated intercultural exchanges, with new ideas spreading through intergroup relations.[5] Therefore, the platform for the promotion of any religion was already erected, at least mentally, and one of the requirements for the successful implantation of religious practice was the commitment and determination of the agents of conversion to achieve their goals.[6] It spread slowly at first and became one of the fastest-growing religions in the twentieth century.[7]

---

1. Shaheed, "UN Expert Says Anti-Muslim Hatred Rises to Epidemic Proportions."

2. Jikeli, "Discrimination of European Moslems," 77–96.

3. Kane, *Beyond Timbuktu.*

4. Tukur, "Islam Came to South."

5. Cartwright, "Spread of Islam in Ancient Africa."

6. Robinson, *Muslim Societies in African History.*

7. Clarke, *West Africa and Islam.*

Recent events among the Yorùbá—notably the rise of Christian Pentecostalism, the increasing use of religion for political purposes, and fights over symbols such as the hijab—are creating complications and division among segments of the population.[8] Many intellectual productions have examined the relationship of Islam with the Yorùbá, but most of the conclusions, or the theoretical models of evaluation, are changing because of the impact of modernity, contestations for power, and aggressive interreligious rivalries. This chapter presents many important issues, including a brief history of Islam in Yorubaland, Yorùbá Islamic practices in a global context, the Yorùbá Muslims in the diaspora, and the response of Yorùbá Muslims to the global narrative on Islam.

The introduction of Islam to the Yorùbá occurred in a globalizing world, coming slowly and probably in multiple directions. Scholars differ in their assessments of when Islam originated among the Yorùbá.[9] Some scholars argue that it came around the seventeenth century, while others advocate for earlier or later dates,[10] but they all emphasize the impact of the nineteenth-century jihad and the creation of the Sokoto Caliphate on the spread of Islam, as it sought to extend its reach beyond the Hausa states.[11] One account of the introduction of Islam into Yorùbá culture is the association of the beginning of the religion with the influx of Malians into the Yorùbá space around the fifteenth and sixteenth centuries.[12] In this association was the relevance of extensive regional connections that moved goods and religion across a wider savanna belt and down to the forest.[13] Once the people within contiguous regions had access to the Islamic community—including the exchange of commodities—the spread of Islam became facilitated and clusters of traders and missionaries emerged in different parts of the Sudanese empires. The argument is that around the sixteenth century, they were traveling long distances and spreading out to reach places such as the Yorubaland.[14]

At various times from the sixteenth century onward, Islam arrived in different Yorùbá locations, gaining converts in the Oyo Empire, the Lagos area, and other places.[15] These careful yet effective ways of introducing the religion later resulted in the rapid spread of Islam in the twentieth century. The spread cut across different Yorùbá cities once the expansionists had carefully succeeded in winning people to their side. In short, the history of the religion among the Yorùbá was part of a much wider network. Coincidentally, by the nineteenth century, Christianity was simultaneously spreading among the people. The consequence is that today, the Yorùbá have millions of people practicing both religions and developing mutual tolerance.[16]

---

8. Lawal, "Nigerian Schools in the Throes of Hijab Crisis."

9. Doi, *Islam in a Multi-Religious Society*.

10. Gbadamosi, *Growth of Islam among the Yoruba*.

11. Obayemi, "Sokoto Jihad and the 'O-Kun' Yoruba," 61–87; and Mason, "Jihad in the South," 193–209.

12. Badawi, *Ma'a Harak ul-Islam fi Ifriqiyah*.

13. Adelabu, "African Christianity."

14. Lasisi, "Muslim Traditional Rulers in Nigeria," 31–41.

15. Ogunbado, "Islam and Its Impact in Yorubaland," 1–18.

16. Nolte et al., "Research Note," 541–561.

Yorùbá Islamic Practices in Local, Regional, and Global Contexts

Yorùbá Islam

Just like language, when a religion moves away from the territory it initially originates from to other territories that practice it through evangelization, it amounts to a variation in the religious tenets. This was the same phenomenon that occurred when Islam got to Yorubaland. For the Yorùbá people, Islam was a religion, a form of devotion to Allah. It was not imbibed by many as a way of life, for instance, as it was for the Hausa people. In other words, the Yorùbá accepted Islam but not all its attendant civilizations. While the Yorùbá accepted the worship of Allah, many lived in ways that were assumed to be contrary to some of Islam's established practices. To critics, the Yorùbá erroneously believed that Islam encompassed the Yorùbá culture, especially regarding behavioral dispositions, respect for one another, festivals, traditions, customs, and a host of others. The term *Yorùbá Islam* can be coined to assess and analyze the variations in the way the Yorùbá practiced the religion compared to how it should be practiced according to the Quran and *Sunnah*, the scriptures of the Holy *Qur'an* and the sayings of Prophet Muhammad.

Perhaps the major factor that accounted for the intermixing of Yorùbá traditions and Islam was that the Yorùbá believed that no new religion was capable of totally overturning their ways of life but could only be practiced side by side with other belief systems. The Yorùbá themselves had an established religion and were fervent adherents. Another reason was the erroneous belief that Islam was all-accommodating as well as the common view that Islam took or only accepted indigenous cultures that were compatible with its tenets and ways of life, as Muhib Opeloye explains it.[17] Put differently, Islam rejected aspects of indigenous culture that underlined the belief in and supremacy of Allah (Olódùmarè in the Yorùbá language).

Tawhid, an Arabic word that explains the way Muslims are to believe in Allah, is often missing among or taken for granted by the Yorùbá Muslims—hence why they are not tagged "true Muslims." Although research has revealed that many Yorùbá Muslims attempted to practice the religion in its undiluted form when it was introduced to the land, it did not last long.[18] Yorùbá Islamic clerics wanted to gain attraction and followership, so some of them engaged in what is called *Shirk*, which denoted the simultaneous worship of Allah with other gods. However, notable Islamic scholars failed to reach a consensus about the definition of *Shirk*. To some of them, *Shirk* occurs when one intentionally worships through the profession of belief in other lesser gods, but it goes beyond that. *Shirk* encompasses the use of material things, such as amulets and charms, as a form of protection. This form of religious practice is commonplace among the Yorùbá Muslims of today. Abdulganiy Oloruntele notes that there are now Muslim *olóògùn* in Yorubaland, otherwise known as "Muslim herbalists," who believe that communicating with God through sorcery is permissible and that the killing of animals for rituals, aside from those firmly established in the Quran, is acceptable as well. According to him, "Muslim clerics also

---

17. Opeloye, "Yoruba Muslims' Cultural Identity Question," 2–5.
18. Rufai, "Emergent Issues in Heterodox Islam," 117–120.

engage in both acts of healing ordinary diseases and exorcism of anyone under supernatural bondage. Their methods connote the combination of Islamic as well as Yorùbá practices of exorcism. The clerics organize congregational supplications for their clients, reciting or repeating some chapters or verses of the Qur'an, or prophetic prayers in various forms, to liberate the client from the evil forces."[19]

Some scholars may call these practices evidence of religious syncretism; however, Islam does not encourage syncretism that undermines the *Tawhid*—that is, the belief in the oneness of Allah. In other words, Islam is on the one side, while one's traditional culture is on the other. It could be argued that the factor that contributes to this development is that religion changes and accepts shifting cultural dynamics over time. While Islam accepts modern development, it remains the same in the manner of worship. In the view of most Islamic scholars, one's indigenous culture does not supersede one's practice of Islam.

However, there is still a prevalence of the intermixing of Yorùbá (religious) traditions and the Islamic religion, which led to the emergence of the term *Yorùbá Islam*. This best explains why some Yorùbá Muslims grace Yorùbá traditional festivals, even when Islam forbids participation in such. Muslims are known to participate in masquerade festivals and some wear masks. Yorùbá Muslims accept Islam if it is compatible with their ways of life. As against the Islamic scripture, Yorùbá Muslims often believe that the true practice of Islam lies in one's heart; that is, they believe that Allah judges one's intention only. This belief is further accentuated in the rise of Sufism among Yorùbá Muslims. It could be argued that Sufism, which is different in doctrines and ideologies from Alu Sunnah—another Islamic group based on the unorthodox teaching and practice of Islam—influenced the practices of religious syncretism among Yorùbá Muslims. Most Yorùbá Muslim clerics who engage in what they call "Islamic divination" are largely "Sufists," which are seen in the many sects such as the famous Tijjaniyah and Qadiriyyah, among a host of others.

Muhsin Balogun contends that the prevalence of religious syncretism is further compounded by the prevalence of the "Yoruba Muslim Clerics" who are also referred to as "Àwọn Alfa Oní Jálàbí."[20] Balogun argues that this practice only shifts Yorùbá Muslims away from the true tenets and practices of Islam.[21] However, such practices are getting more popular because such Islamic clerics are commonplace. Islam has now been redefined by Yorùbá Muslims who have intermixed their traditional practices with the tenets of Islam. Afiz Oladimeji Musa and Hassan Ahmad Ibrahim offer insights into the representation of Islam in Yorubaland. In their essay, they argue that in the first instance, the pattern in which Islamic practices have been shaped by the twin factors of pragmatism and dynamism has facilitated the swift acculturation of Islam among the Yorùbá.[22] They argue that Islam, on getting into Yorubaland, was variegated in its practices to suit the lifestyle of Yorùbá Muslims,[23] citing the case of "Jálàbí." The Yorùbá take their spiritual activities seriously, and in the face of Islam, the new religion, there

---

19. Abdulganiy, "Evil Forces and Shirk among the Yoruba Muslims," 55–65.
20. Balogun, "Syncretic Beliefs and Practices," 50.
21. Balogun, "Syncretic Beliefs and Practices," 50.
22. Solagberu, "Impact of Sufism," 405.
23. Solagberu, "Impact of Sufism," 405.

must be a similar phenomenon, especially in the aspect of spirituality. In the event of any disaster, the Yorùbá often seek divination, using the traditional means of *àkọsẹ́jayé*, a practice used to know a child's fortunes. These traditional practices were embedded in Islam for it to gain widespread acceptance.

Thus, the concept of *jálàbí* among Yorùbá Muslims serves to fill the vacuum of traditional Yorùbá divination. One can argue that jalabism has been seen as a sort of strategy to consolidate the acceptance of Islam among Yorùbá Muslims who are still not weaned off from their traditional practices. Rather than a Muslim visiting Babaláwo, they go to "Alfa oní Jálàbí," who makes divination on their behalf. However, these practices are condemned, according to a consensus of Muslim scholars. Yet, it has continued to gain prominence. Some of these "jálàbí practices" involve the use of Quranic verses, albeit in an often radical departure from the tenets of Islam. It is pertinent to note that some of these limitations also involve the misreading of the Quran and the disruption of the verses. Perhaps, one of the most distorted and disrupted chapters of the Holy Quran by the Jálàbí Alfas in Yorubaland is *Suratul Yasin*. Lateef Adetona dwells on this and argues that most Yorùbá Muslims have identified with *Suratul Yasin* as a means of "supplication and healing."[24] However, he notes that "this is a clear departure from the right precepts of the Sharīah on the beneficial uses of portions of the Qur'ān. . . . There are many cases which involve misuse of the Sūrah through bastardisation of its contents, i.e. twisting, alternating and missing out some of its wordings."[25]

In an essay, G. O. Gbadamosi reveals that the appointment of Imams in Yorubaland does not often follow due Islamic process.[26] The Islamic position of the Imam established that the most knowledgeable assume the mandate. However, what has been the case, in some instances, as noted by Gbadamosi, is that Imamship has now become a thing of hereditary right, in a simulacrum to the ascension of monarchy in Yorubaland. Therefore, it can be deduced from the foregoing that this aspect further showcases the reconstruction of Islam by Yorùbá Muslims.

Similarly, J. Lorand Matory asserts that Islam has radically departed from what it is meant to be among Yorùbá Muslims.[27] He notes that there have been obvious instances of interweaving between Islam and traditional religion, and he draws references to various cases of similarities between the Yorùbá Orìṣà religion and Islam, harping that there is a Yorùbá maxim to that effect. According to him, the interaction between Islam and èsìn ìbílè ("traditional religion") is not a face-off between primordial and discrete elements, but a mutually constituting dialogue well precedent in the Islamic world. A Yorùbá proverb represents their coexistence itself as primordial:

Ifá [the ranking divination priesthood] is as old as life
Islam is as old as life
It was at noon day that Christianity came in.[28]

---

24. Musa and Ibrahim, "Islamization and the Representation of Islam," 210–215.

25. Musa and Ibrahim, "Islamization and the Representation of Islam," 210–215.

26. Gbadamosi, "Imamate Question among Yoruba Muslims," 231.

27. Matory, "Rival Empires," 495.

28. Matory, "Rival Empires," 495.

Cross-Cultural Practices

In *Resurgent Islam and the Politics of Identity*, Ali Mazrui argues that there are two ways of interpreting Islam.[29] The first centers on a critical interrogation of the rules guiding the religion and its complex political functions in the context of a theological design. This means that Islam favors the recommendations ingrained within the Quran concerning purity, perfection, and devotion. In essence, the religion's injunctions are allowed to determine the actions and activities of its adherents.[30] Muslims build healthy relationships around the injunctions, and their social engagements can be determined by the prescriptions recommended in the Qur'an or the ones associated with the teachings of Islam and the sayings of Muhammad, the Prophet of Islam. In this argument, the Quran will impact the Yorùbá who accepted Islam, and communities of worshippers and individuals can take whatever they find appropriate from the Quran, as the Yorùbá has done.

Mazrui suggests that the other available method of interpreting the religion is through the interrogation of its historical antecedence.[31] Here, the interpreter is not usually concerned with the doctrinal characteristics of the religion but centers on the examination of the social activities of Muslims and the ways through which they have managed to survive over time. Indeed, when one passes a provocative comment on Islam, one is engaging in what Mazrui calls "historical Islam interpretation."[32] The history is not local, and global traffic in fundamentalism can generate hostility.[33] For instance, the conversation on Islam among the Yorùbá can include data drawn from varying locations from Syria to Indonesia. Allah is supreme over local leaders.[34]

Meanwhile, the cultural mix of Islam among the Yorùbá has been impressive. It is impossible not to admit that Islam and its culture have transformed the Yorùbá and connected them to a much larger world. This has also provoked a variation in the practices, especially as some do believe that there is no such thing as "liberal Islam." In essence, the evaluation of Islam also rests on how ideas drawn from it have been appropriated among the Yorùbá over time. It is part of the appropriation of culture that present-day Yorùbá Muslims conduct marriages by drawing from indigenous practices and mixing them with those accepted in Islam.[35] This is one example of how Islam encourages flexibility and openness to Yorùbá cultural and religious practices. It is a conventional understanding that the lived philosophy of the Muslims in Yorubaland points to acculturation and enculturation. Islam appealed to the Yorùbá because the religion never preached against all the various Yorùbá cultural norms in practice. Islam supported many aspects of the existing cultures of the Yorùbá, such as dressing and polygamy. This made

---

29. Mazrui, *Resurgent Islam.*

30. Ul Haq, "Social Order in Islam," 39–66.

31. Mazrui, *Resurgent Islam.*

32. Mazrui, *Resurgent Islam.*

33. Ward, "Cleric Said to Be behind Tunisian Beach Massacre Is Living on Benefits in Britain"; and Furness, "Hate Preacher Abu Qatada Can Be Deported."

34. Bin Khaled al-Saud, "Spiritual Teacher and His Truants," 736–754.

35. Peel, *Christianity, Islam, and Orisa-Religion,* 150–171.

it possible for converts to adopt the ideologies of Islam, as it does not place them in a precarious situation of losing their cultural identity.

Having established that the line between religion and Arab-Islamic culture can be blurred among Muslims in some other parts of the world, we must clarify that the Yorùbá exhibit some differences that ironically portray them to other believers, especially in parts of northern Nigeria, as "theologically inferior" and not "true Muslims." Yorùbá cultural or social behaviors do not always fall within the preserve of Islam. Many Muslims believe in Òrìṣà and Ifá. Although Ifá, the compendium of Yorùbá's oral history, epistemology, philosophy, and spirituality, can offer moral advice, it does not prevail on humans to decide how they run their social or cultural affairs, if they show a good sense of moral rectitude.[36] Thus, one can be a Muslim and accommodate Ifá, since Ifá is not opposed to Islam. For example, Ifá does not give explicit guidance on marriage. Marriage could be monogamous or polygamous; it is principally left to a man's choice, for Ifá understands that every human action has corresponding consequences. Hence, the number of wives that can be accumulated is a human invention because it is humans who react to their social realities, and people's choice of marriage can be interpreted as their reaction to their socioeconomic realities. What we, therefore, call culture is the accumulation of human behavior that has been consistently practiced. When Islam came to Yorubaland, the form of marriage system popular among them was polygamy, and because Islam does not object to polygamy for Muslims, one can understand how it was easy to align this view with the Ifá message.

In addition, the naming culture is another inheritance that Yorùbá Muslims draw from Islam. Across the world, people give names to their children, plants, and animals. However, a name as a phenomenon (or nomenclature) has different cultural understandings. The Yorùbá naming culture is predominantly anthropomorphic, as many African naming systems have been. And since Islamic culture also has a unique naming system, it became easy for Yorùbá Muslims to incorporate these cultural practices.[37] However, their cultural basis for naming is different. While the Yorùbá consider their environment and considers family history for direction, the culture of naming among Yorùbá Muslims accepts this in addition to adopting Islamic names. Thus, although they accept the naming culture of Muslims, Yorùbá Muslims still offer their children their cultural names as a sign of commitment to their heritage.[38]

The evolution of Islamic titles in Yorùbá was born out of the need to honor deserving members of the faith who were perceived to play strategic roles in the propagation of the religion in their respective communities. The individuals who hold these Islamic titles are known to have gone an extra length to show their support for the development of the religion in their respective communities. The conferment of chieftaincy titles is one of the ways through which an individual's status in Yorùbá society is improved. From the *Olorí ẹbí*, who serves as a local family head, to *Baálẹ*, who acts in the capacity of compound heads, the sociopolitical strata of Yorùbá were strategically structured before the coming of Islam.[39] In the preexisting Yorùbá

---

36. Abimbola, *Ifa Will Mend Our Broken World*.

37. Oyewumi, *What Gender Is Motherhood?*, 193–209.

38. Fakuade, Friday-Otun, and Adeosun, "Yoruba Personal Naming System," 251–271.

39. Raheem, "Alhaji Azeez Ajagbemokeferi and His Da'wah Activities."

culture, the conferment of chieftaincy titles came in one of two ways. The first was through heredity, which followed that a chieftaincy title was confined to a particular family or set of families within the community. Hereditary chieftaincy titles carried more weight and responsibility, as it was through this that the paramount ruler, like the Ọba, was chosen. The second manner took the form of honorary titles accorded to individuals for their various contributions to the development of the community. This can be bestowed on any individual who was perceived to have deserved such titles, irrespective of family background or origin.

In the same vein, the Islamic institution in Yorùbá societies embarked on parallel conferment of titles on individuals who made a great impact on the growth and development of Islam. As obtainable with the traditional titles, Islamic titles were not for indigenes alone but also extended to non-indigenes who contributed to the growth and development of the religion. The most prominent among such titles was the Bàbá Àdínnì, otherwise known as the patron of the Islamic religion. This position is not a spiritual one, as it is conferred on individuals with respectable standing in the community. The Bàbá Àdínnì serves as the overall head of all other titleholders, but his office is limited to nonreligious issues alone.

Another title introduced into the Muslim structure is the Balógun Mùsùlùmí, which is accorded to anyone who is perceived to be influential and faithful to the Islamic leadership and the congregation. The Balógun Mùsùlùmí title is modeled according to the prevailing Balógun title in Yorubaland, which is conferred on the strongest warrior. From the Islamic point of view, the Balógun Mùsùlùmí is a "warrior" in his own right simply for the fact that he provides the material and funds needed for the successful propagation of the religion within his community. The bearer of such a position will automatically get the respect of the traditional ruler of the community as well as other authorities.[40]

Worship

The worship of the Supreme Being among the Yorùbá shares some features with Islam. Apart from the similarities of worshipping a "cosmic force" who is naturally unscathed with or without recognition by humans, the Yorùbá believe that worshipping a particular god does not mean the abandonment of other gods and goddesses.[41] The Òrìṣà could be worshipped and venerated for appeasement and be sent on errands. It, therefore, means that the relationship between humans and the divine is a symbiotic one.[42] The worship of these Òrìṣà comes at designated times, except for emergencies where their veneration is prescribed by Ifá. Even though some people settled for some of these Òrìṣà relating to their patrilineal history, there is nothing that suggests every member of the society or family gives religious attention to these beings, at least from historical and anthropological evidence.[43] This is one area of significant difference between Islam and the Yorùbá religion.

---

40. Doi, *Islam in Nigeria*, 236.

41. Idowu, *Olódùmarè*.

42. Barber, "How Man Makes God in West Africa," 724–745.

43. Neimark, *Way of Orisa*.

From the foregoing, it is apparent that the concept of religion and worship between Yorùbá and Islam is conceived differently but are similar in some ways. The synchronization of Islam by the Yorùbá was made possible in part because of the ability to accept multiple belief systems, so also is the idea of transferring one's ideological convictions from one religious identity to the other. The Òrìṣà devotees could become Muslims. The Ìjẹ̀ṣà did not have an Oǹdó person invading their space to spread the gospel of Ògún; neither did someone from Óṣogbo invade Ẹdẹ for the ecumenical rendition of Ọ̀ṣun. Thus, one could accept ideas from the outside, and with sufficient advantages offered, a person could gravitate toward different philosophies. It was this social condition that influenced various interpretations of many scholars about how the Yorùbá maintained their indigenous practices while embracing Islam.[44]

To understand that it is a social behavior, some instances of Yorùbá diasporan Muslims who have a strong attachment to their Yorùbá identity will be discussed. It is observed how the

Figure 9.1. "Alfa Iyanrin," by Dr. Kazeem Ekeolu. A Muslim cleric is imitating *Ifá* divination to foretell the future.

---

44. Gbadamosi, *Growth of Islam*.

Ìmàle of Brazil interspersed Islamic ideas with their indigenous spiritual systems to organize a rebellion.[45] During the confrontation between the Fulani and Yorùbá at Óṣogbo in the 1840s, many individuals on the battlefield were Muslims who depended on Yorùbá charms.[46] As such, it is more fitting to address the situation of Muslims in the Yorùbá world as an intermixing of two religions, a kind of syncretism that happens at the intersection of two different religions. One is that the target religion, in this case, Islam, would begin to appropriate attributes that are originally ascribed to Òrìṣà. The fact that Òrìṣà intermixed with Islamic religion and culture is spreading in the diaspora community without proselytization is indicative of this profound syncretism.[47] Second, the semantic implication of employing the word *syncretism* suggests an update of cultural and religious behavior by the people who have accepted the new religion; in this case, the Yorùbá who have embraced Islam represents a good example of this development. Some embrace Islam among the Yorùbá, while there are also those people who cling to their indigenous spiritual identity, but the reality remains that the ideas and philosophical dispositions of those who have embraced Islam have been influenced by said religion and its cultural undercurrents.

Perception of Justice and Separation

Matters of justice and law are deferred to the Islamic culture in traditionally Islamic countries. The legal system is structured on the propositions and pronouncements known as the Sharia. Generally, Muslims accept the fact that Sharia is the accumulation of spiritual positions and injunctions on the nature of human engagements within their immediate social environment and across it. Even when it appears inconsequential that the supreme entity whose realization is in immaterial form gives positions about the legal system of a people, it is believed in the Islamic culture that the assignment of law construction exclusively lies with Allah. The situation is different among the Yorùbá, as they have a social justice system that differs philosophically from what is found in Islamic civilization. Conflict resolution takes a very different form among the Yorùbá; this is indicative of their understanding or position about human relationships. They manage conflict in ways that would promote social togetherness and create a healthy environment where relationships are mended progressively. Except during the introduction of Western-centered civilization, the Yorùbá did not patronize physical court edifices where internal infringements were solved, infractions settled, and contradictions smoothed out. Their laws were corrective and not punitive, and this gave way to the creation of a society that was meant to promote justice and equity, although dictates of power and patriarchy sabotaged this from time to time. Solutions to interpersonal disputes were found through the appropriation of societal laws.[48]

But Sharia jurisprudence, which is centered on the prescriptions of Allah about the proscriptions of certain human engagements, shares an entirely different behavior among Muslims.

---

45. Robinson, *Muslim Societies in African History*.
46. Peel, "Syncretism and Religious Change," 121–141.
47. A. Ogunnaike, "Bilad al-Brazil," 1–21; and Capone, "'Orisha Religion,'" 219–232.
48. Charles, "Trial by Ordeal," 62–74.

Social infrastructure is built with cultural traditions that link religion and morality. Therefore, one is naturally condemned to social justice if one commits excessive misconduct, over the belief that nature always has a way of intervention—the spiritual aspect of their justice. It is, therefore, not uncommon to find a Yorùbá person committing acts of injustice against Ògún, Òsun, Alálẹ̀ (the forebears), Olódùmarè, or any of the deities in the pantheon of Yorùbá Òrìṣà. This developed from the thinking that these icons of their religion and culture have a way of intervening.[49] Any Yorùbá Muslim in the contemporary world who still shares that orientation will always commit people to Allah's judgment, over the impression that only He can fight for the oppressed.

In the alternative, however, it is not uncommon to find people who go to the necessary symbols of authority in traditional Yorùbá society when seeking justice or retribution. There are the family heads that settle domestic issues and vested authority representatives in the environment that they would approach if the conflicts were above domestic. This behavior is transposed into the Islamic culture for the Yorùbá Muslims and has seen to the systematic ways of resolving conflicts among the Yorùbá Muslims of today, irrespective of where they are. Matters of infractions are taken to the symbols of authority in Islam for the position of Sharia on them. The leaders, serving as interpreters, use their cultural discretion to redress the issues.

The Pluralizing Mix of Yorùbá Islamic Songs

In some ways, the Yorùbá culture has been mixed with Islamic civilization, resulting in the production of Yorùbá Muslim songs. Since the 1950s, there has been the proliferation of a uniquely imposing music genre created as a catalyst for sociocultural redefinition and political transformation. Although there are different music genres available among the Yorùbá from before the invasion by external civilizations, these are blended with a modern style that appears like a hybrid, characterized by its infusion of Yorùbá praise poems, chants, and word plays to produce a different form. However, the Yorùbá music genre fújì has a significant attribute, in that it was the exclusive creation of the Yorùbá Muslims.[50] The reason for the innovation of this genre is based on the evaluation that the Islamic world entertains the music pattern that only follows the Islamic culture. Because they are products of a different one, therefore, their best reaction was to create an alternative model that would answer the question posed by their social experience without dissociating itself from their culture. Subsequently, the fújì music genre was filtered by superfluous cultural traditions so much that its religious import was unmistakably waning. As a response to this, purely Islamic music that follows the recommendations of Islam emerged and became more popular in the twenty-first century.

Yorùbá Muslim songs are exemplary because they are considered philosophical instruments for the negotiation of political and moral dialectics. Although fújì was developed from wéré (a music genre developed as a response to Islamic culture),[51] the modern genre is conceived as the modifications of the fújì genre or the reversion to the former one in more developed ways.

---

49. Raheem and Famiyesin, "Controlling the Boundaries of Morality," 231–247.

50. Klein, "Allow Peace to Reign," 1–22.

51. Ọlátúnji, "Modern Trends in the Islamized Music of the Traditional Yorùbá," 447–455.

Therefore, its redefinition is characterized by the integration of instrumental music, and the socioreligious music genre has been employed as materials of entertainment during important social activities and engagements such as naming ceremonies, freedom for apprentices, marriages, and funerals, among others.[52] Importantly, it has been used as an instrument of social activism in recent years where the artist dwells on some sociopolitical challenges confronting the nation and indirectly calls out the corresponding authorities.[53] In some other cases, blatant acts of terrorism are criticized for obvious reasons.

Although Islam has been identified with the terrorization of the nation, the Yorùbá Muslims are a relatively peaceful people, and they consider the perpetual instances of confrontations of the fundamentalists in the religion as a blemish on their culture and identity, hence their employment of the music genre and medium to challenge culprits in those horrendously provocative engagements. Beyond the local appeal of these songs, some have found themselves in a transnational environment, as the Yorùbá Muslims in these places play indigenous Islamic songs and, by implication, leave a trace of the religion and their own culture anywhere they go.[54] As Muslims, the implications of this are that they would not be generally associated with condemnable engagements.[55]

Sufism and Yorùbá Epistemology

Definitional exactitude naturally should remain the first important thing to do when examining Islamic philosophy in association with the Yorùbá epistemic perception. Because there have been inevitable contradictions in the proposed definitions offered by various scholars, we will adopt Oludamini Ogunnaike's definition in his educative work, *Sufism and Ifá*, where he rules that the concept means "divine essence."[56] It primarily dwells on the integration of Islamic principles and the observation of the prescriptions of the Prophet. The foundational basis for the adoption of this philosophy springs from the conviction that some divine configurations or forces determine the conditions of the universe. To attune oneself to the frequency of the universal energies means that one answers the demands of the Supreme Being that is responsible for its creation. Beyond this, however, has been the conviction that previous individuals who have made commendable progress in making themselves relevant in religious practices will experience spiritual blessing. Looking at this from a deeper reflection, one realizes that Sufism centers on the personal convictions of individuals resulting from their association with nature, questioning their positions, and making logical inferences from their evaluation and examination of things.[57] In actuality, Sufism does not especially rely on concepts as immobile and constant truth. Instead, their personal experience and observation are promoted beyond the politics of doctrine.

---

52. Barber and Waterman, "Traversing the Global and the Local," 240–262.
53. Klein, "Fújì," 145–149.
54. Klein, *Yorùbá* Bàtá Goes Global.
55. Klein, "Allow Peace to Reign."
56. Ogunnaike, "Sufism and Ifa."
57. Knysh, *Sufism*.

A careful observation of Yorùbá spirituality and epistemology reveals that it is shaped by their dependence on truth as found with individuals and not doctrinal expressions. There are no strong doctrines to be especially followed by the devotees of the Yorùbá religion. Individuals are mostly encouraged to search for their truth because they accept that people differ in their spirit and social composition. Yorùbá emphasizes personal experience, and this forms the background for their relative freedom in relating with others and even embracing philosophical constructs that are not from their cultural traditions. The Yorùbá who have been converted to the Islamic religion have historically blended the philosophy of Sufism with their Yorùbá epistemic source to produce a more compelling worldview. Because the Sufi philosophy provides the platform for humans to question events and arrive at an end through reasoning, many Yorùbá adherents of the religion combine their indigenous perspectives so that they can understand and interpret the nature of knowledge.[58] Once communication between them and nature is facilitated, many people associate the potency of their words, deeds, and accomplishments with their initiation of unbreakable relationships with God. The Yorùbá also believe in God, and they use this approach in their relationship with Olódùmarè. Sufism does not condemn any perspective to truth; while it allows the appropriation of Islamic ways as better ways of knowing or seeking truth, it recognizes that all people can get to the truth through their personal experience, meditation, and other means.

It is imperative to include that Sufism has changed the ideology of Yorùbá Muslims. It has further made them embrace some of the practices of the Yorùbá traditional religion. The initial concept of Sufism connects a sort of mysticism and the ability to connect to one's creator, Allah, without using orthodox means. For the Sufists, the worship of Allah lies in the heart and is more important than the physical activities of Islam, such as Solah and the like. In various instances, there are multiple similarities between the concept of Sufism among the Yorùbá Muslims and the Yorùbá traditional religion, especially in the aspect of sorcery and divination, which Islam prohibits. As Abdur-Razzaq Solagberu notes, the impact of Sufi theories has influenced the perception of the Yorùbá people.[59] These theories have further disrupted the basic tenets of Islam. One factor that greatly contributed to the acceptance of Sufism among Yorùbá Muslims is its compatibility with the Yorùbá traditions.

Unlike Sufism, Sunni (also known as Sunnites or Ahlus Sunnah), another major sect in Islam, based its major practices and ideologies on the basic tenets of Islam. Often erroneously, the followers of this sect, sometimes called Sunnis, are usually described as "extremists." This is because a large group of followers offers no remorse or understanding of the parameters of individualism and often want believers (Muslims) to practice Islam in the way and manner it was practiced by the Prophet (PBUH) and his followers, without accounting for the various circumstances that could have hindered this. In recent times, the Yorùbá call the Sunnis "àwọn alákatakítí," which describes them as a sect that takes Islam as if it is something of life and death. Therefore, while Sufism offers liberalism that is comfortable among Yorùbá Muslims, Sunnism does not. According to Sunnism fervent adherents, Islam should be practiced in the

---

58. Olúkáyòdé, Èlàl'òrò.

59. Solagberu, "Impact of Sufism on the Culture of the People of Ilorin," 400–410.

manner the Holy Prophet practices it, whereas Sufism offers some understanding of the differences between humans.

With the prevalence of Sufism in Yorubaland, Muslim clerics are branded as mystics, and adherents of Sufism have been termed "Sufi mystics." Sufi practices go beyond the normal comprehension of everyday Muslims. These Sufist Yorùbá Muslim clerics have a huge followership that is often acquired through the performance of mystic miracles. After their deaths, these Yorùbá mystic sheiks are sometimes deified. Among a plethora of Yorùbá Sufi sheikhs, Shaykh Musa Ibrahim Ajágbemọ́kèfèrí stands out. In an analysis of his Da'wah activities (his means of Islamic propagation) by Kamaldeen Olawale Suleiman, it was noted that Shaykh Ajágbemọ́kèfèrí had mystic powers that were used to condemn idolatry practices and assisted people spiritually and physically.[60] He was nicknamed "Ajágbemọ́kèfèrí" because of the way he contested and won Yorùbá diviners and herbalists. His source of mysticism is unclear, but his identification as a Sufism is enough to fill in the gaps. The Sunnis would have frowned at the approach of Shaykh Ajágbemọ́kèfèrí because they do not think there is such a thing as Islamic mysticism. However, the presence of Sufism in Yorùbáland has contributed to the rise and popularity of Islam, perhaps in a way different from "Arab Islam."

The Instrumentality of Globalization in Appropriating Islam

Owing to the Yorùbá disposition to naming culture, Islam was referred to as *ẹ̀sìn* ìmàle , which translated either as "a difficult religion" (because of the language barrier and learning by rote) or "the religion of the Malian immigrants"—that is, a religion introduced by people from Mali. Introduced to them by the Malians via their neighbors to the north and immigrants differentiated by identity, the Yorùbá had thought that Islam was indigenous to Mali, hence their christening of the religion as *ẹ̀sìn* ìmàle. Ọ̀yọ́-Ilé attracted the first Malian traders, and through the persistence of the latter, the evangelization of Islam became possible among the Yorùbá. The globalization of trade and economy, the cross-border transmission of cultural heritage, and the universalization of values all enhanced and fast-tracked the appropriation of Islam among the Yorùbá.[61] City-states like Iwo, Iseyìn, Lagos, Sakí, Ikirun, Ede, Osogbo, and some others began to be influenced in the sixteenth century.

The acceptance of Islam is attributed to the offering of a better religious alternative to the Yorùbá.[62] Ahamad Ogunbado argues that because Islam influenced the Yorùbá cultural praxis significantly, the embrace of the religion was inevitable:

> To start with, Islam transformed the Yoruba religion. It is known that the Yorubas believe in the Supreme Being of God, the creator, but they have numerous deities who serve as intermediaries between them and God. They associate other beings (gods) next to God and worship them instead directly worshipping God. The presence or coming of Islam found this idea of Supreme Being in Yorubaland. It was therefore easy to

---

60. Sulaiman and Adeyemi, "Role of Shaykh Jamiu Larubawa Dandawi," 84–100.

61. Ryan, *Imale*.

62. Ogunbado, "Islam and Its Impacts in Yorubaland," 1–18.

introduce the concept from the Islamic perspective. Islam professes the oneness of the Almighty Allah and negates polytheism in all forms. Furthermore, Islam changed the attitude of the Yorubas from seeking help from such other gods as ogun, sango, oya and others. *Those gods could not even help themselves much less others.*[63]

The act of worship is decidedly different from the act of propitiation or persuasion. Worship "is the response of the creature to the Eternal."[64] Islam did not appropriate the Yorùbá gods and goddesses with the angels, so they took ideas around worship and general beliefs about the power of God.[65] But this is not the sense in which one finds it among the Muslims or the Judeo-Christian family. One cannot deny the instrumentality of globalization in the facilitation and adoption of Islam, especially by cultural groups that already have their indigenous spirituality. Ogunbado continues, "Ifa (oracle) consultation is Islamized to *Istikhara* (inquires prayer). Celebration of oriṣa festival is transformed or replaced with celebrating eid-el-fitri and eid-el-kabir. Women and men outlook is modified as polygamy is curtailed or modified into 'four at a time' while prefixed oriṣa names were changed to 'Olu' (Ọlọrun) plus Bunmi, becomes Ọlọrunbunmi. Traditional shrines and ritual sites were replaced with Central Mosques in major Yoruba town and cities."[66]

By arguing that the consultation of the oracle is already shortchanged with Istikhara,[67] Ogunbado perhaps intends to deliberately contradict himself, because those who accept Islam wholeheartedly among the Yorùbá do not always mix their adopted religion with indigenous belief systems and vice versa.

The period associated with the emergence of Islam among the Yorùbá coincided with the time when there was trade exchange, cross-cultural unity, and transnational bonding between the Yorùbá and Muslims from Mali and elsewhere. Muslims who came to the Yorùbá world because of trade were embraced for their economic importance, which was an addition to the religion with which they have come. For Islam to succeed, those who brought the system must show some concern to the people they wanted to convert, as this would increase their chances of being accepted by their hosts, which would help in the proliferation of the religion. Indeed, the first step taken was the decision of these Muslims to combine their military forces with those of the people they were with so that they could be instrumental in their victory during the war. In essence, the spread of Islam among the Yorùbá can be explained under these two processes. Once they mixed with people, they intermarried, procreated, and attracted followers after they won their loyalty. The Lagos situation where Muslims were supportive of one group against another during the power tussle between Kòsókó and his brother is indicative of this.[68] Thus, globalization helps in the facilitation of the religious hybridity we have among the Yorùbá today.

---

63. Ogunbado, "Islam and Its Impacts in Yorubaland." (emphasis is mine).

64. Underhill, *Worship*, 3.

65. Neimark, *Way of Orisa*.

66. Neimark, *Way of Orisa*.

67. Ogunbado, "Islam and Its Impacts in Yorubaland," 9.

68. Balogun, "Syncretic Beliefs and Practices."

Globalizing Yorùbá: The Islamic Effect

Yorùbá Islam has long been connected to global trends. Today, Muslims are found in all major cities of the world. As far back as the era of the transatlantic slave trade, the impact of Islam had spread across the Atlantic. Arguably the most cited example is the "Imale rebellion" in Brazil. The conflict that happened in Bahia, Brazil, in 1835 has been examined from different perspectives. While some scholars like Joao Reis have interrogated the war from a socioeconomic angle,[69] many others have done so from a political aspect.[70] One thing remains constant in relation to the historic infraction in the country and that is the fact that the uprising involved Yorùbá Muslims as a response to the racial prejudices and laws that were targeted at their identity. It is, therefore, important to examine how Muslims from this cultural group became dominant and significant in Brazil. In addition to the amount of material that has clarified the issue, we hasten to add here that Islamic culture was very much on the ground before the ascension of Europeans to African soil. For reasons not detached from their contiguity, North African countries found closeness across the Sahara Desert with West Africa, and they maximized the opportunity by extending a business, and later religious, relationship to them. That Muslims had penetrated the interior of the Yorubaland means that their mixing had birthed several Yorùbá Muslims who participated in the Atlantic slave trade.

Although there were Muslims who already established their presence and influence in Bahia and contributed to the overall peace in the place, at the ascension of Yorùbá Muslims, popularly referred to as Nagos (called Ànàgó among some Yorùbá groups),[71] their different approach to the practice of Islam created for them a new identity and singled them out from others. Conversion to Islam happened, implying that the Nagos participated in proselytization, thereby increasing the religious demographic. Yorùbá Muslims in this new environment were recognized for using amulets worn around their neck, to provide protection or wade away unseen forces.

Salvador, a popular urban community in Brazil, was a supportive environment for a growing Muslim population. There were freedmen in greater numbers, and slaves were transported to the city. Thus, the fact that they professed the same religion created mutual understanding and they connected through the networks created by religion. Proselytization was possible because the Ìmàle (Yorùbá Muslims) stood on the shoulders of the freedmen to spread the religion.[72] In as much as they gave the impression that they could protect their collective interests, people were attracted to Islam, and Yorùbá identity became the driving force. Before long, they established a compelling root that could challenge the existing social structures that gave room for racialization and the marginalization of unimaginable proportions. They grew in influence and organized all their activities to prevent them from the potential onslaught of the political system if they were discovered. They, however, were seriously monitored clandestinely because

---

69. Reis, *Slave Rebellion in Brazil.*

70. Graden, "Act 'Even of Public Security,'" 249–251.

71. Goody, "Writing Religion, and Revolt in Bahia," 318–343.

72. Lovejoy, "Background to Rebellion," 151–180.

Figure 9.2. "Unity in Worship," by Michael Efionayi. Yorùbá Islam is practiced similarly in the Yorùbá world, usually based on unity and brotherhood.

the government was also apprehensive of what they could do. Muslims within the community were both circumspect and tactical. There were secret organizations of prayers used as a diversionary tactic for the discussion of plans and intelligence. Necessary rituals that were expected of Muslims, such as the observation of salat, participation in Ramadan, and committing the Quran to memory, were all carried out by the people.

The rebellion began with a considerably strong foundation, where the freedmen consolidated the aspirations of the slaves to embark on a revolt. The former, who had sought ways through which they could challenge the Brazilian authority for their political ascendancy, incited others using the religion as their mobilizing agenda. It is naturally characteristic of every rebellion that it is preceded by discreteness. Meetings, mobilizations, and strategizing demanded that actions were done without public knowledge, as it can bring aspirations into ruin or jeopardy. Unfortunately, they were revealed along the process through entirely unanticipated means. Their secret plans were exposed to the public because of the indiscretion of some members of the group. At the last moment, the authority discovered the freedmen's plans and increased its security measures. Considering the magnitude of their planning, it was unrealistic to retreat even after their plans had been exposed. They, therefore, continued and began to unleash their terrors by confronting the leadership of the country. It was apparent that they intended to achieve their freedom agenda, but it was more unbecoming that they could not consider a contingency plan to realize their ambition. As a result of their indiscretion, some Yorùbá and then the Black people in the country lost their lives instantly, which became the ultimate price to pay.

Thus, the unsuccessful Ìmàle rebellion came with unforeseen consequences, among which was the increase in the security attention given to the Black community, not intending to protect them but to monitor their eventual activities. Leaders of the rebellion, including but not limited to Manoel Calafate, Elesbão do Corma, Ahuna, and many others, were either killed, punished, or deported back to Africa to prevent similar future occurrences.[73] Islam among the Yorùbá served different purposes at different times. For those in the Yorùbá world, they used the religion first as an instrument to increase their economic positions and later to consolidate their political agenda for domination. While it served a different but related purpose among the diasporan Yorùbá community, by organizing themselves using their cultural identity and epistemological perception in Bahia, they transformed Islam to suit their sociopolitical purposes.

Colonial Africa revealed the political side of Islam. By the time the European imperialists entered the African political space, they were forced to accept the fact that the occupation of the continent would be determined by their ability to withstand the challenges of competition and conscious politicization with Muslims because the latter had gained influence and popularity by globalizing Yorùbá culture. The penetration of the Yorùbá culture and people by Islam reliably came through regional networks, predictably because of their geographical proximity. The contention among Europeans in central and northern Africa, which would eventually escalate the acrimony between European countries in World War I, contributed to the manner and speed in which the Yorùbá accepted Islam. By the time there was a mass embrace of the religion by the Yorùbá, the mixing of Islamic and Yorùbá cultures became widespread. Yorùbá Muslims christened their children into Islam while wearing Yorùbá attire and enjoined them to engage in some Islamic activities while they performed some cultural duties, such as partaking in masquerade festivals. Funerals of the departed members were done the Islamic way, while the process was simultaneously garnished with indigenous styles and systems.

---

73. Reis, *Slave Rebellion in Brazil.*

Generally, whereas European perceptions of Africans were rooted in the white supremacist evaluation that Africans were of lower intellectual status, they did not perceive the dangers of the waves of Islam already sweeping the Yorùbá at a meteoric speed. Dr. Barot, in Alfred Le Chatelier, *L'Islam dans l'Afrique*, for example, points to the power of belief based on traditional religion and not Islam.[74] Islam developed a defensive mechanism against colonial conquest. This worked to the advantage of the Yorùbá who were already immersed in Islamic culture and zealously practicing the religion. To illustrate how divergent their opinions were on the matters of domination of Africans, the "Scramble for Africa" between 1884 and 1885 was concentrated on finding diplomatic solutions to the occupation challenges. The French, especially, feared losing their colonial territories to competing European countries, as reflected in their belligerent reactions to Germany when it was calculated that the latter posed a threat to their economic existence in Africa. They even clashed in Wadai and Tibesti in Central Africa.[75]

Notably, the French were exceptionally protective of their colonies, and whenever they evaluated the need to challenge the domination of another European state, they created a rivalry-enhancing atmosphere where they consciously dragged others until they achieved their ambition. The ascension of France was inspired by their incorporation of the existing religious arrangements into their political philosophy, if the latter did not disrupt their economic advancement.[76] The French and Muslim communities were united in their degenerating understanding of Africa as they accepted the fact that Africans needed salvation. While the former appeared extremely distant from those people they intended to "help," the latter were more accommodating, for the Muslim crusaders in Africa created the impression that Muslim brotherhood transcends geographical and racial territories. A Muslim in Morocco, for example, is seen equally as a Muslim in Chad, and all of them can mix without fear of alienation. The French were not unaware of this reality, and they considered opening their arms to Muslims as a matter of political necessity.[77]

This situation was a clear indication that while Islam was perceived negatively by some Europeans, certain European countries did not conceive Islam and its adherents as such in Africa, as they were a significant political ally calculated to influence the success of the French agenda on a global scale because they had begun to spread in influence and value by then. During these European clashes, Africans, even when they were the reasons for the altercations between the European countries, were aware of the power relations and power politics happening around them. Before this time, the slave trade was seriously embarked upon by the same Europeans, and how Africans were treated during the encounter was a clear statement of devaluation and degeneration, for slavery worked to underscore that Africans were backward and primitive people. Because Europeans considered them unsuitable for contemporary dignity, and Islam related to them and preserved their human dignity, it is clear why these Africans gravitated toward Islam en masse more than toward French culture. Of course, the French were barely

---

74. Le Chatelier, *L'Islam dans l'Afrique*.

75. Le Chatelier, *L'Islam dans l'Afrique*.

76. Levtizion and Pouwels, *History of Islam in Africa*.

77. Robinson, *Muslim Societies*.

concerned about the values, philosophy, or religious practices absorbed into African societies. Instead, they were focused on exploiting African economic systems.

Mali became an example of a West African country where Islam would continue to radiate. The fact that it was colonized by the French complemented their goals of occupying space. Mali was essentially open to Islam and its culture, regardless of French political control, because the Muslim clerics worked to expand the religion; however, the latter was equally diplomatic. The relationship kept with the country was founded on political coordination and mutual understanding between the two. The irony was lost on Europeans that the religion with which they identified an image of radicalism was to be seen as an ally with whom they would have to engage diplomatically. Therefore, it is understandable that the penetration of Yorubaland by Islam was relatively easy. Having been confronted with their internal contradictions and ravaging challenges that necessitated them to seek alliance from anyone ready to provide it, the people were magnetized to the religion. Although the penetration of Yorùbá by various Islamic clusters was preceded by the time of the internal contradictions between the French and Germans during their quest for colonial occupation and control, it was one of the determining factors that decided the embrace of the religion by the Yorùbá. Muslims had successfully established themselves and built an impression that they were not a threat to Yorùbá politics or culture. It was considered useful to those who brought the religion. Also, to the Yorùbá, there was nothing strange in allying with the Muslims; therefore, the globalization of Islam and Yorùbá culture was not seen as a contradiction.

The world wars were another factor in the acceptance of Islam among the Yorùbá. Europeans had graduated from enslavement to colonization in Africa, especially during World War I. The previous altercations and contentions served them additional grievances that complicated World War II. Outsiders, especially Africans and some others who saw the gruesome hands and the unity of ambition of Europeans in Africa, concluded that Europe was an essentially peaceful and exceptionally tranquil continent. They did not understand that underneath the veil of enslavement, colonization, and cultural supremacy that united Europe against Africa was an overly gluttonous ambition to control one another on the continent.

Meanwhile, Muslims have never ceased to seek cracks in the walls of Europe to gain an advantage to negotiate global politics. The fact that there was no peace among European countries became a metaphor for the pronouncement of God's dislike for civilizations that stand in the way of Islam or impede its growth.[78] Muslims, therefore, sought to take the root of diplomacy, one of which was the provision of their economic support system for African polities that supported and opened their arms to the religion. This happened among the Yorùbá in Ọ̀yọ́-Ilé, Lagos, Ikirun, Osogbo, and many others. It was a strategy to create a better image of the religion for the people. Coupled with the fact that Europeans had condemned Muslim activities by labeling them purists and extremists, the image was not shared by Africans who had witnessed the ever-accommodating nature of Islam and believed that the religion was just a victim of European optics. It, therefore, meant that European allegations against Islam were unfounded and Africans yet again expanded their embrace of Islam. A world where European

---

78. Robinson, *Muslim Societies.*

countries were fighting themselves and attacking Muslims out of fear only served to affirm the assumption already implanted in African minds that the world was approaching an apocalypse because of Allah's displeasure with people who did not accept him. It was logical to accept Islam at this point.

Undeniably, through Islam's penetration of the Yorùbá and their culture, the religion has immensely contributed to the globalization of Yorùbá identity. In the seventh century AD, Islamic culture began its evangelizing crusade, making critical efforts for the expansion of the Islamic culture to all cultural traditions of the world.[79] This is an impressive feat because, in the process of widening its geographical and cultural reach, it became a strategic spectacle that the world observed with admiration and reflection because the people who transported Islamic culture and religion showed fecundity through the revelation of their historical accomplishments. For example, the popular numerical system adopted globally is a product of Islamic invention.[80] There are also notable intellectuals from the Islamic world who have contributed to global knowledge systems.[81] It is on this basis that their name as a people has been written with indelible ink in human history. Therefore, their absorption into Yorùbá culture brought about symbiotic advantages. The Yorùbá became attuned to global awareness because they experienced new cultural traditions in Islam. They developed a sense of unity presumably because their association with others has forced them to understand the place of common identity.

Globalization carries its risk. Many Yorùbá Muslims have been accused of supporting the fundamentalist agenda associated with the so-called clash of civilization between the West and Islam. Globally, the attacks on the United States on September 11, 2001, led to negative attacks on Islam and people of different civilizations.[82] Even though Islam's religious philosophy is engraved in the heart of its adherents, it did not prevent the large population of Muslims, including the Yorùbá Muslims, from condemning these heinous acts. More importantly, there was global solidarity from Muslims around the world with the American people during this period.

The arguments on the association of Islam with terrorism have become part of the conversation among the Yorùbá. Defenders of the American empire believe that the radicalization of Islam means that Muslims cannot be trusted, and as such, there has since been a variety of criticism and condemnation produced in every sphere to diminish the status of Islam and its culture. Muslims feel attacked by the numerous despoliations of their cultural and religious identity over the actions of those they consider fundamentalists, and their corrective approach has been to show better sides in global politics. Yorùbá Muslims project the acceptance of globalism and migrate to the United States and other Western societies. The constant message in mosques is that of tolerance. For example, Muslims in Osogbo have continued to show solidarity with the people of different faiths, those in Abeokuta have been tolerant of others, and those in Lagos have continued to be receptive to others.[83]

---

79. Lambton, *Breakdown of Society*.

80. Al-Daffa', *Muslim Contribution to Mathematics*.

81. Rashed, *Ibn al-Haytham's Geometrical Methods*.

82. Rabasa et al., *Muslim World After 9/11*.

83. Nolte, Ancarno, and Jones, "Inter-religious Relations in Yorubaland," 27–64.

Pilgrimage

Since Islamic culture was introduced to the Yorùbá world, people from the cultural group have embarked on a pilgrim journey to Mecca. One of the underlying advantages of this is that it allows one to see the world from the lenses of other people. It provides the opportunity for people to cross-examine their cultural framework with those from other countries so that they can update their knowledge and develop equitable philosophy to be used among others. One of the five pillars of Islam mandates that people consider traveling to Mecca as an act of worship.[84] This creates the opportunity for people to expand their horizons. The realization that people are different in cultural orientation and social principles justifies the fact that individuals should have a variety of experiences. Religiously, going on the journey makes a believer pious once again because the Sharia considers it a genuine act of sacrifice. The people are offered the golden opportunity to strengthen their relationship with God and stand the chance to be qualified for unimaginable transformations in their lives. Going on Hajj unlocks the key to the facilitation of the process of their worldly request. It is a single religious practice that brings people of diverse human experiences together under the same umbrella, and its philosophical import is the way it levels everyone.

Another advantage of this pilgrimage is the opportunity to expand one's knowledge of the world. Having access to another country means that people build strong relationships founded on trust and respect that can facilitate social and personal relationships. The sojourners could introduce products they have to the people and the people have the same opportunity, making the business benefit mutual. Considering the injunction that validates the Hajj expedition, people who have better financial capacity are recommended to take the journey, as it is one of the fundamentals of Islam. They are expected to use their economic ability to spread love and affection to those with comparatively lower economic standards. The ultimate reason for the initiation of such projects is to correct some social and economic anomalies endemic in human society. With this principle of giving, the religion becomes a unifying force among its adherents. The Hajj, therefore, provides the platform for the evolution of some social behaviors built to enhance crucial elements of globalization, which, among other things, is the creation of bodies that would address specific issues and concerns.

Looking at the different types of organizations with Islamic identity among the Yorùbá today, one would understand that they have deep connections with traditional Islamic countries. Funded opportunities are usually available for those who are Muslims, and this extends to those who are Yorùbá Muslims.[85]

Conclusion

While clarifying otherwise contentious concepts, this chapter has traced the progeny of Islam into the Yorùbá world using historical data. In the process, it became necessary to explore the

---

84. Peters, *Hajj*.

85. Weiss, "Muslim NGOs, Zakat and the Provision of Social Welfare," 1–38.

dynamics of the religion vis-à-vis the ways it spread among the Yorùbá, the sociopolitical exigencies that mandated the adoption of the religion, and the attendant challenges in the process. As indicated, the association of philosophical similarity between the Yorùbá and Islamic conception of worship is flawed in its foundation because the Yorùbá of the preexternal invasion conceived the phenomenon of religion and worship differently. Their different perceptions of these concepts subsequently determined the attitudes and general reactions they have to civilizations that share contrastive views. To emphasize, this does not mean their religions or cultural identity are entirely asymmetric; there are some areas of convergence where they meet, and this is underscored by the reality that cross-fertilization of ideas and thought are especially easy among the Yorùbá who considered embracing Islam. Islam has survived among them until the present moment based on the understanding that cultural osmosis and religious exchanges of ideas are possible.

During its expansionist experiment, Islam is fortunate that some global events were taking sweeping dimensions that would subsequently affect the ways people conceived the religion. While the Islamic civilization is not morally innocent in the business of human trafficking, it, however, did not reach the commercial scale that the Europeans did for four hundred years. Both Arabs and Europeans engaged in the slave trade. Meanwhile, the impression that people had when the colonization project was ongoing was that there was a peaceful relationship among the European countries pillaging the African goods, both humans and materials, while in the real sense, they nursed malicious confrontations against one another, such as the fight for the control of Morocco and Central Africa between the French and the Germans. Incidentally, these issues became reinforcing arguments used by Muslims in their crusading campaign to unearth the avarice, gluttony, and greed that characterized European colonization and validated the portion of their scripture that proclaims Allah's wrath on unbelievers.

Banking on these opportunities, Islam grew exponentially and became the preferred religious destination of many West African people, including the Yorùbá. As a corollary to their acceptance of the religion, there has been the introduction of a different perspective to the worship or conception of God, and it has reshaped their views. Islam has contributed greatly to the globalization of Yorùbá people. It developed into an instrument of protest and activism and became a force of unity that helped in the creation of a unique identity. Islam has a fair record of positive and negative additions it has brought to the people. The fact that it continues to contribute to their collective development is a testament to its potential and importance. Through it, a genre of music performance has been created and has been used on several occasions as material for forging peace and bringing about needed tranquility.

Remarkably, colonialism played an integral role in the practice and spread of Islam among the Yorùbá. It protected and enhanced the growth and preservation of the religion,[86] allowing it to spread and develop hybridity that made it possible for the emergence of Yorùbá Islam.

---

86. Ochonu, "Colonialism within Colonialism," 95–127.

10 Christianity in the Yorùbá World

Following the British Act of 1807 that gave institutional backing to the abolition of the transatlantic slave trade, the domino effects of this decision continued for the rest of that century and beyond. Among these were the creation of captive territories in parts of Africa (particularly in Sierra Leone and Liberia), the return of African captives to this location, the onward movement of some of these populations to their homelands, the advent of Christian missionaries, the spread of Western civilization, and the eventual incorporation of African peoples into various European empires.[1]

On the spread of Christianity and the Yorùbá version of it, the role of the returnees and the European missionaries cannot be recorded in a footnote of history.[2] Throughout the presence of Christian missionaries among the people, several events and frictions, which emanated from what was perceived as the alienation of Yorùbá culture and practices and the racial marginalization of the people in the order of things in the church, led to breakaway versions of Christianity among the people.[3] These groups, which later formed a new denomination of Christianity in Nigeria, leaned toward incorporating the Yorùbá worldview into their Christian practices and were distinguished from orthodox establishments.[4]

This chapter includes the trajectory and activities of Christian denominations like the African Church, the Aladura group, Cherubim and Seraphim, and others that adopted a different version of Christianity that came as a rebellion against the original practice in which they were introduced. The chapter takes a trip through the trajectory of Christianity in Yorubaland, the issues at the bone of contention, the making of Yorùbá Christendom, and how this has evolved. It investigates the evolution of the religion in Yorubaland, as its evolutionary condition cannot be insulated from its beginning, established by pioneers such as Bishop Samuel Ajayi Crowther. Consequently, the chapter explores the growth of Pentecostal churches and their flexibility in the contemporary era.

Generally, it is perceived that some observable doctrinal changes exist, as well as notable differences from what the initial missionary religious community brought during the nineteenth

---

1. Lawrance, Osborn, and Roberts, *Intermediaries, Interpreters and Clerks.*
2. Ralston, "Return of Brazilian Freedmen to West Africa," 577–593.
3. Pobee and Ositelu, *African Initiatives in Christianity.*
4. Webster, "Attitudes and Policies of the Yoruba African Churches," 225–251.

century. In the early twentieth century, it became more glaring that the Christian religion introduced by the Europeans had received substantial modifications, enough to speak to the idea of Yorùbá Christianity.[5] If Christianity could be merged with Yorùbá philosophy, this chapter interrogates the common ground where the two meet and their points of departure to see how the Yorùbá have successfully navigated the hurdles in preserving both traditions.

The widespread knowledge about the introduction of Christianity in Africa is that it coincided with the era of the slave trade. Europeans who came intending to extract Africans and make them slaves in the Atlantic did so with missionaries who sought to evangelize Africans. This creates an impression that the introduction of the religion among the Yorùbá comes from the project of exploitative globalization. The Yorùbá encountered European transnational traders and missionaries at the same time. The European traders who came for slaves and the ones who were there for the Christianization agenda had the same attitude of superiority complex. Their actions were not in contravention of each other but were complementary. Europeans were responsible for introducing Christianity to Africans and initiating commercial-scale slavery exchange that birthed the assumption that the arrival of Christianity in the continent could be linked to the time of the slavery expedition.[6] Despite being shrouded in controversy, the success of establishing the religion hinged on many factors, of which language and geography were critical.[7]

Africa was, and still is, home to linguistically heterogeneous identities that posed critical challenges to the introduction of a new idea, no matter how promising. Their differences in language presuppose that they are culturally and religiously pluralistic. Whether the Christian religion was introduced by the Europeans or circulated into the heart of the continent through the agency of their indigenous converts, it required knowledge of the language of communication. The contributions of the freed slaves from Sierra Leone provide the basis for this argument. While the enslaved Africans were en route to the Atlantic world, their migrations were not limited to bodily movement alone; their culture, ideas, native philosophies, and others were transported through the same route of the transatlantic slave movement. The sustained means of communication in the people's language enhanced the transmission of their ideas beyond their indigenous geography. Besides this, the Europeans' intention to substitute the African ideas and epistemologies with their cultural infrastructure fueled them to create a political and economic atmosphere where the globalization project would be instantly fast-tracked. Once the people were convinced of a potentially different religious and cultural perspective, it was easier for them to embrace those religious beliefs associated with the new ideas introduced. This was a demanding task.

Another important factor that ultimately determined the conversion process was the question of the African geography and, by extension, the accommodating climate in some quarters. It was because some African geographies have unique ecological conditions that limited the early missionaries' ecumenical assignments to specific environments.[8]

---

5. Peel, *Religious Encounter and the Making of the Yoruba*.

6. Antwi, "Church Involvement in the Trans-Atlantic Slave Trade," 1–19.

7. Hastings, *Church in Africa*.

8. Alanamu, "Indigenous Medical Practices," 5–27.

History of Christianity in Yorubaland

The spread of Christianity was part of a global process. The emergence of Christianity in Yorubaland can be traced to the arrival of the European missionaries who sought to take their Christianization agenda to different parts of the world. The arrival of these missionaries was the aftermath of the slave trade that disconnected many of the Yorùbá victims from their sociocultural origins. It was a further motive to prepare the territories for eventual colonization. However, it is important to note that the Christian missionaries were at the center of eradicating the slave trade; they believed Christianity would only be accepted when the slave trade ended.

However, the European missionaries met highly structured religious and cultural systems upon arriving in Yorùbá territories. The Yorùbá had been practicing their religion for centuries,[9] and the traditional religion had shaped their value systems and norms and defined their sociopolitical institutions. The Christian missionaries encountered great difficulty and resistance in penetrating the religious and cultural structure and propagating and establishing the new religion of Christianity. The major factor that contributed to this was the basic tenets of Christianity rooted in the belief in the oneness of God, the Father, which can only be accessed through Jesus Christ, His Only Son. Christianity negates the idea of "religious inclusivism," which underlines the notion that all ways to access God (Olodumare, according to the Yorùbá people) remain valid.[10] The Yorùbá further believe there is no "true" way to worship God. Scholarly attention further notes that this aspect of religious inclusivity accounted for the Yorùbá people's initial tolerance for the missionaries and the dialogue with them. When the Christian missionaries first set foot on Yorùbá territories, they enjoyed a warm reception shaped by the beliefs of the Yorùbá to welcome strangers. The whole idea of the Yorùbá religious system was to foster humanity.

In Nigeria, Christianity did not start from Yorubaland. The credit was given to the Benin people who embraced the Portuguese missionaries in the sixteenth century. Notably, in the nineteenth century, Christianity returned to Nigeria through Yorubaland. The chief actors in the propagation of Christianity in this century were former Yorùbá slaves who traced their origins from Sierra Leone to Yorùbá kingdoms.[11] They became valuable protagonists in the Christianization agenda of the Yorùbá people. This set of agents later became prominent figures in the work of evangelization. The European missionaries also discovered that to penetrate the Yorùbá kingdoms, it was necessary to use more Yorùbá missionaries; they believed this would lead to faster assimilation. This does not interpret that the activities of Yorùbá missionaries enabled the smooth progress of Christianity in Yorubaland. They also faced stiff resistance in their various attempts to get more converts.

As time passed, the Yorùbá missionaries could not fill the vacuum, and they were left with no choice but to call for reinforcements. One of the letters written to ask for the coming of more European missionaries had this in it: "For Christ's sake, come quickly. Let nothing but sickness

---

9. Fatokun, "Christian Missions in South-Western Nigeria," 107.

10. Fatokun, "Christian Missions in South-Western Nigeria," 107.

11. Fatokun, "Christian Missions in South-Western Nigeria," 110.

prevent you . . . do not neglect me with this burden. It is more than I can bear."[12] This call, tagged the "Macedonian call," culminated in the arrival of missionaries like Reverends Thomas Birch Freeman of the Methodist Missionary Society, who arrived in Nigeria on September 24, 1842, and Henry Townsend of the Church Missionary Society, who arrived on December 17, 1842.[13] Both men became influential figures in the propagation of Christianity in Yorubaland. Christianity was established in Yorubaland with the arrival of the Methodist Missionary Society in Abeokuta in 1842.[14] The society was swiftly joined by the Catholic Missionary Society in the same year. Besides the need for evangelization, the missionaries tried to introduce Christian "civilization," which was deeply rooted in many Western ideas. These two missionaries were evangelicals and thus "were deeply interested in changing features of Yoruba society."[15]

Echoing J. D. Y. Peel, most Christian evangelicals had plans to change societal architecture; they were not interested in the idea of propagation alone.[16] Therefore, the two missionary sects attempted to sideline or relegate part of the existing Yorùbá culture and replace it with European ones. Many Yorùbá sociopolitical institutions, such as polygamy, among others, were criticized. This attitude of the Christian missionaries toward existing Yorùbá knowledge systems was counterproductive in the long run. First, the concept of European civilization was strange to Yorùbá culture. One of the underlying differences was the primacy of individualism against the principle of collectivism. Second, even the Western education introduced by the missionaries disrupted some of the existing Yoruba education geared toward the production of the "total person," or Omoluabi, in the Yorùbá parlance.

There is a further need to discuss the position of Abeokuta in the context of Christianity in Yorubaland. Abeokuta has been referred to as the "Citadel of Christianity" because most of the early missionaries who played significant roles in the propagation of Christianity settled in there.[17] Also, Abeokuta earned this reputation due to the welcoming hands of the people. Even with the fact that the missionaries came to steer them away from the traditional belief in their ancestors, they were not at all hostile to them. One notable event that attests to this fact occurred when a leading Chief, Sodeke, hosted the duo of Thomas Birch Freeman and Henry Townsend in one of their visits to the town. Sodeke even linked the arrival of the Christian missionaries to the fulfillment of an Ifá prophecy that predicted the coming of the Christian missionaries through sea would spell a boom for the Egba people and would further place them on the pedestal of unrivaled growth and development.[18] After the missionaries arrived at Egbaland, a confirmation was made by Ifá that the missionaries were the fulfillment of the prophecy.[19] This declaration made Abeokuta fertile soil for the germination of Christianity and for the rest of Yorubaland.

---

12. Walker, *Hundred Years in Nigeria*, 14.

13. Fatokun, "Christian Missions in South-Western Nigeria," 107.

14. Falola, "Missionaries and Domestic Slavery," 181.

15. Falola, "Missionaries and Domestic Slavery," 184.

16. Falola, "Missionaries and Domestic Slavery," 184.

17. Falola and Adediran, *Islam and Christianity*, 112.

18. Adewale, "Role of Ifa," 26.

19. Walker, *Romans of the Black River*, 46.

The relationship between the missionaries and the adherents of the traditional religion was cordial. The latter did not hold back their children from mingling with the missionaries, and some of the traditional priests even gave the missionaries custody of the children. This cooperation was influential in the success of Christianity. Samson Adetunji Fatokun recalls an incident where the Aláké of Egbaland sent his son for the priesthood.[20] The missionaries contributed to the development of Egbaland, especially in the aspect of social welfare. The changes occurring in Egbaland at that time aroused the interests of other neighboring Yorùbá kingdoms in the Christian missionaries. As S. A. Adewale puts it, "When the neighbouring chiefs and rulers heard of the fame and progress of Abeokuta, which she earned through the missionaries, they appealed to the ruler of Abeokuta to allow the missionaries to come to them. Hinderer (Revd) went on mission from Abeokuta to Ibadan at the request of the chief of Ibadan. The Oni of Ife sent an urgent message asking for missionaries. . . . Messages also came from the chiefs of Ketu and Ijaye of Abeokuta to ask for the missionaries to preach the gospel news among their people."[21]

Thus, Abeokuta became the point for the spread of Christianity to some other cities, such as Ibadan and Oyo.[22] When Christianity was gaining ground in those places, the missionaries had pluralized. Ajayi identifies five mission societies at that time: the Church Missionary Society, the Wesleyan Methodist Society, the Foreign Mission Committee of the United Presbyterian Church of Scotland, the Foreign Mission Board of the Southern Baptist Convention of the United States, and the Catholic Society of African Missions of France.[23] Islam had been thriving before the arrival of the Christian missionaries, who could still plant the seeds of Christianity. The arrival of the Christian missionaries brought some social changes.[24] The missionaries further influenced agricultural changes.[25]

As Christianity gradually spread across Yorùbá territories, it was easy to mix it with indigenous cultural practices. Elements of Yorùbá culture in the Christian acts of worship became noticeable.[26] Evangelization did not completely take away the Yorùbá ideology of religious pluralism, hence the simultaneous practice of Christianity and Yorùbá traditional religion. Also, some of the Yorùbá Christians were resistant to the subtle imperialism that came with Christianity; as a result, they began to introduce African concepts into church practices, particularly in the aspect of worship, music, dancing, dressing, and drumming.[27] Yorùbá Christians still hold to the cultural belief of the burial rites.[28]

In a bid to get more followership, missionaries discriminated between the traditional priests and themselves. Even when these priests had coexisted with Muslim preachers, the missionaries

---

20. Fatokun, "Christian Missions in South-Western Nigeria," 110.

21. Adewale, "Role of Ifa," 30–31.

22. Balogun, "Emergence and Contributions of Christian Missions," 25.

23. Ajayi, *Christian Missions in Nigeria.*

24. Balogun, "Emergence and Contributions of Christian Missions," 27.

25. Balogun, "Emergence and Contributions of Christian Missions," 27.

26. Omobola, "Influence of Yoruba Culture," 587.

27. Omobola, "Influence of Yoruba Culture," 588.

28. Omobola, "Influence of Yoruba Culture," 591.

found this challenging. The missionaries also began to attack some of the customs of the Yorùbá people.[29] The Babaláwo were initially reluctant to engage the missionaries because some of them were interested in learning the white man's ways. However, as the attacks became prominent, the traditional priests also retaliated. This was worsened by the missionaries' condemnation of the traditional religion as leading to eternal damnation. According to J. D. Y. Peel, "The mission's strategy depended on the construction of 'heathenism' as a system homologous to Christianity, in which some elements would be retained (e.g., God, the idea of saviour or mediator, the value of 'peace', alafia) and others replaced (Orunmila by Jesus, sacrifice by prayer or by Christ's Sacrifice)."[30]

For the missionaries, Christianity could not exist side by side with the traditional religion, which was described as paganistic. While the missionaries strategized on how to get more converts, the traditional priests also strategized on the methods to incorporate new ideologies in the Yorùbá religion to prevent the massive loss of adherents.

Early Conversion: The Realities of Globalization

A careful observation of this history reveals that the introduction of Christianity to the Yorùbá people did not come without challenges. Therefore, it seems that one of the most constant challenges for promoting cross-border trading or exchanging vital resources is the sturdy wall of cultural and religious pillars between two civilizations. For one, these people had been conditioned by their cultural traditions and whose conversion, even when it did not encounter resistance, would inevitably trigger social eruptions. Even the awareness of the unnecessary side effects of embracing a new religion propelled many Yorùbá to negate and reject the religion. Their negation was not in the sense of casting aspersions or violently condemning Christianity; after all, there had been the infiltration of Yorùbá by Islam several years before Christianity arrived. Their reservations about Christianity were caused by their cultural and philosophical expediency. In fact, what could pass as Yorùbá religion was a general practice that accommodated the pluralism of ideas. Once there was a meeting point between their ancient religion and whatever external practices were introduced, the people were especially tolerant.[31] The missionaries also observed these developments. They noticed that the indigenous cosmic referent could be substituted for the Christian God, and modifying their religion, if it did not reduce the spiritual importance of their system, was a clever decision. It was a moral fact that the Yorùbá showed a good sense of tolerance even when external agencies of conversion trampled upon their religion.

However, the fate of Yorùbá Christianity would be tied to Sierra Leone because the freed African slaves who began the ecumenical assignment among the Yorùbá had an ancestral connection with Yorùbá origin. The Yorùbá people were influential in the Christian community in Sierra Leone so much that they adopted the Yorùbá language as a lingua franca.[32] Separating

---

29. Peel, "Pastor and the Babalawo," 347.

30. Peel, "Pastor and the Babalawo," 347.

31. Nolte, Ogen, and Jones, *Beyond Religious Tolerance*.

32. Johnson, *History of the Yorubas*.

Figure 10.1.
"Yoruba Pastor."
Instead of foreign
cassocks, the pastor
wears Yorùbá attire and
preaches in the Yorùbá
language. Christianity
was "domesticated"
in the Yorùbá world
beginning in the 1900s
with the emergence of
African Independent
churches. Yorùbá
Christianity today
extends to Europe and
the Americas to serve
the faith of resident
Yorùbá communities
and families. Drawing
by Dr. Kazeem Ekeolu.

the Christianity of Sierra Leone and that of the Yorùbá people was a difficult engagement. The quest for independence from the British Christian identity in Sierra Leone led to the Africanization of Christianity. The Yorùbá were active in the evolution of their cultural traditions as pressure from within continued to influence their decisions to Africanize the church. For one, Islam already had a major presence among the Yorùbá in Lagos, and its success was partly because it was not in contention with many of the Yorùbá cultural engagements, even though it did not accept them as a matter of religious principles.[33] It was necessary that if Christianity would equally thrive like Islam, it must recognize the sanctity of mixing the religion with indigenous elements. The missionaries were not ignorant of the transition of the religion, from being marginally recognized to being an important factor in the redefinition of the Lagos identity.[34] Christianity became popular in the contest for relevance with Islam.

For a religion that has a worthy competitor in Islam, the challenge of convincing people to accept the faith was enormous. Seeking a better way to promote their religion and make it more attractive to the people, the missionaries considered taking a progressively dynamic method.[35] They became aggressive in their evangelization, introducing something analytically and preferentially better than what Islam had offered. The establishment of schools for the enhancement of the people's education was one strategy they employed. Although Islam had introduced informal education to the people where they taught them numeracy and literacy in Arabic, they could not erect a bridge between the religion and the people's culture. If there had been the codification of Yorùbá or the creation of the alphabet, as later done by Bishop Ajayi, perhaps it would have taken a different growth chart among the Yorùbá. Eventually, the bishop's creativity rescued the Christian cause among the Yorùbá. The missionaries' introduction of schools and the efforts for the codification of the Yorùbá language brought about access to education with utilitarian advantages.[36]

Most of the abovementioned situations were conversion experiences in the Yorùbá urban communities, especially in areas like Abeokuta, Lagos, and Ibadan, which added to ongoing globalization. The contributions of the white missionaries and their Yorùbá counterparts were complementary and reinforcing. They both made efforts to register their presence in a society with the competing religions of Islam and the indigenous religion. Notably, reaching the hinterland was much easier for the Yorùbá missionary agents. Even in the cities, the efforts of early Yorùbá converts who had been duly recognized by the church could not be underrepresented. Through their cultural knowledge and awareness of the environment, what these Yorùbá Christians did to promote the religion was impressive. More than it could be described, they penetrated the hinterland and contributed immensely with their labor and money.

For the Yorùbá people who embraced the religion, they understood it could redefine their general philosophy as a people. In the same measure, they understood that social development was possible if the Christian religion was planted successfully into the people's hearts. They became crusaders of the religion because of the reality that their success would bring social

---

33. Jimoh, "Growth and Development of Islam in Epe," 1–18.

34. Lawal, "Islam and Colonial Rule in Lagos," 66–80.

35. Omotoye, "Christianity as a Catalyst."

36. Thani, *Spread of Christianity.*

projects, such as the creation of schools. This suggests they sought to globalize their society, using Christianity as an instrument. If they could win more converts, they could present their demands to missionary authorities. They understood the motivations of the white missionaries and realized that the only thing that could encourage them to expand their evangelical activities would be concrete evidence that the people had opened their arms to the religion. If the Christian demographic was not encouraging, it was of no financial and social benefit for them to embark on projects that would help the people survive eventually.

For example, a particular canon, James Adedeji Okuseinde, increased the missionary works in Ìbàdàn.[37] He was committed to expanding Christianity and understood that when the community embraced the religion in larger numbers, it would be easier to persuade the missionaries to establish schools and religious centers and embark on other developmental projects so that the Yorubaland would eventually be transformed. The struggle for the conversion of the people, therefore, demanded greater efforts. Apart from being figures of hope and symbols of protection, they needed to make themselves available for issues bordering on the lives of their members.

The expansion of Christianity among the Yorùbá rested on several conditions, among which was the demonstration of loyalty to the missionary as a message to convince them of their readiness. They needed to have Western education, knowing that it was the direction in which the world was moving. Having acquired the education themselves, they wanted to replicate similar development among their people to place them on the right trajectory and prepare them for future encounters. For this reason, Bishop Samuel Ajayi Crowther demonstrated his intellectual capacity by reducing the Yorùbá language to writing. He relied on his knowledge of the English language and familiarization with the Yorùbá culture to create something that would become the foundation for educational growth and systems.[38] The dedication to the cause of laying the foundation for the religion meant that it would come with transformational changes.

Yorubanizing Christianity for a Globalization Agenda

One thing usually marks the place of human efforts, no matter how tiny they appear, and that is the fact that though the general outcome cannot be determined, the possibility of its future impact can never be in doubt. When people make conscious efforts in whatever endeavor, they may be denied the opportunity to experience the outcome by unforeseen circumstances, but their efforts cannot be considered futile altogether. Contexts and situations are two important determinants of the usefulness of efforts. Context because there are certain human situations where efforts produce immediate and material results. The ones who make their efforts as contributions to the course of action are recognized and sometimes celebrated with definite titles or social accolades. However, situations in other circumstances could warrant that the efforts made by an individual would not attract necessary social attention because the results do not

---

37. Mepayeida and Popoola, "Roles of Indigenous Missionaries," 1–7.
38. Ney, "Samuel Ajayi Crowther and the Age of Literature," 37–52.

immediately materialize, but that they have made significant efforts is usually exposed by the tide of time.

In some cases, the people who belong to the latter category do not always get the chance to witness the outcome of their efforts. If they are alive during the transformation inspired by their efforts, they may not be able to derive from the eventual benefit. The Yorùbá Christians who were making conscious efforts to redefine the identity of the religion and make efforts to Africanize the faith were unaware of the propensity and magnitude of what they were doing. While being genuinely patriotic to their Yorùbá identity, most of them had no idea of how massive their contributions would eventually become. When Bishop Ajayi Crowther, Canon James Adedeji Okuseinde, evangelist Thomas Bako, and John Olubobokun were making conscious efforts for the Yorubanization of the religion, they would never have imagined that they were planting a reorientation that would not only redefine the religion at the global community but also would carve out a unique identity for their movement.

Around 1925, the Yorùbá people initiated a philosophical evacuation from orthodox Christianity to create a formidable Christian identity that would bear the mark of Yorùbá origin.[39] This form of Christianity, even though it would retain the ideological convictions of the religion, would be a departure from the known identity of Christianity that centered on European interpretation. In other words, some indigenous Yorùbá spiritual practices would be transported into Christianity through the bridge of ethnoreligious identity constructed through protest. The Aladura Church was founded in 1925, the Celestial Church of Christ in 1947, and the Cherubim and Seraphim in 1925, all evidence of the protest and rethinking of Christianity received from the foreign missions. From their creation, the leaders of these new churches survived on the goodwill of the people by building a new infrastructure that catered to people's beliefs.[40] At least, they were not part of the missionaries who condemned everything African, chastising people who leaned toward indigenous culture. Although the early converts, predominantly slaves in Sierra Leone, had assimilated the culture of the Europeans even during their short experience under them.

There was some kind of symmetry between the Yorùbá religio-cultural infrastructure and Christianity, especially with the attributes of the Supreme Deity. For instance, how to worship God could differ. Yorùbá society placed a premium on the use of drums, songs, and dance during veneration. It was a religious practice that the enslaved Africans also took to the Atlantic environment.[41] Perhaps the slaves in Bahia, Salvador, and other transatlantic environments provided the possibility of the Yorùbá indigenizing the Christian religion and weaving out a unique identity from it when they made their presence felt with their distinctive approach to the observation of religious rites. In what would be cheerfully realized among the Yorùbá in the twentieth century, they introduced indigenous practices to Christianity. These pioneering churches spread their influence as part of the attempt to institutionalize Yorùbá identity.

The Yorùbá introduced their Yorubanized Christianity in various diaspora countries, and a few of them will be examined now. The Aladura churches are subdivided into four

---

39. Omoyajowo, *Makers of Church*.

40. Raheem, "Martin Luther versus Us," 49–72.

41. Udo, "Vitality of Yoruba Culture in the Americas," 27–40.

denominations: Cherubim and Seraphim (1925), the Christ Apostolic Church (1930), the Church of the Lord Aladura (1930), and the Celestial Church of Christ (1945).[42]

The Aladura in the United Kingdom: The Cherubim and Seraphim (C&S)

One of the defining characteristics of the African Traditional Religion is its appropriation of indigenous songs during worship. The Yorùbá people are perpetual believers in the potency of spoken words, which may, however, be realized in different forms.[43] The spoken expression is developed to become the musical sounds rendered for specific purposes in different contexts.[44] Songs are just carefully worded versions of spoken words that are artfully accompanied by drums, specifically on given occasions. Even drums have their sociospiritual uses among the Yorùbá. Many icons of religion are invoked through the manipulation of drums by designated experts. All these were potent instruments combined by the Yorùbá people to worship and perform the veneration process of their intended divinities, although orthodox Christianity has discredited this during the energetic evangelization of the African people. However, the descendants of these African practices would not maintain a long distance from their indigenous epistemological perception, and they instinctively considered its rejuvenation, revitalization, and resuscitation when they had the freedom to reconstruct the Christian identity in the United Kingdom. According to Caleb Oladipo, one of the foremost researchers in African Christianity, Aladura church members reincarnated the African Traditional Religion and found a creative means of injecting their spirituality into the Christian faith.[45]

The account of the C&S church in the United Kingdom, offered by Hermione Harris, provides the basis for this examination. According to her, the denomination was introduced to the United Kingdom in 1967 by Yorùbá immigrants whose spiritual conviction was affiliated with the white garment church in the Nigerian environment.[46] Considering the newness of the British environment and maybe the social and economic searches that ostracized them from others, the need to organize prayer sessions became expedient. As they shared a common cultural identity, the opportunity to reach individuals was readily forthcoming, and they maximized it to organize a prayer session that was attended by a handful of Yorùbá people. The fact that they were in the diaspora community did not weaken their resolve for their dependence on spiritual engagement. They understood that there were opportunities within their church to secure help from their commitment to prayers and other practices unique to them. Originally beginning in 1965, although in very small numbers, they attracted members from different quarters in the United Kingdom. The information about their presence spread quickly, and many Yorùbá who were already seeking something to represent even shreds of identity surfaced for the church activities. Before long, the British community became aware of their presence.

---

42. Omoyajowo, *Makers of Church*.

43. Bernard, "Beyond Spoken Words," 39–53.

44. Omojola, "Rhythms of the Gods," 29–50.

45. Peel, *Aladura*.

46. Harris, *Yoruba in Diaspora*.

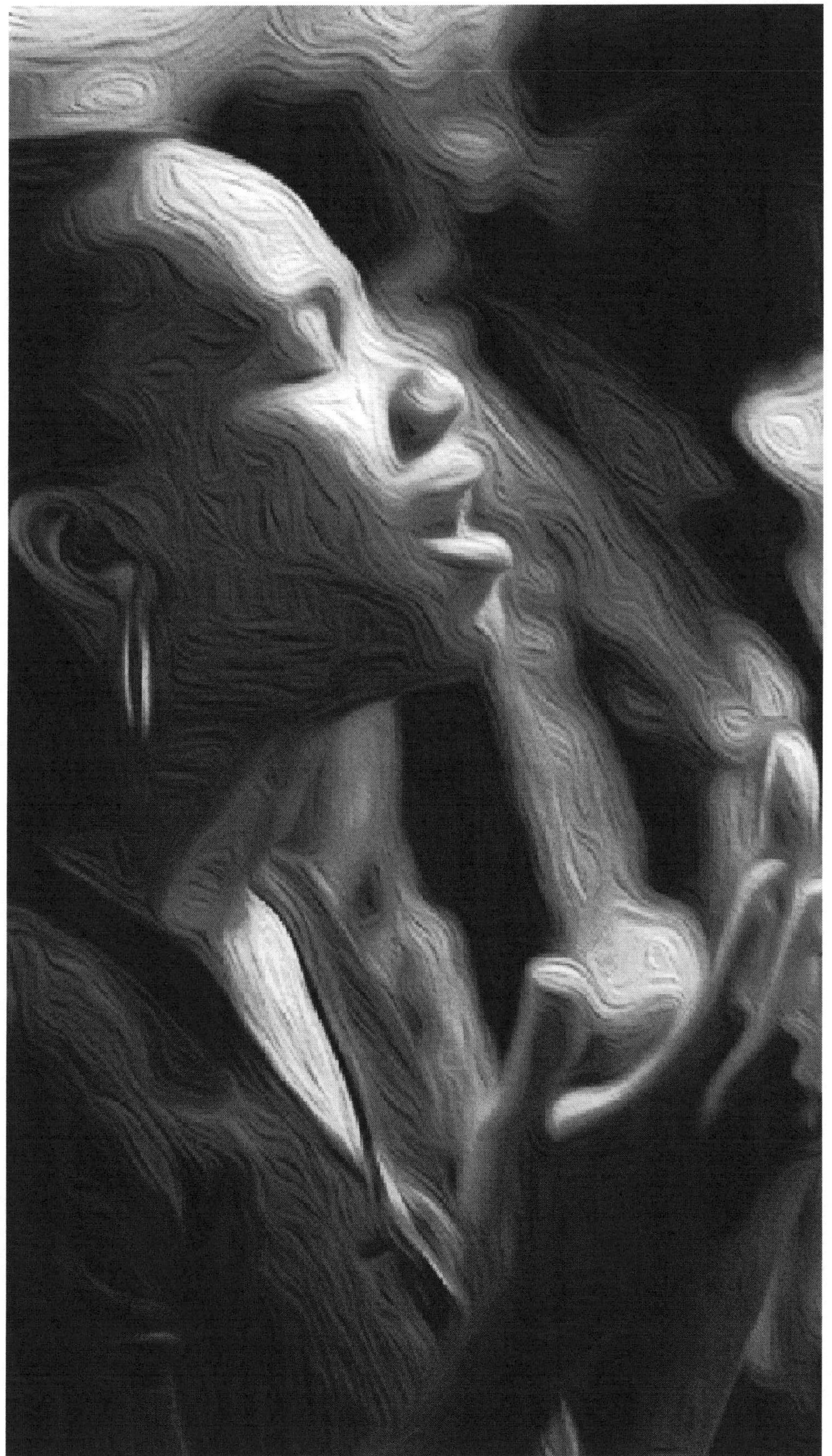

Figure 10.2. The intensity of church worship is common among the Yorùbá at home and in the diaspora. The largest Pentecostal churches in Nigeria are today mostly owned and dominated by the Yorùbá, with major branches in the Yorùbá diaspora and a large Christian following. From the Toyin Falola Private Collection.

The moment the people became certain that introducing a Yorubanized Christianity was not in negotiation, all the materials needed to enhance their dream became paramount. To begin, they purchased their properties so that the prospect of expansion would be set on the right trajectory. Soon, the interjection of different social or cultural practices lent credence to the identity of the religious community. They became the rallying point for the Yorùbá as long as they demonstrated a sense of attachment. When people experienced personal difficulties in the form of spiritual challenges or social problems, they sought consolation from members because it gratified them and made them feel appreciated. The C&S became, in part, a social network for the Yorùbá converts, where it was easier for them to find solutions to their challenges. Job opportunities were created, and business connections were established, and as this became the actual practice, it strengthened their political agenda for common purposes. Many Nigerians with limited connections in the country saw the religious community in the United Kingdom as a better prospect to unify their identities. Moreover, because the diaspora community could be depressingly challenging, the emergence of the church reduced the potentiality of such dramatic situations.

The Aladura Church in the United States: Christ Apostolic Church (CAC)

Introduced in the 1920s, the CAC was another creative component of Yorubanized Christianity that made significant advancements in the diaspora community.[47] This section will examine their activities and engagement in the United States of America and how their common identity became the unifying force protecting their international image. Like other Yorùbá-inspired Christian identities, the CAC began from the perspective of Africanist ideologists, whose radical positions against the class-conscious white missionaries ignited their passion for independence. Over their disagreement with doctrinal positions, they evolved to form their religious identity, which would cater to Africa's reality, as opposed to the cultural undercurrents of the Europeans. It was expected that there would be differences between the religious understanding of the African people and that of white people because it was sometimes impossible to dissociate the place of culture in religious constructions. So, when orthodox Christianity, for example, frowned against polygamy during their evangelization, it was obvious that the doctrine would be successfully established in a Yorùbá society that reserves no condemnation for an individual's choice of marriage if it caters for one's well-being. Through the power of divine language, the Yorùbá believe that even outrageous conditions can be upturned.

Lydia Akande's research provides an inkling about the establishment of the CAC in the United States.[48] According to her, the foundational beginning of the church coincided with the immigration of a CAC pastor, Prophet S. K. Abiara, when he arrived in Brooklyn to begin the ecumenical assignment.[49] However, what was different from the style or focus of the reincarnation of Christianity in America was that it was meant to expand the coverage of Christianity, according to the pastor. Unlike the one introduced in England, the pastor functioned under the

---

47. Alokan, *Christ Apostolic Church.*

48. Akande, "Impact of Christ Apostolic Church on Yoruba Diaspora," 15–26.

49. Akintayo, "Christ Apostolic Church, Agbala Itura," 51–56.

divine instruction of the Christian God to continue his work in the American environment. As racial identities in America are plural, it was considered an act of worship to take God's words to those who had not been introduced to evangelism. Although American society was proportionately diverse, the pastor's actual target was the Nigerian (or African) community, so the quest for economic extension was not quelled in the New World. Expectedly, the Yorùbá people in New York were attracted to the religion and aligned their spiritual beliefs and focus with the CAC. Before long, the CAC registered an imposing presence in the United States.

The Aladura Church in Benin Republic: The Celestial Church of Christ (CCC)

In 1947, the CCC was founded by Prophet Samuel Bilewu Joseph Oshoffa, its first general overseer. Although Oshoffa was born to Yorùbá parents, the political undercurrents of the Yorùbá precolonial period influenced Dahomey (now the Republic of Benin), which explains the location of his ecumenical project.[50] He was a talented carpenter and had attracted people's attention because of his ingenuity. Oshoffa, who had also been exposed to the Christian culture of the orthodox identity, was said to have received a divine message during his meditation in the forest.[51] It coincided with the day of the sun's total eclipse in West Africa, which became the claim of the defining moment of communication between the founder and the celestial community. As the story goes, being a carpenter, he was ordered to fetch ebony wood in the forest. However, the subsequent outcome of that divine instruction was that he spent more than the logical period in the forest, and it stretched from a day to a period of forty days and nights in a Jesus-esque experience. During the spiritual encounter with the angels, he was instructed to establish a religious denomination under Christianity, where he would then embark on the evangelization of the world through the proclamation of the Word.[52]

The religion gained ground with more prominence, especially in Porto Novo, Republic of Benin, making sure that God's pronouncements remained as credible as expected. Like the other Aladura identity, the denomination galvanized the support of the Yorùbá epistemology as the foundation for enhancing its expansionist experiment. Benin Republic was significant for the continuation of the practice because it aided the spread of the religion to places like Nigeria, the founder's ancestral home. The doctrinal expressions in the religion are deviations from orthodox Christianity, making its acceptance wider than was initially imagined. The advancement of these Aladura churches gives the impression that the Yorùbá people were waiting for an opportunity to consolidate their indigenous spiritual systems, possibly with European ones, so they would have a hybrid identity that would confer legitimacy on them and give them a sense of ownership. Abandoning all cultural dictations, such as the practice of polygamy or monogamy as considered useful by the individual, or the prescription to abandon the use of words and their potency under the erroneous impression that it was primitive or clannish, was an indulgence that the Yorùbá people would not find helpful to their cultural course of actions.

---

50. Farrell, "Church Rooted in African Mixes."
51. Farrell, "Church Rooted in African Mixes."
52. Crumbley, *Spirit, Structure, and Flesh*, 54–55.

Even with the concentration on one's indigenous epistemic perception, restoring Christian values was not impossible. In Benin Republic, it became apparent that the Africanness in the CCC could not be contained; therefore, the people were more persuaded by a religious practice that reinforced their interest rather than one that showed disdain for their cultural traditions.

The Pentecostal Community and Its Global Presence

When discussing their involvement in the globalization agenda of the Christian faith, the Yorùbá have gone far in the indigenization of Christianity. The Redeemed Christian Church of God (RCGG) is one branch of African Pentecostal movements that has made giant strides in the advancement of the Christian religion globally. Founded by Reverend Josiah Olufemi Akindayomi, the denomination began its evangelizing crusade in 1952 after discovering that the Christian faith must be attuned to the circumstances of the Yorùbá people. RCCG identifies with virtually all the tenets of orthodox Christianity and adds some indigenous flavor to it. There is the belief in water and spirit baptism, healing without medicine, among others.[53] They are associated with the African identity that rejects the European construction of religious doctrines and has become globally influential today. They have become a firebrand representation of the Christianization agenda, for they have made imposing contributions to the Nigerian and African religious market and globally.[54] Andrew Rice was aware of their widening influence when he said RCCG is "one of [Africa's] most vigorously expansionary religious movements, a homegrown Pentecostal denomination that is crusading to become a global faith."[55]

Another Pentecostal movement is the Living Faith Church Worldwide, popularly known as "Winners Chapel."[56] Founded in 1981, it has made an impact in the contemporary global religious world, as its presence is in approximately sixty-five countries. The founder, Bishop David Oyedepo, claimed to have encountered God in a personal revelation where God instructed him to go to the world to challenge devilish activities and engagement with the substitution of holiness and godliness.[57] He was direct in the divine instruction, so much so that the proposed strategies to start the ministry were unveiled to him through the same revelatory process. The church was founded on the core principles entrenched in the theological positions of the Pentecostal. From all indications, the faith is Africanized, and the spread of its expansionist agenda confirms the assumption that it shows a remarkable commitment to the global redefinition of Christianity. Having its headquarters in Canaanland in Ota, Ogun State, Nigeria, the church wields great influence globally today.[58]

From a closer observation of the growth of religious groups and denominations that have their philosophical root in Yorùbá ideology, one can see that they have a common desire to Christianize the globe using their African potential. It is not an overstatement that today, every

---

53. Owoeye, "Healing in Some Pentecostal Churches," 99–101.

54. Ukah, *Globalisation of Pentecostalism*.

55. Rice, "Mission from Africa."

56. Lindhardt, *Pentecostalism in Africa*, 115.

57. Living Faith Church Worldwide International, "Mandate."

58. Kuponu, "Success and Empowerment in Living Faith Church Worldwide."

major country of the world has adherents of these denominations, only in different capacities. The efforts of pioneer Yorùbá pastors, especially people like Bishop Crowther, have yielded an impressive result because Aladura church establishments have occupied important places around the globe. Those who appeared deeply connected to the Yorùbá epistemology have attracted increased attention from their Nigerian environment and the international community.[59] Ghana, Togo, Benin Republic, South Africa, notable countries from the East African region, the United States, Canada, and European countries (especially the United Kingdom), among others, continue to feel the presence of this Yorubanized Christianity; that they continue to forge ahead explains their irrevocable commitment.[60]

From the preceding, it can be deduced that the spread of Yorùbá churches to Africa, America, and the rest of Europe accounted for the globalization of Yorùbá ideas and ideologies. By the time Christianity further settled among the Yorùbá people, there was evidence of the incorporation of most of Yorùbá culture. However, this incorporation did not lead to religious syncretism. This means that indigenous belief systems contradicted the tenets of Christianity when not included. In the general sense, Christianity was against acts that invalidated the Holy Scripture; nevertheless, some aspects of Yorùbá culture found their way into Christian worship and migrated to other territories, influencing the spread of Yorùbá ideologies.

Religion is one of the diverse ways that account for a cultural mix. Christianity was accompanied by Western culture, which often dictated the tune of evangelism. Therefore, when some of these Yorùbá churches were gradually set up in the United Kingdom, the United States, and elsewhere, it was easier to propagate the ideologies within the Yorùbá culture through acts of worship. By establishing churches, so-called Nigerian Yorùbá missionaries accounted for the spread of the Yorùbá language and culture. For instance, the acts of exorcism or spiritual cleansing, now commonplace in churches in Europe, were the original concepts of Yorùbá churches and missions. Despite this relative success, Kim Esther Kinibe notes that there has been a shift in how the Westerners embrace Nigerian Yorùbá missionaries because they often make the same mistake of civilization, an idea some Westerners do not like.[61] Europeans in the Netherlands have even described these missions as "migrant churches,"[62] although this has not affected the establishment of churches in Europe by the Yorùbá missionaries.

Akintunde Oyetade also notes that the proliferation of Yorùbá churches in London accounted for the preponderance of the Yorùbá people and the Yorùbá culture. He puts it squarely: "The majority of the Yorùbá in London are Christians who actively participate in church activities."[63] He further seems to contend that the propagation of Yorùbá ideologies is hinged on church activities, especially as most of these activities would be carried out in the

---

59. Gerloff, "Churches of the Spirit," 208–220.

60. Burgess, Knibbe, and Quaas, "Nigerian-Initiated Pentecostal Churches," 97–121; Adeboye, "Transnational Pentecostalism in Africa," 439–465; Adogame, "Engaging the Rhetoric of Spiritual Warfare," 493–522; and Oshun, "Aladura Evangelists in Britain."

61. Knibbe, "Nigerian Missionaries in Europe," 479.

62. Knibbe, "Nigerian Missionaries in Europe," 479.

63. Oyètádé, "Yoruba Community in London," 78–79.

Yorùbá language to a Yorùbá audience, and the English language would only be spoken at regular intervals.

Similarly, Hermione Harris traced the establishment of Yorùbá churches in Europe to Yorùbá students who traveled overseas for education and formed Christian groups during their course of study, which later grew into churches heavily influenced by some aspects of Yorùbá practices.[64] For instance, the C&S Church in the United Kingdom practiced exorcism. The church's spiritual powers knew no bounds. It is on record that a church member made this statement: "This Church is based on spiritual power. Without spiritual power, there would be no church."[65] The idea that the church should underscore spirituality could be hinged on the fact that the Yorùbá are highly spiritual people seeking spirituality in every way. Before the arrival of Christianity, the Yorùbá sought spirituality through the means of divination. Since Christianity now forbids the Yorùbá Ifá divination, there is a need for a Christian-like spirituality; after all, the concept is not strange to the new religion.

Also, there is the concept of revelation, especially among the Aladura churches, which look like a rebrand of the Yorùbá practices of revelation. Harris notes, "The purpose of Aladura possession, unlike traditional Pentecostalism, is to transmit messages from God about members' lives so that appropriate prayer and remedial ritual action may be undertaken."[66] The introduction of Yorùbá concepts in Christianity ultimately provides a viable method for the globalization of the Yorùbá language and culture.

The Spread of Yorùbá Gospel Songs

The use of songs is a significant way the Yorùbá people express their indigenous views and cultural imaginations. Songs serve many useful purposes. The Yorùbá use songs to ward off evil, strengthen mutual understanding, initiate conflict and resolve it, entertain, and teach. The common understanding that everyone recognizes the significance of songs makes their use central to the attainment of societal goals. However, the importation of external civilizations has not challenged and changed this orientation, notwithstanding its ferocious efforts to do so. It has only reinforced it. Song is one legacy of the Yorùbá that is given a redefinition just so that it fits into the social and political exigencies motivated by the impact of modernization. No matter how evolved the world becomes and irrespective of the overbearing circumstances and influence of externally inspired pressures, morality remains one of the social legacies that the Yorùbá cannot disconnect from their cultural bloodstream. The realization that humans need a strong moral character to navigate their way through the world has inspired their resolution to use songs because of the potentiality of their influence. When accompanied by necessary musical instruments, songs serve the dual purpose of entertainment and pedagogy and fulfill the other functions they are programmed to do.

The evolution of the indigenous imaginations weaved into their songs to become what we identify as gospel songs in the contemporary world are motivated by the desire to remain

---

64. Harris, *Yoruba in Diaspora*, 28.

65. Harris, *Yoruba in Diaspora*, 63.

66. Harris, *Yoruba in Diaspora*, 147.

  GLOBAL YORÙBÁ

Figure 10.3. Christianity and money-making. Inscriptions such as those in the image: "This church eliminates witches and enemies" and "contribute N1000 to the Church for God to give you N10,000 in return" are some of the methods used by prosperity preachers during sermons to raise funds. Drawing by Dr. Kazeem Ekeolu.

relevant in the religious circle. Once the Yorùbá had domesticated the Christian religion and creatively fleshed out a distinct religious identity from it, it became inevitable that they created other essential things to enhance their agenda. An identified and typical behavior among the Yorùbá across the world is their propensity to be sold to music, dance, and clap during worship or mere domestic engagement. They transferred this behavior to the Atlantic and have even re-created a space for it in the United Kingdom. This means that songs are integral to their cultural traditions, which cannot be jettisoned irrespective of the circumstances. It makes sense that there evolves a distinct music culture among them, which would be an instrument of evangelization and would serve the moral ambition of the religion accordingly. Meanwhile, the reincarnation of these Yorùbá songs is an effective strategy to preserve their cultural legacy. A closer evaluation of the Yorùbá gospel songs will show the relationship between a Christian desire for evangelization and the protection of their Yorùbá identity.

Although the interest is not in the songs produced by members of the Aladura doctrine, owing to the impressive works of various scholars in that field, the connection between these songs and the Yorùbá indigenous imaginations that have resurfaced through them will be traced. Creating a religious brand from the Christian culture that was suited for the Europeans and breaking boundaries as a result demanded that there was a different identity that could only be linked to the created brand. It means that while Yorùbá Christianity was becoming a global property because of the unshaken dedication of the expansionary wings, some elements of the Yorùbá culture must accompany it; hence, the making of the gospel. The fact that it was directed to make a global impact, despite the understanding of the limitation of the Yorùbá language, affirmed the assumption that its religious import could not be undermined. It was a known strategy used to promote the Yorubanization agenda. One begins to make sense of all these the moment it is realized that in every international community where Yorubanized Christianity has a significant presence, a handful of Yorùbá people are vehicles of transference, transportation, and a transformation of the religion. If these practitioners embrace the Yorùbá gospel songs, they become a collective property that even outsiders want to claim.

If one is familiar with the religious landscape of Nigeria, one would have no challenge understanding the argument raised above. In the Eastern part of the country, where the Yorùbá language is not their cultural identity, there are situations where they adopted their gospel songs because they have made their presence felt and their contributions impactful. This develops rather meticulously from the imagination of orthodox Christianity, not as a combative opponent of the indigenous African knowledge but as a complementary agent in advancing the course of humanity. For example, this is indicated by the constant concentration of these gospel songs on Jesus. Their songs continue to demonstrate the capacity to initiate a dialogue between the two expressions of human cultures. The Christian understanding of the place of Jesus is not opposed, and because of the recognition of its validity, adherents have embraced the religion and the cultural properties that come with them. When one comes across Yorùbá gospel songs, one realizes that they are instruments of cultural negotiations that provoke sober reflection about the meeting point of the said faith and one's indigenous culture. For example, Tope Alabi, a popular Yorùbá gospel singer, has strong connections to indigenous knowledge and ontology. Perhaps even to her ignorance, she has employed different indigenous terms to refer to God and Jesus Christ in her songs.

This shifts our attention to a particularly electric Christian gospel song, "Ọlọ́wọ́gbọgbọrọ," premiered by Nathaniel Bassey.[67] "Ọlọ́wọ́gbọgbọrọ" is one of the appellations of Olódùmarè (God in Yorùbá religion). Like that found in the Christian religion as recorded in Psalm 136:12, it means "the one with the long-stretched arm." Although Bassey has a south-south ancestral origin, he was born and raised in Lagos, a Yorùbá cultural society. His song became a countrywide gospel production that steered people into trancelike situations during worship. Like many other Yorùbá songs, it is outstanding because of its cultural persuasion. The impact of the Yorùbá culture is felt even when not pronounced in the way other religions conduct their engagement. *Ọlọ́wọ́gbọgbọrọ* is an indigenous appellation whose origin can be traced to an Ifá verse. It is one of the praise verses dedicated to the adoration of Olódùmarè, the Supreme Being, among the Yorùbá people. The cultural significance of this is that the promotion of this indigenous epistemological perception is underlined by the intention for a dialogue, the facilitation of common ground, and an understanding of where the import of the religion would not be displaced, despite being in synchronization with the indigenous ones.[68] This comes from the evaluation of the two religions and the identification of their meeting points. Despite being extracted from their indigenous legacy, the import of the song has a modern and contemporary appeal.

Diffusion of different sorts has permeated the contemporary musical culture of religious identity, and this is where space equally accommodates different music nomenclature. Gospel highlife and gospel hip-hop, among others, are different variants of the same construct. In the same category, Yorùbá gospel songs can be conveniently identified and examined within the context of Yorùbá epistemic perception that is merged or poignantly reincarnated in the Christian culture. Also, the concept of the enemy in the biblical world is not taken for granted, as enemies take a profound position in the theological philosophy of Christianity. It links its beginning to Satan in the Christian culture, where the latter became antagonistic to God's superiority. The experience created a cultural imperative that strengthened the formulation of a religious outlook where satanic engagements are viewed with suspicion and heavy rejection, to the extent that Christians are encouraged to consciously dissociate themselves from engagements that can facilitate unity between them and the condemned creature, Satan. The Yorùbá people have something philosophically similar but theologically different from this. However, the discrepancy does not stop contemporary Yorùbá Christians from imposing the cultural attributes of one on another, if it satisfies their desire to exalt the Supreme.

The cultural transposition of the indigenous designate, Èṣù, for example, shows the determination of the Yorùbá people to transport the cultural systems and structures attendant with the Yorùbá Èṣù on the target civilization. Once they have successfully, although unabashedly, shortchanged the character of Èṣù on their Christian identity, they have created a cultural vacuum that must be filled by their appropriation of the indigenous characteristics of the alien one, or vice versa. Inevitably, this leads to the phenomenon of the enemy as accepted in the Christian religion and culture, whereas the cultural understanding of the enemy and its theological position as a social phenomenon usually collapse to produce a profound result. One of such is

---

67. Bassey ft. Adenuga, "Olowogbogboro."
68. Peel, *Christianity, Islam, and Orisa-Religion.*

Figure 10.4. "Yoruba Christianity in the World," by Michael Efionayi.

that in their musical artistry, people instinctively frame the existential crisis initiated by the presence of an enemy. The prevalence of Yorùbá songs that dwell only on the spiritual chastisement of an enemy reflects their cultural thinking. They do not, therefore, conceive their songs as mere verbal aesthetics that show the world the fecundity of Yorùbá cultural traditions. Instead, they are considered appropriate instruments for the continuation of their spiritual warfare with their enemies, whose leadership role is imposed on the orthodox Satan. At least, this is the most constant impression one gets when discussing gospel songs that dwell on an enemies-friends dichotomy.

In different circumstances, these same songs are employed as materials for praising the Creator in the Yorùbá way, garnishing the song with indigenous embellishments in a way that makes it contemporary. This is signaled by the reference to Nathaniel Bassey's praise songs. The cultural beginning of this engagement dates to the pre-European and pre-Arabic invasion of the African cultural space. Even when the gospel culture is exclusively European, it has gone through a process of domestication and is used to serve a familiar and common purpose.[69] The

---

69. Ajibade, "New Wine in Old Cups," 105–126.

extended relationship between orthodox Christianity and the Yorùbá traditions has not denied them their claims to indigenous knowledge structures and epistemologies, for these are carefully transferred, transformed, and transplanted into the Christian culture. Moreover, because this has continued without stopping, Christianity coming from the people has been given a different and unique identity. Some of these singers are considered now, but it is important to reiterate that their association with indigenous powers is realized in the continued reference to the Christian God as the foundation of their strength.

One of the five foremost Yorùbá gospel singers is evangelist Bola Are, born in 1954 into a Christian family that shared the African culture. Being one of the Yorubanized Christianity, the CAC was the sole foundation of Are, who came into prominence in 1977.[70] Many of her songs are praises and encomiums on the God Almighty. However, what is unique about them is that the Yorùbá religious identity is preserved in her songs because of the presence of cultural ideas that have a symbolic relationship with Yorùbá origin. In fact, for these people, it was nearly impossible to dissociate their praise songs from being linked to their indigenous system. Yorùbá people permeate their social and spiritual philosophy in words, aphorisms, and proverbs, as these become agencies of cultural transmission. They develop their younger generation through the system that makes it impossible for the latter to construct an identity different from the one to which they have been introduced. However, because of the pressure of Christianity, they are left to navigate the Christian culture through their methods and principles. One of her popular tracks, "Agbára Èṣù Dà Níbi tí Jésù Gbé Ń Joba," lends credence to the argument raised above. It emphasizes the re-creation of images using the Christian religion as the template.

Another important Yorùbá gospel figure is Lara George, born and raised in Lagos State, Nigeria. The presence of Lara George in the Yorùbá gospel music industry is a testament to the fact that cultural identity is more socially and genetically transmitted than consciously learned, except for the human social behavior that can be excused as a component of social constructs that are attracted through interaction with members of the society. Lagos State is not so engrossed in the untainted culture of the Yorùbá world because it is a reasonably secular and multicultural urban settlement. Due to its secularity, cultural ideas are usually updated with many other cultural values. However, George modeled several of her songs along the Yorùbá cultural identity. She began her gospel career as a member of a music choir while she was a student at the culturally perforated University of Lagos, and a careful evaluation of her songs indicates a deep-rooted relationship between them and the Yorùbá culture. One of her tracks, Yorùbá "Ẹ̀yin L'oba," which she produced in 2016, is related to the praise and worship among indigenous Yorùbá people.[71] It is like "Olówógbogboro," and in a way, it appears like Are's "Agbára Èṣù Dà Níbi tí Jésù Gbé Ń Joba."

Tope Alabi is another Yorùbá gospel music icon whose songs demonstrate her indigenous knowledge and ontology. Born in 1970, she was raised in an environment dominated by the Yorubanized Christian culture, which profoundly influences the structure of her songs.[72] She

---

70. Yes FM, "Evangelist Bola Are," 4:21.

71. George, "Eyin L'oba."

72. Ayeni, "Everything You Should Know about Veteran Gospel Artiste, Tope Alabi."

indulges so much in the Yorùbá system of praise that one questions if these cultural icons have a specific divine mandate for the Yorubanization of orthodox Christianity in the first place. The materials of praise Alabi uses are products of the Yorùbá environment. In singing praises of Olódùmarè, she does not separate the Yorùbá indigenous God from the one introduced by the Europeans, as is the case among many Yorùbá believers in Christianity. She has become an important force in the advancement of Yorubanized Christianity because she is known across and beyond the continent for the enchantment of her songs.

These gospel singers are religious icons, and they get international attention and presence because Yorùbá churches are planted in different corners of the world. This suggests that all those of Yorùbá ancestry with a Christian identity in the diaspora would carry their favorite singers to their new environment, where they can expand their works and, invariably, popularity. From Nigeria to Ghana, Senegal to Uganda, the length and breadth of the continent where Yorùbá Christianity is practiced, it is instructive to reiterate how widespread and imposing they have become with their religious activities. These gospel songs continue to function as means of evangelization, and this has been convincingly demonstrated within and outside Nigerian society.

Conclusion

This chapter examined the extent to which the Yorùbá have indigenized the Christian religion by transposing some of their cultural traditions and expressions into the religion. This was done by tracing the history of Christianity in Yorubaland and how the pioneer members of orthodox Christianity used their intellect and wisdom to create a unique identity for themselves through the religion. One valuable take from this is that religion does not remain the same in ideologies when it moves along territories. When it gets to a new territory, it is often incorporated with the culture of the place. It birthed the idea of a Yorubanized Christianity, which denotes the infusion of some aspects of Yorùbá culture into the new religion. This intermix of cultures (Christianity is also treated as a religion and culture, being that it is a way of life) sometimes led to religious syncretism, which was the case with Christianity in the early years of its existence in Yorubaland. However, as the Yorùbá became more enlightened that Christianity negates polytheism, they dropped some acts of syncretism but retained cultural aspects that aligned with the Christian acts of worship. This chapter also shows that the language barrier is one factor that influenced the Yorubanization of Christianity. Even when this factor almost impeded the spread of Christianity, in the long run, it led to the acceptance of Christianity. For instance, English Christian songs were replaced with Yorùbá Christian songs that spread across countries, further contributing to the globalization of Yorùbá culture, ideas, and ideologies.

This chapter also discussed the influence of Yorùbá missionaries in the propagation of Christianity and how they ultimately ended the problem of conversion that the European missionaries faced. The latter identified that the use of Yorùbá missionaries would connect with the Yorùbá people as well as boost the evangelization process. Initially, this did not address the problem because the Yorùbá missionaries stuck with orthodox Christianity and were no different from their European counterparts, except for using the Yorùbá language. In addition, the willing agencies of conversion, predominantly the Yorùbá converts who were returned from

Sierra Leone, understood that the possibility of winning the people into the Christian religion depended on the utilization of a familiar strategy that would factor in their native culture, as that would facilitate easy conversion and fast-track the process of acculturation.

Immediately after returning from Sierra Leone, where they had acquired adequate linguistic competence and outstanding intellectualism, they developed a religious identity that catered only to their indigenous ontological perception. Even when the orthodox Christian adherents from the West felt that this was a departure from the orthodox system, they needed people to embrace the religion first and do some repair to whatever damage was caused in the process of introduction. They were helpless, as the individuals who were ready for the evangelization of the Yorùbá had placed them in this tight condition. The Yorùbá pioneers did not carve this Yorùbá identity because they were intransigent to the doctrinal expressions inside the Bible. Instead, they understood that these people needed to be integrated into the Christian religion through diplomacy, and this diplomacy dictated that they saw themselves in the new religion as active and not passive contributors. In this sense, even those who still show their loyalty to indigenous worship hybridize it with the Christian religion.[73]

As a result, it has brought about innumerable advantages to the people because if those white missionaries gave the pioneers the moral support needed to enhance their goals, it was inescapable that the needed financial consolidation for the proliferation of their faith would follow. One may ask, What would these early Yorùbá Christians need money for in the incorporation project? The subtle answer is that one of the bishop's first steps was the codification of the Yorùbá language into classifiable orthography. Indigenous education was set on a purposeful pedestal. Once this was done, these people could not but be convinced about the significance of the Christian religion to their general socioeconomic development. Such innovation was necessary for different reasons.

Islam's ascent into the Yorùbá world preceded that of the Western missionaries, and because they had already established their faith, the atmosphere of competition was becoming almost a lost battle for the Christian faith. Therefore, the Christians needed to do something creative and flexible so that they could challenge the Islamic religion from converting everyone. Furthermore, because the religion was yet to convert the people's language into writing, the effort to do this became immediately yielding. The Yorubanized religion spread across the world today can be attributed to the education provided by the British.

It was also proven that the global expansion of Yorùbá churches was a viable means of spreading Yorùbá cultural ideologies. The religious activities in these Yorùbá churches showcased evidence of the Yorùbá culture, especially in aspects such as divination, revelation, and a host of others. These doctrines drawn for the Yorùbá indigenous systems influenced acts of worship in other countries outside the Yorùbá territories and showed how the non-Yorùbá people have unconsciously assimilated some Yorùbá ideologies. Another attestation of how Yorùbá ideologies have spread globally is that most of the powerful Pentecostal churches in the world, such as the RCCG, were founded by the Yorùbá people. In all, the arrival and eventual spread of Christianity in Yorubaland influenced the globalization of Yorùbá ideologies and cultural systems.

---

73. Oha, "Yoruba Christian Video Narrative," 121–142.

11 Religion and Globalization

Introduction

Many strong threads hold every society together. Among the Yorùbá, religion is important and a nonnegotiable factor because of its historical, social, and cultural relevance that cannot be underestimated. The African society is a giant twist of culture, religion, institutions, and norms intertwined to bring the peculiarities that are celebrated or much debated in contemporary days. The Yorùbá are one of the forerunners of the reflectors of these African attributes, and it would be too misleading to discuss them and not talk about their religion. The reason is that the metaphysical and epistemological worldview of the Yorùbá is finessed through the anvil and the hammers of indigenous religions, the *Òrìṣà* religion, Christianity, and Islam. Aside from Òrìṣà worship, the religious practices of the Yorùbá people have grown largely toward Christianity and Islam.

Interestingly, the coexistence of Òrìṣà worship, Christianity, and Islam in Yorùbá society have influenced one another, forming new cultures drawn from these religions. Hence, this chapter will explore how Òrìṣà practices have influenced other religions and cultures globally while also examining the contemporary Yorùbá situation and the influence of Christianity and Islam. These will be discussed along with the ideas of globalization and its effect on them, as well as the transnational practices of the religions elsewhere.

The comprehensive understanding of spirits, the pantheon of Òrìṣà, ancestors, destiny, and other aspects of religious understanding help the Yorùbá to make sense of their history, reality, present, future, persons, and other paraphernalia of life. Religion has been the reliable lens through which people saw the world, and its complexity of logic and illuminations leave lesser errors. This is because, unlike many other religions, Yorùbá religious systems have strong aspects that complement logic, science, sociology, philosophy, and other life ramifications that are almost perfect enough to serve the people.[1] Having been practiced for many years with its adjoining epistemology, it captured changes and created a reservoir of wisdom for those who seek it. For instance, *Ifá*, which has left the shores of West Africa, is a complex whole consisting of science, culture, sociology, history, algorithm, mathematics, philosophies, and all one can imagine. Without any attempt at overstating the strength of Ifá practice and worship, it serves

---

1. Adegbindin, *Ifá in Yorùbá Thought System.*

as an ancient manual that the Yorùbá use to navigate life and its adjoining phenomenon. The 256 *Odu Ifá* touch on various aspects of life, and people often consult its wisdom before making important decisions.[2]

Seeing the relevance of the Òrìṣà and Yorùbá religious systems, one would not be surprised that its riches will survive contemporary cultural appraisals and live beyond the pangs of civilization and cultural diffusion. So as not to be distracted from the main discourse of this chapter, the question is, What is the face of the Yorùbá religion in a globalized world? How can one explain the globalization of the corpus of the system and the religious practices within the confines of the contemporary belief system? The role of the Yorùbá religion in the lives and culture of the people will not allow its extinction or total displacement; hence, globalization has only transformed exposure to religion and redefined manners of practice. Therefore, the inquest of this chapter is the interaction between this religion, its riches, and globalization.

Similarly, the practice of Islam and Christianity, as received by the Yorùbá, has evolved over the years following interactions with the Yorùbá culture and beliefs. The Yorùbá have made themselves undisputable stakeholders in the propagation of Pentecostal faith across the world, as they have one of the largest Christian memberships and biggest auditoriums in the world. There is a unique and changing Christian faith quite different from those in other parts of the world, and these varieties among the Yorùbá are being transported outside the locality of the people.

Globalizing Yorùbá Religion

Yorùbá religion transcends Nigeria, Benin, or Togo and has become a transnational affair. The various agents of globalization passed the knowledge and practice of the religion across Africa and the world hundreds of years ago. Given the level of its interaction with globalization processes, it would be wrong to view religion only from an Africanist standpoint. The transportation of the religion beyond the shores of Africa is categorically noticeable during the Atlantic slave trade, making Òrìṣà an Afro-Atlantic religion with a transnational status. From the end of the nineteenth century, the transnational level of religion became more manifested, especially in the Americas, with the emergence of what could be considered Yorùbá-derived religion.[3]

International understanding of the core values of the religion, which served as the foundation of the contemporary interaction with agents of globalization, started with some travelers, missionaries, and explorers' accounts and memoirs that presented the religion from the measure of what they could perceive. Despite traces of European bias in the construction of African history at that stage, the accounts that conceptualized the practices and the instruments of religion threw the discussions on Yorùbá religion open for intellectual conversations. After this, more understandings began to rise, and upon the processes of the decolonization of African history, lost perspectives are being reconstructed. One could see the ideological development in W. H. Clarke's early description of the Yorùbá as "rather a peculiar;" he later adjusted

---

2. Eesuola, "Odu Ifa Ose Meji," 24–34.

3. Capone, "Orisha Religion in a Transnational Perspective," 135–152.

his views to "refined heathen" after understanding the reverence to a Supreme Being whom he believed they accessed by some inferior Òrìsà that served as mediators.[4]

Aside from the new perspectives on the practices elsewhere in those years, the nineteenth century is particularly important, being a definitive century for outright post–slave trade globalization of the religion. It was the period when Islam, Christianity, colonialism, and European culture started having more aggressive and organized infiltration into Yorubaland, and the intermodifications and assimilations of all the new cultures started taking place. This period opened the door to Yorùbá religion and Islam, especially after the jihadist invasion of the Yorùbá states and the collapse of the Oyo Empire. Similarly, the accelerated missionary activities among the Yorùbá in Lagos, Abeokuta, and other parts of the Yorùbá states foregrounded further systematic assimilations of the practices. Colonization, Western education, and onward interaction are bringing new faces and understanding of the religion. Coupled with the influence of culture, one would see that the practices of Christianity and Islam in Africa are largely influenced by these interactions with a similar effect of the Yorùbá religious dogmas.

Aside from these, the Yorùbá religion has gotten to the global stage with an increasing level of intellectual discussion, exchanges, conferences, and relationships that hinge on cultural exposure and understanding. The religions ceded across the world and particularly in the Americas emerged to have cultural influence within the contemporary sphere. Ideas imported to the coasts of Nigeria were reformed with some basic cultural and religious dispositions and their exportation has expanded the practice and knowledge of the religion. In essence, globalization, as a two-way relationship, has made foreign influences visible in contemporary Yorùbá religious practices. There is evidence of the injections of Yorùbá religious belief systems influencing some foreign ideologies and practices. Hence, reciprocal flows of globalization have introduced the Yorùbá to global perspectives with some significant alterations to Òrìsà religions practices by globalizing forces. As Iheanacho states, "Many western societies now have at one end, originally, religious buildings and institutions converted into warehouses, while at the other end of the city, foreign religions which were hitherto alien to the societies are flourishing. In the main, globalization accelerators—Internet, television, telephone and other facilities of the information revolution age expose all peoples of the world to new cultures and religious practices."[5]

Many may not be Christians, Buddhists, or Muslims but their worldviews could be identified to correspond with any of the religions or a predominant religion in the society they interacted with. There is an innate religious culture in every religious practice, and it is possible to deposit its residuals in the subconscious of the people. For this reason, the idea of globalization may not be to say that many have picked up *ópèlè* or the worship of Yorùbá gods; it is largely that there is an adoption of Yorùbá religious cultures. This is why some Islamic or Christian practices in Nigeria or Africa may preach against the Yorùbá people's gods but have some form of the Yorùbá religious cultures in the inclination of their particular practices. This means globalization may be blowing up not only Yorùbá religious practices globally but also its religious

---

4. Clarke, *Travels and Explorations in Yorubaland*.

5. Iheanacho, "Globalisation Challenges and Change Factors," 84.

cultures. Viewing the process of the transnationalization of the religion and its translocal circulation from the angle of its cultural infusion would properly fit into the globalization scheme. It is on this note that syncretism is properly facilitated.

Cuba is one of the countries that shows the two ways in which one can see the globalization of religion in the sense of some actual outright framework practices and not as mere religious cultural influences. The origin of the Yorùbá religion in Cuba was the arrival of the considerable number of Yorùbá slaves who were forcefully taken to the country to work. They brought their religion and practices with them. The Spanish colonialists imposed Catholicism on the people and slaves taken to Cuba, generating a syncretic religion known as Santeria.[6] Santeria has both religious materials and cultures of Yorùbá religion and Catholicism. In terms of cultures emanating from religious practices, Santeria influenced the musical culture of Cubans with the lyrics and melodies traceable to Yorùbá religious music, dances, and rituals. Rumba, Son, and Salsa have heavy Yorùbá influence and their melodic and lyrical composition bear evidence.[7] The Cuban folk dances are directly linked to those identifiable with the Yorùbá Òrìṣà. Given that many of the Yorùbá people's cultural values are religiously motivated, adopting these cultures is synonymous with the prevalent culturalized religious values. Santeria religion has a dominant effect on Cuba's culture, demonstrating the existing religious culture of the Òrìṣà.

In practice, the recognition of the pantheons of Òrìṣà, the gods and goddesses of the Yorùbá religious systems, represent and dominate different aspects of life such as wisdom, fertility, love, and others. There is an adoption of the ritual, festivals, and offerings as they exist in Nigeria. Divination is another part of the Santeria religion that shows the direct adaptation of the Òrìṣà religion.[8] For instance, some worshippers use a divination board upon which cowry shells are thrown, an exact adaptation of divination practices among the Yorùbá Òrìṣà worshippers. The rituals and processes by which priests and priestesses are initiated are also adapted from Yorùbá religions.

The syncretic influence on culture is also largely seen in Brazil through the practice of Candomblé, which is also a syncretism of Yorùbá religion and Catholicism.[9] The religious culture of the Yorùbá is thereby extended to many of the Brazilian ways of life, including their musical lifestyles and dancing patterns. This influence on Cuba and Brazil is also seen in fashion and styles and artworks. The reflection is further seen in contemporary crafts across America and some parts of Europe in textiles, sculptures, and pottery designs.[10] Many American languages and words have been influenced by cultural habits and have been translocated. The religious culture further touched on the American languages like the Caribbean and dishes such as the Brazilian Acaraje and Sancocho of Cuba. Cuba, Brazil, and the Americas are just case studies of how religious practices and cultures have been globalized. There is evidence of these facts, cultures, and practices across the world, allowing the religion to gain a globalized and

---

6. McMillan, "Santeria," 41.

7. Manuel, Bilby, and Largey, *Caribbean Currents*.

8. Brandon, "Lucumi Divination," 167–188.

9. Neeley, *Contemporary Afro-American Voodooism*.

10. Areo and Kalilu, "Origin of and Visual Semiotics in Yoruba Textile Adire," 22–34.

international status. It is a two-way exchange; as much as Òrìṣà influences other cultures, it has also received considerable influence from various sources, religions, and cultures.

Outside the historical exposure of the Yorùbá and their kingdoms to colonialism and other historical forms of globalization, the people have constantly traveled across the world, depositing their religious and cultural ideas. The Yorùbá are not only mobile, visiting different parts of the world, but are also receptive to other perspectives and influences. Their receptiveness has allowed cross-cultural relationships and influences for centuries, so much so that the contemporary Yorùbá culture and religion are becoming gradual simulations of foreign cultures. In many instances, the influence is seen heavily in the customs and activities, altering how they perceive their surroundings. As a result, there is a gradual shift in some fundamental thoughts from Yorùbá religious epistemology. Some ideas of the Òrìṣà have been dropped and newer ones are incorporated. This simulation is not surprising, as it is a process simultaneously going on in other cultures because the continuous nature of globalization and the world's transformation into a global village has meant that religious identities, perspectives, value systems, doctrines, and institutions that were previously alien are now active, especially in Yorubaland.

The world is becoming a global village, and there is almost no religion that has not experienced significant changes. Òrìṣà worship has also been gradually adjusting to fit into the context of the global village, allowing the world access to its understanding and making its outright adoption feasible. The first evidence of the change could be seen in the transiency of the religions and activities towards contemporary characteristics, exemplified in the changes in the religion and Yorùbá traditional societies from a "simple state of cultural homogeneity and agrarian life, with sacred oriented leadership and institutions"[11] to contemporary complexity. Hence, there is a change in the religiously incited social value systems and perspectives. For instance, the introduction of foreign religious perspectives undermined responsibilities that were previously important for existing religious systems. This lowered the standards of religious sanctity and conservativeness, which created room for new patterns and doctrines of religious practice. These doctrines removed the exclusivity of religions in specific parts of the world and posed challenges to traditional beliefs, presenting newfound foreign systems as alternatives. No matter the cloak of negativity this might wear, it makes the Yorùbá religious system more relatable and accessible to the global audience.

Further evidence of the ideological transformation of the religion as a reflection of the preparedness for global access and reflection of globalization is the introduction of elements of capitalism to the religious culture. The contemporary practice and systems of the Yorùbá religion have grown to be more materialistic than its usual state—a foreign concept and concept transported into the religious system.[12] The conceptual change is also found in modern religions like Christianity and Islam, as they have moved from fundamental teachings of a simple, nonmaterialistic, and conservative lifestyle to one prioritizing materialism. "Worship the Lord with your substance" has always been present in the Òrìṣà worship system; it was not in the

---

11. Iheanacho, "Globalisation Challenges," 83.

12. O'Connor and Falola, "Religious Entrepreneurship," 115–135.

light of transactional operations as evident in globalized cultures. Hence, the Òrìṣà worship and Yorùbá traditional religious practices have become globalized culture too.

Capitalism as a characteristic of globalized culture has resulted in the distraction of Yorùbá religious practices from institutional issues, philosophical discourse, and its metaphysical fronts to personal aggrandizement and wealth accumulation. Those who explore the riches of the religion and its practices tend to tailor it toward status, wealth, and personal advantage. Those who have not attained wealth are either meant to believe that this will happen soon or that they have committed some wrong for which they must make amends. This has affected the understanding and the patronage of *Aje*, the deity and goddess of wealth, to the accumulation of wealth without further philosophizing the concepts around it. The concept of *Orí* now has more relatability with fortune than it should.

No matter how much the level at which Òrìṣà worship has been diabolized from an ethnocentric perspective, the religion is built on strong moral codes and values. The newly introduced individualistic mindset has not grown positively in the African circle, and the effect is seen in the people's religious practices. While Aje is getting a negative coloration with the presence of a capitalist approach to Yorùbá religion, the adjoining cultures are not respected. The concept of Aje extends to hard work, as many do not believe wealth would always fall on one's lap. There is a philosophical stance that Aje does not discriminate. As one of the *oríkì* states, "Ó ya'lé asínwín, ó ṣọ asínwín d'olówó; ó ya'lé aṣiwèrè, ó ṣọ aṣiwèrè d'ènìyàn pàtàkì," which means that "Aje gets to the house of the madman and turns him into a wealthy person; it gets to the house of the crazy and turns him to a person of status." However, it emphasizes hard work before wealth, as seen in the proverb "Ìṣẹ́ l'ógun iṣẹ́," translated as "work is the antidote of poverty."

In addition, it warns that one should not be too desperate in anything, including the accumulation of wealth, as seen in the proverb "A kìí kán' jú tu olú ọ̀rán, nítorí pé igba ẹ́ kò tó sè l'ọ́bẹ́," which loosely translates to mean that one does not collect mushrooms in desperation because two hundred pieces does not guarantee they will fill the pot. In other words, a desperate acquisition does not result in a favorable end. However, these values are being forgotten with the introduction of a capitalist mentality to the religion, which has extensively increased the incidences of ritual killings for wealth and personal advantages. There are postulations of ritual killings in religious practices, but there have been rare establishments of the facts. And in those strong cultures, the rituals are often not for personal benefit. In essence, the value systems portrayed by the religion have been relegated to the background to fit into contemporary frivolities in some cases.

The broad usage, practice, and understanding of religion have been open to people of different origins because of their adaptability to languages. Globalization is evidenced in the Yorùbá religion by moving it away from the exclusive use of the Yorùbá language to communicate religious teachings. In opening up to different languages—even without abandoning one's language—many religious institutions have adopted English as their primary language for communicating during religious gatherings, and those that can hold the values and still communicate in their languages do so. The usage of the Caribbean dialect is an example. The simulation of the English language to fit into the context of Òrìṣà worship has allowed for the invitation of intellectual engagement with religion from across the world, as well as global inquiries into the language. English linguistics enhances the epistemological property of the religion, enabling its widespread exportation.

Despite the positive influence of adaptability to languages, the religious institutions that retain the Yorùbá language sometimes do so to remain connected with an audience that does not understand English. Yorùbá language and traditional practices are interconnected; many religious rites and doctrines were originally conceived in Yorùbá. The declining use of the Yorùbá language has affected traditional religious practices, and the meanings of religious rites and doctrines have been reduced. Messages are influenced by foreign languages as meanings are lost in translation.

Another consequence of globalization is the change in the roles and freedoms of women within their respective religious faiths. Global advances in women's rights have had major influences on religious practices, and women have assumed leadership roles in various religious faiths. Women are leading congregations, attaining positions of status, and performing rituals and rites. The Western world, in particular, has integrated the ideas of women's liberation and equal rights into their religious philosophies and practices. Women have more choices available to them, and they rarely surrender in the face of inequality and religious subjugation. These religious philosophies and practices have encouraged women to attain positions of leadership, which is less common in Yorùbá religious contexts. There are cases of renowned women leaders in the traditional Yoruba religion, and their heroic actions have been recorded in history.[13]

Globalization often involves a two-way transfer of information, and the Yorùbá have transferred their own religion and Yorubanized versions of Christianity to other parts of the world. Other religious practices have also arrived in Yorùbáland from other parts of the world, notably from India. One such example is the Baha'i Faith, which was introduced in the 1920s during the colonial administration.[14] Enoch Olinga, a well-known Nigerian, contributed to the development of this religion in 1950, and a National Spiritual Assembly was chosen in 1956.[15] The religion has promoted the importance of other faiths and defended the equality of all people.

The One Love Family, founded in 1987 by Sat Guru Maharaj Ji, is another religion among the Yorùbá. Maharaj Ji asserted that he had received a command from God to deliver humans from global poverty and suffering. His religion believes that nature and natural elements, such as the sun, air, and fire, are essential to their faith and humanity. Its worshippers are vegetarians who wear red and white clothing, revering their guru as a master and as God on earth. This faith has faced constant criticisms due to Maharaj Ji's claim to be a divinity on earth, but it has flourished and continued to gain followers among the Yorùbá people and other ethnic groups—even beyond Nigeria.[16]

In essence, the discourse on Yorùbá religion and globalization tilts toward transformation in practices and religious cultures. The first aspect of the religion is the adoption of other practices in other religions and cultures into the framework of the Òrìṣà worship. The second is how

---

13. Olajubu, *Women in the Yoruba Religious Sphere.*

14. Universal House of Justice, *In Memoriam*, 802–804.

15. Hands of the Cause Residing in the Holy Land, "Bahá'í Faith," 22, 46.

16. Nwosu, "Religion and the Crisis of National Unity in Nigeria," 141–152.

Figure 11.1.
Egungun Orisa by Moses Ogunleye, the continuity of Yorùbá Òrìṣà in today's world. The Egúngún is a society of masqueraders with masks that often represent a person's spirit. Egúngún festivals are held across the Yorùbá world with colorful attires worn by masquerade families.

some of the practices in the traditional religion of the Yorùbá people influence foreign religious practices. The third is the reflection of these instances elsewhere, outside the coast of Nigeria. However, globalization also takes the form of new religions, such as Santara and Candomblé, that have developed because of these syncretisms. On the other side, a more appropriate approach to understanding how the religion has become globalized is the level of the globalization of the cultures attached to it, to other parts of the world or practices, and the extent to which it has adopted globalized cultures. It is viewed from three major lenses: practice adoption, cultural adoption, and emerging syncretism.

The Power and Impact of the Internet

In the twenty-first century, the Internet has revolutionized almost every aspect of human life, changing outlooks and approaches to various issues while enabling the emergence of a completely different world. The United States led the world in the adoption of advanced communications technology—the world had more than 150 million Internet users in 1998, and more than half of them lived in the United States.[17] The Internet's effects are easily seen in the way that information is organized and communicated, and it has also introduced changes to religion. Different religions of the world have been rapidly globalized through the Internet; information has been shared across borders, doctrines have been refined, and religious fallacies have been disproven. The major religious practices of the Yorùbá have been part of this phenomenon. It is worth examining how Americans leveraged the Internet to globalize religions, especially in the context of the Yorùbá religion. This can be done by considering the Internet and the Yorùbá Òrìṣà religion, and then the Internet and the propagation of other religions among the Yorùbá. Such inquiry provides insights into the Internet's role in the globalization of the Yorùbá religion.

The Internet has been successfully used to propagate Òrìṣà worship (also called Lukumi in some communities), the Yorùbá-based religion associated with Brazil, Cuba, and the United States.[18] When Òrìṣà devotees brought the Yorùbá religion to the Internet, they expected to leverage the technology as a medium for connecting Òrìṣà communities around the world. The Internet extended the reach of Òrìṣà religious beliefs, which had initially grown through local channels of communication, including religious festivities and personal interactions. Communication technology has opened up a new range of nonphysical interactions between devotees.[19] These devotees were a minority within the larger group of practitioners, but their actions worked to globalize the Yorùbá religion. Within these minority groups, many considered the Internet to be a significant medium for unveiling the legacy of their religion and the past of its worshippers, sharing such information with other individuals online. Some adherents leveraged the Internet to reorganize societal perceptions of Òrìṣà, educating those who were willing to learn. Miguel Ramos explains what drew the early devotees of Òrìṣà to the Internet: "For others, it was a means of keeping in touch with their religious elders or family. Most saw the

---

17. Shapiro, "Internet," 14–27, 21.
18. Ramos, "Connecting through a Medium."
19. Ramos, "Connecting through a Medium."

Internet as a positive medium for clarifying social stigmas, exchanging information, elucidating the misinformed, and expanding the U.S. Lukumí/Òrìṣà knowledge base. Some even went as far as predicting that cyberspace would eventually transform Lukumí devotion and ritual processes; the possibility of online rituals and ceremonies in the cyber world!"[20]

Reports have identified the first known website about Òrìṣà, *Orishanet*, which was active in 1995. Between 1995 and 2000, there were at least one hundred websites hosting Lukumi or Òrìṣà-related content.[21] It can be assumed that through private communications, including email correspondence, people shared the information even more widely. As these measures propagated the Òrìṣà religious beliefs, they affected the religions themselves.

Some of the earliest internet research conducted on Òrìṣà religion vis-à-vis was done by Stefanía Capone, an Italian anthropologist.[22] She published an article discussing her research that elaborately categorized Internet users within the Òrìṣà cyberspace. Capone explained that when she began her research, only three platforms with Òrìṣà-related messages existed: two were websites hosting Òrìṣà content, and the third was a discussion group. She believes that these venues, which hosted discussions and debates, were "the perfect terrain to observe the transformation that Afro-Diasporan religions undergo as they cross their traditional geographical boundaries and become universal religions."[23] In her classifications of these Internet users, called *Cybersanteros*, Capone notes that some had been drawn to the Internet by the prospect of monetary gains. These people were motivated by the idea of "attracting new clients or new godchildren." Described as *Recruiters*, they were active participants who engaged in different online discussions to bolster their credibility as experts—by sharing Òrìṣà knowledge, they could acquire new patrons or clients.

Capone describes the second group as *Lost Souls*. These people were "secessionists" who had broken ties with their religious mentors and godparents, although they wished to continue acquiring knowledge and practicing Òrìṣà worship. The members of a third group were the *Suspicious Ones*, who sought to verify the information and used the Internet to confirm what they had been told by their godparents and religious leaders. Capone's final group was the *Autodidactic*, who were the "cyber-authority, and have enormous knowledge of Òrìṣà and Lukumi." She suspects that they had gained knowledge from the works of scholars because of the quality of their discussions and the authority with which they spoke. They were considered to possess the ultimate sources of knowledge for Òrìṣà and Lukumi.[24] Capone concludes that the Internet would not "alter the traditional exchanges between priests and religious houses that are characteristic of the Diasporan traditions."[25] However, she also believes that the Internet would introduce and expand how the religion was practiced. In her opinion: "Cyberspace will expand the number of ways in which people may join these religions and provide new tools that will ultimately prove beneficial to all Afro-Diasporan religions by making them appealing to

---

20. Ramos, "Connecting through a Medium."

21. Ramos, "Connecting through a Medium."

22. Capone, "Les Dieux sur le Net," 47–74.

23. Capone, "Les Dieux sur le Net," 47–74.

24. Capone, "Les Dieux sur le Net," 47–74.

25. Capone, "Les Dieux sur le Net," 47–74.

non-African people who will subsequently adopt an African religious identity while retaining their own cultural an ethnic personae."[26]

The Internet is a source of unregulated and uncensored information, which enabled more dubious activities that targeted the devotees of Òrìṣà and Lukumi. Fraudulent users offered illegitimate religious services and made exaggerated promises to unsuspecting victims. In the mid-1990s, unqualified and inexperienced people were already posing as *Olórìṣà*, claiming to hold unique knowledge that was necessary to correctly practice the Òrìṣà religion.[27] These fake priests preyed on people who were looking for easy answers and magical solutions.

As the Internet became more widely used by devotees collaborating and spreading Òrìṣà knowledge, their discussions became politicized. Different groups began to see each other as competitors. Ramos explains how this derailed the initial Òrìṣà agenda: "Political and hegemonic agenda soon made their presence felt as well, and the initial collaborative intentions of some of these Internet pioneers were increasingly frustrated by other Lukumís or Òrìṣà groups that competed with them, disrupting the original dreams of achieving cohesiveness, collective ascendancy, and societal acceptance for the religion. What was originally conceived as a valuable tool to disseminate information and clarify historical social misconceptions was increasingly becoming a brutal field where individual and collective agendas were played out. The anonymity of the new medium made these exploits possible."[28] The Internet quickly became a battleground where rivals struggled for dominance, and it became difficult for individuals to find reliable information about Òrìṣà.

George Brandon is another scholar who has researched the history of Òrìṣà information on the Internet, studying whether religious transmission is affected by the Internet and the concepts of orality and literacy.[29] He asserts that the concepts of orality and literacy needed to be redefined—using definitions that are meaningful to the Yorùbá religion—for a complete picture of the multiple guises and intricate exchanges that were instrumental in the transmission of Yorùbá religious traditions. With these new definitions, one can identify how the ideas have developed on the Internet. Brandon identifies another category of Internet users who sought information about the Òrìṣà religion: the *Border-crossers*. In Brandon's view, the decentralized nature and open-access protocols of the Internet make it possible for these individuals to switch between various religious traditions without encountering any resistance. He conceded that although these Border-crossers have their own religious identities, they still attempt to forge connections between their beliefs and Òrìṣà tradition. Brandon believes these attempts will spark discussions on different Òrìṣà platforms.

Joseph Murphy has also researched how the Internet has influenced Òrìṣà traditions, and he asserts that the transmission of Òrìṣà traditions from local to virtual has exerted tremendous influence on the Òrìṣà religion.[30] Murphy believes that Òrìṣà traditions and the Internet have each enabled changes in the other. His analysis identified significant websites related to Òrìṣà

---

26. Capone, "Les Dieux sur le Net," 47–74.

27. Capone, "Les Dieux sur le Net," 47–74.

28. Ramos, "Connecting through a Medium," 4.

29. Brandon, "From Oral to Digital," 463–464.

30. Murphy, "Òrìṣà Traditions," 470–484.

information and divided them into five categories. The first group was organizational and connected to preexisting Òrìṣà associations and communities. The second group was individual, and these sites were used as self-portraits by Òrìṣà priests and priestesses to illuminate the Òrìṣà influence in their daily lives. The third group of devotional sites acted like virtual altars to present and encounter Òrìṣà with a devotional mindset. The fourth group, academic sites, were championed by scholars who shared their ongoing research into Òrìṣà. The fifth and final group Murphy identified was commercial, and these sites engaged in financial transactions linked with Òrìṣà rituals and worship items.

In writing about these five categories, Murphy states, "Each site displays, and at times merges, the concerns of institution and identity building, information dissemination, and commerce. Their number and exponential growth signal new trends in Òrìṣà traditions, expansion beyond borders conceived in Africa or the African Diaspora."[31] Like the researchers before him, Murphy was cautious of those who deliberately misused the Internet. He warned that the Internet continues to tilt "towards atomizing the traditions rather than building strong communities."[32]

One subject that needs further exploration is the demographics of Internet users who engage with the Òrìṣà and Lukumi religions. The Internet has provided an easy method of globalizing Òrìṣà traditions, but care is necessary to avoid losing important information. In the major centers where Òrìṣà traditions are practiced, Internet access is limited not only among highly experienced devotees but also among the general population. In Nigeria, the majority of experienced Òrìṣà devotees are expected to be above forty years old. These people do not enjoy widespread Internet access. In the rare cases where such devotees are online, they may not be savvy enough to engage in authoritative discussions about Òrìṣà religion.[33] According to Ramos, the Internet remains unconnected to the daily lives of these experienced devotees. If this is true and Òrìṣà tradition is actively being discussed online, then the majority of those who share such information may not be experienced enough to provide accurate perspectives. They may also come from other demographics that have less detailed knowledge or less comprehensive experience with the religion.

Furthermore, English has been the dominant language of the Internet until recently. Discussing and engaging in Òrìṣà enlightenment talks have previously required some level of English literacy, especially if globalization is being leveraged to share the information with new territories. In the major areas inhabited by Òrìṣà devotees, people rarely encounter the English language, and they are not expected to master it. These are challenges for the globalization of the Òrìṣà religion through the Internet, not because of the concept but because of the rapid distribution of content. Unchecked misinformation could quickly devalue the revered Òrìṣà religion. Ramos explains, "There is no doubt that cyberspace discussions are being guided by a group of greatly inexperienced newcomers to the religion. For a religion that places so much emphasis on tradition, oral transmission of religious knowledge, priestly hierarchy, years of experience, and respect for these years, this is a highly contentious issue."[34]

---

31. Murphy, "Òrìṣà Traditions," 471.

32. Murphy, "Òrìṣà Traditions, " 472–475.

33. Adeleke, "Digital Divide in Nigeria," 333–346.

34. Ramos, "Connecting through a Medium, " 13.

Ramos analyzed the historical traffic to www.eleda.org and found that many people considered the Internet to be instrumental for attaining knowledge and education about Òrìṣà, but most of those who visited were not seeking online rituals, religious instructions, or knowledge. The website's most visited pages displayed images of religious arts and aesthetics, and the next most heavily visited pages provided contact information for providers of retail services.

Although some users are leveraging the Internet to expand and propagate global knowledge of the Òrìṣà religion, larger numbers of people are solely concerned with the adornment and arts of the religion. The Internet and the Òrìṣà knowledge have influenced each other, but practitioners may continue to prefer face-to-face interactions when it comes to issues of worship and sacrifices. The global communications network, like any other tool, can be applied for good or ill purposes. Some individuals have spread misinformation, and others have debunked false knowledge and enlightened the public with trusted information from accurate sources. Òrìṣà devotees must follow a similar route, paying less attention to those who are misusing the Internet and placing a greater emphasis on redirecting earnest users to worthwhile sources of information. According to Ramos, "In all probability, the Internet may never successfully replace the traditional networks and the personal contacts that have historically served as the primary means by which devotees join the religion. As an impersonal medium, it cannot provide the most important means of communication for the Lukumí: individual, one-on-one, face-to face interaction. Nonetheless, the Internet will surely contribute as an additional resource for those seeking that personal aspect that cannot exist in cyberspace. As such, it will unquestionably be used and misused."[35]

Seeing the influence and power of the Internet on the state of the Òrìṣà religion, one would understand the propagation of the religion as a global culture and religion, taking contemporary forms and norms. One would agree that the Internet has become too vulnerable and the pendulum of its impact could fall on the more negative side than the positive, but it cannot be disputed that it is the only futuristic approach to Òrìṣà globalization. Today, the world relies on the Internet to get almost everything done. Since its discovery, it has been positioned as core to human existence, and being disconnected from it is almost like being disconnected from oxygen. It might not be physical death but that of ideologies and information. This is not to be unnecessarily ceremonious of the power of the Internet; it is just the reality of contemporary society.

Cultural diffusions and acquisitions have been made more possible by the advent of the exploration of the Internet. Similarly, the Internet has expanded religions' followership, devotions, and interterritorial practices. During the 2020 COVID-19 lockdown, the world adjusted largely to the possibilities of the Internet for communication, and the potency of that reliance has become stronger today. Religious activities increasingly adopted the culture of teleconferencing and fellowships. Teleconference and virtual worship and consultation of the Òrìṣà and Ifá became a habit during this period, and as the phenomenon has grown after the pandemic, it is projected to have a similar effect on the Òrìṣà religious practices forthwith. Hence, the

---

35. Ramos, "Connecting through a Medium, " 24.

 GLOBAL YORÙBÁ

Internet makes the global spread of the religion faster. Social media, blogs, videos, and other Internet platforms increase the visibility of the religion for better global outreach.

In addition, while we understand the dangers associated with exposure to global cultures on Yorùbá religion and the possibilities of losing the value systems, it should be realized that the Internet is one of the best ways to preserve the knowledge and tradition of the religion. First, the contribution of the preponderance of religious ideas, either within a community or all over, ensures that the truth about the worship can be accessed by the people. Second, there is a tendency to reconceptualize misconceived religious ideologies and practices. This is because the Internet is taking a shot at a universal promotion of the right practices, philosophies, and dogma of the religion. It also allows the understanding of the developed variations and syncretic religions that have developed from it.

The promotion of Internet and technology-based artistry in relation to the Yorùbá religious system can also not be underestimated. Recently, there has been an increase in Afrocentric artistry, some of which are steps toward the further development of Afro-futurism. The use of computer-based tools and artificial intelligence to generate pieces with Òrìṣà religious inspirations is gradually increasing. This will further create some visualization of the religious characters and knowledge. For instance, individuals like Oluseni and Ade Okelarin, visual artists and photographers, have tried to use some information about the Òrìṣà, tools, and artificial intelligence to re-create the image and personality of some of the Yorùbá Òrìṣà.[36] Aside from the terra-cotta representations and the artworks around different shrines, these technologies are almost the closest to human depiction and imagery of the personalities. One must, however, be conscious of the fact that these artistries are not in any way the right depictions of the gods but only show some of the features of the gods with some contemporary cultural attributes. There are many other depictions and reimaginations of the Yorùbá Òrìṣàs and the religious properties by artists and virtual artists. The impact of the Internet in this is the projection of the possibility of exploring the Yorùbá religious values for the purpose of imagination and advancement of Afro-futurism.

Varieties of Survival and Contemporary Òrìṣà

Festivals across the World

Ifá and Òrìṣà traditions have extended beyond the boundaries of Nigeria and West Africa and are practiced in places like Brazil and Cuba, where their rituals are even more elaborate and glamorous. The practice of the religion and the celebration of its relevant festivals originated in Nigeria, but the continuous practice and celebration of Òrìṣà is encouraged in the diaspora. Many of these practices and celebrations have undergone contemporary changes and adjusted to new cultural identities in their immediate surroundings.

---

36. Shoks, "I Asked A.I. to Show Me What Yoruba Orishas Looked Like."

Although Trinidad is a major location for Òrìṣà worship and the celebration of related annual festivals,[37] some practices have evolved beyond their Yorùbá origins. In Trinidad, all the Òrìṣà have been combined under a single roof, without associating Òrìṣà to individual families or ritual spaces.[38] Among the Yorùbá, each Òrìṣà is identified with a specific family or community that encourages them to be more involved with the practice and celebration of festivals. There are situations in Trinidad where an Òrìṣà might have a dedicated shrine, but there are also representations of other Òrìṣà within the ritual space. For instance, at the Marabella shrine of Ìyálórìṣà, there are dedicated stools for Jàkùta, Ṣọ̀pọ̀ná, Èṣù, Ọ̀sanyìn, Ògún, Kangun, and many other Òrìṣà.[39] Celebrations invoke all the Òrìṣà, with an expectation that the major ones will manifest on the days that have been dedicated to them.

The Ọ̀ṣun festival is observed annually in Trinidad to honor all the Òrìṣà, but there are some distinct changes to the celebration, especially regarding the public observance of festivals. Among the Yorùbá in Nigeria, there are public ritual festivals to celebrate Ṣàngó in Oyo,[40] Ògún in Ondo,[41] and Ọ̀ṣun in Osogbo.[42] These public rituals are rarely seen in Trinidad. Instead, many of the qualities in the Nigerian observance of ritual festivals occur during the annual Òrìṣà feast in Trinidad.[43] Some of the ritual items from Yorubaland have also been replaced based on the materials locally available for devotees: olive oil is used instead of palm oil, candles replace clay-and-oil lamps, and the celebration of Ògún does not involve a sacrificial dog.[44]

Only active shrines organize Òrìṣà feasts between the end of the Christian Easter celebration to December. Individual shrines ensure that their days for celebration do not clash during this season, but multiple feasts can still occur simultaneously. These events are organized by the priest or priestess of a shrine, working with the shrine's elders and the spiritual children of the priest and priestess.[45] It is common for devotees to attend each other's feasts. Nondevotees may be allowed inside the palais, but they are forbidden from entering the inner sanctum of the Chapelle.[46] In the three weeks leading up to a feast, hosts are expected to fast and abstain from unclean things as a form of ritual preparation. Within this period, hosts continuously table their prayers before Òrìṣà and ask for guidance and support. Participants who would make offerings to the Òrìṣà are also admonished to engage in this form of ritual preparation.

During the weekend of the feast, the ritual sequence of flag planting begins. This ritual raises various colored flags to invite the blessings of Olódùmarè. It usually involves taking down and

Facing, Figure 11.2. Gelede mask. Gelede remains a significant masquerade performance among the Yorùbá. It is performed as a tribute to *Iya Nla* (powerful great mother) in the Yorùbá-Nago communities spread across Nigeria, Benin, and Togo. Many of these masks can be found in Western museums, which helps connect the Yorùbá in the diaspora with their roots and heritage. Mask by Ademola Fakeye.

---

37. Hernandez-Ramdwar, "Religion and Tourism in Trinidad," 110.

38. Aiyejina and Gibbons, "Orisa (Orisha) Tradition in Trinidad," 35–50.

39. Aiyejina and Gibbons, "Orisa (Orisha) Tradition in Trinidad."

40. Oderinde, "Lore of Religious Festivals," 1–12.

41. Opare, "Functional Analysis of the Ogun Festival in Ondo."

42. Elizabeth, "Appraisal of Osun Osogbo as a Festival Theatre," 326–336.

43. Aiyejina and Gibbons, "Orisa (Orisha) Tradition in Trinidad."

44. Aiyejina and Gibbons, "Orisa (Orisha) Tradition in Trinidad."

45. Houk, *Spirits, Blood, and Drums.*

46. Aiyejina and Gibbons, "Orisa (Orisha) Tradition in Trinidad."

replacing flags from previous years. Funso Aiyejina and Rawle Gibbons describe the flag-planting ceremony thus: "In this ceremony, the old flags by the stools are replaced which involves the ritual cleansing of both flags and poles and the ritual revitalization of the Orisa energies inside the holes in which the poles will stand. Also, at this time, those Orisa/powers such as Esu who require to be fed outside the compound are fed in the bush."[47]

The ceremony often takes place over five nights, usually starting on a Sunday, and each night is devoted to a specific Òrìṣà. Each night's ritual opens with an invocation to Èṣù, who is believed to be responsible for transmitting the feast's rituals to the other Òrìṣà and Olódùmarè. The invocation of Èṣù also involves an admonition to maintain peace during the ceremony.

The flag-planting ceremony involves music, songs, dances, and possession—these activities are filled with spiritual energy. Aiyejina and Gibbons describe the celebration of the feast and the energy that follows:

> The success of a feast depends on the degree of the Òrìṣà-energy in evidence. On a primary level, this is determined by the spiritual knowledge and preparedness of the officiating priest/priestess who is usually the owner of the shrine. In addition, there is the degree of spiritual energy contributed by the children of the shrine and visiting devotees which can be felt in their participation in the singing and dancing. Most significantly, complementary to the singing, the performance of the drummers is very crucial to the success of a feast. Although there are individual Orisa devotees who can manifest possession in the absence of music, possessions during a feast are directly related to the quality of the drumming, singing, and the presence of spiritually-primed mediums in the congregation.[48]

Within the shrine, dancers arrange themselves in a circle, which signifies the circularity of the Yorùbá worldview about the repetitiveness of events, and they move counterclockwise while opening with the Èṣù Barago song. Their movement continues until the officiating priest or priestess begins another song, and then the dancers spin, bend, touch the earth, and get back up to begin moving clockwise.

The coordination of this movement is normally so synchronized that dancers are only seen moving out of formation when they are possessed, accompanied by songs and drumming that increase in tempo and a crescendo of chants for the possessing Òrìṣà. This continues until the dancer has been completely possessed by the Òrìṣà, at which point the possessed person delivers the Òrìṣà's divine message and healing rituals are performed. When the possessed devotee is an inexperienced novice, others may prepare them to shoulder the physical and spiritual possession of the Òrìṣà. After the possession, if the devotee wishes to be initiated, the initiation rituals and rites are performed to welcome the manifesting Òrìṣà, encouraging it to settle in their body.[49]

---

47. Aiyejina and Gibbons, "Orisa (Orisha) Tradition in Trinidad," 46.
48. Aiyejina and Gibbons, "Orisa (Orisha) Tradition in Trinidad," 46.
49. Aiyejina and Gibbons, "Orisa (Orisha) Tradition in Trinidad."

There can be no Òrìṣà without Ifá. Both are interlocked and travel together. Yorùbá diviners, the Babaláwo, are scattered in different parts of the world. Examples of Ifá devotees and schools are many. One example, based in Nigeria, is used here, with connections to other parts of the world. This is the Ifá Heritage Institute, established in Nigeria in 2008 to recognize Ifá's crucial role in the cultural and religious identity of the Yorùbá. This institution recognizes Ifá's influence around the world and emphasizes the importance of preserving the Ifá religious system and divination practices. Oyo is one of the strongholds of Ifá practice in Nigeria, and the Ifá Heritage Institute is a postsecondary institution located in the city. It is the world's only higher education institution dedicated to the study of Ifá and other indigenous components of Yorùbá culture and religion.

The Ifá Heritage Institute was established after the 2005 United Nations Educational, Scientific and Cultural Organization (UNESCO) declaration that Ifá was one of the eighty-six world traditions regarded as masterpieces of humanity's oral and intangible heritage. With its declaration, UNESCO urged every nation of the world to support the preservation and cultivation of these traditions. In Nigeria, it resulted in the creation of the Ifá Heritage Institute. The institute's objective is "the preservation and propagation of Ifá as an indigenous African body of knowledge within the settings of a modern and contemporary educational system."[50] UNESCO facilitated the establishment of the institute through a grant from the Japanese government—it was not just a means of preserving Yorùbá tradition but also a way to create a repository of knowledge for the global study of Ifá and Yorùbá religion and cultural heritage. To globalize the traditional Yorùbá religion, the Ifá Heritage Institute admits students from various parts of the world. Its specifically structured curriculum meets the academic needs and accommodates the different perspectives of local and international students.

As a method of inclusion, the school has five groups of faculties, with each focused on different parts of Yorùbá religion and culture. The Department of Ifá Studies introduces local and international students to the basics of Ifá divination, studying "chanting and interpretation of Ifá stories." This department focuses on preserving the orality of Ifá. Part of its usual activities include memorizing verses from each of the 256 Odù of Ifá, the meaning of each verse, and how they are applied. These verses contain 204,800 stories that deal with different parts of Yorùbá mythology, medicine, history, philosophy, and other topics, which introduces students to Yorùbá culture and epistemology.[51]

The Ifá Heritage Institute recognizes that the practice of Ifá transcends Nigerian borders—there are vibrant Ifá practices in Cuba, Brazil, Benin, Togo, and other parts of the world. The institute's Department of Languages accommodates the teaching of Spanish, Portuguese, and French along with Yorùbá and English languages.[52] These languages are taught to encourage students to learn and interpret oral and written Ifá divination. Local and international students

---

50. Ifa Heritage Institute, "Welcome."

51. Ifa Heritage Institute, "Welcome."

52. Ifa Heritage Institute, "Welcome."

are all required to learn Yorùbá and English. However, they can also choose one of the other languages for learning and interpreting Ifá's oral tradition.

The institute includes the Departments of Medicine and Performing Arts. The former teaches the intricacies of indigenous medicine and its application. Students learn how to identify important trees, herbs, roots, and bark. They are also taught how to diagnose specific illnesses and how to apply the right herbal medicine to cure them.[53] These studies demonstrate the beauty and comprehensiveness of biodiversity in Yorùbá flora and fauna. The Performing Arts Department teaches the basics and complexities of dance and music that are associated with the Òrìṣà and Ifá locally and in the diaspora. The institute's final department studies indigenous technology, which exposes students to the machinery, tools, mechanisms, and materials that are used to produce indigenous innovations like calabash carving, metalworking, blacksmithing, and textile production.

The Ifá Heritage Institute is one small step in the preservation of Yorùbá heritage, and it educates and enlightens local and international students who are interested in the practices and rites of Ifá divination. Its work has actively contributed to the globalization of the Yorùbá religion.

Ìjọ Ọ̀rúnmìlà

Ifá and Òrìṣà are now being repackaged into different modes of worship and institutions. An example is the Ìjọ Ọ̀rúnmìlà, also known as the Indigenous Faith of Africa. Olorunfunmi Oshiga formed Ìjọ Ọ̀rúnmìlà Ato in 1920 after claiming to have received a vision and direction from Ọ̀rúnmìlà, the Yorùbá god of wisdom. Oshiga worked to establish a religious organization based on the Ifá corpus and beliefs, breaking from the Anglican Church in Nigeria to form a church that represented and defended Yorùbá religious values.[54] In 1932, Oshiga worked with sponsors and followers to erect a center of worship at Ebute-Metta, Lagos, to provide a site for people to worship and respect Yorùbá culture. Oshiga's church was founded shortly afterward, and other churches and businesses followed, including Chief James Adeyemi Adeshina's group in Ijebu Ode. Adeshina's group adopted the name Ìjọ Ọ̀rúnmìlà Adúláwò for their organization after the British authorities rejected their original proposed name, Ìjọ Akọ́dá, which meant the "first church."[55]

In Nigeria and the diaspora, the Ọ̀rúnmìlà church claims to have attracted around two million followers that adhere to its tenets and teachings. There are exaggerated claims regarding the numbers of Òrìṣà worshippers. The Òrìṣà faith is now using physical campaigns and media outlets to spread its messages and bring in new followers. These efforts included Odù Ifá and Ìwúre Àárọ̀'s radio shows on Radio Lagos and other publicity initiatives. Church branches have been established in London, California, New York, and Florida, along with around twenty-one

---

53. Ifa Heritage Institute, "Welcome."

54. Oguntola-Laguda, "'Pentecostalism' and African Religious Movements," 191–205.

55. Aderibigbe and Medine, *Contemporary Perspectives on Religions*.

sites in Nigeria and eighteen in the Benin Republic.[56] Christians and Muslims are allowed to join the movement, which explains why services were changed from Sunday to Saturday, accommodating Muslims and Christians who attend the mosque on Friday and church on Sunday.

The organized leadership of the Ọ̀rúnmìlà church has established protocols for dealing with their congregation. The Olúwo, who acts as the high priest, is the most senior member of the church. The Olúwo leads the congregation during religious services and takes charge of the group's other duties and activities. He is assisted by other officials, including the Akọ́dá Awo, the direct deputy of the high priest, and the Aṣèdá Awo, the second in rank after the Akọ́dá Awo. The Abẹ̀ṣẹ̀ Awo acts as the churchwarden.

There are significant differences in these approaches, but the services and associated activities are conducted in a manner that resembles Christian worship in African and Anglican churches. Sermons are based on Ifá beliefs, scriptures, and exhortations that influence moral standards and instruct worshippers on proper behavior. The religion also involves a standing choir directed by an *Apènà*. The Apènà and the clergy in charge of the service lead the procession into the auditorium to begin the service with hymns. These hymns continue until the end of the service, assisting with other parts of the ceremony. Group members visit a babaláwo for prayers, divination, and other rites, which include the breaking of kola nuts and *obì pupa*.

Oyotunji Village in the United States

Oyotunji means "Oyo rises again," and it stands as a metaphor for the reincarnation of the Oyo Empire in the diaspora. The Oyotunji settlement has become a symbol of an unbending spirit and a sign of endurance that leads followers to overcome all the challenging trials that characterize a racialized society. Because it was modeled after its Yorùbá archetype, the village is meant to tow the political and social systems of the Yorùbá, with a religious identity that differentiates its members from those within the environment. They are determined to rise and continue to lead a purposeful life not only because they have no alternative but because they appreciate their identity and associate their survival with the renewed existence of their cultural identity. For this reason, Oyotunji invokes the greatness of their ancestors and it complements their undying commitment regardless of negative downsides and challenges. Nothing affirms their pride and hope in the Yorùbá cultural and religious identity more than the inscription posted in Sheldon, South Carolina, before entering the Oyotunji Village: "You are leaving the United States. You are entering Yorùbá Kingdom. In the name of His Highness King Efuntola, Peace. Welcome to the Sacred Yorùbá Village of Ọ̀yọ́ Tunji. The only Village in North America built by priests of the Òrìṣà Voodoo Cults as a tribute to our Ancestors. These priests preserve the customs, laws, and religion of the African Race."[57]

Officially created in 1970, the Oyotunji Village has become a force of Yorùbá identity that makes international awareness of the Yorùbá people and their epistemological design. The

---

56. Oye-Laguda, "African Religious Movements and Pentecostalism," 49–59.
57. Mccray, "Oyotunji Village."

religion and culture of the people, going by the above inscription, are modeled after the indigenous ones practiced many miles away from the New World. Yorùbá religion was transported to the Atlantic world through the agency of the enslaved Africans and, therefore, became adapted by different diasporan civilizations. Holdovers of the indigenous knowledge systems and spirituality are the crux of this international practice, and the Oyotunji Village continues to break grounds in the institutionalization of Yorùbá religion and epistemology. In essence, the village represents the retracement of the African identity and heritage in ways that show the prioritization of African history and identity, despite the prevailing challenges. It depicts an Afrocentric orientation inherent in their endurance and unbending spirit despite consuming challenges. Although the inhabitants of the village are conscious of the influence of a foreign culture and environment, they are committed to the restoration of African history irrespective of the overbearing circumstances.

Walter Eugene King, the founder of Oyotunji Village, was born in 1928 in Michigan and experienced the warmth and greatness of the Yorùbá religion through his initiation into Santeria in Cuba.[58] He was not ignorant of the apparent marginalization and the attitude of the supremacy of the white community over its dark-skinned counterparts. This segregation formed the basis of interpreting the racially lopsided New World and planted in him the determination to come up with a uniquely stronger plan for the resuscitation of the Yorùbá struggling identity. He became very fond of the Yorùbá Òrìṣà, and in satisfaction of his ambition, he created a temple where these Òrìṣà were worshipped and venerated. The village is a preferred destination for those who seek a spiritual connection to their African roots. It has grown in number and impact, and before the end of the twentieth century, Oyotunji Village registered itself as a force of Yorùbá religious and cultural identity in the Atlantic environment. Regardless of its recency, the Oyotunji Village has made a mark in its representation of Black struggles through different realizations. As such, the founders of the community usually make different efforts for the advancement of their cause by drawing from the philosophy entrenched in the Cuban community for the exhibition of grandeur in the Yorùbá systems and institutions.

The Dediabolization of Yorùbá Religion in Global Space

The effect of globalization on religion has been its transformation to fit with contemporary norms and introduce new perspectives. This has been evident in the new practices of Òrìṣà religion both in Africa and other places across the world. However, it is unfortunate that the preponderance of Christian and Muslim devotees and practices within the Yorùbá community has resulted in the diabolization and derogation of the core values of the Òrìṣà worship. To allow the quick spread of Christianity and Islam in the early days of their introductions into the system, the preexisting Yorùbá Òrìṣà religion was painted in a bad light to attract a saving alternative to the people. Hence, the practices were outrightly demonized and the monopolization of Christianity and Islam as the access to God and as the legitimate religions grew. The growth has been evident since the end of the nineteenth century to the contemporary period.

---

58. Mccray, "Oyotunji Village."

Often, the Yorùbá people are divided between Christianity and Islam, with Òrìsà worship as a minority third religion that the majority denies in the open. There is now a social antagonism of Òrìsà worship, with reference to the worshippers as "pagans" and "heathens" who cannot have a favorable afterlife. Ironically, a religion that developed from a particular people and has been responsible for making sense of life and the relationship with God is seen as an abomination to God. Although social antagonism is expected, seeing that it has grown between the Christian faith and Islam devotees, the Yorùbá traditional religion serves as the common enemy of the two.

The demonization and diabolization of the Òrìsà worship was also enforced by the exposure of the Yorùbá people to the slave trade, missionary activities, and colonialism. At the close of the nineteenth century, the religion was regarded as uncivilized and primitive. Hence, this ideology was cemented in the institutional foundation of the modern Yorùbá society that heralded the "civilized" world of the Yorùbá people. Generation after generation thereafter continued to pick up the negativity posture to the practices of Òrìsà, witchcraft, and rituals, including festivals.

The attempt to sell colonization and exploitation of the people through Christianity became one of the biggest deceptions in the history of the Yorùbá people. The colonialists believed that their job was to take the people to the Christian light. With such mindsets, they attacked the religion with such velocity. Some African clerics who were among the missionaries were commissioned to conduct inquiries on the traditional religion as practiced by the people with the end game of demonization.[59] Bishop Emmanuel Moses Lijadu, an evangelist and catechist under the employment of the colonialists, claimed to understand the Ifá corpus and provided biblical verses to antagonize the content of the Odus in a book he wrote in 1908. The attempt to demonize the religion was not successful, but he decided to be initiated into the Ifá cult to have access to the core knowledge and understanding of the religion. Matthew and Victor Taiwo capture the aftermath of the initiation thus:

> This time at the mastering of the knowledge of the religion and ascertaining the true and potent efficacy of Ifa as a thing of pride and utter usefulness for human development rather than the intended truth manipulation and deliberate demonization and condemnation by his European masters. Lijadu literally offered to be realistic and honest, and so opted not to be a quisling destroying the legacy of his own people to the satisfaction of his masters. And so he chose to write the truth he discovered in his learning of the efficacy and potency of the religion. Thus, he became the hero of the Ifa deity rather than go back to his masters. In spite of this, the castigation of and aspersions on the traditional religions continued unabated by the Europeans. Such was the absolute contempt and derogation at which the Yoruba traditional systems were held by the Europeans.[60]

Many Nigerians and Yorùbá were Lijadus at the first instance of his engagement, but many could not become the second phase of his development in the contemporary Yorùbá society.

---

59. Taiwo and Taiwo, "Religion Sectarianism," 165–173.
60. Taiwo and Taiwo, "Religion Sectarianism," 169.

This is because the influx of cultures and the preponderances of an overwhelming conviction through globalization has allowed that knowledge to fade away with difficulty in getting the true versions of them upon inquiries. The demonizing convictions are more upheld by the Yorùbá themselves in contemporary Yorùbá societies. The Muslims see an average Òrìṣà worshipper as a pagan and infidel, with some extremists believing to have some jihadist duty to wipe them off. The Christians find them as an abomination, referring to Exodus 20:3–4, which states, "Thou shall have no other gods before me, thou shall not make unto thee any graven image, or any likeness of anything that is in heaven above, or that is in the earth beneath, or that is in the water under the earth." These convictions are not toward Òrìṣà worshippers alone but also are from Christians to Muslims and vice versa. However, the ideology is stronger against the Òrìṣà worshippers.

The postcolonial posture of the Nigerian nation and leaders of the Yorùbá people were adjusting to the ideology. The traditional leaders, who were the hallmarks and vanguards of the religion, were stripped of their influences from the colonial periods and official business, and a reduced reflection of the religious heritages and social sentiments became constantly and consistently against it.

In addition, Nigerian literature and creative arts began to follow the demonization views of the religion, positioning the Christian expression of faith as the light and those of the Yorùbá traditional religion as darkness. Some Nollywood productions in their early days were separated between celebrating the religious heritage and the misconception of the traditional religion. In many typical Yorùbá movies, human problems are often caused by the acts of the Yorùbá religion faithful, and the solutions are often provided by either Islamic or Christian endeavors and prayers. The message was clear: Satan and demons are worshipped through the Òrìṣà worship and God is either a God of Christians or that of the Muslims but can never be that of the Òrìṣà worshippers.

Òrìṣà worship has a lot to do with the social and cultural constructs of the Yorùbá people, and while the ritual practices may not be obvious on the surface, the cultures continue. However, despite the castigation of the practices and patronage of the traditional religious institutions, there have been records of patronage of the shrines, *abòrìṣàs*, and *babaláwos* outside the churches and mosques. The Yorùbá have not been able to express their Africanness in full in churches and mosques, save some cultural permission. But some of the people, especially the aging demography, still discreetly consult the Òrìṣà and the Ifá priests.[61]

One of the misconceptions of the Yorùbá religious system is the confusion between polytheism and monotheism. To the new religions, polytheistic practices are considered paganism. However, could one call the Yorùbá traditional religious system pagan worship? First, many of the religious examinations of other religions are largely ethnocentric or biased opinions. Where a Buddhist explains the credibility of Muslim or Christian gods through the principles of Buddhism or where a Christian discredits the worship of Allah based on Christian standards of religion is an erroneous but unpreventable understanding of other religious cultures. The same way cultural relativism is the right approach to understanding various cultures, relativism is

---

61. Ntombana, "Trajectories of Christianity and African Ritual Practices," 104–119.

    GLOBAL YORÙBÁ

important in understanding religions too. Hence, debasing Òrìṣà worship practices and beliefs based strictly on Quranic and biblical teachings would not be the right approach to appreciating the Yorùbá traditional religion. As a result, one cannot rightly get the justification for a religion based on the understanding of other religions. The idea of describing a religion as pagan is more of a subjective examination of the other religions.

Paganism is inferred from *paganus*, the Latin word for "village" or "peasant" and has an extensive meaning of worshipping a false God, and heathens are those who worship idols and refuse the acknowledgment of the true God.[62] Using this context to understand the traditional religion of the Yorùbá people is misleading in the sense that there is a subscription to a Supreme Being through whom all things get their meanings. Olodumare is the Supreme and Omnipotent appellation of God in the Yorùbá cosmetology and takes the role of God in the understanding of the Christian God. There is an adoption of this name among the Yorùbá Christians and Muslims to still reference God within the context of their respective modern religions despite it being an indigenous understanding.

Òrìṣà worship recognizes the supremacy of Olodumare over the universe and everyone. Some of the mythological accounts of the creation of heaven and earth have shown some similarities in the understanding of the role of Olodumare and the Christian God in the creation stories. Jozy Egunjobi captures this succinctly thus: "The universe was a vacuum several million years ago. God—Olodumare—asked the Sea to manifest on the planet. Another several million years later, Olodumare saw that the sea was lonely and then sent Orunmila (a deity or Òrìṣà—spirit of wisdom or divinity of destiny and prophesy or god of divination), the oldest son of Olodumare from heaven with some soil and five chicken which function is to help Orunmila in spreading the soil on the Sea. Hence, comes the earth. For the Yorùbá people therefore, it was at Ile-Ife that the earth first started."[63]

The Yorùbá religion has both monotheistic and polytheistic postures, as, in addition to Olodumare, the Supreme God, the Pantheon of 401 Òrìṣà, each with specific roles, are used to invoke the blessings of God. Olodumare does not have organized priesthoods, nor is he worshipped in shrines or temples. Instead, personal relationships are established with him, allowing people to pray to him for blessings. The Òrìṣà are, however, physically approachable through their shrines and are relevant in the day-to-day lives and activities of the devotees. Egunjobi describes the Òrìṣà as "emissaries of Olodumare and they rule over the forces of nature and the endeavors of humanity."[64] He further explains the understanding thus: "The Nigerian scholar J. Omosade Awolalu as cited by George Brandon (2019) divided the Òrìṣàs into three categories: primordial divinities (who existed long before the creation of the world), deified ancestors (who lived in this world after it was created), and personified natural forces and phenomena (any element of the natural world that has manifold and useful functions for human beings has a spirit dwelling in it). These categories are not rigid, and in some cases they overlap."[65]

There is also a belief in the contemporary religious philosophy among the Yorùbá people that the *ìṣègùn* tradition, Yorùbá indigenous medical practice and pharmacology, being that it relies heavily on the Òrìṣà religious cultures, is diabolic and primitive. Medical alternatives provided by globalization, in terms of modern medicine, are portrayed as the right medical sources. The logic behind this inference is better to the extent of the impossibility of getting the right dosage but worse to the extent of Eurocentrism. African traditional medical practices are

---

62. Ezesuokwu, "Phenomenological Approach," 41–54.

63. Egunjobi, "Yoruba Psycho-Spiritual Heritage."

64. Egunjobi, "Yoruba Psycho-Spiritual Heritage."

65. Egunjobi, "Yoruba Psycho-Spiritual Heritage."

based on science epistemologically understood from culture and understanding of nature. It is a herbal system and has been effective for curative and preventive medicines for hundreds of years before exposure to modern medicine.

The *oníṣègùn, eléwé ọmọ*, or *alágbo* are experts in the traditional health care system with a reliance on the nuances of the traditional religion. There are different prescriptions for different sicknesses, and the professionalism of the experts is taken seriously in society. There have been explorations of the medical knowledge of the traditional Yorùbá medicines and rejuvenation of the practices and items in more contemporary forms. Although many Yorùbá, despite their conversion to Christianity or Islam, have found themselves exploring the traditional medical options, safe for some zealots who believe that everything should be avoided altogether. There is nothing fetish in the scope of diabolism in this practice, even with the relations of some of the practices with Òrìṣà worship. In cases where the understanding of the illness is beyond the medical knowledge of the experts or believed to be more spiritual, the Òrìṣà are appealed to with rituals, a similar practice in modern religions.

The contemporary religious reference to Ifá and Babaláwo has taken a diabolic twist based on the spread of globalized religious culture. Ifá, however, is a corpus of philosophy, religion, and divination. The corpus is a sophisticated epistemology often passed through oral means or binary systems and sacred texts known as *Odu Ifá*. It preaches the principles of harmony, interconnectedness, and balance in life with an understanding of the existence of a divine force permeating the universe and overseeing the activities of humans. Divination, wisdom, and rituals are, therefore, the means of understanding and accessing the force. Ifá worship is both ethical and spiritual and does not have any similarities or traces of Satanism or diabolism. It is built on integrity, a good heart, a virtuous lifestyle, compassion, respect, and honor. Contemporary inquiries into Ifá by scholars have shown the ingenuity of the beliefs and knowledge and exonerated it from the ethnocentric imprisonment of its goodwill through early European historians and writers.

Another religious figure that has been diabolized in the contemporary Yorùbá religious worldview is Èṣù, an Òrìṣà, which has been used interchangeably for Satan. This is a false and wrongful understanding of the god and its worship in Yorùbá mythological understandings. Èṣù as a deity is far from the Satan positioned by the religions of modern societies. Èṣù can be seen as one of the temperamental and powerful gods in the Yorùbá religious system, but also one of the most respected and skillful.[66] One of its duties was to enforce the laws of nature and order and, as such, create balance in society. Èṣù was associated with communication and relations, taking messages from Olodumare and other Òrìṣà, even from heaven to those who dwelled on earth, and helping humans convey their sacrifices to heaven. Èṣù has two hundred names, reflecting the flexibility of its nature and characters. With the relationship between Orunmila and Èṣù, the latter is said to supervise the passage of the chapters and, as such, could transform into 256 forms.[67]

Funso Aiyejina, as referenced by Ikechukwu Kanu, describes Èṣù thus:

---

66. Kanu, "Hellenization of African Traditional Deities," 1–9.

67. Kanu, "Hellenization of African Traditional Deities."

In Yoruba philosophy, Esu emerges as a divine trickster, a disguise-artist, a mischief-maker, a rebel, a challenger of orthodoxy, a shape-shifter, and an enforcer deity. Esu is the keeper of the divine ase with which Olodumare created the universe; a neutral force who controls both the benevolent and the malevolent supernatural powers; he is the guardian of Orunmila's oracular utterances. Without Esu to open the portals to the past and the future, Orunmila, the divination deity, would be blind. As a neutral force, he straddles all realms and acts as an essential factor in any attempt to resolve the conflicts between contrasting but coterminous forces in the world. . . . He supports only those who perform prescribed sacrifices and act in conformity with the moral laws of the universe as laid down by Eledumare. . . . Without his intervention, the Yoruba people believe, no sacrifice, no matter how sumptuous, will be efficacious. Philosophically speaking, Esu is the deity of choice and free will.[68]

Akinwumi's explanation of Olubayo's tracing of the etymological explanation of the name of Èṣù is apt in gaining insight into the original personalities and characteristics of the Òrìṣà. He states that Olubayo

affirms that the etymology of the word "Esu" is difficult to decode but submits that the word might have been derived from the combination of the Yoruba prefix "E" and the verb "Su" (i.e., to harmonize or bring together). According to him, the combination of the Yoruba prefix "E" and the verb "Su" becomes "Esu," which connotes "one who harmonizes" or "one who brings people or issues together for harmonious existence." He therefore argues that Esu may be likened to an entity that makes people or things coexist peacefully. Though the veracity of this theory cannot be ascertained, one can deduce from it that it implies a superhuman being that connects other beings and has implicit relationships with individuals. . . . It may also refer to a being that consolidates and harmonizes the society which may as well imply that he is someone that is positive in nature.[69]

Èṣù's flexibility, strong will, creation of balance, temperament, and ability to cause problems for people in the bid to enforce instructions, laws, and orders made it easier for the Christianity adaptability of Satan, the fallen angel, to Èṣù. Èṣù was never a fallen angel; it is a respected *Òrìṣà* with the ability to do both good and evil.[70]

These are a few of the many instances in which the Yorùbá Òrìṣà religion has been demonized and diabolized in contemporary globalizing societies. The effect of this has led to several reconstructions of the beliefs and practices as well as societal postures of the people. Many of the assertions are wrong representations but the effect of globalization cannot be entirely curtailed. Hence, there is a need for knowledge reconstruction, and the globalization of such reconstructions must be done to invite transnational reorientations toward the Òrìṣà knowledge.

---

68. Kanu, "Hellenization of African Traditional Deities." See also Aiyejina, *Esu Elegbara*.

69. Akinwumi, "Esu Elegbara in Yoruba Mythology," 293. See Olubayo, "Esu Elegbara."

70. Aiyejina, *Esu Elegbara*.

Globalizing and Changing Christianity

The traditional practice of Òrìṣà religion is not the sole form of worship practiced by the Yorùbá, and the number of traditional practitioners has been steadily declining, especially among young people.[71] Christianity and Islam are more widely accepted as religious beliefs. These religions have been adapted to accommodate the worldviews of the Yorùbá: different denominational practices of Christianity have been adjusted for Yorùbá practitioners.[72] The Christian religion, after its continuous spread in the nineteenth century among the Yorùbá people, has been taking new shapes to adjust to the local belief system, turn to the local religion itself, and welcome globalized cultures and ideas. The initial churches introduced to Yorùbá societies were the Orthodox churches, including the Anglican Church, Roman Catholic, Baptist, and Methodist, among others. Pentecostalism, as a Christian wave taking the faith across the globe, has taken over the practice among the Yorùbá people. Pentecostal Christianity among the Yorùbá started taking a significant turn upon the emergence of Aladura Christianity.

Aladura, Pentecostal, and the Woke/Gen Z Churches

Aladura Christianity is more like a syncretic religion that took up the Yorùbá cultural and traditional ideologies within the church systems. The influence of the culture and tradition of the people on this Christianity is largely superficial and does not signal the complete altering of the core practices and characteristic of the Aladura churches. The first set of devotees of the Aladura churches adopted two basic principles of the Yorùbá religious philosophies, which include belief in spiritual forces that are mostly demonic and the effectiveness of ritual in Christian practices.[73] It is important to note that the adoptions transcended these two basics as other cultural practices found their way into the church.[74]

The traditional Yorùbá system has "an intentional stance" on spirituality, and it is often difficult to separate the society from continuous reliance on the belief in their strong existence.[75] This attitude is even reflected in contemporary Christian practices among the Yorùbá people. The reason for this is that there is always a subscription to some cause-and-effect logic that everything must either be inspired by some spiritual or human activities. So, the Bible's teaching that Christians do not fight against the flesh but against principalities and power has Yorùbá cultural relevance, and the adoption of many of the biblical teachings on the malevolent acts that could be caused by malevolent spirits has been amplified among the Yorùbá people even up to today.

Ritual systems are particular in the construction of the Yorùbá religious beliefs and cannot be separated from them. The reflection was seen at the onset of the Aladura churches and manifested in contemporary Christian churches. This was adopted into the ways prayers and

---

71. Peel, "Yoruba Religion," 1–24.

72. Omobola, "Influence of Yoruba Culture in Christian Religious Worship," 584–595.

73. Ray, "Aladura Christianity," 266–291.

74. Ray, "Aladura Christianity," 266–291.

75. Ray, "Aladura Christianity," 266–291.

offerings are made to God. The Yorùbá mindset of blessings, *ire, ebo,* and sacrifices took a new form in Yorùbá Christianity. Aladura rituals took the form of spiritual diagnoses, prayers, offerings deprivations as sacrifices, and giving of substances to God or some people in the expectations of *ire* from God. Like the Òrìṣà worship system, people approach the religious head and give some prescriptions of what to do to resolve the issue. They, however, still retain the core doctrines of orthodox Christianity, as Benjamin Ray captures thus:

> Having myself listened to a number of Aladura sermons, I can attest to the fact that Aladura preachers can preach strenuously about such "orthodox" Christian themes as other-worldly salvation, the final Judgment, and the autonomy of God's will. That is, in attending to the problems of life in this world, the Aladuras do not reduce Christianity to a "this-worldly" religion but emphasize an important instrumental or "worldly" function already contained within it. The emphasis in religious worship therefore falls upon God's redeeming action in this world and upon "the right kind" of worship. While affirming the other-worldly salvational goals of Christianity, many Aladura perceive Christian salvation more broadly as something that can also be obtained here and now, and largely through personal ritual and moral effort. There is the widespread assumption that "salvation . . . means a state of wholesomeness [i.e., well-being] in man." To achieve this state requires gaining access to God's saving powers and defeating the evil forces of this world. This, indeed, is entirely in keeping with a biblical view of the efficacy of ritual action and the power of the Holy Spirit.[76]

The Aladura religious culture includes the use of visions, prayers, and dreams to access the spiritual realm, an important exercise for the devotees. In the Celestial churches, for instance, there is a belief that there is a spiritual presence and space in the church that serves as a conduit to heaven; hence, the grounds are sacred and sleeping on the floors of the ground brings about revelations that offer solutions to life's problems.[77] Candles are placed around the church premises to consecrate the environment. They are placed across cardinal points that are relatable to four angels and at the high altar, a place believed to attract the hovering of the angels, especially during service.[78] There is also an *Ile Anu* (Mercy Ground) beside the church, to typify the retreat of Christ to the wilderness. The ground is believed to be spiritually sophisticated and serves as the point where special requests are made to God, holy water is obtained there, and other important spiritual activities take place.[79] This symbolizes the average reference to the shrines of the Òrìṣà and many of the reverences accorded to the activities there.

There are several reflections on the importation of the beliefs in other churches regarded as Aladura churches. The Aladura churches continued to split up to form different varieties of faiths and denominations. Today, Pentecostalism is the primary form of Christianity among the Yorùbá people, and several of the contemporary forms are outdating the old forms of the Aladura churches. Since 1970, there have been thousands of Pentecostal denominations and

---

76. Ray, "Aladura Christianity," 269–270.

77. Ray, "Aladura Christianity," 277–278.

78. Ray, "Aladura Christianity," 277–278.

79. Ray, "Aladura Christianity," 277–278.

churches across Nigeria, with several of them among the Yorùbá people. As of 2001, there were more than 1,018 identified Pentecostal churches in Nigeria; with several of them attended by the Yorùbá who reside there, in Togo, in Benin, and in the diaspora. Emphasizing Kalu Ogbu's nine typologies of Nigerian Pentecostal churches, Benjamin Diara and Nkechinyere Onah explain them thus:

(1) Interdenominational Fellowships (2) Evangelistic Ministries, e.g. Deeper Life Bible Church, (3) Deliverance Ministries, specializing in exorcism (4) Prosperity or Faith Ministries e.g. Zoë Ministry, Idahosa's Church of God Mission (5) Intercessors for Africa; (6) Missionary and Rural Evangelism, e.g. The Christian Evangelical Social Movement, Christian Movement Foundation (Rural Evangelism Outreach [REO] Ministry belongs to this group); (7) Bible Distribution Ministries, e.g. Gideon Bible International whose members must be born again and must be active in their churches; (8) Classical Pentecostals such as Assemblies of God Mission, Four Square Gospel, etc. (9) Children Evangelism Ministries whose branches have mushroomed nationwide from late 1980s. The demarcating lines between the Pentecostal groups are between fellowships and churches and between holiness and prosperity groups.[80]

The churches and Christianity among the Yorùbá respond to cultural change and diffusion. This translates to the continuous adaptability of the churches to contemporary social norms and behaviors. Many of the churches, such as the Redeemed Christian Church of God, which has one of the largest Pentecostal memberships across the world, and Winners Chapel, which has the largest church building across the globe, and many others, have been undergoing systematic changes that are in line with the emerging public.[81] These churches constitute the modern churches consisting of a change in beliefs and culture from the old Pentecostal churches and the Aladura group of churches. These churches form the mainline churches among the Yorùbá people and Nigeria in general.

A growing trend exists among the mainline churches and their faithful in the contemporary and modern form of Pentecostalism among the Yorùbá.[82] The tension has called for the care of not losing the values of Christianity to the susceptibility to globalization and contemporariness and, as such, the call for caution in the Christian religious approach has been increasing.[83] The fear has been that allowing too many global cultures in the church would attract what some regard as unbiblical and negative practices. This could take the form of unintentionally accepted cultures like "rocky dance" and "holy kiss" among the devotees and in the church.[84] This has caused continuing concern and debates among the Nigerian mainline churches.

Sticking to the dogmas as presented by the mainline churches has raised the question of prioritization and adaptability to the socioeconomic well-being of their members. Many of the Nigerian mainline churches provide spiritual solutions and directions toward ways to

---

80. Diara and Onah, "Phenomenal Growth of Pentecostalism," 395.

81. Diara and Onah, "Phenomenal Growth of Pentecostalism."

82. Diara and Onah, "Phenomenal Growth of Pentecostalism," 395.

83. Diara and Onah, "Phenomenal Growth of Pentecostalism," 395.

84. Diara and Onah, "Phenomenal Growth of Pentecostalism," 395.

Figure 11.4.
"The search for the true God," by Dr. Kazeem Ekeolu. There is an intense religious competition among the Yorùbá, as all major religions are represented.

overcome poverty. They are largely welfare oriented in some instances but tilt more toward spiritual development and compliance. However, the continued change in socioeconomic questions has been shedding off some members from the mainline churches looking for what would fit into their contemporary demands. As a result, different churches have been arising to serve as answers to these questions and meet the need of many people. Although several of them did not intentionally emerge to serve these purposes, their styles and practices could be seen as solutions.

As an extension of the modern churches, the Yorùbá people and Nigeria in general are witnessing the emergence of what could be regarded as "woke churches" or "Gen Z" churches. These are new-generation churches largely populated by the youth. They are the raw reflection of the influence of globalized cultures and the assimilation of the styles of Christianity from Europe, America, and other parts of the world. There are contemporary styles of worship, dressing, preaching, and acceptable doctrines among devotees. They step quite away from the conservative perspectives of the old churches toward morality, social relations, social functions, and personalities. The concept of what is moral is largely retained but not in conservative strictness, in the sense that there is a progression toward more inner compliance to God and His commandments than physical appearance.

These Christians are more politically and socially active, becoming drivers of social development. For instance, while it is unlikely to see a male with weaved hairstyles, braids, or other female hairstyles in many of the not-too-contemporary churches, it is seen often among the Gen Z churches. This is because the churches are leaning toward globalized systems of Christian practices, especially in the Western world. However, there are still some touches of Yorùbá cultural influences in the modes of worship, songs, dancing, and other activities. The churches can be seen as a response to disillusionment orientations caused by some touches of cultural orientations and values and tilt toward accommodating the mindsets, aspirations, and concerns of the younger generations. The Gen Z and woke churches have become means of drawing the youth to God without losing the touch of youthfulness. They provide spiritual food that fits into the experiences and worldviews of the young ones across the country.

The progression of the changes in the Christian practice among Yorùbá could be explained in steps:

1. The Orthodox churches comprised of received faith from the foreign missionaries.
2. The emergence of the Aladura Churches, including Cherubim and Seraphim (C&S) Church, Christ Apostolic Church (CAC), the Apostolic Church Nigeria (TACN), the Celestial Church of Christ (CCC), the Brotherhood of the Cross and Star (BCS), the Eternal Sacred Order of the Cherubim and Seraphim (ESOCS), and the Faith Tabernacle Congregation (FTC).
3. Other Pentecostal churches that include those that emerged from the Aladura faith, and the modern churches.
4. Woke or Gen Z churches.

The contemporary Christian practice is now a syncretism of African religious and cultural influence, globalization cultures, and received Christian doctrines and practices. The growth moves with the social and cultural changes and responds well to the interactions of the people.

Influence of the Internet on Yorùbá Christianity

The Internet has allowed Yorùbá Christianity to host a public interface by serving as a platform for sharing sermons, biblical newsletters, and other educational materials to be accessed by congregations and the interested public. In his article "'Get on the Internet!,'"[85] Kwabena Asamoah-Gyadu identifies two groups of churches—older, Pentecostal and modern, more evangelical—that are active on the Internet. He explains that the more modern evangelical churches are concerned about actively engaging with the Internet, especially to globalize their doctrines and modes of practice. The older churches that adhere to more Pentecostal beliefs do not share similar sentiments. Asamoah-Gyadu argues that older churches are rarely keen to use the Internet to reach global audiences or spread their denominational doctrines. Instead, they use the Internet to remain connected with their current followers, either at home or abroad.[86]

The modern, more evangelical churches are leveraging the Internet as a tool for evangelization. They consider the Internet to be a platform for preaching the gospel that serves as a medium for reaching larger audiences, especially outside their existing geographic areas of influence. Some denominations consider the Internet to be a tool for rescuing the "lost souls" whom they believe are using the Internet in an ungodly way.[87]

The modern churches' effective adoption of the Internet appears to have brought down denominational barriers to religious worship, facilitating the evangelical Christian conversion of souls to Christ. The Internet has created a shared area of worship that serves people around the world, transferring the beliefs, ethos, and doctrines of Yorùbá churches to other parts of the world. It has also brought the doctrines of other denominational practices closer to the Yorùbá people.

The Redeemed Christian Church of God has actively brought Yorùbá Christianity to other parts of the world, and it has absorbed influences from the outside world in turn. Like many churches, the RCCG quickly realized that it needed to extend beyond a local audience. In some respect, this outreach fulfilled its alleged covenant with God to bring the gospel to the whole world. As a religious organization, its mission to globalize the Christian religion and its doctrines became part of an expansionist agenda. One of the first steps taken in this direction was the search for a transcultural identity.

The RCCG adopted its current name as part of an effort to assimilate into a transcultural world. The founder of the church had no contact with Western education or ideals; his roots were in the Aladura Christian faith, and early communication in the church primarily involved the Yorùbá language.[88] Because the prospective audience for the church's teachings was a translocal group that spoke diverse languages, it needed to adopt a general language. This probably informed the predominant use of English for communicating the gospel to its global audience. Asonzeh Ukah states, "The opening up of the church to cross cultural influences was the

---

85. Asamoah-Gyadu, "'Get on the Internet!," 225–242.

86. Ramos, "Connecting through a Medium," 25.

87. Ramos, "Connecting through a Medium," 26.

88. RCCG started as the *Egbe Ogo Oluwa* in 1952 by Reverend Josiah Akindayomi.

result of recruitment of people with university education. The expanded worldview brought about by the coming together of the local and the global generated new 'global' tensions exemplified in the person of Adeboye. He was reluctant and skeptical, according to official sources, of taking up the mantle of leadership of a 'tribal church,' it was his responsibility to articulate and negotiate the uneasy waters of global cultural flows and networks, introducing new forms of actions and performances, new opportunities and allowing new practices to develop."[89]

Some religious doctrines also encourage their adherents to migrate around the globe. For Christians, especially Pentecostals, there has been a consistent emphasis on sending missionaries into new territories to share their beliefs. Hundreds of devotees are specifically trained for mission work in Bible schools, and they are ordained to conduct mission journeys into Australia, North America, and Europe. The goal of these journeys has always been to spread the gospel of salvation, but they have a specific focus on recovering people from apostasy and atheism, commissioning new branches of the mother church in these parts of the world.

These missionary journeys have supported the growth of Pentecostal churches in Nigeria. The Redeemed Christian Church of God conducts similar activities. In the 1970s, the church had a structure in place to recruit and train Christians for specialized mission journeys and other elite responsibilities. Christ the Redeemer's Ministry was a special wing of the church created to bring innovative external ideas into the church, and it trained mission leaders to be sent to other countries.[90]

Mission leaders brought the doctrines, practices, institutions, and ideas of the RCCG into different countries and cultures. Similar strategies were employed to disperse RCCG doctrines across Nigeria and around the world. In this context, Ukah explains that the RCCG of the 1980s did not originally design a model strategy for the world; instead, the church worked with its mobile elites who pursued professional and academic opportunities and achievements around the world. Ukah also notes that in Nigeria, the church's advances into northern and southeastern territories did not initially follow a specific template; its growth was enabled by the zeal of its graduating students who carried church doctrines, institutions, and practices to these areas through the National Youth Service Corps. Graduating students set up campus fellowships in their respective states that spread the ideas of the church and laid the foundation for its new branches. This helped to grow the church and establish strong RCCG footholds in different parts of the country.

Similar activities played out on the international level. There was no direct template for the translocation of the church, but those who pursued economic, academic, and professional opportunities became conduits for transmitting the gospel of the RCCG around the world.[91] The need for fellowship was driven by these Nigerians who wanted to continue the practices of worship they had learned in Nigeria. The RCCG also had a standing rule that compelled devotees to create new churches in regions that were not already served by existing ones.

---

89. Ukah, "Redeemed Christian Church of God," 277.

90. Ukah, "Redeemed Christian Church of God."

91. Ukah, "Redeemed Christian Church of God," 280.

Globalizing and Changing Islam

Islam and Yorùbá Culture and Tradition in Contemporary Practice

Yorùbá Islam is an ideological variance of the large Islamic practices as seen across the world. The marriage between the Islamic practices and Yorùbá religion and culture has brought about a syncretism characterized by the integration of Yorùbá cultural practices such as music, ideologies, dance, and attire into Islamic rituals and worship. The Yorùbá people in Nigeria, Benin, and Togo have a rich cultural heritage that has been shaped by their history and geography and cannot be separated from their adopted Islamic practices. After Islam was introduced to the Yorùbá people, especially through the Hausa jihadist movements toward the Ọ̀yọ́ Empire, it started wearing new identities particular to the people and involved the integration of Yorùbá cultural practices and beliefs into Islamic worship. There are several conventional Islamic practices, ceremonies, teachings, and lifestyles that are influenced by culture and traditions. Although some may not agree with syncretism, it is important to make Islam more befitting of the culture and admit more Yorùbá people who may feel disconnected from the religion due to its foreign origins.[92]

Over time, large undertones of the Yorùbá religion became noticeable in Islam. The Yorùbá, with their rich cultural and historical heritage, were able to fuse certain parts of their cultural ways into Islam. History had it that as early as the 1800s, notable families of traditional religious worshippers in Yorubaland shared a cordial relationship with the early Yorùbá Muslims. It was not uncommon to have a family give out their sons to the latter just to learn the new religion. Through this method, culture was transmitted, and large parts of the Yorùbá religious practice rolled into Islam. For example, the bata drum, a traditional Yorùbá drum, is often used in Islamic worship to accompany singing and chanting. This blending of Islamic and Yorùbá musical traditions can be seen in the manners of worship and songs of popular modern Islamic musicians and preachers. Drums are now being played in Maulud celebrations and other events. Aside from this, Yorùbá culture has influenced contemporary Islamic practice in the use of Yorùbá language and proverbs in Islamic preaching and teaching. This became necessary as many Yorùbá Muslims felt more comfortable learning and practicing Islam in their native language. Several Yorùbá societal positions to revere notable personalities are adopted in Islamic societies. Titles like Baba Adinni, Iya Adinni, and Balógun Adinni, among others, now exist within mosque positions and dignitaries.

Yorùbá customs and traditions are built on respect for ancestors, the elderly, and heroes. This is why several of the Òrìṣàs who were largely demigods are revered for their human and spiritual accomplishments. The bravery of Ogun is celebrated severally when hunters sing special songs, known as *sun rara*, as well as through folktales, folklores, and other mediums of worship. This extends to the building of shrines, festivals, and memorial ceremonies for them. Today, these practices are associated with Sufi Muslims, a variant of the faith that is largely the

---

92. Ojo, "Entrepreneurship in Islamic Practices," 270–273.

description of Yorùbá Islam. Similar honors are bestowed on many Islamic clerics, and tombs, which are gradually turning into shrines, have been built for their Sheikhs and Waliyy.

In addition, special dates relating to an Islamic figure have been set aside to venerate the Sheikhs and Waliyy. This is further strengthened by the Yorùbá customs of respect for elders and leaders, and it is one example of worship that is exerting an influence. The Shaykhs, also known as the religious leaders of Islam, have given greater significance through the Sufi system—they act as spiritual and religious guides for the public. The graves of these Shaykhs are frequently visited after their passing as a kind of *ziyarah* to the saint.[93] The shrines of Sidi Boumediene,[94] Bilqis Sungbo of Ijebu (Queen of Sheba),[95] and Muhammad Jimoh, who was regarded as the Mahdi of Ijebu Ode, are a few of such sites.[96]

Several Islamic practitioners in contemporary Yorùbá societies adopt the use of armbands and amulets with *tira*, Quranic verses, and Arabic verses. This is an adoption of the popular traditional protective measures in which enchanted *ìgbàdí* and *ìfúnpá* are used for personal protection or other purposes. Aside from this, the cultural subscriptions of the people cannot be separated from their Islamic practice, a reality seen in southwestern Nigeria. Islamic customs originally used the Sharia law to resolve disputes. Islamic courts were established to issue rulings in accordance with the Quran, along with the teachings of the Prophets, and this system existed in some parts of Yorubaland. Colonialism in Nigeria created a new legal structure that initially limited the scope of the Sharia courts in criminal matters and controlled the civil application of Sharia law. In Nigeria, a Sharia court was established to hear Islamic cases in the north, offering a unique punitive code for criminal law that acknowledged the religion's importance in society.[97]

To encourage peaceful coexistence, many Yorùbá Muslims are adopting more liberal views as a response to the ethnic and religious diversity of people of other faiths. Proponents of liberal Islam hold that all people have the right to practice their religion, free from outside intervention. This attitude is justified by Quranic verse 109, verse 6, which states, "To you your faith, to me my religion." The "Medina Document," a peaceful cohabitation agreement between Prophet Mohammad and the Jews of Medina, is a well-cited source to support their beliefs. Liberal Islam has accommodated people with different beliefs due to immigration and the spread of several new religions, and it has accepted the preexisting practitioners of the Yorùbá indigenous religion.

Various movements have challenged these practices due to their incorporation of Yorùbá beliefs. Many individuals have questioned the justification for using the Quran for healing due to its external links with the Islamic faith. In some customs, Quranic verses or chapters are written on *wàláà*, a slate that is typically black in color and cleansed with water before it is given to those in need of healing. The writing and reading of Suratu'l-Kafirun are also applied as a

---

93. Eickelman and Piscatori, *Muslim Travellers*.

94. Andezian, "Worshipping in Times of Crisis," 99–118.

95. Doi, "Muslim-Christian-Traditional Saint in Yorubaland," 261–268.

96. Doi, *Islam in Nigeria*, 217.

97. Ostien and Dekker, "Sharia and National Law in Nigeria," 553–612.

remedy or antidote for insanity and other severe illnesses.[98] The celebration and observance of Eid al-Fitr, Id al-Kabir, and the inclusion of Maulud Nabiyy are combined with Yorùbá religious activities.[99] Similar differences are seen among the Yorùbá Muslims in neighboring African countries like Togo, Ghana, Benin, and other West African countries; the Muslim society in these places has also been largely influenced by Yorùbá religious practices taken there by the Yorùbá that settled outside Nigeria. In Benin, for instance, many Yorùbá Muslims engage in ancestor worship and the veneration of various spirits and deities.

The influence of Òrìṣà and Ifá worship on the Islamic practices among the Cuban Yorùbá is also unique. Cuban Muslims wear *ilẹ́kẹ́*, typically associated with Ifá and *Òrìṣà* devotees, as a form of protection and spirituality. Additionally, many Cuban Muslims still perform Ifá divination alongside Islamic prayer, beliefs, and practices. It is a typical scene for Yorùbá Muslims to have an altar for Ifá in the home.[100] Similarly, Muslims in Trinidad and Tobago have been largely influenced by the Yorùbá dress sense, such as the brightly colored clothing and head wraps. These attires are mostly worn to religious gatherings and ceremonies.

Among the Brazilians, particularly in the Bahia areas, Yorùbá religion and culture merged with Islamic practices as evident in the Capoeira dance prominent among Brazilian Muslims. The dance is a martial art dance that originated in Brazil but has strong roots in Yorùbá dance and music. Capoeira is often performed during Islamic festivals and celebrations. This dance teaches self-defense and is similar to the traditional Yorùbá ẹ̀kẹ́ /ìjàkadì. A major similarity between these two is the mode through which it is practiced as well as the songs played.

The religious cultural change did not only happen to the Islamic religion; the influences were two-way. There is an obvious heavy bearing on the Yorùbá traditional and cultural practices that may not be separated. The cultural assimilation of the Islamic culture process involves the incorporation of Islamic practices, beliefs, and symbols into the existing Yorùbá religious and cultural systems, establishing new culture different from the pre-Islamic Yorùbá traditions. For instance, in the same way traditional names exist among Muslims of contemporary Nigeria, Islamic names are becoming more popular among Òrìṣà worshippers. For instance, the name *Bello*, among the Yorùbá people, is an adoption of the Islamic name *Belal* or *Bilal*. This has been claimed to be drawn from the Hausa's assimilation of Islamic name systems—Fatimo from *Fatima*, Yusufu for *Yusuf*, and other Islamic-adapted names.

Islam-influenced contemporary Yorùbá practices can also be seen in countries like Benin, Togo, and the Caribbean (especially Trinidad and Tobago and Jamaica), where Yorùbá descendants live. This influence is seen in aspects such as the traditional Yorùbá divination system of Ifá. This act of divination has been modified in some places to align with Islamic beliefs and practices. This system, known as "ifá *ìmàle*," involves the use of Islamic prayers and incantations during divination sessions. It also includes slaughtering livestock for healing and warding off evil spirits. These are done by some set of Alfa called Alfa Jalabi. They also read the palm and water bodies to diagnose their patients for spiritual treatment.

---

98. Opeloye and Jimoh, "Yoruba Muslims of Nigeria and the Glorious Qur'an," 65–83.

99. Doi, *Islam in Nigeria*, 151–152.

100. Janzen, "Islamic Impact on Afro-Cuban Religion," 55–72.

In countries such as Trinidad and Tobago and Jamaica, Islamic schools have been established that teach Yorùbá traditional practices alongside Islamic beliefs and practices. Here, the students learn basic Islamic tenets enshrined with Yorùbá beliefs from their *Mualims*. Students learn how to pray in Arabic and Yorùbá languages effectively. This reflects in the annual Ogun festival in Trinidad and Tobago, where Islamic prayers and the recitation of Quranic verses are parts of the rites offered.[101]

Contemporary Islam

Just like the traditional religion of Òrìsà worship and Christianity, Islamic practices have been influenced by globalization efforts and cultural diffusions. The Yorùbá people are often known to be liberal Muslims because of their acceptance of globalization, their relationship with other faiths, and the adoption of other religious cultures that influence their Islamic tenets.

Unlike the Hausa people who are predominantly Muslim and had little infiltration of Christian faith and little or no traces of traditional religion in their societies until recently, and the Igbo, who are largely Christians and traditional worshippers, the Yorùbá people have a fair share of the three religions coexisting within the same system. Given the people's direct access to Western cultures and the demography, the changes to their Islamic religious practices are unsurprising. A contemporary Yorùbá Muslim can be seen in both churches and shrines, and there would not be the level of surprise as seeing a Hausa Muslim in a church. More so, the Islamic restriction of social relations, positions, and interactions is not as restricted among Yorùbá people. There is a popular Yorùbá song among the Yorùbá Muslims that states thus:

> Awa o s'oro ile wa o
> Awa o s'oro ile wa o
> Imale o pe, o ye
> Imale o pe ka wa ma s'oro
> Awa o s'oro ile wa o.[102]

The translation of the above song goes thus:

> *We will observe our family traditions*
> *We will observe our family traditions*
> *Islam does not forbid us*
> *Islam does not forbid us from observing our traditions*
> *We will observe our family traditions.*

Islamic practices among the Yorùbá people of West Africa reflect the long period of globalization, the adoption of Internet facilities, modern education, and the strong use of the English language in religious gatherings and discourse. The Yorùbá Muslims put Islamic education and

---

101. Fatima, "Trinidad and Tobago's Ogun Festival," 670–687.

102. Balogun, "Syncretic Beliefs and Practices."

Western education side by side to let the two permeate together to get the present social construct. It is a strong reflection of the culture, other religions, globalized cultures, and tenets of Islam.

Conclusion

As the world becomes more globalized, there continues to be a transmission of religions and religious practices from the Yorùbáland to other parts of the world. This makes it important for other countries to become more accepting of different religious practices. Historically, the religious practices of indigenous people in non-Western regions were treated as potential threats and solely viewed from a security perspective. This approach ignores the significance of these religions and the religious faith of their adherents, who want to be treated as equals. The traffic in religious ideas is endless, and new formations and practices will continue to emerge.

PART 3

Modernity, Postcoloniality, and Globalization

Introduction

The relationship between the traditional Yorùbá lifestyle and modernity has often stirred up interest among academic scholars and historians.[1] Some of the frontline questions regarding the interaction between the two include the following: What is the relevance of the Yorùbá traditional lifestyle or cultural inclination to contemporary challenges posed by modernity? In recent times, does Yorùbá traditional culture impede or fast-track the adoption of modern behaviors and thoughts? Has the adoption of modern thoughts and behaviors positively or negatively affected the Yorùbá traditional culture?

Two perspectives have emerged as a way of understanding the potential for the coexistence of the two. The first holds the view that modernity has negatively affected indigenous traditional culture and that to reclaim it, cultural revivalism must occur.[2] This revivalism is expected to address the detriment of precolonial cultures and the problems that arose within and between them as a result of modernity by "reclaiming and revitalizing indigenous traditions that have been degraded and suppressed in the wake of colonialism."[3] This perspective, championed by Kwame Gyekye, believes that colonialism is the root of modernity negatively affecting indigenous culture. He believes colonialism has violently disrupted traditional cultures and further aggravated the situation by imposing Western thoughts and behaviors as well as social organization on indigenous people. Hence, the solution to this, Gyekye believes, is revitalizing cultural norms, for this is the only way through which genuine modernization can be achieved.[4]

The second perspective is more of a criticism of the stance of Kwame Gyekye and his cultural revivalism agenda. Scholars of this perspective believe that the conflict between indigenous culture and modernity can best be resolved when there is a "clean break with the premodern past."[5] Their approach is more critical of reviving indigenous culture, as they believe such an agenda has lost relevance, especially amid contemporary indigenous challenges. Their standpoint is that cultural revivalism only derails focus from key contemporary issues by supporting

---

1. Euba, "Dress and Status in 19th Century Lagos," 139–157.
2. Gyekye, *Tradition and Modernity*.
3. Gyekye, *Tradition and Modernity*.
4. Gyekye, *Tradition and Modernity*.
5. Hountondji, *African Philosophy*.

the reemergence of behaviors and thoughts that interfere with technological and scientific advancement brought about by modernity. Hence, they argue that to move forward, there must be a clean break from the beliefs, attitudes, and ways of living from the premodern past by indigenous people and their communities so they can address contemporary demands. To them, the modernization of indigenous communities demands more of a psychological shift to align with contemporary problems and not a romantic embrace of thoughts and ideas from historical societies.

What these two perspectives bring to the fore is the debate regarding a future that calls for either a revival of cultural ways and an abandonment of modern behaviors in favor of progress within Yorùbá communities or, on the other side, a break away from indigenous culture and a total adoption of more current behaviors and ideas to solve contemporary issues. However, choosing between these two perspectives raises a dilemma, as none can effectively guarantee progress among the Yorùbá or any set of indigenous people. For one, indigenous ways and cultures define a people, and although there might have been some significant changes in their cultures over time, an abandonment of what defines them for a borrowed culture, informed by modern thoughts, achieves no progress. On the other side, a stack embrace of traditional thoughts and ideas in disregard for contemporary ideas and solutions posed by modernity will only slow the advancement of indigenous people. Hence, what seems to be the optimal course of action, and what this chapter will address, is the coexistence of modern thoughts and traditional Yorùbá culture. It is believed that the existence and practice of Yorùbá culture are not mutually exclusive to the adoption of modern thoughts and ideas. Therefore, not only are both simultaneously possible to implement in society; rather, an embrace of the two is needed for effective and efficient development. Under these provisions, it is important to consider how Yorùbá culture and modernity have been interacting in the recent past. This can be viewed in how the flow of cultures and modern ideas have been migrating, the cultural responses that have occurred among Yorùbá people, the emergence of popular culture in Yorùbá and broader societies, and the impact these have had on Yorùbá culture.

Global Transactional Flows

Today's world is punctuated by different, mind-blowing, and exciting innovations circling almost all the corners of the earth and making it possible to spread and receive various philosophies, innovations, and cultures. With the Internet, it has become simpler to ensure the spread of people's culture, religions, values, and morals, and even more importantly, to receive the cultures of the different parts of the world, sift them, and apply aspects from those that are considered relevant or desirable to one's way of life, thoughts, and behaviors.[6] The spread of local culture and adoption of foreign thoughts and ideas has been described as global transactional flow because it establishes an unconscious symbiotic relationship of give and take of local and foreign cultures.[7] Although one could argue that the extent to which one local community

---

6. Hongladarom, "Global Culture, Local Cultures," 389–401.
7. Crane, "Globalization and Cultural Flows/Networks," 359–381.

adopts the culture of another local community is unequal, it is more important to appreciate the constant flow rather than the equality of the flow. Although it is a marvel that cultures across distant places or even in relative proximity to each other can share and appreciate pivotal aspects of their identity and ways of living, this does not change the relative elasticity of groups in adopting new traditions and the inequality existent across the globe in access to resources. Nevertheless, there is no doubt that the effects of global transactional flows are rapidly changing the world into a singular worldwide society.

Regarding the occurrence and awareness of these exchanges about Yorùbá people, these transactional flows have not eluded them.[8] They have also, since the colonial period, given their culture—voluntarily or forcefully—to other parts of the world and have taken back and applied to their way of life—in like manner—the cultures of these parts of the world.[9] The urge to cross-fertilize various worldviews and local perspectives is what defines global transactional flows. Though these interchanges may be situated and balanced, in their midst is often the implication that local identities are most times eroded and replaced by an undefined global attachment. This is fueled by an implication of these flows, which is that cultural concepts, beliefs, attitudes, preferences, and their meanings have been redefined whether within or outside the context in which they originally apply, so they can fit into a more general and global perspective. It has also given room for both active and redundant participation in the local society, in part because of the wave for the establishment of a global village. This, in turn, has seen how foreign ideas have affected local ideologies, arts, production, and culture.

Before there could be smooth global transactional flows, there had to have been tools and agencies in place that served to trigger their achievement. Tools and agencies are meant in this context to identify the various methods by which local ideas were transmitted to the global space and how the foreign ideas were brought and localized. One of these important agencies or tools is the mass media. In recent times, the mass media has grown to be a powerful force because of the influence it has over people and institutions, as well as the influence it can allot those who use it to their advantage or those who are portrayed positively by it.[10] With the mass media, stories and histories have been told the way they ought to be told or the way the controllers of the media want them to be told. And given the attachment of the hordes to the mass media, it is not surprising that the content that it generates is easily believed.[11] Also, since the mass media has gone global,[12] it makes it easier for people in different parts of the world to connect and get a taste of the stories or way of life of another region. Hence, it became easy for foreign ideas and perspectives to be learned in Nigeria, and among the Yorùbá, especially through films, music videos, and reality shows.[13] Local ideas, too, are transmitted through the same channels to foreign citizens. For instance, different Hollywood movies depict Western ways

---

8. Oladipo, "Intercultural Flow."

9. Udo, "Vitality of Yoruba Culture in the America," 27–40.

10. Edwards, *Mediapolitik*.

11. Dellavigna and Kaplan, "Fox News Effect," 1187–1234.

12. Matos, "Globalization and the Mass Media," 1–14.

13. Akpan, "And the Beat Goes On?" 105–120.

of life and ideologies and are based on the day-to-day happenings within the West.[14] However, these movies are consumed not only by the West but also by citizens of other countries. In Nigeria, especially among the youths, there even appears to be a preference for these movies because of the action and the sexual obscenity that many of them depict.[15] By watching these movies, youths learn the ways of Westerners—their ideologies and their everyday habits. Nigerian Nollywood movies, too, largely depict local ideologies, culture, and everyday happenings of Nigerians, and in this context, the Yorùbá people.[16] These movies are consumed not only by Yorùbá people or Nigerians but also by foreign citizens. Through this, local ideologies and cultures are seen by foreign citizens, and the appropriation of the identity of these local cultures may happen.

Aside from mass media, social media has been another powerful and important enabler of global transactional flows.[17] No doubt, social media has gone global, connecting people from different regions and local communities.[18] Many define social media as the virtual version of the global village sought by globalization. Every day on social media, much information is exchanged, through which people inform and are informed of the happenings in local communities they might not even know exist. Within this exchange of information, there are intercultural social communication links formed by both foreign and local citizens. Intercultural social communication links that have been established make cultural identities and ideologies the subject matter of their intermittent discussions. The cultural peculiarities about a particular local community, their ideas and traditions, are shared on the Internet where foreign citizens can have access to them and are encouraged to do the same, to bond with local communities. This way, there is a global transactional flow of cultural peculiarities. One example of how these global transactional flows have influenced local communities is marriage. Through social media, the practice of a marriage proposal whereby a man goes down on one knee in public to ask for a lady's hand in marriage has been copied by the Yorùbá people from Europe and America. This practice which was not situated among the Yorùbá people is now being considered a standard practice, such that every young man is expected to publicly go on a knee and ask a lady to marry him.

What this shows is that cultural flows across borders occur daily and that gradually, changes are happening in local communities. What, however, determines the extent of these changes is the cultural responses given to a particular foreign idea. Hence, if the cultural response is positive, the chances are that a foreign practice will enjoy wide acceptability and practice. On the other hand, if the cultural responses are unwelcoming, it is likely that such foreign practices are not seen among the local communities. As such, the next section of this work explores the cultural responses toward foreign practices received via global transactional flows to understand the materialization of change within indigenous communities.

---

14. Lysonski and Durvasula, "Nigeria in Transition," 493–508.

15. Oyesomi and Salawu, "Influence of Sexualisation of Women," 12059–12072.

16. Ibagere, "Globalization and Nollywood," 1–10.

17. Gainous and Wagner, *Tweeting to Power*.

18. Kollock and Smith, *Communities in Cyberspace*.

Cultural Responses

The operations of global transaction flows of cultures, ideas, and thoughts do not indicate an automatic adoption of learned cultures. The global flow of culture is only but a part of the symbiotic transmission of ideologies and ideas. What determines the successful flow is the extent to which the learned culture is being adopted. For a learned culture to be successfully adopted, it must enjoy a positive local cultural response. Many foreign thoughts and practices have, in the past, enjoyed wide acceptance among the Yorùbá people and have become a part of their daily lifestyle. For instance, the practice of proposal in the way it is being done today was never a part of the Yorùbá ante-marriage behavioral custom. This practice was learned through the operation of global transactional flow and enjoyed wide acceptability and positive cultural response among the youths and so has become a norm today.

Aside from this, there are areas where cultural responses to learned practices have been significant, some of which are considered below. One area where a cultural response to modern practice is significant is in moralizing childbirth outside marriage, especially with no genuine intention of marrying the father or mother of the child. This practice is common among male celebrities who do not genuinely yearn to set up a family but want to bear children. They look for female counterparts who have agreed to become their "baby mama"—that is, bear them children without nursing the need for marriage. From this arrangement, the baby mama provides natal care for the children while the celebrity shoulders the financial and fatherly responsibilities.[19] Originally, the response to this kind of practice was one of resentment, especially as it contradicts the traditional marriage system of the Yorùbá people, who do not embrace childbirth outside wedlock. The women who had initially been involved in these kinds of relationships were condemned and seen as promiscuous, but with time, the cultural responses began to change. People started accepting them, especially since the celebrity, in this case, the father, acknowledges the legitimacy of the children. Now the practice has become well-known and accepted, especially among the young and wealthy people in Yorubaland. One implication of this, however, is that it erodes the sanctity of marriage and reduces the necessity to build up families as traditionally conceived among the Yorùbá people. Moreover, in the context of this conversation, what is of particular interest is the movement of the cultural response from the initial intolerance to the later stage of embrace. Cultural responses to borrowed practices among the Yorùbá people are not static, and provided that the practice lingers long enough, adoption is possible.

Another practice gradually finding its way into the Yorùbá culture through global transactional flows is homosexuality and gender identification. Due to the complex cultural and historical attitudes toward nonheterosexual relationships and conception of gender, the cultural responses among the Yorùbá people toward this are worthy of discussion. In the Yorùbá traditional setting, there is only the recognition of two genders—the male and the female.[20] The strong belief in the singular existence of these two genders is what informs their marriage and

---

19. For an interesting study of this trend, see Raheem, "Having His Baby and Not Being His Wife," 41–55.
20. Case, "Yoruba Culture, Religion, and Gender."

Figure 12.1.
"The rural in the
modern," by Moses
Ogunleye. Despite
contemporary
modernity and
globalization, older
ways of living remain.
The Yorùbá world
retains its heritage
anywhere they reside.

Moses Ogunleye J.
2021

sexual orientation. Hence, it is expected that a man should marry a woman and vice versa. Also, the conception of gender is only that which has been biologically assigned to every individual at birth and does not give room to a psychological orientation of belonging to a gender other than that which has been naturally assigned to individuals. However, this conception is not the same as what applies in the global context, especially in America and Europe. It is believed that though a person might have been biologically selected as part of a particular gender, if the person does not psychologically identify with that gender, he or she can decide to convert or identify with a different gender.[21] This conception is what informs one's sexual orientation and identity. Hence, it is not uncommon to see a woman identifying as a man because she does not feel a sense of belonging to her biologically assigned gender. Also, it is common to see people of the same gender getting married and consummating their marriage, and these practices are recognized and backed by law.[22] In fact, in Europe and America, there are laws against discrimination of people in the LGBTQ community.[23]

Given global transactional flows, this orientation of identifying with a gender other than the biologically assigned one started to find its way among the Yorùbá community; before long, some people started to consciously believe they could also identify as a different gender or marry someone of the same gender.[24] The cultural responses to this orientation, however, became forceful, as it became inconceivable to condemn and abandon the natural selection of one's gender and alter the work of the Supernatural Being.[25] The cultural responses were not only cold; those who showed leanings toward touring that sentimental line were condemned and in different situations were distanced from it. These cultural responses happened not just among the Yorùbá people but also among the other two major ethnic groups in the country. This cold acceptance of LGBTQ orientation was what informed the law against homosexuality in Nigeria signed in 2014, which carries a maximum sentence of fourteen years imprisonment for those caught in the act.[26] There is no doubt that though global transactional flows often trigger an acceptance of culture with foreign orientation among the Yorùbá, there are situations, like homosexual culture, when such is not the case, especially when disregard is given to fundamental cultural ideologies. The cultural responses that homosexuality as a modern practice or orientation received within the African landscape were largely because it contradicts the core principles of the Yorùbá worldview about biological identity. Furthermore, it challenged the indigenous beliefs about human design attributed to irrefutable and inalterable works of the Supreme Being.

The cultural responses to changes in the structure of marriage, especially as it concerns divorce or related issues, are also worthy of discussion. Traditionally, marriage is seen as the union not just between the husband and the wife but also between their families.[27] The Yor-

---

21. Masters et al., "Homosexuality in Perspective," 54–56.

22. Hull, *Same-Sex Marriage*.

23. Kuntz et al., "Human Values, Legal Regulation," 120–134.

24. Afe, Ogunsemi, and Oyelekan, "Social Distancing Toward Gays and Lesbians," 546–557.

25. Rodenbough, "Being LGBT in West Africa."

26. Refworld, "Same Sex Marriage Prohibition Act 2013."

27. Mahmud, "Study of the Yoruba Traditional Marriage," 40–52.

ùbá traditional setting also embraces polygamy, especially when the husband is financially stable. This facet of a marriage going beyond the two people in different capacities adds another dimension of complex relationships among people and society. This explains why in situations where the husband takes another wife, rather than outright divorce, an amicable solution that involves the dialogue of the partners' families is sought. This also explains why, though in Nigeria bigamy is a marital offense, it is one of the least enforced provisions of the law.[28] The response to issues like bigamy and polygamy, even despite the modernity in Yorùbá culture, has shared in this complicated nature. Rather than a total condemnation, the response has been more of acceptance even though the culture in which the idea of one man to one woman is borrowed heavily encourages divorce and condemns polygamy. What this explains is that it is possible, through global transactional flows, to borrow the cultural practices of a particular people and yet still have a different cultural response to its application.

Competing/Contesting Values

Though global transactional flows allowed many cultural practices, ideologies, and thoughts to be received locally, it is, however, not the case that all these ideas and thoughts were applied or even flourished. These incoming or festering ideas must be viewed and placed within the local contexts in which they are to survive; whereas many are positively recognized, others are not well received by the people for factors relating to the surrounding culture and preexisting ideas. The Yorùbá people have strong moral and value systems that guide their daily activities, and oftentimes, these values compete with modern practices. This section takes time to view some of the present-day practices to better elaborate on the nature of hostile interaction that can occur between them and the established culture.

The Yorùbá people had a unique family structure that was embedded in communalism. The family structure or system embraced an encompassing philosophy of oneness and projected active interactions, sharing, praises, and, of course, punishments.[29] It was built and revolved around a hierarchical structure where age and experience determined the leadership and decisions being made, not just for the nuclear and extended family but also for the society.[30] The family structure in place served as an agent of socialization and embodied the philosophy that was the initial contact and training ground for children. This explains why it remains common among the Yorùbá to hear phrases that categorize one's immediate family as the first point of learning. For instance, it is common for the Yorùbá to say *"ilé la ti ńkọ́ ẹ̀ṣọ́ r'òde,"* which literally means that good behaviors and lessons are learned at home before interactions with the society. The family and communal system also places the training and upbringing of a child not just on its immediate family but also on the community itself.[31] In this sense, the responsibility to nurture a child becomes communalistic. This nurturing by the family and members of

---

28. Bigamy is an offense under section 370 of the Criminal Code Act. See Lateef and Adegbite, "Bigamy and Dearth of Prosecution in Nigeria," 91–118.

29. Hallen, "Yoruba Moral Epistemology," 296–303.

30. Ajayi, "Effects of Globalization on Yoruba Family Values," 207–227.

31. Omobola, "Community Parenting and the Concept of Child Abuse," 309–316.

the community is welcome by the nuclear family of the child, such that in situations where the child misbehaves and is corrected by any member of the society, there are no questions raised about what authority the member of the communal society has over the child to correct him or her. The family system of the Yorùbá people is important and epitomized to the extent that people believe that its sanctity must be preserved because it is the smallest unit and the root of society's formation, and that whatsoever corrupts the family system could reflect on the communal life of the society.[32] This explains why the preservation of a good family name or reputation is highly praised in the community, and those who have shown traces of destroying the family and communal system have been ostracized.

However, with globalization and the incursion of modernity, the values placed on good names and a good family structure began to wane. For one, the borrowed culture from Europe does not conceive communalism as a way of life, and this is reflected in the relationship between members of families and the community in which they find themselves. The Western family system is entirely nuclear and usually kept small. When borrowed, however, this system conflicts with the family system structure in Yorubaland. For those who adopted this Western family system, the implication has been a reduction of family values and an abandonment of the communal lifestyle that characterized the Yorùbá family system. Now, especially outside the rural areas, families no longer uphold the values that reflect the traditional culture of the Yorùbá people. Families are now nuclear in composition and the community is no longer responsible for the upbringing of a child. The cherished value system that rewarded good names beyond riches is now being abandoned. This has culminated in the Yorùbá community and family system losing the fundamental structure that defines good and harmonious living among the people.

It also used to be the case that Yorùbá people were the personification of their traditions and culture. One would easily notice the demeanor, candor, and identity of a Yorùbá person because of the cultural personalism the person inculcated. A typical Yorùbá person embodied the values and philosophy of the Yorùbá culture through language, appearance, food, and comportment. This is what set the person apart, and this is what he or she took pride in. However, as modernity set in and a new wave of cultural identity swept through, the Yorùbá cultural personalism was dropped because of the uncontrolled desire and preference to want to key into the narrative of the Western world and its values. Since the West and everything that comes from it has always been seen as having superior quality or standard, a conflict of values and representation of culture inevitably emerged. On the one hand, the traditional Yorùbá culture is intertwined with the daily lives of the typical Yorùbá person and, on the other, the Yorùbá man is faced with a new Western cultural identity that he has been made to believe is superior to his own. The struggle of choice did not persist for long, especially since traditional Yorùbá culture is intricately tied with traditional religion, which has been tagged to be devilish and evil, through the instrument of propaganda from other religions. The dilemma then is whether to choose to uphold his culture and the remnants of traditional religion found within it amid an obvious and intense campaign against the religion or to take a step away from the culture

---

32. Shitta-Bey, "Family as Basis of Social Order," 79–89.

and adopt the Western cultural identity. Although this alternative system does not embody his religion, it nevertheless has been projected to have prospects for the future and for those who follow it.

Emerging Popular Culture

Through global transactional flows, there has been an exchange of cultural values between Yorùbá people and other parts of the world. While there are countless instances where these cultural exchanges have had essential positive consequences on Yorùbá people, there are also instances where the effects have not been so heartwarming. Nevertheless, it is important to recognize trends among the future and emerging members of the community, as there has been an emergence of popular culture among Yorùbá people, especially the youth. The intricacies of these emerging popular cultures are that they simultaneously cut between having a positive influence on the minds and value conception of Yorùbá youth and having a damning negative influence on reshaping the perspective of these same youth. In this context, popular cultures are the cultural influences and changes in food, language, clothing, music, and the overall daily activities and practices that are considered ideal and an adaptable model for the society, or at least the youths and young adults, to follow. Jack Nachbar and Kevin Lause, in explaining the easy adaptation and connection with popular culture, stated that popular culture, due to its omnipresence status, is the easiest thing for a population to adapt.[33] They explain that the relationship of popular culture with many societies is so tight that it can be likened to that which exists between fish and water, surrounding a society the same way that water surrounds fish, and, once adopted, is crucial to the survival of that society.[34]

The argument of the Frankfurt school of thought on popular culture as being deliberately created and propagated to spread and ensure the dominance of capitalism may be relevant, especially as popular culture among the Yorùbá people is discussed.[35] Some have even tried to locate the ideals of the creation of popular culture in Marxism,[36] arguing that it is another type of dominant ideology that secures and promotes capitalism. An argument that has also been put forward is that popular culture tends to place focus on consumerism, which is tainted by the availability of money, without which people cannot engage in it.[37] The cultural industry that is an important trigger of popular cultures is known to create content, which has great exchange as well as use value.[38] Hence, to push their content out, they create a content fetishism, with the idea of indirectly forcing the likeness of the content among the consumers and discouraging the probing of the source or reason for the content.[39] The Frankfurt school believes that this gives the creators the power to manipulate and control the contemplation of the general consumers

---

33. Nachbar and Lause, *Popular Culture.*
34. Nachbar and Lause, *Popular Culture.*
35. Schuetz, "Frankfurt School and Popular Culture," 1–14.
36. Berger, "Marxism and Popular Culture," 146–159.
37. Kolo and Yağbasan, "Popular Culture in Nigeria," 124–139.
38. Kolo and Yağbasan, "Popular Culture in Nigeria," 124–139.
39. Street, Inthorn, and Scott, *From Entertainment to Citizenship,* 8–23.

by distracting them from the process and purpose of a popular culture and consequently creating a mass culture, which undermines conventional practices and beliefs.[40] This way, each individual loses touch with the traditional community and institutional ideal and begins to find relevance and identity amid the existing mass culture. The Frankfurt school also believes that the cultural sector, through the creation and spread of popular culture, is undermining a better society, especially since the consumers of the knowledge being created are unaware that they do not hold any responsibility toward the culture being consumed.[41] The culture industry, in its pursuit of profit, deliberately creates false needs without adequate consideration of what humans truly need by deliberately adjusting the realities and inclinations of people to fit into specific needs that tally with the created popular culture.[42] The masses yearn for the content of the industry without realizing it to be a miscalculated yearning to the detriment of their human needs. Before long, they become too engraved in the popular culture and they adopt it as the right way and the source from which they draw inspiration for their daily activities.[43]

The explanation of the Frankfurt school on the emergence of popular culture rightly explains the obsession with popular culture in Yorubaland, especially among the youths. For one, the creative industry has constructed the illusion of needs so the youth can always key into trending issues as a way of projecting themselves in good light. One of the tools used in the propagation and promotion of culture is major media outputs, such as music, one of the biggest triggers of emerging popular cultures in Yorubaland. Flourishing locally and in the entirety of Nigeria, the music industry is at the forefront of championing this need and market for content by projecting popular cultures through music videos and lyrics. In recent times, the industry has taken up different shapes and has transcended local boundaries.[44] Major players have transported many of the Yorùbá cultural ways, such as Yorùbá dressing styles, Afrocentric rhythms, and language in lyrics, among others, to the outside world, but more importantly, they have brought more than enough Western cultures into the music industry. This is obvious in their representation of what the good life is and how to make waves to succeed in the present world. Before this bridge into Western music, music in Yorubaland used to be a melodic expression that required the major players to gather the skills of instrument playing, dramatization, and miming.[45] This melodic expression in Yorùbá communities was tied to the activities and major way of life of the residents. Daniel Agu explains that music used to be a fascinating experience, especially since people directly associated it with the cultural, social, political, and religious systems in place and, most importantly, enjoyed the protection of the tradition.[46] In such ways, tying music to the physical, psychological, and spiritual identities of the people was easily done.[47]

---

40. Strinati, *Introduction to Theories of Popular Culture.*

41. Corradetti, "Frankfurt School and Critical Theory."

42. Kolo and Yağbasan, "Popular Culture in Nigeria," 124–139.

43. Ugor, "Small Media, Popular Culture," 387–408.

44. Premium Times, "How Big Is the Nigerian Music Industry?"

45. Babátúndé and Olúbòmẹhìn, "Traditional Music," 61–74.

46. Agu, "Advancing Music Scholarship," 216–224.

47. Kolo and Yağbasan, "Popular Culture in Nigeria," 124–139.

The attention and standard given to music were one of a kind because many traditional communities established their musical traditions in ways that imbibed their cultural values, morals, and character formation from childhood. And this embodiment of values and morals was what was projected every time people gathered at the entertainment centers, which were often at the village square. However, with the diffusion of "modernity" so came the emergence of a different method of melodic expressions. The establishment of religious houses and formal training centers like schools, for instance, affected the traditional structures for the training and practice of music, and there began to be the emergence of unfamiliar and unorthodox melodic expressions facilitated by the exposure these new institutions brought. With the acceptance of a Western way of life and systems, there was an unconscious acceptance of popular cultures, especially those projected through music. The emergence of these popular cultures became a thing of interest for the youth, and even elite Yorùbá people were fascinated by the classical music of the Western world.

This newfound interest in music began to force changes in some of the traditional structures in place for making, training for, and practicing music. For one, audience members that gathered to watch and listen to the traditional melodic expression of their peers in the village square began to reduce. Unorthodox entertainment centers like halls and event centers were erected to serve as a replacement to the village centers, and germane aspects of traditional musical performance and training that embodied the cultural heritage of the people were neglected, and this caused a change in the response and interactions of people with their culture and traditions. What used to be an established system of musical arts education and practice began to wane in importance, and the youth started paying less attention to the beauty and pattern of these melodic expressions. The Western institutions reinforced these behaviors as they promoted alternative modes and styles of expression. The churches and schools, especially, tagged the expression of traditional melodic music as demonic and banned any practices of such among their members and learners. In schools, there was an intentional restriction against this traditional music, and the curriculum in place appeared to favor Western-oriented music that neither embodied the cultural inclination of the Yorùbá people nor foregrounded their value orientation. This way, a new structure that accommodated popular culture arose, and within this new structure, the youth created meta-territories and social spaces without barriers.[48] These meta-territories have thence served as the platforms through which popular cultures emerge and are sustained. These meta-territories and social spaces have empowered the youths as change-makers in their societies to redefine acceptable standards of behaviors, popular values, and codes of conduct.

Impact on Yorùbá Culture

To assert that modernity has not had a huge impact on Yorùbá culture is far from the truth. Though no one can deny the transactional flows of Yorùbá culture to the West and vice versa, the cultural responses of the Yorùbá people have been majorly hinged on adjustment. As

48. Ugor, "Small Media, Popular Culture," 387–408.

Figure 12.2. "The City People," by Dr. Kazeem Ekeolu. Highly "modern Yoruba" nuclear family living in Lagos, with children who do not speak the Yorùbá language.

aspects of foreign cultures wedge their way into Yorùbá society, they bring with them different meanings and relationships to other elements of culture that can conflict with values and ideas, leading to important conversations among people in the environment and with those in external locations. It is through these conversations that groups understand other cultures and assess the placement of these cultures to their own. While globalization has encouraged a sort of open-mindedness and assimilation, it can be asserted that the reason for a larger embracing of popular and foreign culture is probably largely due to the perceived superiority of most things "white" or Western. Not only is Western culture promoted most often through social media and mass media, as opposed to other cultures of the Global South, but the engrained history of colonialism and its remaining structures promote the authority and necessity of the guiding ideologies and trends of these countries. Hence, in situations where there are contesting orders of happenings with the way of life of Yorùbá people, provided that such orders of happenings stem from the West, the result, most times, has been an abandonment or modification of Yorùbá culture to fit into the new order of happenings. This, however, is not to say that there have not been positive impacts of modernity on Yorùbá culture. There are instances where the embrace of modern systems has added finesse and attractiveness to Yorùbá culture. Such instances, however, remain largely few compared to the instances of responsive modification of the culture. Below, we consider some of the impacts—both negative and positive—of modern systems on Yorùbá culture.

The positive side of the meeting of modern systems and Yorùbá culture has been the yielding of some sort of coagulation that has resulted in the betterment of Yorùbá culture. For instance, there has been an advancement in the aesthetic maintenance of the cultural items and structures of the Yorùbá people. Many historic sites have coincidentally been fashioned toward modern tastes with contemporary equipment, which guarantees longevity and, of course, a more appealing look.[49] Pamela Eze-Uzomaka and Akintunde John Oloidi document a reference point on the positive impact of aesthetic improvement on the Yorùbá culture, particularly on historic structures. They write that through embracing modernity, the palaces of the Ẹwi of Ado Ekiti and Onígede of Igede Ekiti have been refashioned with contemporary architectural designs and fittings to meet modern state and international standards.[50] The impact of this modernity is felt not only on the palaces of the cultural rulers but on the local communities themselves, where they are now characterized by modern infrastructures that make life easier for the inhabitants rather than the distinctive remote settings and amenities of the communities.

The embrace of modernity by Yorùbá culture has also given room for the adjustment of some cultural practices, especially as they have to do with rituals involving the use of human beings. For some aspects of Yorùbá religious cultures, to appease or worship the gods, there might be an inconsiderate sacrifice of human lives, mainly those with lower social status.[51] However, with the diffusion of modernity and the embrace of agents of civil practices like formal education, many of these sacrifices involving human lives were abolished, and the ritual items were replaced with other significant ritual items. Aside from this, the admixture of Yorùbá culture and modernity has granted the establishment of cultural institutions in various governmental capacities, all geared toward the preservation of Yorùbá culture.

These institutions in government are besieged with the responsibility to represent and attend to the cultural interests of the people. They are also responsible for regularizing and formalizing cultural practices to meet national and international standards. Also, through these institutions, there has been a far-reaching propagation of the cultural practices of the Yorùbá people. For instance, the ceremonies initially celebrated in small towns with conservative gatherings have now been publicized through media institutions and avenues at both the national and international levels. The Osun Osogbo festival is now being broadcast on national television and followed on social media platforms.[52] In Ekiti State, the Ekiti State Cultural Troupe, asso-

---

49. Oloidi, "Impacts of Modernization on Cultural Heritage Management."

50. Eze-Uzomaka and Oloidi, "Modernization and Its Effect on Cultural Heritage," 81–93.

51. Ojo, "Slavery and Human Sacrifice in Yorubaland," 379–404.

52. Ibagere and Adeseye, "Promoting the Development of Indigenous Faith," 130–140.

ciated with television and radio houses, has been involved in broadcasting different cultural events and practices happening in every town of the state.[53] This, no doubt, helps to trigger greater interest in Yorùbá culture among the youths of the state; keep the diaspora community of Ekiti indigenes in the know about their various cultural practices; and inform, educate, and entertain other listeners within and outside the state.

The positive impact of modernity on Yorùbá culture is also demonstrated through contemporary medicinal practices. Traditionally, Yorùbá people have always had the knowledge and ability to categorize, diagnose, and cure many of the diseases and illnesses that spring up among them. Meanwhile, because of the firm belief in spiritual superiority and powerfulness,[54] there were some illnesses and diseases whose occurrences were ascribed to the doings of spiritual forces; hence, people who came down with such sicknesses and diseases were abandoned or killed to allegedly purge the community.[55] But practitioners have received enlightenment in the aspects of these diseases and illnesses as well as introductions of modern medicine and prevention guidelines to tackle each. Instances like premature death, miscarriages, and chronic illness that were once believed to be caused by witches or other spiritual forces as punishment on the victims are now being considered from a different perspective. More specifically, it used to be the case that people with sickle cell anemia were wrongly categorized as *àbíkú*[56] in Yorubaland. They were believed to have come from the world beyond to be given birth and live for a short while, tormenting their parents and loved ones through their constant sicknesses and later dying at a very young age. However, with modernity, it later came to light that people with sickle cell amenia are not the same as the *àbíkú* in Yorubaland and that having a child with sickle cell amenia can be prevented if the parents know their genotypes and their compatibility before marriage and the conception of children.[57] This change in understanding, not only with this disease but also others, happened primarily because of the modern research and experiments into the causes of these occurrences and investment into what could be done to prevent or cure them.

Another aspect that modernity has positively impacted is its interaction with processes of traditional skill exhibition and profession. The use of contemporary tools to fast-track and fine-tune the production of many cultural materials have increased in value. For example, sculptors in Yorubaland that would have ordinarily used cultural materials and tools to make their products have been able to leverage modern-day tools and methods to increase the quality and quantity of their production while reducing the labor and material wastage that comes with the skill.[58] This demonstrates just one way how Yorùbá culture has been known to be flexible and accommodating of other cultural inclinations, ensuring its survival.

However, it is not the case that there have not been negative impacts of modernity on the culture, irrespective of the fact that the culture is well accommodating. The negative impacts

---

53. Ibagere and Adeseye, "Promoting the Development of Indigenous Faith," 130–140.
54. Borokini and Lawal, "Traditional Medicine Practices," 20–33.
55. Amusa and Ogidan, "Yoruba Indigenous Medical Knowledge," 977–986.
56. Lawal, "Indigenous Knowledge and Practices in the Management of Sickle Cell Anaemia," 531–556.
57. Ilechukwu, "Ogbanje/Abiku and Cultural Conceptualizations," 239–255.
58. Eze-Uzomaka and Oloidi, "Modernization and Its Effect on Cultural Heritage," 81–93.

far outweigh the positive ones stated above, such as in the realm of traditional religion. With the introduction of Christianity and Islam among the Yorùbá, there has been a simultaneous reduction in the devotees of traditional religion and the prestige accorded to it. Since Christianity and Islam have been adopted, there has also been a renunciation of Yorùbá cultural practices because of the propaganda that the religion only embodies evil and that those who partake in its activities are made for damnation. In many areas in Yorubaland, especially in relatively modern societies, traditional festivals and rites are treated with indignation, and the devotees of the religion are categorized as evildoers and idol worshippers.[59] More so, youths are actively discouraged from participating in any festival or activities relating to the traditional religion. To further this obscenity toward Yorùbá cultural religion, many traditional religious structures and items that signify or embody the Yorùbá traditional belief system are being pulled down or abandoned. Buildings like groves or shrines that house Yorùbá deities are either being deserted or pulled down, religious titles seen as fetishes are rejected, and there is less contact with and presence of the Yorùbá traditional religion in both local and modern communities in southwestern Nigeria. Eze-Uzomaka and Oloidi point to a sad incident in Ekiti State where the Ayoba historical hill, which once served as a cultural and archaeological site, was bulldozed and the site was used to construct the governor's office.[60]

In the same vein, modernization has also triggered an abandonment of Yorùbá traditional names. It used to be the case that children's names in Yorubaland followed the traditional occupation of their family or the family's deities. It was common to see children with names like Ifatunmbi, Ifayemi, Ogunmodede, Ayanyemisi, and many more. However, these names are now being abandoned and replaced with modern and Western names or those with connections to Christianity or Islam. Hence, it is not uncommon to now find names like Jesutunbi, a replacement for Ifatunbi, or Oluyemisi, a replacement for Ayanyemisi. There are even more common modern names like Fred, Collins, and Josh whose meaning cannot be situated within the Yorùbá epistemology but are being answered to by children of Yorùbá parents.

Furthermore, naming ceremonies that were once the purview of traditional priests are now being conducted by clerics of modern religions. Notably, traditional materials like salt, kola nut, and bitter kola in Yorùbá naming ceremonies are being gradually replaced with items such as money, water, the Bible or Quran, a pen, and a book. This transition symbolizes a conscious effort to disassociate from the Yorùbá Òrìṣà religion. Also, it reflects an aspiration for the newborn to grow up embracing knowledge and learning, particularly through Western education.

The effects of modernity on the Yorùbá religion have also been seen in the traditional structures put in place to nurture and train children both formally and informally. Notably, this has manifested in the reduction of local games that embody Yorùbá values used to correct or approve societal behaviors. Before in Yorubaland, there were series of tales by moonlight, where children gathered to listen to their elders express the history of their culture, share stories that were designed to teach the right paths to take as they grow up, and enforce good or disprove bad behaviors among them and in the society. These games helped to instill values and morals

---

59. Chitakure, *African Traditional Religion Encounters Christianity*.
60. Eze-Uzomaka and Oloidi, "Modernization and Its Effect on Cultural Heritage," 81–93.

in the children and even among the peers with whom they came in contact. It helped them have a working memory of their culture, Yorùbá proverbs, religions, history, and more.[61] However, it is no longer the case that these games are in place; they have now been replaced by computer games, cell phones, and other modern games, which have eradicated the values and morals that are characteristics of the traditional tales by moonlight games of the past. Today, children are left to learn only from what little their parents tell them about their culture and history, if any, and from what they can pick up from the religious and educational institutions around them.

While these changes have materialized in various ways, they are embedded in the working of the society; other impacts on the indigenous culture of Yorùbá people are more outwardly visible, such as their mode of appearance. It used to be the case that Yorùbá people valued the ornamental adornment of their bodies with local and traditional materials, and these materials would have symbolic meaning within the community they were being used. It was common to promote Yorùbá traditions with dresses like *gbáríyẹ́*, *kaba*, *kẹ́ḿbẹ́*, *agbádá*, *sọ́ọ̀rọ́*, and many more. There were instances of tribal marks, body paintings, local bracelets, and hairstyles signifying the identity and affiliation of people in Yorubaland. For instance, hairstyles and modes of dressing were used to show the status and age of people in the community. This, however, is no longer the case. There has been a neglect of this ornamental adornment, body painting, traditional wear, and hairstyles for those inspired by modern lifestyles. Even though these changes represent a loss of value in the traditions of the community, they are also believed to promote excessive nudity and immoral lifestyles, which run contrary to what Yorùbá culture and its people stand for. Menial acts such as modes of greeting and respect have also been pruned among the youth. Prostrating and kneeling to greet elders by young men and women have been replaced with handshakes and the waving of hands in society. This is part of the fallout of modernization that Yorùbá culture has met, and these effects are rapidly eating deeper into the value systems of Yorùbá people.

Along this same line, another aspect of the effect of modernity on Yorùbá culture is on communication—both verbal and nonverbal. Yorùbá people have always devised ways of communicating covertly while ensuring that a third party not meant to receive the message does not understand. This has been done through various methods like fire, the sound of bells, and giving specific traditional items (*àrokò*) to the person for whom the message is intended.[62] For instance, in the Old Oyo Empire, where a calabash with parrot eggs was sent to the Aláàfin, it signified both the rejection of the Aláàfin by the gods and the people and a command to vacate the throne. It was also the case that others were given instructions, corrections, and advice through proverbs while speaking to the person intended to get the message. These served as a strong means of communication among the Yorùbá, and they embroidered the Yorùbá culture. These acts demonstrated a delicacy and a philosophy of community so as not to impose rudeness or distaste among members of society. This attitude and practice have changed as communication expectations have evolved to be quick, direct, and acceptable over devices rather than through face-to-face contact. Modernization has led to the neglect of many of these means of

---

61. Ajila and Olowu, "Games and Early Childhood in Nigeria," 137–147.
62. Ògúndèjí, "Communicative and Semiotic Contexts of Àrokò," 145–156.

communication, as they are now being replaced with social media for individual and communal purposes.

There is also the abandonment of traditional professions for modern jobs. Professions like farming, weaving, blacksmithing, divination, hunting, archery, and many more that require the application of indigenous technologies and skills are now considered archaic and are largely neglected for roles in urban societies. Children and youth are discouraged from apprenticeship and advised to search for white-collar jobs in urban communities. As these traditional sources of material gathering and skill learning are eroded, so are the fruits of these labors, such as food preparation, clothing, weapons, and other ancestral products and practices. With the adoption of modern and urban lifestyles, there is most prominently the abandonment of indigenous delicacies, which are nutritious and significant in the Yorùbá culture. The replacement for these delicacies is fast food and canned products, which have a history of triggering different health issues. These serve as reinforcements of the capitalist lifestyles, through an emphasis on feeding individual people and less communal settings, as well as encouraging modern work lives that do not permit or encourage people to take time to cook or benefit their health in their chase for profit.

It can be concluded that global transactional flows have had various effects on indigenous Yorùbá culture. How these flows interact reinforces many concepts instituted under the colonial rule of Yorubaland, which have also benefited its inhabitants and continue to negatively impact their quality of life. It is critical, however, to draw attention to the application of such modern practices, especially those that seek to destroy the core of the Yorùbá culture. In effect, this is a necessary step to evaluate and understand the evolution and survival of various traditional beliefs and practices and enable scholars and the like to educate and explain the detriment posed by such circumstances.

Conclusion

Yorùbá and modernity have exposed us to the structural breakdown characterized by the application of modern thoughts and ideologies in Yorùbá communities. It has also exposed us to how it is possible to sustain cultural practices or improve them through the scientific and technological advancement of modernity. At this crossroad, however, what is important is the continuous progress of Yorùbá people. Progress within Yorùbá communities will naturally demand two actions: The first is changing and adopting or abandoning some traditional thoughts and behaviors. The second is adapting to or borrowing contemporary ideas from other cultures. However, it is important to advance the need for caution. While modernity unarguably brings advancement in science and technology, its quick and easy adoption should not be used to measure progress among the Yorùbá people. It is not entirely true that the most successful societies are those basking in the behaviors and thought characteristics of modernity. It appears that to the Yorùbá people, traditional life and ideas have more to offer in the aspect of values and morals as they make their way around the maze created by modernity. Hence, it becomes critical to allow the adoption of modern thoughts, behaviors, and ideas after subjecting them to values and morals that guide Yorùbá people and their communities; only then can these elements lead Yorùbá people toward solutions to contemporary issues.

Colonialism and the Yorùbá 13

The consolidation of the Yorùbá as a distinct identity—possessing its narratives, logic, rhetoric, and understanding—is also historically tied to the empire-building strategies of colonial Europe. In colonial and postcolonial Africa, European interests facilitated cultural conquest and economic plunder by pushing to homogenize "native" cultures. This encouraged a mythmaking process that was foundational for the construction of ethnic identities in Africa.[1] By exploiting these ethnic differences for economic advantage, the colonial order left unstable foundations for national progress in the postcolonial years.[2]

Ethnicity can be conceived as a group of people consciously defining themselves and forging common identities through notions of shared ancestry and solidarity across kinship lines. Although ethnicity can be artificially constructed, it can also legitimize identities proposed by various subgroups that acknowledge mutual connections, including religion, language, history, or oral traditions. Oluwaseyi Oyekan notes that the conception of ethnicity opens the door for exploitable flexibility, allowing "a limitless claim to ethnicity by various groups."[3] This flexibility supported the mythmaking efforts of Nigeria's earliest ethnic nationalists, following earlier examples set by the colonizers, which rallied loyalists to dominant ethnic groups in a newly independent country.

This flexibility also allows present-day Yorùbá subgroups to identify as Yorùbá. The influences of intergroup contact and migration, along with the common dynamic trajectory of cultural development in a multiculturalist environment, have led to some similarities in the forging of newly constructed identities. The Yorùbá, as a distinct identity, has emerged from several pockets of commonality that exist between various groups to present a holistic uniformity.

It is also possible that the politicized rhetoric and strategic mobilizations of the colonial period led to the "permanency" and legitimacy of the Yorùbá as an identity. Many Yorùbá emerged as nationalist and ethnocultural leaders, particularly after colonialism, during the demands for independence and in Nigeria's First and Second Republics. Even during the nineteenth century, it is possible to identify this ideological unification at work. One example is the

---

1. Oyekan, "Mythmaking, Identity Formation," 2.

2. Oyekan, "Mythmaking, Identity Formation," 2.

3. Oyekan, "Mythmaking, Identity Formation," 2.

rise of Ibadan after the waning of the Old Oyo Empire. Ibadan's tremendous political power, its military might, and its victories against invading Fulani from Ilorin established the political groundwork for a cultural Yorùbá identity to develop.[4]

Ibadan rose to prominence in the 1830s. As Bolanle Awe notes, its prominence is attributable to "confused conditions consequent upon this event [crisis]," along with Ibadan's opportunistic "ability to exploit the situation."[5] The Fulani of Ilorin had invaded northern Yorubaland, and the Old Oyo Empire was no longer able to protect its territory. Ibadan's success at repelling Ilorin attacks, which recovered some towns that the Fulani had captured, led to a cultural camaraderie that was born from the exigency of survival. To quote Awe,

> The Yoruba [the different and independent city-states] themselves were tired of a life of sudden raids and surprise attacks; they were therefore ready for a stable peace and would willingly support Ibadan's move to secure this. Moreover, there was at the back of their minds an awareness of a common bond binding them together; the Oyo-Yoruba in particular were anxious to preserve what was left of their country and to revive the Oyo-Yoruba community such as had existed in the Old Oyo Empire. . . . Indeed the move to effect permanent peace and unity within Yoruba country through the agency of Ibadan had many supporters in the Oyo-Yoruba world . . .[6]

Awe uses the term *Oyo–Yoruba* in a political context, identifying the existing belief that the Oyo–Yoruba were a form of proto-Yoruba. However, there was an implicit awareness of a connection between the Yorùbá's independent subgroups, which made it more practical to unite against an external threat.

In the Yorùbá world, the tussle for leadership between Ibadan, Ijaye, Egba, and Ijebu implied an existing relationship. However, the relationship had been established by contemporary groups that shared an understanding of which leadership claims could be made or fought for. The development of a present-day Yorùbá identity—the blueprints for ideas that were cultivated and enacted by nationalist leaders championing the Yorùbá cause and the framework that drove their campaigns to success—relied partly on patterns of mobilization that were inherited from the colonizers.[7]

The Yorùbá now have enough of a national and international presence to discuss the Yorùbá diaspora, identifying Yorùbá heritage that exists in Dahomey and other parts of West Africa. As discussed in part 1 of this book, Yorùbá influence spread across the Atlantic to the Caribbean Islands and parts of the Americas. The growth of this presence makes it worth considering how colonialism influenced the formation of Yorùbá.

More importantly, cosmopolitanism has set itself as a mode of cultural survival and interculturality among nations of the world, which carries implications and tenors of Euro-American imperialist tendencies. It is important to understand how colonialism plays residual roles in the identities that the Yorùbá have created for themselves. Euro-American or Western modernity,

---

4. Law, "West African Cavalry State," 1–15.

5. Awe, "Ajele System," 47.

6. Awe, "Ajele System," 47.

7. Okwudiba, *Ethnic Politics in Nigeria*. See also Mbah and Mwangu, "Sub-Ethnic Conflicts in Nigeria," 681–688.

which itself is steeped in colonial modernity, has left threads of influence linking colonialism with the formation and maintenance of Yorùbá identities. Identity and culture are perpetually unfinished products—they are in a continual process of refinement—and the Yorùbá have defined culture in fluid ways to capture their lived experiences.

Colonial Conquests as Global Forces

The Yorubaland that extended across almost all of present-day Nigeria's southwestern region served as a major gateway for establishing colonial influence in Nigeria. The Yorùbá were a major point of contact for acquiring and selling slaves through the notorious transatlantic trade, exploiting Africa's material and human resources.[8] Badagry and other ports were popular slave markets operated by Nigerian intermediaries, which linked coastal areas with the hinterlands. Other groups and ethnicities, including northern Yorùbá groups, had noted these activities; Mohammed Bello of Sokoto referred to them as "Yarba" who captured slaves from the north and sold them to Christians in the south.[9]

The British Empire's acquisition of Yorùbá territory is a story of global invasion, products from the industrial revolution used to subdue Yorùbá people, and treaties that introduced the conventions of written documents and diplomacy with the mechanisms of duplicity and betrayal. During this process, local authorities aligned with the forces of global imperialism. The process narrated the use of force, the language of domination, and shifts in the motivations of wars—in the nineteenth century, armed conflict transformed from Yorùbá activity linked with state formation to become conquests that incorporated the territory into Britain's sea-based empire of modernization.

After the British government positioned naval patrols along the West African coast, especially around Fernando Po,[10] John Beecroft was appointed to oversee their operations. The activity was not limited to patrols—the British government sought to extend its influence into Africa and replace the slave trade with more "legitimate" commerce. In 1849, Beecroft supervised the expansion of British political and economic interests in Fernando Po, Lagos, and other West African societies along the coast.[11] Another consul was appointed to manage the British government's interests in Lagos to support these efforts. Missionaries rapidly established outposts in the surrounding territory, and the British government built its influence in what is now known as Nigeria.

British activity continued into the Niger Delta region, opposing the slave trade. Around 1836, British officials came into conflict with cities along the Bonny River after arresting several slave ships, including four Spanish vessels.[12] Residents still regarded the slave trade as a lucrative source of income, and they were outraged by these actions. Despite this opposition, the British government gained influence in other cities along the coast and extended into more

---

8. M'baye, "Economic, Political, and Social Impact," 607–622.

9. Apter, "Yoruba Ethnogenesis from Within," 356–387.

10. Sundiata, *From Slaving to Neoslavery.*

11. Mulligan, "Nigeria, the British Presence in West Africa," 273–301.

12. Mbaeyi, "British Navy," 211–228.

Figure 13.1. "Monogamy," by Moses Ogunleye. One of the changes of the era was the formation of a new Western-educated elite that took to the idea of monogamy while retaining the values of extended families.

336

remote regions, supported by treaties secured through force and conquest.[13] British influence grew among coastal Yorùbá communities and spread to internal regions. Explorers and Christian missionaries also supported the British government's penetration of Yorubaland. When these forces arrived at Badagry in 1842, their activities extended toward Abeokuta over the next four years, from where they made inroads into other Yorùbá subgroups.

The British Empire was officially working to abolish the slave trade, and that was their justification for using force to support their political interests in West Africa. The British annexation of Lagos in 1951 was a significant step for British colonialism among the Yorùbá. Many Yorùbá settlements, especially Lagos, had been troubled by local instability that provided a foothold for British colonial rule. British colonialists exploited an existing dispute between local leaders, Kosoko and Akintoye, to consolidate their authority.[14]

Kosoko had driven Akintoye to Badagry and gained sole control of Lagos. Under Kosoko's authority, Lagos continued trading slaves, and its policies were hostile to Egba immigrants and British traders. In Badagry, public sentiment was divided between Akintoye and Kosoko, which the British used to their advantage. By fostering dissent, the British could undermine Kosoko, his support for the slave trade, and his opposition to British officials and traders.[15]

Britain allied with Akintoye, and its bombardment of Lagos instigated a civil war followed by an intervention from the British navy.[16] The initial resistance from Kosokó and his men was strong, but Beecroft intensified the attacks on Lagos beginning December 26, 1851. Kosoko was eventually deposed and sought refuge in Epe. Afterward, British officials made Akintoye sign treaties that established Lagos as a British colony in 1861.[17]

Through Beecroft and other officials, the British Empire extended into other areas, including Abeokuta. Britain's influence among the Egba was strengthened by the dynamics between Lagos, the Egba, and the immigration issues that had festered under Kosokó. Missionary activities also opened new pathways for establishing British influence in Abeokuta. Other Yorùbá subgroups had been menacing Abeokuta and the Egba, which made them more receptive to the idea of European intervention.[18] Beecroft and Townsend signed agreements with local chiefs to oppose slavery, which provided opportunities for British intervention in Egba affairs whenever those agreements were violated.[19] These interventions not only allowed the British to influence the affairs of the Egba but also created new opportunities for missionaries and European traders in Egbaland.

The agreements signed by the Egba and their chieftains were carefully prepared traps by Townsend and Beecroft. These leaders desperately needed arms and ammunition to defend against the Dahomey attacks of 1850–1851. Agreements with Britain could also allow the Egba to access trade in Lagos while retaining their independence, allowing them to secure additional

---

13. Mbaeyi, "British Navy," 211–228.

14. Ikime, "Colonial Conquest and Resistance," 251–270.

15. Ikime, "Colonial Conquest and Resistance," 251–270.

16. Ikime, "Colonial Conquest and Resistance," 251–270.

17. Adekoya, "Succession Dispute," 207–226.

18. Davies, "Political Economy of the Egba Nation," 74–101.

19. Ikime, "Colonial Conquest and Resistance," 251–270.

support.[20] The Egba were allowed to maintain political and economic independence if they cooperated with the British and the missionaries.

The illusory independence of the Egba was tested when political tumult surfaced in 1897; Egba leadership found itself at odds with the British government. Lagos governor Sir Henry McCallum needed Egba leadership to acknowledge the British political structure that had been established. As a result, the Egba United Government was established. The Aláké headed this government, and different kings and rulers from various towns became members of its council. Other prominent leaders from Muslim and Christian communities were also council members.[21]

Ibadan was another Yorùbá city subjected to colonial rule. Its transformation was driven by internal and external factors. Migrating warlords had displaced Ibadan's original Egba occupants and drove them to settle in Abeokuta. As Ibadan grew in strength, it became a source of concern for its neighbors. However, it successfully fended off challenges from the surrounding towns to expand its sphere of influence. The growth of Ibadan was so dramatic that the settlement was called the "London of Negroland," estimated by Alvan Millson, the assistant colonial secretary at the time, to contain one hundred thousand residents.[22] Ibadan also developed political and social structures that would influence future events.

Ibadan's military foundation was an integral part of its state formation—existing simultaneously as a source of strength and a potential weakness in its engagements with colonial powers. The political and military conflicts within Ibadan also played out in its social and familial interactions; chiefs imposed military values and mindsets on their families. Their war experience and desire for respect in civilian life added to Ibadan's internal political tensions.[23]

Ibadan's civil disorder created an opportunity for the British government. Ibadan chiefs signed a coercive treaty with the British in August 1893, ostensibly to end regional wars and promote peace in the Yorùbá region. This agreement fully incorporated Ibadan under the British administration. After that, the British Empire monitored the western outposts and outskirts of Ibadan with its constabulary of Hausa soldiers.[24] These agreements did not initially pacify the chiefs of Ibadan—they saw the armed conflict as their primary occupation in the region.

Balogun Akintola believed that the agreement with the British was a mere formality.[25] However, the Royal Niger Company responded to his disposition and his refusal to claim the title of Baálẹ̀ for a second time by annihilating Ilorin's forces and bringing the settlement under its direct control.[26] The ambitions of Ibadan's chiefs were cut short; they no longer needed to wage war, and a change of occupation was necessary for their survival. After these developments, the British government continued to increase its influence in the eastern part of the region.[27]

---

20. Byfield, "Taxation, Women, and the Colonial State," 250–277.

21. Byfield, "Taxation, Women, and the Colonial State," 250–277.

22. Watson, "Murder and the Political Body," 25–48.

23. Watson, "'Ibadan – A Model of Historical Facts,'" 5–26.

24. Watson, "'Ibadan – A Model of Historical Facts,'" 5–26.

25. Akinyele, *Ìwé Ìtàn Ìbàdàn* (Exeter: James Townsend, 1959).

26. Akinyele, *Ìwé Ìtàn Ìbàdàn*.

27. Watson, "Murder and the Political Body," 25–48.

A similar tactic was applied with the Ekiti and Ijesa, who had been in an enduring war with Ibadan. The Ekiti Parapọ̀ War was a notorious war of attrition that had been raging without victory or compromise.[28] The British assumed the role of peacemakers, preparing a treaty and compelling the warring parties to sign documents that placed them under the authority of the British governor in Lagos.[29] British officials subsequently appointed a resident officer in charge of the Ekiti-Ijesa axis in 1897. The Ekiti and Ijesa were fully brought under Britain's authority in 1910.[30]

Battles between the Ijebu and Egba prevented the British from engaging the Ekiti and Ijesa further. Sixteen years of war and confrontations between the Ijebu and Egba, which had begun in 1879, had taken their toll.[31] The Ijebu did not have a good relationship with the Europeans, and their position was clear: they opposed the missionaries and all European activities. British officials needed to address Ijebu hostility and end resistance against Lagos. Ijebu trade routes were important for extending British influence to the east, and missionary activities were only allowed in Ijebu territory after 1889.[32]

Concern over the Ijebu treatment of missionaries became an underlying factor that eventually invited a British military expedition.[33] Although James Johnson had persuaded Awùjalẹ́ Túnwàṣe to open routes for missionary travel, they were charged £50 and later compelled to travel through Oyo. Acting Governor Denton visited the Ijebu in 1891, but he was met with hostility, and they refused to discuss trade routes.[34] British officials were embarrassed and insulted, which they would not tolerate.

A British reaction was inevitable after Carter was appointed governor of Lagos in 1982; he supported an aggressive stance toward the Ijebu. Carter tested the pride of Awùjalẹ́ and demanded an apology for the insult to Acting Governor Denton, insisting that Ijebu delegates had to travel to Lagos. Although the Ijebu met Carter's demands, he also expected them to sign a treaty that allowed the British to use Ijebu trade routes without any charges or fees.[35] The Ijebu delegates, surprised by this request, refused to sign the treaty. However, Carter found other Ijebu who had settled in Lagos, compelled them to sign the treaty, and insisted that the document was binding.[36]

Carter's treaty was a one-sided agreement that was only intended to assist in dominating the Ijebu—it provided official justification for an Ijebu expedition in 1892.[37] Allegations of a broken agreement allowed the British to forcibly open Ijebu trade routes, expand Britain's political power, and allow missionary activities in areas where they had previously been embarrassed.

---

28. Ikime, "Colonial Conquest and Resistance," 251–270.

29. Ikime, "Colonial Conquest and Resistance," 251–270.

30. Akintoye, *Revolution and Power Politics*.

31. Ikime, "Colonial Conquest and Resistance," 251–270.

32. Ikime, "Colonial Conquest and Resistance," 251–270.

33. Oguntomisin, "Impact of the Ijebu Expedition," 1–12.

34. Ikime, "Colonial Conquest and Resistance," 251–270.

35. Ikime, "Colonial Conquest and Resistance," 251–270.

36. Ikime, "Colonial Conquest and Resistance," 251–270.

37. Inyang and Bassey, "Imperial Treaties," 19–46.

The Ijebu mounted stubborn resistance with around ten thousand soldiers,[38] but they were defeated by the sophisticated machine guns, rifles, and maxim guns of the British forces.

The British could not completely control Yorubaland until the renowned Oyo Empire, now considerably diminished in size, was brought under their administration. British efforts to control Oyo began with a set of treaty agreements. By the time the British colonizers arrived, Oyo had lost much of its initial influence to internal and external challenges. Oyo had endured a sixteen-year war, the Dahomey attack of Oke-Ogun, Ilorin's activities in Iseyin, and the growing strength of its former vassal Ibadan.[39] The Aláàfin of Oyo had been weakened to the point that he was eager for peace; he could no longer raise sufficient forces to oppose Ibadan, Dahomey, or Ilorin.

In the face of these realities, Aláàfin Adeyemi I formed an allegiance with the missionaries without any intent to propagate the Christian religion. The Aláàfin wanted to use the global forces of Christianity and colonialism to resolve the struggles for dominance between Yorùbá city-states. The hope was that Britain would drive off Dahomey and Ilorin while keeping the powers of Ibadan in check. British officials did not directly fulfill these ambitions but introduced three treaties that stabilized the situation.[40]

In 1886, missionaries and British officials introduced a treaty that enforced peace in the region.[41] The Aláàfin and other regional leaders signed the agreement. In 1888, Governor Moloney of Lagos presented another treaty to bind the Aláàfin exclusively to Britain—if any other European powers sought a treaty with the Aláàfin, they would need to obtain permission from Lagos. In 1893, the British officials attempted to make Oyo into a proper British Protectorate; the Aláàfin signed a third treaty that ceded powers to British officials.[42]

Despite these treaties, Aláàfin Adeyemi believed his sovereignty would continue without interruption. On the other hand, British officials were determined to demonstrate their complete control over the Aláàfin and waited for the right opportunity. This opportunity came in the form of an incident that occurred in Òkèihò, which the Aláàfin resolved in accordance with long-standing cultural obligations.[43] The Aláàfin dispensed justice using laws and customs that had been in effect since before the arrival of the colonialists.

The British used the Òkèihò incident to ridicule the Aláàfin and place him under constraints that diminished the prestige of his office. When the Aláàfin refused to accept this treatment, British authorities commenced the bombardment of Oyo in 1895, using the disregard of their treaties as a justification. Military force humiliated Oyo and took control of its empire. Oyo and the Aláàfin resisted, but they could not oppose British artillery. The Aláàfin fled the palace and realized he was powerless before the British.[44]

<hr>

38. Smith, "Nigeria-Ijebu," 179–184.

39. Akintoye, *Revolution and Power Politics*.

40. Ikime, "Colonial Conquest and Resistance," 251–270.

41. Awe, "End of an Experiment," 221–230.

42. Adegbite, "One in Heart," 105–122.

43. Ayandele, "Mode of British Expansion," 22–43.

44. Ikime, "Colonial Conquest and Resistance," 251–270.

Oyo's bombardment had disgraced a legendary seat of power and diminished all the glories it had accumulated.[45] As discussed in chapter 5, before its internal and external crises, Oyo was a force to reckon with; it existed as an enduring political power that controlled other subregions. Oyo was a great empire with many warriors, formidable societies, and respected customs. British weaponry had rendered it obsolete. The Aláàfin ultimately decided to join the British government, allowing colonial rule to be established in Oyo. This was a new phase of politics for the Oyo people. The Aláàfin, "Ìkejì Òrìṣà," was now a subject of the colonial government. This was a humbling reversal for an empire that had colonized settlements and demanded tributes.[46]

The British continued to assert dominance over Yorubaland through treaties and military bombardments.[47] In 1906, they declared that the entire area—presently known as southern Nigeria—would be known as the Southern Protectorate. It later became part of a larger body during the 1914 amalgamation, establishing Nigeria as a single colony under the control of the British government.[48] The British introduced an indirect rule system that exploited preexisting institutions and structures for their colonial administration.

The Yorùbá during Colonialism: Roles and Relevance

The colonial government intended to accumulate political strength and economic power to gain a competitive edge against other colonizing powers. The slave trade had ended, but European proponents of legitimate trade remained focused on Africa's abundant resources. Europeans could develop new markets for their products by colonizing Africa while profitably extracting raw materials. The British government in West Africa looked for a cost-efficient way to accomplish these goals, which leveraged the political and social systems already in place.

The British system of indirect rule provided an answer to the issue the British described as the "Native Question."[49] In answering this question, Lord Lugard introduced a system of colonial administration that exploited traditional institutions and systems of government in Africa. The Yorùbá participated in colonial governance through the indirect rule system, assuming roles and responsibilities under the colonial administration. Yorùbá "Native Chiefs" controlled Yorubaland, exerting their authority under the directives and discretion of the colonial government.[50] In Oyo and other parts of Yorubaland, the British government established councils of chiefs. The Oyo Council of Chiefs was composed of the resident, the Aláàfin, and seven other chiefs that administered their people under British rule. A similar council was set up in Ibadan that also held authority over Ife-Ilésà. In 1900, councils were formed for the Ekiti and Ilésà. The Ọwá of Ilésà and other chiefs served on their council, and Ekiti had about fifteen chiefs that were regarded as top-tier kings for their council.[51]

---

45. Folayan, "Egbado and the Expansion of British Power," 70.

46. Adeyeri, "Colonialism Within and Without," 227–245.

47. Folayan, "Egbado and the Expansion of British Power," 70.

48. Eric, "Amalgamation of Nigeria," 66–68.

49. Mamdani, "Indirect Rule," 145–150.

50. Iyer, "Direct versus Indirect Colonial Rule in India," 693–713.

51. Atanda, "New Oyo Empire."

Native authorities and their councils became more important after Sir William MacGregor argued that their jurisdiction should be extended to other, smaller towns.[52] This was followed by the Native Councils Ordinance of 1901, which gave more autonomy to Native Chiefs.[53] As the role of native authorities became more influential over the years, more Yorùbá leaders were included in their administrative activities.

The Yorùbá were politically relevant and major proponents of the Christian faith that gradually changed the social structure of Nigerian society. This relationship dates to the annexation of Lagos, which established colonial rule in Nigeria. The Yorùbá were involved in several movements that spread Christianity throughout Nigerian territory. Their efforts included the leadership of Bishop Ajayi Crowther and Yorùbá, who served as converts, evangelists, and bishops that established new Christian communities in Nigeria.[54] The spread of Christianity in Lagos, its growth in Badagry, and its acceptance in Abeokuta were integral to the influences it exerted over social orders of the time. Yorùbá converts were key drivers for the creation of *Aládúrà* churches, which showed a local acceptance of the Christian faith and the belief that the Christian God could solve all their problems.[55] Although Yorùbá Christians eagerly accepted the ideas of miracles and healing according to biblical teachings, their understanding differed from that of the missionaries who had taught them.[56] Christianity was more widely accepted in the southern part of Nigeria.

The concentration of colonial activity in Lagos and southern parts of Nigeria meant that the Yorùbá were a primary source of labor for British officials. By assuming new roles as clerks and office assistants, the Yorùbá quickly claimed important roles in the colonial administration.[57] They were also instrumental in retrieving commercial goods from the colony's more remote regions for export. Yorùbá individuals were an important part of Nigeria's educational development.[58] During the colonial period, educational institutions were often established in the southwestern territories. The Yorùbá were not completely cooperative with these processes— they opposed various colonial policies. However, missionary efforts in southwestern Nigeria led to establishment of secondary schools. Tertiary education, offered by Yaba College[59] and University College Ibadan, also gave Yorubaland an educational advantage.[60]

Efforts toward Independence

Nigeria's struggles for independence were an ongoing effort that predated the 1960 attainment of self-rule. The battle for independence was waged through various forms of resistance

---

52. Atanda, "New Oyo Empire."
53. Perham, *Lugard*, 445.
54. Barnes, "Samuel Ajayi Crowther."
55. Ray, "Aladura Christianity," 266–291.
56. Dairo, "Christianity and Healing."
57. Derrick, "'Native Clerk,'" 61–74.
58. Akinwale, "Yoruba Traditional Education System," 141.
59. Hargreaves, "Idea of a Colonial University," 26–36.
60. Hargreaves, "Idea of a Colonial University," 26–36.

Figure 13.2. "Misinterpretation," by Dr. Kazeem Ekeolu. A new generation of Yorùbá scholars began to reinterpret the colonial interpretation of their cultural practices, arguing that outsiders had misunderstood their people and cultures.

mounted by different Nigerians. Yorùbá leaders forcibly opposed the colonization of their territory; Yorùbá societies were not ready to cede their powers to foreigners and become second-class citizens in their own country. Kosoko resisted the establishment of British authority in Lagos, and other Yorùbá leaders—including those in Ijebu, Ibadan, and Oyo—also fought to oppose colonial authority over their lands and trade routes. Although these leaders fought to retain their sovereignty and refused to compromise their independence, they lacked the military strength to oppose British forces. They eventually succumbed to unfair treaties and military conquest, but they should be counted among Nigeria's earliest nationalists.

Other Nigerian citizens demanded independence in response to unfavorable policies and unjust taxation. The 1918 Adubi Uprising opposed heavy taxation in Egbaland and the British exploitation of free labor.[61] The protestors demanded that British officials recognize local sovereignty, allowing communities to return to their original social structures. Early nationalist efforts were demands for independence, but they saw little success. Nigerian self-rule was eventually attained through more constructive struggles for independence by educated Nigerians, including the Yorùbá, who had been exposed to other cultural approaches. The introduction of higher education, Nigerian participation in both world wars, and exposure to European cultures nurtured a sophistication among Nigerians that led to successful demands for independence. The Yorùbá were a major component of these efforts.

Political consciousness was a major driver of Nigerian independence. Nigeria's educated elite, including the Yorùbá, knew that the public needed to understand the political environment. People needed to understand how and why they should speak against colonialism with a single voice, and this education required political consciousness. During the colonial era, this consciousness was mainly achieved through newspapers. The press served as a public consciousness, narrating colonial activities and discussing the impact of policies from Nigerian perspectives.

Lagos and Yorubaland were hubs for Nigerian media and press outlets circulating political information. This was facilitated by the concentration of colonial activity in Lagos, providing information and insights into government activities. Nigeria's first newspaper, founded by Reverend Henry Townsend, was Ìwé Ìròhìn. It was established in Abeokuta in 1859, and it reported the activities of British officials and discussed British history and heritage in Nigeria.[62] The newspaper was written in Yorùbá and was published twice a month, providing a summary of national events and colonial activities with a focus on Christianity.

Ìwé Ìròhìn did not do much to advance the cause of nationalist activism; it mainly propagated British commercialization, politics, and Christianity.[63] It was later challenged by the establishment of an Anglo-African newspaper, which was also actively distributed among the Yorùbá, publicizing the various injustices and activities of the colonial government.[64] The *Lagos Times*, *Gold Coast Colony Advertiser*, *Lagos Observer*, and *Lagos Standard* were other newspapers that nurtured a Nigerian political consciousness. These publications expanded the media landscape by providing information for colonizers, Nigerians, and Lagos residents.[65] These newspapers redefined Nigeria's political environment and enabled social change, providing early support for West Africa's most influential nationalist movements.

Nigerian newspapers publicly called for constitutional development in 1914 and provided ongoing updates on these efforts and the governance processes in their country.[66] The importance of these newspapers encouraged additional Nigerian publications, many of which were owned and operated by the Yorùbá. Newspapers successfully encouraged the development

---

61. NAI. CSO 26/3, File No. 21790, Assessment Report, Imala District, Abeokuta Province. January 4, 1928–March 2, 1928.

62. Enemugwem, "Impact of the Lagos Press," 13–24.

63. Enemugwem, "Impact of the Lagos Press," 13–24.

64. Enemugwem, "Impact of the Lagos Press," 13–24.

65. Enemugwem, "Impact of the Lagos Press," 13–24.

66. Enemugwem, "Impact of the Lagos Press," 13–24.

of political consciousness among the Nigerian people. The Yorùbá-educated elite was part of different movements and organizations that began calling for greater Nigerian participation in governance. These efforts began in 1914, and they later fought for complete independence— their efforts intensified in the 1940s.[67] One such organization was the Nigerian National Democratic Party, founded by Herbert Macaulay (Olayinka Badmus Macaulay) in 1923. The party influenced the political environment in Lagos and worked to secure council seats in Lagos at different levels of government.[68]

The Nigerian Youth Movement, originally known as the Lagos Youth Movement, was another group that demanded greater Nigerian representation and encouraged political development within the country.[69] After the MacPherson Constitution laid the foundation for regionalism in Nigeria, the Yorùbá established the Action Group to serve as a political party and as a platform to work toward ending colonialism in Nigeria.[70] These groups mobilized Nigerians, especially in Lagos, to pressure British officials, and their efforts ultimately led to Nigeria's independence.

Colonial Influence on the Yorùbá

Yorùbá culture is a fluid confluence of internal and external forces. The very idea of tradition among the Yorùbá is ambiguous, involving a generative openness.[71] Yai, in describing these, conceives of àṣà as "the set of behaviours, deeds, and habits that characterize it after it has been subjected to a historical process of deliberate choice."[72] This deliberate choice is a process of selecting, rejecting, and negotiating historical precedence and all it has to offer. This process can be idiosyncratic, and it can be a receptacle, a conduit, or a product of external cultural influences.

To cite David Doris, tradition "denotes an empowering repetition of historical precedence," but it also "entails a moment of difference or departure from that precedence."[73] This ambiguity, fidelity, and departure simultaneously define what tradition means for the individual and the community. Individual acts of fidelity, rejection, and compromise alter tradition in ways that can become accepted as conventions. To quote Doris fully, the ambiguity rests in the fact that the community's choices thus "constitute and transform the cultural field of 'tradition'; further, the historical authority of that tradition is perpetually being invoked in the present to justify acts of transformative choice."[74]

---

67. Ubaku, Emeh, and Anyikwa, "Impact of Nationalist Movement," 54–67.

68. Ubaku, Emeh, and Anyikwa, "Impact of Nationalist Movement," 54–67.

69. Ubaku, Emeh, and Anyikwa, "Impact of Nationalist Movement," 54–67.

70. Ubaku, Emeh, and Anyikwa, "Impact of Nationalist Movement," 54–67.

71. Yai, "Tradition and the Yoruba Artist," 32–36; Doris, "Unfunctioning Baby," 115–138; Adeeko, *Arts of Being Yorùbá*; and Afolayan, "Tunde Kelani and the Art of Being Yoruba," 1–13.

72. Yai, "Tradition and The Yoruba Artist."

73. Doris, "Unfunctioning Baby," 115–138.

74. Doris, "Unfunctioning Baby," 115–138.

Adeleke Adeeko proposes the idea that an openness rests at the core of Yorùbá culture, and Adeshina Afolayan explains this openness as flexibility that facilitates a relationship between tradition and creativity through deliberation. In this case, creativity is the ability to negotiate with historical precedent in ways that sustain, promote, or depart from the previously established to institute new norms. These acts draw from the charged atmosphere of continuity that ensures cultural longevity, channeling and bringing new aspects of culture into focus via creativity. Through its participants, Yorùbá culture opens up to other cultural influences, in whatever forms that Yorùbá people may channel them. Navigating this openness is where the vital flexibility lies—Afolayan sums it up by stating that culture or tradition for the Yorùbá "enables an openness, deriving from the sense of incompleteness, which facilitates the willingness to interact with and accommodate cultural others. The concept, in its fluidity, therefore makes it impossible for the Yoruba culture to be self-contained. *Àṣà* evolves even more cogently at the juncture where tradition engages creativity, especially for the Yoruba artist(e). Culture as an unfinished phenomenon would definitely have an implication for artistry and creativity as generative phenomena. The Yoruba understands tradition as a process of deliberate and voluntary 'picking' that cognitively involves the idea of creativity and even historical practices and awareness."[75]

Yorùbá people act as conductors who dictate the ebb and flow of culture as it emanates from experience. The newness of cultural contact that births, institutionalizes, or marginalizes new patterns of existence is normalized by the fact that it is performed every day. For the Yorùbá, culture is formed and maintained as a continuous process, even as it strives toward and achieves some measure of solidity within such fluidity. Cultural custodians add and subtract from the system and ensure fluidity—to the extent that they are cosmopolitan. The ambiguity Yai speaks of is a guarded acknowledgment of how culture maintains its integrity by being flexible enough to accommodate foreign influences. This flexibility and ambiguity affect the relationship between colonialism and the Yorùbá. Colonialism and its afterlives influenced the Yorùbá world, and the nature of the relationship between the Yorùbá and colonialism can be identified within the dominant features of African pre- and postcolonial history. This offers insights into the ambiguity and flexibility at the heart of Yorùbá identity and culture.

Trade between Europe and the Yorùbá existed in several forms from the fifteenth century—including the notorious transatlantic slave trade. However, it was not until the nineteenth century that colonialism spread to the southwestern Yorùbá territories as an institutionalized form of cultural contact and multiculturalism. Colonialism differed from other forms of cultural contact in Yorùbá history, most notably in the manner and intensity of the changes it brought. In the 1800s, before the arrival of the colonialists, Yorùbá city-states like Ibadan primarily traded agricultural goods. Ibadan also had weavers, tailors, tanners, blacksmiths, and various organized industries that processed food for consumption and trade.[76]

Yorùbá nation-states also traded palm oil, which was exported in exchange for merchandise like guns and ammunition. Awe observes that the weaponry was "all imported items, which

---

75. Afolayan, "Tunde Kelani and the Art of Being Yorùbá," 1–13.
76. Awe, "Militarism and Economic Development," 65–77.

came from the coast, mainly through the Ijebu and Egba countries, to Ibadan. The demand for these firearms stimulated, in particular, the production of palm oil, which, in the era of legitimate trade, became the main trade good exchanged between West Africa and Europe."[77] Rum, textiles, and salt were also traded between these West African precolonial nations and the Coast, often exchanged for livestock, shea butter, and the enslaved.[78] It was a two-sided relationship between colonizing nations in Europe and colonized nations in Africa.

The relationship between Yorùbá textile markets and Western cloth manufacturers was another instance of commerce facilitating cultural contact. The history of Yorùbá garments and their design choices show a degree of mutual influence with European cultures and their economies.[79] To quote Steiner, "The textile trade between Europe and Africa in the 19th and early 20th centuries was a back-and-forth process in which European textile producers responded to African desires, and in which African consumers reacted to European stylistic and commercial proffers."[80] Cultural contact at the level of clothing choices facilitated a symbiotic relationship between different cultures and fostered a degree of multiculturalism. Multiculturalism itself is a synonym for cultural flows and interflows beyond local or territorialized boundaries. When one culture's sartorial tradition influences the economy of another, it provides an impetus for creativity in both groups, which has subsequent effects on demand and supply.

Steiner's perspective not only acknowledges the flows and interflows between cultures but also uses these dynamics to negate the narrative that African cultures had a one-way relationship with Europe. Some accounts incorrectly position African cultures solely as receiving and being influenced by Europe. However, European cloth makers—and their related European economies—were affected by the aesthetic and stylistic influences of Yorùbá tastes. By articulating this contribution, Steiner establishes the role of the Yorùbá in a global cultural process, furthering a narrative of their participation in a global economy. This is merely one example of such interactions and their contributions to the narrative of precolonial and colonial Yorùbá contact with a globalizing world.

Several other forms of trade-driven cultural contact existed between southwestern Nigeria and Europe. These were mostly mutually beneficial, but colonialism introduced a new format for cultural contact. The incursion and subsequent institution of colonialism in modern-day southwestern Nigeria, the homeland of the Yorùbá, was openly imperialistic. The arrival of the colonizers and their aggressive agenda for colonization had several implications for the self-perception of the Yorùbá and their perception in the global arena. The forces of colonization calcified connections that were forming in a Pan-Yorùbá identity, uniting disparate or different ethnic subgroups under a single identity. This development was a consequence of efforts to repel or preclude external invasion, and it was encouraged to assist imperialist schemes.[81] Mythmaking proved to be useful in these efforts.

---

77. Awe, "Militarism and Economic Development," 65–77.

78. Awe, "Militarism and Economic Development," 65–77.

79. Steiner, "Another Image of Africa," 91–110. See also Oyeniyi, *Dress in the Making of African Identity*.

80. Steiner, "Another Image of Africa," 91.

81. Falola, *Falola Reader*.

Figure 13.3. Chief Sunday Adeniyi Adegeye, popularly known as King Sunny Ade, is a foremost Nigerian *Juju* musician of Yorùbá descent who is regarded as the first Nigerian to be nominated for a Grammy and has collaborated musically with major international artists such as Stevie Wonder. Painting by Michael Efionayi.

British colonizers encouraged the unification of Yorùbá groups by inventing an origin myth that reframed existing narratives to position the Aláàfin of Oyo, the ruler of the Oyo, as the divinely recognized origin of the Yorùbá race. This had two advantages for the British: the myth made it easier to manage conflicting subgroups in the region so that they could be exploited economically, and it supported the British indirect rule system that allowed the Southwest to be controlled politically.[82] This cultural revisionism and mythmaking were crucial for the British. Oyekan explains that it provided a "single, cultural symbol of authority in alliance with which the colonialists expected to establish acceptance to their rule."[83] Oyekan also notes that this "invention of the myth of the Aláàfin occurred at a time when the powers of the Aláàfin had waned drastically, with Ibadan on the ascendancy. Ibadan had to be bypassed because it was a more recent settlement with little pedigree, founded by warriors, and of little mythological and historical value to colonial objectives."[84]

This strategic reframing of history also altered the Yorùbá identity in a global context. Not only did it build homogenized coalitions but it also provided the schematics for future associations, enabling a Pan-Yorùbá identity in the present. This is an optimistic interpretation of the prospects for this colonial invention—the colonial effort was not entirely in favor of creating a Pan-Yorùbá identity since the effort was neither altruistic nor undertaken to benefit the Yorùbá themselves. This reworking of history was solely for the colonizers' economic benefit.

Abiodun Afolabi has examined these activities vis-à-vis British taxation policy in Yorubaland, describing it as an economic strategy that sought out two outcomes: "to derive revenue for the mother country and to make the Crown Colony of Lagos and the Western Protectorate as financially self-sustaining as possible."[85] The goal of a self-sustaining colony was largely to reduce expenses for the British Crown, and the colonial mission itself was largely capitalist. Whatever benefits the Yorùbá reaped happened despite these policies and not because of them.

The British strategy hoped to provide stability by reframing historical legacies to benefit the colonizers. They worked to keep the peace between Yorùbá subgroups to enable exploitation and the plunder of their cultures. The colonizers also allowed enough instability and tension between rival groups to prevent them from creating a united opposition. In the long run, it was a stability that supported "divide and rule tactics" to undermine the burgeoning Yorùbá identity.

Colonizers profited from the export of farm produce and other natural resources. One such export was cocoa, which Yorùbá farmers produced for the international community. The United States was the largest consumer of cocoa, which facilitated an asymmetrical global interaction that was parasitic and exploitative. British authorities managed the exportation of cocoa for the benefit of British chocolate manufacturers, which revealed the monopolistic schemes of the imperial administration. For example, "the head of the British chocolate firm was the chairman of the Cocoa Board. While production was in the hands of the Africans, the marketing of cocoa in England, America and other countries was entirely in the hands of British merchants who

---

82. Falola, *Falola Reader*.

83. Oyekan, "Mythmaking, Identity Formation and Ethnic Nationalism," 12.

84. Oyekan, "Mythmaking, Identity Formation and Ethnic Nationalism," 12.

85. Afolabi, "Colonial Taxation Policy," 63.

formed a pool."[86] These arrangements created an international monopoly that cheated Yorùbá farmers out of their rightful compensation. Abiodun provides a clearer picture of the manipulation: "The Yoruba cocoa producers, like their counterparts in other West African economies, were forced to accept the lowest prices for their cocoa. The West African Cocoa Board was absolutely in the hands of the British officials and capitals. The African cocoa producer had no representation in the Board. In Western Nigeria, the Yoruba cocoa planter had become the victim in a tripartite relationship between the planters, the middlemen and the European firms."[87]

The colonial relationship between the British and the Yorùbá allowed the latter group to strengthen its presence in global markets, but this relationship was founded on the principles that established colonialism and indirect rule as systems of cultural appropriation, imperialism, and economic plunder.

The Yorùbá's global involvement was mostly cosmetic—more ornamental than beneficial. Regional benefits were a weak echo of the regional exploitation that occurred over the same period. The Nigeria Cocoa Marketing Board, which received its mandate in 1947, was inimical to those for whom it had ostensibly been created. Instead of working to benefit cocoa producers, it became a self-dealing instrument of control. The board channeled a share of export profits into its coffers, reducing the amount that farmers earned on the sale of their produce. The board also flouted its mandate to "keep in trust for the producers" the "difference between world prices (less government export and produce duties, freight etc.) and prices guaranteed by the Board, which constituted its surplus."[88] The income that cocoa producers received from global markets was a minor fraction of the total revenues. Abiodun has astutely observed that "the degree of exploitation was intense and the Board had subtly assumed the role of a tax collector."[89]

Colonial control strategies may have elevated the awareness of African cultures, like that of the Yorùbá, but it was done exploitatively. Colonialism brought advancements like Western education that overshadowed and replaced legitimate forms of alternative education. The Yorùbá were presented to global society as victims of underdevelopment needing European modernity. The narrative supported the premise of Euro-modernity as a complement to colonialism. Euro-modernity was a product of colonialism, and the Enlightenment was a cultural product of eighteenth-century Europe. These concepts were presented as a cultural renaissance that overcame the limitations of traditional African systems, and a similar mindset is possessed by Africans who are seen as the beneficiaries of colonial projects like Western education. It is easy to identify the multicultural orientation of Yorùbá writers like Wole Soyinka and D. O. Fagunwa or to point at appropriative tendencies in the artistry of more contemporary writers like Femi Osofisan and Ola Rotimi.

Wole Soyinka's works have been attacked as elitist and Westernized by critics such as the trio of Onwuchekwa Jemie, Ihechukwu Madubuike, and Chinweizu. Their criticism was based on Soyinka's aptitude and uncritical penchant for cultivating and transferring European

---

86. Afolabi, "Colonial Taxation Policy," 63.
87. Afolabi, "Colonial Taxation Policy," 67.
88. Afolabi, "Colonial Taxation Policy," 71.
89. Afolabi, "Colonial Taxation Policy," 71.

cultural references and mythologies into his works. According to Soyinka's critics, this alien-ated his audience and misrepresented his cultural background as a Yorùbá and a Nigerian.[90] They called him Euro-assimilationist and attacked his mode and design of universalism, dis-counting colonialism's influence on his experiences as a Yorùbá in a colonial state, which had impressed him and others from his cohort through Western education.

Some critics discount the influences of colonialism apart from the physical. Soyinka's schol-arship beyond the shores of Nigeria was expected to have a negligible influence on his intel-lectualism and creativity. However, he was educated at the University of Leeds in England after completing his studies at University College Ibadan. To summarize his oeuvre, when he received the 1986 Nobel Prize, he was the only Yorùbá, the only Nigerian, and the first African from the sub-Saharan region to receive such recognition. By criticizing him for being Euro-assimilationist, his attackers show an expectation of cultural insularity against the globalizing forces of colonialism.

Globalization initiated a cultural mobility reflected in the creative and intellectual choices of writers and their works, showing cultural nationalism or global solidarity. Critics disre-gard how Soyinka counterbalanced alleged Euro-assimilationist tendencies with the Yorùbá cultural legacies that enabled him to be perceived as the creator of mythopoeic literary texts. Regardless of alleged pandering to European mythology, Soyinka's indigenous culture served as a foundational structure for launching into the world, observing it and presenting univer-salist propositions. This endeavor was fast-tracked by colonialist forces that had their conse-quences.

Soyinka has also been criticized for his socialist ideology and the way his works place the agency of the individual above that of the collective. In allowing the individual to initiate com-munal salvation, Soyinka's works are believed to downplay the importance of the collective. Such criticisms conveniently displace how Soyinka has drawn on his Yorùbá cultural heritage, which identifies the individual and the collective as mutually inclusive. This interplay occurs even when he addresses a global audience, emphasizing how the individual (or the focus on the individual) functions as a satirical tool to explore social rot fostered by colonial and postcolo-nial misrule.[91]

Daniel Fagunwa, another prominent Yorùbá writer, has displayed the kind of hybridity expected from colonialism's impact in Nigeria as a process of forced enculturation. To quote George's assessment of Fagunwa's cultural aesthetics, "In addition to being cast as a precur-sor to subsequent writers of Yorùbá origin—indeed as a master ancestor to the institutional category we have come to call modern African literature—Fagunwa's writings are generally acknowledged as compelling narratives dealing with the process of Black Africa's march into modernity."[92] Fagunwa is an emblematic reflection of the consequences of colonialism, Chris-tianity, Western education, and the consciousness of technology. Many of these themes of glo-balization appear in his work.

---

90. Lindfors, "Beating the White Man," 475–488. See also Chinweizu and Madubuike, *Toward the Decolonization of African Literature.*

91. Balogun, "Wole Soyinka and the Literary Aesthetic," 503–530.

92. George, "Compound of Spells," 78.

While Fagunwa deals with profoundly indigenous themes through characterization and plot, he also gestures toward Christian theology. His concern with African modernity naturally exhibits a globalist subjectivity—a consciousness of African indigenous heritage and Western cultural particulars. Olakunle George explicitly identifies the coupling of religious fanaticism and worldly pragmatism in Fagunwa's novels: "Several commentators have drawn attention to the specifically Christian-missionary dimension of the novel (Bamgbose, *Novels*; Ogundipe-Leslie; Olabimtan). There is no question whatsoever that Fagunwa's work is inconceivable outside of the history of Christian missionary work in black Africa."[93] Fagunwa's heroic protagonists always invoke the essence of the Christian God, despite their investments in the traditional nuances of cultural and magical life. There are constant appeals to a Christian god in Fagunwa's work, through characters that request divine intervention during times of trouble and through the acknowledgment of Christian supremacy in a way that is absent from Yorùbá cosmology. These themes pay homage to Christian theology while striving to marry a consciousness of Western modernity and its globalist claims with Fagunwa's core traditional heritage.

This perceived tension in Fagunwa's works has been challenged by critics such as Afolabi Olabimtan, who asserts that the hybridism "suggests that Fagunwa's novel serves the onslaught of Christian indoctrination." George states that Fagunwa's constant demonstration of the "transcendence of God" reflects a superimposition of Christian theology over pagan worship,[94] but he also concedes that it is a dilemma that globalization dragged to the doorstep of Yorùbá elites who were introduced to Western traditions through colonialist actions. That the story is written in Yorùbá, a traditional language, points to a cultural awareness that has remained strong in the face of globalization pushed by colonialism and its legacy. Soyinka's complementary strategy merges worlds to develop a global, even universalist appeal, and Fagunwa's cultural and Christian politics complement each other to situate his work for global and local acceptance; it invests and proselytizes within both cultural streams.

Fagunwa is often cited as a prime example of these influences from colonialism, particularly in the way that Christian theology jostles for superiority inside and outside the imagination of indigenous Yorùbá life. Africans in general, and the Yorùbá in particular, have contributed to global Christianity in the present day—these contributions were shaped by a colonial administration that facilitated missionary work in present-day southern Nigeria and hindered it in the North. Given these influences, it is understandable that Fagunwa's style suggests and capitalizes on parallels with Yorùbá beliefs. Traditional African religion is presented as a mode of cosmic understanding and appreciation or communication with a divine force, and the contours of Christian belief hold religion as "a matter of ultimate concern . . . a case of veritable engagement with life's meaning, and . . . an encounter with the *mysterium tremendum*."[95]

When considering Yorùbá contributions to the current trajectory of global Christianity, Fagunwa represents the cohort of those who manifested this hybridism in more pragmatic terms through literary and imaginative thinking. Ogbu Kalu's work on the Africanization of

---

93. George, "Compound of Spells," 91.
94. George, "Compound of Spells," 92.
95. Wariboko, Falola, and Kalu, *Christianity Missions in Africa*, iii.

Christianity indicates several modes of hybridization in present-day global Christianity stemming from the indigenization of the religion as it permeated Africa and Yorubaland. For the missionaries and colonial administrators working to integrate Christianity into African cultures, it was easier to draw comparisons between Christianity and traditional religions that had been described as pagan. Ironically, this invention has returned to the global space and influenced the broader form of Christianity.

Conclusion

In reflecting on colonialism's effects on the Yorùbá and Yorubaland, the precolonial period offers a gateway to juxtaposing current influences with Yorùbá social constructs from before colonialism. The Yorùbá had faced different challenges that threatened their peace and unity, and they responded by developing traditions and ways of life to accommodate their historical journey. The implantation of colonialism, which none of them invited, was a swift change that impacted the unity and culture of the Yorùbá.

The Yorùbá did not respond passively to colonialism; they first mounted various forms of resistance and later took active roles in the colonial administration. They worked in almost every sector, becoming relevant, noticed, and appreciated throughout the colonial government. Some of the most prominent voices agitating for Nigerian independence were Yorùbá, working to achieve their goals from a more constructive and informed perspective.

Colonialism wrought major changes in Nigeria's social history, and its influence is still felt in the present day. The Yorùbá were part of the cultural and social changes that birthed a new Nigeria, reforming the Yorùbá perspective to operate on a larger scale. The colonists brought new languages, fashions, religions, and customs, and the Yorùbá became further inserted into the Western world.

14   Cultural Icons and Progress Narratives

Introduction

Worlds are like systems, and like all systems, they are made of constituted parts whose immanence ties directly to their functionality as part of a whole.[1] This analogously relates to the idea of cultures as systems as well as constituting force for the making of the lifeworld, and indeed they are. If cultures are foundations or gradients upon which participants or people anchor their beliefs and can view the world, or templates around which they can mobilize their subjectivities and anchor their subject positions,[2] it is because the groundwork has been made possible by preexisting forces. Culture itself is never created in a vacuum. Neither is it monolithic, fixed, or unchanging.

If we assume that the maxim "the only constant thing is change" has universal significance in its experiential application, we can argue the same for culture as a human phenomenon that seeks to and remains relevant over time. These shifts can be minute or enormous. The shifts are often inputs by in-group and out-group forces that constitute, functionally at least, the immanent parts of culture. Thus, it is true that the efforts of many members of any society are required in creating practices that, through routine, become rituals. Through their ritualization, that is, practices that institutionalize them, they become part of folklore that eventually provides a base for the development of heritage that becomes legacy, and so on.

What is being proposed here is not different from the several theorizations and explanations of the history of modern humans as well as the growth and transformational development of existing human cultures. In the literature on African tragedy and African religion, the arguments that privilege growth from everyday observation to the circadian routine and then to performative rituals that become institutionalized practices carried over the years to form culture are prevalent, just to cite a common instance. More often, these arguments emphasize the creative movement from the individual to the collective and then back, which seems to be a tested formula for culture-making and growth.

---

1. By worlds, I do not refer to the human world as a single phenomenon but the various existences that make it up and that give it the unifying sense that has been ascribed to it as the abode of the human species.

2. Relph, "Pragmatic Sense of Place," 24–31.

Therefore, it is easy to trace such a brand of organic development to many cultures in the world, partly because humans all have one source point, a theory put forward by archaeologists that have traced existence to Africa, and partly because the human race is more or less a prime example of how the difference in diversity works—that is, how diversity can instruct on the unique ways cultures are structurally different and similar. This kind of world is that which practicalizes sociological understandings of the human species and the environment they have made home, where each society is considered constituted of several contributing factors and is thought impossible to exist in isolation. That is, every part is important as a single and connected entity. Hence, society is almost always the result of its several competing and harmonized parts.

This idea of culture as organic, anchored in individual and collective inputs, and defined by rituals that become institutionalized practices, as well as that of the organicity of worlds, is sacrosanct to the idea behind this chapter. The changeability that keeps a culture progressive, continuous, and contiguous is responsible for its elasticity, fluidity, and wide- and free-ranging nature. For the Yorùbá, even in the global outlook, the focus of this chapter is no different. Such changeability sits at the core of Yorùbá culture as a mode of living and a systematic and practicable definition of being.

According to Adeleke Adeeko, whose book *Art of Being Yorùbá*[3] addresses this issue squarely and provides much conceptual clarity, being Yorùbá is complex. Adeshina Afolayan, who draws on the book's postulations to address Yorùbá cinema and Tunde Kelani's approach to Yorùbá beingness as a filmmaker and auteur,[4] observes that at the heart of Yorùbá culture and its definition of what it means to be culturally Yorùbá, being (that is the essence of humanity) is fluid. David Doris also offers an insightful contribution to this amorphous and equally concrete nature of Yorùbá beingness, by describing the idea of personhood in Yorùbá as an ontological signifier/entity as well as a social formation whose very existence has immense implications for what and whom Yorùbá are.[5] These views owe much of their ideological foundations to the idea that the personhood of the Yorùbá individual often manifests as an ambiguity. This seemingly contradictory and even nebulous conception is often clearer when juxtaposed or inserted within the discourse of Yorùbá's conception of culture, tradition, or *àṣà*—that is, those rituals, routines, and institutional practices that have come to sum up a tradition.

In drawing on Olabiyi Yai, Doris, whose view is in line with the focus here, argues further on the subject of Yorùbá beingness and personhood by locating it within Yorùbá conception of tradition. His position is that "àṣà contains an essential ambiguity."[6] Quoting him further, Doris argues that Yorùbá's conception of tradition through the idea of *àṣà* "denotes, to be sure, an empowering repetition of historical precedent, but at its linguistic and conceptual core, it also entails a moment of difference (ìyàtọ̀) or departure from that precedent."[7]

---

3. Adeeko, *Arts of Being Yorùbá*.

4. Afolayan, "Tunde Kelani and the Art of Being Yorùbá," 1–13.

5. Doris, "Unfunctioning Baby," 115–138.

6. Doris, "Unfunctioning Baby," 115.

7. Doris, "Unfunctioning Baby," 115–116.

This difference and even the simultaneous fidelity to and breakaway from the precedent are components of the ambiguity that defines *àṣà* or tradition for the Yorùbá. This ambiguity is a result of fluidity. The very linguistic conception of the term itself supports this thesis: *àṣà* derives from *ṣà*, which means to choose or select, which draws on exclusionary and inclusionary methods or discrimination, to use Doris's choice. Hence, it is not surprising that for the Yorùbá, beingness, anchored or defined by choice and individuating acts, can inform, comprise, and change/alter cultures and the traditions that make it. According to Doris, "The historical authority of that tradition is perpetually being invoked in the present to justify acts of transformative choice."[8] To translate in the context of this work, this means that the ambiguity that defines beingness also implicates individuals in their furthering of culture through specific actions or inactions.

Thus, there is flexibility to the idea of tradition and culture for the Yorùbá, which means there is also elasticity to what being a Yorùbá means. To quote Afolayan, whose views on the matter help to clarify the direction being pursued, there is flexibility "at the core of the Yorùbá concept of *àṣà* that facilitates a flexible relationship between traditionality and creativity."[9] This flexibility allows for Olabiyi Yai to consider *àṣà* as "permanently open to innovation informed by preceding phases in the process."[10] *Àṣà*, thus, is conceived by the Yorùbá as "a set of behaviors, deeds, and habits that characterize it after it has been subjected to a historical process of deliberate choice."[11] This historical process is in perpetual continuity, as are, consequently, the behaviors, rituals, and routines that define it. Likewise are the subjective positions it births and the lifeworld it sustains. This endless loop of influence is why this statement by Afolayan captures the crux of Yorùbá's conception of culture that there "is no essential understanding of what it means to be Yorùbá that has endured over time beyond the historical iterations of those gestures, motions, ideas, practices, objects, and so on over cultural time."[12] In other words, the culture and the people—both complementary forces helping to define each other—are continually revised: subjectivities and culture as a system of practice.

Two things are of importance here: The first is channeling Edward Relph's idea that culture is a vantage point from which several aspects of human life (spirituality, cosmic consciousness, materiality, science, epistemic practices, rituals and folklore, interactivity, etc.) are pooled together to enhance a better and harmonized circadian experience for individuals. To take this conception and frame it within the fluid structure that shapes Yorùbá *àṣà* allows us to see these aspects as continually changing, fluid, shifting, and persistently improved upon. Second, this highly fluid, unstable, and revisable nature of culture reflects on those participating in the making of culture. As said earlier, culture does not just materialize and is a result of strategic choices and processes, even when they are a priori to the performative moment or instance of creative endeavor—even at that, they can be revised, which coincides with the fluidity of culture resulting from internal and external factors.

---

8. Doris, "Unfunctioning Baby," 116.

9. Afolayan, "Tunde Kelani and the Art of Being Yorùbá," 1.

10. Yai, "Tradition and the Yorùbá Artist," 32–35.

11. Yai, "Tradition and the Yorùbá Artist," 34.

12. Afolayan, "Tunde Kelani and the Art of Being Yorùbá," 12.

Figure 14.1. "Some Prominent Yoruba Writers," by Dr. Kazeem Ekeolu.

The fluidity that marks cultural processes is a result of the strategic efforts of those who are involved in the project of culture-making. The centrality of individual actions to culture-making finds credence in the idea that actions at individual levels can alter, maintain, and constitute tradition. It thus stands to reason, as posited by Afolayan, that there is an instructive relation between tradition and creativity because creativity is one of such individuating modes of contributing to culture-making, building, and maintenance.

This position helps to clarify the focus of this chapter on the idea of cultural icons and their contributions to the identity of Yorùbá as a product of local and global forces as additions to progress narratives. This translates to a preoccupation with the place of creatives or artists of whatever medium their industry is defined by and which provides outlets for cultural consciousness, awareness, revitalization, and progress. Focusing on four selected creatives working across the literary and filmic creative traditions, this chapter explores the ways these individuals partake in culture-building and tradition-making in a way that images the Yorùbá as an individual or culture whose beingness and cultural core, respectively, is constituted of local and globalizing forces. This approach helps to reveal how the creative activities and inputs of these icons have reflected on them as cultural ambassadors and on their creative enterprises as progress narratives. It uses, as its starting point, the flexibility, openness, and ambiguity at the center of Yorùbá tradition and the flexible relationship between tradition and creativity as operational within the Yorùbá cultural space. These icons are Isaac Delano, Daniel O. Fagunwa, Akinwunmi Isola, and Adebayo Faleti.

The idea here, which provides methodological clarity for the chapter, is to explore these individuals as cultural icons by examining some of their works in connection to how they have troubled, clarified, and exemplified the flexibility and ambiguities that define Yorùbá being, culture, and creativity-tradition tropes, as well as the progress of the collective in relation to globality and modern forces. This is done by examining the ideas they work with while relaying them back to common ideas pursued and lived by the Yorùbá culture. It is the view that this approach will not only reveal how they have been seen in the light of icons who work explicitly with cultural materials that have contributed to what is known of the Yorùbá and who they are but also how these contributions reflect upon them as cultural activists. Thus, in doing this, attention will be paid to each individual while using select works to answer the questions at the heart of this chapter.

Chief Isaac Delano

For Isaac Delano, three things are sacrosanct: First is locating Yorùbá culture within a broader global framework, within modernity, to be precise. That is, unraveling what to make of the relationship between colonial/Western modernity and Yorùbá culture, and in what ways the latter has been impacted. Second, Delano's works are as critical as they are celebratory of the Yorùbá culture, which stands as one of the most defining features of his approach toward furthering cultural narratives. In other words, at the heart of some of his works are tempers of frustration about what has befallen the culture or the direction it has been forced toward. However, running concurrently with this is a deep reverence for the culture. Third, the materials Delano works with, the world he cultivates in narrative forms, and his mode of creatively reworlding the Yorùbá cultural space manifest ambivalence or evoke a conundrum that troubles the idea of what it means to be Yorùbá in a modern world.

Born in the early twentieth century, Delano grew up to be a political activist whose activism found acute resonance in his writing. A career writer whose nationalist agitations translated on and off the pages of books, as he was also a broadcaster, Delano pushed the boundaries of cultural nationalism with his fixation on representing and spotlighting Yorùbá culture and history. Owing to his preoccupation with the Yorùbá world in all its entireties, Delano invested his linguist and lexicographer's know-how in manipulating the orthography and essence of Yorùbá language for astute cultural and national politics. Delano was also a radio broadcaster and a teacher, both of which influenced his authorship of narratives and journalistic entries that have dignified him as a cultural and political nationalist.

With this eclectic background, Delano would document Yorùbá history, language tradition, and religion with the view of making a stand against the corrosive and hegemonic influences of Western tradition fostered upon the Yorùbá by the colonial regime. Hence, his writings and much of his activism articulated a counterhegemonic posturing by way of explorative and expository narratives. These narratives focused on core aspects of Yorùbá cultural space, like its pantheon, heroes, political and knowledge systems, heritage, oral history, and folk practices. His choice for both the English and the Yorùbá language dramatizes the political fervor of his positionality to the issues he has contended with, as well as his understanding of the flexibility and ambiguity that lies at the heart of Yorùbá culture and its relation to modernity. Thus, in his advocacy for cultural practices through his writings, he also pointed out deficiencies in extant indigenous routines and prefigured the inadequacies of some of the essentialist decolonization propositions, opening up the Yorùbá world for both scrutiny and appreciation—the kind that can ignite change. In essence, Delano's positionality to tradition as a kind of mouthpiece for the Yorùbá culture and its interplay with change-inducing forces (like modernity) unveils him as a representative voice. In representing the changes that affect Yorùbá culture, Delano acts in the capacity of a chronicler of cultural progress and the alterations that enable this. In addition, he faults or celebrates these changes but serves them up to the watchful public in the hope that, perhaps, witnessing these changes will make compatriots of the public.

Delano's works hold all these at their center as an oeuvre. Given his preoccupation with the place and fate of Nigeria and, more precisely, the Yorùbá world within the vortex of modernity, it is arguable that Delano was as concerned with the dynamic of the local versus global that has come to shape discourses of globalization and cultures in a rapidly modernizing and globalizing world. His notable works such as *Atúmọ̀ Èdè Yorùbá, Òwe Lẹsin Ọ̀rọ̀: Yorùbá Proverbs, Their Meaning and Usage*, and *Modern Yorùbá Grammar* are pivotal for their insightful, progressive, and representative coverage of the Yorùbá people and culture. They provide instructive and educative clarification and information on the verbal and aesthetic peculiarities of the people. *Atúmọ̀ Èdè Yorùbá* served as a rich lexicon, a dictionary of sorts and the first of its kind. It came bursting with grammar rules that were rich in Yorùbá lexicography, orthography, and cultural oratorical specificities. This dictionary is considered the first of its kind, as it sidestepped the existing fault in Yorùbá language scholarship, which explained Yorùbá grammar and language with English language rules. His reliance on diacritics and tonal marking helped consolidate the autonomy and uniqueness of the language, even if the print technology he used suggested an appreciation and functional deference to the power of modernity.

This is perhaps important in understanding the input and this portrait of Delano—and, indeed, the other icons of this chapter. There is a robust understanding of the unique interaction of modernity and culture while also noticing, earmarking, or striving to maintain the integrity of either. Making recourse to print technology is a gestural acknowledgment of the benefits modernity holds for indigenous modes of cultural transmission, which have always been oral. Yet, this acknowledgment is not total deference in that the same principles constituting orality—to the extent that orality is conceivable as a mode of thought constituted with a priori features and communicative elements[13]—that have shaped the grammar of the Yorùbá language are maintained even in orthographic form and in the dictionary, so much so that print technology and modernity are seen more generally in utilitarian functions as the vessels that they are.

In their exposition on the grammar and sociolinguistic heritage of the ethnic group, the books cement Delano's status as a campaigner for the culture or ethno-nationalist as well as an instructor of the language and traditions of the people. It is no wonder that he was not only appointed as the first administrative secretary of that illustrious group with clear political and cultural agitations, Ẹgbẹ́ Ọmọ Odùduwà, but also honored with several chieftaincy titles. Also, part of his honors is the honorary Doctor of Letters conferred on him in 1976 by Obafemi Awolowo University, previously the University of Ife. Delano's charismatic leadership, which informed his work in the sense of mapping patterns of change and narrativizing them, reflected in several aspects of his life that would find much more meaning on the print page.

It is important to mention that his awareness of modernity—this time a lived experience—played out in his conciliatory role in instituting a stronger relationship between the modern Christianity practiced by Yorùbá and the indigenous religions. His first book, *The Soul of Nigeria*, gained so much weight in this regard and on this matter of cultural and indeed national advocacy since it was part of his corpus that not only championed Pan-Africanist ideals but also helped to preserve Yorùbá culture and its ideas from hegemonic and oppressive cultural and political invasions—as well as their blowbacks.

The Soul of Nigeria exemplifies the range and manner of Delano's activism and insight into the topic of Yorùbá culture and its attempts at or strivings toward modernity. The book, a journalistic entry that doubles as Delano's documentary of his physical and ideological journey across Yorùbáland and culture, is also an archival material mapping the contours and substance of the changes tearing through the heart and soul of the culture. His caveat at the beginning of the collection of tales of his experiences and that of his culture lends much credence to this position: "LET me make it clear at the outset that I do not profess to know all about Yoruba laws and customs. For ten years I devoted such spare time as I have to finding out how our ancestors lived, governed themselves and enjoyed things, before the advent of the white

---

13. Olowookere, "Orality and the Bible," 133–146.

man. Old customs and laws are fast dying out, and in the following pages I have attempted to record in plain and readable form some of the details concerning our origin before they die out altogether."[14]

This excerpt functioning as a caveat helps to set in sharp relief the cultural politics with which Delano occupied himself and his approach toward executing this task. Much of the entries in this book are narratives of cultural evolution and progress, given their focus on the changes manifesting in the heart of Yorùbá culture resulting from global modernity. The narrative offered by Delano grapples with the idea of globality as it dovetails with the Yorùbá cultural locale. Hence, it is as invested in the dialogues of postcoloniality as it is in the agitations for visibility in any multicultural framework. Thus, we have in the book engagements, implicitly and explicitly, the relationship of enlightenment (*ọ̀làjú*) with the idea of modernity and the effacing or developmental contributions of the white man's world. The latter is why another of his famous books is titled *Ayé D'ayé Òyìnbó* (whose literal translation is "the world is now the white person's"). In articulating how a breakaway was initiated, encouraged, and mobilized between the cultural past and future, the narrative acts as a witness to those changes as they continue to influence the present.

Delano's autobiographical exposition and explanatory accounts in *The Soul of Nigeria* affirm his place as a cultural icon and an invested writer in spinning narratives around the idea of cultural progress, even if he questions the latter. For instance, we can agree, based on the trajectory of the essays, that he concerns himself with the place of precolonial Africa—its heritage and legacies—within a modern epoch that displaces some of these legacies, reinvents others, and allows for the kind of syntheses and syncretization that drives culture forward. This very approach centralizes Yorùbá conception of tradition as a culmination of outside and in-group forces. In other places, the placement of a heavy question mark on the rationalizations and superiority of modernity as a sociocultural frame and knowledge system is noticeable.

It would then seem that Delano narrativizes the theoretical base of Yorùbá's conception of what cultural progress is while also making visible how this progress has come about. The book itself simplifies the reach of indigenous cultures toward globality to the extent that the very indexes of modernity Delano sets out to uncover within Yorùbá culture are materials of global modernity as they have evolved from Western modernity and colonialism. It is thus not surprising that Delano chooses to source his autobiographical and journalist materials from spaces outside the aristocratic and royal spaces lived by the proletariat.

His narratives touch on education as he revisits how modern or British education operated as opposed to the traditional mode of learning. He also emphasizes the meaninglessness of the practices to the students, which validates some of the hegemonic outcomes of Euro-modernity in the Yorùbá cultural sphere. His outcome is not only the displacement of indigenous modes of knowing but a call to reevaluate what it means to learn and educate. He emphasizes the shift from a more hands-on approach to individual and community development to a reliance on Western modes of collective responsibility by using the phrase "Talking big grammar does not

---

14. Delano, *The Soul of Nigeria*, 7.

pay. Work with your hands."[15] This view recalls the Yorùbá belief in the importance of hard work However, he also makes sure to emphasize how English and other aspects of reality and the knowledge it entails are merely means to an end, and their absence does not stop cultural participants from making meaning out of their lives through being productive.

Delano touches on cultural routines and beliefs, validating previously thought supernatural occurrences as real while not denying the scientific realm, which paints his aim as validating both as coterminous real occurrences, signifying that his cosmopolitanism is not absent of indigenous sensibilities. His chapter on this phenomenon is illuminating, as he gives firsthand incidences; he recounts narratives of those who have shared their experiences of the mystical with him. He makes judicious recommendations by validating aspects of spirituality and invalidating others—rather than the kind of erasing denunciation peculiar to advocates of modernity in judging the civilization of non-Western cultures. Quoting him is expedient here: "Now there are superstitions *and* superstitions, and some are plausible and people are greatly concerned if we do not lose our heads about them. Others they instinctively distrust, and yet again some that we interpret excitedly and with great hope of fulfillment."[16]

Delano, through chapters like "Medicine Men and Their Cures," "Spiritualism and Witchcraft," and "How Did the Dead Return," argues for aspects of cultures that cannot be explained by Western rationality but are still as genuine as any aspects of material reality. In the chapter "The Gods of Yorùbá," Delano validates traditional rituals and customs in the modern dispensation. He recounts his experiences with traditional science and spiritualism that make a mockery of Western science, where practitioners of the latter make prophecies of death that Western medicine could not avert. He then advocates for the procedures that delineate traditional spiritualism as a mode of knowledge and how practical its mysticism can be.

Evaluating Delano shows that his preoccupation is in questioning the place and effects of modernity of Yorùbá culture while also trying to maintain the legitimacy of Yorùbá cultural legacies against any implied superiority of the Western tradition.

Chief Daniel Olorunfemi Fagunwa

D. O. Fagunwa was a prominent Yorùbá author who pioneered the Yorùbá-language novel. This was an immense feat given the time he started writing and the literary subtradition he helped found, which had immense influence on what is often erroneously described as fantasy novels but which Harry Garuba has rightly argued are novels anchored on animist spirituality.[17] That Fagunwa's novel is also seen as a pioneer of mystical and magic-driven Nigerian narratives is attested to by the derivative relation often drawn between his works and that of the Nigerian literary titan Amos Tutuola.[18] Tutuola's works have remained a veritable reference as source materials and forerunners of Nigerian speculative fiction novels, such as the Ben Okri trilogy. Olakunle George, echoing other scholars who have made similar assertions, points out "it

---

15. Delano, *The Soul of Nigeria*, 19.

16. Delano, *The Soul of Nigeria*, 65.

17. Garuba, "Explorations in Animist Materialism," 261–285.

18. Lindfors, "Tutuola and Fagunwa," 57–65.

has generally become a truism in African literary studies that his work illustrates a significant moment in the sociocultural adventure of Nigeria in particular, and Black Africa in general."[19]

In recent years, Jane Byrce has co-opted these kinds of novels and narratives into the futurist category, claiming that the combination of myth, orality, and indigenous belief systems allows for the "invention of personal mythologies, rewriting of history in the light of future realities and the use of extra-realist or magical phenomena as part of the everyday"[20] ties futurist speculative fictions to those mythic narratives of old. For this reason, she claims such older narratives are invested in futurist imaginations. On this note, Bernth Lindfors's claim is not far-fetched: "Modern scholarship on Tutuola's writing has confirmed that he does indeed owe a great deal to native oral tradition, but few critics have commented at length on his debt to Chief Fagunwa."[21] One of the reasons for this is the reluctance of Yorùbá critics to make this comparison and the availability of Fagunwa's books in Yorùbá.[22] George further asserts, corroborating the view that "in addition to being cast as a precursor to subsequent writers of Yorùbá origin— indeed as a master ancestor to the institutional category we have come to call modern African literature—Fagunwa's writings are generally acknowledged as compelling narratives dealing with the process of Black Africa's march into modernity."[23]

Lindfors's conclusion is yet again not wrong, as it is scarce to find this comparison between Fagunwa's and Tutuola's oeuvre than one is to find reference to Tutuola's inspiration as deriving mainly from the broader Yorùbá tradition—a relation Lindfors's work argues clearly. However, stepping away from the controversy of critical omission and charges of error of oversight as to what the source material influencing Fagunwa is, two things are worth emphasizing: that both Fagunwa and Tutuola are pioneers and that they are also cultural innovators and icons who have brought the global spotlight to the broader culture from where they draw inspiration.

Fagunwa, born in 1903, wrote between 1930, when his most popular novel, Ògbójú Ọdẹ Nínú Igbó Irúnmọlẹ̀, was published in 1938, and 1963, with *Adììtú Olódùmarè* coming out in 1961. Ògbójú Ọdẹ was written and entered as a submission for a literary contest of the Nigerian education ministry, but it would become so much of a literary success that it is recognized as the first Yorùbá novel and as an exemplar of how indigenous languages could not only capture entire cultural worlds but also adequately produce literary creations and propagate literary and cultural knowledge.

Fagunwa's works are invested in representing the indigenous space and its rituals as well as folk beliefs. As such, many of his narratives and literary creations are masterpieces on and of the Yorùbá life. Drawing on orality, myth, and individual inventiveness with cultural materials, Fagunwa constructed worlds that exalted cultural values, epistemologies, and especially philosophies. The very qualities that ascribe to him the eminence of a master ancestor are defined by the uses to which he puts the cultural materials as well as their effect on the culture he represents. For instance, and quite vital, Fagunwa's protagonists are cast in the splendor of heroes.

---

19. George, "Compound of Spells," 78–97.

20. Bryce, "African Futurism," 1–19.

21. Lindfors, "Tutuola and Fagunwa," 58.

22. Lindfors, "Tutuola and Fagunwa."

23. George, "Compound of Spells," 78.

However, these heroes are not conceived of in the Western sense, as they are often peasants, most often hunters, who commit themselves to the service of the community, even if the adventures these commitments demand are also tailored toward self-discovery.

George offers an illuminating submission on the foregoing that buttresses the point here. As regards Fagunwa's heroes and their exploits, George explains that the "modernity that Fagunwa engages in his fiction may be formulated as a chain of ideational inheritances. The first could be said to be the notion of nationhood, the obligation of the patriotic citizen to that putative communal, that is national, self-understanding and advancement."[24] Thus, Fagunwa's approach to the indigeneity-modernity dynamic is in recasting and perhaps even consolidating individual quest as a nationalistic endeavor. This holds immense significance in the period in which Fagunwa's narratives were produced, which is of cultural, ethnic, and national advocacy as made necessary by a global world territorializing its parts, all culminating into a nationalist sentiment pervasive across the colonized nation, even into its postcolonial state.

Fagunwa's heroes are representations of his so-called inherited ideations; they are also his statements about the nature of this world as it existed before colonialism and even as it has managed to survive in the postcolonial world, despite everything. It is, therefore, not surprising that in his novels, one finds hunters relating with the most eminent of beings, both human and spiritual—that is, kings, gods, deities, and spirits. And that such relations are interdependent and the power dynamic unstable—there are many instances his characters overcome or are overcome by spiritual beings—attest to Fagunwa's manner of a cultural campaign, as this is reminiscent of the spiritually charged cultural sphere of the Yorùbá. It also projects classism as a function of several nonhuman forces or conditions. This is a shift from the usual belief in classism being a function of materiality and a product of the physical, which is peculiar to modernity and its mode of rationality.

Emphasizing the relationship between modernity and tradition, Fagunwa establishes links between Christian beliefs as brought about by Western cultural values and indigenous religious systems. While this adds a moral bent to Fagunwa's narratives, which also is not in discord with the folk philosophies of the Yorùbá, it also reworks the tension between indigenous practices and Western ones. His ability to create this harmony in heavily mythic narratives reveals not only his brilliance but also his cosmopolitan nature—that is, his global leanings— even when the foundation upon which he stands to look outward or globally is local.

Exploring the relationship between Christian beliefs and traditional religions (and, of course, espousing all that is between), Fagunwa not only moralizes but is also sentimental "toward improving his reader."[25] To this effect, it has often been said that Fagunwa's aesthetic and moral philosophies are decidedly Christian, and we see this in his continued evocation of the Christian God in his works and the abundance of Christian themes that are employed to interpolate more traditional cultural and mythic codes. This reveals the openness of Fagunwa in his cultural advocacy toward outside influences in defining the Yorùbá world. Apart from this fondness for Christianity, a religion he practiced, he also relied on Greco-Roman mythic

---

24. George, "Compound of Spells," 81.
25. Lindfors, "Tutuola and Fagunwa," 60.

Figure 14.2.
The Yorùbá have a high dress sense and culture that dates back. They have also developed several aphorisms to symbolize or express the importance or otherwise of dress culture. One example says *Kò sí ìgbà tí a dá aṣọ tí a ó r' ílé fi wọ́* (There is no time one decides to make a dress that one does not eventually adorn it). From the Toyin Falola Private Collection.

heritage, which he mixed copiously and inventively with the Yorùbá, a vivid example of cosmopolitan modernism.

Rather than reveal cultural imperialism, this syncretistic and harmonic artistic disposition reveals his even and almost democratic awareness of himself as a modern cultural participant as well as a compendium of the old and new. Thus, in his works are visible descriptions of imageries and characters that draw upon several sources, old and new, local and Western, Christianity and indigenous religion, spirituality and secularity. Also vital and displaying Fagunwa's instructive cosmopolitan awareness is his double emphasis on literacy and orality in the novel Ògbójú Ọdẹ Nínú Igbó Irúnmọlẹ. In this adventure of a hunter, the narrator is an old man who instructs a scribe to pen down his words, for print is certified to keep his words alive for ages to come, compared to a narrative by word of mouth.

It is easy to see this as a hegemonic favoring of the West and its print technology over indigenous modes of transmitting thought and knowledge. Indeed, George reads this situation as rehashing the tensions between orality and indigeneity. However, one can also read this as a progressive legitimation of the several modes of knowledge-making open to the Yorùbá artist and the Yorùbá individual without falling into the pit of reversed racism. It signals the dependence of one mode of experience on the other in the formation of Yorùbá subjecthood. Fagunwa's didacticism comes full circle in the moment of chaos in his works; however, his novel—and works more generally—is a narrative of progress, where hybridity and interplay of differing viewpoints and knowledge modes manifest an intercultural bent.

Although often subtle, sometimes overt, Fagunwa's ability to bring in several materials in his representation of the Yorùbá world manifests the ambiguity often at stake for the Yorùbá conception of àṣà, which relies on in-group and out-group sources in its development over time.

Akinwunmi Isola

Akinwunmi Isola was a Yorùbá playwright, novelist, actor, and scholar of repute. His works as a thespian and as an artist more generally have touched on several aspects of Yorùbá life. Isola, like the previous two icons, also wrote in Yorùbá, translating his English works into the latter, an act that signaled his devotion to representing the epistemological sovereignty of the Yorùbá and their linguistic inventiveness. This act also links up with the philosophy of decolonization as championed by Ngugi wa Thiong'o, who is foremost known for his advocacy of the linguistic turn in African literature. People like Isola not only embody the arguments of decolonization but show how feasible it is while also emphasizing the benefits thereof.

Taking Yorùbá culture as the provenance and province of his work, Isola explored its rich histories, giving special emphasis to women in his bid to not only accentuate the role of women in modern-day Yorùbá culture, thereby having a hand in its progress, but also revise the gradually concretizing gender disparity that Western modernity continues to make possible in modern Yorùbá societies and the nation at large. Isola's first play, *Efúnṣetán Aníwúrà* (1961), is an eponymous narrative where the titular character is portrayed as the fearless and politically savvy women's leader. Revisiting history through this character, Isola asserts his kind of impact on modern Yorùbá. While history is his material, his focus and the intended audience is the present toward redirecting the trajectory toward the future. The innovativeness of the narrative won him the award provided by the Ẹgbẹ́ Ìjìnlẹ́ Yorùbá in 1966. The eventual staging of the play reminded modern-day Yorùbá of the brave Yorùbá woman who made history during her tenure as the Iyalode of Ibadan. The creative reinvention of this character on the page and the theatrical stage revived her as a feminist figure.

Attesting to Isola's vision for the Yorùbá and his cultural advocacy is his rewriting of Ẹfúnṣetán's history in the manner of a strong and formidable woman who struck fear in her detractors and fought for the progress of fellow women, though historical accounts and some historians have emphasized how Ẹfúnṣetán's death was a result of the evil orchestration of men who were part of the ruling council. Isola revised this bit of historical information undermining Ẹfúnṣetán by characterizing her as a powerhouse. In his defense, Ẹfúnṣetán symbolized motherhood and the agency of the woman as a cultural and political office in the making and sustenance of both the smallest and biggest unit of society: family and collective.

Isola's important revision had an immense effect on contemporary understanding of historical figures, as it brought nuance—the same nuance that would be demonstrated by the filmmaker Kelani, who adapted Ẹfúnṣetán on screen, where her death was more dignified beyond the mockery and vile of political sabotage and male connivance. Also, in reconstructing the character of Ẹfúnṣetán, Isola zooms in and gives latitude to the agency of the African woman as it existed in time past, even with the oppressive forces at play then, while also providing a rounder and nonessentializing picture of Yorùbá political and social life.

This strand of political vision is distinctively Isola, as his other plays were equally invested in women figures. Another character of his that has remained vibrant in cultural imagination, thanks to his inventiveness, is Madam Tinubu. Although a slave trader who amassed wealth from this enterprise, Tinubu was also a culturalist and nationalist, and Isola made sure to emphasize this in his tinkering with history to cultivate his literary/cultural ideology. Isola displayed immense creative awareness and ingenuity with his success in portraying such a problematic figure for her strength while not downplaying her faults.

Campus Queen, eventually adapted to the screen by Kelani in 2003, is also about women's empowerment and agency and their benefits to society. While in his previous dealings with women, he exhumed historical figures and inventively marshaled their relevance to contemporary times, in *Campus Queen*, Isola imbibed and exuded the political aesthetic of women's integrality to social architecturing. This he did by inventing a female character in a modern era where femalehood is synonymous with second-class citizenship and women's education is fraught with several oppressive experiences held in play by hegemonic power differentials. Vesting overt political power in the hands of a lady distinguished Isola from his peers and signaled his preoccupation with nationalism and societal progress, which meant historical excavations or contemporary figures were materials he worked with in ensuring and attaining his political and creative goals.

It is thus to the benefit of culture and national growth that he wrote explicit, politically charged cultural stories where the activistic bent remains glaring. *Ṣaworoidẹ* (1999), *Ó Le Kú* (1997), *Agogo Eèwọ̀* (2002), and *Kòṣeégbé* (1995) are his stories that are best known for their onscreen productions. They represent the didacticism, politics, and cultural philosophy of Isola that mirrors that of the Yorùbá. Ṣaworoidẹ relies on cultural legacies, heritage, and structures in satirizing sovereign power and the relationship between rulers, the state, and citizens. Its allegory also applies to the relationship between the Nigerian body polity and the state, especially as regards political power and sovereign control.

It evokes the place of collectivity in checking and checkmating abuse of power, which is what the Ṣaworoidẹ (Brass Bells) stands for. Matthew Brown, whose article focuses on the movie adaptations of the book, conceives of this mode of checks and balances in Isola's story by operationalizing the concept of sovereignty as not only about who controls what space but also "a question of how power is distributed over and within territories, especially with regard to the members of the human species living there."[26] The story criticizes the kinds of political rule practiced by the ruling elites in the society, especially during military rule, while adding the role of necropolitics, which Brown explains as the institutionalization of a political structure where a talking drum adorned with brass bells is "one of several spiritual mechanisms by which the town of Jogbo secures political legitimacy."[27] To quote Brown, whose description of the story points out the structural relationship in the Ṣaworoidẹ's depiction of sovereignty as a kind of necropolitical and sovereign power shaping how authority is deployed in the ruling elites' dealing with the people and the place of democracy in empowering the polity in fighting back:

> He endures several incisions on his head and back, into which a powerful medicine is applied. Incisions are then made on, and the same medicine is applied to, Àyángalú, the court drummer. Meanwhile, an accompanying form of medicine is placed in both the royal crown and the frame of the Ṣaworo Idẹ. If these steps are not followed properly, as only the foremost priests and chiefs know how to do, then no link between the Ṣaworo Idẹ and the wearer of the crown will be forged. And as powerful as that link might be, its absence is equally awesome. Anyone who wears the crown can be destroyed by the Ṣarowo Idẹ whenever it is played by Àyángalú.[28]

This allegoric reference to postcolonial rule, while maintaining cultural legacies and spiritual ethos as founding principles, is an example of the kind of politics Isola invested in. This is because, in the play, the drum becomes a totem of checkmating monarchical and aristocratic power that gives agency to the people against brutish and even usurping elite forces. The same logic works in *Agogo Eèwọ̀* (Gong of Taboo), a sequel to *Ṣaworoidẹ*, in which the gong is depicted as a necropolitical instrument with judicial powers capable of restoring sanity to a society ridiculed by nepotism and elite corruption of the rule of law.

The nature of these stories has caused scholars to attribute to them the category of allegory or royal allegories. Olubunmi Ashaolu, who has critically appraised the *Ṣaworoidẹ* work, confirms that in the story, the relationship between sovereignty, the drum as a spiritual and cultural artifact, and the crown is a great example of how cultural heritage can be excavated to form prime allegorical and political purpose.[29] She cites the talking drum's (*gángan/dùndún*)

---

26. Brown, "Kèlání and the Question," 415–428.
27. Brown, "Kèlání and the Question," 6.
28. Brown, "Kèlání and the Question."
29. Ashaolu, "Critical Study of History," 201–219.

ability to approximate speech as its power in legitimating age-old cultural discourses such as those with spiritual potency enough to displace illegitimate sovereigns or despotic and corrupt rulers.

Adebayo Faleti

Adebayo Faleti, like the other icons, has gained renown over the years because of his investment in Yorùbá culture and his manner of advocacy. The prolific playwright's plays have become major reference points for the philosophies and ways of the Yorùbá and have been adapted into movies, which lend them longevity status in Yorùbá cultural production.

Before dwelling on his creative works, which are deeply historical and promote some of the very principles that constitute Yorùbá conception of *àṣà*, even its fluidity, it is important to mention Faleti's path-breaking efforts. Considered Africa's first newscaster, stage director, and film editor, as well as the country's first Yorùbá TV and radio presenter, Faleti made creative inroads into several artistic genres and creative professions that allowed him to make the template for future generations while also using these platforms to crusade for Yorùbá culture. In addition, when the Nigerian Television Authority was Western Nigeria Television, Faleti was a Yorùbá translator.

His commitment to maintaining the sanctity and legacies of indigenous Yorùbá life in a modernized world can be read as a moralizing tenor. One of his most popular works made into a movie by Kelani, *Thunder Bolt/Mágùn*, not only revived a deeply mystical aspect of Yorùbá ontology and social affair but also perpetuated a kind of nationalist agenda, where interethnic relation is well rendered, and a cosmopolitan sensibility, where modern science and indigenous remedies are placed side by side and portrayed as complementary. In the narrative are several characters from distinct ethnic groups, but rather than impede progress, they impel it. In speaking directly to the Nigerian experience of national development, the story cast an Igbo woman who is stricken purposely with a spiritually induced sickness by her husband, a Yorùbá man. The sickness, *mágùn*, is meant to be an orthodox remedy for perceived or real infidelity—in the case of Ngozi, the husband knows her to be innocent, but goes ahead anyway, drawn greedily by the allure of her wealth. How it works is that a woman plagued with this mágùn leads a man to his death. If she does not lie with another man—her husband will not lie with her because he knows the consequence of what he has done—she eventually dies.

Ngozi, the Igbo wife, becomes a symbol of the story's message. Her plight is caused by a Yorùbá man, Yinka, but it is another Yorùbá man, Dimeji, who selflessly offers himself as the sacrificial lamb. The tense Yorùbá-Igbo relationship the work portrays is integral in the narrative of Nigeria as an invented nation as well as that of its ethnic groups. The brilliant intermixing of sexual politics, oppression of women, nationalism, modernity, indigenous spirituality, medicine, and ethnic relations is visible in the characters and their symbolisms. Ngozi is depicted as the modern woman who is shackled by indigenous morality and its enforcement rules. Yet again, her salvation comes in the same form of indigenous medicine because she is cured by a risky indigenous method enforced and practiced by seasoned herbalists/native doctors. This is a progressive bent taken by the narrative. It is also ingenious that Faleti's cultivation of these dichotomies toward ensuring or narrating their failings and success and, most especially, their complementarity sits at the heart of the fluidity within Yorùbá conception of culture and beingness.

Ngozi's handling by Yinka, her husband, is oppressive psychologically and then bodily. By infecting her with the mágùn curse, Yinka turns her into a vector of pathologies, a threat to other men. Yet, it is another man, Dimeji, who comes to her rescue. While Faleti has constructed a world where men are the alpha and omega, it is the case that the injunction is toward working with antithesis to portray men in diverse light that contradicts the single narrative of men's oppression. This antithetical approach to cultural preoccupation is well used in the narrative. Ngozi, for instance, is warned by an old man in a kind of deus ex machina format: the old man appears like an apparition and warns her of the pathology inside her, although not in clear terms, which is in line with the often-cryptic ways the spiritual world of indigenous African communities communicate with the physical. Here, Faleti gives prominence to Yorùbá cosmogony and spirituality, which, of course, does not downplay the role of science.

There is also an indictment of modernity and its emphasis on material acquisition, coupled with a redemptive approach toward the image of Yorùbá and its purported culture of the occult as indictable ways of assessing wealth. This is beautifully portrayed through Yinka and the route he takes toward acquiring wealth. Rather than through the usual motif of money ritual or human sacrifice for upward social and class mobility, he tries to dispense with his wife to access her material wealth by plaguing her with a mystically powerful disease capable of dealing death to her physically. In essence, the story implicitly argues that the less-than-ideal aspiration toward material wealth is not always through the occult, even if it is conceived of within the usual family—husband-wife—dynamic.

As Afolayan has forcefully quipped, it is as if the story throws "the full weight of the Yorùbá cultural dynamics against the menacing encroachment of European modernity."[30] While this may be true to the extent of the story's politics, it is also the case that it gestures toward unusual conciliations, and this might be easily glossed over with how sharp the dichotomies appear to be. It is not a mistake that Dimeji, who believes in the scientific process, scoffs at the legitimacy of mágùn, and that he offers himself—also out of love—to be a test experiment, particularly so he can publish a scientific paper in refutation of such beliefs. It is also not accidental that Dimeji, after having intercourse with Ngozi, is saved by the herbalist from the full wrath of the implications of mágùn when his mortality is threatened.

Some of the work's greatest assertions are the complementary and unique places of knowledge systems as well as the nationalist sentiment that all people, regardless of race or religious or ethnic affiliations, are good and bad. This narrative best exemplifies Faleti's position as a cultural icon whose creative material bears a cosmopolitan sense of everyday Yorùbá lifeworld. It is important to see this narrative in this light because it is often the case that prevalent narratives at its time of production are fully invested in the ideas of a traditional Africa and often pursue its legitimacy, even to the detriment of portraying other knowledge systems as coeval in the progress of Yorùbá culture.

---

30. Afolayan, "Tunde Kelani and the Art of Being Yorùbá," 8.

There exists an array of cultural icons in the Yorùbá literary space, although only a handful are often made foci of scholarly interrogations. Take, for example, C. L. Adeoye, whose major creative work, *Ẹ̀dá Ọmọ Oòduà*, provides us with the first taste of the Yorùbá cosmological theory in a fictional modality. In it, Adeoye explores the Ifá literary corpus with the popular folktale tradition to provide a fictional narrative that traces the primordial human journey through birth and anchors existence on the metaphysics of predestination. The fiction globalizes the Yorùbá belief system as if adopting John Locke's dogma regarding America and saying, "In the beginning, all the world was Yorùbá." The promotion (or shall we say, selling) of the Yorùbá culture through this work is unprecedented, creative, and original. The audacity of placing the Yorùbá culture at par with, if not superior to, Western cosmologies is of indigenous epistemological relevance.

Conclusion

While it is not possible to exhaust how these icons have made their mark by providing narratives of Yorùbá culture, attempts have been made to show in what ways and how some of their works have addressed, depicted, or even contributed to the discourse of Yorùbá's cultural progress, and what progress even means for the Yorùbá in globalized contexts. Each of these creatives, working with the film medium and print technology as writers, as well as other journalistic means, has shown that the principle of flexibility in the Yorùbá conception of *àṣà* and beingness is not abstract. While they have addressed the related issues of cosmopolitanism as well as globality and its pleasant and untoward influences on local cultures in their discourse of modernity and Yorùbá culture, they have also shown that the relationship between both is dynamic. It is how they have brilliantly explored this dynamic for all its beauty and ugliness while leaving lessons that have broken barriers and boundaries and established new pathways for future generations and future understanding of what it means to be Yorùbá that has resonated enough to etch their names in history.

15 Obafemi Awolowo's Politics in Global Context

Introduction

The Yorùbá in relation to Nigerian political history would be incomplete without a reflection on the contributions of nationalists like Nnamdi Azikiwe, Tafawa Balewa, Ahmadu Bello, Obafemi Awolowo, and many more. It is unarguable that they laid the foundation of Nigeria's political climate today. Their contributions are evident in the political dynamics of the people of their respective regions and how they relate to the rest of Nigeria. The demands for self-governance around the world influenced their social and political philosophy. And their ideologies were based on the connection with their roots, as is the case with ideologies like negritude. The global demands of the Black emancipation movement created a Pan-African nationalism that advocated for self-determination and an urgent need for Black people to be regarded as humans. African nationalism had a global yet Afrocentric motivation about it, but in the end, the aim was for self-determination, self-governance, and freedom from colonialism. The wave of nationalism swept through Africa, in many cases, through its people in the diaspora and African students who encountered Western education and found a sense of camaraderie with students from other parts of Africa. In essence, they had a sense of Black consciousness, which sprouted the ideological, political, and philosophical tussle for independence and social justice. African nationalists consequently began a Pan-African movement that freed each Black nation from Western domination and imperialism. Just like African political history, Nigerian political history is influenced by the efforts of nationalists who later became politicians and heads of state.

The colonial and postcolonial politics of Nigeria cannot be discussed without the political and ideological foundations laid by the nationalists. Like other African nationalists, Nigerian nationalists fought against colonial masters and made demands for self-governance. However, in certain cases, the implementation of their principles and ideologies for governance failed in leading the countries on the right path. This shows a gap between political ideation and political pragmatism. These are the events that defined the efforts and legacies of nationalists across Africa, and Nigeria was no exception.

One of the great African nationalists is Obafemi Awolowo. Awolowo's contribution to Nigerian politics is founded upon his nationalistic views and, importantly, his calls for the expulsion of European power from Africa more generally, and Nigeria in particular. Awolowo's political principles and ideologies have received much scholarly attention over the years, and critics have subjected the man's life and actions to intense scrutiny. What is undeniable in this literature is that Awolowo, like many African nationalists in the 1950s, championed a cause that promoted the national self-determination of African nations by Africans.[1] This threatened the continued economic exploitation and governance of Africa by Western powers. During this period, there was a shocking wave of demands for self-determination that entailed the control of the pace and development of their countries. That is, between 1945 and 1951, there was an enormous clamor for independence motivated by self-determination nationalism. The political consciousness had always been there for Africans, but in colonial politics, the political consciousness was directed toward the political and socioeconomic liberation of Africans.

At this time, the Nigerian concerns were the same as the rest of Africa, but the Nigerian case was unique because of the diversity of the Nigerians and their population. The diversity of the ethnicities of its people influenced the political socialization and organization of the people and what the structure of their self-determination was like at the time. Their ethnic nationality influenced the political ideologies of the nation-state, and as such, it determined how nationalist and postcolonial politics was played. Even though Awolowo was a strict adherent of federalism, he understood the importance of regionalism. Arguably, this was influenced by his Yorùbá background and the understanding that self-determination could not end at the nation-state level. It must be granted to each region of the country. What is pertinent to note is that Pan-African and Afropolitan motivations were noticeable in the politics of Awolowo. That is, the idea of group identity in relation to group interests motivated his political ideology. While many may see him as sectional, making the case that his politics in an Afropolitan context puts the question of identity at the forefront is significant. Nonetheless, the significance of Awolowo's political ideologies and implementations cannot be jettisoned from the political history of Nigeria.

This chapter evaluates African nationalism as a product of the complementarity of Pan-Africanism and Afropolitanism—that is, how identity politics motivated African nationalists to push for self-determination with ideologies derived from their cultures. Additionally, this chapter analyzes the politics of Obafemi Awolowo in relation to Nigeria, Africa, and the globe. More importantly, there are cultural influences on his politics, as seen with his Egbe Omo Oduduwa, Remo Politics and the intricacies of the western region politics. Awolowo's humanism and philosophy of change will also be examined. Critics have written about the context of Awolowo's presumed ethnic pitfalls and his general contribution to Nigerian political history. It is pertinent to reiterate that, unlike many African nationalists who became heads of state, Awolowo failed to implement his ideologies across the country. Awolowo was not availed the chance to govern his country and could be excused for the failure of implementation because at the regional level, where he could implement these ideologies, he did, and it was to great success.

---

1. Awolowo was a major writer who published many books on his ideas on politics and reforms, drawing greatly from the Euro-American ideas on federalism and political institutions. See Awolowo, *Path to Nigerian Freedom* and *The People's Republic*.

African Nationalism: Afropolitan and Pan-African Motivation

Throughout time, humans have assembled through shared languages, geography, and common history. This is how humans have been able to mark the self and the other. This is the foundation of the nominalism of race and ethnicity. Through these groupings, humans have been able to demarcate themselves from others, and it helps to put into perspective that though humanity is a universal phenomenon, race and ethnicity are intersubjective. The consequences are obvious, as history has shown that people can use race, color, geography, and ethnicity to torment others. The problem of the "them" and the "us" in human history can be said to be responsible for a high percentage of the ills and wars that are associated with human existence. The idea of nation, race, and ethnicity has created an artificial chasm and, many times, has caused the exploitation and notion of superiority.

As evident in history, racism and racial extermination are results of the clash between the "us" and the "them," which has caused humanity a lot of casualties, events for which no amount of money for reparations could atone. Some common instances in history are the transatlantic slave trade and colonialism. Though the epoch classification was somewhat at different periods in the history of humankind, they both signify the same thing for Africans. The former exemplifies the inhumane Western enslavement of Africans, and the transportation from Africa through the Atlantic to the West shows the extent to which the West exerted its idea of superiority. The latter, on the other hand, is a furtherance of the slave trade, but this time, it was more significantly a systematic economic and political exploitation of Africans in Africa. Colonialism and imperialism in Africa were fueled by the assumption that Africans were primitive and too crude to govern themselves. It was also an attempt to milk Africa dry of its resources, and with this, Africa became a sociopolitical annex of the West. Through the two phenomena, the West penetrated the sociocultural dynamics of Africans, the geography of Africa, and its indigenous system of governance. The domination and subjugation of Africans was a calculated effort of the West, and the result is indelible such that African history is forever marred by the colonial experience.

Colonialism attempted to replace indigenous African systems with Western systems. The mode of governance and the education system began to change. The religion of the colonial masters was forced on the people or rather adopted by the people to the detriment of their traditional religions. Furthermore, these factors led to the desire among Africans to take an interest in reaching the pinnacle of Western education. The colonial masters, on the other hand, needed several Africans to be educated to rule Africans by proxy. Therefore, the Western system of education was established or implemented across Africa, and scholarships were offered to Africans, which meant some of them had to go to countries like the United States of America, Germany, the United Kingdom, Belgium, and France to further their education. At this point, the coming together of Africans from different backgrounds in a foreign land inspired the African students to join the global demand for the independence of nations under any form of colonialism.

Also, the political consciousness of these students was sprouted by Western education, and with contact with various political ideologies and philosophies, they were able to craft their political ideologies and philosophies, which they believed would help in liberating their people. Furthermore, at this period in the history of Africa, the political consciousness of Africans in the diaspora meant that they were well equipped to demand social and political independence. More significantly, it meant that Africa could no longer be the annex of the West. The reasons are not far-fetched; the West has long exploited Africa, treated Africans inhumanely, and harvested the economic and human capital of Africa to a point where Africans had to create a movement of resistance.

From the foregoing, a simple foundation of African nationalism is offered. For some clarification, African nationalism is linked to Pan-Africanism and Afropolitanism. It is pertinent that a conceptual analysis of these concepts is offered. The notion of Pan-Africanism as a conceptual framework or as an ideology is constructed to mean the following: "The idea that people of African descent share similar histories and struggles, a common destiny, and processes for forming crosscultural unity in areas of history, politics, and economics—has a striking resemblance to the concept of the African Diaspora and reverse migrations."[2]

The central idea of Pan-Africanism is that African people share a unified history and culture that is peculiar to Africans. It is important to note that though many works have expanded the centrality of Pan-Africanism, there was nothing such as an Africa with shared views before the adventures of the West to Africa. That is, the geographical nomenclature called African in culture, politics, and history was a creation of the West or, at the very least, they had an influence on it. The cultural and philosophical diversity of ethnicities in Africa suggests that Africans do not share one common destiny, language, politics, and history, at least not before the Atlantic slave trade and colonialism. Pan-Africanism makes the point that suffering a similar fate at the hands of imperialists, Africans with their various cultural similarities can find a cross-cultural understanding that helps them resist the subjugation of Africans at home and in the diaspora. The essence of Pan-Africanism is to create the notion of an Africa that is united despite its cultural diversity against the world powers. Pan-Africanism is a political agenda. Overall, Pan-Africanism can then be best captured as "the sense that all Africans have a spiritual affinity with each other and that, having suffered together in the past, they must march together into a new and brighter future. In its fullest realization this would involve the creation of an African leviathan in the form of a political organization or association of states. . . . It might involve an almost infinite variety of regional groupings and collaborative arrangements, all partial embodiments of the counter-embracing unity which is the dream of the true Pan-Africanist."[3]

The sense in which Pan-Africanism is instituted creates a union between Africans because of their shared history of racial injustice, subjugation, and colonial exploitations. Pan-Africanism did not start in the 1900s; it has its roots in the agitations of slaves. However, there was a Pan-African renaissance in the 1900s that turned Pan-Africanism into a political movement for Black people, and it became the nationalistic tool for Africans to bring themselves together against the foreign determination of the progress, fate, and development of Africa.

---

2. Falola and Essien, *Pan-Africanism*, 1.

3. Emerson, "Pan-Africanism," 275–290; Markovitz, *African Politics and Society*, 450.

Figure 15.1. "The Lead Figure," by Moses Ogunleye, is an abstract depiction of leadership and followers.

Kwame Nkrumah's consciesism, Leopold Senghor's negritude, and Julius Nyerere's *ujamaa* all capture the political interpretation of Pan-Africanism in different forms. Nkrumah believed in the power of one Africa under one united government. He argued that

we have to prove that greatness is not to be measured in stockpiles of atom bombs. I believed strongly and sincerely that with the deep-rooted wisdom and dignity, the innate respect for human lives, and the intense humanity that is our heritage, the African race, united under one federal government, will emerge not as just another world bloc to flaunt its wealth and strength, but as a Great Power whose greatness is indestructible because it is built not on fear, envy and suspicion, nor won at the expense of others, but founded on hope, trust, and friendship and directed to the good of all mankind.[4]

Like Senghor and Nyerere, Nkrumah subscribes to the idea that there is an African identity that is particular to Africans; therefore, they should unite under a confederation that will represent the interest of all Africans. This is based on the notion that there is a sense of brotherhood between Africans that enables them to live in harmony. Therefore, there is a call for African socialism. In each of their cases, there is the belief that the communal living of Africans a socialism that strictly can be theorized and practiced. There is the argument that African nationalism is not just a political movement but also a cultural movement. Lucidly, the political domination of Africans also involved an annihilation of the cultural practices of Africans. Thus, the Pan-African movement was influenced by reactionary emotion to capture the past or elevate the precolonial principles to rival Western sociopolitical principles. By advocating and later creating a system of government based on precolonial structures, the nationalists intended to socioculturally situate that Africa and Africans do not need foreigners to rule them.

The connection between Pan-Africanism and sociopolitical nationalism is that Pan-Africanism served as the theoretical foundation for self-determination and nationalism. Related to this is the Afropolitan angle of Black cultural and political nationalism. Adeshina Afolayan summarized who an Afropolitan is:

Afropolitans existentially attempt to forge a being, an identity, within a vortex of many cultural dimensions, especially the national, cultural, and racial. Their beingness is characterized by an ontological ambivalence; the self hangs in a cultural limbo of being Ghanaian and being American. An Afropolitan represents a self actively struggling to make a purchase in the global cultural supermarket filled with packages inscribed by multiple choices and locations. While the self of the Afropolitans is forged from many sources and imperatives, the final product is not distinctly African. For the exuberant Afropolitans, "Africa" represents a postmodern text, an open space that permits entries and exits on multiple fronts and without the annoying limitations of geography and the historicity of colonialism.[5]

---

4. Nkrumah, *I Speak of Freedom*, xii.

5. Afolayan, "African Philosophy," 391–403.

Afolayan's capture of the being of an Afropolitan suggests that Afropolitanism is a hybrid of Africanity and globality. That is, Afropolitanism is an ideology that does not concentrate too much on being an African but suggests the nurturing of an African in a global context. Therefore, Afropolitanism is the refusal of continued ownership of victim identity. That is, it looks beyond the history of colonialism and the call to look back. Its discourse is situating Africanness in a global context. To further explicate,

> Afropolitanism refers to a way—the many ways—in which Africans, or people of African origin, understand themselves as being part of the world rather than being apart. Historically, Africa has been defined in the Hegelian paradigm as out of history, as not belonging to the world—as being some region of the planet which has no significance whatsoever in terms of the real history of the human in the world. But of course, that is not true. Afropolitanism is a name for undertaking a critical reflection on the many ways in which, in fact, there is no world without Africa and there is no Africa that is not part of it. So that's the philosophical inflection of the term.[6]

Afropolitanism as a philosophical paradigm is a move against the unfair Hegelian characterization of Africa. Afropolitanism is both a counterargument of dislocating Africa from the global context and an argument for the importance of globality in African thinking and the essence of Africa in the globality. The tenets of Afropolitanism, therefore, negate the very essence of Pan-Africanism. Afropolitanism rejects the victim identity and contributes to global politics and finding your place in the global context, while Pan-Africanism maintains a racial ideology. Mbembe clarifies,

> Pan-Africanism, to a large extent, is a racial ideology. Afropolitanism is not, insofar as it takes into account the fact that to say "Africa" does not necessarily mean to say "black." There are Africans who are not black. And not all blacks are African. So Afropolitanism emerges out of that recognition of the multiple origins of those who designate themselves as "African" or as "of African descent." Descent here, or descendants, or genealogy, is a bit more than just biological or racial, for that matter. For instance, we have in Africa a lot of people of Asian or Indian origin. We have people who are Africans but they are Africans of European origin in South Africa, and other former settler colonies like Angola, Mozambique. We have Africans who are of Middle Eastern origin, for example in West Africa, Senegal, and Côte d'Ivoire. And more and more, we have Africans of Chinese origin. So Afropolitanism differs in that sense from Pan-Africanism because Pan-Africanism was fundamentally rooted in the idea of a belonging to a particular racial grouping, whether that's via Marcus Garvey or others.[7]

Pan-Africanism, unlike Afropolitanism, relies on emotional and sociocultural platitudes.[8] It is a sentimental approach based on returning all that was lost because of slavery and colonialism.

---

6. Mbembe and Balakrishnan, "Pan-African Legacies," 28–37.

7. Mbembe and Balakrishnan, "Pan-African Legacies," 30.

8. Nantambu, "Pan-Africanism," 561–574.

Pan-Africanism functioned as a political movement partly built on emotions.[9] Therefore, it is understandable that Nantambu submits that in talking about Pan-Africanism, it must be seen as Pan-African nationalism.[10] He argues that by focusing on just African slaves or geography, Pan-Africanism plays into the hands of the divide-and-rule technique of the colonizers. Pan-Africanism should involve Africans from all over the world. Nkrumah and Nyerere argued a Pan-Africanism that gives the people a sense of nationhood.[11] Therefore, the template upon which the political and theoretical self-determination was based is Pan-African nationalism. Nantambu argues that

> Pan-African Nationalism is the nationalistic, unified struggle/resistance of African peoples against all forms of foreign aggression and invasion, in the fight for nationhood/ nation building. The primary goal of Pan-African Nationalism is the total liberation and unification of all African peoples under African communalism. Pan-African Nationalism seeks to achieve African nationhood and nationality; human perfectibility based on the seven cardinal principles/ virtues of Ma'at; self-reliance; self-determination; the creation of Pan-African nationalist solidarity and confraternity among all African peoples on the continent and in the diaspora; a cooperative, humanistic, and communal value system; spirituality; the traditional extended family modus vivendi; and polycentrism.[12]

The influence of Pan-African nationalism and Afropolitanism can be seen in the political ideologies of these African nationalists in demanding the seven cardinal principles listed by Nantambu. The struggle for independence had Pan-African nationalist and Afropolitan tendencies and underpinnings, as the nationalists differed on whether to return to precolonial principles or embrace the Afropolitan idea that Africans must face the future and carve out an identity that will not isolate them from the rest of the world. However, it is theoretically and politically pragmatic if Pan-African nationalism and Afropolitanism are merged to create a formidable political and intellectual framework for self-determination and confraternity among African people. Pan-African nationalism, on the one hand, can be a way of retrieving what was lost because of colonialism; on the other hand, Afropolitanism will be the template upon which global relationship with the rest of the world is built. This complementarian stance gives Africans the opportunity to retain the essentialities of their identity while interacting with the rest of the world without romanticizing victimhood. The two ideologies are both political and intellectual, and they have their shortcomings. However, one can merge the praiseworthy attributes of the two and use the result as a template for forming political ideologies that will situate Africa's place in world history.

The significance of the analysis thus far points to a somewhat new approach to studying the works of African nationalists and their contribution to the struggle for political independence and the eventual self-governance of their various nations. Importantly, Nyerere is known for

---

9. Legum, "Pan-Africanism, the Communists and the West," 186–196.

10. Nantambu, "Pan-Africanism."

11. Nyerere, "Speech to Congress," 16–20.

12. Nantambu, "Pan-Africanism," 569.

his call for African socialism that is based on indigenous African principles, which means a return to precolonial African identity. Nkrumah's consciencism advocated for a one Africa that is governed through the African personality but not a return to the way Africa was before colonialism. Nkrumah's position can be said to subtly indicate that though Africans deserve self-determination and human decency, there is the need to forge ahead because by going to precolonial Africa, the people called Africans will redefine that identity because, without the European colonization, they would not have had the identity tied to European institutions. This consideration juxtaposes the theoretical, historical, and political foundation of Obafemi Awolowo's philosophy of change and its praxis.

Obafemi Awolowo: Politics in Global and Local Context

Of all the nationalists mentioned so far, Obafemi Awolowo is the only one who did not have the opportunity to lead his country. Akin Makinde connects this political outcome to his being ignored in the works on political philosophy: "The works of African political writers have attracted the attention of foreign scholars, particularly the works of writers like Kwame Nkrumah of Ghana, Jomo Kenyatta of Kenya, Leopold Sedar Senghor of Senegal, and Julius Nyerere of Tanzania. Perhaps the most productive of them all, Chief Obafemi Awolowo of Nigeria, has not received the same attention as given to the above politicians probably because, unlike them, Awolowo never had the opportunity of being head of state, a situation that might have enhanced the chances of putting his political doctrine into practice."[13]

As a politician, Awolowo employed his political ideologies in ways that many political writers never did. Political writers theorized about the self-determination of African people without the interference of the West. However, unlike Awolowo, many of these political writers went on to become the heads of state of their nations. The unique case of Awolowo has left many to agree with a well-known tribute that Awolowo was the best president Nigeria never had.

In understanding the politics of Awolowo, political readers must learn how the political wave of Black nationalism that influenced other African political writers also influenced him. It is arguable that he is the only one that was able to translate the identity of belonging to an ethnic nation into understanding the politics of diversity of African people and especially his country, Nigeria.

Awolowo's politics was a hybridization of the local realities of his people combined with the new wave of ideological resistance against the colonial occupation of African territories. Therefore, his politics and Awolowo the man were products of global and local politics. Insa Nolte notes that Awolowo was a product and producer of Remo politics: "Along with other provincial politicians, including his fellow Remo man Samuel Akinsaya, Obafemi Awolowo challenged the position of the Lagos-based political elite by advocating a nationalist politics based on mass mobilization in the provinces. Keenly attuned to the political significance of local ideology and practice beyond Lagos, Awolowo combined demands for an Africanization of colonial states

---

13. Makinde, *African Philosophy*, 184.

with a validation, albeit at the cost of democratization, of local political institutions such as chieftaincy and obaship."[14]

What is demonstrated in the assertion of Nolte is that the political awareness and basis of Obafemi Awolowo were greatly influenced by the local politics of Remo, which was transferred to Lagos. Awolowo's nationalist politics was greatly influenced by the communalistic nature of the Remo community.

The influence of Remo politics, as argued by Nolte, cannot be disputed. The progress of Awolowo's politics was not just based on the intimation of the importance of Remo politics. Rather, during the period of nationalists' struggle for independence, Awolowo was seen as a progressive. This is reminiscent of his life and politics. The understanding of the people and the polis is essential in putting forward any form of political agenda. The translation of local politics into regional and national levels is not just about being a product of local politics but creating a sense of belonging for the people that makes them feel a sense of identity. During the period of Awolowo's political elevation, reclaiming identity—and Yorùbá identity—was important to his people, and his ideologies aptly supported that. People saw him as a progressive who would fight for their cause and contribute immensely to nation-building. Segun Gbadegesin explicates thus:

> Progressives in politics subscribe to, and invest heavily in, the forward-looking agenda for the polity and the people. They stake their resources in promoting the agenda and in building and sustaining coalitions around it; and they succeed in selling it to the citizenry. And because the citizens realize that the agenda is for them and in their interest, they embrace it and give their support to those who launch it. Progressives ride to power on the strength of progressive agenda which the people buy into. They retain power as long as the agenda remains attractive to the people and as long as progressives do not lose their ability for effective political strategy. The combined forces of a progressive agenda and an effective political strategy are positive sources of the political power of progressives.[15]

In many senses of the word, Awolowo was a progressive who understood the plights of his people. His nationalism was, indeed, as Nolte pointed out, motivated by local politics, but it was also a motivation toward placing the Yorùbá people as an ethnic group that should be reckoned with in the Nigerian state and globally.

It is not surprising that when Awolowo left Nigeria for London in 1944, he saw an avenue to avail the world of his nationalist politics. Although, his nationalist politics was not entirely motivated by any Pan-African agenda. His regionality of political nationalism simply meant rightly placing the Yorùbá people around the world and in Nigeria on a pedestal that would ensure that they are not discarded from Nigerian or global politics. When Ẹgbẹ́ Ọmọ Odùduwà was created by Awolowo and other intelligentsia in the United Kingdom, the political consciousness of the Yorùbá people was awakened. Rasheed Olaniyi believes that

---

14. Nolte, *Obafemi Awolowo and the Making of Remo*, 19–20.
15. Gbadegesin, "Obafemi Awolowo and the Golden Era," 57–73.

the formation of Ẹgbẹ́ Ọmọ Odùduwà had three-fold fundamental objectives: to foster unity among the Yoruba by promoting its cultural heritage and traditional leadership, to rescue the Yoruba from the threat of other ethnic groups, especially the Igbo, and to empower the Yoruba youths educationally. An overriding objective was to protect the Yoruba from the "danger of Igbo domination." *Ẹgbẹ́ Ọmọ Odùduwà* was conceived by Yoruba intelligentsia studying in the United Kingdom who wanted to infuse "Yoruba nationalism" into the Yoruba-speaking people. According to Ige, "Odùduwà was invoked and brought out from the shadows; his 'children' flocked to where he beckoned."[16]

The establishment of this sociocultural group created nationalist politics that was influenced by ethnicity. The complexity of Nigeria's diversity and the colonial gluing of people who are socioculturally different dictated the nationalist politics of Awolowo. However, there was a global reach because while abroad, the Ẹgbẹ́ Ọmọ Odùduwà spoke to the Yorùbá people and in the diaspora. The politics of identity in this is that although many Yorùbá people became citizens of the world at the time, the creation of Ẹgbẹ́ Ọmọ Odùduwà reminds them of their ancestry and the need to always push for its growth and its progress, including demanding for the self-governance of Nigeria.

The reverberation of nationalists like Nyerere at the time was a return to the cultural essence of being African. However, the irony of this is that there was no single African cultural essence to return to because colonialists created the new countries of Africa with the notions of subjects and citizens. Therefore, there is self-contradiction in this call; it was an act of overromanticizing the precolonial traditional community. This is not to say that there were no principles that would benefit Africans, but the eradication of Western structures is nearly impossible. Awolowo appealed to the historical consciousness of his people. That is, in moving forward, a sense of nationalism based on the race to which they belong is essential, which is implicated in the name of the group "Ẹgbẹ́ Ọmọ Odùduwà." Notwithstanding, the essence is not to dwell in the past but to take what is useful from the past and display its pragmatics in moving forward. Awolowo's Yorùbá nationalism in relation to the connotation of the descendants of Oduduwa is a revisitation rather than a total return, unlike the case of Nyerere. This is why Falola believes that

> the central figure in the translation of Yoruba history to Yoruba politics is Chief Obafemi Awolowo. No modern Yoruba has come near the stature of Awolowo, who is now often described in some kind of mythological way. One scholar describes him as "the first truly heroic, visionary leader of the Yoruba since Odùduwà." The connection between two heroes—Odùduwà and Awolowo—reveals two things: the "creation" of history by Odùduwà and the "use" of history by Awolowo. But the "creation" and "use" of history are connected in the emergence of the idea of the Yoruba nation. Awolowo's political career reflects the careful manipulation of Yoruba history and traditions infused with the ideas of modernization.[17]

16. Olaniyi, "Identity and Solidarity in a Yoruba Diaspora," 111.

17. Falola, "Yoruba Nation," 29–48.

The link between history and Awolowo's political movement meant understanding one's identity in relation to modernity and globality. It may not entirely cover what Afropolitanism stands for, but Awolowo's use of "Odùduwà" creates a political ideology that emanates from Yorùbá past and the implementation in close terms with how the world can benefit the Yorùbá and vice versa. While Afropolitanism reiterates the impossibility of regaining the African identity because of globalization, Awolowo's creation of Ẹgbẹ́ indicated the need to synthesize fragments of the past to the sociopolitical dynamics of 1945 and the global future. The significance of the creation of Ẹgbẹ́ Ọmọ Odùduwà is further corroborated by Segun Gbadegesin: "The Ẹgbẹ́ Ọmọ Odùduwà was not a political organization in the sense of one whose objectives was the canvassing of votes on the platform of a political party. It however had a political objective in the 'propagation of the idea of a modern Yoruba State and a Federal state of Nigeria' through research lectures. The birth of the Egbe in 1945 with is emphasis on education, research and social welfare was a pointer to what an Awolowo political machine would later do for Yorubaland in particular and Nigeria in general."[18]

The points made by Falola and Gbadegesin going forward are important to Awolowo's politics and his philosophy of change in a global context. The very foundation of Awolowo's African nationalism is based on a Yorùbá nationalism in search of a global identity because Awolowo recognized that Yorùbá cannot exist in seclusion from the rest of the world. Therefore,

Chief Awolowo emphasized the imperative for creative use by nationalist leaders of received cultural values imported by colonialism. While showing respect for the cultural achievements of the Yoruba before colonial contact, Awolowo refrained in his policies from romanticizing Yoruba pre-colonial culture by preaching the importance of Western education as a source of enriching the culture of the pro-modern Yoruba. He succeeded in making the old (Yoruba, Edo, Urhobo, etc.) culture and the new (British) culture, which he once characterized in The People's Republic as a "paradoxical heritage," coalesce in the educated Yoruba man and woman, particularly through the programmes that his government implemented in the field of education and cultural enrichment.[19]

R. Sekoni captures the argument made earlier about the synthesis of nationalism and Afropolitanism. Awolowo understood in practical terms that there are systems that can be adopted

---

18. Gbadegesin, "Obafemi Awolowo and the Golden Era," 63.

19. Sekoni, "Awolowo and Culture," 269–283.

from the British to enlighten some of our cultural processes. With this, the Yorùbá will be in constant contact with the world and the world with the Yorùbá.

Awolowo was not just a nationalist; he was a visionary. By 1945, he had written a political treatise that prescribed the remedies to the problems of the colonial Nigerian state. His book *Path to Nigerian Freedom* highlighted his political views and how to rule an independent Nigeria:

> Path to Nigerian Freedom was quickly recognized as the most important and impressive view of Nigeria's future political development produced by a nationalist politician. In thoughtful analysis of colonial rule and local government, Awolowo challenged British-inspired ideas about the difficulties constituted by Nigeria's heterogeneity. Where other nationalist leaders saw the imperative of overcoming tribalism to create a unified nation, Awolowo drew both on his understanding of the emergence of ethnic nations in Europe and the existing phenomenon of Yoruba cultural nationalism to turn his argument around: Nigeria must recognize that it did not constitute one but many nations, including the Yoruba, and each with its own historical trajectory.[20]

The relevance of this political treatise explains the influence of Yorùbá nationalism on Awolowo as well as the influence of his understanding of similar nationalistic agitations in Europe. Awolowo's political view, as pointed out earlier in Nolte's analysis, shows the great influence of local politics in Awolowo's political philosophy, but Awolowo recognized that there is the need to syncretize Yorùbá nationalism into a global context, and global context into Yorùbá nationalism. His support for a federal Nigerian state where each region can control its development is an adoption of a somewhat global practice of federalism, but for Awolowo, he recognized the need for the ethnic nations to acquire autonomy within the union.

Awolowo's Democratic Socialism

Awolowo's political philosophy is not complete without Fabian socialism. During his stay in London, he became greatly influenced by the Fabian Society and its socialism. Fabian Socialism is a British model of socialism that subscribed to the idea that socialism should be a gradual process rather than revolutionary. Akinjide Osuntokun captures the influence of Fabian socialism on Awolowo thus: "As a student during the war, he was influenced by the Labour movement, particularly by Fabian socialism—a kind of socialism that permeated from within rather than the violent revolutionary socialism of communist Russia. Awolowo was impressed by the political culture of Britain and the British liberal tradition and the rule of law. He believed, however, that this way of conducting politics could be applied to Africa only where African culture determined which aspect of it was applicable."[21]

By the time Awolowo and his allies created the Action Group, he had become known for his socialist agenda. However, unlike other nationalists who adopted Marxist theories, Awolowo

---

20. Nolte, *Obafemi Awolowo and the Making of Remo*, 20.
21. Osuntokun, "Obafemi Awolowo," 1–19.

was rather influenced by Fabian socialism, which is why socialism is more of an intellectual construct. That is, his socialism was more academic than it was a revolutionary upturn.

Socialism is entrenched in Awolowo's politics but different from the call for African socialism like the rest of the nationalists. The idea of socialism is foreign to Africans, but the nationalist proposes the African equivalence of it, and for many of them, it is African communal living. Therefore, African socialism is birthed. However, it meant different things to each nationalist. According to Akin Makinde,

Figure 15.3. Chief Samuel L. Akintola, Awolowo's political partner, later a critic and political foe, who served as the deputy and subsequently premier of the Western Region. Mutinous soldiers gruesomely murdered him during a bloody coup in January 1966. Drawing by Dr. Kazeem Ekeolu.

In African context, socialism could mean living together in a spirit of love and brotherhood. It could also mean, as Nyerere puts it, Ujamaa, i.e., "familyhood" or "community spirit." The "foundation" and "objective" of African socialism which has been in Africa all long is, according to Nyerere, the extended family. In Leopold Senghor's sense, Socialism in Africa is "community society founded on the general activity of the group." And he seems to agree with Nyerere when he (Senghor) argues that, because of its communal nature, the Negro African society has traditionally been socialistic. And for Nkrumah, "African traditional society is communal, egalitarian, and humanistic." The root of this is to be found in African tradition . . . but in any of these African conceptions of socialism there is one thing that would be generally accepted, and that is what "living together in a spirit of love and brotherhood." That is what familyhood and community spirit seem to entail.[22]

The idea of African socialism is closely knitted with communism, communalism, and communitarianism. The socialist approach of African nationalists, except for Awolowo, was greatly influenced by Marx and Engels. The Marxist reading of African predicaments is a contextualized theorizing of communism in Africa and the product of which is, as seen with these political writers, socialism that can be Africanized. Their argument was based on the notion that African socialism is rooted in a traditional African way of life. For them, some principles are essentially socialistic in the traditional African sense, and these principles are to be strictly adhered to and implemented as the best medium to govern the people. From Makinde's explication, the conception of the African human person is communally defined, which puts a mark on the intents of African socialism and the place of freedom. However, Makinde points out that

---

22. Makinde, *African Philosophy*, 186.

socialism is foreign to Africa, and the political writers found a nomenclature and concept that may be understandable in a global context. As Ifeanyi Menkiti puts it,

> As Africa engages in a global discourse with other traditions of thought and of practice, especially where these traditions happen to also embrace a collective, or quasi collective, approach to life, it is important that we keep in mind the key question: what constitutes a genuine commonality and what does not? This is so because sometimes despite similarities in surface structure, there is not an underlying unity between two cultural practices. But, sometimes, despite an absence of surface similarities, an underlying unity may yet be found that would surprise the scholarly observer. What items relate to the core, and what items relate to the periphery, becomes then a key question as one adjudicates the perennial problem that what is community for someone, something considered enabling, may, for someone else, be considered oppressive something antithetical to the welfare of the individual. In philosophy as in life, these disagreements could get to be complicated, even quite nasty.[23]

The adoption of socialism can then be seen as Africa trying to engage in global discourses, and the use of "socialism" to encapsulate the African sense of community and brotherhood can be tagged as the attempt to situate the traditional African way of life in a global context. In fact, to these African intellectuals, it was an attempt to show the validity of traditional African principles vis-à-vis Western concepts and paradigms. Whatever the case, African socialism was central to the political prescriptions of these African intellectuals, and later these principles were put to use when the intellectuals became the heads of state of their countries.

The differences between African socialism by other nationalists and the socialism of Awolowo can first be seen from the points of their ideological leanings. Other nationalists take the Marxist route, which interprets their socialism as communism, but Awolowo was more Fabian socialism. The difference between his socialism and that of the Marxist-Leninist is methodological. Makinde believes that

> the issue here is how socialism is to be achieved, whether in African or any other societies. This is a question of methodology. Marxist-Leninist approach to socialism is through a theory of violent revolution, or any means that would lead to the dictatorship of the proletariat. Any means to a desired end is considered appropriate and necessary for, in as much as the ruling class will not voluntarily relinquish their wealth, capital and power, the only thing to do is to abrogate them by force or violence if necessary.... One important difference between Awolowo's socialism and the Marxian socialism is that of methodology. For instance, he does not believe that violence is inevitable in the evolution of a socialist state, and for this reason rejects the Marxist idea of the dictatorship of the proletariat.[24]

---

23. Menkiti, "Community, Communism," 461–473.
24. Makinde, *African Philosophy*, 191–192.

The idea of methodology is a sound point. Awolowo's socialism is based on Plato's tripartite division of the soul. Plato, in his philosophy, divided the human person into three: reason, appetite, and temperament. For Plato, only a man ruled by his reason should be the one qualified to be a ruler. Hence, his idea of "philosopher-king." In a similar style, Awolowo goes further not just by identifying what it takes to be a leader but also by prescribing the attributes needed to be a good follower. Socialism cannot work through radical implementation and imposition on the proletariat. For Awolowo, the proletariat must enjoy their freedom, and the understanding of this use of their freedom can only be possible through a regime of mental magnitude.

Awolowo's democratic socialism is laid on the idea of the mental magnitude. Makinde argues that

> in his search for a supreme value of human existence in social and political organization, Awolowo developed a doctrine known as "Mental Magnitude." The doctrine of mental magnitude is essentially Platonic, with Stoic and Cartesian flavors. It states a tripartite division of man with physical, psychical and divine attributes. It makes a case for a conscious effort to reach that state and stage wherein all the three "levels" of attributes may be jointly employed by homo sapiens to master fate and destiny, and thereby live a happy, healthy, prosperous and full life—a triumphant life (Omoboriowo, 1982, p. 46). Mental magnitude is a philosophical doctrine which derives from a theory of mind and body, with the assertion that the mental is superior to the physical element of person, and should take control over the emotions, desires, and actions of man. Awolowo believes socialism, like democracy, is an attitude of the mind, irrespective of whether we talk of the European mind or the African mind. This is to say that it is a social attitude, imposed, as it were, by the rational mind in general, at all times and everywhere.[25]

He further explicates that

> Awolowo provides a philosophical basis for his universalist doctrine of socialism. We cannot properly appreciate his conception of socialism without understanding his philosophical analysis of the human mind and the importance he attaches to the individual person as an instrument of change. In so far as socialism is seen as a particular attitude of the mind and a way of life translatable into a theory of social, political, economic and moral behaviours of man in a society, mental magnitude, as a philosophical basis of Awolowo's socialism, puts man at the centre of all activities, thus making him the main instrument of social, political, scientific, economic and moral changes. The doctrine of mental magnitude, therefore, leads to a profound metaphysical analysis of man in relation to his mental and physical capabilities and his well-being, both as an individual and as member of a society.[26]

Awolowo's socialism has a philosophical basis that recognizes the importance of the mind. Philosophically, the mind is the seat of reason and mental process. The idea of magnitude is

---

25. Makinde, *African Philosophy*, 172.

26. Makinde, *African Philosophy*, 193.

based on the position that the mind should be groomed and nurtured to be able to participate in the community of rational people. Evidently, rather than revolutionary socialism that takes us backward, Awolowo advocated socialism that is based on the strength of the mental consciousness of the people and their leader. It is through this that the leaders and followers can interact and push their societies forward. The essence of this is ingrained in some of his policies such as education and health care. The doctrine of mental magnitude is lucidly the training of the mind. Like Plato, Awolowo believes in the importance of education. Education became the central point of his agenda. Also, the idea of health care is built on the Platonic notion of the interaction between the body and the mind. Now, one understands why Makinde elucidated that Awolowo's mental magnitude is Cartesian in theory. That is, the mind is the most essential part of the human division, but the mind must exist in a body. The continuous existence of the mind must be caged in a sound body. Therefore, mental magnitude is a cardinal point of Awolowo's democratic socialism. Makinde succinctly puts that

> an essential tool for a good training and discipline of the mind is education which Awolowo makes as the first cardinal programme of his socialist party. Whether in Africa or Asia, Russia or America, education and discipline of the mind are seen as essential to the improvement of the individual and of the society as a whole. An educated carpenter will be more efficient than an illiterate carpenter, and the same can be said of farmers, builders, and even traditional healers. But more importantly, the education and training of the minds of those who aspire to leadership is absolutely essential, particularly the kind that is needed for the cultivation of mental magnitude.[27]

The essence of Awolowo's socialism cannot be fulfilled without reiterating the importance of training the mind, and at the same time, the pragmatics of his democratic socialism is a complementarity of two important cardinal programs: free education and free health care. With this, Awolowo hoped to translate the global standard of governance into the governance of the Western region and Nigeria as a whole. Therefore, mental magnitude is amplified by the sound body. Though this is theoretical, Awolowo was able to translate theory to practice. Makinde argues that Awolowo's socialism is incomplete without health care:

> Awolowo sees the second important cardinal programme in a socialist state as free medical healthcare for all, coming after the first, i.e., free education at all levels. It is believed that only when people have sound mind in a sound body will the remaining socialist programmes naturally fall into place, viz, full employment and integrated rural development. It is at this point that every individual can make his own meaningful contributions to the society by acting as an instrument of social, political, moral or scientific change. What is more, educated citizens would know their rights (as opposed to the uneducated and unenlightened traditional societies), thus preventing injustice either from fellow citizens or the state. And if rulers are themselves of educated and

---

27. Makinde, *African Philosophy*, 195.

disciplined minds, they would know the limit of their powers and the purpose of leadership in a community of equally enlightened people.[28]

Wale Adebanwi adds that "Awolowo's political philosophy was truly egalitarian in ways that could not be understood nor appreciated by the ruling elite who were in no way buoyed by egalitarian ideals. Where Awolowo argues in *The People's Republic* that rights to education and health are among the fundamental rights which each family regarded—and properly so—as inalienable and that these constituted the bases of either voluntary or compulsive entry into political association with other families, he was quick to note that all chief contributing causes of the worst forms of social instability."[29]

It is pertinent to consider some things in the commentaries of scholars on the politics of Awolowo and his socialism. First, Awolowo's elevation of mental magnitude as the central point of his socialism is a plausible point. However, the assumption that it will solve leadership problems is faulty. As seen in political history, the most educated leaders have proved to be some of the most terrible leaders, whether in Africa or America. This is not to argue against the importance of education. Rather, it is to accuse Awolowo's mental magnitude of the failure of Plato's philosopher-king. Plato's philosopher-king is idealistic, and this can be said of Awolowo's mental magnitude too. It is important to train the mind, but the question remains that people can get an education just to oppress others.

Political history suggests that well-read people and intellectuals have found ways to exploit others, and they employ the knowledge from education. Lettered men are also responsible for the misfortunes of unlettered men. Although ignorance is not a defense, Awolowo's mental magnitude doctrine may present what he calls universalist socialism, but his democratic socialism in relation to mental magnitude indicates that the impact of education does not entail the ability to perform absolute good. The cases of corruption in Nigeria and the world over are evidence that educated people are capable of running the resources of the nation aground. However, the defense one would expect is that Awolowo implied that mental magnitude is not just about education but an education that is coated by discipline. It is the discipline of the mind that one should use in judging an educated mind. That is, a trained mind must be disciplined, and education is worthless without humanistic morality.

Nonetheless, human affairs cannot be easily predicted, as Awolowo assumed. Therefore, it becomes less surprising that Awolowo's socialism is theistic, thereby resting on the idea of a universal mind. The success of Awolowo's socialism is limited to the western region of the early postcolonial years. Therefore, the general acceptance of it can be debated, as Awolowo was often rejected at the polls. However, that does not invalidate the pragmatism of his socialism; it is just to point out that socialism, even with a Fabian approach, was seen as a radical political theory to adhere to. What is important is that when Awolowo had the chance to implement his socialist stances, he succeeded in creating a truly democratic socialism where the fate of the people was in their hands; at the same time, they felt connected to their leaders. The evaluation of Awolowo's socialism and mental magnitude aims not to dismiss the reliability or relativity

---

28. Makinde, *African Philosophy*, 196.
29. Adebanwi, "Quintessential Awo," 33–56.

of it. It is just to put the philosophical underpinnings of Awolowo's socialism under intellectual scrutiny.

No matter what position one may hold, Awolowo's democratic socialism seems more plausible than the socialism of other nationalists mentioned in this chapter. The impact of Awolowo's mental magnitude is written clearly in Yorùbá and Nigerian history. Therefore, when intellectuals and political thinkers appraise him as a political prophet, a philosopher, and the best president Nigeria never had, it is because of his many developmental and progressive politics that synthesized global ideology with African history. However, it is unfortunate that progressives are nowhere to be found in the current Nigerian sociopolitical epoch. This is why Awolowo's intellectualized politics and the intentions he had with his socialist programs should be immortalized and revered.

Awolowo's Humanism

African humanism is praised, and many argue that it is overromanticized. But some reject this notion. The idea of African humanism is to put traditional African principles at the forefront of governance, existential debates, and moral evaluation. The romanticization of African humanistic principles is due to the recognition of some moralistic tenets that are strictly African. The two most popular African humanistic principles are *ubuntu* and *ọmọlúàbí*. According to Bola Dauda,

> The ubuntu and ọmọlúàbí precepts remain evident in the everyday lives of the postcolonial Bantu and Yoruba communities in South and West Africa respectively. And they can be developed as a hybrid corpus of unwritten constitutions to redeem the years of slavery, colonization, and the consequent bastardization of African self-image and identity. Thus, beyond the ideological revisionism of the protagonists of negritude and also of the various forms of African socialism, ubuntu and ọmọlúàbí, if developed, seem to represent enduring indigenous systems of African humanism and ethical governance, that is, somehow democratic, equitable, morally responsive, and self-regulating. Given the historical colonial heritage of the African nation-states, ubuntu and ọmọlúàbí are systems of a cohesive and harmonious social order as they both transcend the ideological preoccupation of both communism or capitalism with distribution and production respectively, and the Darwinism of the survival of the fittest either in the free enterprise market or the exploitative struggle between the proletariat and bourgeoisie in the labor market.[30]

The creation of Ẹgbẹ́ Ọmọ Odùduwà qualifies Awolowo as an ọmọlúàbí not just by the creation but by reaching into the deep history of Yorùbá. As analyzed in the words of Falola earlier, the connection between Awolowo and Odùduwà was based on the fact that Odùduwà was the creator of history and Awolowo was the user of history. Furthermore, the central attribute of the ọmọlúàbí principle is *Ìwà* (good character) and Awolowo's mental magnitude is centered

---

30. Dauda, "African Humanism and Ethics," 475–491.

on the ability to be self-disciplined. A leader without self-discipline lacks the moral integrity to lead any community of people anywhere in the world. Awolowo thereby preached the essentiality of *Ìwà* bequeathed from the mental magnitude. Sam Aluko argues that "Awo's art of politics was so ordered that public interest rather than self or private interest prompted his entire public life. He trusted those with whom he related, even when some of them betrayed him, because he believed that without trust, the society would deteriorate into paranoia. Awo had integrity in abundance and, as he often advised us—his associates and followers—the man of integrity would always walk securely while those who took crooked paths would eventually be found out. No one, he always maintained, could truly be successful in life without integrity, soundness, trustworthiness, uprightness, and honesty."[31]

The attributes that Aluko listed are some of the basic tenets of the omolúàbí humanistic principle. As Dauda points out, "Consequently, to reinforce compliance to social norms and values, the Yoruba have names for describing all ethical behaviors: *Olóòótọ́* (the truthful); *Olódodo* (the upright or one with integrity); *Onírẹ̀lẹ̀* (the humble or modest); *Ọlọ́fin tótó* (the one who follows the rules to the letter); *Ẹni tí ò mọ àá-tií-gbọ́* (the one who would not do anything secretly that s/he would be ashamed if disclosed in public); and *Ọmọlúàbí* (the one of high integrity and probity or the paragon of all ethical behavior)."[32]

In summary, Awolowo exhibited the basic tenets of the omolúàbí principle. However, while he can be praised for this omolúàbí ethics, events in history lead his critics and political detractors to crucify him. One of the most significant was the self-contradictory move that made him accept a role in a military government. Because he was a political thinker and writer who wrote treatises on the need for democracy and an egalitarian Nigeria, critics consider it ironic for Awolowo to have partaken in a military government. Osuntokun believes that after leaving prison, Awolowo was carefully selected to be the civilian face of the Gowon military regime because of his political appeal and the people's opinion of him as a leader who was politically persecuted.[33] However, his contribution and participation in a military government that some have accused of the genocide of the Igbo people[34] further polarized opinions about him. Osuntokun believes that

whatever Awolowo did attracted the scrutiny of his political opponents. The Igbo never forgave him for his service to Nigeria during the civil war. Some believed he betrayed them for not taking his Yoruba people out of the federation. Many of his critics simply forgot the ordeal he went through from 1962 to 1967 in the hands of the same people who felt he should support them in the time of their own crisis. Awolowo was not a bitter man, wanting to pay his enemies in their own coin. What motivated him was the desire to save Nigeria from total disintegration.[35]

---

31. Aluko, "Awo as a Humanist," 75–86.

32. Dauda, "African Humanism and Ethics," 483.

33. Osuntokun, "Obafemi Awolowo."

34. Achebe, *There Was a Country*.

35. Osuntokun, "Obafemi Awolowo," 15.

Osuntokun's perception of the event is relative yet laudable: this was war as a fight against the federalism Awolowo wrote extensively for and at the same time went to prison for. Also, by shutting the borders of the eastern states from getting food supply, some have accused him of negating ọmolúwàbí principles. But the question remains: What option had Awolowo, who had been accused of being tribalistic, had other than to demonstrate not only his gratitude to the military government that released him from prison but also his patriotism by playing his part to preserve the unity of Nigeria?[36] It is, however, on record that he resigned after the war when General Yakubu Gowon did not fulfill his promise to return the country to democratic rule.

Conclusion

Awolowo's politics and philosophy can be compared to the best of any political thinker from any region of the world. Though he was unable to govern Nigeria, the practicality of his political philosophy, now known as Awoism, cannot be denied. His political philosophy and doctrine pose many interesting philosophical investigations. However, his theory remains at the intellectual level, as many leaders lack the mental magnitude that Awolowo said is required of a leader. His political philosophy is not restricted to Nigeria or Africa; the praxis of his political philosophy can work in any country in the world. In comparison to the efforts of other nationalists, what makes his socialism underappreciated is the fact that he never became the head of state. The closest he came to rule the country was through the military government, in which he served as the civilian face, minister of finance, and vice president of the military government council. Intellectuals will continue to explore his politics and philosophy because his ideas are interesting and idealistic.

Awolowo became a sage in Nigerian politics and nationalism through the mechanism of global networks, mainly Western education. As the chapter has shown, the creation of the likes of Awolowo in Yorubaland, and indeed in the whole Nigerian colony, including areas where this came belatedly, is significant in the integration of these nations into the global political system and its discourse. By the time these figures were emerging in the post–World War II years, Britain had become the extension of the Nigerian colony, Yorubaland in particular. The traffic between these two spaces, in terms of ideas and migration, took its toll on molding the society and the state that emerged afterward. Yorùbá cities like Abeokuta, Ibadan, and Lagos played strategic roles, not only in the production of Awolowo figures but in their activities. Among these cities, the role of Ibadan is even more pronounced. The next chapter thus focuses on the amalgamation of networks of scholars, writers, and intellectuals in this city and the historical contributions of this city to the intellectual productions in the modern Nigerian state through their activities. This narrative is inherently laden with the production of a global Yorùbá space in many respects, to be explored next.

---

36. Awolowo, *Awo on the Nigerian Civil War*.

    GLOBAL YORÙBÁ

Ibadan 16
THE INTELLECTUAL CAPITAL CITY

Introduction

Cities are constructions of multiple ideas and peoples facilitated by location and a vibrant economy. Location provides the auspicious ambiance for activities that construct the reality of the city. Building on its precolonial pedigree, the city of Ibadan earnestly assumed the typical role of cities around the world from the colonial period onward. Whereas many cities around the world are known for their economic and social attractiveness in terms of big markets, tourism, arts, and entertainment, the Yorùbá city of Ibadan is popular for its intellectual attractiveness. Since the advent of Western education, it has become a melting pot for students, intellectuality, and emerging educated fellows in the colony. This status was boosted when in 1948, the University College, now the University of Ibadan, was added to the few secondary schools located in this city.

Since the establishment of the institution, the first of its kind in Nigeria, and one of the very few in Africa at the time, it has been dominated by several structures of intellectual relations and engagements, increasing the stake of intellectuals residing in the city. In a great departure from its precolonial history, book clubs, publishing presses, schools, and libraries have been major magnetic forces in the modern making of Ibadan. The military prowess of the past is thus transformed into intellectualism during the colonial and postcolonial periods.

The southwestern region of Nigeria, known as the home of the Yorùbá, has always featured prominently in the discussion of the nation and its resources and its capital, whether intellectual, economic, social, cultural, or human. This chapter defines capital along the lines of thought proposed by the French sociologist Pierre Bourdieu regarding capital and society. He conceives capital as resources given to the production or creation of social profit transferable through culture, cultural participants, cultural praxes, and cultural institutions.[1] Here, social profit signals those returns that aid a community's development toward defining the features of their modernity. Culture is paramount in creating and disseminating capital, or the significance of the reflection capital cast back on culture as some kind of net profit. Social capital is "the virtue through which third world communities may develop."[2] Bonds and strong selfless

---

1. Bourdieu, "Forms of Capital," 241–258.
2. Ayokunle and Akinpelu, "Social Capital," 77–88.

ties along familial, kin, or kith lines are the required ingredients.[3] Cultural capital also provides material for the generation of economic capital.

My conception of culture allows for this association, or for one to be able to read this association as a source or enabler of progress for the immediate community of Ibadan and the larger national and global one. It follows the usual definition of culture as a set of dispositions, beliefs, and practices that define a group of people; set them apart from others; form structures that shape identities, individuals, and subjectivities; and provide vantage points for these identities to understand reality and the human condition. The association of humans inevitably generates capital since human activities and identity formation are necessary elements for the kinds of productive endeavors, atmosphere, or culture that can drive growth along cultural and national lines or even poise cultures as noteworthy contributors to global discussions.

Hence, culture, in the way it is being used here, is a baseline without which no other forms of capital exist. Cultural capital, as a type, therefore reflects intellectual capital—where the latter refers to those locally available resources in the manner of folkloric practices, belief systems, and plastic expressions, among others—considering that it not only shapes the latter in whatever form it occurs but also provides the very materials and channels through which intellectuality as a resource is distilled into productive forms. Cultural capital, what Louie Rodriquez determines as "a set of knowledge, skills, and dispositions that are typically passed from one generation to the next,"[4] allows for or produces the networks, materials, folkloric routines, and even institutional practices that foster the generation of knowledge as a capital form, the type that is passed along not only generation lines but also transculturally, and that, in the context of a nation-state as well as that of the transnational global stage, engenders the production of feelings and resources that drive the human condition forward.

Hence, the focus of this chapter is not on the subtle—if technical—difference between cultural and intellectual capital as forms of capital. The interest lies in anchoring the chapter on how capital as a product of knowledge can be sourced from a cultural group, particularly one of its prominent subgroups as a defined geopolitical formation or cultural zone, with immense implications for propagation, generation, and dissemination of knowledge. Essentially, the interest is on how the location of Ibadan as a geopolitically defined cultural subgroup of the Yorùbá, existing or occupying a space in time and a time in space, is responsible for the production of knowledge as a capital form—that is, through those practices, structures, identities, subjectivities, ties, associations, ideologies, and beliefs that constitute a culture type. Particularly of interest is how Ibadan fosters the generation of the kind of knowledge that ripples beyond the local boundaries that determine it as a geopolitically distinct cultural formation in Nigeria and the borders that define the Yorùbá as one of the largest ethnic groups in Africa—at least to the extent that Ibadan is the capital of a state and one of the historical geocultural references of the Yorùbá world, home, and diaspora.

The focus of this chapter will be on how intellectual capital is a product of cultural capital, as well as how Ibadan, as a physical zone, cultural space, and geopolitical place, encourages the

---

3. Ayokunle and Akinpelu, "Social Capital."

4. Rodriguez, "Dialoguing, Cultural Capital," 22.

patterns of living that translate into intellectual productivity, one that contributes to the discourse beyond ethnic and national lines. The distinction between space and place is to signify the place of the abstract and the physical realms where those features that determine Ibadan as unique to all other Yorùbá geographies come to a head. It relies on conceptions of place as the zone of human activities and the (physical) public realm controlled by the state and its civil structures and also on those material and tangible aspects of the everyday cultural reality of Ibadan.[5] Space, on the other hand, is conceived in more abstract terms as the realm of tactical acts of survival and negotiating the conditions of living through the everyday on collective and personal terms.[6] The idea of space here leans toward the conception of an unstable, impermanent, and temporal ideal.[7]

The interest here is particularly not in the politicized manner in which scholars like Michel de Certeau, Homi Barber, Henri Lefebvre, Edward Relph, and Victor Turner have conceived of the difference between space and place, employing conceptually heavy terms like *liminal space*, *third space*, *locus of power*, and the *realm of the beyond*, even though one cannot ignore or refuse the place of politics in how spaces/places are governed and how such governance determines actions since actions produce capital as results. My interest, however, is how the one (space) is located in the other (place) as a protean and makeshift zone of activities and how this affects the production of capital. In clearer terms, space is germane to the conditioning of cultural participants as members of society. It is not only the dais from which individuals continually form a sense of self and their context; through the discourses and expressions that govern it, it also provides a frame of reference for its members. Thus, a cultural space is considered a realm of interactivity with regulations and defining discourses that govern identity and the codes of conduct, which bear lasting implications—in this context in the form of capital. It is thus a frame that shapes actions as members respond to the realities as induced by the structures of the geophysical place. It is from this frame that their collective identities are forged and individual subjectivities maintained that allow for producing relations and expressions that sustain cultural tempers and national progress, particularly when it supports the ties and bonds along filial, kith, or ancestral lines that aid in providing the cohesive atmosphere where resources for progress can be produced. Therefore, in this chapter, the idea is to reflect on how various aspects of Ibadan as a major metropolitan center in Yorubaland situates itself as a cultural space—that is, a vortex of cultural possibilities and material realities through which the kinds of advancements that push forward a group onward toward modernization are achieved.

Consequently, in this chapter, reflections will be on Ibadan as a physical site, geographical place, and realm of the discourse and the activities that constitute it.[8] Also, there will be thoughts along the lines of the function or implication of the historical progress within Ibadan, given its unique situation as one of the important cultural and historical sites of the Yorùbá. These functions will cut across several aspects of culture as it is generally defined, with emphasis on the attitudes, patterns of governance, social philosophies, and even institutionalized

---

5. Johnson, "Geographies," 790–803. See also Ekeh, "Colonialism and the Two Publics," 91–112.
6. See, for example, Marshall et al., *Contemporary Publics*.
7. Dudgeon and Fielder, "Third Spaces within Tertiary Places," 396–409.
8. Johnson, "Geographies."

modes of being and how they have shaped and pushed Ibadan to a position of influence and enabled it to provide the kind of atmosphere that has led to the cultivation and production of intellectual capital.

Hence, the approach is to read parts of the history of the making of and transition of Ibadan from its earliest formation into a precolonial city-state and a modern state in present-day Nigeria to trace connections between the incidences that are involved in this process of the transition and the various forms of knowledge they have produced over time. Given how expansive it will be to trace and discuss all of the various aspects of Ibadan's significant contribution to the Yorùbá, Nigeria, and the diaspora, the discussion is limited to aspects of the past that involve how Ibadan has come to be and those structures that came into place through the process and how these structures provide the impetus for the emergence spaces that have come to be seen as producing various types of knowledge as capital forms, both home and abroad.

In plain terms, some of the historical details and incidences as well as other social processes that culminated in the stature of Ibadan in the precolonial era will be identified. These will be read as forms of capital in the service of generating more capital, and then used to reflect on the present-day influences Ibadan has had in terms of intellectual content and knowledge production. In reflecting on the latter, the focus is largely on the dynamics of the literary and scholarly cultures that grew out of Ibadan, partly because of the need to delimit the scope of this chapter and partly because these aspects lend themselves generously to the discussion at hand, reflecting in precise, interesting, and clear ways how Ibadan, a Yorùbá town, has come to contribute intellectual capital to the nation and beyond.

The Knowledge Value of the Formation of Ibadan

In the discourse of modernity, Nigeria has been characterized as belonging to that cohort of nation-states labeled "fledgling modernities," an idea suggesting modernity as an indicator of progressive growth, a manifestation of many of the symbols of Westernization, and a symbol of advanced civilization. My approach here will be to read between the lines and draw inferences that support my reading of established historical facts as endeavors, processes, and contributions of Ibadan (the place, cultural space, and people) to knowledge. Hence, to start with the intellectual capital of Ibadan, the emphasis is on the knowledge value of those attempts, actions, procedures, policies, and reforms that suggest endeavors toward modernity and how these historical data provide us with insight into how Ibadan has accumulated intellectual value over time. Thus, the approach here should be seen as rethinking and rereading those historical events as instances of knowledge forms, how past actions produced future consequences and allowed Ibadan to generate different kinds of capital and, eventually, an entire knowledge system. It thus means that those past actions are potential or viable knowledge forms that produced in the future other knowledge considerable as capital.

Starting from this premise is paramount because it offers us a view into not only the formation of Ibadan but how this formation, the events that led to it, and the events that its formation enabled have direct and indirect ties to those indexes of modernity. This helps us to see an aspect of the historical significance and import of the historical events that shaped Ibadan. Ibadan proper is one of the largest indigenous cities in Nigeria, occupying a total area of 3,080

Figure 16.1. The entrance to the University of Ibadan, the first tertiary institution founded in 1948. The generations of scholars and professionals the University of Ibadan has produced in the last seven and half decades have formed great minds doing great things in all spheres of human life in the Yorùbá diaspora. Photo by Toyin Falola.

square kilometers.[9] Founded in the 1830s[10] out of a series of crises and "as a consequence of the political crises, wars and migrations of the century,"[11] the city has remained a cornerstone of the Yorùbá heritage. This owes to the city's stature as previously a military settlement that transformed successfully into a thriving city-state, otherwise sometimes considered a Yorùbá country by historians such as Bolanle Awe.[12] Significant also are the concessions and reforms it pursued that allowed such a transition. Thus, the crises, reforms, and concessions have culminated in the production of valuable resources that have not only shaped Ibadan as a trailblazer

---

9. Adeboye, "City of Ìbàdàn," 7–19.

10. Awe, "Militarism and Economic Development," 65–77; and Adeboye, "City of Ìbàdàn."

11. Falola, "From Hospitality to Hostility," 51–68.

12. For recurring uses of this particular designation, see Awe, "Militarism and Economic Development"; Awe, "Ajele System," 47–60.

of a metropolitan city but shaped it in a way that it would become of positive value to pre- and postindependence Nigeria.

While Awe has described this as a "phenomenal rise,"[13] it owes largely to Ibadan's timely actions in the form of sociocultural reforms, campaigns, and governing structures, which cast a light on the actions of persons at group and collective structures, and how these reflect on the generation of the kind of capital that has maintained Ibadan's foothold in the history and discussion of modern Yorùbá, home or abroad. Whether the conditions of its making are confused is not the subject here; rather, it is the relevance of these conditions and their response. Equally vital is reading both as remote causes of Ibadan's capital value to knowledge generation over time and to the image of the Yorùbá, past and present.

One of the crises so referenced in the creation of Ibadan that has amounted to having and retaining its pioneer place in the identity of the Yorùbá is the Fulani jihadist campaign and the Ibadan–Ilorin war. The Fulani made invasive excursions into northern Yorubaland that led to the escapees and other Yorùbá subgroups fleeing the Fulani-ravaged northern Yorùbá settlements to resettle in Ibadan, originally considered a small Ẹ̀gbá village.[14] That it provided security as a war camp is one of the reasons for the population of Ibadan by several individuals and different Yorùbá subgroups. This bears a lasting imprint on and through the Mesìọ̀gọ̀ philosophy and principle and its convivial connotations or import associated with Ibadan or, particularly, the social capital that generates the kind of knowledge that has stood Ibadan ahead of many of its fellow Yorùbá city-states. Because social capital itself involves "investments in social relations with expected returns,"[15] one cannot read a useful relationship between this attempt at social capital through openness and the kind of Ibadan as a distinct sociocultural and geopolitical metropolis that has come to contribute significantly to the image of the Yorùbá.

For instance, we see this investment in the Ibadan norms, social behaviors, and collective values that emerged in the city around ties-making between ethnic groups, fidelities to preexisting kingdoms, and individualism as the basis for collective growth. This refers to the idea that "everybody at Ibadan, irrespective of his place of origin, had equal opportunities, and could acquire wealth, power and status."[16] This view is a well-shared one, with Akintoye claiming that this feature of the social structure of Ibadan ensured that "a man of ability, could, no matter his sub-ethnic or family antecedents, rise to any position in the state . . . [and] so could he, if he was so inclined, acquire considerable wealth as farmer or trader or artisan."[17] Adebanji Akintoye mentioned the absence of the traditional Yorùbá land tenure system, with which land of a particular Yorùbá subgroup was distributed based on lineage. However, in Ibadan, those who made up its polity as individuals were at liberty to use and grow portions of the landscape that was accessible, or they could cultivate as far as they could put in the required work.[18]

---

13. Awe, "Ajele System," 47.

14. Falola, "From Hospitality to Hostility."

15. Awofeso and Ademuson, "Social Capital," 41.

16. Falola, "From Hospitality to Hostility," 52.

17. Akintoye, *Revolution and Power Politics*.

18. Akintoye, *Revolution and Power Politics*.

Thus, Ibadan thrived because of a kind of social policy that sought to attract the best of minds, skillful and resourceful. A good example of this is Balógun Ibikunle, described in 1851 as a middle-aged warrior, a military man "to whom master of arms had to be made to subserve political ends."[19] Awe, using the term *soldier of fortune* to describe men like Ibikunle as an adventurous war chief, was one of those men who, with their popularity as victors, channeled their knowledge and military exploits to the service of the host community. To quote Awe, men like Ibikunle, who would become Òsì Balógun, third in rank to the Balógun, the Ibadan head military honcho, "had visions of restoration of an orderly, powerful Yoruba community maintained by Ibadan arms and enjoying the blessing and moral support of the Aàfin Àtìbà; this was in fact for them another name for an Ibadan empire, which because of the patronage of the Aláàfin would command the support of the other Ọ̀yọ́-Yoruba towns."[20]

These short historical digression points toward an important sociocultural orientation germane to the argument that lies at the heart of this discussion: the very conditions that resulted in the making of Ibadan and that have sustained its ascendancy as a producer of intellectual capital. While shedding more light on how this conclusion is arrived at is the main idea here, it is also important to note that despite the famed hospitality of Ibadan, there are also instances that point to hostility, an argument well-made in my 2009 article "From Hospitality to Hostility: Ibadan and Strangers."

The above premise encourages reading the historical crises that led to the development of Ibadan and to its famed processes of modernity, with modernity here meaning structured reforms toward modern civilization as remote baselines to produce capital, the type that continues to stand Ibadan out from its environs. When the Old Ọ̀yọ́ Empire collapsed, and with it its stature in the Yorùbá community and the peace it afforded, Ibadan stood in place to ensure the protection of Yorùbá cities to the north by using advanced military tactics and reforms to repel the Fulani's advancement and by reclaiming many states back to the Yorùbá fold. Its ability to respond to the dire military solution required at the time, which itself culminated in a rapid, commendable, and well-organized military-dependent state, galvanized the relevance of militarism to the new states that would emerge, either in terms of annexation, being free from Fulani hold, or that willingly moved under the protection of Ibadan.

For instance, militarism allowed for a different—and as at the time—effective distribution of political power and influence within Ibadan and the towns under its protection.[21] More so, it fostered the pursuit of governing procedures and strategies of a state rule that would prove beneficial to both indigenes and the larger Yorùbá nation. A good example is the introduction of the *Ajélẹ́* system, which was employed by Ibadan to administer its empire. Awe would note that while Ibadan's military approach to the Fulani menace and other intra-Yorùbá subgroup wars, like that between Ibadan and Ijaye, allowed for successful campaigns, where riches flowed into Ibadan and made affluent war chiefs and other soldiers who could distinguish themselves, it also allowed Ibadan to resolve another major problem that beset the Yorùbá world. To quote the historian, "Each state within the Yoruba country was faced in varying degrees with the

---

19. Awe, "Ajele System," 52.

20. Awe, "Ajele System," 52.

21. Awe, "Militarism and Economic Development."

problems of military survival, and each responded in its way to this crisis: it is, however, in Ibadan that the Yoruba people came to grips with the problem."[22] This is not in the least significant, going by the nature of the often extended and numerous wars many Yorùbá subgroups as precolonial independent nations were submerged in, and which drastically impeded growth for some (Ijaye and Owu) and constituted an impasse between reconciling state governance and military campaigns and expeditions—given how the latter is as risky and unpredictable in its outcomes for state progress as it involves expending state resources, in all sense of the word.

However, Ibadan's case is unique for many reasons, many of which allowed for the success of this strategy and the founding of state governance, a strangely democratic one in many ways, on militarism—an almost ironic case. On the one hand, its foremost settlers and inhabitants were of the military, as the geospace was a military camp. These individuals were experienced military men with skills and application of the strategies and discipline required to etch out success in the most unlikely of situations. It is only logical that given the ample opportunities Ibadan provided for growth, this would reflect on its success as a rapidly expanding empire. More so, the military nature and origin of the region meant a natural and almost kneejerk disregard for the bottlenecks and bureaucratic impasse that comes with the usual royal administration of Yorùbá societies.

The adoption of militarism as an approach to state rule allowed for the making of institutional reforms and what could be considered constitutional edicts that evoked, relied on, or blended with the demands of a highly militarized atmosphere of the period and region as Ibadan progressed from a camp to a city and a nation of sorts. Save for a few religious titles held in high esteem, Ibadan is said to have denounced the use of and reliance on the traditionally conventional route toward power ascension. In its place was a meritocracy, which meant that preference was given to ability in bestowing chieftaincy titles and other recognitions with social significance and political authority. To use Awe's words on the matter, "competition was thrown open to all freeborn men, and a man's proven ability as a soldier, rather than the accident of birth, became the determinant factor of his success in acquiring a title."[23]

In discussing these initial periods in the formation of Ibadan, the aim is to unveil a reading of the generation of capital that relies on certain historical reforms, social ethos, and efforts at individual and collective levels that can be read as remote forms of capital-making with future dividends that are now visibly seen in the present stature of Ibadan. To posit that these reforms led to a modern-day Ibadan in their short- and long-term life span means that there is a strong relationship between Ibadan as a war-camp-turned-city and as a modern postcolonial metropolitan center, with defined features of modernity, and the types of modern features that have improved the Yorùbá race in many ways, as well as the nation-state of Nigeria and the Yorùbá diaspora.

The emphasis on meritocracy led to the cultivation and even indirect attraction of credible and intelligent persons, who had much to offer and whose pedigree spoke for them. Working this into governance as a reform allowed for upward mobility by individuals; it also encouraged

---

22. Awe, "Militarism and Economic Development," 66.

23. Awe, "Militarism and Economic Development," 65.

a system where accolades and positional benefits like chieftaincy (Balógun, Òsì Balógun, Òtún Balógun, Bàbá Kékeré, etc.) were fluid and mobile. By being anchored on merit and proven value or valor, these positions were kept beneficial to the community as valuable resources and were attractive to those who had value to add or could use capital to generate more capital. It is possible to interpret such chieftaincy titles as endowed positions—that is, they were positions that endowed individuals with the resources they required to use their intellect, war wisdom, experience, valor, might, and sagacity to win campaigns, cultivate the followings that campaigns required, instill trust that was required within the rank and file, and judiciously put to use the spoils of war that were recovered during successful invasions and rescuing of invaded protected towns.

For instance, those who were able to attain such lofty positions during the height of Ibadan's military strength and governing success were required to be both warriors and resourceful people. They were expected to "command a large body of followers whose loyalty would be primarily to him, for the Ibadan army was, in reality, a collection of private personal armies made up of such loyal followers."[24] In this context, each leader had trusted followers, who, in turn, were occupiers of important positions within the army. All had servants who were sometimes prisoners of war and who worked on their establishments, like their farms, leading to massive harvests and production. To quote Awe, who describes this scenario perfectly,

> The bulk of this following would consist of slaves, mainly captives of war, many of whom were absorbed into his household; their presence ensured not only his rise to power, but also his continued enjoyment of that power, because of the very many services they rendered to him. The best of them were recruited into his own private army; while most of these formed the rank and file, a few held important positions as leaders in the army, and in turn had their own personal following of slaves. Most of the remaining slaves worked on his farms, and many Ibadan farms were indeed colonized entirely by these slaves; others did specialized duties, like the Fulani and Hausa slaves who looked after his cattle and horses, the slaves who stayed around his compound and served as messengers, drummers, and praise singers, as well as the women slaves who became his wives and ensured the continuation of his lineage.[25]

With many warriors having this kind of structure determining their relationship to Ibadan, and Ibadan's sociocultural development hinged on this structure, it is not hard to imagine the productivity levels impacting the economic life of Ibadan generally. While it can be argued that such a warrior mindset worked into a community's mode of governance can be pernicious, given the precarious nature of war and its effects on community building—and there are merits to such a stance—it is the case that the growth and development of Ibadan demanded more than the skill of war, as the system in the place itself required a great deal of economic success, if not for nothing, to sustain its expansive population that stretched across Ibadan and the areas within its protective reach.

---

24. Awe, "Militarism and Economic Development," 67.

25. Awe, "Militarism and Economic Development," 67.

Ibadan's openness to outsiders, its noteworthy celebration and exaltation of merit, and its fondness for rewarding ability with profitable recognition naturally drew those with substance and potential, with only further benefit to the region. The conquests, military might and power, and the subsequent stability Ibadan provided because of its successful campaigns naturally was a magnet for economically savvy individuals as well as indigenes from other places seeking stability for their life patterns and trade. It is thus not impossible that the military structure made way for the kind of resources that led to the development of the region. Agriculture, trade, and craft—all of which relied heavily on the intellect to make a useful contextual distinction—were some of the pillars of Ibadan's economic growth that provided an impressive buoyant standard of living, which was directly traceable to the military structuring Ibadan encouraged.

The Ibadan farmers, who were the original settlers, had taken up large swaths of land, and those with whom they shared the lands as welcomed strangers engaged in large-scale farming, growing staple crops like beans, vegetables, cotton, and yams. These lands were tilled and worked by those who made up the retinue and households of the military personnel, given that large households constituted by workers of different ranks signified wealth and were thus common features, given the emphasis on military occupations and the preponderance of individuals who pursued military careers to distinguish themselves, contribute to the society, and scale the economic ladder. After all, in Ibadan, power and wealth often went together.[26] The large influx of people into Ibadan encouraged and galvanized the diversification of economic industry, whereby several types of trade—war related and agro allied, ranging from blacksmiths, weavers, and tailors—became popular. Blacksmithing offers an instructive example of the relationship between the approach to governance by Ibadan and economic growth. This industry is said to have had about seventy workshops. With enough presence all over Ibadan and by being run by refugees from neighboring settlements that had arrived in Ibadan, the workshops, just like the farms, were managed by military personnel with the manpower as part of their lineage.

Patronage by warlords and soldiers meant more production of commodities ranging from metal instruments for warfare and edibles, all of which culminated in the flourishing of a diversified economy buoyed by an appreciable increase in the production of necessities (crops and tools) and by profiting from these productions through marketing them to others outside Ibadan. The need to feed a growing population and the increase in production resulting from expansion through warfare required strategic economic decisions. One is the creation of markets, rural and urban, specialized and generic, with routines and schedules, which led to emphasizing economy-related positions/chieftaincies like *Ìyálójà*. Markets like Ọjà Igbo, Elékùrọ̀, and Ọjà Ọba all had their uses, like markets accessible chiefly by and for goods from the forest, markets for palm kernels, and markets for materials and goods from overseas, respectively. Another is the creation of multiple trade routes that linked the world up with Ibadan. Through this, trade was sustained as materials and production moved in and out of the region.

Two things are apparent: The first is that the structures set in place in organizing a region as a sociocultural space can successfully rely on militarism as a resource; this means as a mode of

---

26. Falola, "From Hospitality to Hostility."

operations and state philosophy, militarism as adopted by Ibadan tests against any assumption in the lines of the implausibility in economic activities relying successfully on military choices. However, it should also be noted that the same militarism did impede economic growth in certain areas, which is only logical given the upsides and downsides of economic strategies.[27] The second apparent thing is that Ibadan's growth was contingent on the needs of the region as determined by its brand of religiosity. Thus, the service of distinguished warriors to Ibadan as a growing nation and the emphasis Ibadan placed on proven merit were self-beneficial since they led to more effort to outdo any initial performance put forward or for which they were known. More so, such progressive application of the self to task and state duty, as well as securing and promoting the well-being of inhabitants and those from other Yorùbá subgroups under the rule and protection of Ibadan, would have positive effects on the state and the several facets that make it up.

Figure 16.2.
The frontage of the University of Ibadan, by Dr. Kazeem Ekeolu.

---

27. For more on how Ìbàdàn's economic reliance on militarism impeded much-needed or possible growth, see Awe, "Militarism and Economic Development."

Another unique way in which Ibadan handled its affairs that leaves much material for reading in the sense of intellectual resources is its mode of managing its territory and harnessing the best gifts of this territory for its gains while also making sure these territories thrive, given the reciprocity between them and their longevity as viable geocultural spaces. The Ajẹ́lẹ́ system, as adopted by Ibadan, is a physical manifestation of the use of human capital backed by the kind of sociocultural nous capable of putting the former to the generation of resources as a knowledge form or product of knowledge. This system, with its multiple influences traceable to preexisting Yorùbá and non-Yorùbá kingdoms, reflected the energy and drive behind the rapid growth of an empire as well as the unique political system and military temper of Ibadan.[28] The Ajẹ́lẹ́ system was a representative type, with a town, out of the several territories under the protection of Ibadan, given out to chiefs in reward for their military services. While some chiefs had more towns allocated to them than others, they were all spokespersons in those towns, often serving as the link between them and Ibadan.

Much authority was given to these chiefs in the administration of their towns, so they often had judicial and administrative power through which they regulated their towns on behalf of Ibadan. The Ajẹ́lẹ́, thus, is the representative of each chief in his allotted town. As a type of political agent,[29] he maintained Ibadan's hold over the towns. One important factor about this Ajẹ́lẹ́ system is that the Ajẹ́lẹ́ need not be from Ibadan as an indigene[30] but be fastidious in representing and pursuing the will and desires of Ibadan as a political unit. To quote Awe, "[The Ajẹ́lẹ́'s] role was to reinforce Ibadan's control in a subject-town; each town, however small, had its own separate Ajẹ́lẹ́ in other to ensure complete and firm jurisdiction."[31] Thus, individuals demonstrate faithfulness and commitment to causes where moral capital values are required, alongside the usual emphasis on cognitive aptitude in managing people, and enforcing leadership qualities derived from a military-style commitment to self-growth and application to duty.

Evident in this political structuring are the cultural values placed on sense and intellect in the pursuit of self-worth through devotion to the collective. So, while Awe argues that the Ajẹ́lẹ́'s commitment was to his overlord or chief and not to Ibadan, the deference of each chief to Ibadan suggests an indirect commitment to the larger political unit. It would then seem that Ibadan rewarded ability handsomely, as the Ajẹ́lẹ́ had enough political clout to command respect from the political leaders of each town where they resided. And that the Ajẹ́lẹ́ had the duty of ensuring economic success and realizing the economic goals of each chief, which reflected on Ibadan since tributes of all sorts had to be sent from the towns managed by the chiefs to Ibadan. This tribute system itself is noteworthy in the context of Ibadan's mode of governance. Taxes were levied from households, who paid it to the ruler of each town, supervised by the Ajẹ́lẹ́, fortnightly. These levies found their way to the chiefs in Ibadan, and they contributed to the financial coffers of Ibadan, where they were largely managed by the Bale for projects or used to compensate the chiefs for their administrative successes.

---

28. Awe, "Ajele System."

29. Awe, "Ajele System."

30. For significant definitions or the changes in the definitions of what an Ìbàdàn person is/has been taken to be over time, see Falola, "From Hospitality to Hostility."

31. Awe, "Ajele System," 54.

Ibadan capitalized on its human resources as well as the potential of its emphasis on ways of being while instrumentalizing these capabilities by founding solid structures based on military discipline and a way of life that required mostly a soldierly philosophy. If it is true that what made up power in Ibadan and enabled its organicity as a civilization in the nineteenth century were "chieftaincy titles and control over a large, disciplined and effectively organized army,"[32] then there is a lot to think about in how these allowed for a particular approach to cultivating unique modes of governance that are themselves facilitators of capital production. And that these same characteristics elicited genuine appreciable qualities as they are signifiers of the kind of merit-based qualities required in individuals to contribute to the power and development of Ibadan allows us to make sense of them as valuable resources—that is, the kind of capital that eventually goes into the production of long-lasting knowledge resources.

Having attempted to sketch out the founding origins of Ibadan and how the resultant sociocultural formation and the civilization that arose from it contributed to the stature of Ibadan as a capital resource of knowledge generation—the type with wide-ranging benefits along economic, social, educational, political, and global lines—the focus shifts to examining other aspects of Ibadan as they have revealed its status as a resource of intellectual capital production.

Ibadan and Education: Literary Circles, Scholarship, and the Making of Intellectual Capital

Ibadan has had a strong influence on the national and diasporic intellectual culture, with its strongest evidence in the realm of literature and creative writing. It is generally agreed that the region sparked what has been dubbed a cultural renaissance through the arts in Nigeria.[33] In postindependence Nigeria, Ibadan stood as the pinnacle of Nigeria's creative and intellectual accomplishments, rivaled only by Nsukka[34] as a historical hub of creativity and intellectualism. This has cemented Ibadan's place as the foremost producer of intellectual content in Yorubaland/Southwest and Nigeria at large. The formation of intellectual culture as it has occurred in Ibadan, and the role of Ibadan in it as a place and space with its distinct character, is immensely significant because, as Olabode Ibironke rightfully frames it, in the event of the anti- and postcolonial agitations that sought and moved to reduce the influence of British power, "the greater force of unification was not to be found in political organizations but in cultural institutions and spaces."[35]

On the one hand, Ibironke's position allows for reading and translating cultural spaces as having far-reaching, strong, and lasting influences within the polity and on governance, ultimately promoting a reflection on the geopolitical spaces within which cultural spaces are cultivated as actors in social formation and, in this case, in the production of knowledge. His submission is also significant because of the educational atmosphere that Ibadan supported, which not only allowed for the founding of the University of Ibadan, formerly known as University College,

---

32. Falola, "From Hospitality to Hostility," 55.
33. See Raji-Oyelade, "Ìbàdàn and the Memory of a Generation," 21–35.
34. Okunoye, "Critical Reception," 769–791.
35. Ibironke, "Ìbàdàn Origins," 550–559.

Ibadan, but also for attracting the kind of resources and human capital that led to the development and promotion of artistry, intellectual content, and, ultimately, knowledge production. For instance, expatriate scholar-teachers like Martin Banham, Ulli Beier, and Janheinze Jahn, among others, were instrumental to the emergence, development, and sustenance of creative groups and communities in the University of Ibadan.

Besides these foreign elements is the social character of Ibadan itself—to follow the argument that alien influences like colonial education and educators are not solely responsible for the fertilization and germination of the robust nature of Nigerian literature as it is traceable to the University of Ibadan and the city more broadly.[36] As argued by Olabode Ibironke, the very character that stood Ibadan out from other southern states in the nation also "accounts for the extraordinary eruption of creativity that was witnessed during the 1960s."[37] Raymond Williams identifies some of the elements of this character by pointing out "that the pursuit of industry and urbane pleasure" coupled with its "defining centers of culture and learning" were primary markers of its emphatic tilt "toward progress, enlightenment, civilization, and liberty."[38] Incidentally, these character elements are the very same principles we can trace and have identified with the beginnings of Ibadan as a war-camp-turned-state. As Ibironke notes, these same attributes can be traced to the creative aesthetics and socially conscious creative groups that were formed at the heart of Ibadan and through the University of Ibadan, such as the Mbari Club that was created by Ulli Beier and named by Chinua Achebe. That the club was located outside the university but within the heart of Ibadan goes to show the influence of the social character of Ibadan as a resource for intellectual growth and production. A description of Mbari Club by Wole Ogundele ties strongly with this part of the social character of Ibadan, which further emphasizes the point:

> MBARI Club was as much a social centre as a cultural-intellectual organization, and its social side needs stressing. It was a place for likeminded people generally interested in the arts and culture to gather freely and informally—something like the Paris Café but with an African character. There was a Lebanese restaurant upstairs which supplied very good food and drinks at any time, and very quickly too. At night members sat in the open courtyard to eat, drink, relax and talk. It was an open house kept strictly informal, with a library that anybody could just walk into, wander around in, and browse to his heart's content. There were paintings and pictures everywhere. This made it possible for people not to have to wait for something to be happening in the place before visiting it. In any case something or other was always happening in the place and it was a magnetic point for the members, the university people, young American Peace Corps volunteers (who made it a place of cultural pilgrimage), and the townspeople generally.[39]

This social spirit of Mbari and the way it integrates with the creative side of the club evokes the character of Ibadan and its ability to allow for a fine and even compensatory blend of

---

36. Ibironke, "Ìbàdàn Origins."
37. Ibironke, "Ìbàdàn Origins," 551.
38. Ibironke, "Ìbàdàn Origins," 551.
39. Ibironke, "Ìbàdàn Origins," 555.

creativity, pleasure, industry, and social awareness. It is in recognition of the place of Ibadan as a strong stimulator of creativity and intellectualism that tags like "Ibadan School" or "Ibadan tradition" as opposed to the "Nsukka school" have been employed in reflecting on the strands of anti-colonial and postcolonial creative dispositions that were predominant in the country a few decades after independence.[40] This period has received critical attention to better understand pre– and post–civil war Nigerian creative writing traditions, signaling their legitimacy as descriptors of a type of intellectualism and artistic philosophy. Emphasizing the place of Ibadan in light of being responsible for influencing a national literary tradition and its accompanying intellectual traditions are Banham and John Ramsaran: "Ibadan has become the centre of literary creativity in the country and has an important part to play in the guidance of a Nigerian literature."[41] It is thus not surprising that the same Ibadan, with its citadels of learning and the accompanying creative spirits, has led to the emergence of several writers of repute, some prominent publishing houses and publications, and path-charting creative groups. Some of these writers have been identified as kindling the foundational spirit that has fermented as Nigeria's and indeed influenced Africa's creative and literary tradition.

In trying to emphasize the integral place of Ibadan in the success that Nigeria's literary tradition has recorded over time, in terms of prestige, longevity, relevance, and political and economic clout, before and after the civil war, Banham rebuts the argument that colonial education contributed immensely by juxtaposing the several college universities the British Empire created across Africa and the Caribbean, and how these colonial universities paled in comparison. The fact that the University of Ibadan has produced several distinguished, world-renowned writers—in the words of Banham, "two of them candidates for Nobels, and one a laureate"—says a lot.[42] This assertion is tendered by Banham in corroborating the argument that Ibadan allowed for the cultivation of art in a particular way that many of its (Nigerian literature) forebears or founding fathers pursued or gave life to.

Explained in another way by Nathan Suhr-Sytsma, despite the university, when it was a colonial institution (University College Ibadan), having introduced modern literature in English, and what Suhr-Systma describes as mediating literary modernity to the pioneering groups, "they came into a sense of themselves as modern African poets and playwrights by developing their cultural institutions."[43]Another interpretation is that this early cohort of writers was able to define for themselves the idiom of their literary sensibilities or what idiom best describes their literary orientations, which meant they could achieve a judicious and seamless blend of cultural nationalist with idiosyncratic modernist stylist/aesthetical aspirations. Hence, this so-called way is defined as the pursuit of or being free to cultivate art as each artist deems fit. Quoting Robert Wren, who has researched Ibadan's role in the cultivation and successful growth of Nigerian literature, Ibironke puts the claim this way: in Ibadan "were a happy coincidence of people whose idea of the arts is that they should be a living form."[44]

---

40. See Okunoye, "Critical Reception."
41. Okunoye, "Critical Reception," 778.
42. Ibironke, "Ìbàdàn Origins," 554.
43. Suhr-Systma, "Ìbàdàn Modernism," 44.
44. Ibironke, "Ìbàdàn Origins," 554.

Already shared by several editors and publishers of Nigerian and, indeed, African literature, this idea that identifies Ibadan's place as being central in the production of literature and literary culture as knowledge forms is not misplaced. For instance, and quite important to note, the division of the direction of the intellectual and cultural consciousness between the Nigerian southwest and southeast writers or literary traditions has often engendered dichotomies along aesthetic and thematic lines that have implications for their source cultures. What is meant here is that the "Nsukka School" tradition, reflected by its creative writers, privileged an Igbo-centered cultural consciousness, while the Ibadan counterpart was the direct opposite. As Oyeniyi Okunoye frames it, "The Ibadan poets are neither drawn from, nor associated with any geo-cultural section of the country."[45]

Okunoye's point reflects an established point about the openness of Ibadan, which dates to its beginning as it is now known, while also demonstrating how this reflects in the city's social character, institutions, and the lives of its people. In another article, Okunoye attributes the creative consciousness of the founding group of writers and intellectuals at the University of Ibadan to being simultaneously fed by private, personal, and collective commitments. He argues in this article that the writers of the founding era, who were students of the University of Ibadan, are best regarded as "self-conscious writers whose work was shaped by shared experiences as well as individual preferences."[46] While we cannot attribute the reason for this creative direction as squarely owing to the historical and cultural atmosphere in Ibadan, one would be missing a crucial point if no connection is made whatsoever, especially in the light of the contrast made with Nsukka and in light of the emphasis made by previous scholars to the place Ibadan occupies in the formation of Nigerian literary culture, its effects on African literature, and the difference between other colonial universities and the growth of the University of Ibadan as regards the nation's literary culture or its global acceptance. The emphasis on idiosyncrasy and personal thematic preoccupations or aesthetics, as mentioned above, emphasizes that the creative culture at Ibadan jettisoned any attempt at shepherding or gatekeeping literature. It recognizes the place of and the premium placed on individual capacity, service to the self (and through that to the collective), and personal ambition in Ibadan as it relates to the mix of industry and artistry, even as the larger community comes to benefit. All these remind one of the same philosophies associable with the development of Ibadan from a war camp to a precolonial state.

It is, therefore, no wonder that this openness typical of Ibadan's approach to individual capacity and industry reflects on and allows for a distinct kind of expansive creative tradition; for diversity in the creative repertoire that it produced; and for a unique and diversified voice among those artists or writers who constituted its earliest creative groups. Naming many of the associated writers of the Ibadan School across generations will reveal this openness in terms of demography as well as in terms of preoccupation and aesthetic choices: Wole Soyinka, Mabel Segun, Abiola Irele, Biodun Jeyifo, Christopher Okigbo, J. P. Clark, Molara Ogundipe-Leslie, and Ayo Banjo, among many others. They not only attended the University of Ibadan

---

45. Okunoye, "Critical Reception," 778.
46. Okunoye, "Captives of Empire," 105–116.

Figure 16.3. Founded in 1829, Ibadan was born out of the ashes of the Old Oyo Empire and held a military character for much of the mid-nineteenth century that salvaged much of the southern fringes of modern-day Nigeria from marauding armies from the Sokoto Caliphate. Painting by Michael Efionayi.

but many of them formed the circles and encouraged the camaraderie upon which Nigerian and a great deal of African literature as knowledge would rest.

For some, the most prominent name and perfect tag used to describe the group responsible for this outburst of creativity or for founding the grounds upon which it fermented is the Mbari Club, formed by writer-intellectuals like Chinua Achebe, Wole Soyinka, and Christopher Okigbo—all of whom also incidentally attended and graduated from the University of Ibadan. Ibadan thus was a meeting point for Nigerian and African writers, both physically and ideologically, spurning several schools and allowing for the cultivation of a high literary culture. So, while it is not without cause that the several luminaries that would define Nigerian and impact African literature (Achebe, after all, is colloquially referred to as the father of African literature, and Soyinka, father of African drama) are traceable to Ibadan, or that many individuals that have come to shape knowledge production in Nigeria and the world as Nigerians have ties to Ibadan, it is important to emphasize in what ways these luminaires capitalized on the resources Ibadan had to offer in founding and promoting an intellectual culture, the kind that enabled maximum production of knowledge far and wide.

As Okunoye argues in "Captives of Empire: Early Ibadan Poets and Poetry," the formation of writer groups in early colonial universities contributed immensely to the development of African literature. This is more so in respect of Ibadan, a fact supported by the idea that "university communities served as institutional bases for African writers,"[47] providing materials for

---

47. Okunoye, "Captives of Empire," 105.

the development of and the kind of social capital required in producing knowledge. The groups formed by the members of the University of Ibadan have been identified as having foundational input in the stature of Nigerian literature and Africa more generally, even as they were supported by the expatriate lecturers who helped conceive the ideas for and financed them. The Ibadan school, or literary tradition as it is also known, is associated with several publications, like *The Eagle*, *The Sword*, *The Weekly*, and *The University Herald*—many of which not only gave room for the emergence of the literary texts that are either now deemed canonical or are seen as earliest works of those writers agreed to be founding fathers of African literary genres.

The creation of a publication like *The Horn* in 1957 is a good example of the point here, with its focus on poetry and poetic expressions by students. The publication started by Banham and J. P. Clark not only gave student poets the platform to showcase their talents and come to terms with a rapidly modernizing Nigeria but allowed for the development of intellectuals and led to the creation of several other publications because it sustained the kind of atmosphere and resources needed to cultivate individual talent and interest in creativity as a tool of reflecting on postcolonial Nigeria and the fate of the African/Black in a Western-controlled world. Furthermore, the publication was edited throughout its run by J. P. Clark, Abiola Irele, Dapo Adelugba, Omolara Ogundipe-Leslie, and Onyema Iheme—names that have become canonized in African literary and intellectual circles for their seminal contributions.

However, it is a journal like *Black Orpheus* that captures the relevance of journals at the University to African literature best since it sought to serve the global Black body, literally and literarily. Started in 1957 by Ulli Beier and Janheinz Jahn, expatriates who had visited and were working from departments at the university, the journal had an international focus. Okunoye captures the value of the journal well by explaining that "the journal made a greater impact in the society that *The Horn*, not only because it had a broader vision and a wider circulation but also because it also enjoyed the financial support of the Paris-based Congress for Cultural Freedom and the government of the defunct Western Region."[48] These two journals, with the kind of talents they attracted, the industry they cultivated and promoted, and the intellectual culture they supported, eventually led to the creation of the Mbari Club.[49] It is in recognition of these that Suhr-Sytsma acknowledges that *The Horn* published and allowed to a good extent "the emergence of three of the most important figures in twentieth-century African poetry, even as they helped to make Ibadan well known for its vibrant inter-arts scene."[50]

The other journals that sprang up in the university and other universities across the country can be said to have been influenced by this culture at Ibadan. Chinua Achebe founded *Okike* at Nsukka in 1971, having studied at the University of Ibadan and having tasted its culture and even facilitated the creation of the Mbari Club. Abiola Irele founded *New Horn* to revive the original *The Horn* journal, while *Idoto* and *Ọpọ́n Ifá*, founded in 1975 and 1976, respectively, would also be associated with the Department of English of the University and its alumni. With this said, it cannot be denied that the creation of the now premier university, the University of Ibadan, set in motion a series of possibilities that eventually culminated in the maturity

---

48. Okunoye, "Captives of Empire," 109.
49. Raheem, "Review: The Mbari Artists," 63–66.
50. Suhr-Systma, "Ìbàdàn Modernism," 41–59.

of a host of acclaimed writers, intellectuals, and people of substance. The university, founded on a generous land provided by the Ibadan community after a series of requests for centers of higher education that could serve the local communities, trained foremost Nigerian thinkers and writers, people who have made their marks on the Nigerian and global intellectual scene.

However, this narrative of influence does not end here. The occasion that the emergence of these people marks, which cuts across several generations, is that of the dawning of a long process of creative production that would add to the stature of Ibadan on account of its contribution to knowledge production and that which emphasizes its hospitability in welcoming people, while also emphasizing industry and self-application to task in ways that would generate capital with intellectual and material values for both society and the self. To cite a good example, the formation of Mbari Artists' and Writers' Club and the journal *Black Orpheus*, as a result of the creative energies of the artists in Ibadan at the time, as well as their (artists) having studied and formed social groups capable of generating social capital within the walls of its university, resulted in the emergence of Mbari publications. The Ibadan-based publication is considered one of the most important African literature publishers. It produced the earliest book-length works of writers like Clark, Soyinka, and Okigbo; it also produced translated versions of francophone African poetry collections by South African poets.[51] This publisher is another instance of the reach and yield of Ibadan as a space of capital-making in service of knowledge production. The publisher marketed to writers all over the continent while also making their works visible on foreign soil, increasing the visibility of homegrown writers to the outside world.

The decades immediately preceding Nigerian independence boast of considerable creative output. To this effect, dialogues such as nationalism, decolonization, anti-colonialism, and anti-imperialism were common themes within the intellectual circles and the art they produced and supported. The proliferation of creative publishers in Ibadan during this time, and the presence of publishers like Cambridge University Press, Heinemann, and Longman, contributed to the creative outpouring from Ibadan. The emergence of other locally owned and controlled ones like Ibadan University Press and Onibonoje Press and Book Industries Ltd., speaks to the thriving environment Ibadan provided for knowledge growth and production. There was also a proliferation of new age publishers like Bookcraft, Kraftbooks, and Evans, among many others.

As a result of this spirit of Ibadan, it was not unusual to find several creative communities and literary initiatives in the city. The environment itself (Ibadan's cultural philosophy of conviviality and emphasis on charisma and personality) had a rich history of promoting creative ways of social bonding that allowed the efforts of these enterprises to thrive. Even after the lull that came with the civil war, where creative production declined, and therefore the creative bulwark that Ibadan provided weakened, with faint echoes limited to the universities, certain aspects of literary production, like poetry, thrived. Surviving what Remi Raji-Oyelade termed

---

51. Suhr-Systma, "Ìbàdàn Modernism."

"acute structural adjustment to self-imposed aridity,"[52] poetic productions and poetry-based creative practices like performances, readings, and even intellectual groups emerged.

The Soyinka-Achebe generation revived the dying embers of a once-formidable literary presence through creative outputs concerned with issues of nationalism and colonialism, signaling Ibadan as a bastion of defense against an imposed death on creativity by the government. As Ime Ikiddeh, who studied the relationship between the civil war and literature in the nation, opines, it would take a decade for literary production, with Ibadan being the center, to remotely resemble what it was before the war.[53] And the productions that arose at the time were focused on remembering, revisiting, and sensitizing the populace on the war; therefore, they are often thematically grouped as creative outputs oriented toward dealing with what transpired during the genocide that led to the war. However, corroborating Ikiddeh is Raji-Oyelade, for the former argues that poetry almost replaced the period that came after the lull. In the case of Ibadan and the role its citadel of learning played, this seems accurate. Quoting Raji-Oyelade, "There is a sense in which it can be said that the most symbolic gesture to encourage and establish the emergence of new Nigerian writers, new voices, who would later be referred to as members of the Third Generation, occurred in the year 1988. The place was Ibadan, and the silent visionary was the scholar and poet, Harry Garuba, then teaching in the Department of English, University of Ibadan."[54]

In one single breath, Raji-Oyelade affirms three things: First is the continued place of Ibadan as a foremost resource for the creation of spaces concerned with knowledge production. Second is Ibadan's emphasis on creativity, industry, self-application, and individualism that serves the collective. Third is its approach to using one or many forms of capital to generate other forms of capital like social for intellectual capital. Raji-Oyelade further corroborates the foregoing by claiming that Ibadan of the 1980s allowed rising and unsure creative artists to find their feet. To emphasize this relevance of Ibadan, he says: "For promising and struggling writers lucky to be in Ibadan at the period, the 1980s was an exemplary decade indeed!"[55]

The university provided the spatial and human resources in the form of teachers and specific courses and groups/clubs where creativity was harnessed and allowed to blossom. One such club was the Poetry Club, which also produced issues edited by students of the department. The spirit of the poetry club itself manifested the kind of spirit already identified with the earliest writing groups in Ibadan by the Achebe-Soyinka generation and thus exhibited the convivial and open nature of Ibadan and its celebration of an even blend of individuality and collectivity. To give an instance, rather than propose a single or focused creative/aesthetic ideology or cultural one, the group allowed for different and divergent expressions of creativity. What was binding was "collective love and individual enthusiasm for the art," which reminds us of Ibadan's emphasis on collectivity and camaraderie and its flair for individual capacity and industry. Drawing this relation does establish a direct connection between how Ibadan had come to be and those state structures, ethos—as well as the institutions they birthed—and

---

52. Raji-Oyelade, "Ìbàdàn and the Memory of a Generation," 21.

53. Ikiddeh, "Literature and the Nigerian Civil War," 163.

54. Raji-Oyelade, "Ìbàdàn and the Memory of a Generation," 21.

55. Raji-Oyelade, "Ìbàdàn and the Memory of a Generation," 25.

modes of expressing the creativity that existed during and after colonialism. However, it hints at the oversight that can occur in the attempt to understand some of the roles Ibadan has played as a resource in the generation of intellectual capital for the Yorùbá and the nation when this link is overlooked entirely.

Over time, the poetry club hosted by the university would accommodate live performances, signifying its expansive poetics and the club's open interpretation of what poetry was as a mode of producing intellectual content. One significant feature of this period, especially by the mid-1980s, was the proliferation of writers that cut across different departments in the university and, in fact, from other institutions. In recognition of this expansiveness, the expression "moving spirit of the loose collective" by Raji-Oyelade becomes appropriate in describing the consciousness that sustained creative outpourings as forms of capital in Ibadan, guided by professors and teachers. Thus, the dispersal of such groups of creativity into the town itself— that is, away from the city—was only both natural and reminiscent of what happened with the Mbari Club and the earliest journals that were collaborations between students and teachers.

With the full transition of Ibadan into the capital city of Ọ̀yọ́ State came more resources and provision of spaces for other intellectual groups that were artistically inclined, such as the Association of Nigerian Authors (ANA), Ọ̀yọ́ Chapter, of which Ibadan served as its capital. So rather than the university serving as its major center of knowledge production in terms of creativity, the entire city began to manifest this potential. The ANA group and its monthly meetings provided space for digesting and producing literary content through readings and focused discussions. Scholars and writers like Harry Garuba, Odia Ofeimun, Tony Marinho, Aderemi Raji-Oyelade, and Wale Okediran, among many others, played important roles in the success of the ANA.

Going forward into the last decade of the twentieth century and then the first decade of the twenty-first, these groups allowed for the emergence of more scholarly forums. Raji-Oyelade describes it as the "moment of deliberate return to the idea of literary criticism and scholarship,"[56] in reference to the tradition started by formidable African intellectual giants like Wole Soyinka, Abiola Irele, Chinua Achebe, Biodun Jeyifo, Isidore Okpewho, Dan Izevbaye, Femi Osofisan, Tanure Ojaide, Ken Saro-Wiwa, Niyi Osundare, Wale Ogunyemi, Omolara Ogundipe-Leslie, and many others. The Premier Circle was founded by Raji-Oyelade, with the help of the late Pius Adesanmi, with scholars like Sola Olorunyomi, Omowunmi Segun, Obododimma Oha, Segun Oladipo, and many more contributing to establish the group where discourses where engaged, with serious intellectual fervor.[57]

Conclusion

The contribution of Ibadan to the intellectual culture and content in Nigeria and globally is a vast topic to cover. However, it makes for an interesting context to understand how Ibadan's history connects and contributes to African literary production and intellectual weight in the

---

56. Raji-Oyelade, "Ìbàdàn and the Memory of a Generation," 28.
57. Raji-Oyelade, "Ìbàdàn and the Memory of a Generation."

global knowledge economy. There are several lessons to be learned and connections to be made into discursively relating or situating the intellectual contribution that Ibadan has made possible as a state to its historical formation. The emphasis here is on the relationships between Ibadan's past and present in terms of its historical formation and its contribution to the generation of intellectual capital. However, the idea of capital itself is taken to be a product of several other interacting capital while also approaching Ibadan as a space and a place, more loosely, to be able to flesh out in what light Ibadan (and its history) have come to serve as resources in the formation of more capital—the intellectual kind. As it has been discussed, some of the ethos and principles that made Ibadan into a stronghold and thriving empire have continued into the present and can be seen, at least, as traces or residues, in the lives and afterlives of those intellectual circles and contents that are or have been generated as capital.

The memory of Ibadan's military lords like Olúyọ̀lé has been revived not in the militarization of the city but in the compression of their activities and achievements in books read all over the world. What Ibadan represents in the intellectual scene, Lagos inhabits in music and performance creativity. The two cities find an intersection in reproducing the creativity produced in literary works from Ibadan, in visual arts and performances set in Lagos. The next chapter investigates how Nollywood—the umbrella body and industry through which these reproductions have been made—has preserved and constructed Yorùbá culture for the wider world.

Nollywood in the World of Creativity 17

Nollywood and Its Creatives:[1] Global Yorùbá and the Decolonial Angle

Creativity transverses the superstructure of human society and, in the process, interprets the workings of state institutions and practices using different media, namely: visual performance, graphics, writings, carving, and even through orality. These have gone through different stages among the Yorùbá from the precolonial to contemporary times. Nollywood, a name adopted for the Nigerian visual entertainment industry by a *New York Times* journalist, Onishi Norimitsu, at the opening of the current millennium, has its root in the stage performance of Yorùbá theater groups. The Yorùbá represent the nucleus of creativity and intellectual production in modern Nigeria.

The focus of this chapter is on the Yorùbá as reflected and refracted by Nollywood within a global ecology. Creativity and creative expression, which Nollywood embodies as a creative institution and as Nigeria's film industry, is central to the conceptions of the Yorùbá—and indeed is, as we will discover in the conceptual relation between àṣà (as creative tradition) and what it means to be Yorùbá (identity) and in the context of a global world (globality). However, before diving into this subject, it is essential to explore ideas whose interconnections provide a solid conceptual point around which the tenor of this work can be built and upon which can be anchored the theoretical premises of this chapter. Also, it is judicious to proceed from what might initially seem a digression, as it will add a refreshing angle to complicate the subject of Yorùbá identity, cultural tradition, and globality regarding Nollywood and Nigerian film production.

Enrique Dussel argues in his seminal article, "Agenda for a South-South Philosophical Dialogue,"[2] that it is essential for philosophers of the Global South (to which Africa and Nigeria belong) to "come together to define and claim for themselves a philosophical practice—generating its topics and methods from its own historical, socio-economic-political realities and traditions."[3] He would later flesh out this philosophy as the "Philosophy of Liberation." In

---

1. I use the word *creatives* here to refer to those engaged in creative practices and, because this is the focus of this chapter, Nigerian filmmakers as well as those involved in the production of the creative expression and industry that Nollywood is.

2. Dussel, "Agenda for a South-South Philosophical Dialogue," 3–18.

3. Dussel, "Agenda for a South-South Philosophical Dialogue," 3.

another of his work equally significant for its conceptual groundwork on interculturality and transmodernity, he enjoins indigenous culture's critical thinkers or cultural innovators to work with what he calls "creative force" in enabling transmodernity and interculturality. This translates to his recognition that ideas and ideology-making, as well as their execution, often fall within the purview of creative enterprises if a true nonhegemonic relationship can be fostered between global cultures.[4] Dussel's injunction is also in recognition and in view of facilitating the production of a pluriversal knowledge ecology and an experiential climate where, to use Dussel's own words, "each culture will be in dialogue with all cultures others from the perspective of a common 'similarity,' enabling each culture to continuously recreate its analogical distinction and to diffuse itself within a dialogical reciprocally creative space."[5] For Dussel, this interculturality allows for the interaction of Global Southern epistemologies, from which knowledge-based discussions can be initiated between the South and the North.

The reason for beginning with Dussel is that he champions a trisected argument that provides direction for "true multiculturalism," a term for an egalitarian relationship between world cultures. The first is the accent placed on the need for a knowledge-driven and knowledge-based cultural exchange between world cultures and from equally egalitarian positions or positions of equal footing. In other words, the basis of multiculturalism in the global polity should be an epistemological interaction that is as pluriversal as possible. This charge toward pluriversalism of epistemic systems and practices leads to the second proposition that can be read off Dussel's injunction: the need for a multicultural framework to foster such pluriversal knowledge-sharing experience and interaction of several epistemic codes. Dussel's proposition gestures toward a more planetary globalism, where there would simultaneously exist several centers of knowledge production—which ultimately means multiple centers of socioeconomic, political, historical, ontoepistemological, and philosophical values that are not in hegemonic relation to one another.

Several terms have been used to describe such situations: Dussel himself has tied it to his concept of transmodernity; Walter Mignolo describes this possibility as a world of pluriversal universalities;[6] and Boaventura Sousa Santos explains such situations as those in which hegemonic and counterhegemonic globalization can coexist.[7] These scholars, although they have globalization as their prime focus and have addressed the matter from different disciplines— for this is what is essentially being dealt with when multiculturalism, human identity, subjectivizing practices, and global knowledge systems are simultaneously topicalized—often converge on the idea that what is at stake in the world of multicultural interaction is the agency of the local—that is, multiple locales. In the cross-cultural and multicultural interrelational lattices that define the vast modern world, the independence and sovereignty of cultures are nonnegotiable—that is, doing away with any form of hegemony that has come to define present-day global interactions and the iterations or miniaturizations of such interactions within multiple social and locale-specific (knowledge) institutions.

---

4. Dussel, "Transmodernity and Interculturality," 28–59.

5. Dussel, "Agenda for a South-South Philosophical Dialogue."

6. Mignolo, "Cosmopolitanism and the De-colonial Option," 111–127.

7. Dale, Robertson, and de Sousa Santos, "Interview with Boaventura de Sousa Santos," 1–22.

This leads to the third proposition, which is that each culture must creatively reach inward into its ontological and epistemological reserves and establish symbiotic relations with others within a mutually beneficial space and through creative practices. According to Dussel, this enables a process of creation and re-creation, as each occasion of interactivity demands—that is, (re)creative cultural practices must be enabled that can harmonically and symbiotically allow for interaction between multiple cultural praxes on the global map. These creative practices would promote epistemic and philosophical values unique to each culture while also serving as the basis for expanding planetary pluriversalism. Dussel argues for diffusing and continually re-creating "specificity" and "uniqueness" within a dialogic reciprocally creative space, which is not oppositional to the elasticity of cultural identity hinged on knowledge-based creative practices in a global matrix. By this, Dussel's position is reflective of conviviality, as well as of the mutability of culture-based identity. Suggested in this particular injunction—which is the prime focus of this chapter—is the role of the "creatives" (re: practitioners of art) doing these (re)creations and the effect of these (re)creations on those experiencing the multicultural interaction.

While it is inarguable that these propositions by Dussel are core tenets or philosophical thoughts upon which decolonial theory has anchored itself, they are also vital to discussions on the place of creative practices like those of Nollywood, both old and new, in fostering the kinds of cross-cultural and multicultural interactions that are devoid of the influences of power plays as maintained by Euro-American cultural hegemony. Hence, it could be argued that this redefinition of power relation underwrites the relationship of creative practices like that of the Nollywood industry to the philosophical directions of decoloniality. However, this relation holds immense implications for the subjects of Global Southern cultures and their subjectivities—elasticity, nonetheless, since cultures and the subjectivities they help in forging are neither monolithic nor rigid and stagnant. This is because cultural uniqueness must be maintained if creatives hope to remain steadfast with the dynamics of the home culture, even as they find themselves in a cross-relation with other cultures and the foreign subjectivities they foster through multiculturalism and other processes of cosmopolitanism. This facet of the interaction remains troubling for cultural studies scholars, and creatives have easily given to essentialist conceptions of culture in their exploration or dealings with the phenomenon of globality.

For instance, it is not without cause—and which Adeshina Afolayan points out in his article on the filmmaker—that Tunde Kelani has been studied as not fully maximizing the potential of multiculturalism (as a framework) in conceiving of Yorùbá subjectivity on the screen as an auteur. Afolayan charges that Kelani's traditionalism impedes his ability to fully conceive of what it means to be Yorùbá in a globalizing world. To quote Afolayan, Kelani, as a filmmaker, "fails to decode the flexibility at the core of the Yoruba concept of àṣà that facilitates a flexible relationship between traditionality and creativity."[8] This flexibility is the expansiveness and mutability that lies at the heart of identity, especially group identity that develops over time and across generations. Kelani is not alone in this challenge, as many filmmakers, especially

---

8. Afolayan, "Tunde Kelani," 1.

those classifiable as belonging to Old Nollywood, can be seen as grappling with the challenge of "mediating between the imperatives of tradition and the exigencies of modernity."[9]

On the one hand, such complications or the oversights they engender degenerate into essentialist perspectives that discountenance the globality of their subjects. In another sense, it can be seen as *trapped* in the game of counterhegemony, which only perpetuates the divide instituted by the specter of colonialism, particularly if it fails to embrace the totality of its subject and pits one aspect of its identity against the other(s)—that is, if it fails to be fully open, convivial, and thus decolonial in its approach. Creative practices aware of this challenge and successfully managing it can ensure the demise of the hegemonic patterns of multiculturalism if they are principally decolonial. They must aim to retain and flesh out the richness of subject positions while fostering the dynamic of the relation between traditionalism and globalism.

The link, which can be traced through a culture's creative repertoires—as many as they may be, depending on discursive context—cannot be easily dismissed, and it underscores a culture's ability to maintain openness and civil and mutually benefiting engagements between its subjects and others in a global framework. This would enhance the production of realities where Global Southern subjects are presented as equal (their identities and everyday practices) to other world subjects without being hegemonically marginalized, erased, subalternized, exoticized, or displayed as the "traditional Other." It presupposes the idea of a "cosmopolitan localism," a situation where each culture is evenly weighted or its subjects are present in equal terms on a global scale.

This cosmopolitanism is devoid of all the pretensions and trappings of Western hegemonic globalism and its fostering of atmospheres where non-Western subjects and cultures are repressed and forcefully reimaged as "other." It is a decolonial kind of cosmopolitanism that can be buoyed through creative industries as containers of culture and purveyors of local— that is, space-specific—identities. By calling it a decolonial kind of cosmopolitanism, this draws on Walter Mignolo's article "Cosmopolitanism and the Decolonial Option" to comment on and reiterate the usefulness of pluriversality as a global project through which the universal narrative of one master localism can be supplanted with that of several localisms. These localisms are in agreement despite their unique individuality, which forms the basis of planetary globalism and the basis of the film industry in making this possible.

However, in referring to this concept, essentially a synonym for a global condition of pluriversality, particular emphasis is placed on the role of creatives and the function of creative industries like Nollywood in this ironic union—that is, the function of the Nigerian cinema in projecting such conditions and images as they deal with Yorùbá subjects, the Yorùbá lifeworld, and its numerous subjectivities. This concept, much like Mignolo's, is acknowledged as loaded with ironies because the idea of cosmopolitanism, especially as traceable to Immanuel Kant, the Enlightenment philosopher, is imbued in the globality narrative that made and maintains the universalism of the West. At the very least, this negates the idea of localism as signifying the tensions between traditionalism and modernism in cultures—that is, their lifeworld, zeitgeist, and imaginaries—as well as the fact that such cultures are often territorialized and bounded.

---

9. Afolayan, "Tunde Kelani," 3.

However, because this kind of localism is decolonial, it can be equally global as it is local without being hegemonic or territorial.

This conception of localism as decolonial is important to the perspective on the relation of Nollywood cinematic culture and the creative choices of its filmmakers in the context of globality and the Yorùbá subject. Thinking of this relationship this way emphasizes the argument—which Mignolo also makes—that localism is a response of creatives and critical intellectuals to Eurocentrism and its power structures.[10] Aside from emphasizing this ideologically vital semantic shift of what localism can mean in a decolonial context, it also clarifies how creative film practitioners in the Yorùbá cultural space can be engaged in a campaign for cosmopolitan localism in their creative attempts as they strive to correct and reimagine, represent or produce, and invent the image of the Yorùbá on a global scale and as a global project and subject.

In touching on the production of the Yorùbá lifeworld or subject as a global project, the emphasis is not on production and invention as the creation of something new entirely but that they contribute to the Yorùbá subjects or, more generally, the Yorùbá people's visibility and the new ways their identities and defining cultural praxes can be seen. As regards creative enterprises like film productions, this can be said to be a production of what Alessandro Jedlowski calls the "Minor Cinema"[11] and a product of what Akinwumi Adesokan conceives of as the "aesthetic of exhortation."[12] This idea of the Minor Cinema as a fitting description for some of the film productions out of the Yorùbá space is apt because this type of cinema represents global minorities by showing how they have been made to disappear as a result of global processes of "colonization/decolonization, industrialization and urbanization, which altered the internal balance of societies and cultures."[13]

The idea of the Minor Cinema, especially as Jedlowski introduced it in his article on Kelani, echoes the philosopher Gille Deleuze's idea that cinema can represent people erased by the processes mentioned above that truncated the natural progression of societies, thereby making several aspects "no longer exist, . . . or not yet."[14] This cinema does this by dramatizing how these identities and their lifeworld have been erased and by "building the foundations for a new, convivial culture able to transmit some of those elements to future generations, while at the same time creating the conditions for these societies' encounter with the rest of the world."[15] Hence, this invention is a morally conscious and politically charged one. Together—as political and moral—they aestheticize cinema so that it can represent people in continually progressive and futuristically productive ways and facilitate a more leveled relationship of specific cultures with the world.

While Jedlowski uses this term to address the work of Kelani as a filmmaker, it is also reminiscent of the Yorùbá movie world more generally, as we have filmmakers like Tade Ogidan

---

10. Mignolo, "Cosmopolitanism and the De-colonial Option," 111–127.

11. Jedlowski, "Minor Cinema and Conviviality," 367–381.

12. Adesokan, *Postcolonial Artists*.

13. Jedlowski, "Minor Cinema," 367–381.

14. Jedlowski, "Minor Cinema," 367–381.

15. Jedlowski, "Minor Cinema."

working with this cinema. This is because the minor cinema, as Jedlowski puts it, contributes to inventing people in places where they have been made absent, a reality familiar to Yorùbá filmmakers and the Yorùbá subject, whose existential experience is subtended by these erasures. Thinking of Nollywood as participating in this kind of intervention echoes Deleuze's rhetorical campaign for the cinema as an aestheticized art: "Art, and especially cinematographic art, must take part in this task: not that of addressing a people, which is presupposed already there, but of contributing to the invention of a people."[16] Deleuze would make this submission to consolidate his idea of the relation between minor cinema as a political cinema and its focus on missing people, which to him is not the "renunciation of political cinema, but on the contrary, the new basis on which it is founded, in the third world and for minorities."[17]

However, unlike Jedlowski, who superimposes one aspect of the minor cinema on the other (moral over political), this type of cinema, which Yorùbá filmmakers like Tunde Kelani and Kunle Afolayan largely represent, is considered to be essentially composed of the moral and the political. Political because of the kind of inventive representation it produces; moral because of the effects it provokes in its immediate world and other publics where it can mobilize/generate across cultural spaces. One can talk of Yorùbá filmmakers as appropriating this cinema in different ways since they are didactic and heavy with moral leanings and since they are invested in representation across global divides. Movies like *Ṣaworoidẹ*, *Aago Kan Òru*, and *Mágùn/Thunderbolt* are as political as they are moral. These movies, engaged as they are with productions of Yorùbá lifeworld, harness what Cheng describes as the "recycling of traditional socio-cultural institutions."[18] It is possible, however, to argue for a superimposition of one aspect of this cinema over the other, particularly when one seeks conceptual grounding in Adesokan's idea of "aesthetics of exhortation," which he describes as "a tradition of aesthetic populism which understands politics as a subcategory of morality, and gauges the impact of a work of art according to how the audience responds to it."[19]

This brand of populism, Adesokan explains, allows for a wider reception of movies by Yorùbá film producers on local and global stages owing to didacticism, which fuels "creating new moral publics through the questions that it raises and the open-ended interactions that they provoke among audience."[20] This is true of Yorùbá filmmakers as creatives whose working materials are cultural and whose cinema manifests the complexity at the heart of Yorùbá identity as regards traditionalism and modernity. A combination of both politics and morals to achieve this idea of decoloniality—for the argument so far has pointed this way—through populism, therefore, speaks to Dussel's emphasis on the importance of the popular space in the reclamation of identities and cultural legacies on the global space,[21] as well as the role of creatives in facilitating this process through production and invention, which aids in enabling the transmodern and pluriversal project.

---

16. Deleuze, *Cinema 2*, 217.

17. Deleuze, *Cinema 2*, 217.

18. Cheng, "Yoruba Ẹ Ronú," 382–399.

19. Adesokan, *Postcolonial Artist*, 81.

20. Jedlowski, "Minor Cinema," 9.

21. Dussel, "Transmodernity and Interculturality."

Locating the premise of this chapter within and thinking it through these existing paradigmatic perspectives places a particular emphasis on epistemology. A knowledge-based approach is imperative in facilitating this brand of multicultural project, where the ontological and epistemological specificities of the Yorùbá space become the basis upon which the global sensibility of the Yorùbá subject as well as the elasticity of the Yorùbá identity are filmed. Where this is achieved, the cinema becomes the bridge through which the necessary fusions of traditionalism and modernism are harnessed as they represent the mix of diverse cultures and lifeworld. So, in their political endeavors that facilitate the invention of the Yorùbá, where they have been made missing on the global scale as part of Global Southern people, and in their founding of morally charged publics as part of this process, filmmakers engage in redefining the nature of multiculturalism, especially from its hegemonic moorings. Their redefined brand of multiculturalism exhibits itself as founded on conviviality, in philosophic (and perhaps moral) terms, and on decoloniality in terms of its politics. This particular position is not strange if we consider conviviality as "a concept that allows us to re-conceptualize the place of African cultures and societies in the world, turning our attention to their intrinsic openness and relationality."[22] More so, this idea of conviviality as bordered on openness and relationality sits at the heart of decolonial thought, as well as that of the political cinema, which Jedlowski has rightly affirmed[23] by averring that "conviviality is something of a programmatic effort that aims at overcoming simplistic dichotomies between the North and the South, 'modernity' and 'tradition,' and Northern wealth and Southern poverty. It is an invitation to overcome narrow conceptions of individuality and sociality to contemplate the intrinsically relational open nature of all human beings."[24]

This conviviality is at stake for the Yorùbá creatives and their conception of identity, especially as represented and invented by its movie industry and its filmmakers, who are part of the industry's creatives by the way they are central to and stand apart from it.[25] As anchors to the cinema working with the philosophy of conviviality, Yorùbá filmmakers are engaged in a pluriversal project: their movies can be read as seeking to activate the transversal leanings of the local or localism. They capitalize on conviviality's emphasis on relationality and openness in a subject's positionality to the world to continually exhibit the elasticity at the heart of Yorùbá's conception of identity, which in the long run supports the idea of a global Yorùbá that would then complicate conceptions of what being a Yorùbá means, on the one hand, and support what Adeleke Adeeko proposes as the openness at the heart of Yorùbá's concept of culture and the subjectivities it supports, on the other hand.[26]

This proposition and Jedlowski's submission (because it largely mirrors mine) references Deleuze's position that the cinema and its politics of inventing people is not a rejection of the

---

22. Dussel, "Transmodernality and Interculturality," 2.

23. Dussel, "Transmodernality and Interculturality," 2.

24. Dussel, "Transmodernality and Interculturality," 4.

25. These distinctions are made to accommodate self-defining categories like those attributed to filmmakers like Kunle Afolayan, who calls his cinema New Nollywood to dissociate himself from the commercialism and capitalist thrust of the "mainstream" or "Old" Nollywood.

26. Adeeko, *Arts of Being Yorùbá*.

political cinema. However, it attempts to find new principles upon which the latter can ferment. These principles are as convivial as they are decolonial since they facilitate patterns of engagement with the world (between different localisms), allow for interactions of "minor" epistemologies and their dialogue with dominant epistemologies (a backbone of Dussel's transmodernity), and participate in the minor modes of production, which as proposed by Deleuze is partaking in the global system of knowledge production, not to oppose it but to change it from within—again a significant part of Mignolo's decolonial argument on multiculturalism.

For Yorùbá filmmakers, what is at play here is a participation in a philosophic enterprise through the cinema, which entails aiming to locate Yorùbá lifeworld as a specific brand of localism in a world where various localisms seek—because of colonial power matrixes that globalized/universalized Euro-American localism as the standard—to remand others in the categories of the local and the native. Here, Afolayan's work on reading Kelani as a Deleuzian philosopher resonates aptly since it essentially re-sounds the idea that filmmakers, in their jostle with the twin issues of modernism and traditionalism or Yorùbá culture and identity or globalism and localism, are grappling with philosophic implications of representing knowledge and people and of different cultures/worlds colliding. To paraphrase Afolayan, cinemas that "enable us to ask fundamental questions about the nature of human society and how we relate together"[27] exhibit how filmmakers can be critical thinkers and philosophers ruminating through images.

In making this argument, Afolayan draws on Deleuze's thoughts about the relationship between philosophy and the cinema, where he establishes a relation between filmmakers and their ability to create images in terms of signifiers as analogously related to thinking through concepts and mental signs as drivers of philosophical thought. Sharing a similar view, the aim is to make sense of how Yorùbá filmmakers' images as signage are bound up in philosophic concepts such as conviviality, decoloniality, and transmodernity in their preoccupation with the Yorùbá culture and identity and how this preoccupation manifests implication for the Yorùbá as a global subject as well as for filmmaking as a creative act caught up in a global knowledge/creative matrix.

Decoloniality and conviviality as philosophical precepts find much resonance in filmmaking from cultures like the Yorùbá. It is not a stretch to relate Mignolo's idea—that localism is often an equalizing attempt by those with the intellectual and critical capital to negotiate global spaces—to the efforts of Nollywood filmmakers in creating spaces for Yorùbá identity in the global network flows defining culture production, thereby displaying the global sensibilities of the Yorùbá subject.

The idea of cosmopolitan localism underwrites the agency of the local through (creative) practices that aid its agenda and re-sound the autonomy of the lifeworld it produces and represents in the global space—hence, the approach of thinking about the relation between the agency of the local and its agential subjects and between creative practices and multiculturalism in the dynamics of Nollywood regarding global Yorùbá.[28]

---

27. Afolayan, "Tunde Kelani," 2.

28. By global Yoruba, I seek to draw attention to the fact that the premise already complicates the dichotomies of global and local, tradition and modernity, and other such epistemic positions and concepts.

The focus of this chapter finds strong credence in (and in how) Santos has conceived of the idea of localizations as a worthy discursive category to globalization—that is, in addressing multiculturalism and cultural production in a global network framework. Santos has argued for reconstituting the language and points of enunciation of the globalism discourse to privilege the local and, hence, localizations or localism as a frame of reference, to privilege all localisms without prejudice or preference. Therefore, what is at stake here is the ability of the local to reach outward into the world without detaching itself from its roots and losing itself in the world. While executing these goals, it should be shown as expansive and progressive, responsive to multicultural influences. Implied and at stake is the role of creative practices in ensuring this agenda of the local. Thus presented, the task here is how Nollywood as a creative enterprise allows the Yorùbá the much-needed cultural visibility in a multicultural global space without hedging cultural significations or kowtowing to foreign influences while also manifesting the globalization of the Yorùbá subject.

Taking Nollywood and the Yorùbá culture as its focus, this chapter discusses how the cultural identity of the Yorùbá is being represented. This is because the importance of this cultural

Figure 17.1. "Screen Addiction," by Dr. Kazeem Ekeolu. A toddler sitting in front of a TV screen watching a Yorùbá movie and learning the Yorùbá language.

and creative industry is immense. Its impact as a cultural industry can be seen in its ability to shape the social form of society since the twentieth century. The significance of this cultural industry in the current time has increased dramatically because of the advent of the Internet culture. Thus, visiting the phenomenon of Nollywood in relation to the Yorùbá cultural sphere would inform on the aspects of the trajectory of the Yorùbá culture since the introduction of Nollywood as a theater institution and an effective industry for cultural production that cater to the rebranding of the image of the global Yorùbá.

Among other things, it addresses the role of this industry in the evolution of the Yorùbá culture, society, and civilization. Therefore, this chapter would help to categorize the movie industry into its appropriate place and educate the global audience about the reliability or otherwise of the institution when digging into Yorùbá culture. Knowing that there have been a series of cultural despoliations that one could perceive in Nollywood production, the economic and other motivations behind them would provide rich resource material where appropriate. For instance, the rise of Nollywood in the twentieth century introduced another dimension to the distribution of culture to the people. Among many other things, it allows people to transmit their culture and traditions into the medium where they consume and detoxify. Ever since its breakthrough into the system of the people, Nollywood has recorded much acceptability beyond what was projected.

Certain determinant factors shape the productions of Nollywood, and this affects the representation of the Yorùbá lifeworld and its perception or import on the global idea of the Yorùbá. For instance, for a considerable number of years, Nollywood became the abattoir where Yorùbá culture either became slain or mutilated for economic benefits. Although some movie producers were relatively fair with their portrayal of Yorùbá identity the way it should naturally be—unprovincial—Nollywood is being considered in relation to how it has become an instrument of identity revolution or impediment, as well as the progression of this industry in terms of production and mechanisms of production.

Old Nollywood, New Nollywood: Where Is the Yorùbá?

The relationship between what is considered the Old and the New Nollywood is significant enough to underscore developments in the Nigerian film industry and cinema culture, as well as its implication for the image of the Yorùbá on the global front. Of specific interest here is how the changes, sometimes debated,[29] reflect on continued imaginings of the Yorùbá subject and culture, especially regarding how they are presented by screen media and what their effectuations as choices by filmmakers signify in the broader context of what it means to be Yorùbá. The focus here is to mark out and understand the image of the Yorùbá as it is shaped by the differences or improvements between Old and New Nollywood, especially concerning the ori-

---

29. The extent of these changes is often debated, implicitly or explicitly. For instance, Haynes maintains that the major change is the creation of multiplex theaters, while others like Adejunmobi have shown areas of convergence and divergence based on narration, narrative strategies, and thematic offerings. Some have even drawn parallels based on grant and the absence thereof for each production.

entations of the movie as defined by specific content framing, aesthetics, and other structural underpinnings.

New Nollywood describes a specific type of cinema, with a different taste in ideology and thematic offerings, as well as its technological sophistication and market strategies. Ryan Connor describes it as "a select group of aesthetically sophisticated films intended for a new tiered distribution, beginning with theatrical release and ending with DVD release."[30] This tiered distribution model has been tied to the innovative use and centering of urban multiplex cinemas at the heart of the distribution networks, a far cry from the production strategies popularly associated with Nollywood, hence the designation, Old Nollywood.

While Connor considers these upscale multiplexes as rich and foremost indicators of what is new about Nollywood, Jude Akudinobi considers these indexes, which Moradewun Adejunmobi describes in terms of an "exertion seeking to achieve congruence between ideology and narrative"[31] as an improvement on the "rough-and-ready production practices, stylistic mélanges, humdrum soundtracks, stilted dialogue, prevalent technical lapses, chaotic straight-to-video distribution, commerce-driven ethos, and proclivity for melodrama, the supernatural, and occult horror" peculiar to Old Nollywood.[32] So, in place of these, we have bold and daring movies, big-budget and complexly themed films, and movies made to be screened at international festivals, streamed by global audiences, inserted in more structured and mainstream global distribution channels and flows, and made to emphasize the metropolitan nature of the Yorùbá space as well as the cosmopolitan nature of its plural ethnoreligious character in the global imagination that had fed off more limiting, traditionalist, and lopsided conceptions of Global Southern ethnicities like the Yorùbá.

The exertion Adejunmobi refers to circumscribing the type of narration and narrative styles New Nollywood filmmakers are all about, which reveal the orientation behind their choices as creatives. Her research on the subject teases out the differences between the old and new filmmaking paradigms from this premise of filmmakers creatively exerting themselves at the level of narration. Her emphasis is on representations of modernity and temporality and neoliberal subjectivity as points of critical departure and convergence between the two Nollywood paradigms. One of the points made in consolidating this is that the Old Nollywood paradigm involves the narration of aspirations toward modernity and the often-complex struggle between achieving this aspiration, particularly where modernity is a set of social symbols defined by certain economic and financial conditions of life. To cite her position, "Old Nollywood films cater to the visual pleasure of desired access to modernity by exhibiting its supposed bounty—grand homes, stylish clothing, and expensive cars—as obtained frequently through vice and debauchery."[33]

Movies produced from the Old Nollywood paradigm are heavy on morals and their didacticism is blatant since part of the complex maneuvers toward achieving the aspirations of

---

30. Connor, "New Nollywood," 55–76.

31. Adejunmobi, "Neoliberal Rationalities," 33.

32. Akudinobi, "Nollywood," 2.

33. Adejunmobi, "Neoliberal Rationalities," 33.

modernity would involve violating society's moral codes. Such movies abound, one of which is *Ololade Mr Money* (acted by Ebun Oloyede), where Ololade engages in money ritual by killing his wife to escape generational poverty and a life of penury to live lavishly and extravagantly. The usual symbols of modernity populate this movie: fancy houses, structures, and gadgets, as well as ostentatious living and apparent lust for material gains. This violation of society's moral code is made more manifest when Ololade is punished with an insurmountable task in the afterlife as his comeuppance for his vile acts in life—even his death in the physical world is mysterious. This is Old Nollywood's manner of resolving egregious defiance of society's moral institutions, which often involves killing or punishing characters with a moral failing of some sort to achieve a more desirable ending.

Such narrative strategies, while soused in morals, also have unintended consequences in terms of the images they portray to the global world. Belief in the supernatural, the occult, and the cultic is one of such, which would naturally cast the Yorùbá world as antithetical to (Western) modernity. Many movies employ this strategy, but to counteract any reading of Old Nollywood as trapped in essentialist traditionalism is the instructive mix of tradition and modernity that shaped such movies, as exemplified by Ololade, whose route to modern wealth is through evil spiritualism. What is, therefore, vital here as a major departure between the old and the new is the aspirational relationship toward modernity upon which the movie is based, the strategies through which the aspiration is achieved, and the consequence of the strategy employed. However, it is worth noting that while Old Nollywood works with an aspiration toward modernity, New Nollywood presents lives living this modern reality.

It can be argued that as a result of ready formulas that present the Yorùbá in a generic, clichéd, and overflogged light—of being spiritual to a fault, of taking a pervasive route toward modernity with heavy spiritual implications, and of being morally scrupulous, even if the society is heavily shaped by moral philosophies—Nollywood became associated with proliferation of weak scripts, lower production values, recycled motifs, lack of innovation, and overproduction. It is not illogical to argue that the replication of familiar themes and lack of innovative strategies in narrating such themes would automatically typecast certain parts of the Yorùbá lifeworld as all there is to the Yorùbá to its international audience, leading to a situation where a part represents the whole.

While New Nollywood, represented by filmmakers like Mahmood Ali-Balogun and Kunle Afolayan, strives for better production values and to differentiate itself from the narrative strategies of Old Nollywood, there are not necessarily changes in the content. This change would affect the aesthetics and strategies of narration, affect, and representation, leading to more quality control in terms of production. Thus, it validates Adejunmobi's idea of "exertion" on the part of the filmmakers as a significant difference between the old and the new in terms of modes of content creation and the various practices involved, like scriptwriting. In the larger scheme, this quality control at the level of content would impact film financing and production, whose function within the film industry is crucial to the sustenance of the image of the Yorùbá that finds its way onto the global stage. While such control would affect existing production styles that catapulted Nollywood to the second most productive film industry based on the number of films produced in any given year during the first decade of the twenty-first century, such effects are hardly seen as unwelcome developments.[34] This is because this overproliferation and circulation of movies mark Old Nollywood, whose crises would gather momentum in 2007, eventually came to a head beginning in 2010, spelling specters of lost revenues for producers and dwarfing the industry in significant ways.

Correcting this anomaly through strategic financing and newer models of production and distribution set apart the movies and filmmakers driving the New Nollywood as rejuvenation and improvement from those practicing old ways of filmmaking. Recognizing this departure, Jonathan Haynes, in his attempt to document and theorize this distinction, explains New Nollywood as a term that caught sometime around 2010 as a response to the crises of Old Nollywood. He argues it entails the strategies embarked upon in correcting these crises and their more contextual implications, like on the economy and the subjectivities it purports to portray.

It is, therefore, not surprising that the term is often employed as a descriptor for the dynamic methods by filmmakers to produce movies with higher budgets, aimed at screening them at international festivals and in multiplex cinemas to have a better handle on the financial aspects of the production and generate better revenue, while also ensuring better international recognition for the movies and those they represent. To cite Haynes, New Nollywood was about "making better films with bigger budgets, films that can survive the aesthetic and technical challenge of being projected in cinemas rather than being released immediately as VCDs (video compact discs, the standard medium for movies in Nigeria) or DVDs for home viewing."[35]

Significantly immanent to the creative repertoire New Nollywood works with or the value it brings to the Nigerian and Yorùbá film industry is the global distribution networks in which New Nollywood inserts itself, which are more defined, structured, and beneficial than those relied upon by the Old Nollywood model of film distribution. There is a progressive and valuable shift from more informal networks of global distributions and channels that are "generally left out of dominant global cultural industry distribution networks"[36] to more integrated pathways defined along and connected to regional and diasporic flows, where their reach to audience becomes more mainstream, enhancing growth and innovation. In this sense, there is a palpable shift from relying on homegrown resources, substantial foreign aid, and less formalized input from foreign bodies in the filmmaking process of Nollywood movies and culture more generally; there is also the avoidance of the implication of using low-cost equipment that is acquired through informal networks that offer little guarantee and immaterial long-term benefits, [37] which need not be said affect the quality of the movie produced, the kind of innovation that produces it, and the type of reality that can be invented—all of which does the Yorùbá lifeworld little to no good.

The distribution channels available to Old Nollywood rely on private contacts in international and diasporic spaces whose positions in the network chain are often amorphous, as they operate as substitutes for more formal and structured channels. Jade Miller, whose work on

---

34. Miller, "Global Nollywood," 117–133.

35. Haynes, "New Nollywood," 53–73.

36. Miller, "Global Nollywood," 118.

37. See Miller, "Global Nollywood," for an extensive discussion on this.

Nollywood network distribution provides important information on the subject, argues that while these contacts foreground that for Old Nollywood, global connection routes do exist, they reveal themselves as patterned after the "logics of informality, opacity and small-scale enterprises that mark the rest of the industry."[38] The connections in which movies produced under the paradigm of Old Nollywood invest as parts of a global chain of an international distributive network are heavily dependent on physical sale formats.

What the above means regarding structure is a heavy reliance on unreliable sales of VCDs and DVDs made in open-air markets and small-scale shops.[39] In the diaspora, largely North America and some parts of Europe like the United Kingdom and Germany, this means anchoring global distribution on small-scale shops. More so, rather than a large-scale distribution of copies of movies, a single copy is often provided through such informal channels and then recopied. To worsen the case, the master copies from which others are made are sometimes made available through sources that are not always associated with the producer of the movie in question, sometimes through acquaintances of the shop owners—all of which culminate in some type of loss for the filmmaker and continues to infantilize the industry in terms of commerce and corporate and international growth. What it means on the creative front—which is tied to the structural—is the continued proliferation of cheaply produced movies, movies produced for the local space and whose appearance abroad is more incidental than deliberate, and movies whose lifecycles are produced with the endemic system of piracy in consideration. This all depends on the level of investment in inventing the Yorùbá cultural space on the screen. Surely, it would be hard to convince a filmmaker to invest resources into a movie that would earn little returns once it hits the physical markets.

New Nollywood impresses the global cinema as improving on these odds. First is the heavy reliance on Internet streaming and corporate partners like IrokoTV and other mega-platforms like Netflix that allows for more controlled returns on investment and a better handle on the menace of piracy that invalidates the efforts of filmmakers, makes the industry unlucrative for investors, and threatens bankruptcy for many. This Internet development, however, should not be seen as entirely benevolent. As Haynes rightfully points out, there are downsides to this upscale in distribution via the Internet. For example, "the markets for Nigerian DVDs in the United States and the United Kingdom have been severely eroded by Internet streaming," and the fees paid by these streaming sites often are meager and unencouraging: "the biggest player in this game is Iroko Partners, which runs the twin Internet channels NollywoodLove.com (via YouTube) and iROKOtv.com. The company claims it pays $3,000 each for the rights to stream the films for three years, but people around the industry say actual payments are usually far less."[40] In addition, there are new platforms on cable TV that have also contributed to the popularization and mainstreaming of Nollywood movies. Channels like Africa Magic Yoruba on DSTV, owned by the South African company Multichoice, are an example of such platforms, although, there are undersides to this, like the disincentivization to purchase hard

---

38. Miller, "Global Nollywood," 125.
39. Miller, "Global Nollywood."
40. Haynes, "New Nollywood," 102.

copies and the underpayment that comes with buying the rights to the movies these channels broadcast.

However, the consensus of film scholars points to the arrival and preponderance of multiplex theaters as one of the major improvements that alternate New Nollywood to Old Nollywood. Although agreeing to the place of the theaters, Haynes refutes most of the other points often raised in defense of New Nollywood as a radical alternative. His argument borders on the idea that besides an improvement as regards multiplex cinemas, other much-discussed advancements like public screenings, premiering films in the choicest venues, and foreign sponsorship are not as new as they are often portrayed. The arguments presented in his article, which traces these developments back to the era of celluloid film productions, have considerable implications for how the Yorùbá is projected.

New Nollywood and its multiplex cinemas signify consumerist subjectivity at play, as they cater to the senses of its audience, which is necessarily cosmopolitan. To quote Connor, they "appear to appeal directly to spectators' senses by promising not only a movie and shopping but also an affective experience closely bound up with global consumerism."[41] This has immense implications for the premise of this chapter, since the presence of such subjectivity and its centralization as (one of) the goal(s) of a filmmaking experience suggests being conversant with the taste and lifestyle patterns of its audience, enough that it is worked as a guiding principle into the cinematic experience or cinema culture each movie furthers.

If the above proposition is not convincing, this excerpt from Adejunmobi's position on the subject where she quotes Barber should clarify it: "Imaginative narrative . . . bears the imprint of the conditions of its production."[42] Adejunmobi argues that each work—here, film—reflects its materiality or the conditions that shape its artifice. To put it in other words, each movie from Yorùbá filmmakers of New Nollywood that takes as its premise the Yorùbá lifeworld is the "outcome of labor performed by an author [filmmaker]" on "ideological materials—that are available in the particular position in society that he or she occupies."[43] These ideological materials are the lifestyle patterns, epistemic specificities, moral codes, social frameworks, economies, and mental frames that shape the Yorùbá lifeworld.

So when Connor refers to such Yorùbá movies and the multiplex theaters in which they are first given life as "exhibits of a metropolitan vantage point that emphasizes subjects such as airline travel, trendy technology, consumer culture, global pop culture, lifestyle brands, high fashion, and luxury goods,"[44] he is drawing our attention to how these affective experiences both reflect and connect to the core of the audience's subjectivities. Agreeing with this premise allows us to understand how the changes that have been upheld reflect the forces of culture and other aspects of the reality at play in the Yorùbá modern and traditional space.

Knowing this, even if we were to agree with Haynes that there is less than meets the eye as regards the supposed differences between Old and New Nollywood and that the major

---

41. Connor, "New Nollywood," 55.

42. Adejunmobi, "Neoliberal Rationalities," 32.

43. Adejunmobi, "Neoliberal Rationalities," 32.

44. Connor, "New Nollywood," 55.

significance is the introduction of urban multiplex theaters, there is still the matter of the influence of this improvement on the filmmaking process itself, which cannot be argued as less radical or dynamic. For instance, at the level of storytelling and ideology, the very processes that have made these structural changes possible are also responsible for the reception of movies tailored to an intended audience. Echoing, albeit partially, Connor's argument that the metropolitan sensibilities that the New Nollywood movies have or espouse, as well as their advertisement of modernity, are signifiers of the modernity of its cinematic subjects and those contextual to it. This partial agreement results from Connor's position that these movies and their materialities do not put forth a coherent or consolidated order of "knowledge and values" but rather an assemblage of signifiers of city life. In other words, they are not adequate representations of the lifeworld they seek to represent but are disconnected constituents of a sign system strategy harnessed to appeal to a group of people.

This statement is ambiguously loaded in its consequences and has unpleasant implications for how cinema can be said to represent or invent the Yorùbá. It does not set New Nollywood apart from the old in its treatment of modernity as separate from traditionalism, as something outside the world of the Yorùbá that must be struggled toward and attained. By implication, it recycles the idea that operating within the nucleus of Yorùbá movies are the usual binaries of modernism and traditional life and that the signifiers of these worlds are separate enough to be distinct. Connor sees New Nollywood movies as replicating these binaries in new ways. This, however, is also not entirely true, as it would imply that the "same cultural and economic signifiers of cosmopolitanism and urban lifestyle"[45] that the New Nollywood screen and narrativize somehow stand apart from the subjectivity of its intended audience or those whose lifeworld it mimics as if they are not integrated.

For instance, the movie *The Figurine*, by Kunle Afolayan, himself the face of New Nollywood, works the cosmic orientations of the Yorùbá spiritual space seamlessly with more urban and cosmopolitan sensibilities. The character ensemble is rich, ranging from more mainstay Yorùbá actors and iconic figures like Adebayo Faleti to crossovers from the English movie industry like Ramsey Nouah and those who find themselves grounded in both the Yorùbá and the English movie worlds, like Jide Kosoko. This cast is significant to the movie's ambitions and can be read to make assertive statements about the lives of those it seeks to invent on the global stage: the Yorùbá. After all, such a kind of character representation makes claims about the sensibilities of the people as wide, convivial, tolerant, and varying, as well as about how the Yorùbá are as diverse in their economic lifestyles as they are when it comes to religion, folk practices, and mythologies. Also important is its cross-cultural and nationalist vibes, giving the mix of cultural and ethnic participants in the movie.

Another significant aspect of the movie is the overarching narrative principle in the myth of Aràròmírẹ, *an invented* Yorùbá goddess who returns to earth intermittently to bless her worshippers, the people of Aràròmírẹ, *with seven years of plenty and seven years of suffering. This goddess is invented because no such goddess exists within the* Yorùbá orisa pantheon; more so,

---

45. Connor, "New Nollywood," 55.

there are copious references to her narrative as folksy and mythic, classifications Yorùbá people hardly ascribe to their spiritual origins. However, even as a narrative organizing principle, the figure and function of Àràròmíṛẹ *are divested of the totalitarian hold that mythologies or cosmic codes and religious spirituality often have in* Yorùbá indigenous cultural spaces. This is because, in the story, we are not sure of what exactly is at play, the spiritual implications of stealing the figurine of Àràròmíṛẹ, *which brings about the fourteen years of bliss and evil, or* whether it is the twin emotions of jealousy and covetousness wrecking the blissful lives of the characters.

There are many things to consider, and making a simple conclusion is impossible. One, the love triangle between the three central characters, Femi, Sola, and Mona, is thick enough to inspire diabolical acts of evil, an angle the story does not in any way discount. Femi, the cautious, bespectacled, asthmatic, and morally straight individual, loves Mona, who prefers the womanizing and promiscuous Sola and is pregnant by him. Sola and Femi are friends and graduates of archaeology with Mona too. The two friends would discover the figurine of the goddess in ruin during their National Youth Service Corps program and make away with it, perhaps because of occupational/disciplinary curiosity, oblivious of the fourteen-year rule associated with the goddess.

The signifiers of Western modernity would come into full view with the upscale lifestyles and success of these characters about seven years later, with each of them doing brilliantly well and living large, so to speak, only for the seven years of misfortune to begin in earnest. For example, Femi is no longer asthmatic during these seven years, and his father, previously diagnosed with cancer, is no longer ill. Mona is now married with kids, Femi is well-to-do, and his friend Sola is also doing great. However, we cannot ascribe the good lives enjoyed by the characters to Àràròmíṛẹ, nor can we attribute the misfortunes that come after to the curse of Àràròmíṛẹ, given Femi's sinister confessions at the end of the movie, revealing that he is the architect of some of the mishaps that befall the trio.

For instance, Femi, the son of a sculptor, requests his dad to make copies of Àràròmíṛẹ to fuel the hysteria of Mona, who considers the figurine the source of the sudden spate of unpleasant occurrences that have befallen the trio, like Femi losing his job and Sola going bankrupt and losing a child, among other things. When Mona throws away the figurine, it reappears— though we are not sure how. The movie tilts toward Àràròmíṛẹ as the culprit when Sola and Femi decide to return the figurine to the village of Àràròmíṛẹ as a possible way of achieving a meaningful resolution. But the movie emphasizes the ambiguity of its world when we see Femi club Sola by the head, with the intent of killing him and having Mona to himself. This, of course, negates the kind of deus ex machina introduced by the Old Nollywood formula where evildoers are killed or punished miserably to give the story a happy ending.

Viewers are forced to see the story from a more physical and logical perspective, especially as Femi begins to reveal how he orchestrated the whole thing. But no matter how sensible this angle reads, it is just not all that logical. Indeed, Femi might have had a hand in the entire ordeal, but to what extent, we are unsure. After all, it is easy to attribute Femi's miraculous healing from asthma to the result of the seven years of blessings, likewise his father's cancer remissions. It is also easy and quite sensible to attribute the return of these ailments during the seven years of curses to Àràròmíṛẹ.

This ambiguity is strategic, but it also reflects the fluid identities and sensibilities of the world it creates. The cosmopolitan Yorùbá cannot be put in neat boxes. This principle of conviviality is manifest as a lived experience of the Yorùbá, who are both religiously inclined and given to unshakable beliefs in the rationality of Western modernity. Ambiguous, maybe, but it is not strange at all. To cite Haynes, who reads the story in a similar light: "The movie is carefully constructed so it can be read either way, as an example of supernatural agency by the goddess Àràròmírę or as a tormented and finally psychotic lover's plot that exploits superstition. The alternative interpretations spiral ironically around one another."[46]

This openness of interpretation comments on the nature of the relationality of Yorùbá people to various worlds and cultural orientations; it also shows how their subjectivities can be influenced by seemingly opposing but complementary social forces. In addition to narrativizing the nature of the relationality shaping the Yorùbá world are other parts of the artifice of the movie, such as the significances of cloth choices, fashion statements, soundtrack, and architectural specificities that buoy the movie, which cut across both cosmopolitan/Western modernity and more traditional lifestyle patterns. Can we then, knowing this, agree that the signifiers of modernity in the movie are either simply inflections of neoliberal subjectivities, as Adejunmobi has argued, or indexes of a consumerist sensibility, or that New Nollywood "advertizes . . . modernity which is not presented as a consolidated order of knowledge and values," as Connor puts it?

Another movie that manifests this blend while also tinkering with the ambiguities that conviviality fosters particularly in plural and open cultural contexts like the Yorùbá is *October 1* (2014), by the same filmmaker. The movie established an openness toward multiculturalism and the kind of relationality that is bound to happen when progress considers the simultaneous modernization and traditionalization of the world. The movie, which is about a prince of *Àkútè* who goes to study abroad, complicates the relationship between modernism and traditionalism. The prince, Aderopo by name, who commits acts of savagery by raping and murdering women, is seen as a victim of a perverse form of modernity (in the form of experiencing horrors in pursuit of Western education and at the hands of Christianity), particularly of homosexual rape by a Reverend Father. The Reverend Father's place in the story is significant for its symbolization of the openness of a deeply traditional Yorùbá society to foreign cultures, even if the outcomes of such progress leave drastic repercussions. We might question the benevolence of a Western culture that seeks to cover its ugly truths, since Danladi, the northerner and inspector charged with solving the murders, is made by the colonial masters not to speak of the real events, partly because of peaceful independence and primarily because it puts the Western image in a pervasive light. The benevolence links to the scholarship that Prince Aderopo won that made him go live with the Reverend Father.

However, we cannot ignore Afolayan's reworlding of the Yorùbá sociocultural sphere in a way that reflects a strong nationalism and emphasizes the modernity of the Yorùbá space where it has been erased and unrecognized, thereby inventing it for all to see. We see Danladi, who is not Yorùbá, given a prominent role. He is welcomed and treated with respect in the

---

46. Haynes, "New Nollywood," 65.

community of *Àkútè*, even if he has to navigate the sometimes-tough terrain of intercultural relations. His role is significant in the movie as he retells the narrative and solves the crime, at least at the physical and human level, with the detective skills learned through modern and Western education. It is, however, also significant that this truth had been uncovered and cryptically revealed by the *Ifá* priest in the often-mysterious manner that knowledge is doled out to inquirers who seek out Ọ̀rúnmìlà for clarity. Thus, sharing the movie's epistemological space are the Western and the indigenous modes of knowledge making, and Afolayan ensured that none supersedes another and that their relevance is contextually defined.

The movie calls attention to the atrophy of foresight and lack of priority that attends to a community's inability to make sense of its epistemic modes of knowledge creation and not the demonization of Western modernity. The movie waxes strong about many things, but one of them is the nature of the world it cast on the screen media: a convivial world, even as far back as colonial times, negating narratives of the antagonistic or dyadic nature of indigenous cultures and subjectivities to forms of modernity or their hostility to progress preindependence. So, while we can agree that changes are indeed underway and continue to manifest between the old and new, and this is shown through an emphasis on high-stakes and big-budget movies screened at national and diasporic theaters and also at international festivals, we also cannot deny that these improvements in situating Nollywood and by extension Yorùbá in a global knowledge ecology reflect on the need to reinvent and on the continued improvement of the image of the Yorùbá on a national and global scale. These structural and strategic changes in the context of a global creative cosmos have implications at the ideological and narrative levels of cinema production. Moreover, because ideology and narration are products of societal occurrences, we can also agree that there is some level of fidelity between the cinematic experience and the lived experience of the Yorùbá, which continues to be the premise of this chapter.

More importantly, it means we can, for instance, see the various awards that *The Figurine* won at the African Magic Academy Awards and recognitions at the Rotterdam International Film Festival, the African Film Festival of New York and the Pan-African Film Festival, Los Angeles, as one of the indexes of the presence of the Yorùbá image as it were on an international stage. It thus stands to reason that we can move from chronicling the changes between Old and New Nollywood to what this means for the Yorùbá who are reinvented along the way.

18 The Yorùbá Nation and Its Borderless Creativity

Introduction

The concept of a nation is embedded in ideas of homogeneity and unity. A nation speaks of a group or community of people who have certain things in common, usually language, culture, and beliefs.[1] Therefore, a nation of people is not necessarily bound by a limited space of geography in which they live next to one another. The case of the Yorùbá, who exist in Nigeria, Benin, Togo, and the Atlantic diaspora, speak to this notion of a nation. Various factors make up Yorùbá nationhood: connection to the same ancestry, shared language, and a religious belief system.[2] This does not conclude that there are no variations to the shared myths about the foundation of the Yorùbá people, their language, or their religious practices. Rather, there is a commonality to these factors among the different Yorùbá communities worldwide. For instance, there is no doubt that the worship of certain Òrìṣà (deities) in some (if not all) Yorùbá communities outside Nigeria, Benin, and Togo have been greatly influenced by the cultures of other inhabitants of those places.[3] Catholic beliefs have interacted with the Yorùbá beliefs in Brazil and some Caribbean countries to create a hybrid. However, this does not nullify the fact that the Yorùbá in places like this share a thing or two in common with those in Nigeria, Benin, or Togo, thereby justifying the grounds for a Yorùbá nation.

The existence of Yorùbá communities in various parts of the world necessitates a nation of people that are not confined by geographical borders. However, the borderlessness of the Yorùbá also entails creative outputs. A discourse on this creativity must start from their belief in the Supreme Being and the pantheon gods who hold an irreplaceable position in the life of Yorùbá people, especially because religion is valuable to the Yorùbá and because it is generally believed by many that creativity emanates from the Supreme Being through the gods.[4]

Like other communities, the Yorùbá have myths of creation that have served as an explanation for why some things are the way they are in the world.[5] From these myths, one can infer that the Yorùbá do not just believe in a Supreme Being that is all-powerful and all-knowing but

---

1. Smith, "Genealogy of Nations," 94–112.
2. Eades, *Yoruba Today*.
3. Koike, "How Orisa Worship," 77–104.
4. Ayegboyin and Olajide, "Olodumare," 488–488.
5. Lawuyi, "Mythical Images," 55–71.

that their God possesses a sense of creativity. They refer to the Supreme Being with names such as *ẹlẹ́dàá*, which can be literally translated as the creator of destiny. According to Babatunde Lawal, the Supreme Being is also referred to as *aláṣẹ*, which connotes "the source of àṣẹ, the enabling power that transforms, creating something out of nothing, changing materials from one state to another, imparting motion to the motionless, and life to the lifeless."[6] It is in this similar vein that the Yorùbá believe that the creativity of the Supreme Being is also reflected in the activities of smaller gods, those they refer to as deities. For instance, the Yorùbá believe that Olódùmarè commissioned Ọbàtálá (a deity) with the responsibility of molding humans.[7]

They project the belief to Ọbàtálá because he is very artistic and highly creative. The Yorùbá hold the belief that the variance in human body structures is a result of the versatile nature of Ọbàtálá's creativity. Physical disability is presented as a creative project. Hence, Ọbàtálá molded humans, but it was not just his sole responsibility; rather, he passed the mold to *Ògún*, who also did his part of adding some features to it before finally passing it on to Olódùmarè, who gave the mold the life it needs to be a living being.[8] This is exemplified in the following praise poem (*oriki*), as offered by Lawal:

He created the child and its mother
After doing good to the father,
He sent for the child to come and collect its own good . . .
He molded the inner surface of the hand called the palm
He molded the underside of the foot called the sole
He molded the massive part of the body called the chest
He created the refractive water ball called the eyes
He molded the small pot called the skull . . .
The-Òrìṣà-has-made-a-work-of-art,
Owner-of-choice-clay . . .

Yorùbá text:

Ọbàtálá
Ò dá'mọ, dá'yàá
Ó ṣe bàbá lóore tán,
Ó ránṣẹ́ sí ọmọ kó wá gba ore . . .
Òun ló dá pẹ́tẹ́ ọwọ́,
Òun ló dá pẹ́tẹ́ ẹsẹ́
Òun ló dá àyà j'àǹkà, tí à ń pè ní ìgbá àyà
Òun ló dá omi lójólójó, tí à ń pè lójú
Òun ló dá orù rẹ́bẹ́tẹ́, tí à ń pé ní Àtàrí . . .
Oòṣọ̀nà, Alámọ̀rere . . .[9]

---

6. Lawal, "Divinity, Creativity and Humanity," 162.
7. Lawuyi, "Obatala Factor," 369–375.
8. Lawal, "Divinity, Creativity and Humanity," 163.
9. Lawal, "Divinity, Creativity and Humanity," 163.

Of course, Ọbàtálá is just one of many deities to whom Olódùmarè has delegated artistic responsibility. Ògún himself exhibits creative dimensions. The Yorùbá have come to accept *Ògún* as the god of "civilization."[10] Indeed, civilization has a lot to do with improvement on what is existing and obtainable. *Ògún* is also referred to as the god of warfare.

Consequently, this creativity is passed on to humans as well. Little wonder the Yorùbá take pride in artistic endeavors like carving, oral poetry, singing, dancing, painting, and more.[11] Perhaps one can argue that they see a reflection of these possibilities in the gods they serve. Lawal posits that to become a professional artist, according to the Yorùbá culture, "training has two aspects, the cultural and technical."[12] The cultural part has a lot to do with understanding the worldview and religious outlook of the Yorùbá because this is vital to their artistic and creative endeavors. The technical part has to do with learning the craft itself.

In contemporary times, although things are a bit different in terms of how learning is done, there is no artistic work with a Yorùbá context whose author or creator is not established in the Yorùbá culture and the technical training required. Wole Soyinka, a Nobel Laureate, has claimed that Ògún is his muse, and some of his works have been dedicated to explicating Ògún.[13] Several of Soyinka's works are steeped in Yorùbá sociocultural context. For the Yorùbá, and as found in Soyinka's works, Ògún has both positive and negative sides. Creativity is embedded in his positive side, while his negative side leads to destruction.[14] Writing on Soyinka's connection to this god of creativity, Yaw Adu-Gyamfi notes that in "Idanre," the title poem of the volume, Soyinka summarizes what the god stands for in Yomba mythology: "God of Iron and Metallurgy, Explorer, Artisan, Hunter, God of War, Guardian of the Road, the Creative Essence."[15] These names emerged from the different legends about Ògún and his exploits among mortals.

Other creative and artistic people of Yorùbá origin in different spheres of artistic production also lay claim to their roots in Yorùbá cultural beliefs. The works of world-acclaimed singers like Fela Anikulapo Kuti and Sunny Ade not only have contexts in Yorùbá culture but have also crossed the boundaries of southwestern Nigeria to many other parts of the world.[16] The same is true of Yorùbá fashion, movies, and many other creative expressions.

This chapter seeks to highlight creative expressions of people with Yorùbá heritage that have crossed the boundaries of southwestern Nigeria and explain the factors responsible for the diffusion of these works into regions where the authors, singers, or artists were hardly known. The chapter answers the question of why people in different regions outside Nigeria, and indeed Africa, have become familiar with the creative expressions of people of Yorùbá origin. Similarly, this chapter considers what can be regarded as creative materials that have their source in the Yorùbá nation. Holistically, the discourse is based on the submission of Aribidesi Usman

---

10. Asante and Mazama, "Ogun," 481–482.

11. Aremu, Ajiboye and Abiodun, "Art and Culture," 737–744.

12. Lawal, "Divinity, Creativity and Humanity," 167.

13. Ebeogu, "From Idanre to Ogun Abibiman," 84–96.

14. Barnes, *Africa's Ogun*.

15. Adu-Gyamfi, "Wole Soyinka's 'Dawn,'" 73–89.

16. Fadipe, "Skin Bleaching," 216–235.

and Toyin Falola: "Yoruba creative arts include hairstyling, body scarification, tattooing, the wearing of beads, and chipping or creating a notch between the upper front teeth, along with other body decoration such as rubbing the body with palm kernel oil and camwood powder. Music, like art and religion, also plays a significant role in Yoruba culture, permeating all aspects of traditional Yoruba societies."[17]

This is not an attempt to analyze every form of art mentioned above but to consider a few that have been selected to locate Yorùbá creativity within the context of its manifestations and acceptance in places and cultures far and near the southwestern region of Nigeria and other Yorùbá communities in West Africa. As fully explained in part 1, Yorùbá communities have been scattered across the globe linked to circumstances of history, trade, colonialism, and even the myth and legend of Odùduwà.[18] The Odùduwà story is one of migration.[19]

The existence of Yorùbá communities outside the popular boundaries of southwestern Nigeria explains the presence of Yorùbá creative production in places outside Nigeria. Of course, inversely, it also explains why creative expressions from the Yorùbá communities from other West African countries are being entertained in Nigeria. However, beyond the communities in these West African countries, Yorùbá people are found in other parts of the world in sizes that are not negligible, which perhaps can be explained under two categories: migration and slavery. Indeed, slavery is also a form of migration, only in this case, it is forced. Before the arrival of the Europeans in Africa, the Yorùbá had always been mobile. This mobility led to the spread of the Yorùbá to other settlements away from their source in Ile-Ife. For instance, the collapse of the Old Oyo led to the migration of Yorùbá people to other new areas.[20]

Slavery was a global phenomenon from the fifteenth century until the early nineteenth century.[21] As part of its mission to conquer new places, European expeditions broke into the African continent and established a transatlantic slave trade that exported people to Europe and the New World.[22] Kingdoms subdued other kingdoms and took their subjects as slaves. The transition of Yorùbá slaves from Africa to the New World was not a palatable experience; it continues to hold a lot of memory. The forceful transitioning of the enslaved to the New World and the harsh conditions they were subjected to in this process were just a tip of what they would encounter in their new habitats. By the time they got to these new places, according to Michele Reid, "The thousands of Africans who arrived in nineteenth-century Cuba may have arrived without material culture, but they carried their personal and group identities with them, and the Yoruba were no exception."[23] It was impossible to have dumped their personal and group identities, as chapter 4 explains concerning epistemology.

Part of their identity was their religious beliefs and the cosmological view of the world. The revival of Orisa was both a spiritual and creative process. New modes of worship and

17. Usman and Falola, *Yoruba from Prehistory*, 295.
18. Akinjogbin, *Cradle of a Race*.
19. Babatola, "Formation of Yoruba Nation."
20. Usman, "Precolonial Regional Migration," 112.
21. Daudin, "How Important Was the Slavery System," 151–157.
22. Stilwell, *Slavery and Slaving in African History*.
23. Reid, "Origins of the Yoruba in Cuba," 116.

Right and facing,
Figure 18.1.
Contemporary
creativity in sculpture
(a collage of major
woodworks). From the
Toyin Falola Private
Collection.

performance must adjust to new locations. The Òrìsàs were named after Roman Catholic saints.[24] Miguel De La Torre describes one scenario as if it was a form of drama: "These Africans being led to a life of bondage, like so many of their descendants, saw no reason to turn to the white Spanish Jesus of the dominant culture. Prevented by their masters from worshiping the gods of Africa, these slaves simply masked their gods with the clothing of Catholic saints. It thus appeared to priests, sea captains, and slaveholders that slaves were praying to Saint Lazarus, for example—but unbeknownst to these oppressors, the slaves were continuing the worship of the òrìsà Babalú-Ayé."[25]

The enslaved Yorùbá also maintained certain aspects of their cultural beliefs, especially those that brought entertainment like singing, dancing, poetry, and other art forms. Marta

24. Herskovits, "African Gods and Catholic Saints," 635–643.
25. De La Torre, *Santeria*, 19, 20.

Moreno Vega notes that "the more than thirteen million Africans who survived the Middle Passage carried with them the creative impulse that continues to weave through the aesthetic vision and expressions of African descendants. . . . Spread throughout the Americas, the Yoruba were successful in transplanting their traditional culture to new environments."[26] Despite the harsh conditions, they were not just content by being molded by their new environment; rather, they infused their new environments with elements of what they brought with them from their homelands. As Lawal points out in his work on the Yorùbá of Cuba, "The practice of Santeria . . . inspired new artistic forms."[27]

Vega takes it a step further when she says, "Embedded in the cosmology of the different African belief systems that traveled to the Americas are the ancestors, including Eéguns (deceased persons) and spirits, and African deities (òrìṣàs, nkisis, and luas). These entities possess divine intelligence and the power to create."[28] This underscores how African slaves in the New World expressed their creative abilities and propagated African arts.

As established in the case of religion, a holistic approach to Yorùbá creativity and especially its different expressions beyond the borders of "traditional" Yorùbá communities will be incomplete without the contributions of diasporic communities in the New World. The decision of the diaspora to hold on to Yorùbá culture is explainable as a way of maintaining ties with their source. Albert Oikelome explains this using Oyotunji Village in the United States as a case study. What is more instructive in Oikelome's exposition are the ritual and cultural activities of this village, which affirm the transcendence of Yorùbá creativity beyond the borders of Africa. Oikelome notes that music and performances are strong cultural icons in this community. Music and performances have been used to further assert and define their identity as the first of Yorùbá heritage before being an African American. The people of Oyotunji in the United States are known for reenacting the Osun-Osogbo festival in their village, according to Oikelome. Shedding some light on the Osun-Osogbo festival, Oikelome notes that "while the location of the central shrine is fixed, the intangible cultural heritage of the festival—the ephemeral and experiential component—may be transported to some extent, and this is precisely what is happening."[29] Oyotunji Village is an example of this transportation. In reenacting the festival, Oikelome notices that some form of hybridity exists in the music form of the Yorùbá people of Oyotunji Village. Perhaps this should not be so much of a surprise, as he submits that "the music in Oyotunji village can be described as cultural hybridity. This consists of the confluence of African American and Yoruba musical styles and the relationships between them. One element of this hybridity was how both sounds were blended to form a new type of music in the Yoruba tradition."[30]

Indeed, the cultural activity of the people of Oyotunji is minute compared to what has been hybridized as a result of the Yorùbá creativity existing in a new atmosphere. Yorùbá people in

26. Vega, "Ancestral Sacred Creative Impulse," 46, 47.
27. Lawal, "From Africa to the Americas," 28.
28. Lawal, "From Africa to the Americas," 48.
29. Oikelome, "Stylistic Analysis of Afrobeat Music," 9.
30. Oikelome, "Stylistic Analysis of Afrobeat Music," 13.

the New World and other Africans have always found ways to connect to their ancestral homelands. Another way by which the Yorùbá diaspora connects to home is through the creative works that come out of Southwest Nigeria. Through the works of notable literary writers like Wole Soyinka and award-winning musicians like the late Fela, Yorùbá in the diaspora can connect to their roots.

These slaves needed to hold on to their gods, and it was instructive that their descendants would remain committed to the religion. The Yorùbá religion is a form of creative expression, and the Yorùbá people, home and abroad, believe that creativity comes from Olódùmarè, who passes it on to humans through the Òrìṣà. Again, this takes the conversation back to the example of Wole Soyinka, who cites Ògún as his muse. There is a fusion of the spiritual and creativity in the Yorùbá religion, and religious practices inspire creative expressions.[31] Duro Ladipo's Òba Kòso (The King Did Not Hang) comes to mind. Ladipo, ironically, was born to Anglican parents but was greatly influenced by his grandfather, who was a Ṣàngó and Ọya worshipper. This would serve as the veritable foundation he needed later in life.[32] While in Ibadan, he was inspired by the activities of Ulli Beier and later returned to Osogbo to replicate the Mbari Mbayo group.

Ọba Kòso highlights the sojourn of the legendary Ṣàngó on earth. Ladipo was very close to his grandfather, from whom he picked a lot of folklore, myths, legends, and many other creative outputs that highlighted the Yorùbá worldview and beliefs, which had a major influence on his creative prowess.[33] It is generally believed that Ṣàngó was the fourth king to rule in the Old Ọ̀yọ́ kingdom.[34] His reign was characterized by war and unrest. At some point, he had two powerful generals—Gbonka and Timi—who proved difficult to handle. Consequently, he pitted the two warlords against each other; this would haunt him, as Gbonka came back to fight Ṣàngó himself. Ṣàngó's followers deserted him in this encounter with Gbonka; seeing this, he fled. Ladipo's Ọba Kòso typifies this history. Some believe that Ṣàngó committed suicide, while some hold the view that he transformed to become the god of thunder that Yorùbá believes in today—hence the name and meaning of Ladipo's play, Ọba Kòso.[35]

Ọba Kòso and other stage plays did not gain recognition and acceptance among the Yorùbá people or Nigerians only; his creative endeavors transcended the shores of the nation. In an article published by Lekan Alabi in 2018, the author highlights some of Ladipo's achievements, which specifically went beyond the shores of his hometown Osogbo and even Nigeria at large. Alabi notes, "With vigorous rehearsals, attention to details, researches, guts, and sheer luck, he broke through the amateur ranks and emerged the notable dramatist whose group, the Duro Ladipo National Theatre would win the first prize at the Berlin Arts Festival in Germany in 1964 and at the first-ever Commonwealth Arts Festival in London, UK, the following year,

---

31. Fahm, "Ijebu Ode's Ojude Oba Festival," 1–11.

32. Raji-Oyelade, Olorunyomi, and Ladipo, *Duro Ladipo*.

33. Beier, *Return of Shango*.

34. Law, "West African Cavalry State," 1–15.

35. Johnson, *History of the Yorubas*, 151–152.

with his epic play, 'Ọba Kòso.'"[36] These are just a few of the international recognitions that Duro Ladipo and *Ọba Kòso* received, not to mention the numerous accolades that came after the death of this Yorùbá icon. A certain record has it that Ọba Kòso was performed over two thousand times before Ladipo's death.[37]

Ladipo and his theater group succeeded in taking their dramas to different joints in Southwest Nigeria and different countries around the world, especially in Europe and America. Ladipo's plays were loved and celebrated for the ingenuity with which they portrayed the Yorùbá myths and culture. Indeed, Ladipo's recognition as the second Sango is justifiable. For one, available record has it that it rained heavily on the day he died, signifying, according to Yorùbá superstition, that there was more to the individual than meets the eye.[38] This belief in the spiritism of Ladipo is tied to his role as Ṣàngó in his play, *Ọba Kòso*. According to one of Ladipo's sons, "My father was more spiritual than human being to the extent that it is going to be a waste of time to attempt to replicate his exploits. As a matter of fact, some Ṣàngó worshippers attest to the fact that he was another Ṣàngó of his generation. I have no reason to doubt these people because, apart from their depth in tradition, what my father used to display on stage could frighten anyone."[39]

The second pointer to his almost-deified portrayal among the Yorùbá people is traceable to his ability to present the Yorùbá culture impressively and appreciably to the outside world, especially Europe and America. It is no longer news that the Western world held (and partly still holds) the view that the African man and his culture are barbaric and that the exposure and civilization being experienced in Africa is traceable to the offerings of white people during colonialism. Though his plays were thoroughly Yorùbá and highly creative, Ladipo also, in a way, attempted to nullify this view. Ladipo paved the way for Nigerian and African acting and cinema and was a trendsetter in the Nigerian theater space.

Another icon in the foundational stage of Nigerian film and theater is Hubert Ogunde, also Yorùbá. His contributions to the Yorùbá/Nigerian operatic tradition revolutionized that scene. Ogunde started the first professional touring company in Nigeria,[40] which is sometimes referred to as the *Alarinjo* theater groups among the Yorùbá people. *Alarinjo* is literally translated as "those who walk and dance from one location to the other."[41] It depicts the creative ability of the Yorùbá people to combine dance with drama, something that has become a popular genre in the theatric world today. Ogunde transformed this genre and took it global. He used this medium to castigate the colonial government at the time and the indigenous Nigerian government when it took over after independence.[42] Consequently, works like *Yoruba ronú* helped him stand out among the other travel theater groups in Nigeria and abroad.

---

36. Alabi, "Remembering the Thunderking of Theatre."
37. DAWN Commission, "Duro Ladipo."
38. Ògúndèjí, "Image of Ṣàngó," 57–58.
39. Sanusi, "Meet Duro Ladipo."
40. Clark, *Hubert Ogunde.*
41. Adedeji, "Alarinjo," 27–51.
42. Olukotun, *Repressive State,* 107.

Ulli Beier: White Skin, Yorùbá Mind

One major way by which Yorùbá creativity has attained its global prominence is through the popularity of its music and its musicians. Many foreigners like Ulli Beier and his then-wife, Susanne Wenger, were attracted to the Yorùbá arts and culture, and their contributions were in no small way instrumental in projecting Yorùbá creativity to the world. Beier was a major contributor to the start-up of the Mbari Mbayo cultural group in Osogbo, alongside Duro Ladipo.[43] It has been said that he left the urban setting of the University of Ibadan to mix with the Indigenous people of Ede and Osogbo, where he attended festivals and other cultural ceremonies. The Center for Black Culture and International Understanding (CBCIU) puts it this way: "But rather than look up to the new Western-educated Yorùbá elite who were bent on modernizing the society from without, Ulli went back to the source of the cultural fire, as it were, for his own edification, education and illumination . . . for it was to the Òrìṣà themselves and their human representatives on earth that Ulli went."[44]

It was during these kinds of events that Beier would take notes and carry out research on Yorùbá creative culture. For instance, at one of the outings, Beier and Duro Ladipo came across the young Chief Ifayemi Elebuibon, who narrated that he had been tasked with the responsibility of getting appropriate poems for some of Ladipo and Beier's performances.[45] Apart from supporting creative endeavors through the Mbari Mbayo group and others, Beier was a prolific writer on the culture and ways of the Yorùbá people. So much was he involved in the Yorùbá culture that he liked to refer to himself as a Yorùbá man.

Beier has been credited to have contributed immensely to the progress of the Yorùbá creative space within and outside Nigeria. According to the CBCIU, Beier was the reason certain Yorùbá creatives could display their talents to the global community. Making a passing comment about this in the article, they stated that "Timi Laoye, an accomplished dundun drummer for whom Ulli arranged a tour of Europe,"[46] helping the reader to see Beier's impact on those he called his friends. More important is how much of an impact Beier had on the Yorùbá creative space and how he was instrumental in helping these creative outputs find international audiences. The CBCIU article notes further: "There is no space here to give a detailed account of his equally deep friendship and association with Kola Ogunmọla, so suffice it to just mention that he played a decisive role in getting foreign grant for Ogunmola's Yoruba stage adaption of Amos Tutuola's The Palmwine Drinkard, a work in the realization of which the theatre arts department at Ibadan and the artist Demas Nwoko (a member of Mbari Club) also played crucial roles."[47]

Beier's efforts in promoting Yorùbá creativity and helping some of his Yorùbá friends and colleagues find an entrance into Europe and America were only part of his significance. He was also the mastermind behind two famous journals, *Odù* and *Black Orpheus*, which gained

---

43. Kennedy, "I Saw and I Was Happy," 8–16.
44. Centre for Black Culture, "Story of Ulli Beier."
45. Adewole, "How I Met Ulli Bier."
46. Centre for Black Culture, "Story of Ulli Beier."
47. Centre for Black Culture, "Story of Ulli Beier."

Figure 18.2. Contemporary creativity in painting (a collage of major works by Moses Ogunleye).

444

popularity and positive notes in literary magazines at the time.[48] The magazines spotlight some of the best poems from most people of Yorùbá origin of this time: "Ulli Beier's literary productions are more or less well-known: the excellent anthology of Yoruba poetry and, the no less pioneering anthology of modern African poetry in English which he did with Gerald Moore; another anthology of essays on modern African literature; plus the founding, editing and publishing of Black Orpheus and Odù, both of which, we now know, he did virtually alone (otherwise, how come the two journals died the moment he left?)."

Whatever Beier did for the Yorùbá culture is a part of the larger contribution attributable to him.[49] It is said that Beier brought Yorùbá culture and art to wherever he was in the world. This accompanies "the numerous essays he wrote and published in notable magazines and journals, all of which centered on the Yorùbá culture, society, and traditions."[50] Mention should also be made of the Iwalewahaus at the Universität Bayreuth. The establishment, which started with the intent to promote cross-cultural interaction between Europe and non-European countries, has today become, among many other things, a hub for Yorùbá creatives to refine their craft and enjoy greater visibility.[51]

A former bank building is the new home for African art and culture in Bayreuth, southern Germany. Iwalewa House offers an exciting insight into the work of contemporary African artists and the chance to meet them. . . . The building even has studios for artists, much to the delight of Maimuna Adam who happens to be in Bayreuth once again. The Mozambican artist is full of praise for the modified concept of the house that has changed its focus from old fashioned exhibitions to show young artistic talent from Africa. . . . A treasure trove that has been put at the artists' disposal is now to be found in the new Iwalewa house—the largest collection of contemporary African art. Among the items in this outstanding collection are barber shop signs which decades earlier advertised hair styles such as the "Lumumba" and "Kennedy" cuts in Nigeria. Original masks, visionary aluminum reliefs, billboards of shoemakers from Mozambique showing the giant ape "King Kong" are also to be found.[52]

There is no doubting the fact that this brainchild of Beier played and continues to play a significant role in spreading the ingenuous creativity that exists in the Yorùbá culture (and, of course, Africa at large). Indeed, many people worldwide are regular visitors to this monumental building that houses some of the most beautiful artworks the world has ever seen, some of which are by or from the Yorùbá nation. This highlights the tireless role of Beier in ensuring that Yorùbá culture and artistry receive recognition among the comity of nations.[53] Coming from the efforts of a white man no doubt gave prominence to the assertion that the Yorùbá people and Africans at large had culture and civilization and displayed a high level of creativity in

48. Currey, "Literary Publishing after Nigerian Independence," 8–16.
49. Abodunrin, "How I Advised Ulli Beier."
50. Tubosun, "Ulli Beier at the British Library."
51. Okeke-Agulu, "From Mbari Mbayo."
52. Welle, "Iwalewa House."
53. Uhakheme, "Osun, Artists Mourn German Scholar Ulli Beier."

their endeavors. And by the twentieth century, Yorùbá creatives had begun to be more confident in showing the world what they had to offer. Paying close attention to the music industry from this time helps to foreground this point.

Pioneers of Unique Genres

Ayinla Omowura was an enigma who grew up and lived in the city of Abeokuta. Although he also frequented Lagos and some other southwestern cities when he gained fame, Omowura's rising is solely traceable to his hometown of Abeokuta. In relation to this discourse on the borderlessness of Yorùbá creativity, Omowura's contribution lies in his ability to pick socio-economic, political, marital, and other issues that affected humans of his time, establish them in deep philosophical Yorùbá thoughts, and channel all these into song.[54] He used proverbs, insults, and metaphors to drive home his point. Despite his "limitation" in the English language and resources, his fame rose far and wide. Ironically, Omowura had expressed his wish to be educated, which he tried to force upon his children. Ironic because even without this Western education that he desired, his music appealed to many people, especially those of Yorùbá heritage.[55] While his genre of music was more popular among the Yorùbá people of southwest Nigeria in his lifetime, his music found greater audiences beyond the country's border only after his death. Of course, he had expressed a wish and belief to one day take his music to Europe and America, and just when Providence smiled on him through his record label, and he was to perform in England, death came knocking and snatched his life at the prime. Festus Adedayo notes, "The desire to one day travel abroad (àbí *London tí ẹ wí ti yá? Bó s'America a jọ ń lọ ni*, etc) featured prominently in his songs."[56]

His death was indeed a loss to the Yorùbá nation. The question is if Omowura had just been a "local champion," would he have had the opportunity of international exposure that presented itself just at the point of his death? Indeed, his crew members, led by his son, eventually took his music to England just as planned before his death. This speaks to what Adedayo said about Omowura's artistry, which was initially denigrated by Yorùbá intellectuals. He submits that "in spite of his limitations and foibles, Omowura remains a great musical beacon in Yorubaland and the eternality of his advocacies and evergreen texture of his songs are beginning to be seen by a Yorùbá world that shut its mind off his melody, musical scholarship and social criticism, simply because of his low class, illiteracy and obsessive identification with the rejects of society."[57]

Interestingly, Omowura was not the original pioneer of the Apala genre.[58] Its invention is often traced to the efforts of Haruna Ishola, who changed the name of the genre from Òṣùgbó to Apala. Ishola, popularly referred to as Baba Gani Agba, changed not only the music genre itself but also the face of it; he gave it the recognition this type of music and those who sang it

---

54. Fadipe, *Ethical Reorientation*.
55. Adedayo, *Ayinla Omowura*.
56. Adedayo, "Ayinla Omowura."
57. Adedayo, "Ayinla Omowura."
58. Broughton, *World Music*, 593.

deserved. Ishola was so popular as an Apala crooner that the government of Nigeria, under the leadership of Shehu Shagari, bestowed him the title of the Member of the Order of the Niger award.[59]

Though his first album was a commercial failure, Ishola refused to be discouraged, and his second album went on to receive public applause and acceptance, so much so that "Haruna Ishola was the undisputable king of Apala Music."[60] Not only was Ishola able to dazzle those around him and the Yorùbá community in southwest Nigeria, but his style of music also became accepted beyond southwest Nigeria and the country itself. Onigegewura writes of him: "Haruna Ishola was also one of the pioneer musicians to tour Europe. Before his epic journey, apala music used to be derided as a local music. I am certain you have heard that *ko sí aye apala ní ilu* oyinbo [Apala music has no place in the white man's country]. Well, that was before Haruna Ishola. He succeeded in taking Apala music to London. He went to Germany. He visited Sweden. He returned to Nigeria via Rome."[61]

Ishola's tour around Europe was a groundbreaking experience that inspired and paved the way for other young Yorùbá musical talents from all over Nigeria.[62] On his return to Nigeria, he sang in the album he released thereafter: *On my way to London ko s'ewu rara!* This further points attention to the excitement and the recognition of the great feat he had achieved. It is also worthy of note that Ishola was accepted into these countries, and he enjoyed his tour because Europeans appreciated the beauty and splendor of his music, which was steeped in Yorùbá culture and lifestyle.

Fela is another artist who contributed immensely to the progress of the Yorùbá creative space within and outside Nigeria. Fela and his music are important to us because, apart from the fact that he is Yorùbá, the Afrobeat genre that he propagated fused with a traditional Yorùbá style of music. Writing about the origin of the Afrobeat genre, Albert Oikelome submits that "various definitions by several scholars agreed that the musical synthesis presented in this genre is defined by a fusion of foreign elements with a socio-stylistic musical framework whose roots lie in traditional Yoruba music."[63]

This globally recognized genius began studying music at Trinity College in London, much to his parent's disappointment, as they wanted him to study medicine. While in school, John Dougan[64] notes that Fela got tired of the European style of music taught in his classes. Consequently, he started a band called *Koola Lobitos*.[65] The James Brown singing style of Sierra Leonean musician Geraldo Pina had an impact on this band. Also, the band was able to combine elements of traditional highlife, especially Yorùbá traditional music style and jazz. Fela's

---

59. 1981 National Honours Awards Recipients, Federal Republic of Nigeria Official Gazette. Lagos: Federal Government Press, October 1, 1981, 1160.

60. Onigegewura, "Death of a Musical Partnership."

61. Onigegewura, "Death of a Musical Partnership."

62. Collins, *Musicmakers of West Africa*, 49.

63. Oikelome, "Stylistic Analysis of Afrobeat Music."

64. Dougan, "Biography."

65. Denselow, "Fela Ransome-Kuti & His Koola Lobitos."

meeting with Sandra Isidore no doubt marked a turning point in his musical career.[66] It was at this point that he realized how he had abandoned a treasure, his real identity, to pursue what should not be regarded as so important.

Against the background of the flashy, sophisticated technology of the American society that awed him, he saw people who were turning to Africa's cultural treasures for inspiration and wisdom. *The Autobiography of Malcolm X*, in particular, convinced Fela to claim and explore his African identity, both personally and with his music. Inspired by the expatriate African musician Ambrose Campbell, he immediately began composing music based on chants, call-and-response vocals, and complex, interacting rhythms. He dubbed the new sound "Afrobeat."[67]

There is no gainsaying the fact that Fela's return to his true identity redefined his place in the music world. Staying true to this identity and the plight of the common man reflected in the language with which he wrote his music—Yorùbá and Nigerian Pidgin mostly—and the lyrics of such songs. The lyrics of "Water No Get Enemy" exemplify these two features in a typical Fela song:

> To bá fẹ lọ wẹ omi lo ma lò
> If you want go wash, na water you go use
> To bá fẹ́ sebẹ̀ omi lo ma lò
> If you want cook soup, na water you go use
> Tó rí bá ń gbóná o omi lẹ́rò̀ rẹ̀
> If your head dey hot, na water go cool on
> Tọ́mọ bá ń dàgbà omi ló ma lò
> If your child dey grow, na water he go use
> Tómi bá pọmọ ẹ́ o omi náà lo ma lò
>
> If water kill your child, na water you go use
> Kò sóhun to lè ṣe kó o má lomi o
> Nothing without water
> Kò sóhun tòlè ṣe ko ma lomi o
> Omi ò lọ́ọ̀tá o
>
> [Chorus]
> (Water, him no get enemy!)
> Omi ò lọ́ọ̀tá o
> (Water, him no get enemy!)
>
> Omi ò lọ́ọ̀tá o
> (Water, him no get enemy!)
> If you fight am, unless you wan die (Water, him no get enemy!)
> I say water no get enemy (Water, him no get enemy!)
> If you fight am, unless you wan die (Water, him no get enemy!)

---

66. Izsadore and Oyekunle, *Fela and Me*.
67. Grass, "Fela Anikulapo-Kuti," 134.

Omi ò lọ́ọ̀tá o
(Water, him no get enemy!)
I dey talk of Black man power (Water, him no get enemy!)
I dey talk of Black power, I say (Water, him no get enemy!)
I say water no get enemy (Water, him no get enemy!)
If you fight am, unless you wan die (Water, him no get enemy!)
I say water no get enemy (Water, him no get enemy!)
I say water no get enemy (Water, him no get enemy!)
Omi ò lọ́ọ̀tá o (Water, him no get enemy!)
Omi ò lọ́ọ̀tá o (Water, him no get enemy!)[68]

This song shows Fela's artistic ability to communicate a profound message to his audience. With one effort, he successfully communicates to a typical Yorùbá audience while not leaving out those who are more at home with the English language and those of the Pidgin English. Yet, Fela can communicate the irreplaceable place of the Black man in the world. Indeed, Fela seeks to drive home the point that the Black man is like water which no sane person should attempt to make an enemy of. Hence, because water is extremely necessary to any living being, it cannot be seen as an enemy by anyone. It is the same thing for the "Black power," Fela says. The Black race is so important that no right-thinking person should choose enmity with this race. If, therefore, the plight of the Black man affects all, why should it be ignored?

Despite his insistent use of both the Yorùbá language and Nigerian Pidgin, Fela's music found a home in different parts of the world, perhaps because his message had a universal appeal—a campaign against oppression and bad governance[69] or because he found a way to marry the foreign and the traditional. Whatever the case, one thing that cannot be denied is the influence of Yorùbá culture in defining his novel approach to music.[70] Aside from the use of Yorùbá elements, Fela, upon returning to Nigeria, founded what he termed the Kalakuta Republic, with a shrine (or an abode) in Lagos. Although the term *Kalakuta* itself is said to have been borrowed from Indian culture,[71] the shrine represented (and still does) what is African and indigenous. Grass notes that "the Shrine encompassed a little community, temporary perhaps, but one that expressed Fela's concept of a liberated African society."[72]

Earlier, Fela's genius was alluded to. The proper reflection of this genius is actually in the universal endorsement of his music and particularly the new genre of music he propagated. Before Fela became popularly accepted, he had embarked on tours in America with his band, showing that his music was already finding audiences even before his global fame. By the time he settled for an infusion of his Yorùbá and African identity into his music, his fame rose higher. So much was his genre of music accepted worldwide that in August 2002, an Afrobeat remembrance

---

68. Fela Anikulapo-Kuti and Africa 70, *Expensive Shit*.

69. Sithole, *Kuti and the Oppositional Lyrical Power*, 1–12.

70. Adu, "Re-inventing Fela Anikulapo Kuti," 68–79.

71. Another popular understanding is that it was the name of a prison cell, Calcutta, Fela inhabited in the Lagos, possibly Alagbon. See Veal, *Fela*, 143.

72. Grass, "Fela Anikulapo-Kuti," 139.

Right and facing,
Figure 18.3.
Contemporary
creativity in masks (a
collage of major masks).
From the Toyin Falola
Private Collection.

450

festival was established in Nigeria and Europe and America.[73] Furthermore, countless movies and documentaries have been made in honor of this legend.[74] His music has been reproduced in different formats and quantities since his demise. Equally important are the awards and recognition attached to his name and music during his lifetime and even at his death. The greatest legacy of the legend must be that Afrobeat continues to live—now in myriad ways—after the death of its most prominent propagator.[75] With every acceptance, popularity, and spread of Afrobeat, Yorùbá art and culture also receives a greater measure of attention.

Perhaps one major musician who broke the barrier against Yorùbá creativity and its borderlessness is Sunday Adeniyi Adegeye, popularly known as King Sunny Ade (KSA). While not the principal musician who exposed the world to Yorùbá's creative abilities, the magnitude of KSA's impact on peoples of other cultures around Nigeria and the world at large is formidable. Just like Fela, KSA also had a stint with Victor Olaiya, which was where KSA began as

73. Oikelome, "Stylistic Analysis of Afrobeat Music."

74. Araújo, "My Friend Fela."

75. Gikandi, "Femi Kuti and Made Kuti."

a professional musician.[76] He would later go on to start his band, the Green Spot, in 1967. His band name was later changed to African Beats and later Golden Mercury. Also, like Fela, KSA had ventured into music against the desire of his parents, who wanted him to be educated in the Western style. He was determined to pursue his destiny through music.

KSA did not remain a local champion—although he indeed has enjoyed fame and popularity in Nigeria—despite that his songs are hugely influenced by the Yorùbá language, and he sang in the Yorùbá language. He eventually entered the global scene, and his music became widely accepted.[77] According to a report that traced the rise of KSA into the international limelight, "In 1975, Ade made his first tour outside Africa, performing in Washington, D.C., Boston, N.Y., and Detroit as part of a U.S. government-sponsored cultural exchange program. It was on his return home from this trip that Ade, a prince by birthright, was dubbed 'king' by Nigeria's musical press."[78]

Indeed, KSA was not the only musician in Nigeria at the time. It shows how much of his genius the American government had recognized to have considered him for the cultural exchange program. This is not a surprise because apart from KSA's ability to serenade his audience, he had magical fingers that could play the guitar in amazing ways. He was also a skillful and natural dancer.

KSA is also credited as the first Nigerian to be nominated for what is perhaps the biggest music award in the world—the Grammy.[79] Again, these recognitions keep coming in even though he sings in the Yorùbá language. His launch into fame in the international scene came sometime in 1982

> when he signed a contract with the British company Island Records, which had introduced Jamaican reggae to the world. By this time Ade's albums on his own label were selling more than 200,000 copies apiece, and Island counted on similar sales for their own first release. In hope of turning Ade into an international star, the company hired as producer a Frenchman with experience in working with African musicians, Martin Meissonnier, and launched a major media campaign in both the U.S. and Britain. Ade's first Island LP, Juju Music, was a remix of a previous Alade label release that simplified the complex juju rhythms to a light funk beat and inserted Meissonnier's own synthesizer part. On both sides of the Atlantic, press coverage of both the recording and an early 1983 concert tour was largely enthusiastic, and the album made it into the Billboard charts in February 1983, just as Ade began a 22-city U.S. tour.[80]

Although this arrangement did not turn out as the British Record Label and even KSA himself had hoped, it was the beginning of greater international recognition for the artist. He eventually dissolved his band and went into what might be regarded as hibernation for a while.[81]

---

76. Awojulugbe, "KSA, Victor Olaiya, Onyeka Onwenu."

77. Pareles, "Music."

78. Online Encyclopedia, "Ade, Sunny (Prince Sunday Adeniyi Adegeye)."

79. Records Nigeria, "King Sunny Ade."

80. Online Encyclopedia, "Ade, Sunny (Prince Sunday Adeniyi Adeyemi)."

81. Raheem, "From the Sublime to the Ridiculous?"

By his return in 1986 and the reassembling of a not-so-new band, his music had gained more acceptance internationally and recorded the success that eluded his initial union with Island Records. He would go ahead to host successful concerts in Britain in 1988 and a musical tour of the United States in 1989. It is instructive that despite the international recognition that KSA has enjoyed, he has stayed true to his Yorùbá identity. Of course, his music, just like others, has been influenced by Western music style. The infusion that exists in his music and his undeniable exotic exposure have not in any way undermined his Yorùbá identity. Buttressing further on this point, Jon Pareles submits that "he also changes his outfits between encores, like a Western rock star. But he hasn't seriously internationalized, or diluted, his music."[82]

Sikiru Ayinde Barrister, the Fuji maestro, is another Yorùbá pioneer of a unique genre. He began his career in 1965, two years before KSA. It is not possible to speak of Fuji music without proper respect paid to Barrister, also popularly called Barry Wonder. It is often believed that Barrister and his friend, Killington, are the fathers of Fuji music. However, Barrister had more contribution to the fame and popularity Fuji music enjoys today. The rise of Fuji like wildfire today is, however, a contrast to the Fuji maestro's background. Barrister started as a very poor man, even after he joined the military. He had been deployed to the eastern part of the country during the Nigerian civil war. At the end of the war and on his return to the Southwest, Barrister had a brief stint with the military but later resigned to pursue a career in music.

At the time of this decision, some other traditional music genres like Apala and Highlife were popular. This was not a deterrent for Barrister, who was already used to the *Wéré* style of music that was common among the Muslims of Southwest Nigeria. Barrister took his local style and made it good enough for international consumption. This, indeed, has been a recurrent theme in the Yorùbá artists considered so far. Although Barrister's music had noticeable traces of Islam and Arabic in particular, it was no doubt largely situated in Yorùbá culture and language.[83]

Barrister's Fuji music became a leading genre in Nigeria and Africa by extension. This music genre, which started in 1966, has failed to frizzle out like Apala, which came before it. The legacy of Barrister lives on even after his death. In the 1970s, Barrister had become the toast of many socialites, especially among the Yorùbá. However, by 1978, he was set to go on his first tour to Britain as a Fuji musician. Kola Ibrahim goes further to iterate the exploits of a relatively young traditional music genre: "Since 1978, he had joined the category of popular artists churning out more than two albums in a year. In 1980, his three albums: 'Fuji Disco,' 'Oke Agba' (a.k.a Fine Bara) and 'Aiye' (a.k.a. Disney World) sold widely, with Oke Agba and Aiye becoming national anthems. By early 1980s, Fuji music had become a household music, with several young artists joining the train."[84]

One thing that remains constant in the narrative of the Yorùbá creative pursuits highlighted here is the fact that their music has an undeniable Yorùbá flavor. Yet rather than being a turnoff for people of foreign cultures within and outside Nigeria, this flavor remains one principal

82. Pareles, "Music."

83. Oyeweso, "Philosophical Contents," 5–18.

84. Ibrahim, "Sikiru Ayinde Barrister."

Figure 18.4.
"Endless Skills," by
Dr. Kazeem Ekeolu.
The abstract art shows a
woman carrying a baby
on her back, another on
her side, and a basket
of goods on her head
without holding it. It
shows strength and
ingenuity: the children
show creation, she is
creative, and while
she migrates with
her creation, water is
borderless.

reason it was accepted and continues to be accepted among people of diverse cultures and orientations. According to Ibrahim, "Aside further taking Fuji to international stage, especially among Africans in diaspora, Barrister also deepened Fuji's support base among the elites. Canadian Fuji, released in 1995/96 signaled the peak of Barrister's career with his popular shows and concerts in 11 cities in North American continent, US and Canada."[85] Canadian Fuji, as referenced, shows that Fuji, in the early 1990s, had found a new home in North America. Fuji was no longer the exclusive heritage of the Yorùbá but had found itself a suitable abode among Canadians. It should not be forgotten that slavery contributed in no small way to the acceptance of African music in Europe and America.[86] African music and that of the Yorùbá, in particular, first found acceptance among the Black people in the diaspora. These would further give the music more wings to spread and more visibility in these new homes. Consequently, Barrister's Fuji also benefited from this. As Ibrahim further espouses about Barrister: "He had undertaken a tour of nine European cities, including show at the prestigious Berlin World Music Festival, in 1993. In the album, Barrister also contributed to debate on the post-June 12 political logjam. He joined the campaign for the immediate release of the winner of June 12, 1993 presidential election."[87]

Artistic expressions of every form in Africa do not just thrive on the creative input of the artist—be it a musician, poet, carver, or drummer—but also determine and, in fact, use as their main ingredient the deteriorating socioeconomic and political state of the artist's immediate and wider community. In other words, artists in Africa and those of the Yorùbá stock assume the role of an activist and sometimes a revolutionist, using their media to chastise erring government officials and pointing attention to the deplorable state of things around them.[88] Barrister was not just an entertainer but also used his music to condemn bad governance.[89] Indeed, one artist of Yorùbá heritage that dedicated his life and music to this kind of way was Fela, profiled above. Fela was so bent on calling out the wrongs of the military government of the day that on one occasion, his eighty-something-year-old mother was thrown to the ground from the second story of a building in Fela's Kalakuta Republic.[90] But Barrister's ability to infuse what was happening in his environment into his music also contributed to how well he was accepted both at home and abroad. If this were not so, Ibrahim's exposé would not have acknowledged that "the release of Barry at 40, Fuji Garbage Series 1 and 2 in 1988, Current Affairs and Garbage Series 3 in 1989, changed the face and nature of not just Fuji music but the music scene in Nigeria. It was like a revolution in the music scene."[91] One way to understand this assertion is also that engaging himself with the concerns of his people through his music gave Fuji music more credibility.

85. Ibrahim, "Sikiru Ayinde Barrister."
86. Berry and Blassingame, "Africa, Slavery," 501–516.
87. Ibrahim, "Sikiru Ayinde Barrister."
88. Raheem, "Role of Nigerian Celebrity Music Artists," 16–38.
89. Adeniji, "Popular Songs as Literary Texts," 336.
90. Schoonmaker, *Fela*, 107, 119.
91. Ibrahim, "Sikiru Ayinde Barrister."

Literary Giants, Yorùbá Roots

D. O. Fagunwa's Ògbójú Ọdẹ Nínú Igbó Irúnmọlẹ is regarded as the first full-length novel published in the Yorùbá language and any indigenous African language.[92] Going by the logic of scholars who believe that African literature is that which is written in the indigenous African language, Fagunwa might as well be regarded as the first African novelist. He would later write other astounding short stories and novels in the Yorùbá language, for instance, *Igbó Olódùmarè* (1949; "The Forest of God"), *Ìrèké Oníbùdó* (1949; "The Sugarcane of the Guardian"), *Ìrìnkerindò Nínú Igbó Elégbèjé* (1954; "Wanderings in the Forest of Elégbèje"), and *Adìitú Olódùmarè* (1961; "The Secret of the Almighty").[93] These are works that will go ahead to shape and sharpen the childhood education of a lot of many Yorùbá children.

Fagunwa's writing digs into Yorùbá folktales and births new and interesting stories. Fagunwa unveils the mysterious, the spiritual, and the cultural in his writings; however, he does not leave out the moral, entertaining, and creative.[94] It might be safe to say he unveiled the magical realism subgenre in Africa, despite that he wrote in the Yorùbá language.[95] While there are critics who frown at Fagunwa's refusal to tackle "contemporary social issues," he is also often praised for his "knowledge of the Yoruba mind, his careful observation of the manners and mannerisms of his characters, and his skill as a storyteller."[96]

Fagunwa's work has influenced other writers that came after him, particularly those who wrote in English. Prominent among them is Wole Soyinka, who translated Fagunwa's first novel, as noted earlier. Another one is Amos Tutuola, whose first work, *The Palmwine Drinkard*, also holds an important place in African literature. Tutuola, also Yorùbá, was born in Abeokuta, Southwest Nigeria. Unlike many other prominent Yorùbá creatives highlighted so far, Tutuola had limited education, even though he eventually wrote in the language of the colonizer—the English language. Many have critiqued Tutuola's works based on what they regard as his "bad English." These critics hold on to the belief that Amos Tutuola's use of the English language is primitive and unrefined.[97] Interestingly, a good portion of these critics are based in Nigeria, whereas the work was positively accepted in parts of Europe and America. As though to render their opinions baseless and insignificant, Taban Lo Liyong, in 1975, opines thus:

> Now, in all that he has done, Amos Tutuola is not sui generis. Is he ungrammatical? Yes. But James Joyce is more ungrammatical than Tutuola. Ezekiel Mphahlele has often said and written that African writers are doing violence to English. Violence? Has Joyce not done more violence to the English Language? Mark Twain's Huckleberry Finn is written in seven dialects, he tells us. It is acknowledged a classic. We accept it, forget that it

92. Lindfors, *Early Nigerian Literature*.

93. Bamgbose, *Novels of D. O. Fagunwa*.

94. Lindfors, "Form, Theme, and Style," 11–15.

95. Irele, "Tradition and the Yoruba Writer," 75–100.

96. Gunner, "African Literature."

97. Ogundipe, "Palm Wine Drinkard," 99–108.

has no "grammar," and go ahead to learn his "grammar" and what he has to tell us. Let Tutuola write "no grammar" and the hyenas and jackals whine and growl. Let Gabriel Okara write a "no grammar" Okolo.[98]

Taban believes that it is the narrow-mindedness that comes with Western education that would make anyone regard Tutuola's work as not literary enough because art is arbitrary and should be welcomed in whatever language or style the artist uses to convey a message. To be bothered about the accuracy of Tutuola's use of the English language is to "turn to that aristocratic type of criticism which magnifies trivialities beyond their real size."[99] Oscar R. Dathorne would have a more aggressive opinion of Tutuola's genius, situating it beyond the boundaries of what is Yorùbá, Nigerian, or even African. According to him. "Tutuola deserves to be considered seriously because his work represents an intentional attempt to fuse folklore with modern life. In this way he is unique, not only in Africa, where the sophisticated African writer is incapable of this tenuous and yet controlled connection, but in Europe as well, where this kind of writing is impossible."[100]

There is no denying that the Yorùbá icons described above have exemplified the borderless transition of creativity from this ethnic community. Other factors like the efforts of white men like Ulli Beier, who took an interest in Yorùbá culture and arts, slavery and colonialism, Western education, and migration have all contributed to the formation and spread of Yorùbá creativity across the borders and nations of the world.

In 1986 when he was announced as the winner of the Nobel Prize for Literature, Wole Soyinka undoubtedly became the pride of Africa, his country Nigeria, and, more importantly, the pride of the Yorùbá people. Born in Ake, Abeokuta, young Soyinka grew up in a family of a Christian father and mother. However, he would choose a different path of spirituality when he grew older. Soyinka was clearly in touch with his people and culture during his youth. He experienced the Yorùbá culture, if not at its purest state; it was close to that. In one of his autobiographies, he narrates how at a very young age, he had followed a moving train of masquerade and his supporters. He was so engrossed by the display of these artists that he strayed miles away from home.[101] Just as Mary Jaggi puts it, "Rebelling against his parents' Christianity, he was drawn to the Yoruba òrìṣà—ancestor or nature worship—of his grandfather, which became a pillar of his art."[102]

By the time Soyinka went to the University of Leeds to study English Literature, it was difficult for him to be wooed away by the foreign culture. Rather than submit to the new culture, Soyinka found common ground between the two. Indeed, some people of African roots have condemned and continue to condemn Soyinka for "desecrating" the African culture with his

---

98. Liyong, "Tutuola, Son of Zinjanthropus."

99. Liyong, "Tutuola, Son of Zinjanthropus."

100. Dathorne, "Amos Tutuola," 66.

101. Soyinka, *Ake, the Years of Childhood*.

102. Jaggi, "Ousting Monsters."

foreign infusions. This has remained a controversial issue even among scholars of repute in the wider literary terrain in Africa. Consequently, there is a dichotomy of views as to what is appropriate—for writers to embrace the foreign culture wholly and use the foreigner's language, which carries its sensibilities, or resort to the use of the mother tongue, which in itself is a form of decolonization and a strong signal to the colonizers about the strength of the African culture and language. Soyinka is not a subscriber to the idea of using his mother language in writing.

An honest observation of Soyinka's writings will reveal the deep-seated Yorùbá sensibilities, just as the same is true of his colleague, Chinua Achebe. Even in writings that were direct adaptations of an existing European play like Brecht's *Threepenny Opera* (*Opera Wonyosi*, Soyinka's version), he remained true to his Nigerian context.[103] It makes the argument of his desecration of the African culture with the foreign infusion a somewhat baseless assertion. The same Soyinka, who is believed to have a pro-white cultural bias because of his writing style, has declared on multiple occasions and platforms that Ògún, the Promethean Yorùbá god of iron, is his creative muse. How Ògún will take his own far away from his source, therefore, begs for an answer.

Soyinka's creativity has exposed more people and cultures to the ways and art of the Yorùbá people. He has been able to take his global audience of readers on a fantastic journey into the Yorùbá culture, even if they have never been to a Yorùbá community or met a Yorùbá person.[104] Making a general comment on the person of Wole Soyinka and his works, Jaggi notes that "Soyinka, who in 1968 translated D. O. Fagunwa's classic Yorùbá novel *The Forest of a Thousand Daemons*, adds: 'I come from a culture which uses language in a very dense way.' For Msika, his plays possess a 'necessary difficulty: they use a variety of western and African idioms, but move between them fluidly, without signposting the boundaries between cultures.'"[105]

Perhaps the biggest sign of Soyinka's ability to dissolve the boundaries that exist between cultures was winning the Nobel Prize for Literature in 1986. He has been referred to as one of the great dramatic imaginations of the twentieth century.[106] Not only have Soyinka's works been creatively appealing and thought-provoking, but his writings have also connected with the people at the level of suffering instilled upon them because of bad governance. In this regard, Jaggi, quoting Helon Habila, reveals that "Soyinka is better known in Nigeria as a political activist than a playwright, though he remains an influence on younger writers. He's been an example for people because he's lived what he believes in."[107]

Soyinka has borrowed heavily from his Yorùbá background to get to where he is today as a world-renowned writer and scholar. Apart from the beauty of translating literary devices like proverbs and idioms to the English language in his writings, he has also rewritten some myths, legends, and the general culture of the Yorùbá people into relatable stories in the English

---

103. Soyinka, *Opera Wonyosi*.
104. Kemi and Chijioke, "Aesthetics of Yoruba Culture," 30–38.
105. Jaggi, "Ousting Monsters."
106. Smith, "Profile of Nobel Laureate Wole Soyinka."
107. Jaggi, "Ousting Monsters."

language.[108] An example is the retelling of the old Yorùbá culture in *The King and His Horseman*. The play profiles the life of one man known as Abobaku—translated as one who dies with the king. In the Old Oyo Empire, an Abobaku was buried with his master, the king, when the king died. In the drama, Soyinka showcases the frictional intersection between the new colonial culture that came into Africa and indigenous traditional African culture, like the death of an Abobaku with his master.[109] While he is mindful of the foreign culture that has come to change everything for the traditional Yorùbá man, he does not fail to portray the pride and ingenuity of the Yorùbá culture through his characters. The theme of Western cultural incursion on the Yorùbá culture is explored further in more of his works.[110]

What is of interest to this discourse remains how Soyinka carries the pride of his Yorùbá culture. For instance, his desire to spread the Yorùbá culture is seen in the effort he put in place in translating Fagunwa's classic novel Ògbójú Ọdẹ Nínú Igbó Irúnmọlẹ̀ as *The Forest of a Thousand Daemons*. The globally applauded novel not only became popular with Soyinka's translation but also became more widely read across the globe, aligning with what Olakunle George meant thus: "As the 1986 reprint informs us, Fagunwa's novel has since been reprinted 24 times."[111] Soyinka's literary genius can be encapsulated in the words of the Swedish Academy, which described him as "one of the finest poetical playwrights that have written in English."[112]

Yorùbá Nation: A Home to Global Fashion

As a way of bringing this discourse to a close, the chapter will consider how fashion, especially that which originates from the Yorùbá people and culture, has also taken wings and become useful in other parts of the world beyond its Yorùbá root. Yorùbá people, without a doubt, are highly fashionable people. This continues to place them in relevant spots when fashion is discussed. In recent times, the Yorùbá clothing material, *aṣọ-òkè*, has received widespread attention among people both at home and abroad.[113] *Aṣọ-òkè*, as the name suggests, is the cloth of the people of the hill—the Oke-Ogun is a part of Southwest Nigeria. Although *aṣọ-òkè* is not limited to the people of Oke-Ogun, it has been said to be more popular among these people. One unique thing about the *aṣọ-òkè* is its relationship with the rich, wealthy, and highly placed in the Yorùbá society. With the ability to embed different designs on the material, it serves as a status symbol to the people who have worn *aṣọ-òkè* in the past.[114] Today, *aṣọ-òkè* is synonymous with weekly occasions among the Yorùbá people. It is not uncommon to hear people in this region in Nigeria speak of "owambe," roughly translatable as "it is there."

Beyond its widespread use for celebrations and events, however, aṣọ òkè has also done well for itself in attracting international recognition. For instance, Chioma Nnadi of the international

---

108. Fagunwa, *Forest of a Thousand Daemons*.
109. George, "Cultural Criticism," 67–91.
110. Dauda and Falola, *Wole Soyinka*.
111. George, "Compound of Spells," 78.
112. Smith, "Profile of Nobel Laureate Wole Soyinka."
113. Idowu, "Inside Nigeria's Million Dollar Wedding Industry."
114. Agbadudu and Ogunrin, "Aso-Oke."

fashion magazine *Vogue* once noted that "if you've been to a Nigerian wedding, then chances are you've seen the mesmerizing handwoven fabric known as aṣọ òkè."[115] Interestingly, the designer Kenneth Ize whom Chioma Nnadi had profiled in the *Vogue* article is not from the southwestern part of Nigeria but had confessed that he watched his mother put on the aṣọ-òkè throughout his growing years. The color, beauty, and durability of the aṣọ-òkè would inspire Ize to do much more to the point of putting this once Yorùbá local fabric on the body of world-renowned tennis player Naomi Osaka. Nnadi is of the view that "in Nigerian culture there are daily rituals around getting dressed and feeling good beyond special occasions. And that's true regardless of your gender . . . [as] 70 percent of . . . menswear is bought by women, among them fashion stars like Naomi Campbell and Imaan Hammam."[116]

It is rather interesting that the aṣọ-òkè, which has become "another fabric" among the Yorùbá people, is held dear among peoples of other cultures. It is important to reemphasize here that the precious assertion by Western scholars and colonialists who came to Africa describing the people's culture as barbaric and backward was undeniably untrue. If the world has come to accept things like the aṣọ-òkè of the Yorùbá people, which had always had a presence, then the people have always had an enviable and admirable culture. Nnadi confessed that "I remember showing a sample of the fabric to Hussein Chalayan, my professor at the time, and he freaked out."[117]

Indeed, there are more instances of the acceptance of Yorùbá-inspired fashion has enjoyed all over the world. Duro Olowu stands tall among notable designers in the world, and what is interesting, despite the undeniable influence of his exposure to many other cultures of the world, is the input of his Nigerian nay Yorùbá root, particularly his experiences as a child who grew up in southwestern Nigeria. Armed with these experiences, Duro Oluwu has bagged many international awards and recognitions in his fashion career—notable of which is the New Designer of the Year at the 2005 British Fashion Week in London, barely a year after he launched his fashion label.[118] Olowu's fashion artistry has also enjoyed the patronage of the former first lady of the United States, Michelle Obama.

Conclusion

The contributions of the Yorùbá to the creative space are too enormous to be relegated to local relevance. What this chapter has tried to do is to highlight some of the contributions of this borderless nation to global creative and artistic needs. By analyzing some of the factors, which include human agencies, that are responsible for the global spread of Yorùbá creativity, this chapter emphasizes the undisputable flavor that the Yorùbá nation adds to the global stage, perhaps one being the Grammy Award bagged by the Yorùbá-born hip-hop star Ayo Balogun, popularly known as "Wizkid."[119]

---

115. Nnadi, "Nigerian Designer."
116. Nnadi, "Nigerian Designer."
117. Nnadi, "Nigerian Designer."
118. Fashion Model Directory, "Duro Olowu."
119. Muhammed, "Wizkid Receives Grammy Plaque."

From Yorùbá origins, new genres of music have been launched into the international community that continue to weather the challenges and needs of contemporary times, although some of the pioneers of these genres are no longer living. Members of this nation have presented their culture to the international community and have been commended with notable awards for the same. The Yorùbá, both home and abroad, continue to prove the colonizers wrong in their assessment of ascribing such adjectives as "unprogressive" and "dark."[120] More importantly, the impact of Yorùbá religious beliefs and activities in sustaining and propagating these creative abilities is evident. Yorùbá creativity has inserted itself into the world.

---

120. Denby, "Trouble with 'Heart of Darkness.'"

19 The Media and Internet Nation

Introduction

The use of the Internet in the twenty-first century is immense and the information dissemination it undertakes has helped the Yorùbá to manage their identities and concerns in a dynamic world. Social media platforms are now forums through which Yorùbá people can share their ideas on culture, language, politics, and intellectualism. Before the Internet, the Yorùbá in the diaspora defined the self partly based on orature. That is, they found themselves in mythologies of home and they defined themselves through oral philosophy.[1] Defining the self and group identity is now beyond the paradigm of myths and reminiscence of what home is like. With the Internet, there is a reconstruction of what being Yorùbá is and how to define the self within this new world.

This chapter situates the Internet in self-definition and group identity of the Yorùbá. The Internet has afforded the Yorùbá in the diaspora a chance to become active participants in the Yorùbá nation. In essence, the Internet has permeated the iron curtains of geography so much that the Yorùbá in the diaspora can get news of home in an instant.[2] The Internet has also contributed to the fluidity of identity, being continually reconstructed, and it is now beyond birth and borders. At present, it is about the willingness to participate in the conglomerate of views, history, and politics that defines who a Yorùbá person is and what a Yorùbá nation is. Yorùbá citizenship is not limited to Nigeria; with this in mind, it is expected that Yorùbá people in every corner of the world find a sense of association in finding people with whom they share cultural heritage. It is this sense of association that propels them to define themselves as Yorùbá in the diaspora and, more importantly, it gives them the sense to be sociopolitically active in the affairs of the Yorùbá nation. As global citizens, they recognize the need to combine multiple identities: the native one, those of their new homes, and newer ones generated by the Internet. With all of these, the idea of what a Yorùbá nation is becomes redefined, and the redefinition reiterates that identity is no longer limited to geography. Unsurprisingly, the Internet has replaced traditional media, which were previously employed by the Yorùbá all around the world. It has given rise to notable individuals and to popular Yorùbá spaces that are

---

1. Ojaide, "Indigenous Knowledge," 11–28.
2. Ogunyemi, "Appeal of African Broadcast," 334–352.

responsible for the proliferation of Yorùbá programs and discussion on everyday themes such as the fight against the invasion of Yorùbá farmlands by Fulani herdsmen, the establishment of Southwest security outfit (Àmọ̀tẹ́kùn), the creation of Oduduwa Republic, the idea of secession from Nigeria, and many more. Yorùbá Internet citizenship not only finds a group identity for the Yorùbá in the diaspora but closes the chasm of information between those who are at home and abroad.

There will always be a clash of group and self-identity: particularism versus universalism. As history and recent events have shown, people of any nation-state can hijack the cause of a group and turn it into a cause for self. The task of elevating a group's cultural heritage and politics should not be left to an individual but should remain the objective of the collective. Similarly, the Yorùbá identity for the Yorùbá people in the diaspora is also a question of choosing between being a global citizen or a Yorùbá citizen. However, with the aid of the Internet, there is a syncretism between universal standards and those particular to the Yorùbá people. Therefore, this chapter will analyze the development of Yorùbá identity through time and space and the current Internet reimagination of being Yorùbá. The political maneuvering of Yorùbá people at home and abroad is important to this work because the negotiation for self-determination is always in the public domain. Although one may be Yorùbá, to self-determine the identity of the Yorùbá nation means political participation and negotiation to either discontinue existing within the Nigerian democracy and demography or to find better living conditions within the Nigerian context. Whatever the case, the Internet contributes more to discussions and negotiations, as many Internet spaces have given people the platform to elevate their interests and find online communities where their identities can be exerted.[3] One aspect of these that should not be taken for granted is the globalization of Yorùbá ethos, cultures, and language through the works and efforts of general Web and social media spaces dedicated to the promotion of Yorùbá sociopolitical affairs.[4]

Concisely, this chapter intends to look at Yorùbá identity, the sociopolitical history of the Yorùbá nation at home and in diaspora, and the contribution of the Internet in promoting Yorùbá values, sociopolitical dynamics, and praiseworthy achievements and blameworthy actions of Yorùbá groups. Finally, this chapter discusses the twenty-first-century Yorùbá nation with retrospect and reimagination of Yorùbá citizenship vis-à-vis group identity and self-determination.[5]

Yorùbá Nationalism and Political Consciousness

It is important to repeat the mythology of Yorùbá origins for two reasons. First, it is invoked in the contemporary language of liberation from Nigeria and justification for secession. Second, the new definitions are not always connected with some mythological ones presented in part 1

---

3. Daniel, "Yorùbá in Diaspora."

4. See "Ilana Omo Oodua Worldwide."

5. This is a new field of research, with limited a database. Much of the evidence for the chapter was drawn from personal observations in the last fifteen years and with close encounters with persons in public office or individuals and groups privy to inside knowledge.

of this book. The older mythologies require reconciling stories, and the newer requires clarifying citizenship. In a summary of a mythological story by Professor Banji Akintoye, who is currently leading a Yorùbá independent movement—the Yorùbá nation is fighting for the creation of a new country:

> The Yoruba have some remarkable graphic myths of creation and of origins. The most widely known Yoruba myth has it that at the beginning of time, when the whole surface of the earth was one watery matter, Olódùmarè (also known as Ọlọ́run, "king of heaven") sent down some heavenly beings to create solid land, as well as plant life and animal life, on the earth. Bringing with them some quantity of earth, one chicken and one palm nut, they came down by a chain and landed on the spot that is now known as Ife in the heart of Yorubaland. They poured the earth onto the water, and thus created a small piece of solid land. They then set the chicken on the land, and as the chicken scratched at it with its claws, the small piece of dry land spread—and continued to spread until all the continents and islands of the world came into existence. The heavenly beings sowed the palm nut, and it sprouted and grew as the beginning of plant life in the world. The heavenly beings themselves became the progenitors of the human race. The place where all this began was named Ife—that is, "the source of the spreading." The Yoruba believe, then, that theirs is the first race of humans, and that all human life and civilization originated in their country.[6]

Akintoye affirms the mythological origins of the Yorùbá people with their creation by Olódùmarè, and there is also the myth of Odùduwà being the progenitor of the Yorùbá people. The stories are necessary for the validation of the Yorùbá nationality and separation from Nigeria. After all, they are "different." They are also, according to Akintoye, the first race to be created. All other "Nigerians" were offshoots.

According to Samuel Johnson, the difficulty in tracing the history and origin of the Yorùbá nation is "involved in obscurity."[7] Kamari Maxine Clarke qualifies this obscurity perfectly: "The Yoruba people of southwestern Nigeria, whom diasporic practitioners regard as the guardians of "traditional" òrìṣà, were classified as an ethnic group by sociologists and anthropologists of the twentieth century. Studies documenting the people, their origins, and their cultural practices often involved the use of intensive fieldwork in which researchers lived with informants and documented their life cycles, ritual practices, ceremonies, and death rituals."[8]

Clarke's idea of the origins of the Yorùbá people deserves credit because the identity of the Yorùbá people is shrouded in their cultural practices and mythologies, which are housed in Yorùbá oral history and philosophy. The mythology must now be clearly stated, removing the earlier emphasis on obscurity to which Samuel Johnson alluded.[9] In Akintoye's presentation, there is no obscurity, but value must underpin the establishment of a Yorùbá country.

---

6. Akintoye, *History of the Yoruba People*, 18.

7. Johnson, *History of the Yorubas*, 3.

8. Clarke, "Transnational Yoruba Revivalism," 723.

9. Johnson, *History of the Yorubas*, 3.

The "nation" in the Yorùbá nation should be analyzed as "a resemblance of a stable community of people of a common language, territory, history, ethnicity and common culture."[10] However, this conceptualization of a nation cannot but help in placing the ideas that are to be discussed in this work. The Yorùbá nation cannot always be described as a "stable community" of people with a shared language, culture, territory, history, and ethnicity. Olatunji Ojo posits that

> scholars investigating Yoruba ethnic identity have justifiably argued that until the nineteenth century the people now called Yoruba, despite their cultural affinities, belonged to multiple ethnicities: Akoko, Bunu, Ekiti, Ijesa, Igbomina, Ijumu, Ikale, Ilaje, Ondo, Owe, Owo, Oworo and Yagba in eastern Yorubaland; Awori, Egba, Ife, Ijebu, Ọ̀yọ́ and Owu in the center; and Ana, Anago, Egbado, Idaisa, Isa, Manigri, Ketu, Ohori and Sabe in the western Yorubaland. Each group had its sub-units: Ekiti was divided into sixteen chiefdoms; Ọ̀yọ́ consisted of the metropolitan, Ibolo, Ibarapa, and Epo districts; Egba had Ake, Gbagura and Okeona divisions; and Ilaje was carved into Ikale, Mahin and Ugbo chiefdoms. Ethnic plurality underpinned centuries of intra and intergroup tension, most notably the century-long Yoruba wars fought between the 1790s and 1893. The wars resulted in mass enslavement and population dislocation.[11]

In the contemporary creation of the Yorùbá on the Internet, the Yorùbá nation has become more of a stable community with a common territory, history, and language. However, the history, geography, and language of the Yorùbá nation were greatly influenced by colonialism. According to Toyin Falola,

> The modern map consigns the Yoruba to the southwestern part of Nigeria, a product of colonial creation reflecting the limitations of maps and the European origins of the modern nation state in Africa. This specific location does not capture the historical geography of the Yoruba-speaking people, although it has had a substantial impact on how knowledge about them has been constituted. The map is true in the sense that the majority of the Yoruba population now lives in southwestern Nigeria. It is incomplete because the colonial map does not include the entire "home" of the Yoruba in West Africa and the African diaspora.[12]

As Falola points out, the modern map is responsible for the demarcation of the Yorùbá nation because European partitions of Africa divided the Yorùbá nation between the current southwestern part of Nigeria and other neighboring countries. What should not be lost in this reading is that this artificial demarcation of people had an earlier form in the nature of transatlantic slavery. The collapse of the Old Oyo Empire also added to the dispersal of Yorùbá people around the world.[13] These two key factors all contributed to why the definition of "nation" as a people with geographical, linguistic, and cultural commonality is easily defeated in the case of

---

10. Babatola, "Formation of Yoruba Nation."

11. Ojo, "'Heepa' (Hail) Òrìṣà," 31.

12. Falola, "Yoruba Nation," 29.

13. Eltis, "Diaspora of Yoruba Speakers," 17–39.

the Yorùbá Nation. To be called Yorùbá nation means that there is a sense of commonality of cultural heritage and linguistic relationship between the people who claim to be Yorùbá; therefore, the definition of the nation given above may not suffice. This definition agrees with the notion that the Yorùbá nation did not exist before the invasion of Europeans and their introduction of the weapon of colonialism into the territory. Thus, the idea of a nation, as in the case of Yorùbá nation, should be expanded beyond geography. It must be inclusive in the classification of who can be called Yorùbá.

Falola claims that Yorùbá identity and the way it has become known intellectually started with the emergence of Christian missionaries in the nineteenth century. He argues that "the intellectualization of the Yoruba as a collective identity (that is, of one nation) dates back to the nineteenth century, thanks to the Christian missionaries and the pioneer Yoruba elite. The Yoruba discovered the missionaries and used the knowledge they provided to discover themselves. By the time Samuel Johnson completed his classic in the 1890s, *Yoruba* had become a widely used name among the pioneer Christian elite to define the people and their land, culture, and language."[14]

Being called Yorùbá and its colonial documentation should not be a universal paradigm for defining the history of Yorùbá identity. The Yorùbá identity and nationhood had a precolonial history, but it began to be intellectualized in the early years of colonialism. Even in the precolonial period, the Yorùbá were scattered over many places. The coming together of these regions, as captured by Samuel Johnson and historians after him, shows that it was then that the Yorùbá nation was birthed on paper. The different groups existed on their terms, but this existence was not peaceful, as there were many civil wars in Yorùbá history to point to the fact that missionary intervention seemed like the only viable solution.

The argument that the Yorùbá nation transcended what is now known as Southwest Nigeria is well established both in the cultural appropriation of Yorùbá people in other places and also in the intellectual memory of Yorùbá around the world. As earlier mentioned, two notable contributors to this were the transatlantic slave trade and colonialism. Defining Yorùbá nation must be done by discounting the imposed and limited parameters of borders and geography. In essence, the Yorùbá nation cannot be solely defined based on geography that is restricted to current Nigeria.[15] What Babatola emphasizes here is that Yorùbá identity is not limited to those who exist or are within the confines of Southwest Nigeria. Rather, Yorùbá people are all over the world and they bear the Yorùbá identity as well. He continues, "The creation of colonial territories over traditional societies which the colonial powers left in Africa with its near fatal consequences on our ethnic identities due to the division of the traditional societies has not ruled out our nationhood as Yoruba people."[16]

What this supposes is that the Yorùbá nation comprises Yorùbá people from all over the world. To corroborate this point, Paul E. Lovejoy argues that the choice of the term *Yorùbá* is

---

14. Falola, "Yoruba Nation."
15. Babatola, "Formation of Yoruba Nation," 4.
16. Babatola, "Formation of Yoruba Nation," 8.

curious because it has Muslim origins and was adopted by Christians in intellectualizing Yorùbá identity.[17] However, Falola claims that

> although naming is important, especially in the politics of the twentieth century, which consolidated ethnic identities in Nigeria, the definition of Yoruba identity is linked to the historical connection to Ilé-Ifẹ in two interrelated ways: first, as the city where the Yoruba believe that they all originated; and second, as the city where their political dynasties emigrated from. The most common myth takes Ilé-Ifẹ. as the original home, where the first humans were created. It was from here that other Yoruba groups and cities derived their own origins. A series of migration stories show how various groups, led by princes who created dynasties, left Ilé-Ifẹ. A common ancestral father, Odùduwà, provides the biological link: all Yoruba claim him as their progenitor. A linguistic unity has also emerged in spite of the fact that the Yoruba language has various dialects.[18]

The Yorùbá in the diaspora and homeland who share Yorùbá principles, mannerisms, mores, and worldviews deserve to be attributed the Yorùbá identity. This helps to accommodate those who lost their roots and are trying to find a way to connect to home; also, it presents the globalization of Yorùbá nation even at a point when the world was not yet described as a global village. Being Yorùbá at the time of the advent of intellectualizing Yorùbá identity, some of the factors considered for the classification of Yorùbá were practices and sociocultural norms that are peculiar to a group of people. Inherited practices and gestures define what the Yorùbá nation is and who the Yorùbá people are. This signifies that being Yorùbá is enshrined in attitudes and beliefs more than in geography. Adeleke Adeeko asserts that "'Ilẹ gbogbo ntorìṣà' (all the earth belongs to orisa), Hubert Ogunde once sang passionately. Denoting, as late as the twentieth century, some areas on the map as Yorubaland contradicts the fluid and acutely self-aware cultural reality of the people such demarcations seek to characterize and restrict. To risk a little exaggeration for the purposes of making a point, there is no land on earth where some people, no matter how few in number, do not strive to be Yoruba."[19]

The relevance of this excerpt further emphasizes the dynamism that is attached to the Yorùbá identity. Yorùbá people all around the world have elevated their sense of belonging so much that people who are not Yorùbá by birth desire to share in the attributes of being Yorùbá. The essentiality of Yorùbá identity is not phenomenologically transcendental, but it is geographically transcendental. That is, geography is not a determinant of the Yorùbá identity but the connection to the group identity in itself.

The Yorùbá nation comprises everywhere around where a concentration of people of Yorùbá descent is found. However, we cannot be drawn away from the fact that the highest concentration of Yorùbá people remains in Nigeria, most especially, Southwest Nigeria.[20] As a result, they have firsthand experiences of the effects of being part of Nigeria. Yorùbá identity since colonialism has become intrinsically linked with Nigerian identity. The Yorùbá identity is

17. Lovejoy, "Yoruba Factor in the Trans-Atlantic Slave Trade," 40–55.
18. Falola, "Yoruba Nation."
19. Adeeko, *Arts of Being Yorùbá*, xiv.
20. Ogundiran, *Yoruba*.

ensconced in the people and how they carry the Yorùbá identity.[21] In consideration of the Nigerian dynamics, the Yorùbá identity is the card by which the Yorùbá nation negotiates its existence within the sociopolitical mapping of Nigeria. Therefore, the interests of Yorùbá people are not achieved through individualistic programs but through group interests. The Yorùbá nation in diaspora and the homeland do their best to better place the interests of the Yorùbá people. The amalgamation of ethnic groups in Nigeria and the region has not stopped the adherence to the ethnic identity of each ethnicity, and the Yorùbá nation is not left out.

The political consciousness of the Yorùbá nation dates to the precolonial era when each town had its king or a head chief.[22] The political institution of the Yorùbá people was in tune with its traditions with the notion that kings were deputies of Òrìṣà. In this sense, the political institution of the Yorùbá people can be associated with natural law theory.[23] The respect and genuflection to kings and traditional rulers were because they were seen as representative of their ancestors and ancient history. However, Yorùbá sociopolitical philosophies served as the institutions in which the actions of the kings and chiefs can be checked.[24] In Yorùbá society, the political philosophy reads thus: "'We are greater than them all.' 'We are more important than everybody else. The tracks of bush animals are difficult to trace.' These were the principles adopted by greedy politicians who managed public affairs in pristine Yoruba society. They were cautioned against playing politics as if hunting animals in the forest. They were warned not to turn political parties to cheating organizations. They were told not to convert public funds to personal use. The greedy did not listen. They did not change. In the end the people said: Go away! We do not want you in this society anymore."[25]

The quote is from *Ọ̀wọ́nrín Méjì*, a canto of *Ifá*. *Ifá* can be seen as the philosophical treatise of the Yorùbá.[26] Therefore, *Ifá* houses the history and philosophies of the Yorùbá and, as such, warns against political indiscipline and corruption.[27] Importantly, it showcases how the Yorùbá are politically conscious enough to demand change when they are being misruled. This may well indicate the métier of Yorùbá people politically. The talk of identity in this case is traceable to the philosophical positions that have shaped Yorùbá people of different generations.[28] The political consciousness of the Yorùbá people is associated with their identity. The precolonial Yorùbá society had its political institutions and ideals that were used in governing the affairs of the people, and these political institutions and ideals depended on the structure of each region. The Yorùbá nation was not in national unity until the intervention of the Christian missionaries. Therefore, each region carved rules, laws, and political philosophies based on the uniqueness of each region and experiences.[29]

---

21. "Ilana Omo Ooduwa Worldwide," https://www.ilanaomooduduwa.org/.
22. Lloyd, "Yorùbá Lineage," 235–251.
23. Lloyd, "Traditional Political System of the Yoruba," 366–384.
24. Alabi, "Law Making in Pre-colonial Yorubaland," 111–124.
25. Oluwole, *Socrates and Orunmila*, 73.
26. Bascom, *Ifa Divination*.
27. Abimbola, *Ifa Will Mend Our Broken World*.
28. Awolalu, "Yoruba Philosophy of Life," 20–38.
29. Watabe, "Traditional Political Organization of Yoruba Town," 1–20.

At the beginning of the colonial era, Yorùbá traditional political institutions were subdued and became only a means to an end.[30] Babatola supports this claim by stating that

> the changing role of traditional rulers in Yorubaland in the turn of twentieth Century led to adoption of indirect rule by the British and much later, the restructuring of Local Government system in Western Nigeria through passage of laws that restricted the involvement of Obas in local administration. Equally, the introduction of competition among Obas and their tussle for leadership to become autonomous due to introduction of Native Courts reduced their prestige and source of income. Though the introduction of the conference of Obas turned them into celebrities, the Yoruba Obas began to compete for traditional grandeur. Indeed, the meetings were opportunities for them to meet at public functions and make demand from British agents toward attracting development to their localities or increasing their income. Invariably, the Obas were relegated to background while the educated elites and politicians took over the affairs of political leadership in the region. At best, the Oba became advisers of the Governor or the Local Government Council Chairmen.[31]

To corroborate, Falola explicates that "in the 1940s, the politicians and nationalists had 'converted' the idea of the nation into a political project. By this time, British rule had firmly consolidated ethnicities, and British Nigeria was fragmented into regions brought together by some kind of federal-oriented policies. The Yoruba subgroups might have been competing, as in the case of the Ìbàdàn and Ìjèbú, but their politicians looking for power in Nigeria had to struggle to unite them if they wanted to compete with their Igbo and Yoruba rivals. The benefits derivable from ethnicity contributed to the creation of the Yoruba 'nation.'"[32]

The salient points from Babatola and Falola are that the adoption of indirect rule in Nigeria put limitations on the relevance of traditional rulers. Over time the influence of the traditional rulers decreased. As a result, individuals from each ethnicity saw it fit to maintain the relevance of their ethnic group in Nigerian politics. Many prestigious Yorùbá sons and daughters have put themselves as representative of the Yorùbá at the national level.

Arguably, Herbert Macaulay was a pioneer of Yorùbá nationalism.[33] The contributions of Macaulay to Nigerian nationalism represent the first phase of Yorùbá nationalism. Macaulay was among the first of his people to stand against British rule.[34] His contribution to Nigerian politics can be seen in the exploits of the parties he founded: the Nigerian National Democratic Party and the National Council of Nigeria and the Cameroons (NCNC).[35]

By the 1940s, due to the worldwide demand for self-governance, there was a heightened sense of nationalism, and the Yorùbá people were not left out.[36] They became champions of

30. Geary, *Nigeria under British Rule*; and Hopkins, "Property Rights and Empire Building," 777–798.

31. Babatola, "Formation of Yoruba Nation," 52–53.

32. Falola, "Yoruba Nation," 37.

33. Babatola, "Formation of Yoruba Nation," 54.

34. Lawal and Jimoh, "Missiles from 'Kirsten Hall,'" 41–62.

35. Sklar, *Nigerian Political Parties*, 41–49.

36. Lawal, "From Colonial Reforms to Decolonization," 39–62.

cultural awareness with a close reminiscence of negritude. The Yorùbá nationalism during this period was cultural and political. First, the nationalism was to ensure that people of Yorùbá descent know their place in the Nigerian space, and second, it was a call to make Yorùbá culturally aware of their heritage. In the 1940s, to better foster the cause of Yorùbá nationalism, *Ẹgbẹ́ Ọmọ Odùduwà* was created. Rasheed Olaniyi writes,

> The formation of Ẹgbẹ́ Ọmọ Odùduwà had three-fold fundamental objectives: to foster unity among the Yoruba by promoting its cultural heritage and traditional leadership, to rescue the Yoruba from the threat of other ethnic groups, especially the Igbo, and to empower the Yoruba youths educationally. An overriding objective was to protect the Yoruba from the "danger of Igbo domination." Ẹgbẹ́ Ọmọ Odùduwà was conceived by Yoruba intelligentsia studying in the United Kingdom who wanted to infuse "Yoruba nationalism" into the Yoruba speaking people. According to Ige, "Odùduwà was invoked and brought out from the shadows; his 'children' flocked to where he beckoned."[37]

The Ẹgbẹ́ Ọmọ Odùduwà was a cultural group with the interests of the Yorùbá people at heart, and to do this, the use of Yorùbá language and indigenous programs to promulgate the agenda of the Yorùbá nationalists was necessitated.[38] Aptly, this is a deviation from Macaulay's Yorùbá nationalism that can be seen as being elitist. Falola explains that at this period in time, nationalists had turned the idea of a nation into a political project with political figures from the major ethnic groups pushing for political movements that revolve around ethnic nationalities.[39] He argues that

> the central figure in the translation of Yoruba history to Yoruba politics is Chief Obafemi Awolowo. No modern Yoruba has come near the stature of Awolowo, who is now often described in some kind of mythological way. One scholar describes him as "the first truly heroic, visionary leader of the Yoruba since Odùduwà." The connection between two heroes—Odùduwà and Awolowo—reveals two things: the "creation" of history by Odùduwà and the "use" of history by Awolowo. But the "creation" and "use" of history are connected in the emergence of the idea of the Yoruba nation. Awolowo's political career reflects the careful manipulation of Yoruba history and traditions infused with the ideas of modernization.[40]

The connection between Awolowo and Oduduwa is that both exemplified the leadership traits needed by the leader of the Yorùbá race. Subsequently, the role of Awolowo cannot be overestimated. First, the creation of Ẹgbẹ́ Ọmọ Odùduwà shows that Awolowo was a leader who wanted to revitalize Yorùbá cultural consciousness. Therefore, the *Ẹgbẹ́ Ọmọ Odùduwà* served as the mouthpiece of the agenda of the Yorùbá nation. In every sense of it, Awolowo's rebranding of Yorùbá nationalism implied that Yorùbá people should occupy a central position

---

37. Olaniyi, "Identity and Solidarity in a Yoruba Diaspora," 111.

38. Arifalo, *Egbe Omo Oduduwa.*

39. Falola, "Yoruba Nation."

40. Falola, "Yoruba Nation," 37.

in the Nigerian political space. Hence, Yorùbá nation as a whole became aware of the intentions of Awolowo, and though there were always pockets of antagonists within his ethnicity, Awolowo was popularly received by the vast majority of his people.[41] Olaniyi claims that "the formation of the Egbe created a forum for the discussions of issues affecting the Yoruba at home and the diaspora. For reasons of politics, personalities and history, not all the Yoruba supported the Ẹgbẹ́ Ọmọ Odùduwà but within few months of its establishment, it spontaneously spread to several parts of Nigeria, as far as Sokoto. Three major factors could be adduced for the spread of Ẹgbẹ́ Ọmọ Odùduwà among the Yoruba migrants in northern Nigeria. These include cultural nationalism; discontent against colonialism and re-homing processes."[42]

The political negotiations of Nigeria created a necessary coexistence of these groups even when it was obvious that they are distinctively different both culturally and ideologically. Because of this, the leading political figures of each ethnic group created political agendas around their ethnic nationality rather than creating an all-encompassing political movement.[43] It is understandable that Awolowo created a Yorùbá cultural movement group that used the Yorùbá language to reach the Yorùbá people of all classes. One may lay the claim that the reason Awolowo's Ẹgbẹ́ Ọmọ Odùduwà became widely accepted and Macaulay's NCNC was rejected was because of the elitist agenda of NCNC that ruled the lower class out of political participation; in addition, Ẹgbẹ́ was solely about the interests of the Yorùbá people. In comparison, the "tribalization" of Nigerian politics is not a new political phenomenon. The foundation of Nigerian politics was laid on the segmentation of ideologies and interests that were dictated by ethnic philosophies and agendas.[44]

The Ẹgbẹ́ Ọmọ Odùduwà suggests that it was a group that was ultimately first about the descendants of Oduduwa before any other thing. Essentially, the group was not a political party at the time of its creation, but it surely informed the Yorùbá people at home and in the diaspora about their political destiny in the emerging Nigerian political space. Awolowo understood the power of culture and language in appealing to the sensibilities of the people. Not only was the group the mouthpiece of a new Yorùbá political dispensation, but it was also a center of the cultural renaissance that was accepted by the elites and all classes of Yorùbá people. The acceptance of this group is also a question of group identity. The Yorùbá people wanted a sociopolitical group that revalidates their group identity, and from the name of the group alone, they understood that this sociopolitical group had ideals that captured their sense of belonging, history, identity, and principles.

Scholars have placed Awolowo as arguably the most important political figure in Yorùbá history. He positioned himself as a Yorùbá leader whose interests were the interests of the Yorùbá people. He submerged his self-definition with the group identity because he understood that without the group identity of belonging to the Yorùbá people, his political ideology could not be instantiated. The creation of the Ẹgbẹ́ Ọmọ Odùduwà was not just the brainchild of Awolowo.

---

41. Arifalo, "Intensification of Ethnic Political Consciousness in Nigeria," 7–33.

42. Olaniyi, "Approaching the Study of the Yoruba Diaspora," 115.

43. Ubaku, Emeh, and Anyikwa, "Impact of Nationalist Movement," 54–67.

44. Schwarz, "Tribalism and Politics in Nigeria," 460–467.

Figure 19.1.
"Demand for Yoruba
Nation," by Dr. Kazeem
Ekeolu. In recent
years, demands for
the Yorùbá to create
their own independent
country have increased,
popularized by several
media outlets.

CAMERA
TF PRODUCTION

By the late 1940s and early 1950s, the influence of the Ẹgbẹ́ Ọmọ Odùduwà became indispensable. Olaniyi believes that "the formation of the Egbe led to ethnic and political consciousness among the Yoruba. There was an awakening among the Yoruba educated and traditional power elite on the 'danger of the Igbo domination.' This created social mistrusts between the two ethnic groups and intensified commercial rivalries in many cities where they co-existed. The activities of the Igbo State Union and the Egbe promoted political consciousness among other ethnic groups in Nigeria, which reshaped intergroup relations."[45]

The political consciousness of each ethnic group was a response to the political consciousness of the other. Each ethnic group saw political consciousness and participation as a way of countering the domination by other ethnic groups. If anything, this captures the sociopolitical relations between the ethnic groups in Nigeria and, as a result, the many political failings as a country.[46] The importance of Ẹgbẹ́ Ọmọ Odùduwà is so immense that it cannot be entirely captured here. The wave of its importance led to Awolowo's creation of the Action Group (AG) in 1951.[47] Awolowo intended to capture the center, but his efforts yielded little or no results at the federal level; however, the party easily captured the western region.[48] It has been said that no political figure captures and utilizes Yorùbá history and its ideologies like Awolowo. However, it looks vague without examples. The use of Ẹgbẹ́ Ọmọ Odùduwà as a mouthpiece of Awolowo's political movement has been reiterated, especially with the idea of group identity and the use of Yorùbá language. One other aspect that should not be overlooked is how his political party, the AG, captured the Old Bendel state, which in the present day is now two states: Edo and Delta. Bendel was a state with groups of people who at one point or another shared ancestry with the Yorùbá people. Therefore, Awolowo's realization of the sibling relationship between ethnic groups within Bendel and the Yorùbá is notable.[49] Undoubtedly, the importance of Ẹgbẹ́ Ọmọ Odùduwà, Awolowo and AG should not be underestimated.

Nonetheless, the review of Awolowo's politics suggests that he was praised in certain quarters,[50] just as much as he was rebuked.[51] By 1957, there was already turmoil between Awolowo and his allies. This inspired the great Yorùbá dramatist Hubert Ogunde to perform his popular play, "Yoruba Ronú." Ajala states,

> Through theater, Ogunde canvassed for pan-Yoruba unity. As noted by Nolte, the dramatic play was sympathetic to Awolowo, thus the proscription of Ogunde's popular performance by the then government of Western region. Yet, the messages in Ogunde's production, promoting a pan-Yoruba political identity, proved popular and desirable for Yoruba political control of Nigeria. The monumental cultural production of Yoruba Ronú was produced during the political crises between Awolowo and Akintola in 1957,

45. Olaniyi, "Approaching the Study of the Yoruba," 124.

46. Bouchat, *Causes of Instability in Nigeria.*

47. Ayoade, "Party and Ideology in Nigeria," 169–188.

48. Awolowo, *Adventures in Power.*

49. Babarinsa, "Ode to Itsekiri and a Game Called Life."

50. Oduguwa, *Chief Obafemi Awolowo.*

51. Achebe, *There Was a Country.*

an incidence that later led to the trial of Awolowo for treasonable felony and his eventual conviction and sentencing to prison in 1964. Through the genre, Ogunde lamented Yoruba's betrayal of their fellow Awolowo and called on the Yoruba to close their ranks and salvage Yoruba society from its political marginalization in Nigeria.[52]

Ogunde's theater is another signifier of the political consciousness of the Yorùbá people.[53] Political crisis and instability have caused the Awolowo name and legacy to be called to question. Falola summarizes that

from then until his death in May 1987, Awolowo struggled unsuccessfully to become the country's head of state. He was jailed by his political enemies in 1962 and released by the military in 1967, after which he became a hero and the most towering Yoruba political figure. If the Yoruba regard him as their hero, the other rival groups regard him as a "tribalist." To Azikiwe, his archrival for the entire duration of Awolowo's career, Awolowo introduced "extreme regionalism" into Nigeria. Critics like Azikiwe focused on the link that Awolowo created between political party and ethnicity, rather than between ethnicity and federalism. They focused on the power that Awolowo wanted to give the Yoruba, rather than the general concept of power devolution that would give each group a considerable amount of power.[54]

The heroism or villainism of Awolowo, whether then or now, were/are based on how he pushed his Yorùbá agenda. His Yorùbá agenda was because he understood that with regionalism, each ethnic group can politically self-define itself without interference from any other group, and no group will be able to dominate the other. The political otherness of the country was and still is very shaky. The mistrust is so deeply rooted that it did not take more than six years of political independence for the country to start seeing the cracks in the relationships between over 350 ethnic groups lumped together by the British.[55] Possibly, if regionalism had been allowed to mature, it could have saved Nigeria from its perpetual sorry history. Sadly, that is now left for debate and open guesses of what could have been. Irrefutably, the political consciousness of the Yorùbá resulted from the political ideals and philosophies of Awolowo, and it has developed over time. The Yorùbá people navigate their Yorùbá identity in constant clash with the Nigerian identity. Those in the diaspora have also contributed immensely to the political consciousness of the Yorùbá nation. An example of this is the fact that Awolowo started brewing the idea of Ẹgbẹ́ Ọmọ Odùduwà while he was in London. At that point, Africans in the diaspora were creating movements that ensured Black nationalism.[56] For Awolowo, Ẹgbẹ́ Ọmọ Odùduwà ensured Yorùbá nationalism.

Yorùbá nationalism became the bedrock of Yorùbá politics. That is, the participation of Yorùbá people in the politics of Nigeria was dictated by their identity. With the analysis of the

---

52. Ajala, "Cultural Patrimony, Political Identity," 479.

53. Adebanwi, *Yoruba Elites and Ethnic Politics in Nigeria*, 61–62.

54. Falola, "Yoruba Nation," 39.

55. Ocheja, *Rise and Fall of the Nigerian First Republic*.

56. Nantambu, "Pan-Africanism versus Pan-African Nationalism," 561–574.

contribution of Hebert Macaulay, Obafemi Awolowo, and the Ẹgbẹ́ Ọmọ Odùduwà, what was evident was that Yorùbá political consciousness was reinvigorated. Despite this reinvigoration, the Yorùbá never controlled power at the federal level. In 1993, the Yorùbá nation at home and abroad stood behind M. K. O. Abiola in his presidential bid because of the many failed attempts of the Yorùbá to capture the presidency. For Falola,

> between the 1950s and 1999, the Yoruba struggled to dominate national politics and produce a president. Awolowo failed in his number one ambition of leading the country. Then came Chief M. K. O. Abiola in the 1990s, not hitherto connected with the politics of the AG (which reappeared as the United Party of Nigeria in the Second Republic, and other new labels in the 1980s and 1990s), but with the hurriedly formed Social Democratic Party. Fed up with a long period of military rule and the deception of its leading officers to hand over power to civilians, the Yoruba united behind Abiola who, as chapter seventeen points out, also received support in other parts of the country. The electoral commission was stopped by the military administration of General Babangida from declaring Abiola as the winner of the 1993 presidential elections, whose results were thereafter annulled. Protracted struggles and protests followed, Abiola died in detention, and the military eventually relinquished power. The country was almost thrown into a second civil war during the 1990s. Members of the Yoruba political class successfully sold the idea to the majority of the Yoruba people that they had become "colonized" by the northerners. Yoruba consciousness around the idea of one "nation" was heightened as never before. In addition, ethnic militias—notably the Oòduà People's Congress—emerged to advocate autonomy or even a secession to create a new country, Odùduwà.[57]

Between 1957 and 1979, the Yorùbá had important roles politically at the federal level. Awolowo served as the finance minister under the Yakubu Gowon military administration, and his role in the Nigeria civil war has received criticism from the Igbo people.[58] General Olusegun Obasanjo also became the military leader of the nation in 1976. More than anything else, the expectations and desires of the Yorùbá were to exert their identity; to do this, they needed to be at the helm of affairs of Nigeria or at least have their nation where they could determine their destiny. So, after many attempts to win the presidency, they had a better shot in the 1993 polls. The Yorùbá nation threw its weight, identity, and wealth behind Abiola. Unfortunately, the military government of Ibrahim Babangida made a U-turn on its promise to hand over the government to a democratically elected government.[59] This event singularly upturned the wheel of fortune of the Yorùbá nation in the most unfortunate ways. At the time, that was the closest they had been to the presidency, and not only have they been denied by refusing to announce Abiola the winner of a free and fair election, but the election was also later annulled accompanied by an eventual arrest of Abiola, which led to his death. The concerns of the Yorùbá

---

57. Falola, "Yoruba Nation," 44

58. Achebe, *There Was a Country.*

59. Omoruyi, *Tale of June 12.*

heightened at this period because the fate of the Yorùbá nation, which hung on Abiola's neck, was thwarted by the actions of military rulers of northern extraction. These events fostered the continued mistrust between the Yorùbá and the Hausa-Fulani ethnic group. There was also a subtle interrelation between group and individual identity. The latter point suggests that the Yorùbá wanted a person who was theirs at the top of government. This Yorùbá nationalistic dream became the dream of Abiola too. He represented the political will of the Yorùbá people; the dream of one became the dream of a whole, and the dream of the whole became the self. In general, it was not strange to assume that the reason Abiola was denied the presidency was because he was Yorùbá.

The Hausa-Fulani ethnic group has always seen the Yorùbá people as rivals who keep stopping them from having a complete grip on Nigeria.[60] Once again, the mistrust between them is not surprising because there is the fear that one ethnic group will want to dominate the other if power is given to its people. Though it is difficult for many to accept, one would believe that this is why the advocacy for regionalism or secession is an applaudable idea. The annulment of the 1993 presidential election was an ironic dash of the slogan "Hope" of the Social Democratic Party, the platform upon which Abiola ran for the presidency.

The political history of the Yorùbá nation is not independent of the Yorùbá nation and the identity of its people and vice versa. In other words, one cannot talk about Yorùbá identity without Yorùbá politics, and the interconnectedness of the two has transformed over time. Therefore, an exposition of the new wave of Yorùbá politics and identity cannot be understood if the history upon which it is grounded is not laid out and analyzed.

Yorùbá Sociopolitical Groups and the Calls for Secession

Many ethnic groups have been able to negotiate their continuous participation in Nigeria through the creation of sociopolitical pressure groups that are ethnically motivated. The creation of the Ẹgbẹ́ Ọmọ Odùduwà represented the political awakening of the Yorùbá. Over the years, many sociopolitical groups have been created in Nigeria along ethnic lines too. Sociopolitical groups like the Movement for the Actualization of the Sovereign State of Biafra, Arewa People's Congress, Northern Elders Forum, Ohanaeze Ndigbo, Pan Niger Delta Forum, and Middle Belt Forum have been formed to fight for ethnic rights.

Many of these groups champion either restructuring or absolute secession. The idea of secession is not new to Nigeria. In preindependence Nigeria, some nationalists nursed the notion of wanting the regions that were forcefully joined under the name Nigeria to go their separate ways.[61] The basis of this move was that many of the ethnic groups forced to coexist under the name "Nigeria" did not share the same history, cultural heritage, political will, and group identity. Those who wanted this understood that the continued existence of the ethnic groups after independence would be difficult and at the same time disastrous. The notion of secession is not a phenomenon that started in 1967. Before independence, there were concerns that if the

---

60. Abegunrin, "Chief MKO Abiola's Presidential Ambitions," 334–352.
61. Tamuno, "Separatist Agitations in Nigeria since 1914," 563–584.

ethnic groups were not allowed to go their separate ways, the country would later come to be at war with itself. Some political activists called for a postponement of political independence because of the problem of ethnic mistrust and tensions.[62] The understanding then was that the ethnic groups should first learn how to live with themselves harmoniously before seeking independence. However, the long history of Nigeria has shown that ethnic groups would not have learned how to live with themselves without first dismantling the notion of ethnicity. And as is also clear, it is impossible to discard the concept of ethnicity. By 1967, the fragility of the coexistence reached its height after a series of coups motivated by ethnicity and the ethnic cleansing of the Igbo in the northern part of Nigeria.[63] This led to the Nigerian civil war, or the Biafran civil war, as many prefer to call it. The war between 1967 and 1970 revealed the fractured relationship between the Igbo and the Hausa-Fulani. It also underscored the politics of access to resources.[64] The creation of sociopolitical pressure groups encouraged and supported separatist agendas in Nigeria. The idea of separation and secessionism is used as a renegotiation of each ethnic group's continued existence and participation in the Nigerian political space.[65]

Like the other ethnic groups, the Yorùbá also created several sociopolitical pressure groups. We have discussed how the Ẹgbẹ́ Ọmọ Odùduwà elevated the nationalism of the Yorùbá. After the annulment of the 1993 election, the Yorùbá were agitated and began to form pressure groups of many interests and focuses. One of these groups was the Oòdùà People's Congress (OPC) in 1995.[66] The Afenifere also existed at the time and represented the ideals of Awolowo.[67] While the Afenifere can be tagged a Pan-Yorùbá voice of reason, OPC was a militia group with the interest of protecting Yorùbá people and their territory. According to Funso Afolayan,

The OPC's message of ethnic pride and vigilantism against crime and its demand for Yoruba autonomy within a confederal Nigeria resonated favorably among the younger generation. The Yoruba, the OPC campaigned, must be prepared to fight and, if necessary, go to war to achieve their objectives and secure their interests within or without the Nigerian polity. The government soon became alarmed as discussion increased among the Yoruba over the possibility or even necessity of seceding from the Nigerian union. This agitation for secession came from the Yoruba's profound sense of alienation from the nation; the siege mentality, helplessness, and hopelessness created by the unabated repression specifically directed against the group by the Abacha regime. Tired of it all, the Yoruba wanted a way out, including, if necessary, by secession. To achieve their objectives, they became the most vociferous in calling for the convening of a sovereign national conference where all the different stakeholders in the Nigerian union would be able to come together to discuss their grievances and renegotiate the terms of the union or agree to go their different ways. This house, they argued, was falling.

---

62. Olusanya, "Olaniwun Adunni Oluwole."

63. Siollun, *Oil, Politics and Violence.*

64. Harnischfeger, "Biafra and Secessionism in Nigeria," 325–359.

65. Akaruese, "Beyond Ethnic Militias," 212–227.

66. Pratten, *Perspectives on Vigilantism in Nigeria.*

67. Adedayo, *As It Is,* 293–320.

The structure the British had delicately put together in 1914 was unraveling. Steps, they argued, must be taken to either rebuild the structure or dismantle it peacefully before the whole edifice collapse in a war of self-annihilation, as happened in Rwanda.[68]

The call for secession is not a new experience in Nigerian history, as the position and explication of Afolayan show that the OPC led a spirited fight for the Yorùbá to secede from the Nigerian state because of the continued trampling of Yorùbá interests. Yorùbá nationalism and calls for secession have taken two forms: the intellectual and the military. For instance, the efforts of a figure like Awolowo take an intellectual dimension, as his political ideologies later came to be known as Awoism. The other dimension of the fight is the militia, which is to organize protests, deploy political violence when necessary, and seek the means to create a police force. The call for secession, however, shows the incompetence of several Nigerian administrations over the years—their recklessness, support, and protection of one ethnic group over the other. The incompetence, insincerity, and unsympathetic nature of the Nigerian government has resulted in ethnic clashes that have left the country with myriads of security challenges.[69]

Today, Yorùbá nationalism is expressed in terms of meeting the challenges in facing the rising insecurity caused by Fulani herdsmen, banditry, and kidnapping.[70] Insecurity has informed the decision of the southwest governors to create the regional security outfit, Amotekun.[71]

Social Media, Yorùbá Citizenship, and Group Identity

The Internet has become a tool of globalization that has made the world reachable through technological devices. The Internet has become an important aspect of defining the self and the other. The Internet is not unique to Nigeria; however, its usage, the issues that are discussed on virtual spaces, and concerns expressed on Nigerian virtual spaces are dictated by Nigerian history, politics, and general conditions that dictate people's existence as Nigerians. The virtual space is representative of the physical world; therefore, topics that affect the physical world are transmitted into the virtual space and are discussed extensively. The issues vary from politics, culture, and religious activities. In this sense, there are also Yorùbá virtual spaces that articulate the personal, political, cultural, intellectual, international, and linguistic problems of the Yorùbá people.[72] These Yorùbá virtual spaces allow Yorùbá people around the world to converge and discuss a variety of issues affecting the Yorùbá nation and Nigeria as a whole. The importance of the Internet in twenty-first-century life is gigantic. As Omachonu Omatta succinctly puts it,

There is no doubt that the Internet, more than any other media, has widened the information landscape in the global world. This holds true because of the unprecedented and

---

68. Afolayan, "Politics, Ethnicity, and the Struggle for Autonomy," 307.

69. Anyebe, "Reflection on Ethnic Militia in Nigeria," 972–983.

70. Sahara Reporters, "Igangan Attack"; and Olu-Adeyemi, "Deprivation, Frustration and Aggression," 1–13.

71. Rasheed, "Real Significance of Amotekun."

72. Oloruntoba-Oju, "Youth Language in Virtual Space in Nigeria," 1–4.

emerging rapid connectivity from the widespread availability of Internet technology. The Internet remains a major medium through which information on world affairs (politics, economy, education, religion, culture, business, medicine, etc.) is disseminated. It is a bearer of messages that influence our dispositions and ways of thinking. With users being active participants in online activities, the Internet cannot be considered a passive venue for the dissemination of information. It not only shapes the everyday lives of users, but it is also constantly in the making. There is no doubt that networking through the Internet has proved indispensable. It is common to say that we live in a global village. The Internet globalizes the local and localizes the global in such a way that one can read about events happening elsewhere; and activities in one's backyard are circulated with dispatch beyond frontiers. It has become a medium that erases time and space. Various religious, marginal cultural, and diasporic groups are making their voices heard on the Internet, through self-representation; rather than outsider representation.[73]

What Omatta captures here is that Internet spaces are the replacements of traditional physical spaces by which people of a group come together to talk about their living conditions. For example, in older Yorùbá societies, deliberations and decisions are made by gathering at the palace of the *ọba*, the market square, or the compound of a clan's head. This was how issues about security, economics, wars, and politics are ironed out. In addition, the cultural representation and definition that these physical spaces represent dictate the factors of Yorùbá identity. The *Ẹgbẹ́ Ọmọ Odùduwà* in the 1940s created cultural and political awareness for the Yorùbá people through the Yorùbá language and with the use of traditional media. Yorùbá groups in the twenty-first century, with the availability of the Internet, have switched the mode of Yorùbá citizenship. Virtual spaces through the Internet have created a connectivity between home and diaspora. There is also a systemic erasure of diaspora and home through the Internet. This collapse of the walls of diaspora and home is what changes the identity of the Yorùbá in the diaspora.

The argument is not that people stop being Yorùbá, but it is a claim that the Internet has helped them become Internet citizens (netizens) who can combine the identity of their new homelands, their homelands, and global identity. The Internet, with its connectivity of the regions of the world together, has helped to make issues that are locally inclined globalized, and it has localized global issues. That is, with the Internet, people around the world are not just aware of their immediate environments; they have become aware, informed, and conscious of the culture, politics, and history of the other. Therefore, the Internet reveals the other to the self and the self to the other. Virtual spaces help people to become citizens of the world. There is the question of identity in terms of particularism and universalism. Yorùbá people in the diaspora or at home are left to grapple with the definition of their identity in this global village. The uniqueness of being Yorùbá should not limit anyone from participating in discussions about the issues of the world while still maintaining the unique identity of being Yorùbá. It is

---

73. Omatta, "Ethics of Representation and the Internet," 785.

pertinent to state that the particularity of Yorùbá identity is at first necessary before the universalism of existing in a world that is now a global village.

The Yorùbá in the diaspora is aware of the task of self-definition. It is when the self is defined that the self can objectively interact with the other. The Yorùbá nation and its people are not just netizens; they have mastered the art of using the Internet to propagate the sociopolitical demands of the Yorùbá people. The Internet is now being used for the cultural gospel and elevation of Yorùbá ethos, language, and politics. For example, the "Yoruba Gbòde" page on Facebook is known for promoting cultural heritage.[74] Ẹgbẹ́ Ọmọ Odùduwà used language to elevate the sociocultural consciousness of the Yorùbá people during a period that was significant to the sociopolitical awakening of the Yorùbá nation. A page like Yoruba Gbòde is engaging in a similar orientation. Although it is apolitical, Yoruba Gbòde transports the Yorùbá language and heritage to the rest of the world through the Internet, lessening the possibility for the Yorùbá language to become extinct or endangered. Pages like Yoruba Gbòde are many on the virtual spaces, and what they do for Yorùbá nation is as immense as the efforts the Ẹgbẹ́ Akọ́ mọlédè àti Àṣà Yoruba has achieved over the years.[75]

The creation of Yorùbá netizens is an interesting aspect of Yorùbá existence and identity. Just as we have studied so far in this chapter, Yorùbá identity is about the participation in the traits, norms, and ethos of being Yorùbá. With Yorùbá netizenship, to be a Yorùbá citizen now entails actively participating in online discussions on matters concerning the Yorùbá nation. A large population of Yorùbá nation is now in virtual spaces, and opinions and decisions are formed and made through new media. The Yorùbá diaspora are often the creator or in charge of these pages and this is a way of taking their Yorùbá identity beyond territories. The Internet also helps in the transterritorializing of Yorùbá nation and Yorùbá identity. Arguably, the Internet is a platform for cultural representations. For the Yorùbá in the diaspora, the Internet is now the home for them and it is the platform on which they get the news of home and self-identify with pages like "Yoruba Gbòde" and other more political cyberspaces. Omatta argues that

> diasporic groups are able to find ways of being at home online thus avoiding the nostalgia of disconnection from their lands of origin. The point at issue is not whether indigenous or diasporic groups make a home in cyberspace, but to what extent online homing is authentically a home. This is the aspect that appears problematic in indigenizing Internet technology. Normally, home is associated with a place and to be identified as belonging to a home implies being part of a place. This idea of home is now contradicted by online homing, which is not dependent on physical place. Invariably, the idea of home has been transformed.[76]

The Internet is now home for the Yorùbá in the diaspora, and the idea of attaching identity to a place is erased. By constantly using the Internet and being able to see their kinsmen and ethnic group on Internet spaces, the Yorùbá diaspora is transforming the conceptualization and intellectualization of Yorùbá identity. Through Internet spaces, Yorùbá diaspora can connect

---

74. Facebook, "Yoruba Gbode."

75. "Egbe Akomolede Yoruba."

76. Omatta, "Ethics of Representation," 792.

with home and register their presence. They also create cyberspaces to address the issues concerning the people of their homelands. In many cases, people in the diaspora who create these cyberspaces have never stepped on their home soil, but they feel the need to be connected to their roots and their politics. The metaphor of home soil is also being reconstructed, as the Internet can now be home for millions of Yorùbá people in the diaspora. So they do not need to connect with the physical space of home but with the cyberspaces. Yorùbá in the diaspora can go on pages like Yoruba Gbòde and Yoruba Nation on Facebook and feel at home by seeing issues of Yorùbá heritage and politics being discussed.

Participation in being Yorùbá no longer involves being in the physical space where Yorùbá people are gathered. Now it involves participating in online forums and cyberspaces. Through these forums and cyberspaces, the Yorùbá diaspora can contribute to the Yorùbá nation financially, intellectually, and politically. This reimagination of identity is important because it gives the Yorùbá diaspora a sense of inclusion. Just as some members of Ẹgbẹ́ Ọmọ Odùduwà were at the time in the diaspora, the Yorùbá diaspora netizens can find a sense of nationalism in their efforts to make their kinsmen politically relevant in Nigeria. With the efforts of the Yorùbá diaspora, it is evident that they contribute immensely to supporting the political demands of the Yorùbá people in Nigeria. The Yorùbá diaspora is politically sought-after for endorsement and sponsorship, and this often mars the integrity of the Yorùbá diaspora. Politicians often can use them to get to political positions and then embezzle government funds or, in certain cases, ignore the demands of the Yorùbá nation they had promised to fulfill. Also, with Internet spaces, anonymity and authenticity are put into question. The creators of Yorùbá cyberspaces are most times anonymous, which can make them susceptible to posting news, history, and politics about homes that may be totally untrue; this then brings in the question of the authenticity of intentions.

Omatta believes that

the many instances of the conundrum surrounding the idea of authenticity establish the difficulty experienced when considering the authenticity of representation on the Internet. The mediated nature of online material is indisputable. This mediatedness allows producers to remove things from their original context by way of abstraction. This can happen in such a way that what netizens see on the Internet is some steps removed from what it should be. A lot of simulations and imitations can occur with online materials. We have noted before that the Internet does not provide an easy way to determine authenticity. This difficulty doubles as netizens attempt to judge the authenticity of online representations because of the increasing virtuality of cyberspace. The ability to evaluate also depends on the kind of user one is. There are users whose ability to judge the authenticity of online representation is attenuated. We should also not forget that the line separating the authentic from the false is not clear either in online or offline representations.[77]

---

77. Omatta, "Ethics of Representation," 791.

The Yorùbá diaspora is susceptible to misrepresentation of views; the authenticity of, say, a new article about home cannot be easily verified, and as such it is always difficult to know what to believe and what not to believe, what to react to, and what not to react to. But as Omatta suggests, the authenticity of things about home to get concerned about has to do with the kind of Internet user one is. The Nigerian cyberspace, as with cyberspaces of other nations, is filled with "fake news" and cultural representations that are not entirely true; it is then left to individual users to determine what they are going to allow to dictate their affiliation with home.

The Yorùbá nation since the precolonial era has always been one that wears the pride of its identity like a badge, and its people are always proud to belong to the nation. The politics and existence of the Yorùbá through space and time have shown that Yorùbá history and culture dictate their political participation in the Nigerian political space. This continuous existence within the Nigerian geography also determines the identity of the people of the Yorùbá nation even amid clamor for the creation of the Odùduwà Republic—a country that will be established on the Yorùbá nationalistic principles. The Yorùbá diaspora has witnessed some of the leading voices on the call for secession and their contribution to the cultural heritage and sociopolitical concerns of the Yorùbá nation within the Nigerian space. However, they are redefining the concept of Yorùbá citizenship through the Internet. They are participating in the politics of home through the Internet. They have also created cyberspaces that ensure that they keep a connection with home. Internet citizenship redefines the self and the other for the Yorùbá diaspora, and it is in this redefinition that they can situate their place in the world and the Yorùbá nation. They contribute culturally and politically to the growth of the Yorùbá nation through the Internet. Although many of their progenitors constituted self-definition and self-determination in different ways, what the new age Yorùbá diaspora are doing is relative to the twenty-first century, and as such, they are the twenty-first-century reincarnates of their ancestors. The contributions of Yorùbá diaspora to Yorùbá nationalism have always been immense, which is reflected in the call for Oduduwa Republic. The active participation of Yorùbá diasporic groups, both in terms of contributing finances and propagating the agenda to the rest of the world, is all similar to the events surrounding the creation of Pan-Yorùbá sociocultural groups. The Yorùbá diaspora has transformed the physicality of home and these social groups with virtual spaces and cyber forums.

Although there are commendable effects of this reimagination of identity and the global presence of the Yorùbá nation, it is pertinent to note there are always going to be persons who want to take advantage of unsuspecting Yorùbá people just for their individualistic ambitions and greed. Nonetheless, the transformation of Yorùbá citizenship in the Internet age is laudable, and the efforts at revitalizing and evangelizing the Yorùbá cultural heritage are applaudable.

Tellingly, the Internet age has brought about major transformations among the Yorùbá people, like every other culture. The digital revolution of the current century has propelled changes in the way people live all over the world. It has created a fictional community whose culture, norms, and traditions are seldom dictated by any known entity, such as the state and the elders. The overall achievement of this will be determined in years to come. In the meantime, it is appropriate to mention that the democratization of the cultural space by technological advancements of this age has two broad spectra of implications for cultures like that of the Yorùbá people. On the one hand, it can transform the status of these cultural groups and preserve their language identity; on the other, it is equipped to exacerbate their recession into history. Considering the rate at which information is produced and consumed in this current age, it is hard to tell the extent to which the preservation of cultures and languages like Yorùbá could retain their original form. In any case, it should also be brought to light that no living entity is static, not even culture as a living organism that mutates in response to the evolving social milieu. Nevertheless, this part of the book examines the impact of this age on the Yorùbá culture.

Conclusion

Yorùbá beyond Borders   20

Introduction

As a language, culture, people, and religion, Yorùbá has transcended beyond what it was some five hundred years ago. It has attracted several features of different varieties, which this book endeavors to cover by first laying a foundational understanding of Yorùbá in its evolutionary history and providing perspectives on its permeation toward other realms and states. Although the Yorùbá are primarily found in West Africa, especially in Nigeria, they can also be found in Benin and Togo and have a remarkably rich cultural heritage that has been sustained for centuries.[1] Today, the Yorùbá as a people are scattered across the globe, and Nigeria is only one of the primary places where they are concentrated in an overwhelming number. Other countries have been identified as additional primary and secondary concentrations. This phenomenon has enabled the growth of Yorùbá communities and settlements.

Undoubtedly, there is almost no set of people that grew out of the ground to become citizens or people of a society. People have been linked with several forms of migration, and despite the existence of modern civilization, globalization, and distinguishing international features, this migration syndrome cannot be stopped. Although this book may not see the complete overhauling of a set of people and their attributes by some powers, given the existing territorial integrities that have become the core of foreign policies and international relations, such identification switching could occur gradually or through the rare achievement of a global citizenry. Following this path, the Yorùbá people will continue to decentralize into small and large populations of people around the world, taking up proper international multiple identities.

The idea of Yorùbá and beyond is also reflective of Yorùbá's cultural diffusion across all cultures. Despite assertions that African cultures are gradually evaporating in the wake and domination of foreign cultures, it would not be wrong to note that the diffusion is mutual, in the sense that even if some people do not entirely identify as Yorùbá, there are traces of cultural influence on them and their cultures across the world. The best instance is the modification of cultural properties found in Yorùbá-dominated areas to create a hybrid culture. For example, the idea of Yorùbá English or Nigerian English, although not welcomed in official settings and conversations, is gaining ground in Nigeria and some other places where Yorùbá is spoken.

---

1. Smith, *Kingdoms of the Yoruba.*

Yorùbá is spoken by an estimated figure of 47.5 million people in Nigeria alone, with millions of others in West Africa, Europe, and America.[2] Today, the language is the focus of teaching and research in several universities and academic engagements across the world. There is a high chance of full metamorphosis of the language taking the proper position in the global politics of language, especially because of its preservative and diversity characteristics.

Similarly, Yorùbá religion goes beyond the borders within which it was practiced, taking on new faces and changing the aura around other religions to fit into its characteristics. Yorùbá religious practices and adjoining cultures, such as the veneration of ancestral spirits, divination, philosophizing, and ritual ceremonies, have become prominent among non-Yorùbá people worldwide, resulting in a broader and global understanding and appreciation of Yorùbá culture. Yorùbá philosophical perspectives and worldviews have made significant contributions to global knowledge systems, from art and literature to politics and economics.[3] The Yorùbá worldview, which emphasizes the interconnectedness of humans and nature, has provided a unique perspective on issues related to sustainability, climate change, environmental preservation, and other global concerns.

Hence, the concept of Yorùbá beyond borders is an inquiry into the permeating extent of the Yorùbá in whichever form or strata it is perceived, whether as a demography, language, culture, religion, or any other instance of classification. Following other discussions as relayed previously, this chapter will ask questions around these processes, the current state of things, and some contemporary interactions that have put several values in question. It would reposition the understanding of Yorùbá in the international phase, exposing its identity as such and the state of its language. These and other inquiries made in this chapter would answer some contemporary questions and notions drawing from the aforementioned stances, facts, and established knowledge from the previous chapters as well as new endeavors.

Seeing that the human mind and societies are preoccupied with enough subjects, one must ask whether the emerging agitations for the creation of a Yorùbá nation would be the right step, despite the arguments proffered by the proponents or the presentation of a front to promote an increase in Yorùbá consciousness among people and across the world. More so, academics and scholarship have been among the fortes for the cultivation, spread, and preservation of ideas and knowledge, aside from the ancient scholarly system, like the *Ifá* corpus, embedded in the Yorùbá system. It is high time people started exploring contemporary scholarship and expanding the scope of the preexisting ones.

Yorùbá Migration and International Identity

Yorùbá has transcended beyond being a phenomenon relatable to just a set of people and has gained international identity in terms of ideology, language, religion, and culture. It has become the subject of academic and intellectual engagement, as well as evidence of cultural legacy representing the uniqueness of the African continent and all it stands for. With a language

---

2. World Data Info, "Yoruba Speaking Countries."

3. Coker, "Modernity and the Recycling of Indigenous Knowledge," 65–76.

population put at over 47.5 million, one would understand that the people who have identified themselves as Yorùbá are not just indigenes of Nigeria but a nationality that goes beyond territorial specification.[4] However, before the contemporary alternatives to communications that are rapidly making the world a global village, migration was the most necessary, effective, and commonly adopted method of cultural diffusion in different ways.[5] Across the Atlantic, the Caribbean, and some other parts of the world, there is always a Yorùbá people that could trace themselves to any of the original Yorùbá settlements, especially those that existed before the transatlantic slave trade.[6]

At a point, migration was the soul of international identity, and the Yorùbá people, whether voluntarily or involuntarily, moved beyond the shores of western Nigeria. Yorùbá people are among the largest ethnic groups in Africa, with a rich cultural heritage that is deeply entrenched in historical events, traditional beliefs, and customs. As the early chapters of this book show, tracing the origin of the Yorùbá has been based on different perspectives, including myths, migration theories, and archaeological clarifications. Modern-day conversations in the media revive all those stories and mythologies. It is not unusual to probe into the meaning of the word *Yorùbá* in recent times. Often repeated is the proposition that the word originated from the Hausa word *Yar'ba*, which was supposed to mean "being cunning" to describe people from the Old Ọ̀yọ́ Empire whom they had extensive contact with, especially with their significant role in the trans-Saharan trade.[7] Some kings today will posit that the word must have emerged from the Yorùbá people themselves, with some pointer to their migration from the savanna. Irrespective of the various theories that exist, the word *Yorùbá* has become a generally accepted description for the people of southwestern Nigeria.[8]

Academic scholars and historians located in Lagos, Ibadan, Ile-Ife, Ikire, Ondo, and Àkùngbá have shown special interest in the historical events surrounding Yorùbá early history and migration to explain the sociopolitical, economic, and cultural developments that molded the region. The scholars repeat the mythological theories that might have had some factual bearing but also agree that the most likely way of understanding the origin of the Yorùbá people is through migration. There are several migration theories that tend to dwell on external origins and internal movements of people. A theory among some kings posits that the Yorùbá people migrated to their present locations in Nigeria from the Middle East and have settled in their current territorial areas for over four thousand years.[9] Evidence for justification for this inference is the linguistic and cultural similarities between languages that tend to dwell on sounds and spellings. Archaeological findings can differ. The Iwo Eleru archaeological site in Owo in the present-day Ondo State put evidence of life around the areas of the Yorùbá people at

<hr>

4. World Data Info, "Yoruba Speaking Countries."

5. Eltis, "Diaspora of Yoruba Speakers," 17–39.

6. Kanu, "Migration, Globalization," 45–56.

7. Akinjogbin, "Oyo Empire in the 18th Century," 449–460; and Falola, "From Hospitality to Hostility," 51–68.

8. Falola, "From Hospitality to Hostility," 51–68; see Matory, "How to Read African-American Syncretistic Religion," 113–133.

9. Akintoye, *History of the Yoruba People*; and Schlebusch and Jakobsson, "Tales of Human Migration," 405–428.

about twelve thousand to fifteen thousand years ago.[10] Fossil remains scientifically put the people who settled at Iwo Eleru in the late Stone Age. If the people who originally occupied these areas did not migrate within that period, there is a possibility that the Yorùbá people could be traced to alternative local traditions.[11]

Other fascinating inferences of the origin that are repeated today allude to the Nok civilization as the origin of the Yorùbá people, whose preeminence was supposed to have been felt since 1000 BC.[12] The theory presupposes that there is a cultural similarity between the cultural development of the Yorùbá people and the Nok traditions. Some regard Egypt as another consideration for the origin of the Yorùbá because of the large influence the ancient society had on many African societies.[13] Egyptian origin theory suggests that the Yorùbá people originated from ancient Egypt and moved down to current locations in western parts of Africa.[14] This belief is reinforced by the similarities in culture, languages, and arts with the ancient Egyptian people. Additionally, a great resemblance in religious activities, creation myths, and architectural designs, among others, have proven that a cultural link exists between the two.[15] However, various studies and criticism have shown that these similarities could be coincidental or indirectly influenced by cultural acts.[16]

Further inferences are made to Ghana as either the source or one of the mixed origins of the Yorùbá people.[17] Also, scholars have posited that the Yorùbá people of Nigeria have ancestral linkage with the Bantu-speaking people in Central and southern Africa. This is due to the resemblance in linguistic and cultural beliefs, as both cultures use tones to establish different words and meanings.[18] Likewise, both the Yorùbá and the Bantu-speaking people have traditions of ancestor worship, divination, and the use of masks and other forms of art in religious and cultural practices. Based on these factors, some scholars have maintained that the Yorùbá are an offshoot of the Bantu, while others believe that the cultural linkage could be a result of cultural diffusion or independent development.

As this book argues, all the mythologies and inferences speak to the ideas of regional and global networks. The debate on the migration theories of the Yorùbá people continues, but the center of this discussion is the migration of people and culture from the primary and initial settlements of the Yorùbá people to other parts of the world. There might have been records of the migration of Yorùbá people from the southwestern part of Nigeria, Benin, and Togo across other parts of Africa to the Middle East and beyond the oceans, especially considering the advent of trans-Saharan trade and interactions with the Berbers north of Africa. But one of the most remarkable and historical collective migrations of the Yorùbá people is heavily traced

---

10. Usman and Falola, "Summary and Conclusion," 429–450.

11. Harvati et al., "Later Stone Age Calvaria," e24024.

12. Smith, *Kingdoms of the Yoruba*.

13. Wescott, "Ancient Egypt and Modern Africa," 311–321.

14. Agai, "Rethinking Yoruba Culture," 427–450.

15. Agai, "Reflection on the Theory of the Arab Origin," 1–9.

16. Hunwick, "Egyptian Connection," 187–198.

17. Eades, "Growth of a Migrant Community," 37–57.

18. Zakharia et al., "Characterizing the Admixed," 1–11.

to the transatlantic slave trade, during which a port was created in the backyard of the Yorùbá people.[19]

The Yorùbá migration is an important part of Yorùbá history and has contributed to the rich cultural heritage of the world. The migration of the Yorùbá people did not come up suddenly. One major factor that led to Yorùbá migration was political instability. Throughout history, the Yorùbá people have faced political turmoil and conflict, and as these war-torn areas became more volatile, they sought a calmer region to live in. For instance, during the nineteenth century, the Yorùbá were caught up in the wars and conflicts that erupted in the area. This led to the migration of many Yorùbá people to neighboring countries such as Benin and Togo as well as to other parts of Nigeria. Prominent among these crises was the Dahomey War in modern-day Benin.[20] The Dahomey Kingdom was the epicenter of the slave trade. The slave trade was a booming business, which led to frequent raids in neighboring territories, particularly Yorùbá settlements, for more slaves. The Yorùbá felt threatened by this and moved out of endangered areas, seeking safer abodes. Aside from this, the Fulani launched the jihad in the early nineteenth century to establish Islamic rule among the Hausa states. The crises that ensued from this war displaced large numbers of the Yorùbá people, especially those in the northern part. Some of these displaced persons migrated to Ijaye, Abeokuta, and Ibadan to resettle.[21]

Apart from local and interethnic wars, political instability caused by the transatlantic slave trade saw the displacement of captured Yorùbá as enslaved to plantations in far America. In modern-day Brazil, Cuba, Trinidad and Tobago, among other countries in the Americas, significant Yorùbá diaspora communities, cultures, and religions exist with a rich imprint of cultural and linguistic preservation. These communities have been able to maintain and sustain their Yorùbá identities over time, which brought about the presence of Yorùbá people in these places. Yorùbá slaves were sent to the Americas to work on sugar and coffee plantations and mining industries as laborers.[22] Over time and having maintained their cultural heritage under harsh conditions and the imposition of Catholicism in some locations, these Yorùbá slaves and those who were able to escape their masters sustained their cultural heritage through their religious practices, music, and arts, some aspects of which remain today.[23]

Yorùbá identity in the international communities, as seen with the emergence of *Òrìṣà*, was not automatic until the advancement of the Yorùbá diaspora. The advancement of those in the diaspora gradually became established over time. There was evidence of the adjustment of the Yorùbá people to new lifestyles in such places as Havana and Bahia, using their cultures as tools for adaptability.[24] This is also the situation in Central America and the United States of America; identity formation and creolization became more noticeable in the first and second generations of the few Yorùbá populations that found themselves there.[25] In the Americas, the

---

19. Okpevra, "Dynamics of Intergroup Relations," 126–143.

20. Law, "Dahomey and the Slave Trade," 237–267.

21. Falola and Heaton, *History of Nigeria*, 48–50.

22. Ramos, *Black Diaspora*.

23. Fage and Oliver, *Cambridge History of Africa*, 330–332.

24. Falola and Childs, *Yoruba Diaspora in the Atlantic World*, 6–8.

25. Falola and Childs, *Yoruba Diaspora in the Atlantic World*, 6–8.

Yorùbá identity gained traction by seeking out slaves and people who could be considered to have Yorùbá backgrounds. The name "Lucumi" was used as a general reference to those of Yorùbá identity across America and as a collective group under the same label.[26] The convergence of people of Yorùbá origin continued as their identification across America.

Another example is the identification as Nago in Bahia, which comprised people believed to have belonged to Ẹ̀gbá, Ìjẹ̀bú, Ọ̀yọ́, Kétu, and Iléṣà kingdoms. The fall of the Ọ̀yọ́ Empire pointed to the fact that many of the slaves captured from the seventeenth century were under the empire and were sold to Bahia, Cuba, and Brazil.[27] The enslaved promoted common cultural affinities, religions, and languages, coupled with the influence of their present society. Remarkably, since the name "Yorùbá" was arguably not applicable to the generality of the Yorùbá until around the nineteenth century, one could not say that those who were taken away could have been identified as Yorùbá but under different appellations like "Lucumi" and "Nago," across different settlements, instead of taking a Pan-Yorùbá label.

With the arrival, from the nineteenth century onward, in Lagos of some Africans from Brazil, Jamaica, Cuba, North America, and Sierra Leone, who had a reconnection with ancestral locations, the subscription to a Yorùbá identity became concrete.[28] Subsequently, they reestablished identification with the people back home through commercial and political relevance made available by trade, missionaries, and British colonial officials. With the knowledge gained from abroad, traders, writers, priests, and travelers interacted with the immediate Yorùbá society and established some belief systems that increasingly solidified the Yorùbá identity. Therefore, the connection between the African and Atlantic sides led to communication, a sense of community, and the adoption of the Yorùbá identity both on and off the continent of Africa. These migrations constitute a significant impact on the region and beyond.[29]

The migration of the Yorùbá people to Brazil became more prominent before and during the early nineteenth century. The Yorùbá people were taken to Brazil to work on the northeastern part of the Brazilian plantations. The people took their religion, culture, music, and language with them, created a hybrid of each with the preexisting phenomenon and other perpetual influences, settled down, and continued to develop with the circumstances around them. In Cuba, about 30 percent of the population could be said to have African origin, with the Yorùbá people as one of the major groups. From the fifteenth to the nineteenth century, the migration through the slave trade continued to increase the population of the Yorùbá people in Cuba. They brought their culture, religion, and other social convictions that are evident in contemporary society. With the combination of the Òrìṣà religion and Roman Catholicism in Cuba, there arose a syncretic religion called Santeria. This is also reflected in their fashion, music, and contemporary cultures. Some of the people also found themselves in Europe, although the number could not have been comparable to the concentration in the Americas because of their economic usage.

26. Falola and Childs, *Yoruba Diaspora in the Atlantic World*, 6–8.

27. Falola and Childs, *Yoruba Diaspora in the Atlantic World*, 6–8.

28. Falola and Childs, *Yoruba Diaspora in the Atlantic World*, 6–8.

29. Ogundiran, "Yoruba History and Migration."

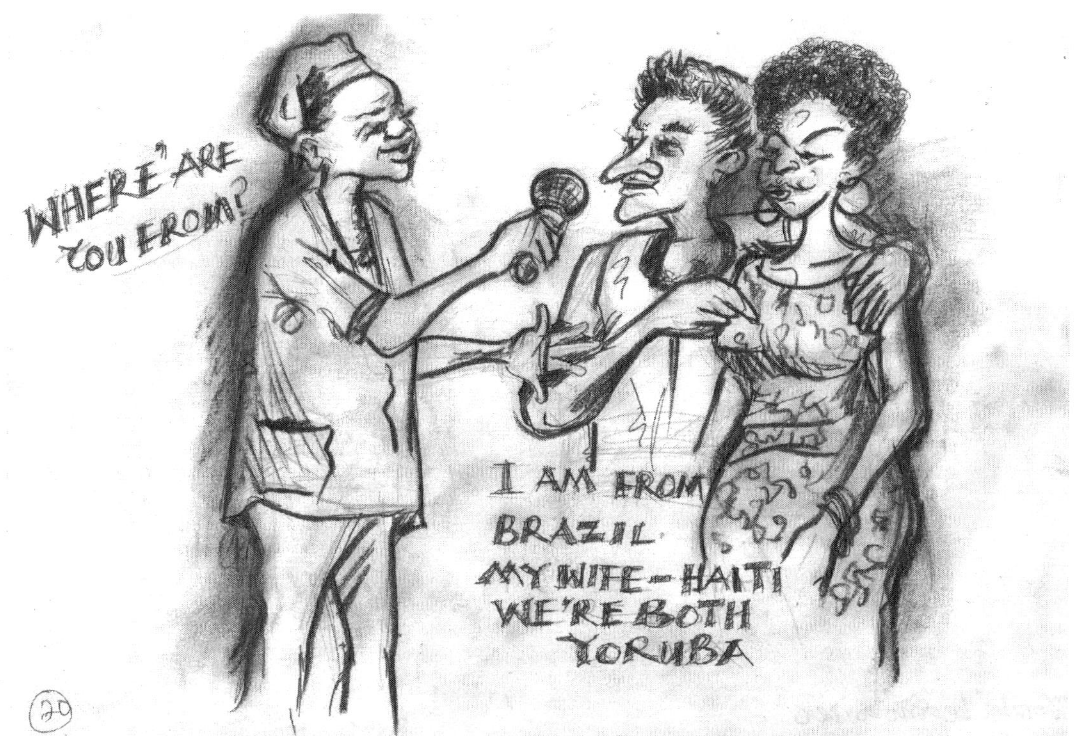

Figure 20.1. "Identity," by Dr. Kazeem Ekeolu. A description of Yorùbá in the diaspora, even though they appear not to look as Yorùbá.

Yorùbá consciousness and identification began to develop across the world as many people were able to either find their roots or develop interaction with the Yorùbá culture. The establishment of the colonial system and institution of modern education across Yorubaland in Nigeria also brought about the further acquisition of identity indexes. Different events and opportunities drew the interest of the people to permeate other parts of Africa, Europe, and the Americas for exploration and other engagements. The colonial system enhanced the economic incentives for migration of the people into high concentration in Lagos, to some other parts of Africa, and across the world. For example, during the colonial period, many Yorùbá people migrated to cities such as Lagos and Ibadan, which were emerging as centers of trade and commerce. Around this time, the availability of wage labor in mining and transportation industries saw more influx of Yorùbá into northern Nigeria for mining activities and to the Railway Corporation in Lagos and Ibadan.

Internal migrations within Nigeria were triggered by emerging opportunities. For instance, the colonial census of 1911 showed that about ten thousand Nigerians had settled in Jos and were employed in tin mines.[30] In 1931, the census showed high migration to Lagos and Ibadan as a result of the railway and created a pathway to traveling outside the country for educational

---

30. Murray, "Migration in the 20th Century," 47–63.

purposes. The Yorùbá were getting to be fully represented in major African countries and cities, notably in all the major cities in West Africa, as in the case of Sierra Leone.[31]

Education and employment further took Nigerians to Europe, America, and Asia. The twentieth century gradually became a golden one for the successful establishment of Yorùbá consciousness across many of these continents and countries. In the twenty-first century, the trend of leaving Nigeria for other parts of the world, especially Europe and the United States of America, has seen a significant increase. The Nigerian migration balance in 2021 was about −0.29, with most of the youth having a growing desire to leave the country.[32] This has affected several industries in different parts of Yorubaland, and the phenomenon seems to be on the rise.

As the Yorùbá leave Nigeria, they are contributing to what this book has characterized as "global Yorùbá." The number of Yorùbá in the diaspora includes those who were outside Nigeria by circumstances of the slave trade, economic activities, employment, education, and professionalism. The generation of Yorùbá identity has been growing, with the Yorùbá in the diaspora being the frontrunners of the Pan-Yorùbá movement, creating the consciousness and reidentification of people of Yorùbá origin. International identification makes more sense with the awareness of how Yorùbá people are dispersed across the world and people who have become natives of foreign nations but could find their roots among the Yorùbá of West Africa. The Yorùbá in the diaspora and those at home who constantly engage in the international space have reinforced the spread of the Yorùbá culture and language, making them a global heritage across the world. It has exceedingly become a thing of pride to identify as Yorùbá, looking at the respect the culture and people have amassed over the years. The continuous creation of cultural centers, acknowledgment of Yorùbá festivals across the world, the tourist interests in Yorùbá cultural and historical locations, and growing efforts toward learning Yorùbá language and epistemology are rapidly creating an international identity for Yorùbá. In addition, the advent of the Internet and social media engagement on Yorùbá cultural properties and interaction have also increased the possibilities of identification with the Yorùbá culture, fashion, style, and lifestyle by people who had no traces of origin with the Yorùbá people.

Philosophical Worldview and Epistemology in the Contemporary World

At a point in Africa's history, what became contentious was the question whether there was an African philosophy and whether it could be possible to say that the people had a mind complex enough to philosophize. As denigrating as it may have been, it sparked a certain level of scholarly discussion in the establishment of the Departments of Religious Studies and Philosophy in African universities. Pioneer scholars of Yorùbá studies insisted that their nation was not that of intellectual darkness with no concrete complexity in the people's mental structure. Although the damage caused in the intellectual prowess of the African people because of this thinking and doubt were doused by many of those who launched the misguided account, it had its impact on individual's perspectives, a phenomenon that the African scholars had to deal

31. Falola and Heaton, *History of Nigeria*.
32. Falola, "Japa!"

with in the process and aim of decolonizing Africa. This was the same problem that the Yorùbá idea of philosophy faced alongside other cultures in West Africa.

Gradually, the world started moving away from the erroneous conception and understanding of African philosophy as not philosophy per se, to seeing the beauty locked in the thoughts of ancient African cultures and beliefs, including other philosophical materials. Scholars have shown the world that African philosophies could be deciphered from the value systems, beliefs, and worldviews of the African people generated from their culture, experience, and unique history. African philosophies could be traced to hundreds of years of evidence of philosophizing. The Egyptian traditions, Ethiopia and Yorùbá, who are the focus of this concluding chapter, had codes of oral traditions and ideas that shaped the general and individual overview of things and influenced the strings of conceptual and environmental appreciation.

The Yorùbá concepts of *Ọmọlúàbí, Orí, Okùn ọmọ* ìyá (brotherhood), *Ìṣẹ́ṣe* (tradition), *Àṣà* (culture), *Kádàrá* (destiny), *Ikú* (death), and *Òwe* (proverb), among others, are the Yorùbá people's philosophical materials that have achieved social construction.[33] The unique concepts of communalism and collectivity, reverence for the ancestors and their spirits, the power of folklore and storytelling, and religious activities are all cords that bind the people and make them a force to be reckoned with globally. Admittedly, compared to other parts of the world, the Yorùbá did not have exposure to literacy early enough, but this does not mean they had not developed a profound philosophical worldview and epistemology for themselves. Recent years have shown that there are global inquiries into the Yorùbá philosophies and adjoining recognitions and attention from philosophers and scholars alike. Several academic programs and universities have African Studies institutions in which studies around Yorùbá thoughts are pivotal to the growing scholarship from such establishments.

The question on the potency of the philosophical worldview and epistemology of a people in this concept is not to compare the contemporary philosophizing processes upon some foreign standards. Would one still say the common and old convictions and philosophies are sustainable upon contemporary variations and complications? Are Yorùbá epistemology and metaphysical conceptions relevant in the current state of science or on subjects like climate change, among others?

Yorùbá thoughts have been responsible for the maintenance of social and individual peace by seizing the minds of children within its philosophical compounds as early as possible, forming a worldview on not only collectivism but also social responsibility and integrity. It points to the concept of Ọmọlúàbí (virtuous individuals), which is a sociophilosophical orientation fundamental to the construction of the Yorùbá communal and social values. Ọmọlúàbí is a Yorùbá societal behavioral model and moral codes that reflect the expected response of people to issues, their ability to make right judgments, and a model that juxtaposes socially accepted characters with individual characters. Olufunmilayo Fabiyi captures the construction of the concept when he describes it as "Ọmọlúàbí, an adjectival Yoruba phrase with 'Ọmọ + tí + Olú-ìwà + bí' as the components can be literally translated as a 'child born by the chief of character,' and such a child is expected to be exactly as his father."

---

33. Adebowale and Onayemi, "Aristotle's Human Virtue," 27–44.

"Ọmọ Àjànàkú *kìn ya àrá, ọmọ tí ẹyá bá bí, ẹyá ní ńjọ,*" meaning that "an Elephant's child can never be a dwarf, a child born by Ẹyá (bush animal) will surely resemble Ẹyá." Hence, the son of the "Ìwà Chief" is expected by the society to be just like his father in terms of impeccable characters, which are expressed in several ways such as (Akanibi and Jekayinfa, 2016) *ọ̀rọ̀ sísọ̀* (spoken word), *ìtẹríba* (respect), *inúrere* (having a good mind toward others), *òtítọ́* (truth), *ìwà* (good character), *akínkanjú* (bravery), *iṣẹ́* (hard work), and *ọpọlọ pípé* (intelligence). The end of Yorùbá traditional education is to make every individual "Ọmọlúàbí." To be "Ọmọlúàbí" is to be of good character. That is why the goal of Yorùbá traditional education has always been to foster strong character in the individual and to prepare each person to become a useful member of the community.[34]

Ìwà, which is "character," is one of the most expected virtues of an Ọmọlúàbí in Yorùbá society. The virtues, although first expected to be impacted by the immediate family and parents, are widely learned from the large group of people that form the society. The training and the upbringing of a child have always been the responsibility of the community, and not just the parents, because the Yorùbá people believe that an error of one could be detrimental to the entire society, and if one person crosses an Òrìṣà or goes against the instructions of the culture, the entire community may bear the brunt. This is most reflected in the Yorùbá adage *Ojú mẹ́rin ló ń bí'mọ, igba ojú ló ń wò ó,* which literally translates as "four eyes give birth to a child but hundreds of eyes train him or her." Those that give birth to a child, the father and mother, and immediate society are the close point of influence on a child, but it is the general duty of society to train that child. There is a logic that societal peace or turbulence is suggested by whether an individual behaves wrongly or rightly in a social contract arrangement. Fabiyi further captures it in Yorùbá wisdom thus:

> Àìmọ̀wà hù ní kò jẹ́ kí ayé gún
> Ọlógbọ́n ni ẹni tí ó kọ́ ẹ́kọ ọgbọ́n mímọ̀wàáhù.
> Ọ̀gbẹ́rì ni ẹni tí kọ́ ọgbọ́n

Meaning that "it is want of knowledge of right conduct that has made the world a horrible place to live in. He is a wise man, who has studied the possession of the act of good, moral conduct. He who has not done so is a novice."[35]

Virtue is promoted from various societal fronts in the Yorùbá society, as well as the religious teachings, no matter how nebulous some foreign influences would like to paint it. *Ifá* corpus has also been a promoter of the *Ọmọlúàbí* character, as it serves as both a religious and philosophical reference of the people. One such reference in the *Odù Ifá* called *Ìwà, Ogbè Òtúrá,* is analyzed by Fabiyi thus:

Òrìṣà lo se *laa ni feere*	It is Obatala who made pawpaw like trumpet
Ó ṣe ẹnu rẹ́ dududu	He made the mouth of the trumpet systematically
Kọ́mọ aráyé ó lè máa ri fọn	For all humans to use for rhythm

---

34. Fabiyi, "Iwa and Omoluabi," 245.

35. Fabiyi, "Iwa and Omoluabi," 247.

Dífá fún Òrúnmìlà	Made *Ifá* reading for Òrúnmìlà
Baba ń lọ rèé gbé Ìwà níyàwó	He wanted to marry Ìwà (character)
Ẹbọ ni wọ́n ní kó wá ṣe	A sacrifice was prescribed for him
Ó gbẹ̀bọ ́mbẹ́ ó rúbọ	He made ẹbọ as prescribed
Ǹjẹ́ Alárá o ríwà ń mi?	King Alárá did you find/see Ìwà (character)
Ìwà là ń wá o Ìwà	We are in search of Ìwà (character)
Ajerò o ríwà ń mi?	King Ajerò did you find/see Ìwà (character)?
Ìwà là ń wá o Ìwà	We are in search of Ìwà (character)
Ọwáràn-gún o ríwà ń mi	King Ọwáràn-gún did you find or see my wife?
Béèyàn lówó láyé	If one is rich in life
Bí ò níwà owó olówó ni	If he doesn't have good character the riches will be lost
Ìwà là ń wá o Ìwà	We are in search of Ìwà (character)
Béèyàn níre gbogbo	If one has all blessings in life
Bí ò níwà ire oníre ni	If he lacks good character all the blessings will vanish.[36]

Òrúnmila and other gods with the fountain of their knowledge and legends are also bound by the social requirement of Ọmọlúàbí through the right ìwà. This is why the *Ifá* corpus in various *odù*, especially the one above, provides an anecdote that seems to show Òrúnmìlà's compliance to it and the consequences of losing the behavioral attributes in the Yorùbá ethical makeup.[37] It is believed that an average Yorùbá person should be strong on humility, respect, integrity, responsibility, and hard work. It is what is believed to be the ideal character of a person and the cornerstone of Yorùbá ethos.

Ọmọlúàbí, as the conception of value, is not strange to other ethical ideologies around the world. The Aristotelian concept of value centered on good living proves that the Yorùbá ideologies, such as Ọmọlúàbí as a principle of virtue, are not just an afterthought but have similarities across the world.[38] Aristotle's conceptions only bear little difference from the tenet of Ọmọlúàbí. According to him, "Ethics is properly conceived, not as a separate inquiry, but as part of political theory."[39] He further retorts that striving for moral excellence in a way that will resort to happiness is the best possible way to live. In Aristotle's view, "happiness"[40] should be the pursuit of a moral agent. Similarly, there is a societal value attached to the principles of Ọmọlúàbí, and adherence to it is believed to be one of the most important options for promoting a favorable society.

The idea of relating the success and failure of the larger society to the virtue of the individual is not only logical but also relevant in contemporary society. More like Ubuntu, derailment from several of the core values that defined the kinds of social contracts that were preexisting in Africa are explanations for the state of the continent in terms of peace, environment, and political situations. Ọmọlúàbí does not do anything to put others in harm's way, and situations like

---

36. Fabiyi, "Iwa and Omoluabi," 246.
37. Fabiyi, "Iwa and Omoluabi," 246.
38. Olanipekun, "Omoluabi," 217–231.
39. Olanipekun, "Omoluabi," 218.
40. Olanipekun, "Omoluabi," 217–231.

that of the COVID-19 lockdowns, consciousness about climate change, and many others would be understandable to an Ọmọlúàbí person, who would see situations as not only his or her problem but will also understand it from the angle of protecting others and society.

Seeing the relevance of the principle, especially with its potency from the contemporary global standpoint, one would understand the influence of Africans in the diaspora and those that have adopted the Yorùbá ethos and culture in several ways, especially in the Americas. It, therefore, gives it a position of being a global concept of a gentleman and virtuous lady. It would be an approach that will take the world toward resolving many of its pending issues. Hence, Pan-Africanists and Africans that are conscious of African values should be conscious of the possibility of forgoing a solution in the name of modernity.[41]

One other concept that has been subjected to debates and controversy is the position of women within the Yorùbá worldview and the social interpretation of their roles. The debate around the role of women has become "global" in private and public conversations in such countries as Cuba, Brazil, and the United States. This debate is relevant by looking at the prevailing feminism consciousness in African society and repositioning the global postures toward recognition women's rights. There is no final word yet on this contentious debate, but some key points are offered here.

Data suggest that the Yorùbá culture and philosophy are not favorable to females, as Yorùbá societies are largely patriarchal. However, this does not make their practices strange to the world, as several Western and global cultures have initially relegated the roles of women and placed heavy societal burdens and discrimination on them.

First, African culture was and is not belittling of women and their positions in society, especially because of their biological nature, but lays emphasis on the social structures of social order and seniority. This has unarguably put women in disadvantageous positions, but the concept of seniority, which is one argument that has circulated,[42] partly determines the nature of the social order of the Yorùbá people and has even made it possible for the germination of feminist ideologies on Yorùbá soils.

The assumption of Yorùbá culture being structurally herculean to women must be understood in context. The categories of humanity and social fiber are not predicated on nature but on seniority, and males do not automatically take superiority over women, especially from the point of birth, except in some few but also important circumstances. Hence, if one interprets or conceptualizes the position of women from European or Western conception, it would lead to "distortions, obfuscations in language and often a total lack of comprehension due to the incommensurability to social categories and institutions."[43] The worldview of the Yorùbá does not always take biological consideration for the determination of social positions, but role allocation and seniority are more favorable compared to many mainstream cultures.

As Oyeronke Oyewumi argues, there is first an emphasis on age and positions in society before any consideration of gender particularization. For instance, the family structure of the Yorùbá community is based on seniority. The father first, then the mother, and finally the

41. Fayemi, "Human Personality," 166–176.

42. Oyewumi, *Invention of Women*.

43. Oyewumi, *Invention of Women*, 319.

Figure 20.2. "Inter-racial marriage," by Dr. Kazeem Ekeolu. Yorùbá and non-Yorùbá are united in marriages and families in different parts of the world.

children in the order of their age, not their nature of birth. A woman exacts authority once she is older than any man, even if he is biologically related or unrelated at all. That is why the concept of àgbàlagbà is taken with seriousness in the Yorùbá social system. Ọmọdé gbọ́n, àgbà gbọ́n, la fi d'ótù Ifẹ́, which means that Ife is created and founded on the wisdom of the elderly and the youth. A combination of generational wisdom is considered important.

In a family, anyone older among the children is taken as égbọ́n, and if she is a female, she could do almost all that could be possibly done despite the gender. The younger ones are scolded for not according to her full respect, and she has the authority to discipline a defaulting young person. This extends to the general social model in every community, as the structures are based on seniority over any other bias, which is why one could easily see and refer to an elderly woman as Ìya wa (our mother) and an elderly man as Bàba wa (our father), even if there are no biological traces. Disrespect to an elderly woman is frowned upon by the entire Yorùbá community and there are adjoining punishments. Oyewumi captures this thus: "Seniority is the social ranking of persons based on their chronological ages. Hence the words egbon refers to the older sibling and aburo to the younger sibling of the speaker regardless of gender. The seniority principle is dynamic and fluid; unlike gender, it is not rigid or static."[44]

Leadership positions, although they could be gender based, have always given representation to women. This is because it is believed that intelligence, strength, and wisdom are not gender

---

44. Oyewumi, "Conceptualizing Gender," 317.

based in the Yorùbá epistemological foundations. Ìyálóde, Ìyáláje, Agbẹ́bí, Ìyá ńlá, Yèyé Ọ̀ṣun, and other female appellations based on religious, professional, or political roles are respected by everyone, and those in such positions are accorded their honors in the order of things. There have been several instances where a woman, such as *Adelé*, could hold the throne instead of a man or wait for the emergence of a new king. An Ondo monarchical mythology points at the creation of the kingdom by a woman king.[45] However, the limitation is seen in how some roles are restricted to males and not females.

In terms of inheritance, women are not entirely excluded from being beneficiaries of their parents' properties. First, the women and the wives of their male siblings inherit the mother's pieces of jewelry and accessories. With the way marriage is structured in Yorùbá society, married women are entitled to property held in trust by the eldest male, who, in most instances, must welcome his sister home when there are issues.[46] This prevents the property from passing to another family or person, seeing that the arrangement in marriage connotes that in every family, there is a centralization of wealth that is controlled by the husband. However, in contemporary times, a married woman can now lay claim to her father's property, and her children also have a direct claim to them. The woman's husband is disregarded and the person who could claim the property is either the woman herself or her children. Unmarried women are given some of their father's property appropriately but widely.[47]

The argument is that since gender discrimination, as the case may be in the Yorùbá system, is not always based on biological nature but on seniority and assignment of social role, then the modern ideas of feminism in its global endeavor are easier to flourish within the Yorùbá system and people. This is seen in the adaptation of Yorùbá culture to several of the values of equality in contemporary society, making it potent in contemporary constructions. A similar thing is seen within some other worldviews of the Yorùbá people.

The Yorùbá epistemological construction is largely predicated on *ọgbọ́n* (wisdom), *ìmọ̀* (knowledge), and *òye* (understanding). These factors could stand on their own but could form just a factor that is fundamental to Yorùbá's conceptualization. *Ọgbọ́n, ìmọ̀,* and *òye* are reflected upon by proverbs, *Ifá* corpus, folklores, and folktales that reenact some of the knowledge-based values, in addition to models of their application in Yorùbá society.[48] Yorùbá proverbs are developed to take care of almost all ramifications as well as provide solutions and directives on logical reasoning that could help one surmount problems. While they uphold the values and riches of the Yorùbá traditions and cultures, they orally handed down wisdom that permeates physics, biology, philosophies, and all imaginable subjects of life. The *Ifá* corpus has also undergone logical and scientific analysis that validates its relevance in the contemporary world. This is to suggest that the epistemological foundation of the Yorùbá is valid within the scope of contemporary subjects and issues today.

Yet another potency of the Yorùbá knowledge system and philosophy is the approach toward medicine and health care services. The medical philosophy of the Yorùbá people tries to create

<hr>

45. Olajubu, *Women in the Yoruba Religious Sphere.*

46. Familusi, "African Culture and the Status of Women," 299–313.

47. Familusi, "African Culture and the Status of Women," 299–313.

48. Ogunyemi, Ogunyemi, and Anozie, "Indigenous African Wisdom and Its Orientation to the Common Good."

a balance between emotional, spiritual, and physical elements that are believed to influence an individual's good health. The people have devised several means of preventive and curative treatments of illness using herbs, plants, natural substances, and sacrifices to heal the sick scientifically and spiritually.[49] The pharmaceutical orientation of the people ascribes special properties to different plants and developed systems around their usages. Several ailments, including diabetes, high blood pressure, arthritis, malaria, and other illnesses have traditional herbal remedies. These medicines are still relevant today, and they have been adopting modern medicinal procedures to make them more contemporary. The pharmaceutical system has been largely adjusted to modern medical culture, and their usage is also being adopted outside Nigeria. As heard several times in Brazil:

> Bí kò sí ewé, kò sí òrìṣà
> Without plants, there are no gods and goddesses
> Plants are powerful agents of the globalization of the Yoruba.

Yorùbá in the Global Politics of Language

Yorùbá language is a global heritage because of the uniqueness of its characteristics and spread. Understandably, the global community has been engaging with the language for decades now, but one must reflect on the position of the language in the global politics of language. Over the years, language has been used as an influential and powerful tool in the determination of international relations. The world is a place of diverse languages, but some languages have become common attributes of nations for effective communications and exchange of ideas and a means by which dominance and influence of power balance are made possible across the world. This could be seen in the deposition of English, French, and other languages in African countries, India, and other countries colonized by European countries. Hence, a particular language becomes either a common feature of some set of people or an instrument that must be had to relate.

Today, some languages have become global lingua franca, as they have been promoted as international languages of science, diplomacy, and business by some of the most powerful nations like the United States, Britain, France, Spain, and others across the world. The promotion of the English language in the global politics of language has given the United States, for example, economic and cultural dominance. The importance of some languages in international relations and diplomacy, the conduct of the businesses of international organizations such as the United Nations, propaganda and media, and education, among others, have influenced the development of different multilingual necessities. These necessities have become a prerequisite for many individuals to function well in various roles and open numerous opportunities across the world. The point at which some languages become dominant in the order of languages in multilingual endeavors is when global language politics becomes more visible.

There are about 1.1 billion speakers of Mandarin Chinese, with 897 million and 193 million native and non-native speakers, respectively, in the world. English has about 983 million

---

49. Borokini and Lawal, "Traditional Medicine Practices among the Yoruba People of Nigeria."

speakers, with 371 million and 611 million native and non-native speakers, respectively. Hindustani has about 544 million speakers, Spanish has about 527 million speakers, and Arabic has about 422 million speakers, among others.[50] This language dominance is influenced first by the number of citizens in a country. China's population exceeds 1 billion people, and it is expected that at least an average Chinese would understand Mandarin, especially because of the language rights policies in place. English and French have more native speakers because of the political factors and the spread of colonization outside England and France. Others are either because of religion or some other influences. English is the most learned language in the world, with around 1.5 billion language learners aside from native speakers; this is followed by French, which has approximately 120 million individuals learning it worldwide.[51]

What, therefore, is the place of Yorùbá language in the global politics of languages? Can the Yorùbá language be considered an endangered language in the face of globalization and cultural diffusion? Because there are over forty million Yorùbá speakers across the world,[52] compared to the number of people who speak and learn English, French, Spanish, Mandarin, and other languages, one can state that the place of the Yorùbá among these languages is not a strong one. Although it would not be right to classify Yorùbá as a minority language from a global perspective, it could be more like it when the level of its use in official and large-scale transactions across the globe is put into consideration.

The spread of the Yorùbá language and its possibility of taking a favorable position in the international politics of language did not just start in recent times; it has been in motion from the point of migrations and slave trade when millions of people, their culture, and languages were taken beyond the shores of traditional locations in Nigeria. Today, Nigeria, Benin, Togo, European countries, the Americas, and almost all continents and countries have Yorùbá-speaking people. The Yorùbá in the diaspora and the exposure of the language to the generality of the world have made the language spoken and understood by a growing number of people. The Yorùbá communities in Europe, South America, and North America have made it possible for the language to be taught and accessed in some of the educational facilities. Today, many of the higher institutions of learning and universities have dedicated efforts to understanding the language and teaching it. In addition, several learning materials, platforms, and systems have been adapted to incorporate the language. There are now textbooks, language exchange programs, and online programs and courses that have been instituted around the language.

The Yorùbá language does not appear as one that would die anytime soon, but its position in the global politics of language is becoming more complicated. Hence, various scholars have asked whether the language can be classified as endangered. Seeing the number of speakers, the growing interest in the world, exchanges, and research into the language, one would conclude that it is far from being an endangered language, let alone facing the possibility of extinction. Also, given its influence on the cultural value of the people in Africa and the rest of the world, it is impossible that such a language would be in danger of dying. Languages face extinction when a considerably fewer number of people speak them as their first language.

---

50. Julian, "What Are the Most Spoken Languages in the World?"
51. McGibney, "What Are the Most Studied Languages in the World?"
52. World Data Info, "Yoruba Speaking Countries."

However, Felix Fabuni and Akeem Salawu, following Wurm's five-level model of language status, classify the Yorùbá language as seriously endangered.[53] Wurm classifies language statuses thus: potentially endangered, endangered, seriously endangered, moribund, and extinct. Wurm classifies Yorùbá to be endangered. The dominance of the English language as the official language of Nigeria, educational language, and social structure constitutes a threat to Yorùbá and the functions it serves in society. Fabuni and Salawu argue that the disposition of the Yorùbá elite toward the Yorùbá language in usage, adoption, and literacy is one of the challenges to the strength of the language and endangers it. They believe that where there is a lesser percentage of illiteracy in Nigeria, the language's potency would not be as strong as it is today and that the irony is that while literacy is gradually reaching the desired rate, it is harming the Yorùbá language. They note the attitudes of the elite or literates thus:

> This is conspicuously demonstrated in the elite attitude towards the use of Yoruba language. English is regarded as a symbol of social structure. The age-long prohibition of "vernacular" is still firmly operational in a large percentage of Yoruba elite homes. Their children must learn and always speak English. Apparently, Yoruba is still existing in Nigeria today because of high-level of illiteracy. If we have a low percentage of literacy, the language will be gone. Parents want their children to speak and learn English. Whereas, language gives us the ability to think differently and retain the mentality. Total abandonment of the Yoruba language brings total dislocation and loss of identity.[54]

The concerns raised by Fabuni and Salawu are real but should be viewed from a different perspective.[55] While recognizing that there is a considerably high number of people of Yorùbá origin who cannot speak a word of the language (although) in a small percentage, many of the elites have been the major drivers of the globalization of Yorùbá language knowledge. They have increased the chances of the language being studied and understood beyond the shores of Africa.

Fabuni and Salawu further emphasize that the financial inducement and economic advantage of the language have been dwindling in recent times, as one of the primary requirements, even implied in most cases, is the ability to understand the English language.[56] As a result, many families' emphasis on being in tune with the present demands of the nation and the international community has been reduced. Among the elite in Nigeria, the pursuit of higher education is primarily motivated by financial incentives and economic well-being, with subjects such as the Yorùbá language not deemed lucrative and thereby affecting the choice of subjects and paths for their children. Consequently, the labor market for graduates in Yorùbá is limited in most cases to teaching or mass media, except for just a few individuals who have been able to break the limitations.[57] In addition, the perpetual pressure to conform to global economic

---

53. Fabuni and Salawu, "Is Yoruba an Endangered Language?" 18.
54. Fabuni and Salawu, "Is Yoruba an Endangered Language?" 18.
55. Fabuni and Salawu, "Is Yoruba an Endangered Language?" 18.
56. Fabuni and Salawu, "Is Yoruba an Endangered Language?" 18.
57. Fabuni and Salawu, "Is Yoruba an Endangered Language?" 18.

Moses Ogunleye E.
2021

policies has discouraged people from learning the Yorùbá language, causing a gradual erosion of language identity within the community. The traditional Yorùbá lexicon for market transactions, as practiced among the people, is rapidly disappearing as they are supplanted by English loanwords. The upshot of these developments as evidence of deterioration is a marked increase in code-switching and code-mixing among Yorùbá people, leading to further dilution of their linguistic heritage.[58]

More issues have been raised specifically in the lack of language rights protection in Yorùbá-speaking societies like Nigeria, which is gradually becoming easy for language loss. The process of language acquisition has been heavily affected because of the uncontrolled effect of language domination from globalized ideologies.[59] In addition, one of the institutions that could have protected the continuous growth of the Yorùbá language across the world is religion. Unfortunately, the Yorùbá traditional religion has been relegated to an evil third language among the Yorùbá people, and the wave of other religions has become too heavy for the language to bear in the Americas, Europe, and Africa.

Adewole argues that the African languages in Nigeria, including the Yorùbá language, are going through cultural xenocentricism (preference for borrowed/foreign culture), with the people themselves as major agents of this phenomenon.[60] In addition, where the Yorùbá language is being spoken, there is language denaturing due to the belief that Yorùbá is seriously endangered and also the heavy influence of foreign languages on it. As a result of these incidents, one might align instances in different ways, such as the creation of Yorùbá English and its subsequent influence on other languages and cultures, or one may also decide that the language is merely endangered but not seriously endangered, as in close to extinction.[61]

However, one can channel these pointers of extinction-endangerment to some of the factors that militate against the status of the Yorùbá language in the global politics of languages. They reduce the possibilities of competing with major languages that dominate the global space. Yorùbá language is not in a strong position in the global politics of language, but efforts could be made to enhance the chances. Research and scholarly endeavors into the language have shown its potency, and this could be a foundation for the proliferation of the language.

Contemporary Survival of Yorùbá Religion

It has been established in the previous chapters that what would pass as the Yorùbá religion is beyond the older African traditional religion, preexisting in the various Yorùbá communities some centuries ago. Contemporary Yorùbá religion includes the resultant religions and syncretism occasioned by the interrelations of cultures, religions, and globalization. The context of Yorùbá religion is, therefore, broader than the worship of *Òrìṣà* and includes the emergence of Yorùbá Christianity and Yorùbá Islam too. In addition, this context is also beyond the

Facing, Figure 20.3. "Footprints," by Moses Ogunleye. The Yorùbá are rooted in the southwest region of Nigeria, but their footprints and presence can be found in different parts of the world, such as West Africa and the Americas.

---

58. Fabuni and Salawu, "Is Yoruba an Endangered Language?" 18.

59. Fabuni and Salawu, "Is Yoruba an Endangered Language?" 18.

60. Adewole, "Cultural Xenocentricism," 193–212.

61. Adewole, "Cultural Xenocentricism."

Yorùbá religious practices outside Nigeria, Togo, Benin, and other African Yorùbá settlements but reflects on the Atlantic connections and Yorùbá as practiced and understood in the Americas, Europe, and other parts of the globe. *Òrìṣà* worship, Yorùbá Christianity, and Yorùbá Islam as the major religious identities that have grown from syncretic operations have spread across the world.

Syncretism and the adjustment of tenets of a certain religion to the values of the society, as well as the injection of prevailing religious practices, is a continuous process. As shown in previous chapters, the development of Yorùbá Christianity and Yorùbá Islam would continue with the imports from civilization and globalization values and interactions. However, the two religions do not face any form of ideological death but a bit of ideological adjustment. The variety of Islam and Christianity, as practiced by the Yorùbá people, is expected to survive the trends as long as the mainstream religion subsists and the Yorùbá people and their cultures are not wiped off. However, one may not be able to say the same about the survival of the traditional Yorùbá religion despite its spread in some pockets across the Americas and Europe. The wide subscription to Christianity and Islam, alongside the mutual condemnation of the *Òrìṣà* worship in the ethos of these religions, especially in the primary societies in Nigeria, Togo, and Benin, continually put *Òrìṣà* worship in danger.

Generally, the Yorùbá religion suffers from the challenges that face African religions. It has been a difficult task to accord African religion and the scholarship around it to the international mainstream of intellectual interactions. One must remember that African nations had to battle with different forms of ideological colonization: African religious practices have been one of the primary victims of this phenomenon. One of the pioneers of the International Association for the History of Religions in West Africa, J. O. Awolalu, observed that it took much effort and delay until 1975 before the first paper on African religion was accepted in the Thirteenth Congress of the Association.[62]

An ideology that has a limited mechanism of being studied across cultures stands the risk of being ignored. The religion has not fully adopted the contemporary styles and modes of idea inheritance and spread. Several of the practices of the Yorùbá *Òrìṣà* religion are determined by the level of their secrecy. Certain facts and practices of the religion are kept secret from many people. Those who could easily have access to the secrets are regarded as *Awo* (fraternity), and those who do not have the right to secrecy are *ọ̀gbẹ̀rì*. Outside the fraternity, people are only armed with the knowledge of worship and basic understanding enough to worship *Òrìṣà*, but certain mysteries and knowledge are kept within the fold of the *Awo*. The activities around *Orò* practice, the knowledge around *eégún*, and other Yorùbá practices are not known to the generality of the people. The reason for this secrecy is to preserve the integrity of the values attached to the practice. For instance, posting the processes of engaging an *Orò* on Twitter would be disrespectful to the values associated with the practice.

While secrecy is appreciated, it makes many of the practices distant from the people, with only the peripheral of the practices fully revealed. Two Yorùbá adages have already forestalled this questionable cultural practice:

---

62. Awolalu, "African Religion as an Academic Discipline," 426.

Òrìṣà tí a bá fi pamọ́ fún ọmọdé máa ń parun ni
(*An Òrìṣà* practice that is hidden from children will perish)
Òkú kìí fi ara pamọ́ fun ẹni tí ó ma wẹ̀ ẹ́
(*A corpse does not hide any part of itself from those who will bathe it*)

Practices that, if widely known, could lead to the abuse of the core values of some religions can be made secret, but some of today's youth must be trusted enough to keep those secrets in their hands, while some other practices should be made open for people to access. In addition, poor recording and adoption of written means of passing religious knowledge of the Òrìṣà amount to limitations in the spread of the practices.[63]

Political and societal factors across the world have brought about hostility toward the practices of Yorùbá traditional religion and Òrìṣà worship. Some of the government policies in these countries do not put into perspective the need for the survival of the Yorùbá religion. In Nigeria, emphasis is often placed on the use and operations of Christianity and Islam in public occasions, places, and documents. Public facilities often have churches and mosques without any provision for traditional worshippers. Hence, the demeanor of the government and the society, caused by the reduced number of traditional worshippers, is doing more damage to the sustainability of the Òrìṣà worship across the globe.

However, religion has found new interests across the globe, giving one a stronger hope of its survival, although not in the original forms in which it was inherited. Cultural appreciation across the world has been notable, and some countries where the Òrìṣà religion is practiced have been able to establish a connection with Yorùbá societies and roots in Nigeria to promote the religion and increase the sustainability of its values in recent times. The Ọọ̀ni of Ife, Ọọ̀ni Adeyeye Babatunde Enitan Ogunwusi Ojaja II, has embarked on different visits to countries whose people have Yorùbá origin and practice Òrìṣà worship and its syncretized forms. On March 19, 2023, the Ọọ̀ni gave a Certificate of Yorùbá Territory to the Quilombola Territory, signifying the preservation of the Yorùbá cultures and Òrìṣà worship in Brazil.[64] On March 23, Brazil had the commemoration of National Òrìṣà Day, a development that is absent in many parts of Nigeria, the supposed primary country for the religion.[65] Ọ̀ṣun State is an exception, where there is a public holiday (Ìṣẹ́ṣe) in which all public institutions, including schools, government ministries, parastatals, and more are closed. It is a holiday set aside for the collective observance of the Yorùbá Òrìṣà in the state.

For Yorùbá religion to survive, it must be practiced in such a way that will adapt to contemporary practices and cultures. The combination of social changes and culture, as well as some elements of globalized trends that do not jeopardize the tenets of the practices, would need to be adopted. One of the instances in the internationalization of the Òrìṣà practice is granting audience on international media and constant promotion of the positive information around them. When religion syncs with contemporary ideologies, one can be sure of its survival. In

---

63. Omotoye, "Study of African Traditional Religion," 21–40.
64. Akinyemi, "Ooni Visits Brazil."
65. Agency Report, "Ooni Inaugurates National Orisa Day in Brazil."

essence, it must be ready to adapt to modern cultures to open up the brackets of people who have access to religious practices.

The development in Quilombola territory and other international Òrìṣà worshipping societies is not only encouraging but also points to one of the survival requirements of any religion. Religions cannot exist in a vacuum; they must touch on the core values of the people and give adequate regard when so needed. To see communities and societies dedicated to the promotion and the preservation of Òrìṣà worship across the globe tells one of the readiness to sustain the legacies. Despite attempts at revival, the knowledge, practices, and doctrines of the Yorùbá traditional religion are dying gradually in West Africa and, most importantly, Nigeria, the supposed origin and location of the religion. There is a need for a community that would be the primary strength of the religious practices. Community support allows the religion to be duly rooted in a conduit of people, which leads to the conduct of festivals and important events that bring about the reenactment and reinforcement of religious beliefs and traditions. Cuba, for instance, has a surprising 80 percent of the people subscribed to the worship of one Òrìṣà or the other and the practice of the Santeria religion.[66] There are museums, festivals, and other events that reinvigorate the communal perspectives toward the religion, as well as festivals that strengthen the social bonds of the believers. The effect of this is that the continuous waves of globalization and cultural diffusion would not negatively wash off the practice but could only create one amendment of beliefs to fit into the general attitudes of the society at a specific time.

Increasing research into Òrìṣà worship is an avenue not only to inquire into the religion and its doctrines but also to promote the understanding of its beliefs. It allows blowing up the religion to a global perspective of intellectualism and avail the world of the opportunity to understand and subscribe to it. The Institute of African Studies, University of Ibadan, Nigeria; the Centre for Black Culture and International Understanding, a research center in Óṣogbo, Nigeria; the Oyotunji African Village in South Carolina, USA, a cultural and religious center targeted at the preservation of the religion, especially in the United States; the Odù Ifá Institute at Atlanta, Georgia, USA, which is dedicated to promoting studies in *Ifá* and adjoining religious practices; and the Ifá Heritage Institute at Ilé-Ife are a few of the various institutions dedicated to promoting Òrìṣà worship. However, there is a need to promote more Pan-Yorùbá scholarship and research institutions across the world. This will allow proper exposure to the tenets of the Òrìṣà religion and increase its chances of contemporary adaptation.

Respective governments of Òrìṣà-worshipping societies must see the need to provide political respect for the promotion and sustainability of the Yorùbá traditional system. Much has been done by the Brazilian, Cuban, and other governments of Òrìṣà-practicing societies in the Americas, but the Nigerian, Togolese, and Benin governments have not taken deliberate political steps to ensure the sustainability of the culture. For instance, religious zoning into political offices in the Nigerian space is always between Christians and Muslims, and there is often a general public subscription to Muslim-Christian or Christian-Muslim tickets for elections into public offices at the federal level and in Yorùbá-populated states or regions. The 2023 election got to a level of momentum as the ruling party, the All Progressives Congress, presented

---

66. Ariyo, "Exploring Yoruba Santeria Religion in Cuba."

president and vice president candidates who were both Muslims. This development was faced with several condemnations because of the failure to reflect or represent the interests of the Christians. The question, therefore, arose: What would be the disposition of the people if any of the candidates is an Òrìṣà worshipper?

In the political order of things, especially in the Yorùbá regions, there is a need to capture the interests of traditional religion at the peak of affairs so as not to make the religion look too abstract. This touches on the protection of the religious rights of the people, especially regarding traditional Yorùbá religious worship. Subscribers to the worship are often not respected and unprotected in society, with heavy stigmatization that has made them leave their desired religions for either Christianity or Islam. Religions cannot exist in a vacuum, as the people are core to their successful sustenance. In a society where the rights of the people to practice a religion are not protected, the religion stands the risk of losing its sustainability. Although there are constitutional provisions that tend to protect these practices, proactive steps must be taken to further ensure strict adherence, especially in the case of Òrìṣà worship.

Institutions, persons, and activities that were supposed to uphold the practices of the Òrìṣà worship and promote its values in their respective societies have degenerated. Traditional leaders in Nigeria lost a huge grip on the domination of culture and tradition from the limitation of their powers during the colonial period. The weakness of influence and its limitation of the traditional religious institutions to mere museums, sightseeing locations, and ceremonial title holders delimit the position of the religion in society. In addition, there is a need to "traditionalize" the traditional officeholders. The position is supposed to be the representation of the traditional regions and cultures of the people and not a ceremonial entity. While the holders could practice any of the modern religions, knowledge and practices of the traditional Yorùbá religion should also be a prerequisite to the appointment and selection of traditional leaders.

Yorùbá Consciousness or Yorùbá Nation?

A nation is characterized as the general subscription of a certain set of people to similar and common history, ethnicity, language, and inhibition of a traceable geographical region. Hence, there is a sense of identity that evolves from the mutual subscription to the above subjects and an increased sense of belonging. In this context, Yorùbá could be seen as a nation with shared factors among its people and mutual reinforcement. There is the presence of a shared trauma by the people and their forebears, which brings about a stronger sense of togetherness that is passed from generation to generation.

However, a nation transcends the context of shared values and history but also some sort of country or state independent of others. This brings about the agitation of a Yorùbá nation in Nigeria, a call for secession, and the independence of the Yorùbá people from the general structure of the country. The call for a Yorùbá nation largely comes from the claims that the Yorùbá are marginalized by the federal government, with some beliefs that the country has been in favor of one ethnic group or region over the others. It also comes from the dissatisfaction with the Nigerian government over the political consideration of southwestern Nigeria as well as the unchecked invasion of the places and compromising the Yorùbá people's security. As a result, there has been a back and forth on ethnic tolerance across the country, and many of the Yorùbá nation agitators believe that the independence of the nation would reduce the challenges to the barest minimum.

The Yorùbá have been victims of the invasion of Fulani herdsmen and bandits as well as Yorùbá criminals who disguise themselves as Fulani. One of the highlights of the attacks was the Owo massacre of June 5, 2022, where no less than forty people were ambushed and killed in St. Francis Catholic Church, Owo, a town in Ondo State. The Ìgángán attack in Oyo State on June 5, 2021,[67] and other attacks on what was seen as the Yorùbá territory are other examples. It is important to note that while some are agitating for outright independence of the Yorùbá people, others are requesting further restructuring of Nigeria to encourage more independence. However, what has been causing fuse is the demand for the outright separation of the Yorùbá nation or the Odùduwà Republic.

Without comparing the agitation with those of other parts of the Nigerian state, one must ask whether secession is the right step to solving the effect of the collective problems of Nigeria on places that identify as Yorùbá states. Considering the state of things, the current agitations for secession, even in the face of the attacks and risks, are more idealistic than realistic. Truly, a state must be responsive in terms of both its function and the structural identification of the people; the failure of the former would likely bring about the destruction of the latter. Secession in Nigeria, especially regarding claims from the southwestern part of the country, is like stating that one only gets to take a bath after walking a dusty path, although even if one walks on tarred roads, other body metabolism and factors would require the necessity of cleaning oneself. Before the question of secession of the Yorùbá Republic can be answered in the affirmative, one must ask if the need for such is core to the survival of the Yorùbá people and if the issues facing the people are caused by virtue of identifying as those people. The national issues are truly the country's functional problems, but they are not strong enough to cause a structural breakup. The Yorùbá nation has benefited from the political setting of the nation in many ways, as it has been considered when there are decisive political considerations.

The question then remains: Would those functional problems be resolved after the nation's secession? Corruption, underdevelopment, and insecurity are not ethnically sensitive, the way some people would like to paint them. Corruption is a local affair that generates to the helms of affairs; therefore, so far as Nigerians, even Yorùbá people, are not conscious of stopping it, it would be the first challenge faced by any potential new nation. Insecurity in the nation is not solely ethnic based but emanates from deprivation of the basic things of life as well as religious extremism. The Yorùbá people are almost half-Christian and half-Muslim, so where the people are more religiously inclined, it means that the new nation would always be the target of any insurrection.

The Yorùbá people in Nigeria are far too deeply rooted in the Nigerian structure and represented duly in almost all parts of the country. Also, there is a heavy cultural interaction and influence that promotes a central system and contemporary styles that fit in with all kinds of ethnicity. This is because the historical context and background of the Yorùbá people have a link with other parts of the country. There have always been times in the past whereby trade,

---

67. Kabir, "Igangan Attack."

wars, cultural exchange, and many other factors were in place, and their existence subsisted in contemporary Nigeria. Thus, it is hard to put the Yorùbá people of Nigeria in such isolation when their identification is not challenged.

The nation has not reached the level whereby the continuous existence and interests of the Yorùbá people are jettisoned, and what is needed now is to embrace the approaches that would see to the creation of some level of Pan-Yorùbá consciousness to increase the aura of the culture above others and promote the ìlànà *Yoruba* among the people. To do this, there is a need for concerted and conscious efforts at both the collective and individual levels toward the promotion of cultural heritage, education of the modern generations, and representation in the economic and political framework of the country. Promoting awareness of Yorùbá as a culture and identity will increase the sense of community and prepare the people for any challenge they may face. If several of the tenets of the culture are upheld as expected, the Yorùbá part of the country might not suffer from the pangs of leadership ineptitude in the country.

Conclusion

Unarguably, Yorùbá has grown beyond borders in every way it can be conceptualized. When one sees that Yorùbá is best understood when taken as a concept and ideology, it would be easy to conceptualize its tenets and how much it has permeated beyond the borders of Nigeria and Africa to gain international identity. The Yorùbá people have migrated to every part of the world; there are almost no cities across the world that do not have one Yorùbá or someone of that origin. The music, dance, and fashion have grown beyond a Nigerian affair to gain international relevance. Despite being largely African, the concept of Afrobeat is predominated by Nigerian artists who have paved the way and set the pace for others to follow. Today, Yorùbá as a people, culture, religion, and every other perspective imaginable has become a global affair and reference.

Bibliography

Abdel-Salam, Osman Hashim. "The Evolution of African Monetary Institutions." *Journal of Modern African Studies* 8, no. 3 (1970): 339–362.

Abdulganiy, Oloruntele Oladimeji. "Evil Forces and Shirk among the Yoruba Muslims in Nigeria: With Special Reference to Ilorin City." PhD diss., University of Birmingham, 2009.

Abegunrin, Olayiwola. "Chief MKO Abiola's Presidential Ambitions and Yoruba Democratic Rights." In *Yoruba Identity and Power Politics*, edited by Toyin Falola and Ann Genova, 334–352. Rochester, NY: University of Rochester Press, 2006.

Abimbola, Kola. *Yoruba Culture: A Philosophical Account*. Birmingham: Iroko Academic, 2006.

Abimbola, Wande. *Ifá Will Mend Our Broken World: Thoughts on Yoruba Religion and Culture in Africa and the Diaspora*. Roxbury, MA: Aim, 1997.

———. *Sixteen Great Poems of Ifa*. Paris: UNESCO, 1975.

Abiodun, Afolabi. "The Colonial Taxation Policy among Yoruba of Southwestern Nigeria and Its Implication for Socio-economic Development." *Journal of the Historical Society of Nigeria* 19 (2010): 62–92.

Abodunrin, Akintayo. "How I Advised Ulli Beier Not to Use Obotunde Ijimere Again." *Nigerian Tribune*, December 5, 2020. https://tribuneonlineng.com/how-i-advised-ulli-beier-not-to-use-obotunde-ijimere-again/.

Abogado, Jannel N. "The Anti-Arian Theology of the Council of Nicea of 325." *Angelicum* 94, no. 2 (2017): 255–286.

Achebe, Chinua. *There Was a Country: A Personal Account of Biafra*. London: Penguin, 2012.

Ade Ajayi, Jacob Festus. *Christian Missions in Nigeria, 1841–1891: The Making of New Elite*. London: Longman, 1965.

———. "The Development of Secondary Grammar School Education in Nigeria." *Journal of the Historical Society of Nigeria* 2, no. 4 (1963): 517–535.

———, ed. *General History of Africa VI: Africa in the Nineteenth Century until the 1880s* (abr. ed.). Paris: UNESCO, 1998.

———. *History and the Nation and other Addresses*. Ibadan: Spectrum Books, 1990.

———. "Towards a More Enduring Sense of History, Being a Tribute to K.O Dike on Behalf of the Historical Society of Nigeria, October, 1983." In *History and the Nation and Other Address*, edited by Jacob Festus Ade Ajayi. Ibadan: Spectrum, 1991.

———. "Towards an African Economic Community: A Historical Perspective." Lecture presented at the Discussion of the Lagos Plan of Action, 1970, 298–299.

Ade Ajayi, Jacob Festus, and Stephen A. Akintoye. "Yorubaland in the Nineteenth Century." In *Groundwork of Nigerian History*, edited by Obaro Ikime, 280–302. Ibadan: Heinemann Educational, 1980.

Ade Ajayi, Jacob Festus, and Ebiegberi Joe Alagoa. "Nigeria before 1800: Aspects of Economic Developments and Inter-Group Relations." In *Groundwork of Nigerian History*, edited by Obaro Ikime, 224–235. Ibadan: Heinemann Educational, 1980.

Ade Ajayi, Jacob Festus, and Robert Smith. *Yoruba Warfare in the 19th Century*. London: Cambridge University Press, 1964.

Adebajo, Sola. "Oku-Riro: Yoruba System for Avenging the Dead." *Nigeria Magazine* (1988): 16–21.

Adebanwi, Wale. "The Quintessential Awo." In *Awo, On the Trail of a Titan: Essays in Celebration of the Obafemi Awolowo Centennial*, edited by David O. Oke, Olatunji Dare, Adebayo Williams, and Femi Akinola, 33–56. Ibadan: BookBuilders, 2009.

———. *Yorùbá Elites and Ethnic Politics in Nigeria: Ọbáfẹmi Awólowo and Corporate Agency*. Cambridge: Cambridge University Press, 2014.

Adebanwi, Wale, and Ebenezer Obadare. *Encountering the Nigerian State*. New York: Palgrave Macmillan, 2010.

Adebowale, Bosede Adefiola, and Folake Onayemi. "Aristotle's Human Virtue and Yorùbá Worldview of Omoluabi: An Ethical-Cultural Interpretation." *African Philosophical Inquiry* 6 (2019): 27–44.

Adebowale, Oludamola. "Significance of Egungun in Yoruba Cultural History." *Life*. February 6, 2020. https://guardian.ng/life/significance-of-egungun-in-yoruba-cultural-history/.

Adeboye, O. A. "Diaries as Cultural and Intellectual Histories." In *Yoruba Identity and Power Politics*, edited by Toyin Falola and Ann Genova, 74–95. Rochester, NY: University of Rochester Press, 2006.

———. "Transnational Pentecostalism in Africa: The Redeemed Christian Church of God, Nigeria." In *Entereprises Religieuses Transnationales en Afrique de L'ouest*, edited by Laurent Fourchard, André Mary, and René Otayek, 439–465. Paris, Ibadan: Karthala, 2005.

Adeboye, Olufunke. "The City of Ibadan." *Yoruba Towns and Cities* (vol. 1), edited by Gabriel O. Oguntomisin, 7–19. Ibadan: Bookshelf Resources, 2003.

Adedayo, Festus. *Ayinla Omowura: Life and Times of an Apala Legend*. Ibadan: Noirledge, 2020.

———. "Ayinla Omowura: 37 Years after the Sybarite." *Cable*, September 27, 2017. https://www.thecable.ng/ayinla-omowura-37-years-sybarite.

Adedayo, Wale. *As It Is: A Journalist's View of Nigeria's Young Democracy*. Ikeja: Journal Communications, 2006.

Adedeji, Joel Adeyinka. "The Alarinjo Theatre (The Study of a Yoruba Theatrical Art from Its Earliest Beginnings to the Present-Times)." PhD diss., University of Ibadan, 1969.

———. "Alarinjo: Traditional Yoruba Travelling Theatre." In *Theatre in Africa*, edited by Oyin Ogunba and Abiola Irele, 27–51. Ibadan: Ibadan University Press, 1978.

Adediran, Biodun. "The Early Beginnings of the Ife State." In *The Cradle of a Race: Ife from the Beginning to 1980*, edited by Isaac A. Akinjogbin. Port Harcourt: Sunray, 1978.

Adediran, Biodun, and A. Lawal. "Islamic Influences on Yoruba Culture." *Mediterranean Journal of Social Sciences* 5, no. 23 (2014): 358–366.

Adeeko, Adeleke. *Arts of Being Yorùbá: Divination, Allegory, Tragedy, Proverb, Panegyric*. Bloomington: Indiana University Press, 2017.

Adefarakan, Elizabeth Temitope. "Yoruba Indigenous Knowledges in the African Diaspora: Knowledge, Power and the Politics of Indigenous Spirituality." Ph.D. diss., University of Toronto, 2011.

Adegbindin, Omotade. *Ifá in Yorùbá Thought System*. Durham, NC: Carolina Academic Press, 2014.

———. "The Interface between the Written and the Oral in Ifa Corpus." *Yoruba Studies Review* 1, no. 1 (2016): 19–40.

Adegbite, Ademọla. "The Drum and Its Role in Yoruba Religion." *Journal of Religion in Africa* 18, no. 1 (1988): 15–26.

Adegbite, Ayodeji Wakil. "One in Heart as They are in Tongue: 'Yoruba,' Land and Environmental Violence in Colonial Southwestern Nigeria." In *Environmental Humanities of Extraction in Africa: Poetics and Politics of Exploitation,* edited by James Ogude and Tafadzwa Mushonga, 105–122. New York: Routledge, 2023.

Adejobi, Emmanuel A. *The Observances and Practices of the Church of the Lord (Aladura) in Light of Old Testament and New Testament.* Lagos: Charity Press, 1965.

Adejunmobi, Moradewun. "Neo-Liberal Rationalities in Old and New Nollywood." *African Studies Review* 5, no. 8 (2015): 33.

Adekoya, Preye. "The Succession Dispute to the Throne of Lagos and the British Conquest and Occupation of Lagos." *African Research Review* 10 (2016): 207–226.

Adekunle, Julius O. "The Wasangari: Politics and Identity in Borgu." *Anthropos* 103, no. 2 (2008): 438.

Adelabu, Abu-Abdullah. "African Christianity: A History of the Christian Church in Africa," *Bethel University,* accessed January 13, 2021. https://www.bethel.edu/-letnie/AfricanChristianity/WesternNorthAfricaHomepage.html.

Adeleke, Richard. "Digital Divide in Nigeria: The Role of Regional Differentials." *African Journal of Science, Technology, Innovation and Development* 13, no. 3 (2021): 333–346.

Adeniji, Abiodun. "Popular Songs as Literary Texts: An Analysis of Fuji Songs." In *Scholarship and Commitment: Essays in Honour of G.G. DARAH,* edited by Sunny Awhefeada and Peter E. Omoko, 336. Lagos: Malthouse, 2018.

Adeniran, Adebusuyi Isaac. "The Migration and Integration of Ejigbo-Yoruba in Cote d'Ivoire." *Nordic Journal of African Studies* 26, no. 2 (2017): 144–157.

Adeoti, Ezekiel Oladele, and James Olusegun Adeyeri. "War and Peace in Eastern Yorubaland: Efon Alaaye and Her Neighbours, 1815–1893." *Global Journal of Political Science and Administration* 2, no. 1 (2013): 1–7.

Adepoju, Aderanti. "Creating a Borderless West Africa: Constructs and Prospects for Intra-Regional Migration." In *Migration without Borders: Essays on the Free Movement of People,* edited by Antoine Pecoud and Paul de Guchteneire, 161–173. New York: Berghahn, 2007.

———. "Migration in West Africa." A Paper Prepared for the Policy Analysis and Research Programme of the Global Commission on International Migration, *Global Commission for International Migration.* September 2005.

Aderibigbe, Ibigbolade, and Adepeju Johnson-Bashua. "Yorùbá Traditional and Contemporary Cultural Perspectives on Homosexuality: Questions of Human and Minority Rights." In *Indigenous Knowledge Systems and Development in Africa,* edited by Samuel Oloruntoba, Adeshina Afolayan, and Olajumoke Yacob-Haliso, 279–301. Cham: Palgrave Macmillan, 2020.

Adesokan, Akinwumi. *Postcolonial Artists and Global Aesthetics.* Bloomington: Indiana University Press, 2011.

Adewale, S. A. "The Role of Ifa in the Work of the 19th Century Missionaries." *Orita: Ibadan Journal of Religious Studies* 12 (1978): 26.

Adewale T. J. "The Ijanna Episode in Yoruba History." *Proceedings of the III International West African Conference Held at Ibadan Nigeria 12th to 21st of December 1949* (1956): 251–256.

Adewole, Adedeji B. "Cultural Xenocentrism, Language Denaturing and the Atrophism of the Yoruba Language." *African Scholar Journal of Humanities and Social Sciences (JHSS-6)* 22, no. 6 (2021): 193–212.

Adewole, Segun. "How I Met Ulli Biere, Duro Ladipo—Ifa Priest, Elebuibon." *Punch,* January 16, 2021. https://punchng.com/how-i-met-ulli-biere-duro-ladipo-ifa-priest-elebuibon/#:~:text=Ifa%20priest%2C%20Chief%20Ifayemi%20Elebuibon,the%20amazement%20of%20the%20professor.

Adeyeri, James Olusegun. "Colonialism Within and Without: The Old Oyo Empire in West Africa." In *Shifting Forms of Continental Colonialism: Unfinished Struggles and Tensions,* edited by Dittmar Schorkowitz, John R. Chávez, and Ingo W. Schröder, 227–245. Singapore: Springer, 2019.

Adi, Hakeem. *West Africans in Britain 1900–1960: Nationalism, Pan-Africanism, and Communism*. London: Lawrence & Wishart, 1998.

Adogame, Afe. *The African Christian Diaspora: New Currents and Emerging Trends in World Chrsitianity*. New York: Bloomsbury, 2013.

———. "Engaging the Rhetoric of Spiritual Warfare: The Public Face of Aladura in Diaspora." *Journal of Religion in Africa* 34, no. 4 (2004): 493–522.

Adu, Funmilayo Modupe. "Re-inventing Fela Anikulapo Kuti: Radical Musicology and Political Expressionism, a Dialectical Interrogation." *International Journal of Research in Commerce and Management Studies* 2, no. 2 (2020): 68–79.

Adu-Gyamfi, Yaw. "Wole Soyinka's 'Dawn' and the Cults of Ogun." *Review of International English Literature* 28, no. 4 (1997): 73–89.

Afe, Taiwo Opekitan, Olawale Ogunsemi, and Abimbola Oyelekan. "Social Distancing toward Gays and Lesbians among College Students in Lagos, Nigeria." *Journal of Gay & Lesbian Social Services* 31, no. 4 (2019): 546–557.

Afigbo, Adiele E. "Fact and Myth in Nigerian Historiography." *Nigeria Magazine*, FESTAC Edition, 122–123 (1977): 81–90.

Afolayan, Adeshina. "African Philosophy, Afropolitanism, and Africa." In *The Palgrave Handbook of African Philosophy*, edited by Afolayan Adesina and Toyin Falola, 391–402. New York: Macmillan, 2017.

———. "Tunde Kelani and the Art of Being Yoruba." *Journal of African Cultural Studies* 32, no. 4 (2020): 1–13.

Afolayan, Funso. "Politics, Ethnicity, and the Struggle for Autonomy and Democracy." In *Yoruba Identity and Power Politics*, edited by Toyin Falola and Ann Genova, 297–315. Rochester, NY: University of Rochester Press, 2006.

Agai, Jock Matthew. "An Investigation into the Ancient Egyptian Cultural Influences on the Yorubas of Nigeria." *HTS Teologiese Studies/Theological Studies* 69, no. 1 (2013): 1–9.

———. "Reflection on the Theory of the Arab Origin of the Yoruba People." *Theologia Viatorum* 45, no. 1 (2021): 1–9.

———. "Rethinking Yoruba Culture in the Light of Yoruba Origins." *Journal for Semitics* 24, no. 2 (2015): 427–450.

———. "Samuel Johnson on the Egyptian Origin of the Yoruba." PhD diss., University of KwaZulu-Natal, 2016.

Agbadudu, Amorosu B., and Florence O. Ogunrin. "Aso-Oke: A Nigerian Classic Style and Fashion Fabric." *Journal of Fashion Marketing and Management* 10, no. 1 (2006): 97–113.

Agency Report. "Ooni Inaugurates National Orisa Day in Brazil." *Punch Nigeria*, March 21, 2023. https://punchng.com/ooni-inaugurates-national-orisa-day-in-brazil/.

Agneta, Pallinder-Law. "Aborted Modernization in West Africa? The Case of Abeokuta." *Journal of African History* 15, no. 1 (1974): 65–82.

Agu, Daniel C. C. "Advancing Music Scholarship in Nigerian Contemporary Music Theory, Pedagogy and Creativity." *Awka Journal of Research in Music and the Arts* 5 (2008): 216–224.

Aiyejina, Funso. *Esu Elegbara: A Source of an Alter/Native Theory of African Literature and Criticism*. Lagos: Centre for Black and African Arts and Civilization, 2010.

Aiyejina, Funso, and Rawle Gibbons. "Orisa (Orisha) Tradition in Trinidad." *Caribbean Quarterly* 45, no. 4 (1999): 35–50.

Ajala, Aderemi S. "Cultural Patrimony, Political Identity, and Nationalism in Southwestern Nigeria." *International Journal of Cultural Property* 22, no. 4 (2015): 471–485.

———. *Yoruba Nationalism: Culture, Politics and Violence in South-western Nigeria (1900–2012)*. Koln: Rudiger Koppe Verlag, 2013.

Ajayi, Daniel Sunday. "Effects of Globalization on Yoruba Family Values." *Nigerian Journal of Applied Psychology* 21, no. 1 (2019): 207–227.

Ajayi, Michael Thomas Euler. "A General History of the Yoruba Country." Part 1, *Lagos Standard*, June 7, 1905.

Ajayi, Oladiran. The Otun Asiwaju of Modakeke on July 15, 1989, at Modakeke High School Hall in a Special Commemorative/Mid-year Lecture to Mark the Creation of Ife North Local Government Area.

Ajayi-Lowo, Esther Oluwashina. "The Same-Sex Marriage (Prohibition) Act in Nigeria." In *The Politics of Gender*, edited by Andrienne Trier-Bieniek. Boston: Brill Sense, 2018.

Ajibade, George O. "New Wine in Old Cups: Postcolonial Performance of Christian Music in Yoruba Land." *Studies in World Christianity* 13, no. 2 (2007): 105–126.

———. "Same-Sex Relationships in Yorùbá Culture and Orature." *Journal of Homosexuality* 60, no. 7 (2013): 965–983.

Ajila, C. O., and A. A. Olowu. "Games and Early Childhood in Nigeria: A Critical Focus on Yoruba Traditional Children's Games." *Early Child Development and Care* 81, no. 1 (1992): 137–147.

Ajisafe, Ajayi Kolawole. *Iwe Itan Abeokuta*. Bungay: Richard Clay & Sons, 1924.

Akande, Lydia. "The Impact of Christ Apostolic Church on Yoruba Diaspora in the New York District." *Ilorin Journal of Religious Studies* 8, no. 1 (2018): 15–26.

Akaruese, Lucky. "Beyond Ethnic Militias: Re-constructing the Nigerian State." In *Urban Violence, Ethnic Militias and the Challenge of Democratic Consolidation in Nigeria*, edited by Tunde Babawale. Lagos: Malthouse, 2003.

Akinjogbin, Isaac Adeagbo. *Cradle of a Race: Ife from the Beginning to 1980*. Port Harcourt: Sunray, 1992.

———. *Dahomey and Its Neighbours 1708–1818*. New York: Cambridge University Press, 1967.

———. "The Growth of Ife from Oduduwa to 1800." In *The Cradle of a Race (Ife From the Beginning to 1980)*, edited by I. A. Akinjogbin, 96–121. Port Harcourt: Sunray Publications, 1992.

———. "The Oyo Empire in the 18th Century—A Reassessment." *Journal of the Historical Society of Nigeria* 3, no. 3 (1966): 449–460.

Akinjogbin, Isaac Adeagbo, Adediran A. Abiodun, and Akanmu G. Adebayo, eds. "War and Peace in Yorubaland 1793–1893." Selections from Papers Presented at the Conference on the Centenary of the 1886 Kiriji/Ekitiparapo Peace Treaty Held at the Obafemi Awolowo University, Ile-Ife, September 21–28, 1989.

Akinjogbin, Isaac Adeagbo, and Emmanuel A. Ayandele. "Yorubaland up to 1800." In *Groundwork of Nigerian History*, edited by Obaro Ikime, 121–133. Ibadan: Heinemann, 1999.

Akinola, Gabriel Akindele. "The Origin of the Eweka Dynasty of Benin: A Study in the Use and Abuse of Oral Traditions." *Journal of the Historical Society of Nigeria* 8, no. 3 (1976): 21–36.

Akin-Otiko, Akinmayowa. "The Significance of Sacrifice in Yoruba Religion and the Scope of Sacrifice to Èsù-Òdàrà, the Mediator Divinity." *Calabar Journal of Liberal Studies* 21, no. 2 (2019): 17–24.

Akintayo, Michael. "Christ Apostolic Church, Agbala Itura, North America: Implication of SWOT Analysis." *International Journal of Research in Humanities and Social Sciences* 1, no. 6 (2013): 51–56.

Akintonde, Moses Akintunde, and Margaret Olugbemisola Areo. "Art and Craft of the Old Oyo: It's Manifestation in the Present Oyo." *Journal of Humanities and Social Science* 15, no. 5 (2013): 54.

Akintoye, Adebanji S. *A History of the Yoruba People*. Dakar: Amalion, 2010.

———. "The North-Eastern Yoruba Districts and the Benin Kingdom." *Journal of the Historical Society of Nigeria* 4, no. 4 (1969): 539–553.

———. *Revolution and Power Politics in Yorubaland, 1840–1893: Ibadan Expansion and the Rise of Ekitiparapo*. London: London, 1971.

Akinwale, Ayanleke. "Yoruba Traditional Education System: A Veritable Tool for Salvaging the Crisis Laden Education System in Nigeria." *Academic Journal of Interdisciplinary Studies* 2, no. 6 (2013): 141–145.

Akinwumi, Olatunji Samuel. "Esu Elegbara in Yoruba Mythology: A Search for Identity." *International Journal of Research and Analytical Reviews* 7, no. 2 (2020): 293.

Akinwumi, Olayemi Duro. "The Oyo-Borgu Military Alliance of 1835: A Case Study in the Pre-Colonial Military History." *Transafrican Journal of History* (1992): 159–170.

Akinwunmi, Olayemi, Okpeh Ochayi Okpeh, and Gwamna Dogara Je'adayibe. *Inter-Group Relations in Nigeria During the 19th and 20th Centuries.* Makurdi: Aboki Publishers, 2006.

Akinwunmi, Tunde M. "Oral Traditions and the Reconstruction of Yoruba Dress." In *Yoruba Identity and Power Politics*, edited by Toyin Falola and Ann Genova, 49–73. Rochester, NY: University of Rochester Press, 2006.

Akinyele, I. B. *Iwe Itan Ibadan ati die Ninu Awon Ilu Agbegbe re bi Iwo, Oshogbo ati Ikirun.* Exeter: James Townsend, 1959.

Akinyele, R. T. "Historiography of Western Yorùbá Borderlands." In *Yoruba Identity and Power Politics*, edited by Toyin Falola and Ann Genova, 96. Rochester, NY: University of Rochester Press, 2006.

Akinyemi, Femi. "Ooni Visits Brazil, Issues Certificate for Quilombola as Yoruba Territory." *Nigerian Tribune*, March 21, 2023. https://tribuneonlineng.com/ooni-visits-brazil-issues-certificate-for-quilombola-as-yoruba-territory/.

Akomolafe, Mohammed A. "Yoruba Ontology: A Critique of the Conceptualization of Life after Death." *Journal of Pan African Studies* 9 (2016): 33.

Akpan, Ndueso. *The Yoruba Concepts of Ori and Human Destiny: A Comparative Analysis.* Germany: Lambert Academic, 2016.

Akpan, Wilson. "And the Beat Goes On? Message Music, Political Repression and the Power of Hip-Hop in Nigeria." In *Popular Music Censorship in Africa*, edited by Michael Drewett and Martin Cloonan, 105–120. London: Routledge, 2016.

Akporobaro, F. B. O. *Introduction to African Oral Literature.* Lagos: Princeton, 2005.

Akudinobi, Jude. "Nollywood: Prisms and Paradigms." *Cinema Journal* 54, no. 2 (2015): 2.

Alabi, Lekan. "Remembering the Thunderking of Theatre, Duro Ladipo." *Guardian.* March 7, 2018. https://guardian.ng/opinion/remembering-the-thunderking-of-theatre-duro-ladipo/.

Alabi, Mojeed O. "Law Making in Pre-colonial Yorùbáland." In *The Yorùbá in Transition: History, Values, Modernity*, edited by Toyin Falola and Ann Genova, 111–124. Durham, NC: Carolina Academic Press, 2006.

Alade, Owoyemi Samuwilu. "An Examination of the Contributions of Muslim Clerics (Alfa) to the Development of the Yoruba Nation since the Nineteenth Century." In *Yoruba Nation and Politics: Since the Nineteenth Century: Essays in Honor of Professors J. A. Atanda*, edited by Toyin Falola and Dipo Olubomehin, 567. Austin, TX: Pan-African University Press, 2020.

Alanamu, Temilola. "Indigenous Medical Practices and the Advent of CMS Medical Evangelism in Nineteenth-Century Yorubaland." *Church History and Religious Culture* 93, no. 1 (2013): 5–27.

Al-Daffa', Ali Abdullah. *The Muslim Contribution to Mathematics.* New York: Routledge, 2017.

Alokan, Adeware. *The Christ Apostolic Church (CAC): 1928–1988.* Lagos: Ibukunola, 1991.

Alonso, Miguel. *The Development of Yoruba Candomblé Communities in Salvador, Bahia, 1835–1986.* New York: Palgrave Macmillan, 2014.

Al-Turaiqi, Abdullah. *The Political System of Saudi Arabia.* Saudi Arabia: Ghainaa Publications, 2008.

Aluko, Sam. "Awo as a Humanist." In *Awo, On the Trail of a Titan: Essays in Celebration of the Obafemi Awolowo Centennial*, edited by David O. Oke, Olatunji Dare, Adebayo Williams, and Femi Akinola, 75–86. Ibadan: BookBuilders, 2009.

Amusa, Saheed Balogun, and Charles Adedeji Ogidan. "Yoruba Indigenous Medical Knowledge: A Study of the Nature, Dynamisms, and Resilience of Yoruba Medicine." *Journal of the Knowledge Economy* 8, no. 3 (2017): 977–986.

Andezian, Sossie. "Worshipping in Times of Crisis: Remembering the Past and Constructing the Present." In *Between the Archival Forest and the Anecdotal Trees: A Multidisciplinary Approach to Palestinian Social History*, edited by Dua' Nakhala, Muna El-Tamemy, and Helda Kojstek, 99–118. Birzeit: Birzeit University, 2004.

Anteby-Yemini, Lisa, and William Berthomière. "Diaspora: A Look Back on a Concept." *Bulletin du Centre de Recherche Français à Jérusalem* 16 (2005): 262–270.

Antwi, Emmanuel K. E. "Church Involvement in the Trans-Atlantic Slave Trade: Its Biblical Antecedent vis-à-vis the Society's Attitude to Wealth." *Studia Historiae Ecclesiasticae* 44, no. 2 (2018): 1–19.

Anyebe, Adam Adem. "A Reflection on Ethnic Militia in Nigeria." *International Journal of Development and Sustainability* 6, no. 9 (2017): 972–983.

Apter, Andrew. "A Comparative Study of Orisa Worship in Two Yoruba Communities." Submitted to Fulbright-Hays Training Grants, Doctoral Dissertation Research Abroad Program (CFDA 84.0022), 3.

———. *Oduduwa's Chain: Locations of Culture in the Yoruba-Atlantic*. Chicago: University of Chicago Press, 2018.

———. "Rituals of Power: The Politics of Orisa Worship in Yoruba Society." PhD diss., Yale University, 1987.

———. "Yoruba Ethnogenesis from Within." *Comparative Studies in Society and History* 55, no. 2 (2013): 135.

Araújo, Joel Zito. "My Friend Fela." *International Film Festival Rotterdam*. Accessed April 12, 2021. https://iffr.com/en/iffr/2019/films/my-friend-fela.

Aremu, P. S. O., O. J. Ajiboye, and B. Abiodun. "Art and Culture as a Viable Currency in Yoruba Traditional Architecture." In *The Sustainable World*, edited by C. A. Brebbia. Southampton: WIT, 2011, 737–744.

Areo, Margaret Olugbemisola, and Razaq Olatunde Kalilu. "Adire in South-Western Nigeria." *African Research Review* 7, no. 2 (2013): 352.

Areo, Margaret Olugbemisola, and Razaq Olatunde Rom Kalilu. "Origin of and Visual Semiotics in Yoruba Textile Adire." *Arts and Design Studies* 12 (2013): 22–34.

Arifalo, S. O. *The Egbe Omo Oduduwa: A Study in Ethnic and Cultural Nationalism (1945–1965)*. Akure: Stebak, 2001.

———. "The Intensification of Ethnic Political Consciousness in Nigeria: The Rise of the Egbe Omo Oduduwa 1947–1951." *Genève-Afrique: Acta Africana* 24, no. 1 (1986): 7–33.

Ariyo, Debbie. "Exploring Yoruba Santeria Religion in Cuba." *Guardian*, January 6, 2019. https://guardian.ng/art/exploring-yoruba-santeria-religion-in-cuba/.

Armstrong, Robert G. "The Collection of Oral Tradition in Nigeria." Retrieved from Professor Jacob F. Ade Ajayi Archives, G.R.O. Box 3 (II).

Asamoah-Gyadu, J. Kwabena. "'Get on the Internet!' Says the Lord: Religion, Cyberspace and Christianity in Contemporary Africa." *Studies in World Christianity* 13, no. 3 (2007): 225–242.

Asante, Molefi Kete, and Ama Mazama, eds. "Ogun." In *Encyclopedia of African Religion* (vol. 1), edited by Molefi Kete Asante and Ama Mazama. Thousand Oaks, CA: SAGE, 2009, 481–482.

Ashaolu, Olubunmi O. "A Critical Study of History and Nationalist Discourse in Nollywood Narratives: Tunde Kelani's Saworo Ide and Agogo Eewo." *Africology: Journal of Pan African Studies* 9, no. 10 (2016): 201–219.

Asiwaju, Anthony I. "Dahomey, Yorubaland, Borgu and Benin in the Nineteenth Century." In *General History of Africa VI: Africa in the Nineteenth Century until the 1880s* (abr. ed.), edited by Jacob F. Ade Ajayi, 699–723. Paris: UNESCO, 1998.

———. "Political Motivation and Oral Historical Traditions in Africa: The Case of Yoruba Crowns, 1900–1960." *Journal of the International African Institute* 46, no. 2 (1976): 116–121.

———. *Western Yorubaland under Colonial Rule 1889–1945: A Comparative Analysis of French and British Colonialism.* London: Longman, 1976.

Atanda, J. Adebowale. *An Introduction to Yoruba History.* Ibadan: Ibadan University Press, 1980.

———. "Kings in Nigerian Society Through the Ages." Inaugural Lecture Delivered at the University of Ibadan, January 24, 1991.

———. *The New Oyo Empire: Indirect Rule and Change in Western Nigeria 1894–1934.* London: Longman, 1973.

Audi, Robert. *Democratic Authority and the Separation of Church and State.* Oxford: Oxford University Press, 2011.

Avi, Paul. *God and the Creative Imagination: Metaphor, Symbol and Myth in Religion and Theology.* New York: Routledge, 1999.

Awe, Bolanle. "The Ajele System: (A Study of Ibadan Imperialism in the Nineteenth Century)." *Journal of the Historical Society of Nigeria* 3, no. 1 (1964): 47–60.

———. "The End of an Experiment: The Collapse of the Ibadan Empire 1877–1893." *Journal of the Historical Society of Nigeria* 3, no. 2 (1964): 221–230.

———. "Militarism and Economic Development in Nineteenth Century Yoruba Country: The Ibadan Example." *Journal of African History* XIV, no. 1 (1973): 65–77.

———. "Praise Poems as Historical Data: The Example of the Yoruba Oriki." *Africa* 44 (1974): 331–349.

Awe, Solomon Kolawole. "Existentialist Concerns in Africa: The Yorùbá Perspectives of Death and Suicide." *Language, Literature and Culture* 2, no. 2 (2019): 41–48.

Awofeso, O. A, and Adefolake O. Ademuson. "Social Capital and Cooperative Society Lending in Ibadan, Oyo State, Nigeria." *Nigerian Journal of Sociology and Anthropology* 17, no. 2 (2019): 41.

Awojulugbe, Oluseyi. "KSA, Victor Olaiya, Onyeka Onwenu—Nigerian Golden Oldies Still Going Strong." *Cable Lifestyle*, August 22, 2016. https://lifestyle.thecable.ng/ksa-kwam-1-victor-olaiya-uwaifo/.

Awolalu, Joseph O. "African Religion as an Academic Discipline." In *Dialogue Issues in Contemporary Discussion*, edited by Ade P. Dopamu, Oluwatosin Awolalu, and S. G. Decamater, 426. Akute: Big Small, 2007.

———. "The Yorùbá Philosophy of Life." *Présence Africaine* 73 (1970): 20–38.

Awolowo, Obafemi. *Adventures in Power: The Travails of Democracy and the Rule of Law* (1 and 2). Ibadan: Evans Brothers, 1987.

———. *Awo on the Nigerian Civil War.* Ikeja: John West Publications, 1981.

———. *Path to Nigerian Freedom.* London: Faber and Faber, 1947.

———. *The People's Republic.* Ibadan: Oxford University Press, 1968.

Ayandele, Emmanuel A. *The Ijebu of Yorubaland 1850–1950: Politics, Economy, and Society.* Ibadan: Heinemann Educational, 1992.

———. *The Missionary Impact on Modern Nigeria 1842–1914: A Political and Social Analysis.* London: Longmans, 1966.

———. "The Mode of British Expansion in Yorubaland in the Second Half of the Nineteenth Century: The Oyo Episode." *Odù: Journal of Yoruba and Related Studies* 3, no. 2 (1967): 22–43.

Ayegboyin, Deji, and S. K. Olajide. "Olodumare." In *Encyclopedia of African Religion* [vol. 1], edited by Molefi Kete Asante and Ama Mazama, 488. Thousand Oaks, CA: SAGE, 2009.

Ayeni, Olamide. "Everything You Should Know about Veteran Gospel Artiste, Tope Alabi as She Turns 50." *Fab Woman*, October 27, 2020. http://www.fabwoman.ng/tope-alabi-biography-profile-fabwoman/.

Ayoade, John A. A. "Party and Ideology in Nigeria: A Case Study of the Action Group." *Journal of Black Studies* 16, no. 2 (1985): 169–188.

Ayokunle, Omobowale O., and Olutayo O. Akinpelu. "Social Capital and Human Development in Nigeria: The Case of Lalupon Community, Ibadan, Oyo State." *African Identities* 7, no. 1 (2009): 77–88.

Baalbaki, Ramzi. *The Arabic Lexicographical Tradition: From the 2nd/8th to the 12th/18th Century.* Leiden: Brill, 2014.

Babalola, Adeboye, and Olugboyega Alaba. *A Dictionary of Yoruba Personal Names.* Lagos: West African Books, 2008.

Babalola, Emmanuel Taiwo. "Newspapers as Instruments for Building Literate Communities: The Nigerian Experience." *Nordic Journal of African Studies* 11, no. 3 (2002): 403–410.

Babarinsa, Dare. "Ode to Itsekiri and a Game Called Life." *Guardian*, August 26, 2021.

Babatola, Jadesola Tai. "The Formation of Yoruba Nation and the Challenge of Leadership since Pre-Colonial Era." Opening Remarks of the Guest Lecturer at the Lecture on the Formation of Yoruba Nation and the Challenge of Leadership in Honour of Aare Gani Adams. Annual General Meeting of Odua Progressive Union (OPU), Ado-Ekiti, to Yorubas in Diaspora, January 27, 2020.

Babátúndé, Yussuf N., and Oladipo Olúbòmẹhìn. "Traditional Music and the Expression of Yorùbá Socio-Cultural Values: A Historical Analysis." *Muziki* 15, no. 2 (2018): 61–74.

Babayemi, S. O. "Oriki Orile as Sources of Historical Data." In *Oral Tradition and Oral History in Africa and the Diaspora: Theory and Practice*, edited by Ebiegberi Joe Alagoa, 110. Lagos: Centre for Black and African Arts and Civilization, 1990.

Badawi, Abduhu. *Ma'a Harak ul-Islam fi Ifriqiyah (Siding Islamic Movement in Africa).* Cairo: n.p, 1979.

Balami, Ahmed Dahiru, and Hadiza Umar Meleh. "Misinformation on Salt Water Use among Nigerians during 2014 Ebola Outbreak and the Role of Social Media." *Asian Pacific Journal of Tropical Medicine* 12, no. 4 (2019): 175–180.

Ballard, J. A. "Administrative Origins of Nigerian Federalism." *African Affairs* 70, no. 281 (1971): 333–348.

Balogun, Adekunle. "Syncretic Beliefs and Practices amongst Muslims in Lagos State Nigeria, with Special Reference to the Yoruba Speaking People of Epe." PhD diss., University of Birmingham, 2011.

Balogun, Odun T. "Wole Soyinka and the Literary Aesthetic of African Socialism." *Black American Literature Forum* 22, no. 3 (1988): 503–530.

Balogun, Oladele Abiodun. "The Concepts of Ori and Human Destiny in Traditional Yoruba Thought: A Soft-Deterministic Interpretation." *Nordic Journal of African Studies* 16, no. 1 (2007): 116–130.

Balogun, Yetunde Ruth. "The Emergence and Contributions of Christian Missions to the Civilization of Yoruba Kingdoms in the Old Oyo Empire." *International Journal of Arts & Sciences* 9, no. 4 (2016): 25.

Bamgbose, Ayo. *The Novels of D.O. Fagunwa.* Benin City: Ethiope, 1974.

Bangura, Abdul Karim. *Falolaism: The Epistemologies and Methodologies of African Knowledge*, 63. Durham, NC: Carolina Academic Press, 2019.

Barber, Karen. *The Anthropology of Texts, Persons and Publics: Oral and Written Culture in Africa and Beyond.* New York: Cambridge University Press, 2007.

———. "How Man Makes God in West Africa: Yoruba Attitudes towards the '*Orisa*.'" *Journal of the International African Institute* 51, no. 3 (1981): 724–745.

———. *I Could Speak until Tomorrow: Oriki, Women and the Past in a Yoruba Town.* London: Edinburgh University Press, 1991.

Barber, Karen, and Christopher Waterman. "Traversing the Global and the Local: Fújì Music and Praise Poetry in the Production of Contemporary Yorùbá Popular Culture." In *Worlds Apart:*

Modernity through the Prism of the Local, edited by Daniel Miller, 240–262. London: Routledge, 1995.

Barcia, Manuel. *West African Warfare in Bahia and Cuba: Soldier Slaves in the Atlantic World 1807–1844*. London: Oxford University Press, 2016.

Barka, Habiba Ben. "Border Posts, Checkpoints, and Intra-African Trade: Challenges and Solutions." *African Development Bank: Chief Economists Complex*. January 6, 2012.

Barnes, Andrew. "Samuel Ajayi Crowther: African and Yoruba Missionary Bishop." *Oxford Research Encyclopedias of African History*. Accessed June 11, 2021. https://oxfordre.com /africanhistory/display/10.1093/acrefore/9780190277734.001.0001/acrefore-9780190277734-e -278.

Barnes, Sandra T., ed. *Africa's Ogun: Old World and New* (2nd ed.). Bloomington: Indiana University Press, 1997.

Barnet, Miguel. *Afro-Cuban Religions*. Princeton, NJ: Marcus Wiener, 2001.

Barth, Fredrik, ed. *Ethnic Groups and Boundaries*. London: George Allen and Unwin, 1969.

Barthes, Roland. *Mythologies*, translated by Annette Lavers. New York: Noonday, 1972.

Bascom, William. *Ifa Divination: Communication between Gods and Men in West Africa*. Bloomington: Indiana University Press, 1969.

———. *Sixteen Cowries: Yoruba Divination from Africa to the New World*. Bloomington: Indiana University Press, 1980.

———. *The Yoruba of South Western Nigeria*. New York: Holt Rinehart and Winston, 1969.

Bassey, Nathaniel, ft. Wale Adenuga. "Olowogbogboro." Written and produced by Rotimi Akinfenwa, *YouTube*, June 27, 2017. https://www.youtube.com/watch?v=oSUKLIpYY-8.

Bassia, Olumbe. "Marriage Rites among the Aku (Yoruba) of Freetown." *Africa: Journal of the International African Institute* 24, no. 3 (1954): 251–256.

Bauer, Henry H. *Scientific Literacy and the Myth of the Scientific Method*. Urbana: University of Illinois Press, 1992.

Beier, Ulli. "Before Oduduwa." *Odu: Journal of Yoruba and Related Studies* 3 (1956): 25–32.

———, ed. *The Return of Shango: The Theatre of Duro Ladipo*. Bayreuth: Iwalewahaus, 1983.

———. *Yoruba Myths*. Cambridge: Cambridge University Press, 1980.

Berger, Arthur Asa. "Marxism and Popular Culture: The Cutting Edge of Cultural Criticism." In *Symbiosis: Popular Culture and Other Fields*, edited by Ray B. Browne and Marshal William Fishwick, 146–159. Bowling Green: Bowling Green State University Popular Press, 1988.

Berkey, Jonathan P. *The Formation of Islam: Religion and Society in the Near East, 600–1800*. Cambridge: Cambridge University Press, 2003.

Bernard, Oluwabunmi T. "Beyond Spoken Words: The Yoruba Indigenous Communication Practices." *Ife: Journal of the Institute of Cultural Studies* 11 (2015): 39–53.

Berry, Mary F., and John W. Blassingame. "Africa, Slavery, and the Roots of Contemporary Black Culture." *Massachusetts Review* 18, no. 3 (1977): 501–516.

Bicchieri, Christina, Ryan Muldoon, and Alessandro Sontuoso. "Social Norms." *Stanford Encyclopedia of Philosophy Archive*. March 1, 2011. https://plato.stanford.edu/Archives/win2018/entries /social-norms/.

Bin Khaled al-Saud, Abdullah. "The Spiritual Teacher and His Truants: The Influence and Relevance of Abu Mohammad al-Maqdisi." *Studies in Conflict & Terrorism* 41, no. 9 (2018): 736–754.

Biobaku, Saburi O. *The Egba and Their Neighbors, 1842–1872*. London: Oxford University Press, 1965.

———. "Historical Sketch of Egba Traditional Authorities." *Africa: Journal of the International African Institute* 22, no. 1 (1952): 40–42.

———. *The Origin of the Yoruba*. Lagos: Nigeria, 1971.

———. *Sources of Yoruba History*. Oxford: Clarendon Press, 1973.

Bitiyong, Billy. "The Chiefs." In *Nigeria Since Independence: The First 25 Years, Vol I*, edited by Yusufu Bala Usman, 145–155. Ibadan: Heinemann, 1989.

Blier, Suzanne Preston. "African Creation of Myths as Political Strategy." *African Arts* 37, no. 1 (2004): 41.

Boaz, Danielle N. *Banning Black Gods: Law and Religions of the African Diaspora*. University Park: Pennsylvania State University Press, 2021.

Bonney, Norman. "The Monarchy, the State and Religion: Modernising the Relationships." *The Political Quarterly* 81, no. 2 (2010): 199–204.

Bonney, Norman, and B. Morris. "Tuvalu and You: The Monarch, the United Kingdom and the Realms." *The Political Quarterly* 83 (2012): 368–373.

Borokini, Temitope I., and Ibrahim O. Lawal. "Traditional Medicine Practices among the Yoruba People of Nigeria: A Historical Perspective." *Journal of Medicinal Plants Studies* 2, no. 6 (2014): 20–33.

Bose, Pablo. "Dilemmas of Diaspora: Partition, Refugees, and the Politics of 'Home.'" *Refuge: Canada's Journal on Refugees* 23, no. 1 (2006): 58–68.

Bouchat, Clarence J. *The Causes of Instability in Nigeria and Implications for the United States*. Independently Published, 2019.

Brandon, George. "Lucumi Divination, the Mythic World and the Management of Misfortune." *Anthropologica* 54, no. 2 (2012): 167–188.

———. *Santeria from Africa to the New World: The Dead Sell Memories*. Bloomington: Indiana University Press, 1993.

Brandon, George Edward. "From Oral to Digital: Rethinking the Transmission of Tradition in Yorùbá Religion." In *Orisa Devotion as World Religion: The Globalization of Yoruba Religious Culture*, edited by Jacob Olupona and Terry Rey, 463–464. Madison: University of Wisconsin Press, 2008.

Braziel, Jana Evans, and Anita Mannur, ed. *Theorizing Diaspora: A Reader*. Malden: Blackwell Publishers, 2003.

Brennan, Vicki. *Singing Yoruba Christianity: Music, Media, and Morality*. Bloomington: Indiana University Press, 2018.

Brenner, Louis. "Reviewed Work: Dahomey and Its Neighbors, 1708–1818 by Akinjogbin." *African Historical Studies* 1, no. 2 (1968): 300.

Britannica, The Editors of Encyclopaedia. "Nigerian Theatre." *Encyclopaedia Britannica*, May 2, 2018. https://www.britannica.com/art/Nigerian-theatre.

Broughton, Simon. *World Music: The Rough Guide*. London: Rough Guides, 1999.

Brown, Matthew. "Kèlání and the Question of Sovereign Cinema." *Journal of African Cultural Studies* 32, no. 4 (2020): 415–428.

Bryce, Jane. "African Futurism: Speculative Fictions and 'Rewriting the Great Book.'" *Research in African Literatures* 50, no. 1 (2019): 1–19.

Burckhardt Jacob. *Judgments on History and Historians*. Boston: Beacon Press, 1958.

Burrow J. W. *A History of Histories: Epics, Chronicles, Romances and Inquiries from Herodotus and Thucydides to the Twentieth Century*. New York: Alfred A. Knopf, 2008.

Burgess, Richard Hugh, Kim Esther Knibbe, and Anna Quaas. "Nigerian-Initiated Pentecostal Churches as a Social Force in Europe: The Case of the Redeemed Christian Church of God." *PentecoStudies* 9, no. 1 (2010): 97–121.

Byfield, Judith. "Taxation, Women, and the Colonial State: Egba Women's Tax Revolt." *Meridians* 3, no. 2 (2003): 250–277.

Campbell, Colin. *The Myth of Social Action*. Cambridge: Cambridge University Press, 1998.

Canizares, Baba Raul. *Shango: Santeria and the Orisha of Thunder*. Plainview: Original, 2000.

Capone, Stefania. "Les Dieux sur le Net: L'essor des religions d'origine africaine aux Etats-Unis." *L'Homme* 151 (1999): 47–74.

———. "The 'Orisha Religion' between Syncretism and Re-Africanization." In *Cultures of the Lusophone Black Atlantic: Studies of the Americas*, edited by Nancy Priscilla Naro, Roger Sansi-Roca, and David H. Treece, 219–232. New York: Palgrave Macmillan, 2007.

———. "The Orisha Religion in a Transnational Perspective." *Social Compass* 69, no. 2 (2022): 135–152.

Cartwright, Mark. "The Spread of Islam in Ancient Africa." *World History Encyclopedia*, May 10, 2019. https://www.worldhistory.org/article/1382/the-spread-of-islam-in-ancient-africa/.

Case, Menoukha. "Yoruba Culture, Religion, and Gender." In *The Wiley Blackwell Encyclopedia of Gender and Sexuality Studies*, edited by Nancy A. Naples. Hoboken: Wiley-Blackwell, 2016.

Castor, Fadeke. *Spiritual Citizenship: Transnational Pathways from Black Power to Ifa in Trinidad*. Durham, NC: Duke University Press, 2017.

Centre for Black Culture. "Story of Ulli Beier." *Centre for Black Culture*. http://centreforblack culture.org/content/story-of-ulli-beier.php#top.

Charles, Omotayo K. "Trial by Ordeal: Untangling Indigenous Methods of Trial and Justice in Colonial Ondo." *Journal of Black Culture and International Understanding* 6/7 (2020/2021): 62–74.

Chen, Ping. *Modern Chinese: History and Sociolinguistics*. Cambridge: Cambridge University Press, 1999.

Cheng, Ying. "Yoruba Ẹ Ronu: Tradition, Youth and Cultural Citizenship in Tunde Kelani's Films." *Journal of African Cultural Studies* 32, no. 4 (2020): 382–399.

Chinweizu, Onwuchekwa Jemie, and Ihechukwu Madubuike. *Toward the Decolonization of African Literature*. Washington, DC: Howard University Press, 1983.

Chireau, Yvonne. *Black Magic: Religion and the African American Conjuring Tradition*. Los Angeles: University of California Press, 2003.

Chirila, Alexander. "The River that Crosses an Ocean: Ifa/Orisha in the Global Spiritual Marketplace." *Qualitative Sociology Review* X, no. 4 (2014): 116–151.

Chitakure, John. *African Traditional Religion Encounters Christianity: The Resilience of a Demonized Religion*. Eugene, OR: Wipf and Stock, 2017.

Clark, Ebun. *Hubert Ogunde: The Making of Nigerian Theatre*. Oxford University Press, 1979.

Clark, William Robinson, Henry Nutcombe Oxenham, and Edward Hayes Plumptre. *A History of the Christian Councils: From the Original Documents, to the Close of the Council of Nicaea, AD 325 – Vol. 1*. Oxford: Oxford University, 1876.

Clarke, Kamari Maxine. *Mapping Yoruba Networks: Power and Agency in the Making of Transnational Communities*. Durham, NC: Duke University Press, 2004.

———. "Transnational Yoruba Revivalism and the Diasporic Politics of Heritage." *American Ethnologist* 34, no. 4 (2007): 721–734.

Clarke, Peter B. *West Africa and Islam: A Study of Religious Development of Islam in West Africa from the 8th to the 20th Century*. London: Longman, 1982.

Clarke, William H. *Travels and Explorations in Yorubaland 1854–1858*, edited by J. A. Atanda. Ibadan: Ibadan University Press, 1972.

Clift, K., and Denise Rizolo. "Vaccine Myths and Misconceptions." *Journal of the American Academy of Physician Assistants* 27 (2014): 21–25.

Cohen, Abner. "Politics of the Kola Trade: Some Processes of Tribal Community Formation among Migrants in West African Towns." *Africa: Journal of the International African Institute* 36, no. 1 (1966): 18.

Cohen, Peter F. "Orisha Journeys: The Role of Travel in the Birth of Yorùbá-Atlantic Religions." *Archives de sciences sociales des religions* 47, no. 117 (2002): 17–36.

Coker, Oluwole. "Modernity and the Recycling of Indigenous Knowledge in the Ifá Literary Corpus." *Ọyẹ*: Journal of Language, Literature and Popular Culture 1, no. 1 (2019): 65–76.

Cole, Festus. "Sanitation, Disease and Public Health in Sierra Leone, West Africa, 1895–1922: Case Failure of British Colonial Health Policy." *The Journal of Imperial and Commonwealth History* 43, no. 2 (2015): 238–266.

Cole, Patrick. *Modern and Traditional Elites in the Politics of Lagos.* New York: Cambridge University Press, 1975.

Coleman, James. *Nigeria: Background to Nationalism.* Berkeley: University of California Press, 1958.

Collins, John. *Musicmakers of West Africa.* Washington, DC: Three Continents, 1985.

Connor, Ryan. "New Nollywood: A Sketch of Nollywood's Metropolitan New Style." *African Studies Review* 5, no. 8 (2015): 55–76.

Coquery-Vidrovitch, Catherine, and Paul E. Lovejoy. *The Workers of African Trade.* London: Sage, 1985.

Cordwell, Justin M. "The Art and Aesthetics of the Yoruba." *African Arts* 16, no. 2 (1983): 56.

Cornelius, Janet. "'We Slipped and Learned to Read': Slave Accounts of the Literacy Process, 1830–1865." *Phylon* 44, no. 3 (1983): 171–186.

Corradetti, Claudio. "The Frankfurt School and Critical Theory." *Internet Encyclopedia of Philosophy*, November 18, 2022. https://iep.utm.edu/critical-theory-frankfurt-school/.

Crane, Diana. "Globalization and Cultural Flows/Networks." In *The Sage Handbook of Cultural Analysis*, edited by Tony Bennett and John Frow, 359–381. Thousand Oaks, CA: SAGE, 2008.

Crumbley, Deidre H. *Indigenous Institution Building in an Afro-Christian Movement: The Aladura as a Case Study.* Ann Arbor, MI: University Microfilms International, 1991.

———. *Spirit, Structure, and Flesh: Gender and Power in Yoruba African Instituted Churches.* Madison: University of Wisconsin Press, 2008.

Currey, James. "Literary Publishing after Nigerian Independence: Mbari as Celebration." *Research in African Literatures* 44, no. 2 (2013): 8–16.

Curtin, Philip D., ed. *Africa Remembered: Narratives from West Africans from the Era of the Slave Trade.* Madison: University of Wisconsin Press, 1967.

———. *The Atlantic Slave Trade: A Census.* Madison: University of Wisconsin Press, 1969.

———. "The End of the 'White Man's Grave'? Nineteenth-Century Mortality in West Africa." *Journal of Interdisciplinary History* 21 (1990): 63–88.

———. *The Rise and Fall of the Plantation Complex: Essays in Atlantic History*, 2nd ed. Cambridge: Cambridge University Press, 2005.

Dairo, Afolorunso Olalekan. "Christianity and Healing: The Yoruba Experience." In *Religion, Medicine and Healing*, edited by G. Aderibigbe and D. Ayegbonyin, 6–12. Ikeja: Free Enterprise Publishers, 1995.

Dale, Roger, Susan Robertson, and Boaventura de Sousa Santos. "Interview with Boaventura de Sousa Santos." *Globalization, Sciences and Education* 2, no. 2 (2004): 1–22.

Danesi, Marcel. *Popular Culture: Introductory Perspectives*, 4th ed. Lanham, MD: Rowman and Littlefield, 2019.

Daniel, Eniola. "Yorùbá in Diaspora Declare Support for South West Security Arrangement." *Guardian*, February 1, 2021. https://guardian.ng/news/yoruba-in-diaspora-declare-support-for-south-west-security-arrangement/.

Darkwa, Benjamin Dompreh. "Missionaries and the Politics of Quinine in the Gold Coast (1939–1943)." *Journal of Research om History of Medicine* 11 (2022): 115–128.

Dathorne, Oscar R. "Amos Tutuola: The Nightmare of the Tribe." In *Introduction to Nigerian Literature*, edited by Bruce King, 66. Lagos: University of Lagos, 1971.

Dauda, Bola. "African Humanism and Ethics: The Cases of Ubuntu and Omolúwàbí." In *The Palgrave Handbook of African Philosophy*, edited by Adeshina Afolayan and Toyin Falola, 475–491. New York: Macmillan, 2017.

Dauda, Bola, and Toyin Falola. *Wole Soyinka: Literature, Activism, and African Transformation.* New York: Bloomsbury, 2021.

Daudin, Guillaume. "How Important Was the Slavery System to Europe?" *Slavery & Abolition: Journal of Slave and Post-Slave Studies* 42, no. 1 (2021): 151–157.

Davies, Lanre. "The Political Economy of the Egba Nation: A Study in Modernisation and Diversification, 1830–1960." *African Nebula* 7 (2014): 74–101.

DAWN Commission. "Duro Ladipo." *DAWN Commission,* June 2, 2016. http://dawncommission .org/duro-ladipo/.

Delano, Isaac. *The Soul of Nigeria.* New York: AMS, 1978.

De La Torre, Miguel A. "Dancing with Ochún: Imagining How a Black Goddess Became White." In *Black Religion and Aesthetics: Religious Thought and Life in Africa and the African Diaspora,* edited by Anthony Pinn, 113–134. Cambridge: Cambridge University Press, 2009.

———. *Santeria: The Beliefs and Rituals of a Growing Religion in America.* Cambridge: Wm. B. Eerdmans, 2004.

Deleuze, Gilles. *Cinema 2: The Time-Image,* translated by Hugh Tomlinson and Robert Galeta. Minneapolis: University of Minnesota Press, 1989.

Dellavigna, Stefano, and Ethan Kaplan. "The Fox News Effect: Media Bias and Voting." *Quarterly Journal of Economics* 122, no. 3 (2007): 1187–1234.

Denby, David. "The Trouble with 'Heart of Darkness.'" *New Yorker,* November 6, 1995. https:// www.newyorker.com/magazine/1995/11/06/the-trouble-with-heart-of-darkness.

Denselow, Robin. "Fela Ransome-Kuti & His Koola Lobitos: Highlife-Jazz and Afro-Soul (1963–1969) Review—Afrobeat Pioneer's Early Work." *Guardian,* April 7, 2016. https://www .theguardian.com/music/2016/apr/07/fela-ransome-kuti-his-koola-lobitos-highlife-jazz-and -afro-soul-1963-1969-review.

Denton, Chad. *The Fall of Empires: A Brief History of Imperial Collapse.* Yardley: Westholme Publishing, 2020.

Derrick, Jonathan. "The 'Native Clerk' in Colonial West Africa." *African Affairs* 82, no. 326 (1983): 61–74.

Dianteill, Erwan. "Deterritorialization and Reterritorialization of the Orisa Religion in Africa and the New World (Nigeria, Cuba and the United States)." Translated by Karen George, *International Journal of Urban and Regional Research* 26, no. 1 (2002): 121.

Diara, Benjamin C. D., and Nkechinyere G. Onah. "The Phenomenal Growth of Pentecostalism in the Contemporary Nigerian Society: A Challenge to Mainline Churches." *Mediterranean Journal of Social Sciences* 5, no. 6 (2014): 395.

Diop, Cheikh Anta. *The African Origin of Civilization: Myth or Reality.* New York: Lawrence Hill, 1974.

———. *Precolonial Black Africa: A Comparative Study of the Political and Social Systems of Europe and Black Africa, From Antiquity to the Formation of Modern States.* Translated by Harold J. Salemson. Westport, CT: Lawrence Hill, 1987, 216.

Doi, Abdurahman I. *Islam in a Multi-Religious Society: Nigeria, a Case Study.* Kuala Lumpur: A. S. Noordeen, 1992.

———. *Islam in Nigeria.* Zaria: Gaskiya, 1984.

———. "A Muslim-Christian-Traditional Saint in Yorubaland." *Practical Anthropology* 6 (1970): 261–268.

Doortmont, Michel R. "A Concept of Yoruba History: Samuel Johnson and the Classics." Paper Presented at a Seminar of the Institute of African Studies, University of Ibadan, December 16, 1987.

Doris, David T. "The Unfunctioning Baby and Other Spectacular Departures from the Human in Yoruba Visual Cultures." *Anthropology and Aesthetics* 49, no. 50 (2006): 115–138.

Dougan, John. "Biography: Fela Kuti." *All Music.* Accessed September 11, 2021. https://www .allmusic.com/artist/fela-kuti-mn0000138833/biography.

Drewal, Henry John. "The Arts of Egungun among Yoruba Peoples." *African Arts* 11, no. 3 (1978): 18–19, 97–98.

Drewal, Margaret T. *Yoruba Ritual: Performers, Play, Agency.* Bloomington: Indiana University Press, 1992.

Dudgeon, Pat, and John Fielder. "Third Spaces within Tertiary Places: Indigenous Australian Studies." *Journal of Community and Applied Social Psychology* 16 (2009): 396–409.

Dussel, Enrique. "Agenda for a South-South Philosophical Dialogue." *Human Architecture: Journal of the Sociology of Self-Knowledge* XI, no. 1 (2013): 3–18.

———. "Transmodernity and Interculturality: An Interpretation from the Perspective of Philosophy of Liberation." *TRANSMODERNITY: Journal of Peripheral Cultural Production of the Luso-Hispanic World* 1, no. 3 (2012): 1–26.

Eades, J. S. "The Growth of a Migrant Community: The Yoruba in Northern Ghana." In *Changing Social Structure in Ghana*, edited by Jack Goody. London: Routledge, 2018, 37–57.

———. "Kingship and Entrepreneurship among Yoruba in Northern Ghana." In *Strangers in African Societies*, edited by William A. Shack and Elliot P. Skinner, 169. Berkeley: University of California Press, 1979.

———. *The Yoruba Today.* Cambridge: Cambridge University Press, 1980.

Eason, Louis Djisovi Ikukomi. *Ifa: The Yoruba God of Divination in Nigeria and the United States.* Trenton: Africa World Press, 2008.

Ebeogu, Afam. "From Idanre to Ogun Abibiman: An Examination of Soyinka's Use of Ogun Images." *Journal of Commonwealth Literature* 15, no. 1 (1980): 84–96.

Edward, Ojo Oluranti, and Saibu Israel Abayomi. "Understanding the Socio-Cultural Identity of the Yoruba in Nigeria." *Journal of the Historical Society of Nigeria* 27 (2018): 8.

Edwards, Lee. *Mediapolitik: How the Mass Media Have Transformed World Politics.* Washington, DC: Catholic University of America Press, 2001.

Eesuola, Olukayode S. "Odu Ifa Ose Meji: Orunmila's Cosmological (De) Construction of Political Violence Stereotype in Ibadan, Nigeria." *Journal of African Interdisciplinary Studies* 5, no. 2 (2021): 24–34.

Ẹgbẹ́ Akọ́mọlédè àti Àṣà Yoruba. Accessed July 15, 2021. https://www.egbeakomoledeyoruba.com/index.php.

Egharevba, Jacob U. *A Short History of Benin.* Ibadan: Ibadan University Press, 1968.

Egunjobi, Joyzy Pius. "The Yoruba Psycho-Spiritual Heritage and Its Implication for Counselors." *Academia.* Accessed October 15, 2021. https://www.academia.edu/41913730/the_yoruba_psycho_spiritual_heritage_and_its_implication_for_counselors.

Eickelman, Dale F., and James P. Piscatori, eds. *Muslim Travellers: Pilgrimage, Migration, and the Religious Imagination Vol. 9.* Berkeley: University of California Press, 1990.

Ekeh, Peter. "Colonialism and the Two Publics in Africa: A Theoretical Statement." *Comparative Studies in Society and History* 17, no. 1 (1975): 91–112.

Ekundare, R. Olufemi. *An Economic History of Nigeria 1860–1960.* London: Methuen, 1973.

Elizabeth, Olaniyan Modupe. "An Appraisal of Osun Osogbo as a Festival Theatre." *European Scientific Journal* 10, no. 11 (2014): 326–336.

Ellis, Alfred B. *The Yoruba Speaking Peoples of the Slave Coast of West Africa: Their Religion, Manners, Customs, Laws, Language, etc.* Lagos: Pilgrims, 1974.

Eltis, David. "The Diaspora of Yoruba Speakers, 1650–1865: Dimensions and Implications." In *The Yoruba Diaspora in the Atlantic World*, edited by Toyin Falola and Matt D. Childs, 17–39. Bloomington: Indiana University Press, 2004.

Emerson, R. "Pan-Africanism." In *African Politics and Society*, edited by Irvin L. Markovitz. New York: Free Press, 1970.

Enemugwem, J. H. "The Impact of the Lagos Press in Nigeria, 1861–1922." *Lwati: A Journal of Contemporary Research* 6, no. 1 (2009): 13–24.

Eric, Paul. "The Amalgamation of Nigeria: Revisiting 1914 and the Centenary Celebrations." *Canadian Social Science* 12 (2026): 66–68.

Esguerra, Diana. *The Oshun Diaries: Encounters with an African Goddess*. Shropshire: Eye, 2019.

Euba, T. "Dress and Status in 19th Century Lagos." In *History of the Peoples of Lagos State*, edited by Ade Adefuye, Babatunde Agiri, and Jide Osuntokun, 139–157. Lagos: Lantern, 1987.

Ezesuokwu, Johnpaul Ejike. "Phenomenological Approach to the Nature and Sources of African Traditional Religion." *Oracle of Wisdom Journal of Philosophy and Public Affairs* 6, no. 2 (2022): 41–54.

Eze-Uzomaka, Pamela, and Akintunde John Oloidi. "Modernization and Its Effect on Cultural Heritage in South-Western Nigeria." *AFRREV IJAH: An International Journal of Arts and Humanities* 6, no. 2 (2017): 81–93.

Fabiyi, Olufunmilayo Omolola. "Iwa and Omoluabi: A Philosophical Analysis of the Yoruba Ethical Concepts on Rape Culture." *Journal of African Studies and Sustainable Development* 4, no. 4 (2021): 245.

Fabuni, Felix Abidemi, and Akeem Segun Salawu. "Is Yorùbá an Endangered Language?" *Nordic Journal of African Studies* 14, no. 3 (2005): 18.

Fabunmi, Michael A. *Ife Shrines*. Ife: University of Ife Press, 1969.

Facebook. "Yorùbá Gbode." *Facebook*. Accessed November 8, 2021. https://www.facebook.com /groups/yorubagbode/.

Fadipe, Israel A. *Ethical Reorientation in Ayinla Omowura Music*. Germany: Lambert Academic, 2016.

———. "Skin Bleaching and Women Sexualisation: A Discourse Analysis of Fela Kuti's *Yellow Fever* and Ayinla Omowura's *Oro Kan Je Mi Logun*." *EJOTMAS: Ekpoma Journal of Theatre and Media Arts* 7, no. 1–2 (2019): 216–235.

Fadipe, Nathaniel A. *The Sociology of the Yoruba*. Ibadan: Ibadan University Press, 1970.

Fage, John D., and Roland Anthony Oliver, eds. *The Cambridge History of Africa, Volume 4: c. 1600– c. 1790*. Cambridge: Cambridge University Press, 1975.

Fagunwa, Daniel. *The Forest of a Thousand Daemons—A Hunter's Saga*. Translated by Wole Soyinka. San Francisco: City Lights, 2013.

Fahm, AbdulGafar O. "Ijebu Ode's Ojude Oba Festival: Cultural and Spiritual Significance." *SAGE Open* 5, no. 1 (2015): 1–11.

Fakuade, Gbenga, Joseph Friday-Otun, and Hezekiah Adeosun. "Yoruba Personal Naming System: Traditions, Patterns and Practices." *Sociolinguistic Studies* 13, no. 2–4 (2019): 251–271.

Falola, Toyin. *The African Diaspora: Slavery, Modernity, and Globalization*. Rochester, NY: University of Rochester Press, 2013.

———. *Alternative History: The World of Yoruba Chroniclers*. Ann Arbor: Mpublishing, University of Michigan Library, 1993.

———. *The Collected Works of J. A. Atanda*. Austin, TX: Pan-African University Press, 2017.

———. *Cultural Modernity in a Colonized World: The Writings of Chief Isaac Oluwole Delano*. Austin, TX: Pan-African University Press, 2020

———. *Esu: Yoruba God, Power, and the Imaginative Frontiers*. Durham, NC: Carolina Academic Press, 2014.

———. *Ethnicity in Nigerian Politics*. Lagos: Oxford Publishers, 2010.

———. *The Falola Reader on African Culture, Nationalism, Development and Epistemologies*. Austin, TX: Pan-African University Press, 2018.

———. "From Hospitality to Hostility: Ibadan and Strangers, 1830–1904." *Journal of African History* 26, no. 1 (1985): 51–68.

———. "Japa!, By Toyin Falola." *Premium Times*, September 2, 2022. https://www .premiumtimesng.com/opinion/551986-japa-by-toyin-falola.html?tztc=1.

———. *Key Events in African History: A Reference Guide*. London: Greenwood, 2002.

———. "Missionaries and Domestic Slavery in Yorubaland in the Nineteenth Century." *Journal of Religious History* 14, no. 2 (1986): 181.

———. *The Political Economy of a Pre-Colonial African State: Ibadan, 1830–1900*. Ile-Ife: University of Ife Press, 1984.

———. "Pre-Colonial Origins of the National Question in Nigeria: The Yoruba Identity as a Case Study." *Africa* 12–13 (1990): 3–24.

———. "Ritual Archives." In *The Palgrave Handbook of African Philosophy*, edited by Adeshina Afolayan and Toyin Falola, 703–728. New York: Palgrave Macmillan, 2017.

———. *Violence in Nigeria: The Crisis of Religious Politics and Secular Ideologies*. Rochester, NY: University of Rochester Press, 1998.

———. "The Yoruba Caravan System of the Nineteenth Century." *International Journal of African Historical Society of Nigeria* 24, no. 1 (1991): 188.

———. "The Yoruba Nation." In *Yoruba Identity and Power Politics*, edited by Toyin Falola and Ann Genova, 29–48. Rochester, NY: University of Rochester Press, 2006.

———. "Yoruba Town Histories." In *A Place in the World: New Local Historiographies from Africa and South Asia*, edited by Axel Harneit-Sievers, 67. Netherlands: Brill, 2002.

———. "Yoruba Writers and the Construction of Heroes." *History in Africa* 24 (1997): 157–158.

Falola, Toyin, and Biodun Adediran. *Islam and Christianity in West Africa*. Ile-Ife: University of Ife Press, 1983.

Falola, Toyin, and Akintunde Akinyemi. *Culture and Customs of the Yoruba*. Austin, TX: Pan-African University Press, 2017.

———. "Introduction." In *Encyclopedia of the Yoruba*, edited by Toyin Falola and Akintunde Akinyemi, 4. Bloomington: Indiana University Press, 2016.

Falola, Toyin, and Matt D. Childs, eds. *The Yoruba Diaspora in the Atlantic World*. Bloomington: Indiana University Press, 2005.

Falola, Toyin, and Kwame Essien, eds. *Pan-Africanism and the Politics of African Citizenship and Identity*. New York: Routledge, 2014.

Falola, Toyin, and Ann Genova, eds. *Orisa: Yoruba Gods and Spiritual Identity in Africa and the Diaspora*. Trenton: African World, 2005.

———. *Yorubá Identity and Power Politics*. Rochester, NY: University of Rochester Press, 2006.

Falola, Toyin, and Matthew M. Heaton. *A History of Nigeria*. Cambridge: Cambridge University Press, 2008.

Falola, Toyin, and Christian Jennings, eds. *Africanizing Knowledge: African Studies across Disciplines*. New Brunswick, NJ: Transaction Publishers, 2002.

Falola, Toyin, and Dare Oguntomisin. *The Military in Nineteenth Century Yoruba Politics*. Ile-Ife: University of Ife Press, 1984.

Falola, Toyin, and Olajumoke Yacob-Haliso, eds. *Gendering Knowledge in Africa and the African Diaspora: Contesting History and Power*. New York: Routledge, 2017.

Familusi, Olumuyiwa O. "African Culture and the Status of Women: The Yoruba Example." *Journal of Pan African Studies* 5, no. 1 (2012): 299–313.

Farrell, Cecilia. "Church Rooted in African Mixes 'Best of All Religions' into One." *Washington Post*. August 24, 1991. https://www.washingtonpost.com/archive/local/1991/08/24/church-rooted-in-africa-mixes-best-of-all-religions-into-one/94b71e0f-7219-4ff5-b8f8-3094ab059722/.

Fashion Model Directory. "Duro Olowu." *Fashion Model Directory*. Accessed April 10, 2021. https://www.fashionmodeldirectory.com/designers/duro-olowu/.

Fatima, A. "Trinidad and Tobago's Ogun Festival: A Syncretic Blend of Two Cultures." *Caribbean Quarterly* 62, no. 4 (2016): 670–687.

Fatokun, Samson Adetunji. "Christian Missions in South-Western Nigeria, and the Response of African Traditional Religion." *International Review of Mission* 96, no. 380–381 (2007): 107.

Fatunmbi, Awo Falokun. *Ela: The Ifa Concept of Altered States (The Metaphysical Foundation of Ifa)*, vol. 5. Scotts Valley, CA: CreateSpace, 2014.

———. *Inner Peace: The Yoruba Concept of Ori*. New York: Athelia Henrietta, 2005.

———. *Ori: The Ifa Concept of Consciousness (The Metaphysical Foundation of Ifa)*, vol. 4 Scotts Valley, CA: CreateSpace, 2014.

Fayemi, Ademola Kazeem. "Human Personality and the Yoruba Worldview: An Ethico-Sociological Interpretation." *Journal of Pan African Studies* 2, no. 9 (2009): 166–176.

Feeley-Harnik, Gillian. "Issues in Divine Kingship." *Annual Review of Anthropology* 14 (1985): 273–313.

Feinberg, H. M. "Reviewed Work: Benin and the Europeans 1485–1897." *African Historical Studies* 4, no. 2 (1971): 405–410.

Fela Anikulapo-Kuti, and Africa 70. *Expensive Shit* (CD Track 2: "Water No Get Enemy"). Soundworkshop Records, SWS (LP) 1001, Nigeria, 1975.

Finn, Geraldine. "The Politics of Spirituality: The Spirituality of Politics." *Feminist Theology* 11, no. 3 (2003): 333–345.

Finnegan, Ruth. *Oral Literature in Africa*. Cambridge: Open Book, 2014.

Flint, J. E. "Nigeria: The Colonial Experience from 1870 to 1914." In L. H. Gann and P. Duignan (eds.), *Colonialism in Africa 1870–1960*, Vol 5, edited by L. H. Gann and P. Duignan, 225–239. Cambridge: Cambridge University Press, 1969.

Folayan, Kola. "Egbado and the Expansion of British Power in Western Nigeria." *Genève Afrique: Acta Africana* 13, no. 2 (1974): 70–93.

Freund, Bill. *The Making of Contemporary Africa*. London: Macmillan, 1984.

Frisvold, Nicholaj De Mattos. *Ifá: A Forest of Mystery*. London: Scarlet Imprint, 2016.

Fuglestad, Finn. *Slave Traders by Invitation: West Africa's Slave Coast in the Precolonial Era*. New York: Oxford University Press, 2018.

Fukuyama, Francis. "End of History?" *The National Interest* 16 (1989): 3–18.

Furness, Hannah. "Hate Preacher Abu Qatada Can Be Deported, Home Secretary Says." *Telegraph*, April 17, 2012. https://www.telegraph.co.uk/news/uknews/defence/9209676/Hate-preacher-Abu-Qatada-can-be-deported-Home-Secretary-says.html.

Fwatshak, Sati U. "Reconstructing the Origins of the People of Plateau State: Questioning the 'We Are All Settlers' Theory." *Journal of the Historical Society of Nigeria* 16 (2005/2006): 122–140.

Fyle, Magbialy. "The Yoruba Diaspora in Sierra Leon's Krio Society." In *The Yoruba in the Atlantic World*, edited by Toyin Falola and Matt D. Childs, 369. Bloomington: Indiana University Press, 2005.

Gainous, Jason, and Kevin M. Wagner. *Tweeting to Power: The Social Media Revolution in American Politics*. New York: Oxford University Press, 2014.

Garcia-Navarro, Lulu. "Brazilian Believers of Hidden Religion Step Out of Shadows." *NPR*, September 16, 2013. https://www.npr.org/sections/parallels/2013/09/16/216890587/brazilian-believers-of-hidden-religion-step-out-of-shadows.

Garuba, Harry. "Explorations in Animist Materialism: Notes on Reading/Writing African Literature, Culture, and Society." *Public Culture* 15, no. 2 (2003): 261–285.

Gbadamosi, Gbadebo O. "The Imamate Question among Yoruba Muslims." *Journal of the Historical Society of Nigeria* IV, no. 2 (1972): 231.

Gbadamosi, Tajudeen G. O. *The Growth of Islam among Yoruba, 1841–1908*. London: Longman, 1978.

Gbadegesin, Segun. *African Philosophy: Traditional Yoruba Philosophy and Contemporary African Realities*. New York: Library of Congress, 1991.

———. "Obafemi Awolowo and the Golden Era of the Yoruba." In *Awo: On the Trail of a Titan: Essays in Celebration of the Obafemi Awolowo Centennial*, edited by David O. Oke, Olatunji Dare, Adebayo Williams, and Femi Akinola, 57–73. Ibadan: BookBuilders, 2009.

Geary, William M. N. *Nigeria under British Rule*. New York: Routledge, 2013.

George, Olakunle. "Compound of Spells: The Predicament of D. O. Fagunwa." *Research in African Literatures* 2, no. 1 (1997): 78–97.

———. "Cultural Criticism in Wole Soyinka's Death and the King's Horseman." *Representations* 67 (1999): 67–91.

Gerloff, Roswith. "Churches of the Spirit: The Pentecostal/Charismatic Movement and Africa's Contribution to the Renewal of Christianity." In *Christianity in Africa and the African Diaspora: The Appropriation of a Scattered Heritage*, edited by Afe Adogame, Roswith Gerloff, and Klaus Hock, 208–220. London: Continuum, 2008.

Gijanto, Liza. "Abolition and the Rise of the Aku: Creating Ethnicity through Colonial Policy on the Gambia River." Presented at Society for Historical Archeology, Albuquerque, available at Digital Archeological Record, 2018.

Gikandi, Halima. "Femi Kuti and Made Kuti Continue Afrobeat Legacy in Two-Part Album." *World*, April 12, 2021. https://www.pri.org/stories/2021-04-12/femi-kuti-and-made-kuti-continue-afrobeat-legacy-two-part-album.

Gonzalez-Wippler, Migene. *Powers of the Orishas: Santeria and the Worship of Saints*. New York: Original Publications, 1992.

Goody, Jack. "Writing Religion, and Revolt in Bahia." *Visible Language* 20, no. 3 (1986): 318–343.

Gotesky, Rubin. "The Nature of Myth and Society." *American Anthropologist* 54, no. 4 (1952): 523–531.

Graden, Dale T. "An Act 'Even of Public Security': Slave Resistance, Social Tensions, and the End of the International Slave Trade to Brazil, 1835–1856." *Hispanic American Historical Review* 76, no. 2 (1996): 249–251.

Grass, Randall F. "Fela Anikulapo-Kuti: The Art of an Afrobeat Rebel." *Drama Review* 30, no. 1 (1986): 134.

Gunner, Elizabeth Ann Wynne. "African Literature." *Britannica*. Accessed April 10, 2021. https://www.britannica.com/art/African-literature.

Gyekye, Kwame. *Tradition and Modernity: Philosophical Reflections on the African Experience*. New York: Oxford University Press, 1997.

Hallen, Barry. "Yoruba Moral Epistemology." In *A Companion to African Philosophy*, edited by Kwasi Wiredu, 296–303. Hoboken: Wiley-Blackwell, 2004.

Hands of the Cause Residing in the Holy Land. *The Bahá'í Faith: 1844–1963: Information Statistical and Comparative, Including the Achievements of the Ten Year International Bahá'í Teaching & Consolidation Plan 1953–1963*. Israel: n.p., 1963.

Hargreaves, John. "The Idea of a Colonial University." *African Affairs* 72, no. 286 (1973): 26–36.

Harnischfeger, Johannes. "Biafra and Secessionism in Nigeria: An Instrument of Political Bargaining." In *Secessionism in African Politics: Aspirations, Grievance, Performance, Disenchantment*, edited by Lotje de Vries, Pierre Englebert, and Mareike Schomerus, 329–359. Cham: Palgrave Macmillan, 2018.

Harris, Hermione. *Yoruba in Diaspora: An African Church in London*. New York: Palgrave Macmillan, 2006.

Harvati, Katerina, Chris Stringer, Rainer Grün, Maxime Aubert, Philip Allsworth-Jones, and Caleb Adebayo Folorunso. "The Later Stone Age Calvaria from Iwo Eleru, Nigeria: Morphology and Chronology." *PLoS ONE* 6, no. 9 (2011): e24024.

Hastings, Adrian. *The Church in Africa, 1450–1950*. Oxford: Clarendon, 1994.

Haynes, Jonathan. "New Nollywood: Kunle Afolayan." *Black Camera* 5, no. 2 (2014): 53–73.

Headrick, Daniel R. "The Tools of Imperialism: Technology and the Expansion of European Colonial Empires in the Nineteenth Century." *The Journal of Modern History* 51, no. 2 (1979): 231–263.

Hernandez-Ramdwar, C. "Religion and Tourism in Trinidad." *Social Crimonol* 2, no. 2 (2014): 110.

Herskovits, Melville. "African Gods and Catholic Saints in New World Negro Belief." *American Anthropologist* 39, no. 6 (1937): 635–643.

———. *The Myth of the Negro Past*. New York: Harper & Brothers, 1941.

———. "The Social Organization of the Afrobrazilian Candomble." *Phylon (1940–1956)* 17, no. 2 (1956): 147–147.

Hongladarom, Soraj. "Global Culture, Local Cultures and the Internet: The Thai Example." *AI & Society* 13, no. 4 (1999): 389–401.

Hopkins, Anthony G. *An Economic History of West Africa*, 2nd ed. New York: Routledge, 2020.

———. "Property Rights and Empire Building: Britain's Annexation of Lagos, 1861." *Journal of Economic History* 40, no. 4 (1980): 777–798.

Houk, James. *Spirits, Blood, and Drums: The Orisha Religion in Trinidad*. Philadelphia: Temple University Press, 1995.

Houk, James Titus, III. "The Orisha Religion in Trinidad: A Study of Culture Process and Transformation." PhD diss., Tulane University, 1992.

Hountondji, Paulin J. *African Philosophy: Myth and Reality*. Bloomington: Indiana University Press, 1996.

Hughes, Ted. "Myth and Education." *Children's Literature in Education* 1, no. 1 (1970): 55–70.

Hull, Kathleen. *Same-Sex Marriage: The Cultural Politics of Love and Law*. Cambridge: Cambridge University Press, 2006.

Hunt, Carl M. *Oyotunji Village: The Yoruba Movement in America*. Washington, DC: University Press of America, 1979.

Hunwick, John O. "The Egyptian Connection: Myth or Reality?" *History in Africa* 23 (1996): 187–198.

Ibagere, Elo. "Globalization and Nollywood: Carving a Niche on the Global Plane." *International Journal of African Society, Cultures and Traditions* 2, no. 4 (2015): 1–10.

Ibagere, Elo, and Bifatife Femi Adeseye. "Promoting the Development of Indigenous Faith Tourism in Nigeria through the Mass Media." *International Review of Humanities Studies* 2, no. 2 (2017): 130–140.

Ibidapo-Obe, Akinola. "Battle of Three Ancestors and the Jurisprudence of Black Africa." An Inaugural Lecture of the University of Lagos delivered at the JF Ade-Ajayi auditorium, University of Lagos, Akoka, 2021.

Ibiloye, Emmanuel O. "The Enduring Impact of the 1804 Fulani Jihad on Igbomina Society." *Journal of African Studies and Development* 4, no. 4 (2012): 105–106.

Ibironke, Olabode. "The Ibadan Origins of Modern African Literature: African Writers Series, Mbari Club & the Social Character of Ibadan." *History Compass* 13, no. 11 (2015): 550–559.

Ibrahim, Kola. "Sikiru Ayinde Barrister: The Unforgettable Pioneer of Fuji." Cable, Lifestyle. December 16, 2016. https://lifestyle.thecable.ng/sikiru-ayinde-barrister-fuji-legend/.

Idang, Gabriel E. "African Culture and Values." *Phronimon* 16 (2015): 97–111.

Idowu, Emmanuel Bolaji. *Olódùmarè: God in Yoruba Belief*. London: Longmans, 1962.

Idowu, Torera. "Inside Nigeria's Million Dollar Wedding Industry." CNN, December 16, 2017. https://edition.cnn.com/2017/12/15/africa/nigerian-wedding-industry/index.html.

Ifa Heritage Institute. "Welcome." *Ifa Heritage Institute*. Accessed August 15, 2022. https://ifaheritage.org/curriculum.php.

Iheanacho, Ngozi N. "Globalisation Challenges and Change Factors in the Religions of Africa: The Nigerian Experience." *International Journal of Theology and Reformed Traditions* (2012): 84.

Ikiddeh, Ime. "Literature and the Nigerian Civil War." *Presence African Editions* 98, no. 1 (1976): 163.

Ikime, Obaro. *Can Anything Good Come Out of History?* Ibadan: Bookcraft, 2018.

———. "Colonial Conquest and Resistance in Southern Nigeria." *Journal of the Historical Society of Nigeria* 6, no. 3 (1972): 251–270.

Ikuemonisan, Bababo. *The Kingdoms "Olugbo of Ugbo" and "Ooni of Ife." A Controversy of Manipulation of History or Fact from Antiquity.* Munich: Grin Verlag, 2020.

Ilana Omo Oodua Worldwide. "Ilana Omo Oodua Worldwide." *Facebook.* Accessed July 11, 2021. https://www.facebook.com/IlanaOmoOoduaTV/.

Ilechukwu, Sunday. "Ogbanje/Abiku and Cultural Conceptualizations of Psychopathology in Nigeria." *Mental Health, Religion and Culture* 10, no. 3 (2007): 239–255.

Ilesanmi, Thomas Makanjuola. "The Traditional Theologians and the Practice of Orisa Religion in Yorubaland." *Journal of Religion in Africa* 21, no. 3 (1991): 216–226.

Iliyasu, Garba, et al. "A Multi-Site Knowledge Attitude and Practice Survey of Ebola Virus Disease in Nigeria." *PLoS ONE* 10 (2015): 136–148.

Imbua, David, Otoabasi Akpan, and Ikechuckwu Amadi, eds. *History, Culture, Diasporas and Nation Building: The Collected Works of Okon Edet Uya.* Bethesda, MD: Arbi Press, 2012.

Inyang, Anietie A., and Manasseh E. Bassey. "Imperial Treaties and the Origins of British Colonial Rule in Southern Nigeria, 1860–1890." *Mediterranean Journal of Social Sciences* 5, no. 20 (2014): 19–46.

Irele, Abiola. "Tradition and the Yoruba Writer: D. O. Fagunwa, Amos Tutuola and Wole Soyinka." *Odu* 11 (1975): 75–100.

Isah, Murtala Bindawa, et al. "Coronavirus Disease 2019 (COVID-19): Knowledge, Attitudes, Practices (KAP) and Misconceptions in the General Population of Katsina State, Nigeria." *UMYU Journal of Microbiology Research (UJMR)* 6, no. 1 (2021): 24–37.

Iyer, Lakshmi. "Direct versus Indirect Colonial Rule in India: Long-Term Consequences." *Review of Economics and Statistics* 92, no. 4 (2020): 693–713.

Izsadore, Sandra, and Segun Oyekunle. *Fela and Me.* Ibadan: Kraft, 2019.

Jaggi, Maya. "Ousting Monsters," *Guardian,* November 2, 2002. https://www.theguardian.com/books/2002/nov/02/theatre.artsfeatures.

Jaja, Jones M. "Myths in African Concept of Historical Reality." *International Journal of Educational Administration and Policy Studies* 6, no. 2 (2013): 9–14.

Janzen, J. M. "The Islamic Impact on Afro-Cuban Religion." *Latin American Research Review* 27, no. 2 (1992): 55–72.

Jedlowski, Alessandro. "Minor Cinema and Conviviality: Tunde Kelani's Film Worlds in Comparison." *Journal of African Cultural Studies* 32, no. 4 (2020): 367–381.

Jegede, Ayodele Samuel. "The Yoruba Cultural Construction of Health and Illness." *Nordic Journal of African Studies* 11, no. 3 (2002): 322–335.

Jenkins, Richard. *Social Identity* (4th ed.). London: Routledge, 2014.

Jikeli, Gunther. "Discrimination of European Moslems: Self-Perceptions, Experiences and Discourses of Victimhood." In *Minority Groups: Coercion, Discrimination, Exclusion, Deviance and the Quest for Equality,* edited by Dan Soen, Mally Shechory, and Sarah Ben-David, 77–96. New York: Nova Science, 2012.

Jimada, Idris Sha'aba. *The Historical Background to the Establishment of Patigi Emirate: C. 1810–1898.* Pategi: Amedu Bello University Press, 2016.

———. *The Nupe and the Origins and Evolution of Yoruba c. 1275–1897.* Zaria: Abdullahi Smith Centre for Historical Research, 2005.

Jimoh, Mufutau O. "The Growth and Development of Islam in Epe, Lagos State, Nigeria, 1851–2010." *Ilorin Journal of Religious Studies (IJOURELS)* 6, no. 2 (2016): 1–18.

Johnson, Paul. *History of Christianity.* New York: Touchstone, 2012.

Johnson, Peter. "The Geographies of Heterotopia." *Geography Compass* 7, no. 11 (2013): 790–803.

Johnson, Samuel. *The History of the Yorubas: From the Earliest Times to the Beginning of the British Protectorate.* Lagos: CSS Bookshops, 2009.

Julian, George. "What Are the Most Spoken Languages in the World?" Fluent in 3 Months. Accessed April 2, 2023. https://www.fluentin3months.com/most-spoken-languages/.

Julius, Adekunle O. "Borgu and Economic Transformation 1700–1900: The Wangara Factor." *African Economic History* 22 (1994): 1–18.

Kabir, Adejumo. "Igangan Attack: Police Confirm 11 People Killed in Oyo Community." *Premium Times,* June 7, 2021. https://www.premiumtimesng.com/news/headlines/466053-igangan -attack-police-confirm-11-people-killed-in-oyo-community.html?tztc=1.

Kajiru, Ines, and Isaack Nyimbi. "The Impact of Myths, Superstition and Harmful Cultural Beliefs against Albinism in Tanzania: A Human Rights Perspective." *Potchefstroom Electronic Law Journal (PELJ)* 23, no. 1 (2020): 1–27.

Kane, Ousmane. *Beyond Timbuktu: An Intellectual History of Muslim West Africa.* Cambridge, MA: Harvard University Press, 2006.

Kanu, Ikechukwu Anthony. "The Hellenization of African Traditional Deities: The Case of Ekwensu and Esu." *AQUINO Journal of Philosophy* 1, no. 3 (2021): 1–9.

———. "Migration, Globalization and the Liquidity of African Traditional Religion." *Journal of African Studies and Sustainable Development* 2, no. 6 (2019): 45–56.

Kaoje, AminuU, et al. (2016). "Awareness, Knowledge, and Misconceptions of Ebola Virus Disease among Residents of a Rural Community in Sokoto, Northwest Nigeria." *Annals of Tropical Medicine and Public Health* 9, no. 2 (2016): 105–111.

Kemi, Megbowon Funmilola, and Uwah Chijioke. "Aesthetics of Yoruba Culture in Soyinka's Death and the King's Horseman." *Studies of Tribes and Tribals* 15, no. 1 (2017): 30–38.

Kennedy, Jean. "I Saw and I Was Happy: Festival at Oshogbo." *African Arts* 1, no. 2 (1968): 8–16.

Ki-Zerbo, Joseph. *General History of Africa I: Methodology and African Prehistory*, abr. ed. Paris: UNESCO, 1990.

Klein, Debra. "Allow Peace to Reign: Musical Genres of *Fújì* and *Islamic* Allegorize Nigerian Unity in the Era of Boko Haram." *Yearbook for Traditional Music* 52 (2020): 1–22.

———. "Fújì: Indigenous and Islamic Popular Music Fusions in Nigeria." In *Bloomsbury Encyclopedia of Popular Music of the World*, vol. 12, edited by Heidi Carolyn Feldman, David Horn, John Shepherd, and Gabrielle Kielich, 145–149. New York: Bloomsbury Academic, 2019.

———. *Yorùbá* Bàtá Goes Global: Artists, Culture Brokers, and Fans. Chicago: University of Chicago Press, 2007.

Knibbe, Kim. "Nigerian Missionaries in Europe: History Repeating Itself or a Meeting of Modernities?" *Journal of Religion in Europe* 4, no. 3 (2011): 479.

Knysh, Alexander. *Sufism: A New History of Islamic Mysticism.* Princeton, NJ: Princeton University Press, 2017.

Koike, Ikuko. "How Orisa Worship (Re)constructs the Black Relationships: Cultural Interactions among African Americans and Nigerian Yoruba (in Japanese)." *Zinbun* 97 (2007): 77–104.

Kollock, Peter, and Marc A. Smith. *Communities in Cyberspace.* London: Routledge, 1999.

Kolo, Bilal Rabiu, and Mustafa Yağbasan. "Popular Culture in Nigeria: The Case Study of Nigerian Music Industry." *Kastamonu Şletiıim Araıtİrmalarİ Dergisi* 5 (2020): 124–139.

Kopytoff, Jean Herskovits. *A Preface to Modern Nigeria: The Sierra Leonians in Yoruba 1830–1890.* Madison: University of Wisconsin Press, 1965.

Kumari, Ayele. *Isese Spirituality Workbook: The Ancestral Wisdom of Ifa Orisa Tradition.* Independently Published, 2020.

———. *Iyanifa Woman of Wisdom: Insights from the Priestesses of the Ifa-Orisa Tradition, Their Personal Journey, and Plight for the Divine Feminism.* Scotts Valley, CA: CreateSpace, 2014.

Kuntz, Anabel, Eldad Davidov, Shalom H. Schwartz, and Peter Schmidt. "Human Values, Legal Regulation, and Approval of Homosexuality in Europe: A Cross-Country Comparison." *European Journal of Social Psychology* 45, no. 1 (2015): 120–134.

Kuponu, Selome I. "Success and Empowerment in Living Faith Church Worldwide, Nigeria." Paper Presented at the Postgraduate Colloquium, Department of History of Religions, University of Bayreuth, Germany, February 2, 2006.

Lambton, A. K. S. *The Breakdown of Society: The Central Islamic Lands from Pre-Islamic Times to the First World War.* Cambridge: Cambridge University Press, 1970.

Lange, Dierk. "Origin of the Yoruba and 'The Lost Tribes of Israel.'" *Anthropos* 106 (2011): 579–595.

Lasisi, Rashid O. "Muslim Traditional Rulers in Nigeria: The Alaafin of Oyo during the Last Phase of British Colonialism, 1945–1960." *Journal of Muslim Minority Affairs* 17, no. 1 (1997): 31–41.

Lateef, Misbau A., and Kehinde Adegbite. "Bigamy and Dearth of Prosecution in Nigeria." *OAU Journal of Public Law* (2017): 91–118.

Latour, Bruno. *We Have Never Been Modern.* Cambridge, MA: Harvard University Press, 1991.

Law, R. C. C. "The Constitutional Troubles of Ọyọ in the Eighteenth Century." University of Lagos, School of African and Asian Studies Seminar Papers, October 31, 1968.

Law, Robin. "The Career of Adele at Lagos and Badagry." *Journal of the Historical Society of Nigeria* 3, no. 2 (1978): 59.

———. *Contemporary Source Material for the History of the Old Oyo Empire, 1627–1824.* Toronto: York/UNESCO Nigerian Hinterland Project York University, 2001.

———. "Dahomey and the Slave Trade: Reflections on the Historiography of the Rise of Dahomey." *Journal of African History* 27, no. 2 (1986): 237–267.

———. "A Lagoonside Port on the Eighteenth-Century Slave Coast: The Early History of Badagri." *Canadian Journal of African Studies* 28, no. 1 (1994): 32–59.

———. *The Oyo Empire c. 1600–c. 1836: A West African Imperialism in the Era of the Atlantic Slave Trade.* London: Oxford University Press, 1977.

———. "Trade and Politics behind the Slave Coast: The Lagoon Traffic and the Rise of Lagos, 1500–1800." *Journal of African History* 24, no. 3 (1983): 321–348.

———. "A West African Cavalry State: The Kingdom of Oyo." *Journal of African History* 16 (1975): 1–15.

Lawal, Adebayo A. *Nigeria Culture, Politics, Governance and Development.* Ibadan: Connel, 2015.

Lawal, Babatunde. "Divinity, Creativity and Humanity in Yorùbá Aesthetics." *Literature & Aesthetics* 15, no. 1 (2005): 161–174.

———. "From Africa to the Americas: Art in the Yoruba Religion." In *Santeria Aesthetics in Contemporary Latin American Art,* edited by Arturo Lindsay. Washington, DC: Smithsonian Institution, 1996, 28.

Lawal, Iyabo. "Nigerian Schools in the Throes of Hijab Crisis." *Guardian,* February 14, 2019. https://guardian.ng/features/nigerian-schools-in-the-throes-of-hijab-crisis/.

Lawal, Musediq O. "Indigenous Knowledge and Practices in the Management of Sickle Cell Anaemia among the Yorùbá in Osun State, Nigeria." *Etnoantropološki Problemi / Issues in Ethnology and Anthropology* 14, no. 2 (2019): 531–556.

Lawal, Najeem A. "Positions of the Chiefs." In *Nigeria Since Independence: The First 25 Years, Vol I,* edited by Yusufu Bala Usman, 69–87. Ibadan: Heinemann, 1989.

Lawal, Olakunle A. "From Colonial Reforms to Decolonization: Britain and the Transfer of Power in Nigeria, 1947–1960." *Journal of the Historical Society of Nigeria* 19 (2010): 39–62.

———. "Islam and Colonial Rule in Lagos." *American Journal of Islam and Society* 12, no. 1 (1995): 66–80.

Lawal, Olakunle A., and Oluwasegun M. Jimoh. "Missiles from 'Kirsten Hall': Herbert Macaulay versus Hugh Clifford, 1922–1931." *Lagos Historical Review* 12 (2012): 41–62.

Lawrance, Benjamin N., Emily Lynn Osborn, and Richard L. Roberts, eds. *Intermediaries, Interpreters, and Clerks: African Employees in the Making of Colonial Africa.* Madison: University of Wisconsin Press, 2006.

Lawuyi, Olatunde B. "Mythical Images, Historical Thought, and Ondo Religion: The Oramfe Myth as Clue to Ondo-Yoruba Identity." *Africa: Rivista trimestrale di studi e documentazione dell'Istituto italiano perl'Africa e l'Oriente* 45, no. 1 (1990): 55–71.

———. "The Obatala Factor in Yoruba History." *History in Africa* 19 (1992): 369–375.

Le Chatelier, Alfred. *L'Islam dans l'Afrique Occidentale*. Paris: G. Steinheil, 1899.

Legum, Colin. "Pan-Africanism, the Communists and the West." *African Affairs* 63, no. 252 (1964): 186–196.

Levine, Martin P., and Richard R. Troiden. "The Myth of Sexual Compulsivity." *The Journal of Sex Research* 25, no. 3 (1988): 347–363.

Levtzion, Nehemia, and Randall L. Pouwels, eds. *The History of Islam in Africa*. Athens: Ohio University Press, 2000.

Lijadu, Emmanuel M. *Orunmila!* (reprinted). Ekiti: Omolayo Standard, 1972.

Lindfors, Bernth. "Amos Tutuola and D. O. Fagunwa." *Journal of Commonwealth Literature* 5, no. 1 (1970): 57–65.

———. "Beating the White Man at His Own Game: Nigerian Reactions to the 1986 Nobel Prize in Literature." *Black American Literature Forum* 22, no. 3 (1988): 475–488.

———. *Early Nigerian Literature*. New York: Africana, 1982.

———. "Form, Theme, and Style in the Narratives of D. O. Fagunwa." *International Fiction Review* 6, no. 1 (1979): 11–15.

Lindhardt, Martin. *Pentecostalism in Africa: Presence and Impact of Pneumatic Christianity in Postcolonial Societies*. Leiden: Brill, 2014.

Lindsay, Lisa A. "The Transatlantic Journey of South Carolina Freedman James Churchwill Vaughan." *Black Perspectives*. February 26, 2017. https://www.aaihs.org/author/lalindsa/.

Living Faith Church Worldwide International. "The Mandate." *Living Faith Church Worldwide International*, August 11, 2021. https://faithtabernacle.org.ng/about.

Liyong, Taban Lo. "Tutuola, Son of Zinjanthropus." In *Critical Perspectives on Amos Tutuola*, edited by Bernth Lindfors. Washington, DC: Three Continent, 2019.

Lloyd, Peter C. "The Traditional Political System of the Yorùbá." *Journal of Anthropological Research* 10, no. 4 (1954): 366–384.

———. "The Yorùbá Lineage." *Africa: Journal of the International African Institute* 25, no. 3 (1955): 235–251.

Lovejoy, Henry B. *Prieto: Yoruba Kingship in Colonial Cuba during the Age of Revolutions*. Chapel Hill: University of North Carolina Press, 2019.

Lovejoy, Henry B., and Olatunji Ojo. "Lucumí, 'Terranova,' and the Origins of the Yoruba Nation." *Journal of African History* 56, no. 3 (2015): 353–372.

Lovejoy, Paul. "Background to Rebellion: The Origins of Muslims Slaves in Bahia." *Slavery and Abolition* 15, no. 2 (1994): 151–180.

———. "The Yoruba Factor in the Trans-Atlantic Slave Trade." In *The Yoruba Diaspora in the Atlantic World*, edited by Toyin Falola and Matt D. Childs, 40–55. Bloomington: Indiana University Press, 2004.

Lysonski, Steven, and Srinivas Durvasula. "Nigeria in Transition: Acculturation to Global Consumer Culture." *Journal of Consumer Marketing* 30, no. 6 (2013): 493–508.

Mabogunje, Akin. *Urbanization in Nigeria*. London: University of London Press, 1968.

Mahmud, Memunat O. "A Study of the Yoruba Traditional Marriage as a Rite of Passage." *International Journal of African Society, Cultures and Traditions* 10, no. 1 (2021): 40–52.

Majasan, James A. "Folklore as an Instrument of Education among the Yoruba." *Folklore* 80, no. 1 (1969): 41–59.

Makar, Tesemchi. *The History of Political Change among the Tiv in the 19th and 20th Centuries*. Enugu: Fourth Dimension, 1994.

Makinde, M. A. *African Philosophy: The Demise of a Controversy*. Ile-Ife: Obafemi Awolowo University Press, 2010.

Mamdani, Mahmood. "Indirect Rule, Civil Society, and Ethnicity: The African Dilemma." *Social Justice* 23, no. 1/2 (1996): 145–150.

Manchuelle, Francois. "Slavery, Emancipation and Labour Migration in West Africa: The Case of the Sonike." *Journal of African History* 30, no. 1 (1989): 100.

Mann, Kristin. *Slavery and the Birth of an African City: Lagos, 1760–1900.* Bloomington: Indiana University Press, 1997.

Manuel, Peter, Kenneth Bilby, and Michael Largey. *Caribbean Currents: Caribbean Music from Rumba to Reggae.* Philadelphia: Temple University Press, 2012.

Markovitz, Irving. *African Politics and Society: Basic Issues and Problems of Government and Development.* New York: Free Press, 1970.

Marshall, David, Glenn D'Cruz, Sharyn McDonald, and Katja Lee, eds. *Contemporary Publics: Shifting Boundaries in New Media, Technology and Culture.* London: Palgrave Macmillan, 2016.

Marshall, Ruth. "Power in the Name of Jesus." *Review of African Political Economy* 18, no. 52 (1991): 21–47.

Marta, Moreno Vega. "The Yoruba Orisha Tradition Comes to New York City." *African American Review* 29, no. 2 (1995): 201–206.

Mason, Michael. "The Jihad in the South: An Outline of the Nineteenth Century Nupe Hegemony in North-Eastern Yorubaland and Afenmai." *Journal of the Historical Society of Nigeria* 5, no. 2 (1970): 193–209.

Masters, William H., Virginia E. Johnson, Svensk översättning, and Hans-Olof Lisper. "Homosexuality in Perspective." *Cognitive Behaviour Therapy* 11, no. 1 (1982): 54–56.

Matory, J. Lorand. *The Fetish Revisited: Marx, Freud, and the Gods Black People Make.* Durham, NC: Duke University Press, 2018.

———. "How to Read African-American Syncretistic Religion." In *African-American Religion: Interpretive Essays in History and Culture,* edited by Timothy Earl Fulop and Albert J. Raboteau, 113–133. New York: Routledge, 1997.

———. "Rival Empires: Islam and the Religions of Spirit Possession among the Òyóo-Yorùbá." *American Ethnologist* 21, no. 3 (1994): 495.

Matos, Carolina. "Globalization and the Mass Media." In *The Wiley-Blackwell Encyclopedia of Globalization.* Oxford: Wiley-Blackwell, 2012.

Mawar, Nita, Seema Saha, Apoorvaa Pandit, and Uma Mahajan. "The Third Phase of HIV Pandemic: Social Consequences of HIV/AIDS Stigma and Discrimination and Future Needs." *Indian Journal of Medical Research* 122, no. 6 (2005): 471–484.

Mazrui, Ali A. *The Africans: A Triple Heritage.* A Commentary. Washington, DC: WETA, 1986.

———. *Resurgent Islam and the Politics of Identity.* London: Cambridge Scholars, 2014.

Mbaeyi, Paul Mmegha. *British Military and Naval Forces in West African History, 1807–1874.* New York: Nok Publishers, 1978.

Mbah, Peter, and Chikodiri Mwangu. "Sub-Ethnic Conflicts in Nigeria: The Policy Option for the Resolution of the Conflict between Ezza and Ezillo in Ebonyi State." *Mediterranean Journal of Social Sciences* 5, no. 2 (2014): 681–688.

Mbanga, John. "Utilization of Community-Based Association for Alleviating Poverty in Kope-Ope, Iwo, Osun State: A Communication Infrastructure Perspective." *Ibadan Journal of Humanistic Studies* 26, no. 1 (2016): 255–266.

M'Baye, Babacar. "The Economic, Political, and Social Impact of the Atlantic Slave Trade on Africa." *The European Legacy* 11, no. 6 (2006): 607–622.

Mbembe, Achilles. "Afropolitanism." In *Africa Remix: Contemporary Art of a Continent,* edited by S. Njami and L. Durán, 26–30. Johannesburg: Johannesburg Art Gallery, 2007.

Mbembe, Achille, and Sarah Balakrishnan. "Pan-African Legacies, Afropolitan Futures." *Transition* 120 (2016): 28–37.

Mccray, Kenja. "Oyotunji Village [The Village] (1970)." *Black Past.* Accessed October 11, 2021. http://www.blackpast.org/African-american-history/oyotunji-african-village-1970.

McGibney, Sean. "What Are the Most Studied Languages in the World?" *Newsdle,* July 21, 2022. https://www.newsdle.com/blog/most-studied-foreign-languages.

McKay, Ryan, and Harvey Whitehouse. "Religion and Morality." *Psychological Bulletin* 141, no. 2 (2015): 447.

McMillan, Dawn Downing. "Santeria: Syncretism and Salvation in the New World." *Perspectives in History* 20 (2004–2005): 41.

Medine, Carolyn M. Jones, Gbola Aderibigbe, and Ibigbolade S. Aderibigbe, eds. *Contemporary Perspectives on Religions in Africa and the African Diaspora.* London: Palgrave Macmillan, 2015, 16.

Menkiti, Ifeanyi. "Community, Communism, Communitarianism: An African Intervention." In *The Palgrave Handbook of African Philosophy,* edited by Adeshina Afolayan and Toyin Falola, 461–473. New York: Palgrave Macmillan, 2017.

Mepayeida, Solomon, and Timothy Popoola. "The Roles of Indigenous Missionaries and Christians in the Expansion of Christianity in Nigeria, 1860–1969." *Verbum et Ecclesia* 40, no. 1 (2019): 1–7.

Mignolo, Walter D. "Cosmopolitanism and the De-colonial Option." *Studies in Philosophy and Education* 29 (2010): 111–127.

Miller, Jade. "Global Nollywood: The Nigerian Movie Industry and Alternative Global Networks in Production and Distribution." *Global Media and Communication* 8, no. 2 (2012): 117–133.

Mitchell, Stephen. *A History of the Later Roman Empire, AD 284–641.* Malden: Wiley Blackwell, 2015.

Mohammed, Ahmed M. *European Trade, Imperialism and Under Development in Northern Nigeria: 19th and 20th Centuries.* Zaria: Ahmadu Bello University Press Limited, 2016.

Morton-Williams, Peter. "The Oyo and the Atlantic Trade 1670–1830." *Journal of the Historical Society of Nigeria* 3, no. 1 (1964): 25–45.

Morton-Williams, Peter, William Bascom, and E. M. McClelland. "Two Studies of *Ifa* Divination." *Africa* 36, no. 4 (1966): 406–431.

Mudimbe, V. Y. *The Idea of Africa.* Bloomington: Indiana University Press, 1994.

Muhammed, Hawakulu. "Wizkid Receives Grammy Plaque." *Daily Trust,* June 23, 2021. https://dailytrust.com/wizkid-receives-grammy-plaque/.

Mukhtar, Muhammad Jamal Al-Din, and Unesco International Scientific Committee for the Drafting of a General History of Africa. *Ancient Civilizations of Africa (General History of Africa).* Berkeley: University of California Press, 1981.

Mulligan, Michael. "Nigeria, the British Presence in West Africa and International Law in the 19th Century." *Journal of the History of International Law* 11, no. 2 (2009): 273–301.

Murphy, Joseph, and Mei-Mei Sanford, eds. *Osun across the Waters: A Yoruba Goddess in Africa and the Americas.* Indianapolis: Indiana University Press, 2001.

Murphy, Joseph M. "Òrìṣà Traditions and the Internet Diaspora." In *Òrìṣà Devotion as World Religion: The Globalization of Yoruba Religious Culture,* edited by Jacob Olupona and Terry Rey, 470–484. Madison: University of Wisconsin Press, 2008.

———. *Santería: African Spirits in America.* Boston: Beacon Press, 1993.

Murray, M. O. "Migration in the 20th Century: A Historical Perspective." In *The Palgrave Handbook of African Colonial and Postcolonial History,* edited by Martin S. Shanguhyia and Toyin Falola, 47–63. London: Palgrave Macmillan, 2018.

Musa, Afiz Oladimeji, and Hassan Ahmad Ibrahim. "Islamization and the Representation of Islam in Yorubaland of Southwestern Nigeria: An Exploratory Study with Special Reference to Jalabi Phenomenon." *Journal of Islam in Asia* 12, no. 2 (2015): 210–215.

Nachbar, Jack, and Kevin Lause, eds. *Popular Culture: An Introductory Text.* Madison: University of Wisconsin Press, 1992.

Nantambu, Kwame. "Pan-Africanism versus Pan-African Nationalism: An Afrocentric Analysis." *Journal of Black Studies* 28, no. 5 (1998): 561–574.

Naylor, Robin. "A Social Custom Model of Collective Action." *European Journal of Political Economy* 6 (1990): 201–216.

Neeley, Bobby Joe. *Contemporary Afro-American Voodooism (Black Religion): The Retention and Adaptation of the Ancient African-Egyptian Mystery System*. Berkeley: University of California Press, 1988.

Nehl, Markus. *Transnational Black Dialogues: Re-Imagining Slavery in the Twenty-First Century*. Bielefeld: Transcript, 2016.

Neimark, Philip. *The Way of Orisa: Empowering Your Life through the Ancient African Religion of Ifa*. San Francisco: Harper Collins, 1993.

Ney, Stephen. "Samuel Ajayi Crowther and the Age of Literature." *Research in African Literatures* 46, no. 1 (2015): 37–52.

Nkrumah, Kwame. *I Speak of Freedom: A Statement of African Ideology*. London: Heinemann, 1961.

Nnadi, Chioma. "The Nigerian Designer Has Naomi Campbell and Imaan Hammam Rocking His Mesmerizing Handwoven Suiting." *Vogue*. Accessed April 15, 2021. https://www.vogue.com/vogueworld/slideshow/kenneth-ize-nigeria-fashion-naomi-campbell-imaan-hammam.

Noel, James. *Black Religion and the Imagination of Matter in the Atlantic World*. New York: Palgrave Macmillan, 2009.

Nolte, Insa. *Obafemi Awolowo and the Making of Remo: The Local Politics of a Nigerian Nationalist*. Edinburgh: Edinburgh University Press for the International African Institute, 2009.

Nolte, Insa M., Clyde Ancarno, and Rebecca Jones. "Inter-religious Relations in Yorubaland, Nigeria: Corpus Methods and Anthropological Survey Data." *Corpora* 13, no. 1 (2018): 27–64.

Nolte, Insa, Rebecca Jones, Khadijeh Taiyari, and Giovanni Occhiali. "Research Note: Exploring Survey Data for Historical and Anthropological Research: Muslim–Christian Relations in South-West Nigeria." *African Affairs* 115, no. 460 (2016): 541–561.

Nolte, Insa, Olukoya Ogen, and Rebecca Jones, eds. *Beyond Religious Tolerance: Muslim, Christian & Traditionalist Encounters in an African Town*. Woodbridge: James Currey, 2017.

Norton, John. D. "Science and Certainty." *Synthese* 99 (1994): 3–22.

Ntombana, Luvuyo. "The Trajectories of Christianity and African Ritual Practices: The Public Silence and the Dilemma of Mainline or Mission Churches." *Acta Theologica* 35, no. 2 (2015): 104–119.

Nwosu, Nereus I. "Religion and the Crisis of National Unity in Nigeria." *African Study Monographs* 7, no. 3 (1996): 141–152.

Nyerere, Julius K. "Speech to Congress." *Black Scholar* 4, no. 10 (1974): 16–20.

Obasanjo, Olusegun. *My Watch: Early Life and Military*. Lagos: Prestige, 2014.

Obateru, Oluremi. *The Yoruba in History: 11th Century to the Present*. Ibadan: Penthouse, 2003.

Obayemi, Ade M. "Ancient Ile-Ife: Another Cultural Historical Reinterpretation." *Journal of the Historical Society of Nigeria* 9, no. 4 (1979): 152.

———. "Between NOK, Ile-Ife and Benin: Progress Report and Prospects." *Journal of the Historical Society of Nigeria* 10, no. 3 (1980): 82.

———. "The Phenomenon of Oduduwa in Ife History." In *The Cradle of a Race: Ife from the Beginning to 1980*, edited by Isaac A. Akinjogbin, 70–71. Port Harcourt: Sunray, 1978.

———. "The Sokoto Jihad and the 'O-Kun' Yoruba: A Review." *Journal of the Historical Society of Nigeria* 9, no. 2 (1978): 64.

Obichere, Boniface I. "A Contribution to the Study of West African Oracles." Dar Es Salaam—U.C.L.A. Conference on the History of African Religions, University College, Dar Es Salaam, June 1970.

Ocheja, Daniel H. *The Rise and Fall of the Nigerian First Republic: History of Nigeria from Lord Lugard to Gen. Aguiyi-Ironsi (1900–1966)*. Lokoja: Ogun De-Reuben, 2001.

Ochonu, Moses. "Colonialism within Colonialism: The Hausa-Caliphate Imaginary and the British Colonial Administration of the Nigerian Middle Belt." *African Studies Quarterly* 10, nos. 2–3 (2008): 95–127.

O'Connor, Kathleen, and Toyin Falola. "Religious Entrepreneurship and the Informal Economic Sector. 'Orisa' Worship as 'Service Provider' in Nigeria and the United States." *Paideuma* 45 (1999): 115–135.

Odejobi, Cecilia Omobola. "Influence of Yoruba Culture in Christian Religious Worship." *International Journal of Social Science and Education* 4, no. 2 (2014): 584–595.

Oderinde, Olatunde Abosede. "The Lore of Religious Festivals among the Yoruba and Its Social Relevance." *Lumina* 22, no. 2 (2011): 1–12.

Odey, Mike O., John G. Nengel, and Okpeh O. Okpeh. *History Research and Methodology in Africa: Essays in Honor of Professor Charles Creswell Jacobs.* Makurdi: Aboki, 2007.

Odubajo, Adetola Festus, and Bamidele Omotunde Alabi. "The Elite Factor in Nigeria's Political-Power Dynamics." *Journal of Studies in Social Sciences* 8 (2014): 121–139.

Oduguwa, Adedara S. *Chief Obafemi Awolowo: The Political Moses.* Bristol: Trafford, 2012.

Oduyoye, Modupe. *The Vocabulary of Yoruba Religious Discourse.* Ibadan: Sefer, 2008.

Ogen, Olukoya. "Exploring the Potential of Praise Poems for Historical Reconstruction among the Idepe-Ikale in Southeastern Yorubaland." *History in Africa* 39 (2012): 77–96.

Ogot, B. A, ed. *General History of Africa V: Africa from the Sixteenth to the Eighteenth Century.* Paris: UNESCO, 2000.

Ogunbado, Ahamad F. "Islam and Its Impacts in Yorubaland." *Islamic Quarterly* 57, no. 1 (2003): 1–18.

Ogunbile, David Olugbenga. "Comparative Study of Revelation in Aladura Christianity and in Yoruba Religious Tradition in Ile-Ife." Master's Thesis, Obafemi Awolowo University, 1990.

Ogundayo, Biodun J. "Diaspora: Yoruba in Africa." In *Encyclopedia of the Yoruba*, edited by Toyin Falola and Akintunde Akinyemi, 92. Bloomington: Indiana University Press, 2016.

Ògúndèjí, Philip A. "The Communicative and Semiotic Contexts of àrokò among the Yoruba Symbol-Communication Systems." *African Languages and Cultures* 10, no. 2 (1997): 145–156.

———. "The Image of Ṣàngó in Duro Ladipọ's Plays." *Research in African Literatures* 29, no. 2 (1998): 57–58.

Ogundipe, Molara. "The Palm Wine Drinkard: A Reassessment of Amos Tutuola." *Présence Africaine* 71 (1969): 99–108.

Ogundiran, Akinwumi. "Filling a Gap in the Ife-Benin Interaction Field (Thirteenth–Sixteenth Centuries AD): Excavations in Iloyin Settlement, Ijesaland." *African Archaeological Review* 19, no. 1 (2002): 27–60.

———. "Yoruba History and Migration." *Oxford Research Encyclopedia of African History* (2018).

———. *The Yorùbá: A New History.* Bloomington: Indiana University Press, 2020.

Ogundiran, Akinwunmi, and O. Akinlolu Ige. "'Our Ancestors Were Material Scientists': Archaeological and Geochemical Evidence for Indigenous Yoruba Glass Technology." *Journal of Black Studies* 46, no. 8 (2015): 751–772.

Ogunnaike, Ayodeji. "Bilad al-Brazil: The Importance of West African Scholars in Brazilian Islamic Education and Practice in Historic and Contemporary Perspective." *Religions* 12, no. 131 (2021): 1–21.

Ogunnaike, Oludamini. "Sufism and Ifa: Ways of Knowing in Two West African Intellectual Traditions." PhD diss., Harvard University, 2015.

Oguntola-Laguda, Danoye. *Divinities in West African Religion.* Lagos: Intes Training & Educational Services, 2007.

———. "'Pentecostalism' and African Religious Movements in the 21st Century: A Case Study of Indigenous Faith of Africa, Ijo Orunmila." *Journal of Oriental and African Studies* 19 (2010): 191–205.

Oguntomisin, Dare. "The Impact of the Ijebu Expedition of 1892 on the Politics in Epe, 1892–1925." *African Notes* 19, no. 1–2 (1995): 1–12.

Ogunyemi, Kemi, Omowumi Ogunyemi, and Amaka Anozie. "Indigenous African Wisdom and Its Orientation to the Common Good: Responsible Leadership and Principled Entrepreneurship." In *Responsible Management in Africa, Volume 1: Traditions of Principled Entrepreneurship*, edited by Kemi Ogunyemi, Omowumi Ogunyemi, and Amaka Anozie, 1–12. Lagos: Emerald, 2022.

Ogunyemi, Olatunji. "The Appeal of African Broadcast Web Sites to African Diasporas: A Case Study of the United Kingdom." *Journal of Black Studies* 36, no. 3 (2006): 334–352.

Oha, Obododimma. "Yoruba Christian Video Narrative and Indigenous Imaginations." *Cahiers D'etudes Africaines* 42, no. 165 (2002): 121–142.

O'Hear, Ann. "The History of the Okun Yoruba: Research Directions." In *Yoruba Identity and Power Politics*, edited by Toyin Falola and Ann Genova, 111–126. Rochester, NY: Rochester University Press, 2006.

O'Hear, Ann, ed. *Letters from Nigeria, 1899–1900: David Wynford Carnegie*. Madison: University of Wisconsin–Madison African Studies Program, 1992.

Oikelome, Albert. "Stylistic Analysis of Afrobeat Music of Fela Anikulapo Kuti." PhD diss., University of Ibadan, 2008, 13.

Ojaide, Tanure. "Indigenous Knowledge and Its Expression in the Folklore of Africa and the African Diaspora." In *Expressions of Indigenous and Local Knowledge in Africa and Its Diaspora*, edited by Karim Traore, Mobolanle Sotunsa, and Akinloye Ojo, 11–28. Newcastle upon Tyne: Cambridge Scholars, 2016.

Ojo, Gabriel J. A. *Yoruba Palaces: A Study of Afins of Yorubaland*. London: University of London Press, 1966.

Ojo, Olatunji. "The Atlantic Slave Trade and Local Ethics of Slavery in Yorubaland." *African Economic History* 41 (2013): 73–100.

———. "'Heepa' (Hail) Òrìṣà: The Òrìṣà Factor in the Birth of Yoruba Identity." *Journal of Religion in Africa* 39 (2009): 30–59.

———. "The Organization of the Atlantic Slave Trade in Yorubaland, Ca. 1777 to Ca.1856." *International Journal of African Historical Studies* 41, no. 1 (2008): 80.

———. "Slavery and Human Sacrifice in Yorubaland: Ondo, c. 1870–94." *Journal of African History* 46, no. 3 (2005): 379–404.

———. "The Slave Ship Manuelita and the Story of a Yoruba Community, 1833–1834." *Tempo* 23, no. 2 (2017): 360–382.

Ojo, Sanya. "Entrepreneurship in Islamic Practices: A Case Study." *SAGE Business Cases* 8, no. 2 (2019): 270–273.

Ojuade, J. Sina. "The Issue of *Oduduwa* in Yoruba Genesis: The Myths and Realities." *Transafrican Journal of History* 21 (1992): 139–158.

Okediji, Moyo. "Art of Yoruba." *Art Institute of Chicago Museum Studies* 23, no. 2 (1997): 175.

Okeke-Agulu, Chika. "From Mbari Mbayo to Iwalewahaus Conference, Bayreuth—Photos." *Chika Okeke Blog*, October 20, 2013. http://chikaokekeagulu.blogspot.com/2013/10/from-mbari-mbayo-to-iwalewahaus.html.

Okigbo, Charles. "Nigerian High School Students Evaluate Journalism Careers." *Journalism Quarterly* 61, no. 4 (1984): 907–909.

Okonkwo, Rina. "The Nigeria Civil Service Union, 1919–1922." *The International Journal of African Historical Studies* 26, no. 3 (1993): 609–622.

Okpevra, U. B. "The Dynamics of Intergroup Relations in Pre-Colonial Nigeria up to 1800: A Reappraisal of a Lopsided Historiography." *Lwati: Journal of Contemporary Research* 11, no. 1 (2014): 126–143.

Okunoye, Oyeniyi. "Captives of Empire: Early Ibadan Poets and Poetry." *Journal of Commonwealth Literature* 34, no. 2 (1999): 105–116.

———. "The Critical Reception of Modern African Poetry." *Cahiers d'etudes africanines* 176 (2004): 769–791.

Okwudiba, Nnoli. *Ethnic Politics in Nigeria*. Enugu: Fourth Dimension, 1978.

Olademo, Oyeronke. *Gender in Yoruba Oral Tradition*. Lagos: Concept, 2009.

Oladipo, Olufunmilola T. "Intercultural Flow, Movement and Migration of Yoruba Music into America." Paper Presented at the African Studies Association 56th Annual Meeting, Baltimore, November 21–23, 2013.

Oladiti, Abiodun Akeem. "Religion and Politics in Pre-Colonial Nigeria." *Cogito: Multidisciplinary Research Journal* (2014): 72–84.

Olajubu, Oludare. *Iwe Asa Ibile Yoruba*. Lagos: Academy, 1981.

Olajubu, Oyeronke. *Women in the Yoruba Religious Sphere*. New York: State University of New York Press, 2012.

Ọláléyẹ, Samuel K., and Ayọadé Òkédòkun. "The Concept of Death in Yorùbá Indigenous Belief as Depicted by Ifá Divination System in Òyẹ́kú-Pòsé." *African Journal of Religion Philosophy and Culture* 3, no. 1 (2022): 111–128.

Olanipekun, Olusola Victor. "Omoluabi: Re-thinking the Concept of Virtue in Yoruba Culture and Moral System." *Africology: Journal of Pan African Studies* 10, no. 9 (2017): 217–231.

Olaniyi, Rasheed. "Approaching the Study of the Yorùbá Diaspora in Northern Nigeria." In *Yoruba Identity and Power Politics*, edited by Toyin Falola and Ann Genova, 231–250. Rochester, NY: Rochester University Press, 2009.

———. "Identity and Solidarity in a Yoruba Diaspora: The *Egbe Omo Oduduwa* in Northern Nigeria, 1948–1966." *Ife Journal of History* 6, no. 1 (2013): 1–28.

Olaode, Funke. "Lara George: On Finding Fulfilment in Gospel Music, I Have Set Boundaries, I Have Conquered Territories." *ThisDay*, September 22, 2019.

Olaopa, Tunji. *Yorùbá Nation: (Dis)Unity National Politics and the Republican Spirit*. Ibadan Nigeria: Pan-African University Press, 2017.

Ọlátúnji, Michael O. "Modern Trends in the Islamized Music of the Traditional Yorùbá: Concept, Origin, and Development." *Matatu* 40 (2012): 447–455.

Olayinka, Sunday Akintayo. "Religious Heritage and Values Perfecting Peacefulness among the Contemporary Yorùbá." In *Dearth of Integrity: The Bane of Leadership in Nigeria*, edited by Selome Kuponu, 103–121. Lagos: Christian Studies Unit, Department of Religions and Peace Studies, Lagos State University, 2021.

Oloidi, Akintunde John. "Impacts of Modernization on Cultural Heritage Management and Tourism Development in Ado and Igede Ekiti, Ekiti State." PhD diss., University of Nigeria, Nsukka, 2014.

Oloruntoba-Oju, Taiwo. "Youth Language in Virtual Space in Nigeria: Multimodal Affordance, Indexicality and Youth Identities." *Linguistics Vanguard: A Multimodal Journal for the Language Sciences* 6, no. 4 (2020): 1–4.

Olowookere, Daniel. "Orality and the Bible: A Context for Repertoire of the Universe of the Yoruba Mind." *Nigerian Journal of Oral Literature* 2 (2014): 133–146.

Olu-Adeyemi, Lanre. "Deprivation, Frustration and Aggression: An Interrogation of Fulani Herdsmen Terror in Nigeria." *Advances in Social Sciences Research Journal* 4, no. 15 (2017): 1–13.

Olubayo, O. A. "Esu Elegbara in Yoruba Spiritual and Religious Discourse." In *Esu: Yoruba God Power and the Imaginative Frontiers*, edited by Toyin Falola. Durham, NC: Carolina Academic Press, 2013.

Olúkáyòdé, Alèse. *Èlàl'òrò: A Critical Exposition of Yorùbá Philosophical Ways of Reasoning*. Ibadan: Ajé-Olókun, 2011.

Olukotun, Ayo. *Repressive State and Resurgent Media under Nigeria's Military Dictatorship, 1988–98.* Uppsala: Nordic Africa Institute, 2004.

Olusanya, Gabriel. "Olaniwun Adunni Oluwole." In *Nigerian Women in Historical Perspective,* edited by Bolanle Awe. Ibadan: Sankore, 1992.

Oluwole, Sophie Bosede. *Socrates and Ọ̀rúnmìlà: Two Patron Saints of Classical Philosophy.* Lagos: Ark, 2014.

Omari-Tunkara, Mikelle Smith. *Manipulating the Sacred, Yoruba Art, Ritual, and Resistance in Brazilian Candomble.* Detroit, MI: Wayne State University Press, 2005.

Omasanjuwa, Akpojevbe, and Junisa Phebean. "Acrimony in Colonial Liberia." *Journal of Universal History Studies* 3, no. 1 (2020): 1–38.

Omatta, Boniface O. "The Ethics of Representation and the Internet." In *The Handbook of Global Communication and Media Ethics,* edited by Robert S. Fortner and P. Mark Fackler, 785–802. Sussex: Blackwell, 2011.

Omobola, Odejobi Cecilia. "Community Parenting and the Concept of Child Abuse in Yoruba Culture." *Mediterranean Journal of Social Sciences* 3, no. 2 (2012): 309–316.

———. "Influence of Yoruba Culture in Christian Religious Worship." *International Journal of Social Science and Education* 4, no. 2 (2014): 587.

Omojola, Bode. "Rhythms of the Gods: Music and Spirituality in Yoruba Culture." *Journal of Pan African Studies* 3, no. 5 (2010): 29–50.

———. "Singing Yoruba Christianity: Music Media and Morality." *Yale Journal of Music & Religion* 5, no. 2 (2019): 133–135.

Omoruyi, Omo. *The Tale of June 12: The Betrayal of the Democratic Rights of Nigerians (1993).* Nigeria: Press Alliance Network, 1999.

Omotoye, Rotimi W. "Christianity as a Catalyst for Socio-Economic and Political Change in Yorubaland, Nigeria: An Account of a Church Historian." 159th Inaugural Lecture of the University of Ilorin, June 25, 2015.

———. "The Study of African Traditional Religion and Its Challenges in Contemporary Times." *Ilorin Journal of Religious Studies* 1, no. 2 (2011): 21–40.

Omoyajowo, Joseph. *Makers of Church in Nigeria, 1842–1947.* Lagos: CSS, 1995.

Onigegewura, Olanrewaju. "Death of a Musical Partnership: The Story of Haruna Ishola and Nurudeen Alowonle." *Onigegewura Blog,* October 6, 2017. http://onigegewura.blogspot.com/2017/10/death-of-musical-partnership-story-of.html?m=1.

Onilu, Yagbe Awolowo. "Opele = Ifa Divination Chain." *Yagbe Onilu,* October 23, 2017. https://yagbeonilu.com/opele-ifa-divination-chain/.

Onipede, Festus M. "Yorùbá and Their Symbolic Means of Communication: A Pragma-Semiotic Analysis of Ààlè." *Al-Lisan: Jurnal Bahasa* 7, no. 2 (2022): 145–160.

Online Encyclopedia. "Ade, Sunny (Prince Sunday Adeniyi Adegeye)." *Web Archive.* Accessed September 11, 2021. https://web.archive.org/web/20121225030029/http://encyclopedia.jrank.org/articles/pages/196/Ade-Sunny-Prince-Sunday-Adeniyi-Adegeye.html.

Opare, Andrew. "Functional Analysis of the Ogun Festival in Ondo, Nigeria." PhD diss., Kajaani University, 2014.

Opeloye, Muhib O. "The Yoruba Muslims' Cultural Identity Question." *Ilorin Journal of Religious Studies* 1, no. 2 (2011): 2–5.

Opeloye, Muhib O., and S. L. Jimoh. "The Yoruba Muslims of Nigeria and the Glorious Qur'an." *NATAIS: Journal of Nigeria Association of Teachers of Arabic and Islamic Studies* 7 (2004): 65–83.

Oshun, Christopher O. "Aladura Evangelists in Britain: An Assessment of Spiritual Adventurism." Paper Presented at the Centre for the Study of Christianity in the Non-Western World, University of Edinburgh, March 9, 1999.

Ostien, Philip, and Albert Dekker. "Sharia and National Law in Nigeria." In *Sharia Incorporated: A Comparative Overview of the Legal Systems of Twelve Muslim Countries in Past and Present*, edited by Jan M. Otto. Leiden: Leiden University Press, 2010, 553–612.

Osunlakin, Damilola. "Oral Traditions and the Making of Identity in Yorubaland: An Introductory Case Study of Ikire Kingdom." Paper Presented at the International Conference in Memory of Emeritus Professor Jacob F. Ade Ajayi, at the University of Ibadan, Ibadan, August 12, 2019.

———. "Rethinking Cultural Diversity and Sustainable Development in Africa." In *Imagining Vernacular Histories: Essays in Honor of Toyin Falola*, edited by Mobolanle Ebunoluwa Sotunsa and Abikal Borah, 54. Lanham, MD: Rowman and Littlefield, 2020.

Osuntokun, Akinjide. "Obafemi Awolowo: Politician, Prophet, Philosopher and Patriot." In *Awo: On the Trail of a Titan. Essays in Celebration of the Obafemi Awolowo Centennial*, edited by David O. Oke, Olatunji Dare, Adebayo Williams and Femi Akinola, 1–19. Ibadan: BookBuilders, 2009.

Osuntokun, Akinjide, and Tunji Oloruntimehin. "J. F. Ade Ajayi and His Intellectual Contribution to the Study of History." In *J. F. Ade Ajayi: His Life and Career*, edited by Michael Omolewa and Akinjide Osuntokun, 300. Ibadan: Bookcraft, 2014.

Otero, Solimar, and Toyin Falola, eds. *Yemoja: Gender, Sexuality, and Creativity in the Latina/o and Afro-Atlantic Diasporas*. Albany: SUNY Press, 2013.

Owoeye, Saibu Ainde. "Healing in Some Pentecostal Churches in South-Western Nigeria." *European Scientific Journal* 8, no. 30 (2012): 99–101.

Owomoyela, Oyekan. "The Pragmatic Humanism of Yoruba Culture." *Journal of African Studies* 8, no. 3 (1981): 126–132.

Oyekan, Oluwaseyi A. "Mythmaking, Identity Formation and Ethnic Nationalism in Post-colonial Nigeria through the Lens of Yoruba and Igbo Nationalism." *Politikon: South African Journal of Political Studies* 48, no.1 (2020): 2.

Oye-Laguda, Oguntola. "African Religious Movements and Pentecostalism: The Model of Ijo-Orunmila, Ato." In *Contemporary Perspectives on Religions in Africa and the African Diaspora*, edited by Ibigbolade S. Aderibigbe and Carolyne M. J. Medine, 49–59. New York: Palgrave Macmillan, 2015.

Oyemakinde, Wale. "The Chiefs Law and the Regulation of Traditional Chieftaincy in Yorubaland." *Journal of the Historical Society of Nigeria* 9, no. 1 (1977): 63–74.

Oyeniyi, Bukola. *Dress in the Making of African Identity: A Social and Cultural History of the Yoruba People*. New York: Cambria, 2015.

Oyesomi, Kehinde, and Abiodun Salawu. "Influence of Sexualisation of Women in Music Videos on the Body Image of Nigerian Female Youths." *Gender and Behaviour* 16, no. 3 (2018): 12059–12072.

Oyètádé, B. Akíntúndé. "The Yoruba Community in London." *African Languages and Cultures* 6, no. 1 (1993): 78–79.

Oyeweso, Siyan. "The Philosophical Contents of Sikiru Ayinde Barrister's Music." *Journal of Black Culture and International Understanding* 6/7 (2020/2021): 5–18.

Oyewumi, Oyeronke. "Conceptualizing Gender in African Studies: The Eurocentric Foundations of Feminist Concepts and the Challenge of African Epistemologies." In *The Study of Africa: Disciplinary and Interdisciplinary Encounters*, edited by Paul Zeleza, 317. Dakar: Codesria, 2006.

———. *The Invention of Women: Making an African Sense of Western Gender Discourses*. Minneapolis: University of Minnesota Press, 1997.

———. *What Gender Is Motherhood? Changing Yorùbá Ideals of Power, Procreation, and Identity in the Age of Modernity*. New York: Palgrave Macmillan, 2016.

Page, Willie F., ed. *Encyclopedia of African History and Culture Volume 1: Ancient Africa*. New York: Facts on File, 2005.

Pallinder-Law, Agneta. "Aborted Modernization in West Africa? The Case of Abeokuta." *Journal of African History* 15, no. 1 (1974): 65–82.

Pareles, John. "Music: King Sunny Ade and Band, from Nigeria." *New York Times*, May 15, 1987. https://www.nytimes.com/1987/05/15/arts/music-king-sunny-ade-and-band-from-nigeria .html.

Parratt. J. K., and A. R. I. Doi. "Some Further Aspects of Yoruba Syncretism." *Practical Anthropology* 16, no. 6 (1969): 252–256.

Patterson, Amy S. "Religion and the Rise of Africa." *Brown Journal of World Affairs* 21, no. 1 (2014): 181–196.

Paul, Ilesanmi Akanmidu. "The Migration Patterns and Identity of the Okun-Yoruba People of Central Nigeria." *Yoruba Studies Review* 1, no. 1 (2016): 108.

Pecoud, Antoine, and Paul de Guchteneire, eds. *Migration without Borders: Essays on the Free Movement of People*. New York: Berghahn, 2007.

Peel, John D. Y. *Aladura: A Religious Movement among the Yoruba*. London: Oxford University Press, 1968.

———. *Christianity, Islam, and Orisa-Religion: Three Traditions in Comparison and Interaction*. Berkeley: University of California Press, 2016.

———. "The Cultural Work of Yoruba Ethnogenesis." In *History and Ethnicity*, edited by Elizabeth Tonkin, Maryon McDonald, and Malcolm Chapman, 67–89. London: Routledge, 1989.

———. "Kings, Titles, and Quarters: A Conjectural History of Ilesha I: The Traditions Reviewed." *History in Africa* 6 (1979): 110–135.

———. "The Pastor and the Babalawo: The Interaction of Religions in Nineteenth-Century Yorubaland." *Africa* 60, no. 3 (1990): 347.

———. *Religious Encounter and the Making of the Yoruba*. Bloomington: Indiana University Press, 2000.

———. "Syncretism and Religious Change." *Comparative Studies in Society and History* 10, no. 2 (1968): 121–141.

———. "Yoruba Religion: Seeing It in History, Seeing It Whole." *Orita: Ibadan Journal of Religious Studies* 40, no. 1 (2008): 1–24.

Perham, Margery. *Lugard: The Years of Authority 1898–1945*. London: Collins, 1960.

Peters, F. E. *The Hajj: The Muslim Pilgrimage to Mecca and the Holy Places*. Princeton, NJ: Princeton University Press, 1994.

Pétré-Grenouilleau, Olivier, ed. *From Slave Trade to Empire European Colonisation of Black Africa 1780s–1880s*. New York: Routledge, 2015.

Pobee, John S., and Gabriel Ositelu. *African Initiatives in Christianity: The Growth, Gifts and Diversities of Indigenous African Churches—A Challenge to the Ecumenical Movement*. Geneva: World Council of Churches, Geneva, 1998.

Porteres, R., and J. Barrau. "Origins, Development and Expansion of Agricultural Techniques." In *General History of Africa I: Methodology and African Prehistory*, edited by L. Ki-Zerbo, 687–705. Westport: UNESCO, 1985.

Poynor, Robin. "Ako Figures of Owo and Second Burials in Southern Nigeria." *African Arts* 21, no. 1 (1987): 82.

Pratten, David. *Perspectives on Vigilantism in Nigeria*. Edinburgh: Edinburgh University Press, 2008.

Premium Times. "How Big Is the Nigerian Music Industry?" *Premium Times*, February 16, 2023. https://www.premiumtimesng.com/promoted/582338-how-big-is-the-nigerian-music-industry .html.

Rabasa, Angel, Matthew Waxman, Eric V. Larson, and Cheryl Y. Marcum. *The Muslim World After 9/11*. Santa Monica, CA: Rand, 2004.

Raheem, Oluwafunminiyi. "Cosmic Perception of Water in Yorùbá Belief." Seminar Paper Presented in the Department of History and International Studies, University of Ilorin, September 18, 2019.

———. "From the Sublime to the Ridiculous?: Contemporary Nigerian Hip-Hop, Music Consumption and the Search for Meaning (1999–2015)." In *Yoruba Arts, Culture, Entertainment & Tourism in the Age of Globalization & Uncertainty*, edited by Felix Ayoh'Omidire, Shina Alimi, and Akin Adejuwon. Ile Ife: Obafemi Awolowo University, Institute of Cultural Studies, 2020.

———. "'Having His Baby and Not Being His Wife': The Baby-Mama Trend in the Nigeria Entertainment Industry and Marriage Perceptions." *African Notes* 42, nos. 1 and 2 (2018): 41–55.

———. "Inheriting an Artistic Legacy: The Duro Ladipo Museum at the CBCIU (Nigeria) and the Construction of Perpetual Image." Paper Presented at the Annual Conference of the DFG Research Training Group, Identity and Heritage, Technical University, Berlin/Bauhaus Universität, Weimar, Germany, November 19–20, 2020.

———. "Inheriting Sango: The Duro Ladipo Museum at the CBCIU (Nigeria)." In *Practices of Inheritance: Metaphors, Materialization, Power Constellations 3*. Weimar: Bauhaus University Press, 2022.

———. "Martin Luther versus Us: Assessing the Reformation through the Perspectives of an African Class." *African Diaspora Discourse* 2, no. 2 (2020): 49–72.

———. Review: "The Mbari Artists and Writers Club in Ibadan." *Kulturwissenschaftliche Zeitschrift* 4, no. 1 (2019): 63–66.

———. "The Role of Nigerian Celebrity Music Artists in the Anti-Apartheid Struggle, 1970–1990." *Stichproben: Vienna Journal of African Studies* 41 (2021): 16–38.

Raheem, Oluwafunminiyi, and Mike Famiyesin. "Controlling the Boundaries of Morality: The History and Powers of Ayelala Deity." *Yoruba Studies Review* (Special Issue) 2, no. 1 (2017): 231–247.

Raheem, Thanni. "Alhaji Azeez Ajagbemokeferi and His Da'wah Activities." B.A Project, University of Ibadan, 1986.

Raji, Adesina Yusuf, and Peter F. Adebayo. "Yoruba Traders in Cote D'Ivoire: Study of the Role of Migrant Settlers in the Process of Economic Relations in West Africa." *African Research Review* 3, no. 2 (2009): 134–147.

Raji-Oyelade, Remi. "Ibadan and the Memory of a Generation: From the Poetry Club to the Premier Circle." *English in Africa* 32, no. 1 (2005): 21–35.

Raji-Oyelade, Remi, Sola Olorunyomi, and Abiodun Duro Ladipo, eds. *Duro Ladipo: Thunder-God on Stage*. Ibadan: Institute of African Studies, 2003.

Ralston, Richard D. "The Return of Brazilian Freedmen to West Africa in the 18th and 19th Centuries." *Canadian Journal of African Studies* 3, no. 3 (1969): 577–593.

Ramos, Arthur. *The Black Diaspora: Africans and Their Descendants in the Wider World, 1850–1950*. Ann Arbor: University of Michigan Press, 1996.

Ramos, Miguel. "Connecting through a Medium of a Different Nature: The Orishas Go Online." *Journal of Hispanic Theology* Online (2008). http://eleda.org/blog/2009/11/21/connecting-through-a-medium-of-a-different-nature%e2%80%94the-orishas-go-online1/.

Rashed, Roshdi. *Ibn al-Haytham's Geometrical Methods and the Philosophy of Mathematics: A History of Arabic Sciences and Mathematics*, vol. 5. Translated by J. V. Field. New York: Routledge, 2019.

Rasheed, Olawale. "The Real Significance of Amotekun." *Nigerian Tribune*, January 15, 2020. https://tribuneonlineng.com/the-real-significance-of-amotekun/.

Ray, Benjamin C. "Aladura Christianity: A Yoruba Religion." *Journal of Religion in Africa* 23, no. 1–4 (1993): 266–291.

Records Nigeria. "King Sunny Ade—First Nigerian Grammy Award Nominee." *Records Nigeria,* January 16, 2017. https://web.archive.org/web/20181029074021/http://records.com.ng/2017/king-sunny-ade-first-nigerian-grammy-award-nominee/?relatedposts=1.

Refworld. "Nigeria: 'Same Sex Marriage (Prohibition) Act, 2013.'" *Refworld.* Accessed July 14, 2022. https://www.refworld.org/country,,,LEGISLATION,NGA,,52f4d9cc4,0.html.

Reid, Michele. "Origins of the Yoruba in Cuba: Lucumí, Yoruba, Spain, and the Slave Trade." In *Yoruba Diaspora in the Atlantic World,* edited by Toyin Falola and Matt Childs, 116. Bloomington: Indiana University Press, 2004.

Reis, João José. *Slave Rebellion in Brazil: The Muslim Uprising of 1935.* Baltimore: Johns Hopkins University Press, 1993.

Relph, Edward. "A Pragmatic Sense of Place." *Environmental and Architectural Phenomenology* 20, no. 3 (2009): 24–31.

Rice, Andrew. "Mission from Africa." *New York Times Magazine,* April 22, 2009. https://www.nytimes.com/2009/04/12/magazine/12churches-t.html.

Robinson, David. *Muslim Societies in African History.* New York: Cambridge University Press, 2004.

Rodenbough, Philip P. "Being LGBT in West Africa: A Virtual Student Foreign Service Project." USAID, 2014. https://blogs.cuit.columbia.edu/rightsviews/files/2015/03/The-Being-LGBT-in-West-Africa-Project-Final-Report.pdf.

Rodriguez, Louie F. "Dialoguing, Cultural Capital, and Student Engagement: Toward a Hip Hop Pedagogy in the High School and University Classroom." *Equity & Excellence in Education* 2, no. 1 (2009): 22.

Rosenberg, Donna. "The Creation of the Universe and Ife." In *World Mythology: An Anthology of the Great Myths and Epics,* edited by Donna Rosenberg, 509–514. Lincolnwood, IL: NTC/Contemporary, 1999.

———, ed. *World Mythology: An Anthology of the Great Myths and Epics.* Lincolnwood, IL: NTC/Contemporary, 1999.

Rufai, Saheed Ahmed. "Emergent Issues in Heterodox Islam among the Yoruba of Nigeria." *Journal Hadhari* 4, no. 2 (2012): 117–120.

Ryan, Patrick J. *Imale: Yoruba Participation in the Muslim Tradition: A Study of Clerical Piety.* Missoula, MT: Scholars' Press, 1979.

Ryder, A. F. C. "A Reconsideration of the Ife-Benin Relationship." *Journal of African History* 6, no. 1 (1965): 25–37.

———. "The Trans-Atlantic Slave Trade." In *Groundwork of Nigerian History,* edited by Obaro Ikime, 238–250. Ibadan: Heinemann Educational, 1980.

Saakana Amon Saba, ed. *African Origins of the Major World Religions.* London: Karnak House, 1991.

Sahara Reporters. "Igangan Attack: How Fulani Herdsmen Killed Amotekun Commander, Three Others." *Saharareporters,* July 17, 2021. http://www.saharareporters.com/2021/07/17/igangan-attack-how-fulani-herdsmen-killed-amotekun-commander-three-others.

Sandoval, Mercedes Cros. *Worldview, The Orichas, and Santeria: Africa to Cuba and Beyond.* Gainesville: University Press of Florida, 2006.

Sanusi, Sola. "Meet Duro Ladipo, the First Nigerian Actor to Win International Award." *Legit,* April 5, 2018. https://web.archive.org/web/20210523000000*/https://www.legit.ng/1161281-meet-duro-ladipo-nigerian-actor-win-international-award.html.

Saupin, Guy. "The Emergence of Port Towns in Pre-colonial Sub-Saharan Africa, 1450–1850: What Kind of Development Did They Entail?" *International Journal of Maritime History* 32, no. 1 (2020): 172–184.

Schlebusch, Carina M., and Mattias Jakobsson. "Tales of Human Migration, Admixture, and Selection in Africa." *Annual Review of Genomics and Human Genetics* 19 (2018): 405–428.

Schoonmaker, Trevor. *Fela: From West Africa to West Broadway.* New York: Palgrave Macmillan, 2003.

Schuetz, Arnold. "The Frankfurt School and Popular Culture." *Studies in Popular Culture* 12, no. 1 (1989): 1–14.

Schwarz, Walter. "Tribalism and Politics in Nigeria." *World Today* 22, no. 11 (1966): 460–467.

Sekoni, R. "Awolowo and Culture." In *Awo: On the Trail of a Titan. Essays in Celebration of the Obafemi Awolowo Centennial*, edited by David O. Oke, Olatunji Dare, Adebayo Williams, and Femi Akinola, 269–283. Ibadan: BookBuilders, 2009.

Shack, William A., and Elliot P. Skinner, eds. *Strangers in African Societies*. Berkeley: University of California Press, 1979.

Shaheed, Ahmed. "UN Expert Says Anti-Muslim Hatred Rises to Epidemic Proportions, Urges States to Act." *OHCHR*. Accessed March 4, 2021. https://www.ohchr.org/EN/NewsEvents/Pages/DisplayNews.aspx?NewsID=26841&LangID=E.

Shapiro, Andrew L. "The Internet." *Foreign Policy* 115 (1999): 14–27, 21.

Sharma, Arvind. *The Concept of Universal Religion in Modern Hindu Thought*. London: Palgrave Macmillan, 1998.

Shitta-Bey, Olanrewaju. "The Family as Basis of Social Order: Insights from the Yoruba Traditional Culture." *International Letters of Social and Humanistic Sciences* 23 (2014): 79–89.

Shittu, Ayodeji Isaac. "An Ethnographic Reading of Nigerian Migrant Autobiographical Poetry in English." *Ibadan Journal of Humanistic Studies* 28 (2018): 187–204.

Shoks, Oluseni. "I Asked A.I. to Show Me What Yoruba Orishas Looked Like: A Thread." *Twitter*, February 4, 2023. https://twitter.com/OluseniShoks/status/1622038267292958720?lang=en.

Siedlak, Monique Joiner, *Seven African Powers: The Orishas*. St. Augustine, FL: Oshun, 2017.

Siollun, Max. *Oil, Politics and Violence: Nigeria's Military Coup Culture (1966–1976)*. New York: Algora, 2009.

Sirriyeh, Elizabeth. "Modern Muslim Interpretations of Shirk." *Religion* 20, no. 2 (199): 139–159.

Sithole, Tendayi. "Fela Kuti and the Oppositional Lyrical Power." *Muziki: Journal of Music Research in Africa* 9, no. 1 (2012): 1–12.

Sivelä, Jonas. "Dangerous AIDS Myths or Preconceived Perceptions? A Critical Study of the Meaning and Impact of Myths about HIV/AIDS in South Africa." *Journal of Southern African Studies* 42, no. 6 (2016): 1179–1191.

Skinner, Elliot P. "West African Economic Systems." In *Economic Transition in West Africa*, edited by Melville J. Herskovits and Mitchell Harwit, 77–88. London: Routledge, 1964.

Sklar, Richard L. *Nigerian Political Parties: Power in an Emergent African Nation*. Princeton, NJ: Princeton University Press, 1963.

Slave Voyages. "Trans-Atlantic Slave Trade Database." *Slave Voyages*. Accessed May 4, 2021. https://www.slavevoyages.org.

Smith, Abdullahi. "A Little New Light on the Collapse of the Alafinate of Yoruba." History Department Seminar Series, vol. 1. Zaria: Ahmadu Bello University Press Limited, 2011.

Smith, Anthony D. "The Genealogy of Nations: An Ethno-Symbolic Approach." In *When Is the Nation?: Towards an Understanding of Theories of Nationalism*, edited by Atsuko Ichijo and Gordana Uzelac, 94–112. New York: Routledge, 2005.

Smith, Malinda S. "Profile of Nobel Laureate Wole Soyinka." *Africa Society*. Accessed April 10, 2021. https://sites.ualberta.ca/~afso/documents/soyinka.pdf.

Smith, Robert. "Nigeria-Ijebu." In *West African Resistance: The Military Response to Colonial Occupation*, edited by Michael Crowder, 179–184. London: Hutchinson, 1971.

Smith, Robert S. *Kingdoms of the Yoruba*. Madison: University of Wisconsin Press, 1988.

———. *The Lagos Consulate, 1851–1861*. Berkeley: University of California Press, 2022.

———. *Warfare and Diplomacy in Pre-Colonial West Africa*. London: Routledge, 1976.

Smythe, Kathleen R. *Africa's Past, Our Future*. Bloomington: Indiana University Press, 2015.

Sofela, Babatunde. *Egba-Ijebu Relations: A Study in Conflict Resolution in 19th Century Yorubaland*. Ibadan: John Archers, 2000.

Solagberu, Abdur-Razzaq M. B. "The Impact of Sufism on the Culture of the People of Ilorin, Nigeria." *Journal of Muslim Minority Affairs* 32, no. 3 (2012): 400–410.

Sowande, Fela. *Ifa*. Lagos: Forward, 1992.

Soyinka, Wole. *Ake, the Years of Childhood*. New York: Random House, 1981.

———. *Opera Wonyosi*. Bloomington: Indiana University Press, 1981.

Steiner, Christopher. B. "Another Image of Africa: Toward an Ethnohistory of European Cloth Marketed in West Africa, 1873–1960." *Ethnohistory* 32, no. 2 (1985): 91–110.

Stilwell, Sean. *Slavery and Slaving in African History*. New York: Cambridge University Press, 2014.

Street, John, Sanna Inthorn, and Martin Scott. *From Entertainment to Citizenship: Politics and Popular Culture*. Manchester: Manchester University Press, 2013.

Strinati, Dominic. *An Introduction to Theories of Popular Culture*. London: Routledge, 2004.

Suhr-Systma, Nathan. "Ibadan Modernism: Poetry and the Literary Present in Mid-Century Nigeria." *Journal of Commonwealth Literature* 48, no. 1 (2013): 41–59.

Sulaiman, Kamal-Deen Olawale, and Kamil Adeleke Adeyemi. "The Role of Shaykh Jamiu Larubawa Dandawi to the Development of Arabic and Islamic Studies in Ekitiland." *Sri Lankan Journal of Arabic and Islamic Studies* 2, no. 1 (2019): 84–100.

Sundiata, Ibrahim. From Slaving to Neoslavery: The Bight of Biafra and Fernando Po in the Era of Abolition, 1827–1930. Madison: University of Wisconsin Press, 1996.

Sundkler, Bengt, and Christoper Reed. *A History of the Church in Africa*. Cambridge: Cambridge University Press, 2000.

Taiwo, Matthew T., and Victor O. Taiwo. "Religion Sectarianism in Yoruba Land and Threats to Its Millennial Tribal Union." *Randwick International of Social Science Journal* 1, no. 2 (2020): 165–173.

Tamuno, Tekena N. "Separatist Agitations in Nigeria since 1914." *Journal of Modern African Studies* 8, no. 4 (1970): 563–584.

Tarrow, Sidney. "Mentalities, Political Cultures, and Collective Action Frames: Constructing Meanings through Action." In *Frontiers in Social Movement Theory,* edited by Aldon D. Morris and Carol McClurg Mueller, 174–202. New Haven, CT: Yale University Press, 1992.

Tesei, Tommaso. "The Barzakh and the Intermediate State of the Dead in the Quran." In *Locating Hell in Islamic Traditions*, edited by Christin Lange 31–55. Leiden: Brill, 2016.

Thani, Taofeek M. *The Spread of Christianity in Yorubaland of Nigeria: An Historical Perspective*. Malaysia: International Institute of Islamic Thought and Civilization, 2012.

Thompson, Sheneese. "The Proliferation of Yorùbá Religion in the Atlantic during the Nineteenth Century: The Portability of the Orisha." *Yoruba Studies Review* 7, no. 2 (2022): 1–16.

Tine, Adama. "Gambia: Paramount Chief Calls on Yoruba Community to Cherish Tradition, Culture." *All Africa*, April 13, 2021. https://allafrica.com/stories/202104140292.html.

Tishken, Joel E., Tóyìn Fálọlá, and Akíntúndéí Akínyẹmí, eds. *Sàngó in Africa and the African Diaspora*. Bloomington: Indiana University Press, 2009.

Treviño, Linda Klebe, Michael E. Brown, and Stephen J. Wall. "Managing to Be Ethical: Debunking Five Business Ethics Myths [and Executive Commentary]." *The Academy of Management Executive* (1993–2005) 18, no. 2 (2004): 69–83.

Tsang, Martin. "The Art of Sweeping Sickness and Catching Death: Babalú Aye, Materiality, and Mortality in Lukumí Religious Practice." *Journal of Africana Religions* 8, no. 2 (2020): 292–316.

Tubosun, Kola. "Ulli Beier at the British Library." *British Library Blog*, March 23, 2020. https://blogs.bl.uk/asian-and-african/2020/03/ulli-beier-at-the-british-library.html.

Tukur, Sani. "Islam Came to South, before Northern Nigeria—Isa Yuguda." *Premium Times*, April 26, 2013. https://www.premiumtimesng.com/news/131497-islam-came-to-south-before-northern-nigeria-isa-yuguda.html.

Ubaku, Kelechi C., Chikezie A. Emeh, and Chinenye N. Anyikwa. "Impact of Nationalist Movement on the Actualization of Nigerian Independence, 1914–1960." *International Journal of History and Philosophical Research* 2, no. 1 (2014): 54–67.

Udo, Emem M. "The Vitality of Yoruba Culture in the America." *Ufahamu: Journal of African Studies* 41, no. 2 (2020): 27–40.

Ugor, Paul. "Small Media, Popular Culture, and New Youth Spaces in Nigeria." *Review of Education, Pedagogy, and Cultural Studies* 31, no. 4 (2009): 387–408.

Uhakheme, Ozolua. "Osun, Artists Mourn German Scholar Ulli Beier." *GhanaNews*, April 4, 2011. https://www.ghanamma.com/2011/04/04/osun-artists-mourn-german-scholar-ulli-beier/.

Ukah, Asonzeh Franklin-Kennedy. "The Redeemed Christian Church of God (RCCG), Nigeria: Local Identities and Global Processes in African Pentecostalism." PhD diss., zur Erlangung des Doktorgrades an der Kulturwissenschaftlich Fakultätder Universität Bayreuth, 2003.

Ukah, F. K. Asonzeh. *Globalisation of Pentecostalism in Africa: Evidence from the Redeemed Christian Church of God (RCCG), Nigeria*. Ibadan: IFRA, 2005.

Ul Haq, Irfan. "The Social Order in Islam: Basis, Nature and Principles." In *Economic Doctrines of Islam: A Study in the Doctrines of Islam and Their Implications for Poverty, Employment and Economic Growth*, edited by Irfan Ul Haq, 39–66. Virginia: International Institute of Islamic Thought, 1995.

Underhill, Evelyn. *Worship*. Eugene, OR: Wipf and Stock, 2002.

Universal House of Justice. Prepared under the Supervision of the Universal House of Justice (1986). *In Memoriam. The Bahá'í World*, vol. 18. Bahá'í World Centre.

Usman, Aribidesi. "Ila Kingdom Revisited: Recent Archeological Research at Ila-Yara." In *Yoruba Power and Identity*, edited by Toyin Falola and Ann Genova, 130. Rochester, NY: Rochester University Press, 2006.

———. "Precolonial Regional Migration and Settlement Abandonment in Yorubaland, Nigeria." In *Movements, Borders, and Identities in Africa*, edited by Toyin Falola and Aribidesi Adisa Usman, 112. Rochester, NY: University of Rochester Press, 2009.

Usman, Aribidesi, and Toyin Falola. "Summary and Conclusion." In *The Yoruba from Prehistory to the Present*, edited by Aribidesi Usman and Toyin Falola, 429–450. Cambridge: Cambridge University Press, 2019.

———. *The Yoruba from Prehistory to the Present*. Cambridge: Cambridge University Press, 2019.

Usman, Aribidesi A. "Ceramic Seriation, Sites Chronology, and Old Oyo Factor in Northcentral Yorubaland, Nigeria." *African Archaeological Review* 20 (2003): 149–169.

———. "A View from the Periphery: Northern Yoruba Villages during the Old Oyo Empire, Nigeria." *Journal of Field Archaeology* 27, no. 1 (2000): 43.

Valdés-Cruz, Rosa. "The Black Man's Contribution to Cuban Culture." *Americas* 34, no. 2 (1977): 244–251.

Vansina, Jan. *Oral Tradition as History*. Madison: University of Wisconsin Press, 1985.

Vaughan, Olufemi. *Nigerian Chiefs: Traditional Power in Modern Politics, 1890s–1990s*. Rochester, NY: University of Rochester Press, 2006.

Veal, Michael E. *Fela: The Life and Times of an African Musical Icon*. Philadelphia: Temple University Press, 2000.

Vega, Marta Morena. *The Altar of My Soul: The Living Traditions of Santeria*. London: One World, 2001.

———. "The Ancestral Sacred Creative Impulse of Africa and the African Diaspora: *Ase*, the Nexus of the Black Global Aesthetic." *Lenox Avenue: Journal of Interarts Inquiry* 5 (1999): 46, 47.

Vercoulter, J. "Discovery and Diffusion of Metals and Development of Social Systems up to the Fifth Century before Our Era." In *General History of Africa: Methodology and African Prehistory*, edited by Joseph Ki-Zerbo, 706–729. Berkeley, CA: Heinemann Educational, 1981.

Vignoli, Tito. *Myth And Science: An Essay*. New York: D. Appleton and Co., 1882.

Vlach, John Michael. "Affecting Architecture of the Yoruba." *African Arts* 10, no. 1 (1976): 48–55.

Wahab, Bolanle. "African Traditional Religions Environmental Health and Sanitation in Rural Communities." *The Environscope: A Multidisciplinary Journal* 1, no. 1 (2004): 1–9.

Walker, F. D. *A Hundred Years in Nigeria: The Story of the Methodist Mission in the Western Nigeria District, 1842–1942*. London: Carthage, 1942.

———. *The Romans of the Black River: The Story of the C. M. S. Nigerian Mission*. London: CMS, 1931.

Wambua, L. T. "African Perceptions and Myths About Menopause." *East African Medical Journal* 74, no. 10 (1997): 645–646.

Ward, Victoria. "Cleric Said to Be behind Tunisian Beach Massacre Is Living on Benefits in Britain." *Telegraph*, July 6, 2015. https://www.telegraph.co.uk/news/worldnews/islamic-state /11720000/Cleric-said-to-be-behind-Tunisian-beach-massacre-is-living-in-benefits-in-Britain .html?onwardjourney=584162_v1.

Wariboko, Nimi, Toyin Falola, and Wilhelmina J. Kalu. "Editors' Introduction." In *African Christianity: Mission, Ferment, Trauma*, edited by Nimi Wariboko, Toyin Falola, and Wilhelmina Kalu, iii. Trenton, NJ: Africa World, 2010.

Watabe, Shigeyuki. "The Traditional Political Organization of Yorùbá Town: A Case Study of Ayedun-Ekiti in Comparative Framework." *Journal of African Studies* 26 (1985): 1–20.

Watson, Ruth. "Ibadan—'A Model of Historical Facts': Militarism and Civic Culture in a Yoruba City." *Urban History* 26, no. 1 (1999): 5–26.

———. "Murder and the Political Body in Early Colonial Ibadan." *Africa: Journal of the International African Institute* 70, no.1 (2000): 25–48.

Webster, John. "Attitudes and Policies of the Yoruba African Churches Towards Polygamy." In *Christianity in Tropical Africa*, edited by Christian G. Baeta, 225–251. London: Oxford University Press, 1968.

Weiss, Holger. "Muslim NGOs, Zakat and the Provision of Social Welfare in Sub-Saharan Africa: An Introduction." In *Muslim Faith-Based Organizations and Social Welfare in Africa*, edited by Holger Weiss, 1–38. Cham: Palgrave Macmillan, 2020.

Welle, Deutsche. "Iwalewa House: Showcase for African Art and Culture." *Deutsche Welle*. Accessed September 11, 2021. https://www.dw.com/en/iwalewa-house-showcase-for-african-art -and-culture/a-18560680.

Wells, Jonathan. *Icons of Evolution : Science or Myth?: Why Much of What We Teach about Evolution Is Wrong*. Washington, DC: Regnery, 2000.

Wescott, R. W. "Ancient Egypt and Modern Africa." *Journal of African History* 2, no. 2 (1961): 311–321.

Willis, John Thabiti. *Masquerading Politics: Kinship, Gender and Ethnicity in a Yoruba Town*. Bloomington: Indiana University Press, 2018.

Wilson, John K. *The Myth of Political Correctness: The Conservative Attack on Higher Education*. Durham, NC: Duke University Press, 1995.

Wirtz, Kristina. *Performing Afro-Cuba: Image, Voice, Spectacle in the Making of Race and History*. Chicago: University of Chicago Press, 2014.

World Data Info. "Yoruba Speaking Countries." *World Data Info*. Accessed April 6, 2023. https:// www.worlddata.info/languages/yoruba.php.

Yai, Olabiyi. "Tradition and the Yoruba Artist." *African Arts* 32, no. 1 (1999): 32–35.

Yandaki, A. I. *The State in Africa: Critical Study in Historiography and Political Philosophy*. Zaria: Gaskiya, 2015.

Yes FM Ibadan. "Evangelist Bola Are Speaks on Her Musical Career and Inspiration." YouTube video, 4:21. May 26, 2022. https://www.youtube.com/watch?v=6LENSGiou4k.

Yusuf, Hauwa'u Evelyn. "Purdah: A Religious Practice or an Instrument of Exclusion, Seclusion and Isolation of Women in a Typical Islamic Setting of Northern Nigeria." *American International Journal of Contemporary Research* 4, no. 1 (2014): 238–245.

Zakharia, Fouad, Analabha Basu, Devin Absher, Themistocles L. Assimes, Alan S. Go, Mark A. Hlatky, Carlos Iribarren, Joshua W. Knowles, Jun Li, Balasubramanian Narasimhan, Steven Sidney, Audrey Southwick, Richard M. Myers, Thomas Quertermous, Neil Risch, and Hua Tang. "Characterizing the Admixed African Ancestry of African Americans." *Genome Biology* 10 (2009): 1–11.

Zielinski, Sarah. "Ten Ancient Stories and the Geological Events That May Have Inspired Them." *Smithsonian Magazine.* April 4, 2014. https://www.smithsonianmag.com/science-nature/ten-ancient-stories-and-geological-events-may-have-inspired-them-180950347/.

Index

Oyedepo, Bishop David, 264
Oyekan, Oluwaseyi, 333, 349
Oyo, 9, 10, 11, 12, 13, 14, 15, 16, 18, 19, 22, 24, 37, 46,
    49, 50, 55, 56, 57, 63, 64, 66, 73, 76, 104, 105,
    106, 107, 108, 109, 110, 111, 112, 113, 114, 115, 116,
    117, 118, 119, 120, 121, 122, 123, 124, 125, 126, 127,
    128, 129, 130, 131, 132, 133, 134, 135, 136, 137, 138,
    139, 140, 141, 142, 143, 144, 145, 146, 147, 148,
    149, 150, 151, 153, 154, 155, 156, 157, 158, 159, 160,
    161, 162, 163, 164, 165, 166, 167, 169, 170, 177,
    183, 184, 186, 215, 218, 219, 223, 228, 254, 276,
    289, 291, 293, 331, 334, 339, 340, 341, 342, 343,
    349, 409, 437, 459, 465, 489
Oyotunji, 76, 138, 188, 198, 293, 294, 440, 508
Oyotunji Village, 188, 198, 293, 294, 440
Oyo-Yoruba, 334

Palmer, H. R., 51
Pan-African nationalism, 372, 379
Pan-Africanism, 4, 26, 40, 178, 375, 377, 378,
    379, 474
Pan Niger Delta Forum, 476
Pan-Yorùbá, 33, 44, 118, 347, 349, 477, 482, 492,
    494, 508, 511
Pan-Yorubana, 12, 31, 46
Parrinder, Geoffrey, 141
Peel, D. Y., 5, 14, 44, 57, 71, 104, 164, 232, 236, 251,
    253, 255, 260, 269, 301
Pentecostal, 43, 250, 261, 264, 265, 273, 275, 301,
    302, 303, 305, 306, 307
Pentecostalism, 81, 226, 228, 264, 265, 266, 292,
    293, 301, 302, 303
Persia, 85, 141
Pina, Geraldo, 447
Plato, 387, 388, 389
pluriversalism, 416, 417
Port Bouet, 182, 188
Porto Novo, 124, 125, 126, 127, 141, 161, 163, 263
Portugal, 121, 123, 124
Portuguese, 105, 121, 122, 123, 126, 135, 145, 163,
    182, 217, 252, 291

Queen of Sheba, 309
Qur'an. *See* Quran
Quran, 78, 197, 199, 206, 213, 229, 230, 231, 232,
    243, 309, 310, 330

Raji-Oyelade, Aderemi, 405, 411, 412, 413, 441
Ramos, Miguel, 282, 283, 284, 285, 286, 306, 491

Ramsaran, John, 407
RCCG (Redeemed Christian Church of God),
    264, 273, 306, 307
Reid, Michele, 437
Relph, Edward, 354, 356, 395
Remo community, 381
Richards constitution of 1946, 27
Roman Empire, 11, 36, 66
Rome, 36, 47, 197, 447
Royal Niger Company, 338

Sabe, 140, 141, 150, 155, 465
Sahel, 158, 164
Salawu, Akeem, 503
Sancocho, 277
Ṣàngó, 110, 111, 113, 114, 143, 144, 202, 204, 210,
    214, 215, 216, 218, 219, 223, 224, 225, 289,
    441, 442
Santara, 282
Santeria, 21, 100, 194, 196, 202, 223, 224, 225, 277,
    439, 440, 492, 508
Santos, Boaventura Sousa, 416, 423
Saro, 177, 184, 413
Segun, Mabel, 408
Senegal, 185, 272, 378, 380
Senegambia, 19, 176, 185
Senghor, Leopold, 377, 380, 385
Sha'aba, Jimada, 57, 58
Sharia, 236, 237, 248, 309
Sidi Boumediene, 309
Sierra Leone, 16, 19, 22, 25, 38, 57, 64, 101, 126, 131,
    137, 142, 158, 169, 170, 172, 175, 176, 177, 183, 184,
    185, 186, 187, 188, 250, 251, 252, 255, 257, 259,
    273, 492, 494
slavery, 3, 10, 19, 25, 98, 103, 125, 132, 133, 136, 137,
    172, 173, 193, 202, 204, 205, 216, 226, 245, 251,
    337, 378, 390, 437, 455, 457, 465
slave trade, 3, 12, 14, 16, 18, 25, 96, 106, 118, 122,
    131, 132, 133, 135, 137, 157, 161, 163, 164, 170, 171,
    176, 183, 196, 197, 202, 216, 225, 242, 245, 249,
    250, 251, 252, 275, 276, 295, 335, 337, 341, 346,
    374, 375, 437, 466, 489, 491, 492, 494, 502
slave traders, 18, 24, 126
socialism, 384, 385, 387
Sodeke, Chief, 253
Sokoto caliphate, 167
Solagberu, Abdur-Razzaq, 136, 230, 239
Songhai, 123, 142, 145, 155, 157, 158, 159, 161, 184
Songhai Empire, 123, 142, 155, 158, 159, 161, 184

Toyin Falola is Distinguished Teaching Professor and Jacob and Frances Sanger Mossiker Chair in the Humanities at the University of Texas at Austin. Professor Falola has authored or edited more than 150 books on African history, politics, and society. He is the recipient of nineteen honorary doctorates from around the world and has received over forty lifetime achievement awards.